Master The LSAT

with Software, Online Course

JEFF KOLBY

Additional educational titles from Nova Press:

GRE Prep Course (624 pages, includes software, online course)

GMAT Prep Course (624 pages, includes software, online course)

SAT Prep Course (640 pages, includes software)

The MCAT Physics Book (444 pages)

The MCAT Biology Book (416 pages)

The MCAT Chemistry Book (480 pages)

Law School Basics: A Preview of Law School and Legal Reasoning (224 pages)

Vocabulary 4000: The 4000 Words Essential for an Educated Vocabulary (160 pages)

Previous editions: 2008, 2007, 2006, 2005, 2004, 2003, 2002, 2001, 2000, 1999, 1998, 1997, 1996, 1995, 1994

ISBN 1–889057–31–2

11659 Mayfield Avenue
Los Angeles, CA 90049

Phone: 1-800-949-6175
E-mail: info@novapress.net
Website: www.novapress.net

ABOUT THIS BOOK

If you don't have a pencil in your hand, get one now! Don't just read this book—write on it, study it, scrutinize it! In short, for the next six weeks, this book should be a part of your life. When you have finished the book, it should be marked-up, dog-eared, tattered and torn.

The LSAT has the reputation of being one of the hardest entrance exams given; it is a reputation well earned. This should not discourage you; rather it should motivate you to take the test seriously and study for it assiduously. Although the LSAT is a difficult test, it is a *very* learnable test.

This is not to say that the LSAT is "beatable." There is no bag of tricks that will show you how to master it overnight. You probably have already realized this. Some books, nevertheless, offer "inside stuff" or "tricks" which they claim will enable you to beat the test. These include declaring that answer-choices B, C, or D are more likely to be correct than choices A or E. This tactic, like most of its type, does not work. It is offered to give the student the feeling that he or she is getting the scoop on the test.

The LSAT cannot be "beaten." But it can be mastered—through hard work, analytical thought, and training yourself to think like a test writer.

This book will introduce you to numerous analytic techniques that will help you immensely, not only on the LSAT but in law school as well. For this reason, studying for the LSAT can be a rewarding and satisfying experience.

Although the quick-fix method is not offered in this book, about 15% of the material is dedicated to studying how the questions are constructed. Knowing how the problems are written and how the test writers think will give you useful insight into the problems and make them less mysterious. Moreover, familiarity with the LSAT's structure will help reduce your anxiety. The more you know about this unusual test, the less anxious you will be the day you take it.

The LSAT is not easy—nor is this book. To improve your LSAT score, you must be willing to work; if you study hard and master the techniques in this book, your score will improve—significantly.

Note: To use the book's official LSATs under timed conditions, give yourself *exactly* 35 minutes for each of the four sections, with a 10-minute break after the second section. Then use the Conversion Charts to calculate your LSAT score.

One of the four official LSAT tests is presented in three parts to better analyze the test. The three remaining official tests are presented intact at the end of the book.

ACKNOWLEDGMENT

Behind any successful test-prep book, there is more than just the author's efforts.

I would like to thank Scott Thornburg for his meticulous and invaluable editing of the manuscript and for his continued support and inspiration. Further, I would like to thank Jim Vaseleck and Law Services for allowing the LSAT tests to be reprinted.

Reading passages were drawn from the following sources:

Passage page 353, from *The Two Faces of Eastern Europe,* © 1990 Adam Michnik.

Passage page 357, from *Deschooling Society,* © 1971 Harper & Row, by Ivan Illich.

Passage page 364, from *The Cult of Multiculturalism,* © 1991 Fred Siegel.

Passage page 368, from *Ways of Seeing,* © 1972 Penguin Books Limited, by John Berger.

Passage page 373, from *Placebo Cures for the Incurable*, Journal of Irreproducible Results, © 1985 Thomas G. Kyle.

Passage page 377, from *Women, Fire, and Dangerous Things,* © George Lakoff.

Passage page 381, from *Screening Immigrants and International Travelers for the Human Immunodeficiency Virus,* © 1990 New England Journal of Medicine.

Passage page 396, from *The Perry Scheme and the Teaching of Writing,* © 1986 Christopher Burnham.

Passage page 398, from *Man Bites Shark,* © 1990 Scientific American.

Passage page 400, from *Hemingway: The Writer as Artist*, © 1952 Carlos Baker.

Passage page 402, from *The Stars in Their Courses,* © 1931 James Jeans.

CONTENTS

ORIENTATION

- **WHAT DOES THE LSAT MEASURE?**
- **FORMAT OF THE LSAT**
- **WRITING SAMPLE**
- **THE THREE TYPES OF PROBLEMS**

  Games
  Arguments
  Reading Comprehension
- **PACING**
- **SCORING THE LSAT**
- **SKIPPING AND GUESSING**
- **ORDER OF DIFFICULTY**
- **THE "2 OUT OF 5" RULE**
- **HOW TO USE THIS BOOK**

  Shortened Study Plan
- **QUESTIONS AND ANSWERS**

What Does the LSAT Measure?

The LSAT is an aptitude test. Like all aptitude tests, it must choose a medium in which to measure intellectual ability. The LSAT has chosen logic. Other tests, such as the SAT, use mathematics and English.

OK, the LSAT is an aptitude test. The question is—does it measure aptitude for law school? Now if you think analytically and like to fiddle with crossword or logic puzzles, then you will probably warm up to the LSAT. On the other hand, if you think intuitively and synthetically, then you will probably find the medium (Logic) less palatable. Whether the ability to determine the possible arrangements of people around a circular table is an important skill for a lawyer is debatable. Nonetheless, the Law School Admission Council has chosen this type of question to test your aptitude for law school, so you must master their solution.

No test can measure all aspects of intelligence. Thus any admission test, no matter how well written, is inherently inadequate. Nevertheless, some form of admission testing is necessary. It would be unfair to base acceptance to law school solely on grades; they can be misleading. For instance, would it be fair to admit a student with an A average earned in easy classes over a student with a B average earned in difficult classes? A school's reputation is too broad a measure to use as admission criteria: many students seek out easy classes and generous instructors, in hopes of inflating their GPA. Furthermore, a system that would monitor the academic standards of every class would be cost prohibitive and stifling. So until a better system is proposed, the admission test is here to stay.

Format of the LSAT

The LSAT is a three-hour-and-thirty minute test. Only two hours and twenty minutes of the test count toward your score—the experimental section and the writing sample are not scored. There are five parts to the test.

FORMAT		
Analytical Reasoning (Games)	24 Questions	35 Minutes
Logical Reasoning (Arguments)	25 Questions	35 Minutes
Experimental Section	?? Questions	35 Minutes
Logical Reasoning (Arguments)	25 Questions	35 Minutes
Reading Comprehension	27 Questions	35 Minutes
Writing Sample		35 Minutes

The order of the format is not fixed: the sections can occur in any order—except for the writing sample, which is always last.

The LSAT is a standardized test. Each time it is offered, the test has, as close as possible, the same level of difficulty as every previous test. Maintaining this consistency is very difficult—hence the experimental section. The effectiveness of each question must be assessed before it can be used on the LSAT. A problem that one person finds easy another person may find hard, and vice versa. The experimental section measures the relative difficulty of potential questions; if responses to a question do not perform to strict specifications, the question is rejected.

The experimental section can be a game section, an argument section, or a reading comprehension section. You won't know which section is experimental. You will know which type of section it is, though, since there will be an extra one of that type.

Because the "bugs" have not been worked out of the experimental section, this portion of the test is often more difficult and confusing than the other parts.

This brings up an ethical issue: How many students have run into the experimental section early in the test and have been confused and discouraged by it? Crestfallen by having done poorly on, say, the first—though experimental—section, they lose confidence and perform below their ability on the rest of the test.

Knowing that the experimental section can be disproportionately difficult, if you do poorly on a particular section you can take some solace in the hope that it may have been the experimental section. In other words, do not allow one difficult section to discourage your performance on the rest of the test.

Writing Sample

The final section of the LSAT is the writing sample. This part of the test is not scored, but a copy of it, along with your LSAT score, will be sent to the law schools to which you apply.

It is unlikely that a person's writing ability can be accurately measured with thirty-minute essay, especially when it is administered after a three-and-one-half hour, time-pressured test. Many people who write well, but only through repeated revision, will bomb this part of the test. Even natural writers can do poorly. The law schools realize this, so it is unlikely that anyone will look at your essay. Hence, your preparation strategy should be to concentrate your studies on those parts of the test that are scored.

Some claim that the writing sample can make or break an applicant whose score borders between acceptance and rejection, or that it can be used to decide between two people with equivalent LSAT scores. However, your best bet is to study the scored sections and bump yourself out of that situation. Besides, it is doubtful that the writing sample is actually used in that manner. Put yourself in the position of an admissions officer who, working against a deadline, has to make a decision on X number of applicants. Would you want to spend the time (and it would be time consuming) to evaluate and contrast two essays? Keep in mind that these essays are often nearly illegible and painfully dull.

The Three Types of Problems

The LSAT uses three types of problems to measure your aptitude for law school: analytical reasoning (games), logical reasoning (arguments), and reading comprehension.

Games

The game section comprises one-quarter of the test. It contains four games; each has about six questions for a total of about twenty-four questions.

Games are designed to measure your ability to analyze relationships between elements and then draw conclusions based on those relationships.

The game section is the most difficult and most mathematical part of the test. Indeed, the games actually fit into a branch of mathematics called Set Theory—though we won't use any mathematical tools to solve them.

While the entire test should be read with care, the games must be read with extra care. In particular, pay close attention to words that limit relationships, such as "only," "never," "sometimes," "exactly," etc.

Example: ***Game***

Adam, Bob, Carl, David, Eric, Frank, George, and Hank are basketball players.

Frank is the same height as Hank.
George is taller than Frank.
Eric is taller than Adam.
Adam is taller than David and Carl.
Bob is shorter than Carl.

Which one of the following must be false?

(A) George is taller than Hank.
(B) Carl is taller than David.
(C) Adam is taller than Frank.
(D) David is the same height as Carl.
(E) Bob is the same height as Eric.

If George is taller than Frank who is as tall as Hank, then George must be taller than Hank. Hence (A) is true. This dismisses (A). Next, the fourth condition tells us that Adam is taller than both David and Carl; it does not, however, tell us who is taller between Carl and David, nor do any other conditions. Hence (B) is not necessarily false. This dismisses both (B) and (D). Next, no condition relates the relative heights of Adam and Frank. Hence (C) is not necessarily false. This dismisses (C). Finally, Eric is taller than Adam who is taller than Carl who is taller than Bob. Hence, Eric must be taller than Bob. This contradicts (E). Thus (E) must be false, and therefore it is the answer.

We will analyze all the varieties of games that occur on the LSAT—there are surprisingly few different types. You will also be introduced to powerful diagramming techniques, such as Paths, Flow Charts (which would be used to solve the above problem), Generating Formulas, etc. Many students write off the games as being too hard—this is a mistake! Although the diagramming techniques will not make the games easy, they will greatly simplify them. Indeed, because diagramming is so effective, this portion of the test is the most responsive to study.

Arguments

Arguments (logical reasoning) test your ability to understand the validity, or invalidity, of a line of reasoning. On the LSAT, an argument is a presentation of facts and opinions in order to support a position. The style of the arguments varies from informal discussions to formal dissertations.

Some of the reasoning tasks required by these problems include:

- Identifying the author's main point
- Recognizing an argument's logical structure
- Identifying base assumptions of an argument
- Detecting flaws in reasoning
- Drawing conclusions

Some arguments are intentionally poorly written and many are fallacious.

This portion of the test looks as though it came right out of a logic book—hence the name "logical reasoning." Now, logic is the study of the connections between statements, <u>not</u> the truth of those statements. On the LSAT, many students hurt themselves by tenaciously pursuing the truth—favoring answers that make true statements over those that make false statements. Although there will be cases where the truth of an argument is a factor, there will be as many cases where it is irrelevant.

Example: ***Argument***

In the game of basketball, scoring a three-point shot is a skill that only those with a soft-shooting touch can develop. Wilt Chamberlain, however, was a great player. So even though he did not have a soft-shooting touch, he would have excelled at scoring three-point shots.

Which one of the following contains a flaw that most closely parallels the flaw contained in the passage?

(A) Eighty percent of the freshmen at Berkeley go on to get a bachelor's degree. David is a freshman at Berkeley, so he will probably complete his studies and receive a bachelor's degree.

(B) If the police don't act immediately to quell the disturbance, it will escalate into a riot. However, since the police are understaffed, there will be a riot.

(C) The meek shall inherit the earth. Susie received an inheritance from her grandfather, so she must be meek.

(D) During the Vietnam War, the powerful had to serve along with the poor. However, Stevens' father was a federal judge, so Stevens was able to get a draft deferment.

(E) All dolphins are mammals and all mammals breathe air. Therefore, all mammals that breathe air are dolphins.

The original argument clearly contradicts itself. So we are looking for an answer-choice that contradicts itself in like manner. Notice that both the argument and the correct answer will not be true—again searching for truth can hamper you.

Choice (A) is not self-contradictory. In fact, it's a fairly sound argument. This eliminates (A). Choice (B), on the other hand, is not a sound argument. The police, though understaffed, may realize the seriousness of the situation and rearrange their priorities. Nevertheless, (B) does not contain a contradiction. This eliminates (B). As to choice (C), although the argument is questionable, it, like (B), does not contain a contradiction. This eliminates (C). Choice (D), however, *does* contain a contradiction. It starts by stating that both the powerful and the poor had to serve in Vietnam, but it ends by stating that some powerful people—namely, Stevens—did not have to serve. This is a contradiction, so (D) is probably the answer. Finally, choice (E), like the original argument, is invalid, but it does not contain a contradiction. This eliminates (E). The answer is (D).

The two argument sections, each with about twenty-five questions, make up one-half of the test. This is good news because as we analyze these problems you will develop an ability to uncover their underlying simplicity.

Reading Comprehension

Reading comprehension, like the games, comprises one-fourth of the test. The section consists of four passages each with six to eight questions, for a total of about twenty-six questions.

The passages are taken from academic journals. As you would expect, they are usually quite dry. Nearly any subject may appear, but the most common themes are political, historical, cultural, and scientific.

Every prep book for the LSAT takes a unique approach to the reading comprehension section, from speed reading to underlining to pre-reading the questions to . . . . Some methods, however, are at best useless gimmicks and at worst can distract and confuse you. Reading styles are very personal. What *may* work for one person may not work for another. The particular style that you use is not the key to performing well on the passages; rather the key is to master the six types of questions. These are

(1) Main Idea Questions
(2) Description Questions (using the context to determine the meaning of a word or phrase)
(3) Writing Technique Questions
(4) Extension Questions (usually drawing an inference)
(5) Application Questions (applying what you learned in the passage to a different, often hypothetical, situation)
(6) Tone Questions (what is the author's attitude?)

We will analyze these six types of questions thoroughly. Additionally, we will study the use of "pivotal words" in LSAT passages. Armed with this knowledge, you will be able to anticipate the places from which questions will likely be drawn. This will help reduce the amount of material you will have to scrutinize.

Following is a condensed version of an actual LSAT passage.

Example: *Passage*

There are two major systems of criminal procedure in the modern world—the adversarial and the inquisitorial. Both systems were historically preceded by the system of private vengeance in which the victim of a crime fashioned his own remedy and administered it privately. The modern adversarial system is only one historical step removed from the private vengeance system and still retains some of its characteristic features. Thus, for example, even though the right to initiate legal action against a criminal has now been extended to all members of society and even though the police department has taken over the pretrial investigative functions on behalf of the prosecution, the adversarial system still leaves the defendant to conduct his own pretrial investigation. The trial is still viewed as a duel between two adversaries, refereed by a judge who, at the beginning of the trial has no knowledge of the investigative background of the case. In the final analysis the adversarial system of criminal procedure symbolizes and regularizes the punitive combat.

By contrast, the inquisitorial system begins historically where the adversarial system stopped its development. It is two historical steps removed from the system of private vengeance. Therefore, from the standpoint of legal anthropology, it is historically superior to the adversarial system. Under the inquisitorial system the public investigator has the duty to investigate not just on behalf of the prosecutor but also on behalf of the defendant.

Because of the inquisitorial system's thoroughness in conducting its pretrial investigation, it can be concluded that a defendant who is innocent would prefer to be tried under the inquisitorial system, whereas a defendant who is guilty would prefer to be tried under the adversarial system.

The primary purpose of the passage is to

(A) explain why the inquisitorial system is the best system of criminal justice.
(B) explain how both the adversarial and the inquisitorial systems of criminal justice evolved from the system of private vengeance.
(C) show how the adversarial and inquisitorial systems of criminal justice can both complement and hinder each other's development.
(D) show how the adversarial and inquisitorial systems of criminal justice are being combined into a new and better system.
(E) analyze two systems of criminal justice and imply that one is better.

The answer to a main idea question will summarize the passage without going beyond it. (A) violates these criteria by *overstating* the scope of the passage. The author draws a comparison between two systems, not between *all* systems. (A) would be a good answer if "best" were replaced with "better." (Beware of absolute words.) (B) violates the criteria by *understating* the scope of the passage. Although the evolution of both the adversarial and the inquisitorial systems is discussed in the passage, it is done to show why one is superior to the other. (C) and (D) can be quickly dismissed as neither is mentioned in the passage. Finally, the passage does two things: it presents two systems of criminal justice, and it implies that one is better developed than the other. (E) aptly summarizes this, so it is the best answer.

You may have noticed that the three sample problems did not ask any questions about legal issues. Ironically, the LSAT does not contain any legal questions. You may have also noticed that some questions have a rather mathematical appearance.

Pacing

In your undergraduate studies you probably learned to quickly read through reams of material. You were also probably taught to seek out truth and knowledge. This academic conditioning will serve you poorly on the LSAT. The LSAT does not measure your academic knowledge; rather it tests your ability to detect patterns and relationships. Often these patterns are invalid, such as fallacious arguments. **Searching for knowledge and truth can be ruinous to your LSAT score**. Instead, seek out patterns and relationships.

Although time is strictly limited on the LSAT, working too quickly can also damage your score. Many problems hinge on subtle points, and most require careful reading of the setup. Because undergraduate school puts such heavy reading loads on students, many will follow their academic conditioning and read the questions quickly, looking only for the gist of what the question is asking. Once they have found it, they mark their answer and move on, confident they have answered it correctly. Later, many are startled to discover that they missed questions because they either misread the problems or overlooked subtle points.

To do well in your undergraduate classes, you had to attempt to solve every, or nearly every, problem on a test. Not so with the LSAT. In fact, if you try to solve every problem on the test ,you will probably decimate your score. For the vast majority of people, the key to performing well on the LSAT is not the number of questions they answer, within reason, but the percentage they answer correctly.

Scoring the LSAT

The LSAT is designed so that it is nearly impossible for anyone to answer all the questions correctly . A "perfect score" can include as many as 3 wrong answers. The LSAT is scored on a scale from 120 to 180, and 151 is the average scaled score.

In addition to the scaled score, you will be assigned a percentile ranking, which gives the percentage of students with scores below yours. For instance, if you correctly answer 77 of 100 questions, then you will score better than 90% of the other test takers. In other words, you can miss nearly one-quarter of the questions and still be in the 90th percentile. This further substantiates the claim that you need not complete the entire test to get a top score. Since 151 is the average scaled score, it marks the 50th percentile.

The following table relates scaled scores and percentile ranking to the number of wrong answers.

Number of Wrong Answers	Scaled Score	Percentile Score %	Number of Correct Answers
5	180	99	95
10	175	99	90
15	170	97	85
20	165	90	80
25	160	80	75
30	155	70	70
35	150	50	65
40	145	45	60
45	140	30	55
50	135	20	50

Skipping and Guessing

Some questions on the LSAT are very hard. Many test takers should consider skipping these questions. We'll talk about how to identify impossibly hard questions as we come to them.

Often students become obsessed with a particular problem and waste valuable time trying to solve it. To get a top score, learn to cut your losses and move on because all questions are worth the same number of points, regardless of difficulty level. So consider skipping the nearly impossible questions and concentrate on the easy and possible ones.

Which problems to skip varies from person to person, so experiment to find what works best for you.

There is no guessing penalty on the LSAT. **So make sure you mark any questions that you skip!** By the laws of probability, you should answer one question correctly for every five guesses.

Order of Difficulty

Most standardized tests list problems in ascending order of difficulty. On these tests, deciding which questions to skip is easy—skip the last ones. Unfortunately, the LSAT does not conform to this rule. The level of difficulty varies throughout the test. Deciding which questions are hard and therefore should be skipped is an important test-taking strategy; we will talk more about gauging the degree of difficulty as we come to each type of question. For now we can say this, the first question will not be the hardest and the last will not be the easiest.

The "2 out of 5" Rule

It is significantly harder to create a good but incorrect answer-choice than it is to produce the correct answer. For this reason usually only two attractive answer-choices are offered. One correct; the other either intentionally misleading or only partially correct. The other three answer-choices are usually fluff. This makes educated guessing on the LSAT immensely effective. If you can dismiss the three fluff choices, your probability of answering the question successfully will increase from 20% to 50%.

Example: ***"2 out of 5" rule***

During the late seventies when Japan was rapidly expanding its share of the American auto market, GM surveyed owners of GM cars and asked, "Would you be more willing to buy a large, powerful car or a small, economical car?" Seventy percent of those who responded said that they would prefer a large car. On the basis of this survey, GM decided to continue building large cars. Yet during the '80s, GM lost even more of the market to the Japanese.

Which one of the following, if it were determined to be true, would best explain this discrepancy?

(A) Only 10 percent of those who were polled replied.
(B) Ford which conducted a similar survey with similar results continued to build large cars and also lost more of their market to the Japanese.
(C) The surveyed owners who preferred big cars also preferred big homes.
(D) GM determined that it would be more profitable to make big cars.
(E) Eighty percent of the owners who wanted big cars and only 40 percent of the owners who wanted small cars replied to the survey.

Only two answer-choices have any real merit—(A) and (E). The argument generalizes from the survey to the general car-buying population, so the reliability of the projection depends on how representative the sample is. At first glance choice (A) seems rather good, because 10 percent does not seem large enough. However, political opinion polls typically are based on only .001 percent of the population. More importantly, we don't know what percentage of GM car owners received the survey. Choice (E), on the other hand, points out that the survey did not represent the entire public, so it is the answer.

The other choices can be quickly dismissed. Choice (B) simply states that Ford made the same mistake that GM did. Choice (C) is irrelevant. Finally, choice (D), rather than explaining the discrepancy, would give even more reason for GM to continue making large cars.

How to Use this Book

The four parts of this book—(1) Games, (2) Arguments, (3) Reading Comprehension, and (4) LSAT Tests—are independent of one another. However, to take full advantage of the system presented in the book, it is best to tackle each part in the order given.

This book contains the equivalent of a six-week course which meets two hours a day, five days a week. Ideally you have bought the book at least four weeks before your scheduled test date. However, if the test is only a week or two away, there is still a truncated study plan that will be useful.

Shortened Study Plan

Games

Study: Introduction
Linear Ordering Games
Grouping Games
Assignment Games

Arguments

Study: Logic I
Inductive Reasoning
Common Fallacies

Reading Comprehension

Study: The Six Questions
Pivotal Words

The Tests

Questions and Answers

When is the LSAT given?
The test is administered four times a year—usually in October, December, February, and June—on Saturdays from 8:30 a.m. to 1:00 p.m. Special arrangements for schedule changes are available.

How important is the LSAT and how is it used?
It is crucial! Although law schools may consider other factors, the vast majority of admission decisions are based on only two criteria: your LSAT score and your GPA.

How many times should I take the LSAT?
Most people are better off preparing thoroughly for the test, taking it one time and getting their top score. You can take the test as often as you like, but some law schools will average your scores. You should call the schools to which you are applying to find out their policy. Then plan your strategy accordingly. A copy of your LSAT and Grade Point Average will automatically be sent to every school to which you apply.

Can I cancel my score?
Yes. To do so, you must notify the Law School Admission Services within 5 days after taking the test. Although your score from a canceled test will not be reported to the schools you apply to, the cancellation will be.

Where can I get the registration forms?
Most law schools have the forms. You can also get them directly from Law School Admission Services by writing to:

Law Services
Box 2000
661 Penn Street
Newtown, PA 18940

You can also get the forms by calling Law Services at 215-968-1001. Or through the Internet: www.lsac.org

Part One

GAMES

GAMES

- **INTRODUCTION TO GAMES**
  - The Three Major Types of Games
    - Ordering Games
    - Grouping Games
    - Assignment Games
  - Format of the Games
  - Skipping a Game
  - Order of Difficulty
  - Reading with Precision
  - Unwarranted Assumptions
  - Logical Connectives
  - Diagramming
  - Symbols/Record Keeping
  - Diagramming Continued
  - Readily Derived Conditions
  - Obfuscation
- **LINEAR ORDERING**
  - Spatial Ordering
  - Hybrid Games
  - Sequential Games
- **CIRCULAR ORDERING**
- **GENERATING FORMULAS**
- **PATHS AND FLOW CHARTS**
- **GROUPING GAMES**
  - By Twos
  - By Three or More
- **ASSIGNMENT GAMES**
  - Assignment Games vs. Grouping Games
  - Schedules
  - Multiple-Choice Games
- **LSAT SECTION**

Introduction

Most people believe that the game section (analytical reasoning) is the most difficult part of the LSAT. They're right. The games are disproportionately hard for two reasons: First, the questions are complex, convoluted, and subtle. Second, it is the most highly "timed" part of the test. That is, you are intentionally not given enough time to finish.

The game section is also the most contrived part of the test. The possible arrangements of a group of people around a circular table has little correlation with the daily activities of a lawyer. The writers of the LSAT use the games as a litmus test, to see whether you have the intellectual ability to make it in law school.

Although this may sound intimidating, everyone taking the LSAT is in the same situation. You probably have never seen this type of problem during you academic career. No specific college course will prepare you for them, except perhaps mathematics.

Furthermore, games are the easiest problems on which to improve, for two reasons: (1) The process of solving a game is very systematic. (2) There are only a few different kinds of games: just three major categories, plus a couple that don't quite fit. This chapter is dedicated to classifying the major types of games and then mastering their systematic solution.

The Three Major Types of Games

ORDERING GAMES

These games require you to order elements, either in a line or around a circle. The criteria used to determine order can include size, time, rank, etc. Ordering games are the easiest games on the LSAT. Luckily, they are also the most common.

Example: ***Ordering Game***

Six people—Rick, Steve, Terry, Ulrika, Vivian, and Will—are standing in line for tickets to an upcoming concert.

Rick is fifth in line and is not next to Steve.
Ulrika is immediately behind Terry.
Will is not last.

Which one of the following people must be last in line?

(A) Steve
(B) Terry
(C) Ulrika
(D) Vivian
(E) Rick

Clearly, Rick cannot be last since he is already fifth. So eliminate choice (E). Next, neither Terry nor Ulrika can be last since Ulrika must stand immediately behind Terry. So eliminate choices (B) and (C). Finally, Steve cannot be last, either. If he were, then he would be next to Rick, which would violate the first condition. So eliminate choice (A). Hence, by process of elimination, Vivian must be last in line. The answer is (D).

This method of elimination is the most efficient way to solve many, if not most, game questions. We will discuss this method in more detail later in the chapter.

GROUPING GAMES

Grouping games, as the term implies, require you to separate elements—typically people—into groups. Some conditions of the game can apply to entire groups only, some to elements within a group only, and some to both. This added complexity makes grouping games, in general, harder than ordering games.

Example: ***Grouping Game***

Eight people—A, B, C, D, E, F, G, and H—ride to work in three cars. Two cars each take three people, and one car takes only two people.

B rides with H.
G rides with only one other person.
F rides with two other people.

If C rides with B, all of the following are groups of people that can ride together EXCEPT:

(A) A and G
(B) G and E
(C) A, D, and E
(D) A, D, and F
(E) B, C, and H

Combining the conditions *"C rides with B"* and *"B rides with H"* gives the completed car-pool CBH. Now F and G must ride in different car-pools because G rides in a pool of two and F rides in a pool of three. However, the group ADE, in choice (C), could not ride with either F or G because in either case they would form a group of four. Hence (C) is the answer.

ASSIGNMENT GAMES

These games involve assigning characteristics to the elements, typically people. The most common task in these games is to assign a schedule. You probably have had some experience with schedules; you may have written the weekly work-schedule for a business. If so, you know how difficult the task can become, even when only a few conditions are placed on the employees: Bob will work Monday, Tuesday, or Friday only. Susan will work evenings only. Steve will not work with Bob. Add to this that the company must have a full staff weekdays, but only three people can work weekends. Scheduling games on the LSAT are similar to this. Because the conditions can apply to individuals separately, to groups of individuals, to times, to places, etc., scheduling games tend to be the most difficult—save them for last.

Example: ***Assignment Game***

The Mom & Pop liquor store employs five cashiers—Adams, Bates, Cox, Drake, and Edwards—each of whom works alone on exactly one day, Monday through Friday.

Adams will work only on Tuesday or Thursday.
Bates will not work on Monday or Wednesday.
Cox works on Friday.
Drake and Edwards do not work on consecutive days.

Which one of the following is a possible work schedule?

(A) Edwards, Bates, Adams, Drake, Cox
(B) Drake, Adams, Bates, Edwards, Cox
(C) Edwards, Adams, Cox, Bates, Drake
(D) Edwards, Adams, Drake, Bates, Cox
(E) Drake, Edwards, Bates, Adams, Cox

Begin by eliminating (A); it is not a possible work schedule since the first condition states that Adams works only on Tuesday or Thursday. Next, (B) is not a possible work schedule since the second condition states that Bates will not work on Monday or Wednesday. Next, (C) is not a possible work schedule since the third condition states that Cox works on Friday. Finally, (E) is not a possible work schedule since the last condition states that Drake and Edwards do not work on consecutive days. Thus, by process of elimination, we have learned the answer is (D).

We will thoroughly analyze each of the three major types of games. Additionally, we will study some games that don't fit neatly into this classification.

Format of the Game Section

The game section of the LSAT consists of four games, each of which has about six questions—sometimes 5 and sometimes 7. Thus, there are usually twenty-four questions. The section is 35 minutes long.

FORMAT

Game #1 (6 questions ±1)
Game #2 (6 questions ±1)
Game #3 (6 questions ±1)
Game #4 (6 questions ±1)

This means that you have a little less than nine minutes for each game. Or if you skip the most difficult game, as many people should, then you have a little less than 12 minutes for each game. If this sounds fast-paced, you're right. The LSAT is a highly "timed" test, and the game section is the most highly "timed" part.

Lawyers typically have to think quickly on their feet. This section is testing how quickly you can understand the structure of a set of relationships and how swiftly you can draw conclusions from the implications of those relationships.

Skipping a Game

Because games are difficult and time consuming, you should consider skipping the hardest one. **Do not, however, skip parts of each game; rather, skip one entire game.**

The time you save by skipping the hardest game can be used to read and solve the other games more carefully. Reading and solving the problems too quickly is the major cause of errors in this section of the test. The questions come in blocks of 6, so misreading the setup to a game can cause you to miss an entire block of 6 questions.

If you decide to skip the hardest game, you will need, of course, some criteria to determine which game is the hardest. You might think that a game with many conditions is harder than one with only a few conditions. This is not necessarily true. In fact, most often, the fewer the conditions the harder the game. Think of the conditions as clues. If you were a detective investigating a case, the more clues you had the easier the case would be to solve. The same is true for games. Furthermore, some of the conditions are often superfluous or are needed only for the last couple of questions. As mentioned before, ordering games generally are the easiest, grouping games are harder, and assignment games are the hardest.

Order of Difficulty

Unlike most standardized tests, the questions on the LSAT are not listed from the easiest to the hardest. If they were, then deciding which game to skip would be easy—skip the last game. However, this much can be said: the first game will not be the hardest and the last game will not be the easiest; do not, therefore, skip the first game. This is also true of the question-set to a game.

Reading with Precision

We are not accustomed to reading and thinking with the degree of precision required for the games. If I ask you to count from one to four, you will probably respond with: one, two, three, four. But is this the correct response? I said to count from one to four, not from one through four. So the correct response actually is one, two, three. This may seem like "splitting hairs", but it is precisely this degree of precision which must be exercised when reading the conditions of a game.

Typically, when reading, we skim the words looking for the gist of what the writer is trying to convey. However, the conditions of a game *cannot* be read in that manner. They must be read slowly and carefully, taking each word for its literal meaning—and making no unwarranted assumptions.

It may seem at times that the wording of a game is designed to trick you. It is not (except for what will be discussed later in the section *Obfuscation*). A game is a logic puzzle that must be solved by applying the fundamental principles of logic—that is, common sense—to the given conditions. If a word has two different meanings, then two different answers may be possible. For this reason, ambiguity in a game cannot be tolerated.

To avoid ambiguity, the LSAT writers always use the literal or dictionary meaning of a word.

To illustrate, take the little, nondescript word "or." We have little trouble using it in our day-to-day speech. However, it actually has two meanings, one inclusive and one exclusive. In the sentence "Susan or John may come to the party" we understand that both may come. This is the *inclusive* meaning of "or." On the other hand, in the phrase "your money or your life" we hope that the mugger intends the *exclusive* meaning of "or." That is, he does not take both our money and our life.

Unless otherwise stated, the meaning of "or" on the LSAT is inclusive.

Unwarranted Assumptions

When analyzing a game, you must not only take the meaning of the words literally but you must also take the meaning of the sentences literally. **That is, do not make any unwarranted assumptions about what a condition implies.** For example, if the setup to a problem states that five people are standing in a line and a condition states that Craig is standing behind Jane, then you *cannot* assume he is immediately behind her. There may be one or more people between them. For another example, take the word "never" in the sentence "Jane never arrives at work before Kelly." Based on this statement we cannot assume that Kelly always arrives before Jane: they may on occasion arrive at the same time. For a more subtle example, take the sentence "John will go only if Steve goes." We cannot assume that if Steve goes, then John will go too. The sentence implies only that if John left, then Steve must also have left, not necessarily vice versa.

The last two sections are not intended to imply that you should dwell on minutia. Instead, they should alert you to pay attention to the exact meanings of words and sentences. Words are used in their literal sense, not to make the conditions "tricky," but to avoid ambiguity.

Reading with Precision/Unwarranted Assumption Drill

Directions: Each condition in this exercise is followed by a series of deductions. Determine whether each deduction is valid or invalid. Answers and solutions begin on page 38.

1. **A and B are two consecutive elements in a line.**
   a. A is next to B.
   b. A is to the left of B.
   c. C is between A and B.

2. **Of four elements—A, B, C, D—in a line, B sits between A and C.**
   a. B is next to A.
   b. B is next to either A or C.

3. **Only people over eighteen years of age can enter.**
   a. A person eighteen years of age can enter.

4. **John is older than Mary who is younger than Betty, and Robert is not older than Mary.**
   a. Mary is younger than John.
   b. Mary is older than Robert.
   c. Betty is older than Robert.

5. **To be in the theater, each child (a person less than 13 years old) must be accompanied by an adult.**
   a. Johnny who is ten could be in the theater by himself.
   b. John who is thirty-five could be in the theater by himself.

6. **If it is cloudy, then Biff is not at the beach.**
   a. If it is sunny, Biff is at the beach.
   b. If Biff is not at the beach, it is cloudy.
   c. If Biff is at the beach, it is not cloudy.

7. **I will take the LSAT unless I am not prepared.**
   a. I prepared thoroughly, so I took the LSAT.
   b. I prepared thoroughly, but I did not take the LSAT.

8. **On a line A and B are two spaces apart.**
   a. Two people sit between A and B.

9. **Only Bob works evenings.**
   a. Bob works only evenings.

Logical Connectives

While no training in formal logic is required for the LSAT, essentially it is a logic test. So some knowledge of formal logic will give you a definite advantage.

To begin, consider the seemingly innocuous connective "if..., then...." Its meaning has perplexed both the philosopher and the layman through the ages.

The statement "if A, then B" means by definition "if A is true, then B must be true as well," and nothing more.

For example, we know from experience that if it is raining, then it is cloudy. So if we see rain falling past the window, we can validly conclude that it is cloudy outside.

There are three statements that can be derived from the implication "if A, then B"; two are invalid, and one is valid.

From "if A, then B" you *cannot* conclude "if B, then A." For example, if it is cloudy, you cannot conclude that it is raining. From experience, this example is obviously true; it seems silly that anyone could commit such an error. However, when the implication is unfamiliar to us, this fallacy can be tempting.

Another, and not as obvious, fallacy derived from "if A, then B" is to conclude "if not A, then not B." Again, consider the weather example. If it is not raining, you cannot conclude that it is not cloudy—it may still be overcast. This fallacy is popular with students.

Finally, there is one statement that *is* logically equivalent to "if A, then B." Namely, **"if not B, then not A."** This is called the **contrapositive**, and it is very important.

If there is a key to performing well on the LSAT, it is the contrapositive.

To show the contrapositive's validity, we once again appeal to our weather example. If it is not cloudy, then from experience we know that it cannot possibly be raining.

We now know two things about the implication "if A, then B":

1) If A is true, then B must be true.
2) If B is false, then A must be false.

If you assume no more than these two facts about an implication, then you will not fall for the fallacies that trap many students.

We often need to rephrase a statement when it's worded in a way that obscures the information it contains. The following formulas are very useful for rewording and simplifying the conditions of a game.

On the LSAT, as in everyday speech, two negatives make a positive—they cancel each other out.

not(not A) = A

Example:

"It is not the case that John did not pass the LSAT"

means the same thing as

"John did pass the LSAT."

■

The statement "if A, then B; and if B, then A" is logically equivalent to "A if and only if B." Think of "if and only if" as an equal sign: if one side is true, then the other side must be true, and if one side is false, then the other side must be false.

(If A, then B; and if B, then A) = (A if and only if B)

A if and only if B	
A	B
True	True
False	False

Example:

"If it is sunny, then Biff is at the beach; and if Biff is at the beach, then it is sunny"

is logically equivalent to

"It is sunny if and only if Biff is at the beach." ■

"A only if B" means that when A occurs, B must also occur. That is, "if A, then B."

A only if B = if A, then B

Example:

"John will do well on the LSAT only if he studies hard"

is logically equivalent to

"If John did well on the LSAT, then he studied hard."

(Note: Students often wrongly interpret this statement to mean *"if John studies hard, then he will do well on the LSAT."* There is no such guarantee. The only guarantee is that if he does not study hard, then he will not do well.) ■

The statement "A unless B" means that A is true in all cases, except when B is true. In other words if B is false, then A must be true. That is, if not B, then A.

A unless B = if not B, then A

Example:

"John did well on the LSAT unless he partied the night before"

is logically equivalent to

"If John did not party the night before, then he did well on the LSAT." ■

The two statements "if A, then B" and "if B, then C" can be combined to give "if A, then C." This is called the transitive property.

("if A, then B" and "if B, then C") = ("if A, then C")

Example:

From the two statements

"if John did well on the LSAT, then he studied hard" and *"if John studied hard, then he did not party the night before the test"*

you can conclude that

"if John did well on the LSAT, then he did not party the night before the test." ■

These fundamental principles of logic are never violated in either the games or the arguments.* Hence by using the above logical connectives, you can safely reword any statement on the LSAT.

Diagramming

Virtually every game can be solved more easily and efficiently by using a diagram. Unless you have a remarkable memory and can process reams of information in your head, you *must* draw a diagram. Because of the effectiveness of diagrams, games are the best candidates for improvement. A well-constructed diagram can change a convoluted, unwieldy mass of information into an easily read list. In fact, from a well-constructed diagram, you can often read-off the answers without any additional thought. Before we begin studying how to construct diagrams, we need to develop some facility for creating and manipulating symbols.

Symbols

The ability to symbolize sentences is one of the most important skills you need to develop for the LSAT.

A good symbol is complete; it summarizes all the relevant information in the sentence. It is succinct. And it is functional, easy to use. The last condition makes creating symbols an art. A good symbol helps you organize your thoughts and frees your mind from the fetters of indecision.

Five basic symbols are used throughout this book. They are

Symbol	Meaning
&	and
or	or
~	not
—>	If..., then...
( )	parentheses

I. The ampersand symbol, &, connects two statements of equal rank. The two statements

"Rob sits next to Jane" and *"Susan sits next to Adam"*

can be translated as

(RJ) & (SA)

Two statements joined by "&" will be true as a group only when both are true.

---

* It is *conceivable* that these principles of logic might be violated in a reading passage because rhetoric is often quoted there; however, I've yet to see it occur.

II. The symbol "or" also connects two statements of equal rank. The above statement can be symbolized using "or" as

(RJ) or (SA)

For an *or*-statement to be true, only one of the two statements need be true, though both can be. For example, the statement *"it is raining" or "it is not raining"* is true even though one of the statements must be false. This makes an *or*-statement much weaker than an &-statement.

III. Placing ~ in front of any true statement makes the statement false, and vice versa. The symbol ~ can be read as "it is not the case that." For example, the symbol ~(RJ) translates as "it is not the case that R sits next to J."

IV. The *if..., then...* symbol (—>) causes much consternation, even though we are rarely confused by its meaning in everyday speech. It is true in all cases, except when the statement on the left side is true and the statement on the right side is false.* As mentioned in the section Logical Connectives "if P, then Q" is logically equivalent to "if not Q, then not P"; the latter is the contrapositive.

For example, the statement

"if it is sunny, then Biff is at the beach"

is logically equivalent to

"if Biff is not at the beach, then it is not sunny."

Sometimes you can use this equivalency to simplify a convoluted condition. For example, the condition "if Jane does not go, then Steve will not go" can be simplified to "if Steve goes, then Jane goes," or in symbols

S—>J

V. Parentheses clarify a symbol statement's meaning in the same way that commas clarify sentences. The symbol statement A&B—>C is ambiguous; we don't know whether it means

(A&B)—>C

or

A&(B—>C)

Sometimes parentheses are used even when they are not truly needed. For example, the symbol statement ~A&B is not technically ambiguous; however, it is less likely to be misread when written (~A)&B. Now clearly the negation applies *only* to the A.

* For a thorough discussion of "if..., then..." see Logical Connectives, page 26.

Symbol Exercise

Directions: Translate the given statements into symbols. Note: There is no "best" symbol. However, you should choose one that is short yet clear. Solutions begin on page 39.

1. On a line, B is to the immediate right of A. **Symbol:**	8. Four people are standing in a line. If A is last, then A must be next to either B or C. **Symbol:**
2. On a line, B is to the right of A. **Symbol:**	9. Four people are standing in a line. A is next to B if and only if C is last. **Symbol:**
3. On a line, B is to the right of either A or C, but not both. **Symbol:**	10. Of three people, Bob is older than Susan but younger than Ted. **Symbol:**
4. On a line, A is not next to B. **Symbol:**	11. A and B are before C, and C is before X and Y. **Symbol:**
5. On a line, B and A are two spaces apart. **Symbol:**	12. At a table, if Bob sits next to Ted, Alice does not sit next to Carol. **Symbol:**
6. If A, then B. **Symbol:**	13. At a table, Mr. Williams sits directly opposite from Mrs. Adams. **Symbol:**
7. A only if B. **Symbol:**	

Advanced Problems

14. A and B cannot serve on a panel unless they serve together. **Symbol:**	18. Stan will only fly in either plane 1 or plane 2. **Symbol:**
15. John lives two floors above Craig. **Symbol:**	19. No one but union members can work. **Symbol:**
16. Nancy and Tom do not both enter the race. **Symbol:**	20. There are exactly two full working days between the day Mike works and the day Jane works, and Mike always works before Jane during a single workweek. **Symbol:**
17. No one drives without a driver's license. **Symbol:**	

Diagramming Continued

As stated before, diagramming is **the** way to solve nearly every game. This section covers how to construct an efficient and functional diagram. The process is very mechanical.

We begin with the setup to a game. The setup gives the context or background for a game. The elements, often people, are named here, too. We abbreviate names by using the first letter of the name. Kindly, the LSAT writers use names that begin with different letters.

For example, we may be told that six people—Jack, Kathy, Larry, Mary, Nick, and Olivia—are seated, evenly spaced, around a circular table. We let J, K, L, M, N, and O stand for their names.

Next, take the conditions and turn them into symbols. For example, suppose for the above setup we are told that

Jack sits at the "top" of the table.
Jack sits directly opposite Larry.
Mary does not sit next to Larry.

The first condition, "Jack sits at the 'top' of the table," is naturally described as **J = top**. The second condition, "Jack sits directly opposite Larry," can be symbolized as **J<—>L** (where the *arrow* means "sits directly opposite"). Finally, the third condition, "Mary does not sit next to Larry," can be written as **M ≠ L**. [Another possible symbol is ~(ML). You may prefer to use this symbol or to create one of your own. The symbol you choose is irrelevant so long as it is short and functional.]

Adding these symbol statements to our previous work yields the following schematic:

J K L M N O
J = top
J<—>L
M ≠ L

Note, the elements O, K, and N are "independent" because no conditions refer directly to them. In general, independent elements can be placed in more positions on a diagram than dependent elements. Think of independent elements as "wild cards".

Now, we need a diagram to complete our scheme. To this end, draw a circle with three spokes inside, and place it below the schematic:

J K L M N O (K, N, O are "wild")
J = top
J<—>L
M ≠ L

Next, we come to the all-important decision—in what order do we place the conditions on the diagram. The following rules should guide your decision.

1. **First, place conditions which fix the position of an element.**
   Examples: Allison is second from the left.
   Steve works on Monday only.

2. **Next, place conditions which limit the positions an element may have.**
   Examples: Allison is either the second or third person from the left.
   Steve works only the night shift.

3. **Then, place conditions which connect two or more elements.**
   Examples: Allison sits directly opposite Jane.
   Steve works only when Bob works.

4. **Finally, on the diagram designate any place an element *cannot* be.**
   (This is the negative counterpart of rule 2, and it is much weaker.)
   Examples: Allison cannot sit in an even numbered chair.
   Steve does not work when Bob works.

Short Drill on Order of Placement

Directions: Using the guidelines on this page, determine the order in which each of the following sets of conditions should be placed on a diagram. Answers and solutions are on page 41.

1. Six students—John, Kelly, Laura, Mick, Nina, Sean—took a test. The following is known about their grades:

   (A) Neither John nor Laura received a B.
   (B) Mick received either an A or a B.
   (C) Kelly received the lowest grade.

2. Commuters P, Q, R, S, and T board a bus. The bus makes six subsequent stops. Each commuter gets off at a different stop, and at one of the stops no one gets off.

   (A) P always gets off at an even numbered stop.
   (B) Q always gets off second.
   (C) S always gets off after Q, and none of the other commuters gets off the bus at a stop that comes after Q's stop but before S's stop.

3. On one side of a street there are five houses, each of which is home to exactly one of five families: the Howards, Ingrams, Jones, Kilpatricks, Leoffs. The street runs west to east.

   (A) The Leoffs do not live in the last house.
   (B) The Howards live in the second house from the west end of the street.
   (C) The Kilpatricks live east of the Howards but west of the Ingrams.

4. Six people—M, N, O, P, Q, R—are seated around a circular table.

   (A) M sits directly opposite N.
   (B) Neither O nor P sits next to M.

Diagramming Continued

Now let's apply these rules to the conditions of our game. **J = top** is the only condition that fixes the position of an element, so place it on the diagram first:

J

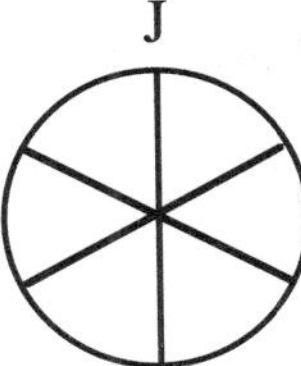

Next, scan the conditions for one that limits the placement of an element. There are none. So the second rule does not apply.

Then, scan the conditions for one that connects two or more elements. The condition **J<—>L** connects J and L. Place it on the diagram as follows:

J

L

Finally, scan the conditions for one that tells where an element can <u>not</u> be. The last condition, **M ≠ L** states that M cannot be next to L. Thus, our final diagram looks like this:

J K L M N O (K, N, O "wild")
J = top
J<—>L
M ≠ L

J

~M ~M

L

This diagram is self-contained. There is no need to refer to the original problem. Looking back should be avoided whenever possible.

Readily Derived Conditions

Before turning to the questions, check whether any further conditions can be easily derived from the given conditions. Suppose in addition to the conditions given in the game above, you were told that K and O do not sit next to each other. You could then deduce that K and O sit on opposite sides of the base axis **J<—>L** since there are only two seats on either side of this axis. Place the derived conditions on the diagram before turning to the questions. Do not, however, spend an inordinate amount of time on this step.

<u>Do not erase</u> previously derived diagrams; they are often useful for later questions.

Keep your symbols and diagrams as simple and functional as possible. **Warning:** Some books suggest diagrams which appear elegant but soon prove too complicated to actually use. A complex "elimination grid" may be very effective in answering the questions, but it probably cannot be constructed and applied to all the questions in less than nine minutes. Your diagrams should be simple and able to evolve with changing conditions.

Obfuscation

To make a game harder, the LSAT writers have two methods available. One is to make the relationships between the elements more complex and subtle. This is the hard way. Working out all the connections possible for a complex condition can be very time consuming, and thinking up a subtle condition can require much creative inspiration. The other way is to obscure the conditions and answers. This is the easy way.

The LSAT writers do not resort to obfuscation as often with games as they do with arguments because games are inherently difficult, whereas arguments are inherently easy. Still, five tactics are occasionally used.

With games, the most common obfuscation ploy is the **leading question.** The question "Which one of the following must be false?" *leads* you to look directly for the *false* answer. However, it is often easier if you reword this type of question as "All of the following could be true EXCEPT?" Then search for and eliminate the true answer-choices.

It is much harder to make a difficult game than it is to solve one. The easiest way to make a game harder is to **convolute the wording of a condition**. For example, the complex condition

"if O is off, then N is off; if O is on, then N is on"

means merely that

"O is on if and only if N is on,"

or even more simply

"O and N are on at the same time."

Often information contained in a condition is obscured by wording the condition in the negative when it would be more clearly and naturally worded in the positive. In these cases, use the contrapositive to rephrase the statement. For example, the condition "If Carl Lewis enters the 100-meter dash, then he will not enter the long jump" may release more relevant information when reworded as "If Carl Lewis enters the long jump, then he will not enter the 100-meter dash."

Adding many conditions to a game can obscure the more important ones. Typically, a game consists of two or three core conditions from which nearly all the questions can be answered. Master these few conditions and you've mastered the game. To obscure this fact, the LSAT writers sometimes **surround the core conditions with other conditions that relate to only one or two questions, if any.**

Another way to make a game harder, or at least longer, is **to word a question so that you must check every answer-choice** (see Indirect Proof, page 51). For example, questions such as "All of the following could be true EXCEPT" often require you to check every answer-choice. Unfortunately, there is no effective countermeasure to this tactic.* If pressed for time, you should skip this type of question. Remember, whether a question is short and easy or long and difficult, it is worth the same number of points.

Advanced Concepts:

The last and most pernicious obfuscating tactic is **to apply subtle changes to the standard wording of a question**. We have already seen an example of a question with the wording "Which one of the following is a complete and accurate list of . . . ?" In this case, the correct answer must include *all* the possibilities. But sometimes (though rarely) the verb "is" is replaced with "could be": "Which one of the following *could be* a complete and accurate list of . . . ?" In this case, the correct answer could include all, some, or even none of the possibilities. Mercifully, this tactic is not often used. But it can occur, so be alert to it.

As you work through the examples and exercises in this chapter, notice how the five tactics of obfuscation are used.

* Rewording the question as "Which one of the following is false?" usually does not help. In fact, the latter type of question is often reworded as the former.

Points to Remember

1. Unless you are one of the few who have a knack for games, you should skip the hardest one. This will leave you with about twelve minutes per game, instead of only nine.

2. The three major types of games are

   Ordering Games
   Grouping Games
   Assignment Games

3. Although the games are not presented in ascending order of difficulty, the first game will not be the hardest and the last game will not be the easiest.

4. Do not assume that a game with many conditions is harder than one with only a few.

5. In general, ordering games are the easiest, and assignment games are the hardest.

6. Read the conditions to a game very carefully, and avoid making any unwarranted assumptions about what they imply.

7. A—>B is logically equivalent to its contrapositive ~B—>~A. It is not logically equivalent to the following fallacies:

   ~A—>~B (Invalid)
   B—>A (Invalid)

8. The following logical connectives are equivalent:

   ~(~A) = A
   (A—>B and B—>A) = (A<—>B)
   (A only if B) = (A—>B)
   (A—>B and B—>C) = (A—>C)
   (A unless B) = (~B—>A)

9. On the LSAT, the meaning of "or" is inclusive, unless stated otherwise.

10. Reword convoluted questions.

11. The questions to a game are independent of one another.

12. Virtually every game should be solved with a diagram.

13. When deciding the order in which to place elements on a diagram, use the following guidelines.

    First: Place any element whose position is fixed.
    Second: Place any element whose possible positions are limited.
    Third: Place any element whose position is connected to one or more other elements.
    Last: Note any place an element cannot be.

14. In general, independent elements can be placed in more positions than dependent elements. Think of independent elements as "wild cards".

15. When answering the questions, refer to the diagram. Avoid returning to the original problem.

16. Before turning to the questions, note any readily derived conditions.

17. Keep your diagrams simple and functional.

18. Do not erase previously derived diagrams.

19. The LSAT writers use 5 methods to obfuscate a game:
    a. The leading question.
    b. Convoluting the wording of a condition.
    c. Surrounding the core conditions with superfluous conditions.
    d. Wording a question so that you must check every answer-choice.
    e. Applying subtle changes to a question's standard wording.

Solutions to Reading with Precision Drill

1. a. **Valid**
   Saying that A is next to B is equivalent to saying that A and B are consecutive.
   b. **Invalid**
   Although A is written to the left of B, we cannot assume that its position on the line is left of B.
   c. **Invalid**
   If C were between A and B, then A and B would not be consecutive.

2. a. **Invalid**
   We know only that B is between A and C, not whether B is next to A. (The ordering could be ADBC.)
   b. **Valid**
   D is the only element which can separate B from either A or C. Therefore, B must be next to either A or C—though not necessarily both.

3. a. **Invalid**
   A person eighteen years of age is not over eighteen.

4. a. **Valid**
   "John is older than Mary" is logically equivalent to "Mary is younger than John."
   b. **Invalid**
   We know only that Robert is not older than Mary; they may be the same age.
   c. **Valid**
   Since Betty is older than Mary who is older than or the same age as Robert, Betty must be older than Robert.

5. a. **Invalid**
   According to the statement, he must be with an adult.
   b. **Valid**
   We know only that children must be accompanied by an adult; the reciprocal relation that adults be accompanied by children need not be true.

6. a. **Invalid**
   We know only that if it is in fact cloudy, then Biff is not at the beach. We know nothing about where he is when it is sunny.
   b. **Invalid**
   Again, we know only that if it is cloudy then Biff is not at the beach. It may be sunny, and Biff may decide not to go to the beach.
   c. **Valid**
   If it were in fact cloudy, this would contradict the premise, "if it is cloudy, then Biff is not at the beach."

7. a. **Valid**
   Generally, "unless" means "if...not." So the sentence can be recast as "I will take the LSAT if I am prepared." (Note two negatives make a positive, so the phrase "if I am *not not* prepared" was simplified to "if I am prepared.") With this interpretation of the sentence, we see that the two statements are consistent. In fact, the second statement necessarily follows from the first.
   b. **Invalid**
   This contradicts the premise of the statement.

8. a. **Invalid**
Many students confuse these two conditions. They do not mean the same thing. "A and B are two spaces apart" means that <u>only one</u> spot separates them.

1 sp	2 sp	
A	___	B

9. a. **Invalid**
"Only Bob works evenings" means only that no one else works evenings. Bob could still work an afternoon shift in addition to his evening shift.

Answers to Symbol Exercise

Statement	Symbol
1. On a line, B is to the immediate right of A.	**AB**
2. On a line, B is to the right of A.	**A...B**
3. On a line, B is to the right of either A or C, but not both.	**A...B...C** (with a line linking A and C)

Explanation: The statement is equivalent to "B is between A and C," which can be symbolized as A...B...C (with a line linking A and C). The line linking A with C, the "flip-flop" symbol, indicates that A and C can be interchanged. The symbol ABC (with a line linking A and C) would be misleading because it implies that B is next to A and C, which cannot be assumed.

4. On a line, A is not next to B.	**~(AB)**

Explanation: Once you become accustomed to the fact that the order could be reversed, you won't need to write the flip-flop symbol.

5. On a line, B and A are two spaces apart.	**A __ B**

Explanation: Many people incorrectly symbolize this as A __ __ B because they read "two spaces apart" as "separated by two spaces" (see Reading with Precision, page 25).

6. If A, then B.	**A—>B**
7. A only if B.	**A—>B**

Explanation: See Logical Connectives, page 28.

8. Four people are standing in a line. If A is last, then A must be next to either B or C.	**(A=last)—>(AB or AC)**

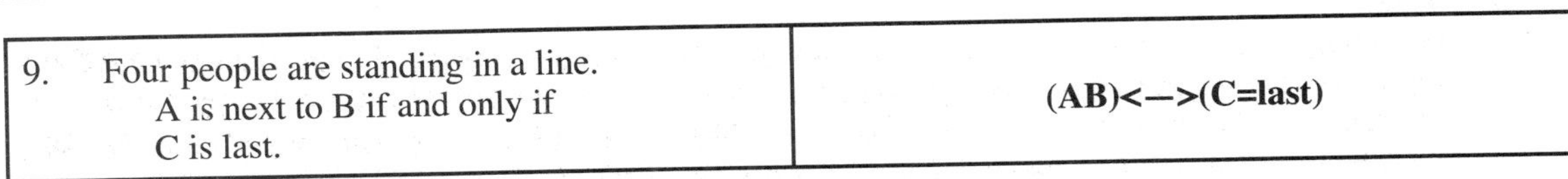

9. Four people are standing in a line. A is next to B if and only if C is last.	**(AB)<—>(C=last)**

Explanation: This is a double implication. That is, if A is next to B, then C is last; and if C is last, then A is next to B. Remember the symbol AB means that A is next to B, though not necessarily in that order.

10. Of three people, Bob is older than Susan but younger than Ted.	**TBS**
11. A and B are before C, and C is before X and Y.	**(A&B) > C > (X&Y)**
12. At a table, if Bob sits next to Ted, Alice does not sit next to Carol.	**(BT)—>~(AC)**
13. At a table, Mr. Williams sits directly opposite from Mrs. Adams.	**W<—>A** (Here, <—> means "opposite to")
14. A and B cannot serve on a panel unless they serve together.	**(A=P)<—>(B=P),** (where P stands for "is on the panel")
15. John lives two floors above Craig.	**J** □ **C** Note that only one floor separates J and C—not two floors.
16. Nancy and Tom do not both enter the race.	**N—>~T** (T—>~N would also work.)
17. No one drives without a driver's license.	**(A=D)—>(A=DL)** (where D stands for "drives" and DL stands for " has a driver's license")
18. Stan will only fly in either plane 1 or plane 2.	**(S=F)—>(S=1 or S=2)** (where F stands for "flying")
19. No one but union members can work.	**(A=W)—>(A=U)** (where W means "works" and U means "is a member of the union")
20. There are exactly two full working days between the day Mike works and the day Jane works, and Mike always works before Jane during a single workweek.	**M __ __ J**

Solutions to Order of Placement Drill

1. (C) first. (B) second. (A) last.

   Condition (C) fixes Kelly's grade; place it first. Next, condition (B) limits the possible grades that Mick received; place it second. Next, none of the conditions connects two or more elements, so Guideline 3 does not apply. Finally, condition (A) states what grade John and Laura did not receive; place it last.

2. (B) first. (A) second. (C) third and fourth.

   Because Q may get off before or after the stop at which no one gets off, two diagrams must be drawn. On each diagram, the elements should be placed as follows: Place condition (B) first since it fixes the position of Q. Next, place condition (A) since it limits the possible stops at which P can get off. Then, place the first part of condition (C) since it connects the two elements S and Q. Finally, place the second part of condition (C) since it states where the elements P, R, and T cannot get off.

3. (B) first. (C) second. (A) last.

   Place condition (B) first; it fixes the home of the Howards. No condition limits where a family lives, e.g., the Jones live in either the first or second house from the west end of the street. So Guideline 2 does not apply, and we turn to Guideline 3. Place condition (C) next; it connects the Kilpatricks with the Howard and the Ingrams. Finally, place condition (A); it states where the Leoffs do not live—the last house.

4. (A) first. (B) second.

   Neither condition fixes the position of any person, nor does either limit the places where any person may sit. So Guidelines 1 and 2 do not apply. Condition (A) connects M and N, so place it first. Condition (B) states where O and P may not be—next to M, so place it last.

LINEAR ORDERING

Introduction

Linear ordering games are the easiest games, and fortunately they also appear the most often. They can be classified according to whether they order elements spatially or sequentially.

- Spatial games
- Hybrid games
- Sequential games

We will study in turn each of the three types of linear ordering games. At the end of most lessons, you will find a warm-up drill. The drills are not remedial. In fact, some are quite challenging. They are designed to bring to the fore some of the subtle issues with which you will have to contend when solving a game, but in a more tractable form. Unlike LSAT games, the drills are presented in ascending order of difficulty. Following the warm-up drill is a "mentor" exercise. A mentor exercise is a full-length game which offers hints, partial solutions, and insight in the right hand column. You should work through each mentor exercise slowly, giving yourself time to study the game carefully. Finally, several full length games are presented for you to solve on your own. If you intend to skip a game when you take the LSAT, give yourself 12 minutes to complete the exercise; otherwise you have only 9 minutes.

It is essential that you time yourself during this exercise, because time is the greatest obstacle when solving games. After studying games for a short while, students often develop an unwarranted self-confidence. Given sufficient time to solve them, many games appear simple. Be forewarned that you must not only master how to solve games—you must master how to solve them rapidly. It is one matter to solve a game with ample time in the quiet and comfort of your home; it is quite another to solve it in a room filled with 100 other people—all racing against the clock.

Spatial Ordering

THE LINE-UP

As the term "line-up" suggests, these games involve ordering elements in a line, from left to right or from front to back.

Before we begin, we need to study the vocabulary peculiar to these games.

Condition	Meaning
A sits next to B. A sits immediately next to B.	Both conditions mean that no one sits between A and B. Although A is to the left of B in the text, that order cannot be assumed on the line. The phrase "immediately next to" is redundant; however, that style is often used on the LSAT.
B sits immediately between A and C. B sits between and next to A and C. B sits directly between A and C.	All three conditions mean that no element separates B from A, nor B from C.
Two spaces separate A and B. A and B are two spaces apart.	Students often confuse these two conditions. They do **not** mean the same thing. "A and B are two spaces apart" means that *only one* spot separates them. 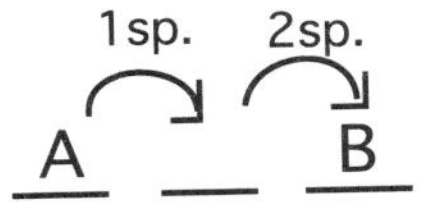 1sp. 2sp. A __ B

It is essential that you master the similarities and distinctions described above. In addition to testing analytical skills, games measure your ability to notice subtle distinctions. Further, since game questions typically appear in blocks of six, misinterpreting even one condition can cost you six questions! Following is a common ordering game; one of this type—or a close variant—has occurred on every recent LSAT.

Line-up Game

There are five people—Bugsy, Nelson, Dutch, Clyde, and Gotti—in a police line-up standing in spaces numbered 1 through 6, from left to right. The following conditions apply:

There is always one empty space.
Clyde is not standing in space 1, 3, or 5.
Gotti is the third person from the left.
Bugsy is standing to the immediate left of Nelson.

1. Nelson CANNOT stand in which one of the following spaces?

(A) 2
(B) 3
(C) 4
(D) 5
(E) 6

2. Which one of the following is a possible ordering of the 5 people from left to right?

(A) Clyde, empty, Dutch, Gotti, Bugsy, Nelson
(B) Bugsy, Clyde, Nelson, Gotti, Dutch, empty
(C) Dutch, Bugsy, Gotti, Nelson, empty, Clyde
(D) Dutch, Clyde, Gotti, empty, Nelson, Bugsy
(E) Bugsy, Nelson, Gotti, Clyde, Dutch, empty

3. If space 6 is empty, which one of the following must be false?

(A) Clyde stands in space 4.
(B) Dutch stands in space 4.
(C) Clyde is to the left of Nelson.
(D) Clyde is to the right of Dutch.
(E) Nelson stands in space 2.

4. Which one of the following spaces CANNOT be empty?

(A) 1
(B) 2
(C) 3
(D) 4
(E) 5

5. If Clyde stands in space 6, Dutch must stand in space

(A) 3 or 4
(B) 5 or 6
(C) 1 or 2
(D) 2 or 3
(E) 4 or 5

Following the strategies developed earlier, we abbreviate the names by using the first letter of the name and then symbolize the conditions. *"Clyde is not standing in space 1, 3, or 5"* is naturally symbolized as **C ≠ 1, 3, 5**. *"Gotti is the third person from the left"* is naturally symbolized as **G = 3rd**. Note: the fact that Gotti is third does not force him into space 3—he could stand in spaces 3 or 4. *"Bugsy is standing to the immediate left of Nelson"* is symbolized as **BN**.

Our diagram will consist of six dashed lines, numbered 1 through 6 from left to right. Summarizing this information gives the following schematic:

B N D C G
C ≠ 1, 3, 5
G = 3rd
BN

_1_ _2_ _3_ _4_ _5_ _6_

Now, we decide the most effective order for placing the elements on the diagram. Following the guidelines on page 33, we look for a condition that fixes the position of an element. There is none. Next, we look for a condition that limits the position of an element. The second condition, *"Gotti is the third person from the left,"* limits Gotti to spaces 3 and 4. This condition, as often happens with ordering games, generates two diagrams: one with the empty space to Gotti's left and one with the empty space to his right:

Diagram I ___ ___ ___ _G_ ___ ___

Diagram II ___ ___ _G_ ___ ___ ___

Next, we look for a condition that connects two or more people. The last condition, **BN**, connects B with N. However, at this stage we cannot place it on the diagram. Finally, we look for a condition that states where a person cannot be standing. The first condition states that Clyde cannot be standing in space 1, 3, or 5. Noting this on the diagram yields

BNDCG (D "wild")
C ≠ 1, 3, 5
G = 3rd
BN

Diagram I _~C_ ___ _~C_ _G_ _~C_ ___

Diagram II _~C_ ___ _G_ ___ _~C_ ___

(Note: D is "wild" because the conditions do not refer to him. Thus D can stand in more positions than any other person.)

This diagram is self-contained. There is no need to refer to the original problem. If possible, always avoid rereading the problem. No further conditions can be derived, so we turn to the questions.

1. Nelson CANNOT stand in which one of the following spaces?

(A) 2
(B) 3
(C) 4
(D) 5
(E) 6

The method of solution to this problem is rather mechanical: We merely place Nelson in one of the spaces offered. Then check whether it is possible to place the other people in the line-up without violating any initial condition. If so, then we eliminate that answer-choice. Then place Nelson in another space offered, and repeat the process.

To that end, place Nelson in space 2 in Diagram II:

_~C_ _N_ _G_ ___ _~C_ ___

From the condition **BN**, we know that B must be in space 1:

_B_ _N_ _G_ ___ _~C_ ___

Now D could stand in space 4, and C could stand in space 6—both without violating any initial condition:

_B_ _N_ _G_ _D_ _X_ _C_ (Where X means "empty.")

This diagram is consistent with the initial conditions. So N *could* stand in space 2. This eliminates choice (A).

Next, place Nelson in space 4. Then Diagram I is violated since G is already in space 4, and Diagram II is also violated since there is no room for the condition **BN**:

B?
___ ___ _G_ _N_ ___ ___

The answer is (C).

As you read the remaining solutions, note the determining power of the condition **BN**.

2. Which one of the following is a possible ordering of the 5 people from left to right?

(A) Clyde, empty, Dutch, Gotti, Bugsy, Nelson
(B) Bugsy, Clyde, Nelson, Gotti, Dutch, empty
(C) Dutch, Bugsy, Gotti, Nelson, empty, Clyde
(D) Dutch, Clyde, Gotti, empty, Nelson, Bugsy
(E) Bugsy, Nelson, Gotti, Clyde, Dutch, empty

This problem is best solved by the method of elimination. To apply this method take a condition; test it against each answer-choice, eliminating any that violate it. Then take another condition; test it against the remaining answer-choices, eliminating any that violate it. Continue until only one answer-choice remains. Many students apply every condition to the first answer-choice, then every condition to the second answer-choice, and so on. This should be avoided since it's inefficient; however, sometimes there is no other option. Because this question type is relatively easy, it often is the first or second question asked.

The first condition contradicts choice (A) since Clyde cannot be first. It does not contradict the other choices. So eliminate (A) only. The second condition contradicts choice (B) since Gotti must be 3rd. It does not contradict the remaining choices. So eliminate (B) only. The third condition contradicts choices (C) and (D) since in neither choice is Bugsy to the immediate left of Nelson. It does not contradict the remaining choice. So eliminate (C) and (D) only. Thus, by process of elimination, we have learned the answer is (E).

To answer this question, we had to test all the conditions; often, however, we will find the answer before testing the last condition.

3. If space 6 is empty, which one of the following must be false?

(A) Clyde stands in space 4.
(B) Dutch stands in space 4.
(C) Clyde is to the left of Nelson.
(D) Clyde is to the right of Dutch.
(E) Nelson stands in space 2.

The structure of this question is awkward—the correct answer will always make a false statement! The question is more tractable when rephrased as "All of the following could be true EXCEPT." Now, merely test each answer-choice against the initial conditions until you find the choice that violates one or more conditions.

Adding the supplementary condition, "space 6 is empty," to the original diagrams gives

Diagram I ~C ___ ~C G ~C X

Diagram II ~C ___ G ___ ~C X

In Diagram I, the only space open for C is space 2:

___ C ___ G ___ X

Clearly, this diagram does not leave room for the condition **BN**. So we eliminate Diagram I.

Next, test each answer-choice against Diagram II, starting with (A). Place Clyde in space 4 as follows:

___ ___ G C ___ X

Now the condition **BN** forces B and N into spaces 1 and 2, respectively, which in turn forces D into space 5. So our uniquely determined diagram is

B N G C D X

This diagram does not violate any initial condition. Hence Clyde could stand in space 4. So eliminate choice (A).

Next, turning to choice (B), place Dutch in space 4:

~C ___ G D ~C X

The condition **BN** forces B and N into spaces 1 and 2, respectively:

B N G D ___ X

But this diagram forces C into space 5, violating the condition **C ≠ 1, 3, 5**. Hence D cannot stand in space 4, and the answer is (B).

The above method of analysis is what mathematicians and logicians call an *"indirect proof"*. To apply the method, assume an answer-choice is possible. Then check whether that leads to the desired result. If not, eliminate it. Then choose another answer-choice and repeat the process. Continue until either the choice with the desired result is found or until only one remains. This method of elimination is not as efficient as the previous one, because typically every condition must be tested against one answer-choice before considering the next answer-choice. Sometimes, however, this is the only method available.

4. Which one of the following spaces CANNOT be empty?

(A) 1
(B) 2
(C) 3
(D) 4
(E) 5

Assume that space 1 is empty. Then in Diagram I, the condition **BN** can be placed in spaces 2 and 3, D can be placed in space 5, and C can be placed in space 6—all without violating any initial condition:

X B N G D C

Thus space 1 *could be* empty. This eliminates (A).

Next, assume that space 2 is empty. In Diagram I, this forces **BN** into spaces 5 and 6:

___ X ___ G B N

However, this diagram does not leave room for C (recall **C ≠ 1, 3, 5**). Diagram I is thus impossible when space 2 is empty. Turning to Diagram II, we see immediately that space 2 cannot be empty, for this would make G second, violating the condition **G = 3rd**. Hence Diagram II is also impossible when space 2 is empty. Thus space 2 *cannot* be empty, and the answer is (B).

5. If Clyde stands in space 6, Dutch must stand in space

(A) 3 or 4
(B) 5 or 6
(C) 1 or 2
(D) 2 or 3
(E) 4 or 5

Adding the new condition, **C = 6th**, to the original diagrams yields

Diagram I ___ ___ ___ G ___ C

Diagram II ___ ___ G ___ ___ C

In both diagrams, **BN** must come before G, and D must come after G, to insure that G is 3rd. This forces D into space 5 in Diagram I and into either space 4 or 5 in Diagram II. In either position, D does not violate any initial condition. Hence the answer is (E).

Points to Remember

1. To apply the method of elimination, take a condition. Then test it against each answer-choice, eliminating any that violate it. Then take another condition; test it against the remaining answer-choices, eliminating any that violate it, and so on, until only one answer-choice remains.

   Do not, as many students do, apply all the conditions to the first answer-choice; then, all the conditions to the second answer-choice, and so on. Such a procedure is inefficient.

2. To apply the method of "indirect proof," assume that a particular answer-choice is possible. Then check whether that leads to the desired result. If not, eliminate it. Then assume that another answer-choice is possible and repeat the process. Continue until the answer-choice with the desired result is found or until only one remains.

   This method of elimination is not as efficient as Point #1, because usually every condition must be tested against one answer-choice before testing the next answer-choice. However, sometimes this is the only method available.

Warm-Up Drills

Answers and solutions begin on page 66.

Drill A

Four people—A, B, C, and D—are standing in a line. For each of the following conditions count the number of orderings possible.

1. A and D are at either end of the line.
2. B is immediately between A and C.
3. B is between A and C.
4. There are no conditions on the people.

Drill B

Four books are arranged on a book shelf. The positions of the books are numbered 1 through 4, from left to right. For each of the following pairs of conditions, count the number of orderings possible.

1. A is left of B.
   B is between C and D.
2. A is first.
   If C is left of B, then C is next to A.
3. C sits to the right of B.
   If B sits next to C, then B sits next to D.

Mentor Exercise

Directions: Each group of questions is based on a set of conditions. In answering some of the questions, it may be useful to draw a rough diagram. Choose the response that most accurately and completely answers each question. Hints, insights, partial solutions, and answers are provided in the right-hand column.

Questions 1-6

On Auto Row there are seven dealerships: Audi, Chrysler, Ford, Hyundai, Mazda, Toyota, Volkswagen. All the dealerships are on the same side of the street, which runs from west to east.

Ford is not next to Mazda.
Audi is the fourth dealership from the west end of the street.
Ford is next to Audi.
Toyota is west of both Audi and Ford but east of Chrysler.

Begin by symbolizing the conditions. *"Ford is not next to Mazda"* is naturally symbolized as **~(FM)**. *"Toyota is west of both Audi and Ford but east of Chrysler"* can be symbolized as **C—>T—>AF**, where the arrow points from west to east. The remaining conditions can be symbolized in like manner, which gives the following schematic:

ACFHMTV (V, H "wild")
~(FM)
A = 4th
FA
C—>T—>AF

The diagram will consist of seven dashed lines, numbered 1 through 7, from west to east. To place the elements on the diagram, follow the guidelines on page 33. First, look for a condition that fixes the position of an element. It is **A = 4th**. This gives

1	2	3	4	5	6	7
			A			

Next, look for a condition that limits the position of a dealership. There is none. Now, look for a condition connecting two or more dealerships. The third condition, *"Ford is next to Audi,"* forces the Ford dealership into either space 3 or 5. This generates two alternate diagrams:

Diagram I

1	2	3	4	5	6	7
		F	A			

Diagram II

1	2	3	4	5	6	7
			A	F		

Finally, look for a condition that states where a dealership cannot be. There is none. No significant properties can be derived from the initial conditions, so we turn to the questions.

1. Which one of the following dealerships CANNOT be next to Chrysler?

(A) Toyota
(B) Ford
(C) Volkswagen
(D) Hyundai
(E) Mazda

1.

Hint!

Use the condition **C—>T—>AF**.

The answer is (B).

2. If Ford is east of Audi, then Hyundai CANNOT be next to both

(A) Toyota and Ford
(B) Chrysler and Toyota
(C) Ford and Mazda
(D) Ford and Volkswagen
(E) Toyota and Audi

2. Since Ford is east of Audi, use Diagram II and again the condition **C—>T—>AF**.

The answer is (A).

3. If Volkswagen is west of Audi, then which one of the following must be false?

(A) Ford is east of Audi.
(B) Volkswagen is west of Toyota.
(C) Volkswagen is east of Toyota.
(D) Hyundai is west of Mazda.
(E) Hyundai is east of Mazda.

3. If Volkswagen is west of Audi, then, from the condition **C—>T—>AF**, we know that Ford must be east of Audi—otherwise Ford, Chrysler, Toyota, and Volkswagen would all be west of Audi, which would violate the condition **A = 4th**. Finally, use the condition **~(FM)**.

The answer is (E).

4. Which one of the following is a possible arrangement of the dealerships from west to east?

(A) C, F, T, A, H, M, V
(B) C, T, F, H, A, M, V
(C) V, C, T, A, F, M, H
(D) C, V, F, A, H, T, M
(E) H, C, T, A, F, V, M

4. This is a straightforward elimination problem: Take a condition. Test it against each answer-choice, eliminating any that violate it. Then take another condition; test it against the remaining answer-choices, eliminating any that violate it. Continue until only one answer-choice remains.

The answer is (E).

5. If Hyundai is west of Ford, which one of the following pairs of dealerships must be next to each other?

(A) Chrysler and Hyundai
(B) Volkswagen and Mazda
(C) Ford and Mazda
(D) Toyota and Audi
(E) Hyundai and Mazda

5.

Hint!

If Hyundai is west of Ford, then, from the condition **C—>T—>AF**, Ford must be east of Audi—otherwise Chrysler, Toyota, Hyundai, and Ford would all be west of Audi, which would violate the condition **A = 4th**.

The answer is (B).

6. **If the Volkswagen dealership is on the east end of the street, then which one of the following must be false?**

   (A) Chrysler is second from the west end of the street.
   (B) Ford is east of Audi.
   (C) Hyundai is on the west end of the street.
   (D) Ford is west of Audi.
   (E) Hyundai is fifth from the west end of the street.

6. This question is hard because it does not give us much information to work with. Volkswagen was a "wild card". That is, its position on the street was independent of the other dealerships—except for Audi. So knowing where the Volkswagen dealership is located will probably tell us little, if anything, about where the other dealerships are located. Furthermore, the question leads us astray by asking *"Which one of the following must be false?"* This prompts us to look directly for the false answer. In problems of this type, however, it is often better to reword the question as *"All of the following could be true except."* Then look for and eliminate the true answer-choices.

We'll use an indirect proof to solve this problem. That is, for each answer-choice, we attempt to construct a possible ordering of the dealerships along the street. The one for which this is not possible will be the answer. Clearly you should save questions like this for last, or skip them all together.

Begin with choice (A). In Diagram II, place Chrysler second from the west end of the street:

1	2	3	4	5	6	7
	C		A	F		V

Next, the condition **C—>T—>AF** forces T into space 3:

1	2	3	4	5	6	7
	C	T	A	F		V

We can place M in space 1 without violating the initial conditions:

1	2	3	4	5	6	7
M	C	T	A	F		V

Finally, this forces the "wild card", H, into space 6:

1	2	3	4	5	6	7
M	C	T	A	F	H	V

This diagram does not violate any initial condition, so (A) could be true. This eliminates (A). Now apply this method to the remaining answer-choices until you find the one that violates one or more of the conditions or until you have eliminated four of the five choices.

The answer is (C).

Exercise

Directions: The following group of questions is based on a set of conditions. Choose the response that most accurately and completely answers each question.

Questions 1-6

A shelf contains six books on six different subjects: Art, Chemistry, Math, History, Physics, and Zoology. The positions of the books are numbered 1 through 6, from left to right.

The zoology book is not next to the math book.
The math book and the history book are exactly two spaces apart.
At most one other book separates the art book from the chemistry book.
The physics book cannot be on either end of the shelf.

1. If the math book is second from the left, then in which one of the following positions could the art book be located?

(A) 2
(B) 3
(C) 4
(D) 5
(E) 6

2. The books located in positions 1, 2, and 3, respectively, could be

I. chemistry, math, and art
II. zoology, art, and math
III. art, chemistry, and history

(A) I only
(B) II only
(C) III only
(D) I and II only
(E) I, II, and III

3. What is the highest numbered position in which the history book can be located, if the zoology and math books are both to the right of it?

(A) 1
(B) 2
(C) 3
(D) 4
(E) 5

4. Which one of the following is a possible arrangement of the six books on the shelf, from left to right?

(A) art, chemistry, physics, history, zoology, math
(B) history, art, math, chemistry, zoology, physics
(C) zoology, history, art, math, physics, chemistry
(D) zoology, chemistry, history, physics, math, art
(E) art, chemistry, math, physics, history, zoology

5. If the physics book is in position 3, then which one of the following must be true?

(A) The chemistry book is in position 6.
(B) The zoology book is in position 1.
(C) The art book is in position 1.
(D) The math book is in position 6.
(E) The zoology book is in position 2.

6. If the history and the math books are both to the left of the chemistry book, then which one of the following must be false?

(A) The art book is in position 3.
(B) The zoology book is in position 4.
(C) The history book is in position 2.
(D) The art book is in position 5.
(E) The chemistry book is in position 6.

Questions 7–10

Seven disks—G, H, L, O, P, S, U—are being inserted in a CD player. The order in which the disks are played is subject to the following restrictions:

L must be played before both O and U.
Exactly two disks must be played between G and P one of which must be L.
H cannot be played first.

7. If G is played third, which one of the following must be played second?

(A) G
(B) H
(C) L
(D) O
(E) N

8. If L and O are played consecutively, which one of the following cannot be true?

(A) S is played second
(B) G is played second
(C) L is played third
(D) O is played forth
(E) H is played sixth

9. What is the maximum number of disks that can separate S from U?

(A) 1
(B) 2
(C) 3
(D) 4
(E) 5

10. If S is played second, which one of the following cannot be true?

(A) G is played sixth
(B) L is played third
(C) U is played seventh
(D) U is played fifth
(E) H is played fifth

The following games appeared on recent LSATs.

Questions 11–12

John receives one grade for each of the following six courses: economics, geology, history, Italian, physics, and Russian. From highest to lowest, the possible grades are A, B, C, D, and E. E is the only failing grade. Two letter grades are consecutive if and only if they are adjacent in the alphabet.

John's grades in geology and physics are consecutive.
His grades in Italian and Russian are consecutive.
He receives a higher grade in economics than in history.
He receives a higher grade in geology than in physics.

11. If John receives the same grade in economics and Italian, and if he fails Russian, which one of the following must be true?

(A) John's geology grade is a B.
(B) John's history grade is a D.
(C) John's history grade is an E.
(D) John's physics grade is a B.
(E) John's physics grade is a C.

12. If John passes all his courses and receives a higher grade in geology than in either language, which one of the following must be true?

(A) He receives exactly one A.
(B) He receives exactly one B.
(C) He receives exactly two Bs.
(D) He receives at least one B and at least one C.
(E) He receives at least one C and at least one D.

Questions 13–17

Seven children are to be seated in seven chairs arranged in a row that runs from west to east. All seven children will face north. Four of the children are boys: Frank, Harry, Ivan, and Joel. Three are girls: Ruby, Sylvia, and Thelma. The children are assigned to chairs according to the following conditions:

Exactly one child sits in each chair.
No boy sits next to another boy.
Ivan sits next to and east of the fourth child in the row.
Sylvia sits east of Ivan.
Frank sits next to Ruby.

13. What is the maximum possible number of different pairs of chairs in which Frank and Ruby could sit?

(A) one
(B) two
(C) three
(D) four
(E) five

14. Which one of the following statements must be false?

(A) Both Harry and Joel sit east of Frank.
(B) Both Harry and Ruby sit east of Frank.
(C) Both Harry and Joel sit west of Frank.
(D) Both Harry and Ruby sit west of Frank.
(E) Both Joel and Ruby sit east of Frank.

15. If Thelma sits next to Ivan, and if Frank sits next to Thelma, which one of the following statements could be false?

(A) Both Frank and Ivan sit east of Ruby.
(B) Both Frank and Ruby sit west of Thelma.
(C) Both Frank and Sylvia sit east of Ruby.
(D) Both Frank and Thelma sit west of Sylvia.
(E) Both Frank and Ruby sit west of Joel.

16. If Frank does not sit next to any child who sits next to Ivan, which one of the following statements could be true?

(A) Harry sits west of Frank.
(B) Joel sits west of Ivan.
(C) Ruby sits west of Frank.
(D) Thelma sits west of Frank.
(E) Thelma sits west of Ruby.

17. If Frank sits east of Ruby, which one of the following pairs of children CANNOT sit next to each other?

(A) Frank and Thelma
(B) Harry and Ruby
(C) Harry and Sylvia
(D) Ivan and Ruby
(E) Joel and Ruby

Answers and Solutions to Exercise

Questions 1–6

This is a spatial ordering problem of above average difficulty. Begin by turning the conditions into symbols. The condition *"The zoology book is not next to the math book"* can be symbolized as **~(ZM)**. Note: although Z is written to the left of M in this symbol, that cannot be assumed on the diagram. We could just as easily have written ~(MZ). The flip-flop symbol could be used to remind us that the order is not fixed, but it would tend to clutter up the conditions. Just remember that the order in all the conditions of this game can be reversed.

Next, the condition *"The math book and the history book are exactly two spaces apart"* can be symbolized as **M □ H**. Don't make the mistake of symbolizing this condition as M □ □ H. The statement "A and B are two spaces apart" means that only one spot separates them. The symbol A □ □ B, on the other hand, reads "A and B are three spaces apart."

Next, the condition *"At most one other book separates the art book from the chemistry book"* can be symbolized as **A □ C**.
max 1

Finally, the condition *"The physics book cannot be on either end of the shelf"* yields **P ≠ 1st, last.**

Our diagram will consist of six compartments—one for each book:

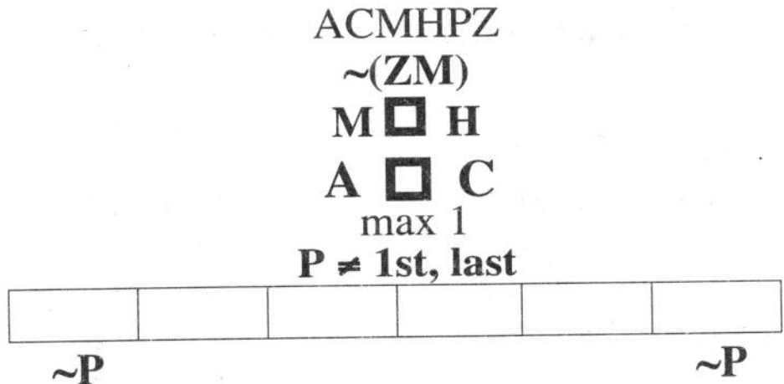

There are no independent elements, no readily derived conditions, and no elements that can be placed on the diagram, so we turn to the questions.

1. This question asks *"Which one of the following could be true?"* This type of question is usually harder to answer than those that ask *"Which one of the following must be true?"* In general, the more information you have, the more likely it is that the order will be fully determined. In such cases, we only need to find one ordering.

On the other hand, the less information you have the less likely it will be that only one order is possible. In these cases there may be many orderings possible, but only one will be listed as an answer-choice. You may spend considerable time working out a possible order, only to be disappointed because it is not listed as an answer-choice. So if you are pressed for time, attempt the remaining *must*-questions before the *could*-questions. You may even want to preview the questions before you begin and then answer all the *must*-questions before tackling the *could*-questions.

I don't use this method myself, though. I find that I tend to lose concentration as I flash from one question to the next, trying to decide which ones are easier. Previewing can also waste precious time. Nonetheless, it may work for you, so experiment with it.

To begin, place the supplementary condition, *"the math book is second from the left,"* on the diagram as follows:

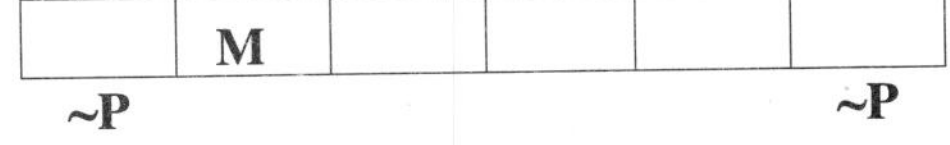

Next, the condition **M □ H** forces H into position 4:

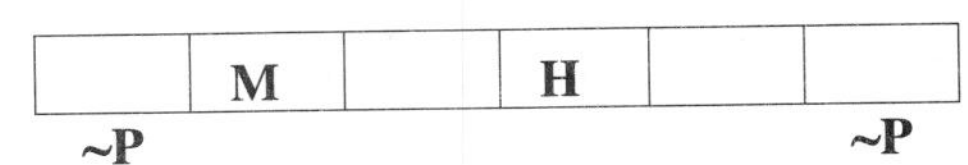

Now, the condition **~(ZM)** forces Z into position 5 or 6. At this point, many students try to juggle the possible positions for Z in their heads. Unless you have a very strong memory, don't do it! Instead, write down a separate diagram for each of the two possible positions:

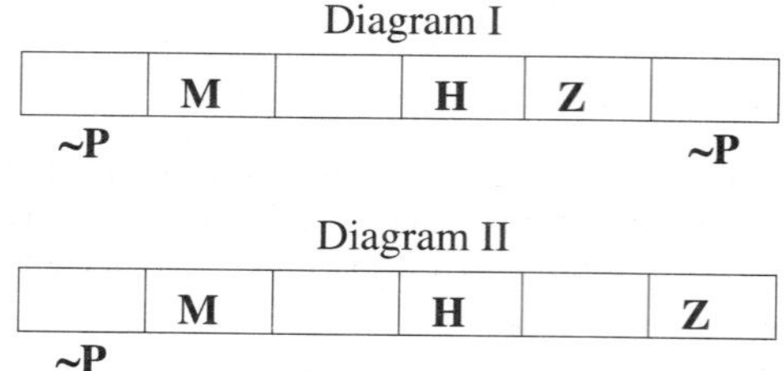

In Diagram I, P must be in position 3, as it cannot be at either end of the shelf:

Diagram I

	M	P	H	Z	

This, however, leaves no room for the condition **A □ C** (max 1). Hence Diagram I is invalid. In Diagram II, P could be placed in position 5:

Diagram II

	M		H	P	Z

Then C and A could be placed in positions 1 and 3, respectively:

Diagram II

C	M	A	H	P	Z

This diagram satisfies all the initial conditions, so it represents a possible ordering. The answer is (B).

2. This is a triple-multiple-choice question. Many students skip these questions, assuming that the LSAT writers have conspired against them. However, a modified elimination method works quite well on these questions.

This question illustrates why you should not erase your previous diagrams. Begin with Statement I. From the final diagram in Question 1, we see that the chemistry, math, and art books could be in positions 1, 2, and 3, respectively. Applying the modified elimination method, we eliminate answer-choices (B) and (C), since they don't contain Statement I. At this point, even if we can't solve this problem, we have significantly increased our chances of correctly guessing the answer.

Turning to Statement II, we try to construct a valid ordering for it. To this end, place Z, A, and M on the diagram as follows:

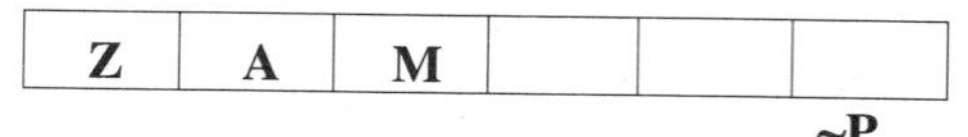

Next, the condition **M □ H** forces H into position 5:

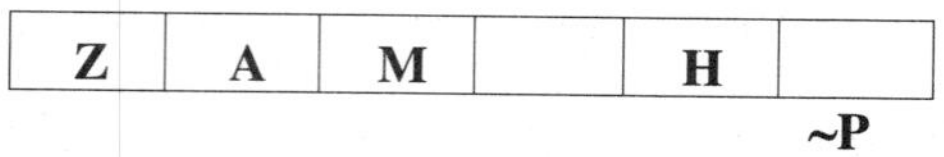

Now, since P cannot be last, it must be in position 4:

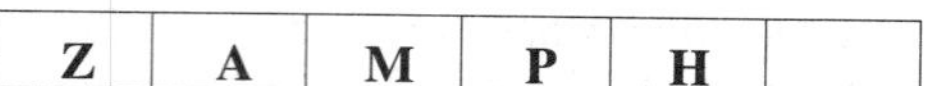

This diagram does not leave any room for the condition **A □ C** (max 1). Hence Statement II is not possible. This eliminates (D) and (E), since both contain Statement II. Therefore, by process of elimination, we have learned that the answer is (A), without having to check Statement III.

3. In problems such as this one, start with the largest number and work your way up the list. The first choice for which you are able to construct a valid order is the answer.

We can quickly dismiss (E) since there are only six spaces and two books are to the right of H.

We can also quickly dismiss (D). If H were in position 4, then the zoology and math books would have to be in spaces 5 and 6. This, however, would violate the condition **~(ZM)**.

Next, if H is in position 3, then— from the condition **M □ H**, and the fact that M is to the right of H—we know that M must be in position 5:

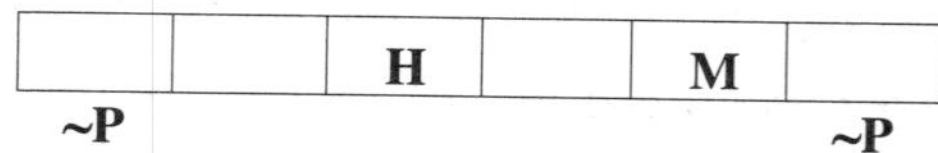

This diagram leaves only positions 4 and 6 for Z. In either case, however, Z would be next to M, which again would violate the condition **~(ZM)**. This dismisses (C).

Next, if H is in position 2, then M must be in position 4:

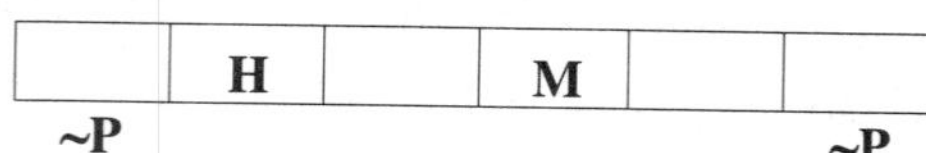

In this case, it is possible to place Z in space 6 as follows:

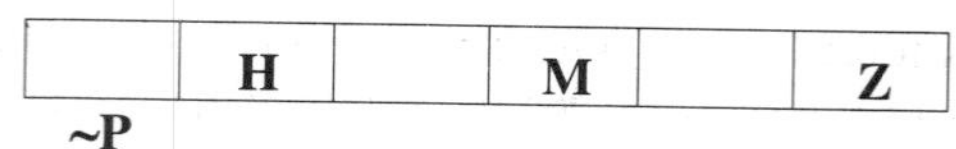

Then, place P in position 5:

	H		M	P	Z

Finally, place A and C in positions 1 and 3, respectively:

This diagram does not violate any initial condition. Hence the largest numbered position that H could occupy is 2. The answer is (B).

4. Never skip problems like this one; they are rarely difficult. We'll use elimination. (A) is not a possible arrangement since it has M next to Z. (B) is not a possible arrangement since it has P last. Neither (C) nor (D) is a possible arrangement since in each case more than one book separates A and C. Hence, by process of elimination, we have learned that the answer is (E).

5. To start, place P in position 3 on the diagram:

		P			

This yields two positions for the condition **M □ H**—2 and 4, or 4 and 6. This generates two diagrams:

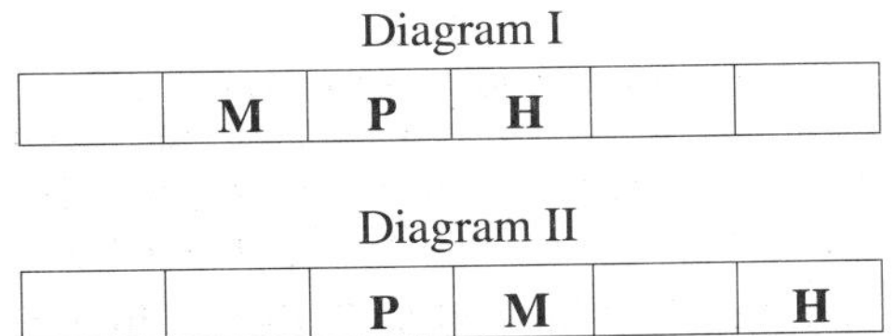

(Note: M and H can exchange places in each diagram.)

Now in Diagram II, the condition **A □ C** (max 1) must be in positions 1 and 2:

Diagram II

A	**C**	**P**	**M**		**H**

This forces Z into position 5, which violates the condition **~(ZM)**. Hence Diagram II is invalid. Turning to Diagram I, we see that the condition **A □ C** (max 1) forces A and C into positions 5 and 6, though not necessarily in that order:

Diagram I

	M	**P**	**H**	**A**	**C**

This forces Z into position 1, which violates the condition **~(ZM)**. Don't forget, however, that we can switch M and H:

Diagram I

Z	**H**	**P**	**M**	**A**	**C**

This diagram satisfies all the initial conditions plus the supplementary condition. It also displays Z in its only possible position. Hence the answer is (B).

Watch out for choice (A). Although C can be in position 6, it need not be: A and C can be flip flopped in the final diagram.

6. In this problem, we have no choice but to apply an indirect proof. Start with (A). If the art book is in position 3, then, from the condition **A □ C** (max 1), there are four positions in which C can be placed—1, 2, 4, 5. We consider each in turn. Position 1 can be quickly ruled out. If C were in position 1, then clearly neither H nor M could be to its left. Similarly position 2 can be ruled out. Next, place C in position 4 on the diagram:

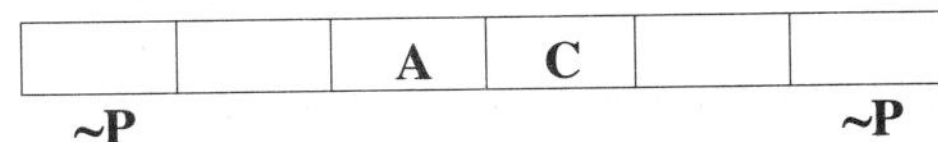

Clearly in this diagram, there is no room to place the condition **M □ H**. Hence C cannot be in position 4. Next place C in position 5:

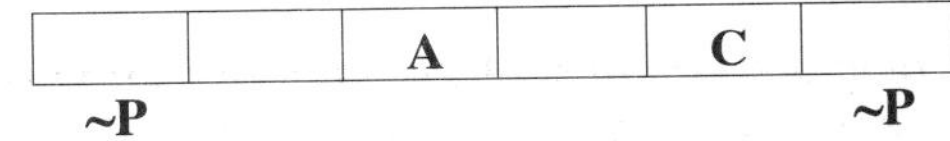

From the new condition, *"both H and M are left of C,"* and the condition **M □ H**, we see that M and H must occupy positions 2 and 4, though not necessarily in that order:

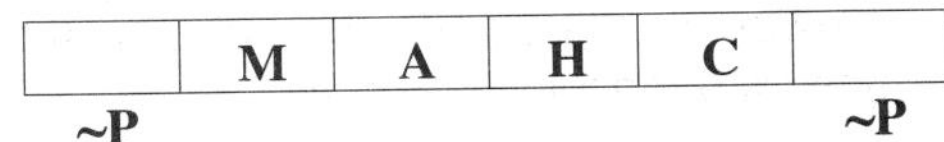

This diagram, however, forces P to be either first or last, which violates the condition **P ≠ 1st, last**. This shows C cannot be in position 5. Hence the art book cannot be in position 3, and the answer is (A).

Questions 7–10

The conditions can be symbolized as follows:

L—>O & U
G ___ ___ P
L between G & P
H ≠ first

1	2	3	4	5	6	7

Note, the flip-flop symbol will not be used in the symbol statement **G ___ ___ P**; just remember that G and P can be interchanged.

7. Since G is played third, the condition G ___ ___ P forces P into space 6:

1	2	3	4	5	6	7
		G			P	

The condition **L between G & P** forces L into spaces 4 or 5. But L cannot be in space 5 since that would leave no room for the condition **L—>O & U**. Thus, L must be in space 4:

1	2	3	4	5	6	7
		G	L	O/U	P	O/U

Finally, since **H ≠ first**, H must be played second. The answer is (B).

8. Suppose S is played second.

1	2	3	4	5	6	7
	S					

Since "L and O are played consecutively" and L is between G & P, the disks G, L, O, and P must be played consecutively. Now, G, L, O, and P cannot be placed in spaces 4, 5, 6, and 7 since that would violate the condition **L—>O & U**. So G, L, O, and P must be place in spaces 3, 4, 5, and 6:

1	2	3	4	5	6	7
	S	G	L	O	P	U

(Note, P and G can be interchanged in the diagram.) However, this diagram leaves no room for H (**H ≠ first**). Hence, S cannot be played second and the answer is (A).

9. The following diagram satisfies all the conditions and has S in space 1 and U in space 7:

1	2	3	4	5	6	7
S	G	L	H	P	O	U

Hence, a maximum of 5 disks can separate S from the U. The answer is (E).

10. Suppose G is played sixth:

1	2	3	4	5	6	7
	S				G	

Then the condition **G ___ ___ P** forces P into space 3:

1	2	3	4	5	6	7
	S	P			G	

The conditions **L—>O & U** and **L between G & P** yield

1	2	3	4	5	6	7
	S	P	L	O/U	G	O/U

However, this diagram does not leave any room for H (**H ≠ first**). The answer is (A).

Questions 11–12

This is a linear ordering game of medium difficulty. The condition *"John's grades in geology and physics are consecutive"* can be symbolized as $\widehat{\mathbf{G\ P}}$, where the flip-flop symbol reminds us that the positions of G and P can be interchanged. The condition *"He receives a higher grade in economics than in history"* can be symbolized as **e > H**. Note, a lower case "e" is used to distinguish it from the letter grade E. The last condition *"He receives a higher grade in geology than in physics"* allows us to drop the flip-flop symbol in the condition $\widehat{\mathbf{G\ P}}$. The remaining condition is symbolized in like manner, which yields the following schematic:

GP

I R

e > H

11. Since John received the same grade in economics and Italian, the condition $\widehat{\mathbf{I\ \ R}}$ becomes $\widehat{\mathbf{e\ \ R}}$. Since he failed Russian, this condition shows that he received a D in economics. The condition **e > H** forces him to have received an E in history. The answer is (C).

12. Since John receives a higher grade in geology than in either Italian or Russian, the condition $\widehat{\mathbf{I\ \ R}}$ becomes $\mathbf{G >} \widehat{\mathbf{I\ \ R}}$. This shows that his geology grade is either an A or a B (remember, he passes all his courses). If his geology grade is A, then from the condition **GP** his physics grade is B. This leaves two places for the condition $\widehat{\mathbf{I\ \ R}}$:

A	B	C	D
G	**P**		
	I	**R**	

A	B	C	D
G	**P**		
		I	**R**

In each diagram he receives at least one B and at least one C. Next, if his geology grade is B, then we get the following diagram:

A	B	C	D
	G	**P**	
		I	**R**

This diagram also has him receiving at least one B and at least one C. Thus, the answer is (D).

Questions 13–17

The condition *"No boy sits next to another boy"* means that the arrangement will be boy/girl/boy/girl . . . , which is naturally symbolized as **Boy/Girl**. The condition *"Ivan sits next to and east of the fourth child in the row"* simply means that Ivan is 5th, which can be symbolized as **I = 5th**. The condition *"Sylvia sits east of Ivan"* forces Sylvia into space 6 or 7. However, since the arrangement is **Boy/Girl**, Sylvia must be in space 6, **S = 6th**. The final condition, *"Frank sits next Ruby,"* is naturally symbolized as **FR**, where F and R can be flip-flopped.

Boys	Girls
FHIJ	RST

Boy/Girl
I = 5th
S = 6th
FR

(West)	1	2	3	4	5	6	7	(East)
					I	**S**		

13.
(A) No. See answer-choice (C).
(B) No. See answer-choice (C).
(C) Yes. As the following diagrams illustrate, Frank and Ruby can sit in chairs 1&2, or 2&3, or 3&4:

1	2	3	4	5	6	7
F	**R**	**H**	**T**	**I**	**S**	**J**

1	2	3	4	5	6	7
H	**R**	**F**	**T**	**I**	**S**	**J**

1	2	3	4	5	6	7
H	**T**	**F**	**R**	**I**	**S**	**J**

(D) No. See answer-choice (C).
(E) No. See answer-choice (C).

14.
(A) No. The following diagram satisfies all the conditions and has both Harry and Joel seated east of Frank:

1	2	3	4	5	6	7
F	**R**	**H**	**T**	**I**	**S**	**J**

(B) No. See diagram to answer-choice (A).
(C) Yes. From Question 13, we know that Frank must sit in chair 1, 2, 3, or 4. Now, since Harry and Joel sit west of Frank, they must sit in chairs 1, 2, or 3. This puts 3 boys in chairs 1 through 4—violating the condition **Boy/Girl**.
(D) No. The following diagram satisfies all the conditions and has both Harry and Ruby seated west of Frank:

1	2	3	4	5	6	7
H	**R**	**F**	**T**	**I**	**S**	**J**

(E) No. See diagram to answer-choice (A).

15. Placing Thelma next to Ivan and Frank next to Thelma yields

1	2	3	4	5	6	7
		F	**T**	**I**	**S**	

Since Ruby sits next to Frank, Ruby must sit in space 2:

1	2	3	4	5	6	7
	R	**F**	**T**	**I**	**S**	

(A) No. See above diagram.
(B) No. See above diagram.
(C) No. See above diagram.
(D) No. See above diagram.
(E) Yes. Suppose in the above diagram that Joel sits in space 1. Then Harry would sit in space 7:

1	2	3	4	5	6	7
J	**R**	**F**	**T**	**I**	**S**	**H**

This diagram satisfies all the conditions and has both Frank and Ruby seated <u>east</u> of Joel.

16. The condition *"Frank does not sit next to any child who sits next to Ivan"* means that Frank does not sit in space 3 or 7. Since the order is **Boy/Girl**, Frank must be in space 1. This in turn forces Ruby into space 2, **FR**:

Diagram I

1	2	3	4	5	6	7
F	**R**			**I**	**S**	

(A) No. See Diagram I.
(B) Yes. Suppose Joel sits in space 3. Then since the order is **Boy/Girl**, Harry and Thelma would be forced into spaces 7 and 4, respectively:

1	2	3	4	5	6	7
F	**R**	**J**	**T**	**I**	**S**	**H**

This diagram satisfies all the conditions and has Joel seated west of Ivan.
(C) No. See Diagram I.
(D) No. See Diagram I.
(E) No. See Diagram I.

17.
(A) No. The following diagram satisfies all the conditions and has Frank seated next to Thelma:

1	2	3	4	5	6	7
J	**R**	**F**	**T**	**I**	**S**	**H**

(B) No. The following diagram satisfies all the conditions and has Harry seated next to Ruby:

1	2	3	4	5	6	7
H	**R**	**F**	**T**	**I**	**S**	**J**

(C) No. See diagram to answer-choice (A).
(D) Yes. Since Frank now sits east of Ruby, the condition **FR** becomes **RF**, where R and F cannot be flip-flopped. From our previous work, we know that Ruby and Frank must sit west of Ivan. Hence, Frank will always be seated between Ruby and Ivan. Thus, Ruby and Ivan cannot sit next to each other.
(E) No. See diagram to answer-choice (A).

Answers and Solutions to Warm-up Drills

Drill A

1. **4 orderings.**

   Two diagrams are possible, one with A first and D fourth, and one with D first and A fourth:

   _A_ _C_ _B_ _D_

   _D_ _C_ _B_ _A_

   Interchanging the positions of C and B in each diagram above results in two more orderings. So there are 4 orderings possible.

2. **4 orderings.**

   Viewed as a group, ABC can be placed either at the beginning or at the end of the line:

   _A_ _B_ _C_ (D)

   (D) _C_ _B_ _A_

   (The circle around D indicates that it was forced into that position by the conditions.) Two additional diagrams result from interchanging A and C in each diagram. So there are 4 possible orderings.

3. **8 orderings.**

   Now B is merely between A and C, not necessarily immediately between them. Thus D may come between A and B or between B and C:

   _A_ _D_ _B_ _C_

   _A_ _B_ _D_ _C_

   Interchanging A and C in each diagram gives 2 more orderings for a total of 4. Combining this with the result in drill 2 gives a total of 8 orderings.

4. **24 orderings.**

Drill B

1. **4 orderings.**

Since B is between C and D, it must be in position 2 or 3:

___ B ___ ___
___ ___ B ___

Next, adding the condition "A is left of B" yields the following diagrams:

Diagram I	A	B	___	___
Diagram II	A	___	B	___
Diagram III	___	A	B	___

Eliminate Diagram I since it clearly violates the condition **CBD.** Next, placing C and D in the remaining diagrams gives the following valid diagrams:

A C B D
C A B D

Finally, interchanging C and D in each diagram gives two additional diagrams. So there is a total of 4 possible orderings.

2. **5 orderings.**

With A first, there are three possible positions for C:

Diagram I	A	C	___	___
Diagram II	A	___	C	___
Diagram III	A	___	___	C

In Diagram I, B or D may be in space 3 or 4. This generates 2 diagrams. In Diagram II, B must be in position 2. If B were in position 4, then from the second condition C would have to be next to A. This gives only one diagram. Finally, in Diagram III, B or D could be in position 2 or 3. This generates two diagrams. So there is a total of 5 possible orderings.

3. **8 orderings.**

There are three possible positions for C:

Diagram I	___	___	___	C
Diagram II	___	___	C	___
Diagram III	___	C	___	___

In Diagram I, place B in each of the possible positions and count the number of diagrams thereby generated. If B is in position 1, then two diagrams are possible. If B is in position 2, then again two diagrams are possible. If B is in position 3, then from the second condition D must be in position 2. So in this case only one diagram is generated.

Next, in Diagram II, if B is in position 1, then two diagrams are possible. If B is in position 2, then by the second condition D must be in position 1. So in this case only one diagram results.

Finally, Diagram III is not valid. (Why?) Counting the above diagrams gives a total of 8 possible orderings.

Hybrid Games

In the ordering games we have studied so far, only one element at a time could occupy a particular position. However, in many ordering games two or more elements can occupy the same position at the same time. These games order elements as groups, rather than as individuals. (Grouping games will be presented later.) As you would expect, this added complication makes hybrid games harder than line-up games. Hybrid games are presented here because their ordering nature is more significant than their grouping nature. Some typical setups to these games are

- Seven books are placed on five shelves.
- A four-story apartment building has four apartments, one on each floor, and seven tenants.
- There are two lines of couples waiting to buy tickets to a play.

When analyzing hybrid games, pay close attention to the number of positions versus the number of elements. Also, pay close attention to the maximum or minimum number of elements that can occupy a particular position.

Hybrid Game

A cupboard has five shelves numbered 1 through 5, from bottom to top; each shelf has two compartments. There are eight items—A, B, C, D, E, F, G, H—in the cupboard, no two of which are in the same compartment.

Items D and E are on the same shelf.
B is on the shelf directly below G.
If a shelf contains only one item, it cannot be directly above or directly below another shelf that contains only one item.
C is the only item on one of the shelves.
There is only one item on the fourth shelf.

1. If H is on the fourth shelf, which one of the following CANNOT be true?

   (A) A is on the second shelf.
   (B) D and E are on the second shelf.
   (C) D and E are on the top shelf.
   (D) C is on the first shelf.
   (E) A is on the third shelf.

2. Which one of the following is a complete and accurate list of the items any one of which could be on the top shelf?

   (A) D
   (B) D, E, G, C
   (C) D, E, G, B
   (D) D, E, G, C, F
   (E) D, E, G, H, F, A

3. Which one of the following must be true?

   (A) If A is on the third shelf, then E is not on the top shelf.
   (B) If E is on the second shelf, then C is not on the bottom shelf.
   (C) If H is on the fourth shelf, then D and E are not on the second shelf.
   (D) If B is on the fourth shelf, then D is not on the third shelf.
   (E) If G is on the top shelf, then H is not on the bottom shelf.

4. If G is on the top shelf and A is on the third shelf, then which one of the following must be true?

   (A) D is on the first shelf.
   (B) E is on the second shelf.
   (C) C is on the fourth shelf.
   (D) Either F or H must be on the same shelf as A.
   (E) F is on the same shelf as G.

5. If A and B are on the second shelf, which one of the following must be true?

   (A) D and E are on the top shelf.
   (B) F is on the same shelf as H.
   (C) A is directly above F.
   (D) C is on the fourth shelf.
   (E) C is on the first shelf.

As in the previous examples, we construct a diagram to help answer the questions. The condition *"D and E are on the same shelf"* is naturally symbolized as **D = E**. The condition *"B is on a shelf directly below G"* can be symbolized as **G/B**. The condition *"C is the only item on one of the shelves"* can be symbolized as **C = alone**. The condition *"There is only one item on the fourth shelf"* can be symbolized as **4th = alone**. Finally, the condition *"If a shelf contains only one item, it cannot be directly above or directly below another shelf that contains only one item"* can be symbolized **not 1/1**. This yields the following diagram:

D = E
G/B
C = alone
4th = alone
not 1/1

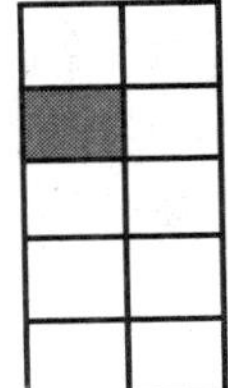

Two readily derived conditions should be noted: There are 10 compartments, 8 items, and C is the only item on its shelf. So two shelves must have only one item each, and no shelf can be empty. Neither of these conditions can be placed on the diagram, so we turn to the questions.

1. If H is on the fourth shelf, which one of the following CANNOT be true?

(A) A is on the second shelf.
(B) D and E are on the second shelf.
(C) D and E are on the top shelf.
(D) C is on the first shelf.
(E) A is on the third shelf.

Add the new condition, "H is on the fourth shelf," to the diagram:

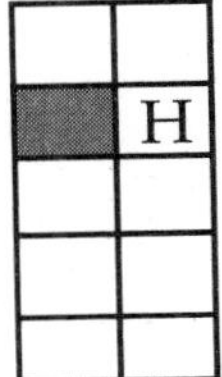

Now we attack the answer-choices, attempting to construct a diagram for each one. The answer-choice for which a valid diagram cannot be constructed will be the answer. Start with choice (A). Place A on the second shelf:

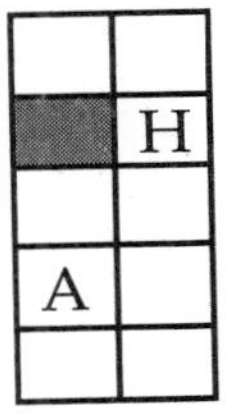

▓	H
A	

Next, place the condition **G/B** on shelves 2 and 3:

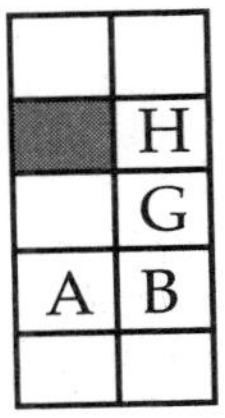

▓	H
	G
A	B

Then, place **D = E** on the top shelf:

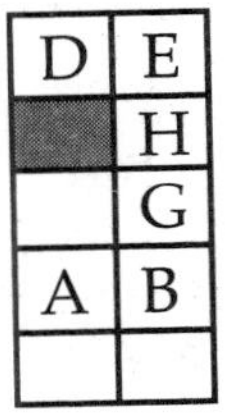

D	E
▓	H
	G
A	B

Finally, place C on the bottom shelf and F on the third shelf:

D	E
	H
F	G
A	B
	C

This diagram does not violate any initial condition. Hence A *can* be on the second shelf. This eliminates choice (A).

Next, attack choice (B). Place the condition **D = E** on the second shelf as follows:

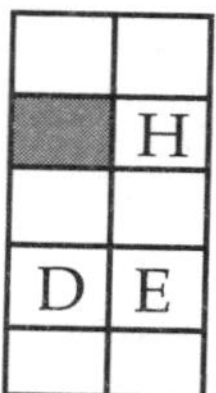

Clearly this diagram leaves no room to place the condition **G/B**. Hence the answer is (B).

As we work through the remaining questions, note the determining power of the condition of **G/B.**

2. Which one of the following is a complete and accurate list of the items any one of which could be on the top shelf?

(A) D
(B) D, E, G, C
(C) D, E, G, B
(D) D, E, G, C, F
(E) D, E, G, H, F, A

The first thing to note about the answer-choices is that they all contain D. So there is no need to check whether D can be on the top—it can. Next, since D and E must be on the same shelf, we eliminate (A). Next, since all remaining choices contain G, there is no need to check whether G can be on the top shelf. Next, since G must be above B, B clearly cannot be on the top shelf. This eliminates choice (C). Finally, C cannot be on the top shelf; if it were, then one shelf with only one item would be directly above another shelf with only one item. This eliminates both (B) and (D). Hence, by process of elimination, the answer is (E).

3. Which one of the following must be true?

(A) If A is on the third shelf, then E is not on the top shelf.
(B) If E is on the second shelf, then C is not on the bottom shelf.
(C) If H is on the fourth shelf, then D and E are not on the second shelf.
(D) If B is on the fourth shelf, then D is not on the third shelf.
(E) If G is on the top shelf, then H is not on the bottom shelf.

This question is long because it actually contains five distinct questions. During the test you should save such a question for last. However, there is a shortcut to this particular question. Notice that answer-choice (C) merely rewords Question 1 and its answer. Hence the answer is (C).

It is not uncommon for the LSAT writers to repeat a question with a different form. Being alert to this can save time.

4. **If G is on the top shelf and A is on the third shelf, then which one of the following must be true?**

   (A) D is on the first shelf.
   (B) E is on the second shelf.
   (C) C is on the fourth shelf.
   (D) Either F or H must be on the same shelf as A.
   (E) F is on the same shelf as G.

Add the new conditions to the diagram:

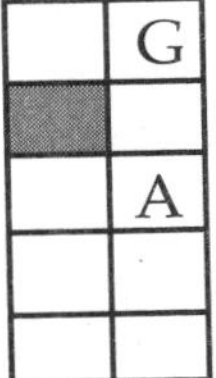

Next, add the condition **G/B** to the diagram:

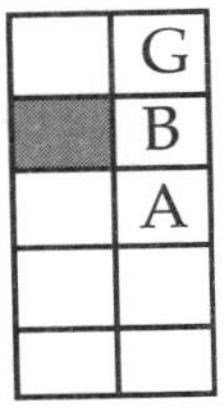

	G
▇	B
	A

Now the condition **D = E** can be placed on either the first or second shelf. We construct a separate diagram for each case:

Diagram 1

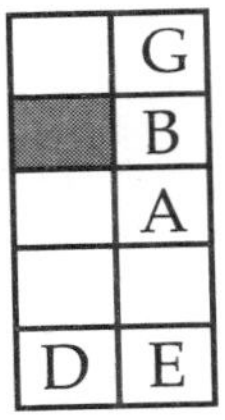

	G
▇	B
	A
D	E

Diagram 2

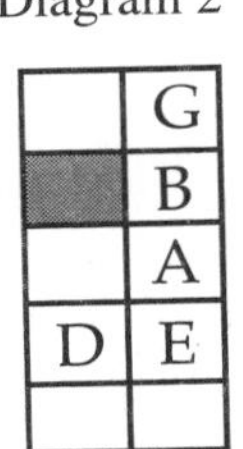

Next, since C must be alone, it must be on the second shelf in Diagram 1 and on the bottom shelf in Diagram 2:

Diagram 1

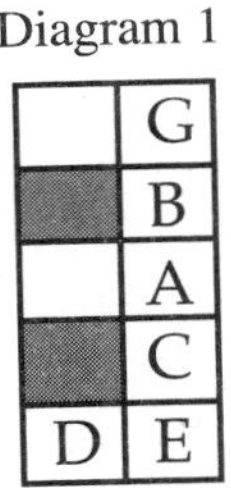

Diagram 2

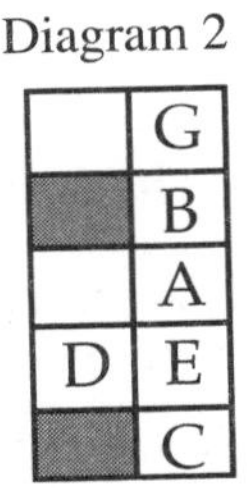

Clearly in both diagrams, either F or H must be next A. Hence the answer is (D).

5. If A and B are on the second shelf, which one of the following must be true?

(A) D and E are on the top shelf.
(B) F is on the same shelf as H.
(C) A is directly above F.
(D) C is on the fourth shelf.
(E) C is on the first shelf.

Adding the new condition to the diagram yields

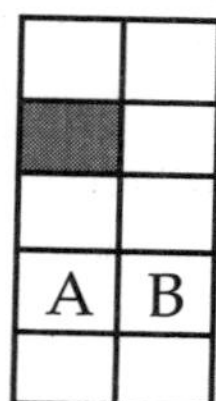

Next, adding the condition **G/B** to the diagram gives

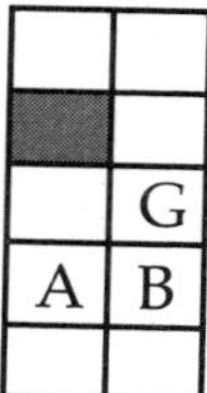

There are two places left for the condition **D = E,** the bottom shelf or the top shelf. We construct a separate diagram for each case.

Diagram 1

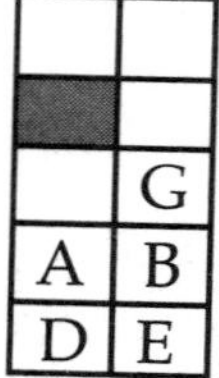

Diagram 2

D	E
■	
	G
A	B

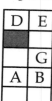

In Diagram 1, the condition **C = alone** must be placed either on the top shelf or the fourth shelf. But in either case this violates the condition that a shelf with only one item cannot be either directly above or directly below another shelf with only one item. This eliminates Diagram 1. In Diagram 2, D and E are on the top shelf. Hence the answer is (A).

Points to Remember

1. Hybrid games order elements as groups, rather than as individuals.

2. When analyzing a hybrid game, pay close attention to the number of positions versus the number of elements. Also pay close attention to the maximum or minimum number of elements that can occupy a particular position.

3. It is not uncommon for the LSAT writers to repeat a question in a different form. You can save time by watching out for this.

Mentor Exercise

Directions: Each group of questions is based on a set of conditions. In answering some of the questions, it may be useful to draw a rough diagram. Choose the response that most accurately and completely answers each question. Hints, insights, partial solutions, and answers are provided in the right-hand column.

Questions 1–4

Six people—Roger, Susan, Tim, Ulrika, Vic, and Walt—are competing for a job at Consolidated Conglomerate. They have been evaluated on a letter scale A, B, C, D, or E, with A the highest possible evaluation.

Exactly two people received Bs.
Only one person received a D, and only one person received a C.
Neither Roger nor Tim received a B.
Susan's evaluation was lower than everyone else's.

This is a moderately hard hybrid game. Half of the elements are "wild", so the situation is very fluid. This makes the game difficult: throughout the problem we will be groping for something concrete.

Begin by symbolizing the conditions. The condition *"Neither Roger nor Tim received a B"* is naturally symbolized as **(R&T)≠B**. The condition *"Susan's evaluation was lower than everyone else's"* can be symbolized as **S=lowest**. The condition *"Exactly two people received Bs"* can be symbolized as **2Bs**. The remaining conditions can be symbolized in like manner. This yields

R, S, T, (U, V, W "wild")
(R&T)≠B
S=lowest
2Bs, 1C, 1D

The diagram will consist of five boxes in a row—with the lettered evaluations listed at the top, the number of each evaluation listed in each box, and restrictions listed at the bottom:

A	B	C	D	E
	2	1	1	
	~R ~T			

One further condition should be drawn before turning to the questions. Since one person is assigned a D and everyone is evaluated above Susan, she must have received either a D or an E. Note this as follows:

A	B	C	D	E
	2	1	1	
	~R ~T		S (D or E)	

1. Which one of the following CANNOT be determined based on the information given?

(A) Ulrika did not receive an E.
(B) At most one person received an E.
(C) At least one person received an E.
(D) Roger did not receive an E.
(E) Tim did not receive a B.

1. Since this question asks for the answer-choice that cannot be determined, we attempt to construct a valid counter-example for each choice. The one for which this is not possible will be the answer.

Choice (A) can be determined from the initial conditions since Susan received the lowest evaluation. Next, choice (B) necessarily follows from the given conditions. (Why?) This eliminates (B). As to (C), suppose that S received a D:

A	B	C	D	E
	2	1	S	

~R

~T

Then both U and V could receive Bs, without violating any conditions:

A	B	C	D	E
	U V	1	S	

Finally, both R and T could receive As and W could receive a C—all without violating any condition:

A	B	C	D	E
R T	U V	W	S	

This is a valid counter-example. Hence the answer is (C)—it cannot be determined from the given conditions.

2. If Vic and Walt received the same evaluation, which one of the following could be true?

(A) Vic did not receive a B.
(B) Walt did not receive a B.
(C) Susan received a C.
(D) Roger received a B.
(E) Roger received a D.

2. Again, this problem requires an indirect proof. With problems like these, don't necessarily start with choice (A). Instead, scan the choices for a likely candidate.

As to (A), it is a poor candidate: we may have to construct a different diagram for each of Vic's four possible positions. The same holds for choice (B). Next, choices (C) and (D) violate the original diagram—eliminate. Finally, (E) is a good candidate because it fixes the position of an element.

Now try to construct a valid diagram, with Roger assigned a D.

The answer is (E).

3. If Vic and Walt received the same lettered evaluation, then which of following must be true?

I. Both Vic and Walt received an A.
II. Both Vic and Walt received a B.
III. Ulrika received an A.

(A) I only
(B) II only
(C) III only
(D) I and III only
(E) II and III only

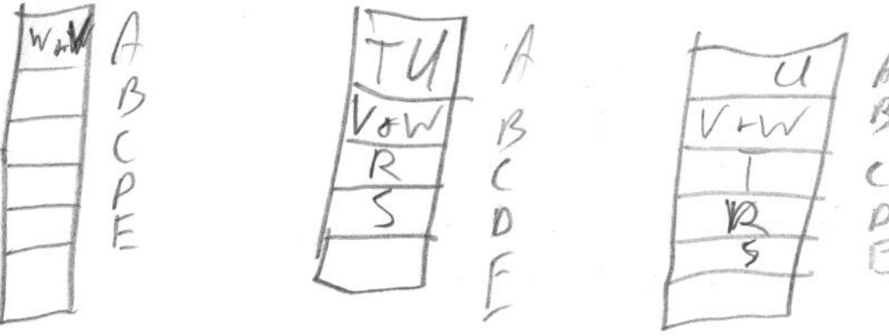

4. If only Vic received an A and Roger received a score higher than Tim, which one of following must be true?

(A) Susan received an E.
(B) Roger received a D.
(C) Ulrika received a C.
(D) Tim received a C.
(E) Susan received a D.

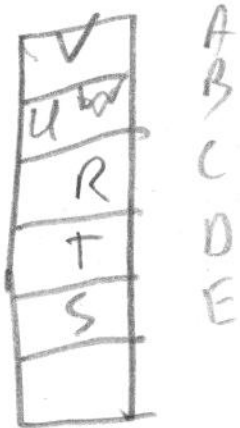

3. Start with I. Place Vic and Walt on the diagram as follows:

A	B	C	D	E
V W	2	1	1	
	~R ~T		S	

Now since Roger, Tim, and Susan cannot receive a B, only Ulrika can be assigned a B. But this violates the first condition, *"Exactly two people received Bs."* So I is false, which eliminates both (A) and (D); they both contain I.

As to II, since Vic and Walt cannot both be assigned either a C or a D (not enough room), they must both receive a B. So II is true, which eliminates (C).

Unfortunately, we have to check III. Given the fluidness of the diagram and the fact that Ulrika is "wild", it is unlikely that III must be true. Nonetheless, you should construct a diagram to check this.

The answer is (B).

4. To start, place Vic in box A:

A	B	C	D	E
V	2	1	1	
	~R ~T		S	

Next, since neither Roger nor Tim can be in box B, one must be in box C and one in box D:

A	B	C	D	E
V	2	R	T	
			S	

But this forces Susan into box E. Hence the answer is (A).

Notice: To solve this problem, we did not need the obfuscating condition *"Roger received a higher score than Tim."* It is not uncommon for the LSAT writers to introduce superfluous conditions. So don't become alarmed if you don't use all the conditions when solving a game. This may indicate an oversight on your part—it may not. Many students, upon discovering that they did not use all the conditions, will fruitlessly check and recheck their work, wasting precious time. If you don't use all the conditions, make a cursory inspection of your work. If no mistakes are found, cut your losses and move on—taking solace in the hope that the unused conditions were extraneous.

Exercise

Directions: The following group of questions is based on a set of conditions. Choose the response that most accurately and completely answers each question.

Questions 1–5

Four couples—JJ, KK, LL, MM—are standing in a line. Their positions are numbered consecutively from 1 to 8, and each person is holding hands with the persons on either side of him or her.

J and J are holding hands.
K and K are not holding hands.
L and L are holding hands.
One of the Ls is at one end of the line, and one of the Ms is at the other end.

1. If M is at position 2 and K is at position 3, then a J must be at position

(A) 1
(B) 4
(C) 6
(D) 7
(E) 8

2. If J is in position 2, it must be true that

(A) M is in position 3.
(B) J is in position 4.
(C) K is in position 7.
(D) L is in position 5.
(E) M is in position 5.

3. If an M is in position 8, which of the following CANNOT be true?

I. The other M is in position 5.
II. The Ks can be in positions 3, 5, or 7.
III. One of the Js is in position 3.

(A) I only
(B) II only
(C) III only
(D) II and III only
(E) I, II, and III

4. If the Ks are separated by at most one other person, then which one of the following groups could be standing in the four even-numbered positions in one arrangement?

(A) The two Js and the two Ls.
(B) The two Ks and the two Ls.
(C) The two Js and the two Ms.
(D) One J, one K, one L, and one M.
(E) One J, the two Ks, and one L.

5. Which one of the following must be true?

(A) At least one J is holding hands with a K.
(B) At least one L is holding hands with a J.
(C) At least one L is holding hands with a K.
(D) At least one M is holding hands with an L.
(E) At least one J is holding hands with an M.

<u>Questions 6–11</u>

Five friends are playing chess. Three are women—Laura, Mary, and Naomi—and two are men—Oliver and Paul. There are three chessboards in a row.

Naomi does not sit next to either Mary or Oliver.
Laura does not play Naomi.
The middle board always has two players.

6. If Mary plays Paul on the middle board and Paul does not sit between two other players, which one of the following is a complete and accurate list of those who might not have an opponent?

(A) Laura
(B) Naomi
(C) Laura and Naomi
(D) Laura and Oliver
(E) Laura, Naomi, and Oliver

7. If Paul does not have an opponent, which one of the following must be false?

(A) Mary plays Naomi.
(B) Mary plays Oliver.
(C) Mary plays Laura.
(D) Laura does not sit between two other people.
(E) Laura sits between Naomi and Paul.

8. If players of the same sex do not play each other and Mary sits between two other players, which one of the following is a complete and accurate list of those players who might be Oliver's opponent?

(A) Mary and Laura
(B) Mary and Naomi
(C) Naomi
(D) Mary, Naomi, and Laura
(E) Mary

9. If players of the same sex do not play each other, which one of the following must be false?

(A) Naomi plays Paul.
(B) Naomi plays Oliver.
(C) Laura plays Oliver.
(D) Paul plays Mary.
(E) Paul does not have an opponent.

10. If the women always play each other, which one of the following must be true?

(A) Laura plays Mary.
(B) Mary plays Naomi.
(C) Laura has no opponent.
(D) One of the women does not have an opponent.
(E) Paul does not have an opponent.

11. How many different people can Naomi play against?

(A) 0
(B) 1
(C) 2
(D) 3
(E) 4

The following game appeared on a recent LSAT.

Questions 12–16

A gymnastics instructor is planning a weekly schedule, Monday through Friday, of individual coaching sessions for each of six students—H, I, K, O, U, and Z. The instructor will coach exactly one student each day, except for one day when the instructor will coach two students in separate but consecutive sessions. The following restrictions apply:

H's session must take place at some time before Z's session.
I's session is on Thursday.
K's session is always scheduled for the day immediately before or the day immediately after the day for which O's session is scheduled.
Neither Monday nor Wednesday can be a day for which two students are scheduled.

12. Which one of the following is a pair of students whose sessions can both be scheduled for Tuesday, not necessarily in the order given?

(A) H and U
(B) H and Z
(C) K and O
(D) O and U
(E) U and Z

13. If K's session is scheduled for Tuesday, then which one of the following is the earliest day for which Z's session can be scheduled?

(A) Monday
(B) Tuesday
(C) Wednesday
(D) Thursday
(E) Friday

14. Which one of the following must be true?

(A) If U's session is scheduled for Monday, H's session is scheduled for Tuesday.
(B) If U's session is scheduled for Tuesday, O's session is scheduled for Wednesday.
(C) If U's session is scheduled for Wednesday, Z's session is scheduled for Tuesday.
(D) If U's session is scheduled for Thursday, Z's session is scheduled for Friday.
(E) If U's session is scheduled for Friday, Z's session is scheduled for Thursday.

15. Scheduling Z's session for which one of the following days determines the day for which U's session must be scheduled?

(A) Monday
(B) Tuesday
(C) Wednesday
(D) Thursday
(E) Friday

16. If H's session is scheduled as the next session after U's session, which one of the following could be true about H's session and U's session?

(A) U's session is scheduled for Monday, and H's session is scheduled for Tuesday.
(B) U's session is scheduled for Thursday, and H's session is scheduled for Friday.
(C) They are both scheduled for Tuesday.
(D) They are both scheduled for Thursday.
(E) They are both scheduled for Friday.

Answers and Solutions to Exercise

Questions 1–5

This is a relatively easy hybrid game. Begin by symbolizing the conditions. The conditions *"J and J are holding hands"* and *"L and L are holding hands"* are naturally symbolized as **JJ** and **LL**, respectively. The condition *"K and K are not holding hands"* can be symbolized as **K...K**. [The symbol ~(KK) would also work well, but the symbol **K...K** is more descriptive because it shows the space between the Ks.] The condition *"One of the Ls is at one end of the line, and one of the Ms is at the other end"* can be symbolized as **L=1st/last** and **M=1st/last**. The diagram will consist of eight dashed lines numbered 1 through 8, from left to right:

JJ
LL
K...K
L=1st/last
M=1st/last

1	2	3	4	5	6	7	8

No significant conditions can be derived from the given information, and no conditions can be placed on the diagram. So we attack the questions.

1. To start, place M and K at positions 2 and 3, respectively:

1	2	3	4	5	6	7	8
	M	K					

From the conditions **LL** and **L=1st/last**, we see that the Ls must be in positions 7 and 8, since M is in position 2:

1	2	3	4	5	6	7	8
	M	K				L	L

Now the condition **M=1st/last** forces the other M into position 1:

1	2	3	4	5	6	7	8
M	M	K				L	L

This yields two possible positions for the condition **JJ**:

Diagram I

1	2	3	4	5	6	7	8
M	M	K	J	J		L	L

Diagram II

1	2	3	4	5	6	7	8
M	M	K		J	J	L	L

Diagram II is impossible, though, because it forces the Ks next to each other, violating the condition **K...K**. Thus Diagram I, which has the Js in positions 4 and 5, is uniquely determined by the conditions. The answer is (B).

2. Place a J in position 2:

1	2	3	4	5	6	7	8
	J						

Then, from the condition **JJ**, the other J must be in position 3, since only L or M can be first.

1	2	3	4	5	6	7	8
	J	J					

Next, since the Ls must be together and one of them must be either first or last, they must be in positions 7 and 8. This in turn forces M to be first:

1	2	3	4	5	6	7	8
M	J	J				L	L

Next, from the condition **K...K**, we see that the Ks must be in positions 4 and 6, which in turn forces the other M into position 5. Thus our uniquely determined diagram is

1	2	3	4	5	6	7	8
M	J	J	K	M	K	L	L

The answer is (E).

3. This question requires an indirect proof. That is, take a sub-statement; then try to construct a valid diagram for it. If this cannot be done, it is an answer—otherwise it is not.

Start with Statement I. If M is in position 5, then, from the supplemental condition *"M is in position 8"* and the condition **L=1st/last**, we know that the Ls must be in positions 1 and 2:

1	2	3	4	5	6	7	8
L	L			M			M

Now, the condition **JJ** forces the Js into either positions 3 and 4, or 6 and 7:

Diagram I

1	2	3	4	5	6	7	8
L	L	J	J	M			M

Diagram II

1	2	3	4	5	6	7	8
L	L			M	J	J	M

In both diagrams the Ks are forced next to each other, which violates the condition **K...K**. Hence Statement I cannot be true. This eliminates (B), (C), and (D), as they don't contain I.

Next, Statement II is time consuming because we will have to check all three positions for the Ks. So skip to Statement III. Place J in position 3:

1	2	3	4	5	6	7	8
L	L	J					M

Then from the condition **JJ**, we know that the other J must be in position 4:

1	2	3	4	5	6	7	8
L	L	J	J				M

Then the Ks can be placed in positions 5 and 7 and the M in position 6—all without violating any conditions:

1	2	3	4	5	6	7	8
L	L	J	J	K	M	K	M

This is a valid diagram with J in position 3. Hence Statement III *can* be true. This eliminates (E). Therefore, by process of elimination, we have learned that the answer is (A), without having to check Statement II.

4. This is a moderately hard problem. The condition *"the Ks are separated by at most one other person"* is somewhat obscure. It is more clearly expressed as *"exactly one person separates the Ks."*

Since the two Js must be next to each other, they cannot both be in even-numbered positions. This eliminates both (A) and (C). The same is true for the Ls, which eliminates (B).

Since the Ks are separated by exactly one person, they must either both occupy even-numbered positions or both occupy odd-numbered positions. But choice (D) places only one K in an even-numbered position. This eliminates (D).

As a matter of test-taking strategy, this is sufficient analysis of the question to mark the answer (E). However, it is instructive to work out a valid order for (E).

To this end, place an M in position 1 and the Ls in positions 7 and 8:

1	2	3	4	5	6	7	8
M						L	L

Next, place the Ks in positions 2 and 4, with M separating them:

1	2	3	4	5	6	7	8
M	K	M	K			L	L

Finally, place the Js in positions 5 and 6:

1	2	3	4	5	6	7	8
M	K	M	K	J	J	L	L

This diagram satisfies all the conditions, which verifies that (E) is the answer.

5. We will consider only the diagram with M at the left end and the Ls at the right end. The diagram with the Ls at the left end and the M at the right end is the mirror image, so it will generate the same answer. (For a discussion of mirror image, see Circular Ordering, page 99.) There are four possible diagrams, one for each of the four possible positions of the condition **JJ**:

1	2	3	4	5	6	7	8
M	J	J				L	L

1	2	3	4	5	6	7	8
M		J	J			L	L

1	2	3	4	5	6	7	8
M			J	J		L	L

1	2	3	4	5	6	7	8
M				J	J	L	L

From the condition **K...K**, we see that in the first diagram there must be a K in position 4, in the second diagram there must be a K in position 2, in the third diagram there must be a K in position 6, and in the last diagram there must be a K in position 4:

1	2	3	4	5	6	7	8
M	J	J	K			L	L

1	2	3	4	5	6	7	8
M	K	J	J			L	L

1	2	3	4	5	6	7	8
M			J	J	K	L	L

1	2	3	4	5	6	7	8
M			K	J	J	L	L

Each of these diagrams has a J next to a K. In other words, at least one J must be holding hands with a K. Hence the answer is (A).

Questions 6–11

This is a hybrid ordering game of medium difficulty. The game is quite fluid since there are no fixed elements. The condition *"Naomi does not sit next to either Mary or Oliver"* is naturally symbolized as **~(NM) and ~(NO)**. The condition *"Laura does not play Naomi"* can be symbolized as **L<-/->N**. Adding a diagram gives the following:

Women	Men
L, M, N	O, P

(P is "wild")

~(NM) and ~(NO)
L<-/->N

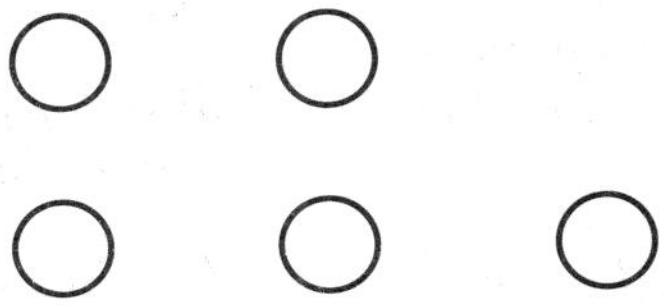

6. Adding the condition *"Mary plays Paul on the middle board and Paul does not sit between two other players"* to the diagram yields

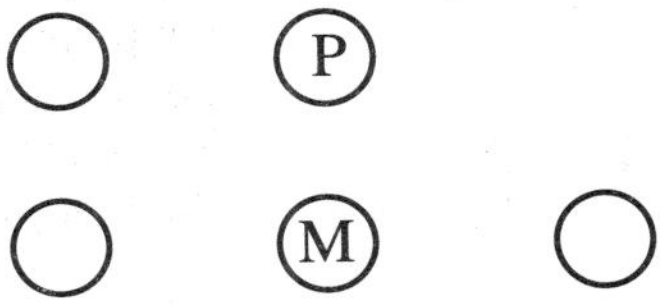

P

M

Now N must sit next to P since she cannot sit next to M, [**~(NM) and ~(NO)**]. This yields

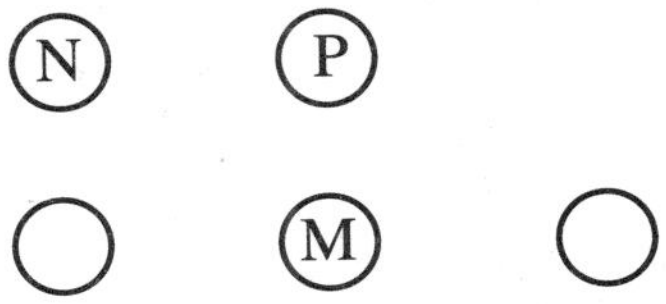

N P

M

Next, the condition **L<-/->N** forces L to the right of M:

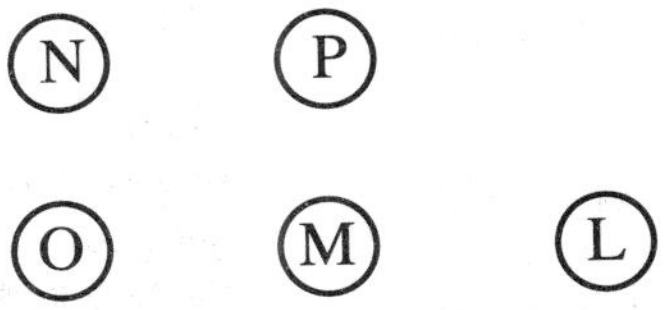

N P

O M L

This diagram is uniquely determined by the conditions. Hence, L and only L will not have an opponent. The answer is (A).

7. Adding the condition *"Paul does not have an opponent"* to the diagram yields

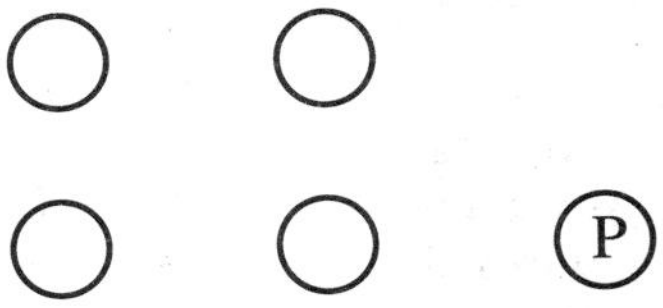

P

Now, we try to construct a diagram for each answer-choice. The one for which this cannot be done will be the answer. Begin with (A). Place M and N on the diagram as follows:

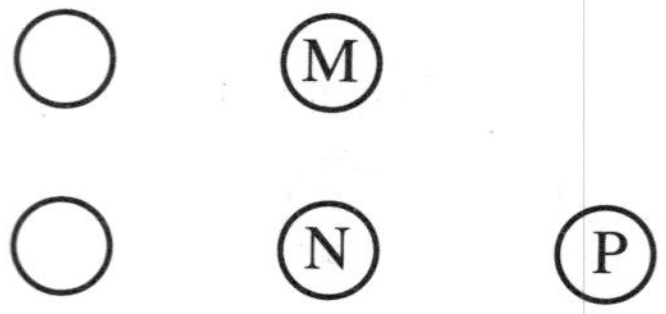

○ M

○ N P

Next, place O and L on the diagram as follows:

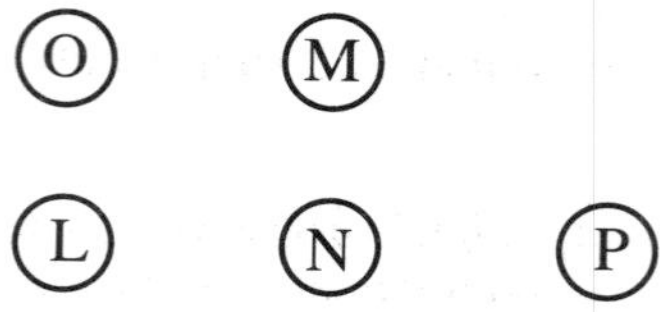

O M

L N P

This diagram satisfies every condition. Hence, Mary can play Naomi. This eliminates (A).

Choice (B) yields two possible diagrams:

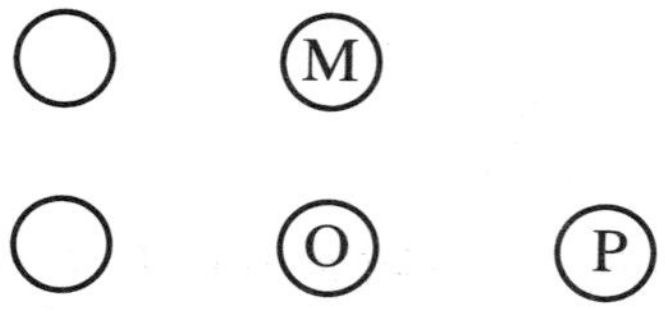

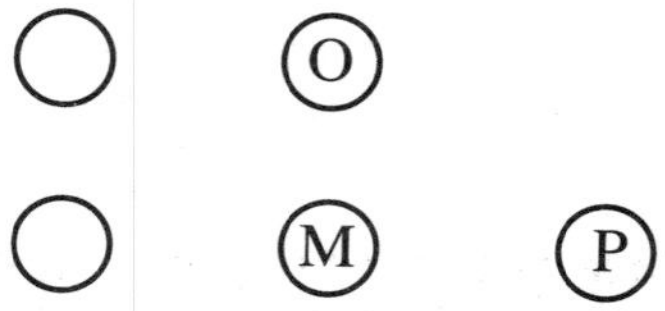

○ M ○ O

○ O P ○ M P

Clearly, in either diagram N must sit next to either M or O. However, this violates the condition **~(NM) and ~(NO)**. Hence, Mary cannot play Oliver, and the answer is (B).

8. Adding the condition *"Mary sits between two other players"* to the diagram yields

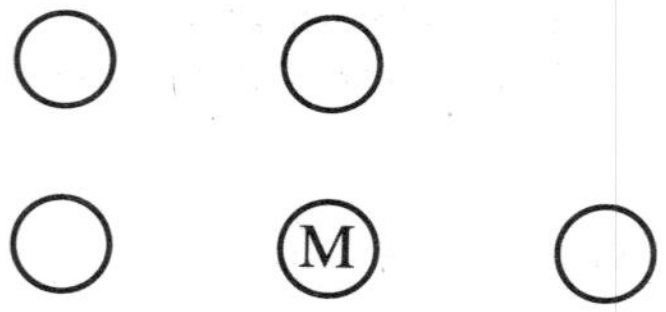

○ ○

○ M ○

Since players of the same sex do not play each other, M must play either O or P. This generates two diagrams:

Diagram I

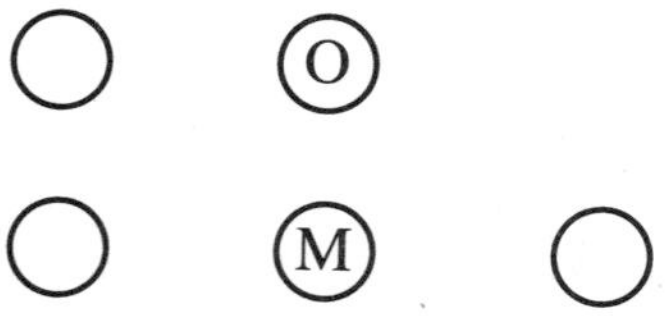

○ O

○ M ○

Diagram II

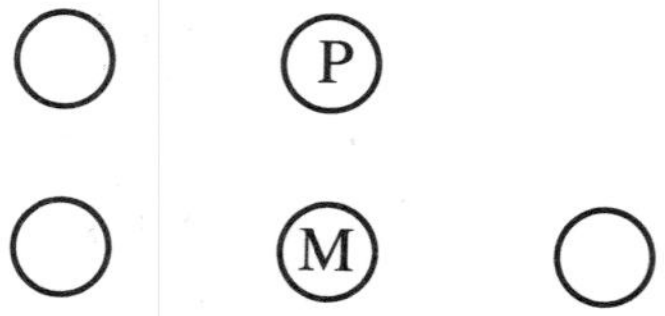

○ P

○ M ○

Diagram I is impossible since it forces N next to either M or O, violating the condition **~(NM) and ~(NO)**. In Diagram II, N must sit next to P since she cannot sit next to M:

Diagram II

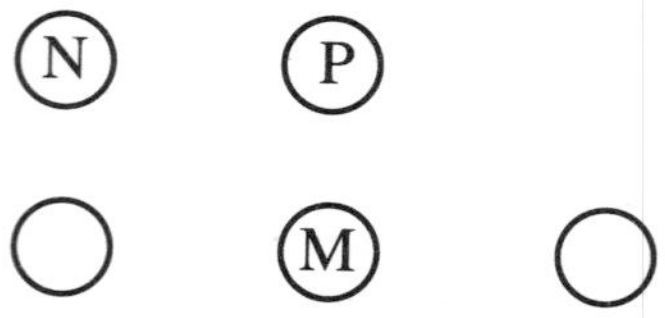

N P

○ M ○

Next, the condition **L<-/->N** forces L to the right of M and O to the left of M:

Diagram II

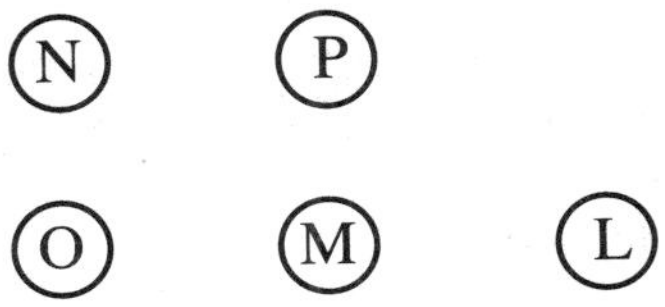

N P

O M L

This diagram is uniquely determined by the conditions. Hence, only Naomi can play Oliver. The answer is (C).

9. This type of problem can be time consuming because we may have to construct a separate diagram for each wrong answer. In these cases, you should quickly survey the answer-choices for a likely candidate and check whether any previous diagrams will help. Now, the final diagram in Question 8 shows that both (B) and (D) are possible. This eliminates (B) and (D). Turning to (E), place P on the diagram:

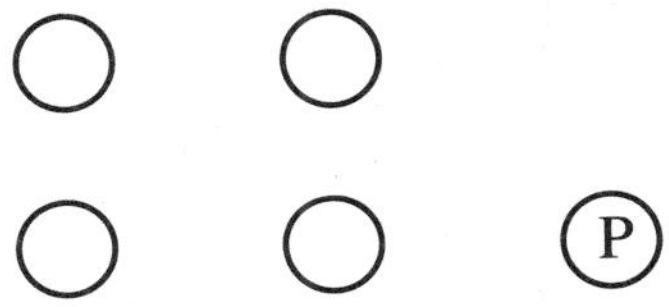

○ ○

○ ○ P

Now, there are three women but only four open seats in the diagram. Hence, two of the women must play each other, contradicting the condition *"players of the same sex do not play each other."* The answer is (E).

10. Since the women must play each other and there are three women, one woman will not have an opponent. The answer is (D).

11. From the condition **L<-/->N**, we know that Naomi cannot play Laura. This eliminates (E). The final diagram in Question 6 has Naomi playing Oliver, and the third diagram in Question 7 has Naomi playing Mary. Next, suppose Naomi plays Paul:

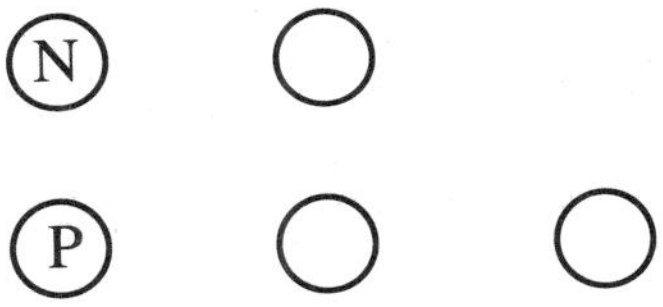

N ○

P ○ ○

Now, Laura could play Mary, which leaves Oliver without an opponent:

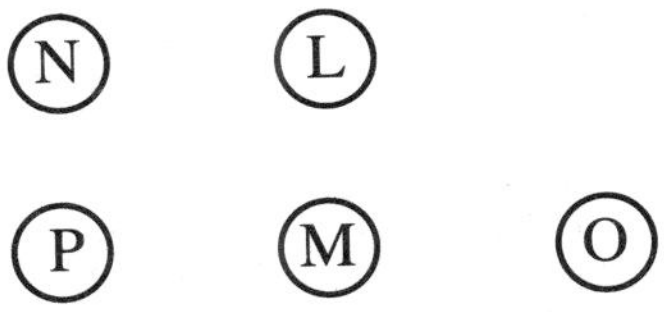

N L

P M O

This diagram satisfies every condition. Hence, Naomi can play Paul. So Naomi can play three different people—Oliver, Mary, and Paul. The answer is (D).

Questions 12–16

Although this game is about scheduling, its structure is actually linear ordering. The condition *"H's session must take place at some time before Z's session"* can be symbolized as **H—>Z**. The condition *"K's session is always scheduled for the day immediately before or the day immediately after the day for which O's session is scheduled"* simply means that K and O must be scheduled on consecutive days; it can be symbolized as **KO** (note, we won't use the flip-flop symbol, just remember that K and O can be interchanged). Symbolizing the remaining conditions yields

H, I, K, O, U, Z
1 day = 2 students
H—>Z
I = Th
KO
M ≠ 2 & W ≠ 2

~2 M	Tu	~2 W	Th	F
			I	

12.
(A) No. Adding H and U to the diagram yields

1 M	2 Tu	1 W	1 Th	1 F
	H **U**		**I**	

This diagram shows that there is no room to place the condition **KO**.
(B) No. Just as in choice (A), there is no room to place the condition **KO**.
(C) No. K and O must be scheduled on consecutive days.
(D) Yes. The following is one of two scenarios that satisfy all the conditions:

M	Tu	W	Th	F
H	**O** **U**	**K**	**I**	**Z**

(E) No. Just as in choice (A), there is no room to place the condition **KO**.

13.
(A) No. Z's session must be scheduled after H's session, **H—>Z**, and only one student can be scheduled for Monday.
(B) Yes. With K and Z scheduled for Tuesday, we get the following unique ordering:

M	Tu	W	Th	F
H	**K** **Z**	**O**	**I**	**U**

(C) No. See explanation for choice (B).
(D) No. See explanation for choice (B).
(E) No. See explanation for choice (B).

14.
(A) No. Following is one of several counterexamples:

M	Tu	W	Th	F
U	**K**	**O**	**I** **H**	**Z**

(B) No. Following is one of several counterexamples:

M	Tu	W	Th	F
K	**U** **O**	**H**	**I**	**Z**

(C) No. Following is one of several counterexamples:

M	Tu	W	Th	F
K	**O**	**U**	**I**	**Z**
			H	

(D) Yes. Place U on the diagram:

M	Tu	W	Th	F
			I	
			U	

This diagram shows that the condition **KO** must be placed on Monday/Tuesday or Tuesday/Wednesday. Hence, one of the days Monday, Tuesday, or Wednesday is left for H and Z. But since H must be scheduled before Z, Z must be scheduled on Friday.

(E) No. Following is one of several counterexamples:

M	Tu	W	Th	F
K	**O**	**H**	**I**	**U**
				Z

15.

(A) No. From the conditions **H—>Z** and **M ≠ 2**, we know that Z cannot be scheduled on Monday.

(B) No. Following are two valid scenarios with U scheduled on different days:

M	Tu	W	Th	F
H	**Z**	**K**	**I**	**U**
			O	

M	Tu	W	Th	F
H	**Z**	**U**	**I**	**K**
			O	

(C) No. Following are two valid scenarios with U scheduled on different days:

M	Tu	W	Th	F
K	**O**	**Z**	**I**	**U**
	H			

M	Tu	W	Th	F
U	**H**	**Z**	**I**	**O**
			K	

(D) Yes. Place Z on the diagram:

M	Tu	W	Th	F
			I	
			Z	

This diagram shows that the condition **KO** must be placed on Monday/Tuesday or Tuesday/Wednesday. Since H must be scheduled before Z, H must be scheduled on Monday or Wednesday, which forces U to be scheduled on Friday.

(E) No. Following are two valid scenarios with U scheduled on different days:

M	Tu	W	Th	F
K	**O**	**U**	**I**	**Z**
			H	

M	Tu	W	Th	F
U	**K**	**O**	**I**	**Z**
			H	

16.

(A) **Yes.** Scheduling U on Monday and H on Tuesday yields the following diagram:

M	Tu	W	Th	F
U	H		I	

The condition **KO** can be placed on the diagram as follows:

M	Tu	W	Th	F
U	H	O	I	
	K			

Finally, placing Z on Friday yields the following valid scenario:

M	Tu	W	Th	F
U	H	O	I	Z
	K			

Note, the supplemental condition *"H's session is scheduled as the next session after U's session"* is not needed for this or any other answer-choice. It is not uncommon for the LSAT writers to introduce superfluous conditions.

(B) No. H cannot be scheduled on Friday since H must be scheduled before Z. Note, Z cannot also be scheduled on Friday since there are already two people—I and U—scheduled on Thursday.

(C) No. Place U and H on the diagram:

M	Tu	W	Th	F
	U		I	
	H			

This diagram leaves no room to place the condition **KO**.

(D) No. This would schedule three people—I, U, and H—on Thursday. But the setup to the game states that exactly one person is scheduled for each day, except for one day when two people are scheduled.

(E) No. H cannot be scheduled on Friday with U since H must be scheduled before Z.

Sequential Games

Unlike spatial and hybrid games, sequential games do not order elements in space. Sequential games can be classified according to the criteria used to order the elements:

- Chronological (before, after, etc.)
- Quantifiable (size, height, etc.)
- Ranking (first, second, etc.)

CHRONOLOGICAL GAMES

Chronological games order elements in a time-sequence. For example, James was born before George who was born before Kim who was born before Sara. In the line-up games that we studied earlier, the elements were ordered spatially. In chronological ordering games, the elements are ordered sequentially. This is true of many of the games that we will study in this chapter. Because these games are sequential in nature, their diagrams can be quite different from those used to solve spatial and hybrid games.

One of the most common and efficient types of diagrams is the flow chart. In these diagrams the elements are connected by arrows.*

Now that we have a second way to diagram linear ordering games, we need, of course, some means of deciding which method to use.

In general, a game with no fixed elements should be solved using a flow chart.

In constructing a flow chart, follow these guidelines:

1. **Look for a condition that starts the "flow".**
2. **Build the chart around the element that occurs in the greatest number of conditions.**
3. **Keep the chart flexible; it will probably have to evolve with the changing conditions.**

An example will illustrate the flow chart method of diagramming:

---

* See Paths and Flow Charts for a treatment of flow charts for non-linear games.

Chronological Game

Eight people—S, T, U, V, W, X, Y, Z—were each born in a different year, 1971 through 1978. The following is known about their ages.

W is older than V.
S is younger than both Y and V.
T is not younger than Y.
Z is younger than Y, but older than U.

1. Which one of the following is a possible sequence of births from first to last?

(A) W V T Y Z U X S
(B) W V T U Y Z X S
(C) U T Y W V S Z X
(D) T W Y S Z U X V
(E) T Y W V S U X Z

2. If S was born in 1975, which one of the following must be false?

(A) V was born in 1973.
(B) V was born in 1972.
(C) Z was born in 1977.
(D) Y was born in 1974.
(E) Z was born in 1974.

3. If S was born in 1976 and X was born in 1973, then the year of birth of exactly how many other people can be determined?

(A) 0
(B) 1
(C) 2
(D) 3
(E) 4

4. If S was born before X, then which one of the following could be true?

(A) Z was born before T.
(B) V was born before W.
(C) U was born before S.
(D) W was born after S.
(E) W was born in 1976.

5. If the condition "S is younger than both Y and V" is dropped, then the year of birth of exactly how many people can be determined?

(A) 0
(B) 1
(C) 2
(D) 3
(E) 4

This game does not have any fixed elements (such as T was born in 1972), so the flow chart method is indicated. We'll use an arrow to indicate that one person is older than another. The condition *"W is older than V"* is naturally symbolized as **W—>V**. The other conditions are symbolized in like manner, giving the following schematic:

1. **W—>V**
2. **Y—>S**
3. **V—>S**
4. **T—>Y**
5. **Y—>Z**
6. **Z—>U**

Now we construct the diagram. Following the guidelines on page 87, look for the element that occurs in the greatest number of conditions. It is Y, so we build the chart around Y. Start with condition 4:

T—>Y

Adding conditions 2 and 5 gives

↗ Z
T—> Y—>S

Adding conditions 1 and 3 gives

```
           ↗ Z
T—> Y—>S
         ↗
W—>V
```

Finally, adding condition 6 gives

```
           ↗ Z—>U
T—> Y—>S
         ↗
W—>V
```

There are no conditions on the element X, so it can not be placed in the diagram. However, we note it below the diagram as follows:

```
           ↗ Z—>U
T—> Y—>S
         ↗
W—>V
     (X "wild")
```

Two properties of the diagram should be noted before turning to the questions. First, if two elements are in different rows and no sequence of arrows connects them, then the diagram does not tell us which one is older. For example, since W and Y are in different rows and are not connected by a sequence of arrows, the diagram does not tell us who is older. However, the diagram *does* tell us that T is older than U, because the arrows "flow" from T to Y to Z to U. Second, the diagram tells us that only T, W, or X can be the oldest, and likewise that only U, S, or X can be the youngest.

1. **Which one of the following is a possible sequence of births from first to last?**

   (A) W V T Y Z U X S
   (B) W V T U Y Z X S
   (C) U T Y W V S Z X
   (D) T W Y S Z U X V
   (E) T Y W V S U X Z

This is a straightforward elimination problem. (B) and (E) are not possible sequences because the diagram shows that Z must be older than U. (C) is not a possible sequence because the diagram shows that T must be older than U. The arrows "flow" from T to Y to Z to U. Finally, (D) is not a possible sequence because the diagram shows that V must be older than S. Hence, by process of elimination, the answer is (A).

2. **If S was born in 1975, which one of the following must be false?**

   (A) V was born in 1973.
   (B) V was born in 1972.
   (C) Z was born in 1977.
   (D) Y was born in 1974.
   (E) Z was born in 1974.

The diagram shows that T, Y, W, and V—not necessarily in that order—were all born before S. So they must have been born in the years '71 through '74. This gives the following *possible* diagram. (Because one of the births, S, is fixed, it is now more convenient to use a *line-up* diagram.)

71	72	73	74	75	76	77	78
T	Y	W	V	S			

Clearly, this diagram shows that Z must have been born after '75. Choice (E), therefore, makes the necessarily false statement. The answer is (E).

3. If S was born in 1976 and X was born in 1973, then the year of birth of exactly how many other people can be determined?

(A) 0
(B) 1
(C) 2
(D) 3
(E) 4

Since two births—S and X—are fixed, we again revert to a *line-up* diagram:

71	72	73	74	75	76	77	78
		X			S		

The original diagram shows that W, V, T, and Y were all born before S, so they must be placed to the left of S on the new diagram. However, we cannot uniquely determine their positions: W and V could have been born in '71 and '72, respectively, or T and Y could have been. So one *possible* diagram is

71	72	73	74	75	76	77	78
W	V	X	T	Y	S		

Clearly this diagram forces Z and U to have been born in the years '77 and '78, respectively. Hence only two other births can be determined. The answer is (C).

4. If S was born before X, then which one of the following could be true?

(A) Z was born before T.
(B) V was born before W.
(C) U was born before S.
(D) W was born after S.
(E) W was born in 1976.

Add the condition *"S was born before X"* to the diagram:

```
              ↗ Z—>U
T—> Y—>S—>X
              ↗
W—>V
```

In this diagram U and S are in different rows and are not connected by a sequence of arrows, so U could have been born before S. The answer, therefore, is (C).

5. If the condition "S is younger than both Y and V" is dropped, then the year of birth of exactly how many people could be determined?

(A) 0
(B) 1
(C) 2
(D) 3
(E) 4

The condition *"S is younger than both Y and V"* anchored the diagram. Without it we get the following diagram:

T—>Y—>Z—>U
W—>V
(X and S "wild")

Because the two parts of this diagram are independent (they are not connected by a sequence of arrows), W and V could have been born before T or after U. Hence the year of birth cannot be determined for any of the people. The answer is (A).

Points to Remember

1. The three types of sequential games are
   - Chronological (before, after, etc.)
   - Quantifiable (size, height, etc.)
   - Ranking (first, second, etc.)

2. Most sequential games can be solved most efficiently with a flow chart.

3. In general, a game with no fixed elements should be solved using a flow chart.

4. When constructing a flow chart, follow these guidelines.
   1. Look for a condition that starts the "flow".
   2. Build the chart around the element that occurs in the greatest number of conditions.
   3. Keep the chart flexible; it will probably have to evolve with the changing conditions.

There will be no mentor exercise in this section.

Exercise

Directions: The following group of questions is based on a set of conditions. Choose the response that most accurately and completely answers each question.

Questions 1-5

Ten children—Anna, Bob, Charles, Don, Emily, Frank, Gina, Hank, Irene, and Jane—are comparing their heights.

Jane is taller than Don.
Hank and Irene are the same height and both are shorter than Don.
Irene is taller than Bob.
Both Anna and Emily are taller than Gina.
Both Charles and Frank are shorter than Gina.

1. Which one of the following can be false?

   (A) Anna is taller than Frank.
   (B) Bob is shorter than Jane.
   (C) Jane is shorter than Emily.
   (D) Frank is shorter than Anna.
   (E) Anna is taller than Charles.

2. What is the minimum number of different heights the ten children can have?

   (A) 3
   (B) 4
   (C) 5
   (D) 6
   (E) 7

3. If Gina is the same height as Irene, then which one of the following can be false?

   (A) Don is taller than Emily.
   (B) Jane is taller than Bob.
   (C) Emily is taller than Charles.
   (D) Gina is the same height as Hank.
   (E) Hank is taller than Frank.

4. Which of the following statements supplies information already contained in the original conditions?

   I. Frank is shorter than Emily.
   II. Jane is taller than Gina.
   III. Charles is taller than Frank.

   (A) I only
   (B) II only
   (C) III only
   (D) I and III only
   (E) II and III only

5. Which one of the following children could NOT be the third tallest?

   (A) Jane
   (B) Hank
   (C) Irene
   (D) Gina
   (E) Bob

The following game is taken from an official LSAT.

Questions 6-7

A law firm has exactly nine partners: Fox, Glassen, Hae, Inman, Jacoby, Kohn, Lopez, Malloy, and Nassar.

Kohn's salary is greater than both Inman's and Lopez's.
Lopez's salary is greater than Nassar's.
Inman's salary is greater than Fox's.
Fox's salary is greater than Malloy's.
Malloy's salary is greater than Glassen's.
Glassen's salary is greater than Jacoby's.
Jacoby's salary is greater than Hae's.

6. If Nassar's salary is the same as that of one other partner of the firm, which one of the following must be false?

(A) Inman's salary is less than Lopez's.
(B) Jacoby's salary is less than Lopez's.
(C) Lopez's salary is less than Fox's.
(D) Lopez's salary is less than Hae's.
(E) Nassar's salary is less than Glassen's.

7. What is the minimum number of different salaries earned by the nine partners of the firm?

(A) 5
(B) 6
(C) 7
(D) 8
(E) 9

Questions 8–11

Six items—H, I, J, K, L, and M—are being packed in a cylindrical carton. The order in which the items are placed in the carton must conform to the following rules:

Both items M and L must be placed in the carton before item H.
Item I must be placed in the carton after items H and K.
Item K cannot be placed in the carton next to item J.
Any red item must be placed in the carton before any non-red item, provided that none of the preceding rules are violated.

8. The items can be placed in the carton in which one of the following sequences?

(A) M, L, H, K, J, I
(B) K, I, M, L, J, H
(C) K, L, M, J, H, I
(D) J, L, K, H, M, I
(E) J, K, M, L, H, I

9. If H and L are the only red items, then the items can be placed in the carton in which one of the following sequences?

(A) L, H, M, K, I, J
(B) L, M, K, H, I, J
(C) L, M, H, K, I, J
(D) L, M, H, J, I, K
(E) L, J, M, H, K, I

10. If M and I are the only red items, which of the following must be true?

(A) J is the last item placed in the carton.
(B) L is the second item placed in the carton.
(C) K is the fourth item placed in the carton.
(D) J is the fourth item placed in the carton.
(E) I is the fourth item placed in the carton.

11. If red items MUST be placed in the carton before non-red items, which of the following cannot be true?

(A) Both K and M are red.
(B) There are two non-red items neither of which is I.
(C) Both H and I are red
(D) There are two non-red items neither of which is H.
(E) Both H and J are red

Answers and Solutions to Exercise

Questions 1-5

Since this game has no fixed elements (i.e., none of the heights of the children are given), a flow chart is indicated. The condition *"Jane is taller than Don"* can be symbolized as **J—>D**, where the arrow stands for *is taller than*. The condition *"Hank and Irene are the same height and both are shorter than Don"* can be symbolized as **D—>(H=I)**. The condition *"Both Anna and Emily are taller than Gina"* can be symbolized as **A/E—>G**. The remaining conditions can be symbolized in like manner, giving the following schematic:

J—>D
D—>(H=I)
I—>B
A/E—>G
G—>C/F

Now we construct a flow chart from these conditions. D occurs in the top two conditions and G occurs in the bottom two conditions; this indicates that there will probably be two charts for this problem. Start with the first condition:

J—>D

Next, add the condition **D—>(H=I):**

J—>D ↗ H
J—>D ↘ I

(The rectangle around H and I indicates that they are the same height.)

Then, add the condition **I—>B**:

J—>D ↗ H
J—>D ↘ I—>B

The conditions **A/E—>G** and **G—>C/F** cannot be added to the diagram, so we build a separate diagram for them:

A ↘ G ↗ C
E ↗ G ↘ F

1. If two elements are not connected by a sequence of arrows or if they are in different diagrams, then their heights are independent of each other. Jane and Emily are in different diagrams, so either could be shorter than the other. The answer is (C).

2. The first diagram generates four different heights (Remember H and I are the same height). Since the second diagram is independent of the first, A, E, and J could be the same height, D and G could be the same height, and B, C, and F could be the same height. So the second diagram does not necessarily add any more distinct heights. The answer is (B).

3. The new condition combines the two original diagrams as follows:

A ↘ [H I G] ↗ C
J—>D—> [H I G] —>B
E ↗ [H I G] ↘ F

Now since E and D are not connected by a sequence of arrows, either could be taller than the other. The answer is (A).

4. From the second diagram, we see that Frank must be shorter than Emily (the arrows "flow" from Emily to Gina to Frank). Hence Statement I *is* contained in the original conditions. This eliminates (B), (C), and (E)—they don't contain Statement I. Note that only (A) and (D) remain and neither contains Statement II. Thus we need not check Statement II. As to Statement III, it is false. In the diagram, C and F are not connected by a sequence of arrows, so either could be taller than the other. Hence, by process of elimination, the answer is (A).

5. From the first diagram, we see that J, D, H, and I are all taller than B. Therefore, B cannot be the third-tallest child. The answer is (E).

Questions 6-7

The condition *"Kohn's salary is greater than both Inman's and Lopez's"* starts the flow:

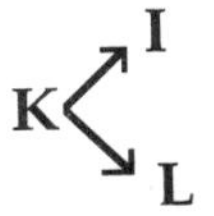

```
  ↗ I
K
  ↘ L
```

Next, add the condition *"Lopez's salary is greater than Nassar's"*:

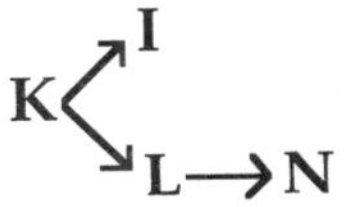

```
  ↗ I
K
  ↘ L → N
```

Adding the remaining conditions yields the following flow chart:

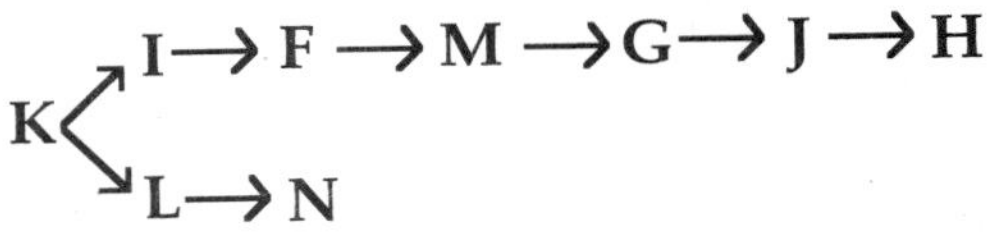

```
  ↗ I → F → M → G → J → H
K
  ↘ L → N
```

6. Suppose Nassar's salary were as low as possible. Then since his salary is the same as that of one other partner, he would have to have the same salary as does Hae. Adding this to the diagram gives

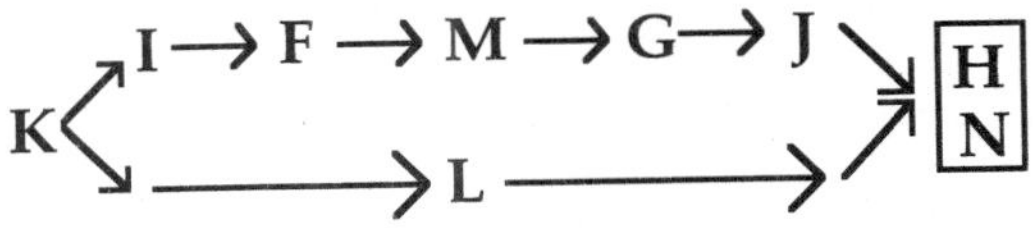

```
  ↗ I → F → M → G → J ↘ [H]
K                        [N]
  ↘ ——————→ L ——————→ ↗
```

Even in this diagram, Lopez's salary is greater than Hae's. The answer is (D).

7. The top row of the original chart shows that K, I, F, M, G, J, and H all earn different salaries. Now L could earn the same salary as I, and N could earn the same salary as F (since they're in unconnected rows). This yields the following diagram

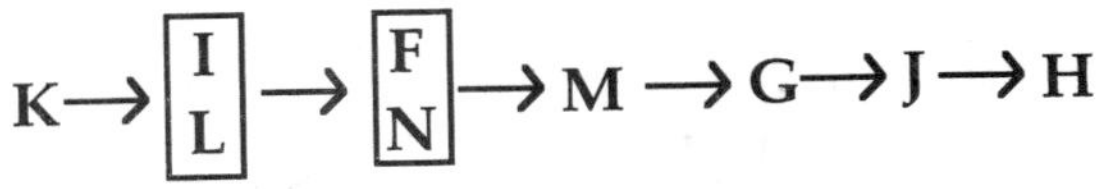

```
K → [I] → [F] → M → G → J → H
    [L]   [N]
```

This diagram clearly displays seven different salaries. The answer is (C).

Questions 8–11

The conditions of the game are naturally symbolized as follows:

1. **M—>H**
2. **L—>H**
3. **H—>I**
4. **K—>I**
5. **~(JK)**
6. **Red items before non-red items (when possible)**

Combining conditions 1 and 3 yields

M—>H—>I

Adding conditions 2 and 4 to the diagram yields

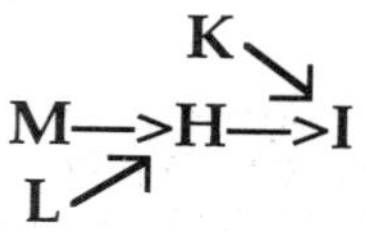

K↘
M—>H—>I
L↗

8. Choices (A) and (E) violate the condition **~(JK)**, eliminate. From the diagram, I cannot come before M, which eliminates choice (B). Choice (D) violates the condition **M—>H**, eliminate. Hence, by process of elimination, the answer is (C).

9. Choice (A) violates the condition **M—>H,** eliminate. Choice (B) has K before H, which violates the condition **Red items before non-red items (when possible)**, eliminate. Choice (D) violates the condition **K—>I**, eliminate. Choice (E) has J before H, which violates the condition **Red items before non-red items (when possible)**, eliminate. Hence, by process of elimination, the answer is (C).

It is also instructive to solve this problem directly. Since L is red, it must come first; and the original diagram becomes

K↘
L—>M—>H—>I

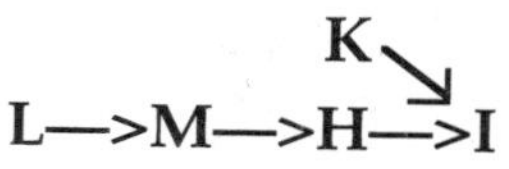

Since H is red, K must come after H:

L—>M—>H—>K—>I

Finally, since J is not red and cannot be next to K, J must be last:

L—>M—>H—>K—>I—>J

This uniquely determined order is choice (C).

10. Since M is red, the original diagram becomes

K↘
M—>L—>H—>I

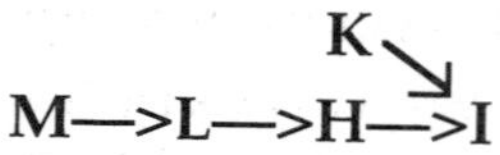

Now, since I is red, J must be placed after I:

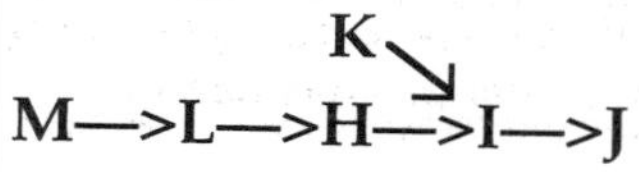

K↘
M—>L—>H—>I—>J

Hence, J is last and the answer is (A). Note, since there is no sequence of arrows connecting K with either L or H, K can come before L, directly after L, or after H. Hence, choices (B) and (C) are not necessarily true.

11. Begin with choice (A). Since both K and M are red, the original diagram becomes

[M / K]—>L—>H—>I

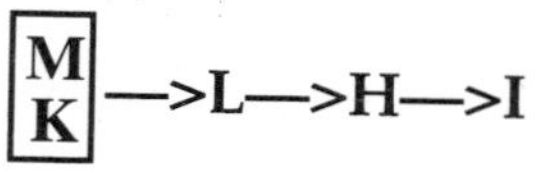

where the box around M and K indicates that they are first and second, not necessarily in that order. Now, J can be placed last in this diagram without violating any condition. Hence, choice (A) can be true, eliminate.

Turning to choice (B), I must be red since neither of the two non-red items is I. Now, the original diagram shows that M, H, K, and L all precede I and therefore must all be red. Hence, J and only J can be non-red. Therefore, choice (B) cannot be true and therefore is the answer.

Circular Ordering

We have thoroughly studied the ordering of elements in a straight line—the most common type of LSAT game. In the next most common type of ordering game the elements are placed around a circle—typically, people who are evenly spaced around a table. Circular diagrams have a few interesting properties not found in linear diagrams.

First, circular diagrams—unlike linear diagrams—are not fixed. That is, circular diagrams do not have a first, second, . . ., or last position. You can envision a circle as derived from a line by bending the line until the left end point (say, the first) and the right end point (say, the last) meet—forcing the first and last elements to become one and the same. Hence there is no beginning or end on a circle.

For this reason, you can initially place an element anywhere on the diagram—it can be fixed only in relation to other elements. It is conventional to place the first element at the top of the circle. Then place any additional elements (where applicable) to the left of it, clockwise around the circle.*

Next, although there is no first, second, etc., on a circle, there is left-right orientation (at least locally). So if a condition states that one element is next to another element but does not state whether it's to the left or the right, then two diagrams that are mirror images of each other will be possible.

However, if there is no mention of the circle's orientation (left or right), then the mirror image of the diagram need not be considered.

For example, if it is given that A is next to B, and it is not specified whether A is to the left or right of B, then only one of the following two possible diagrams need be considered. They will generate the same answer to any question.

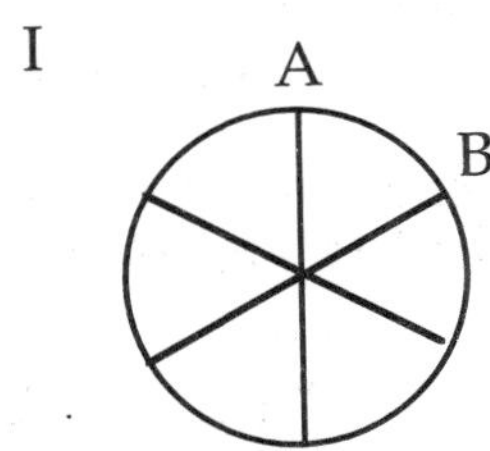

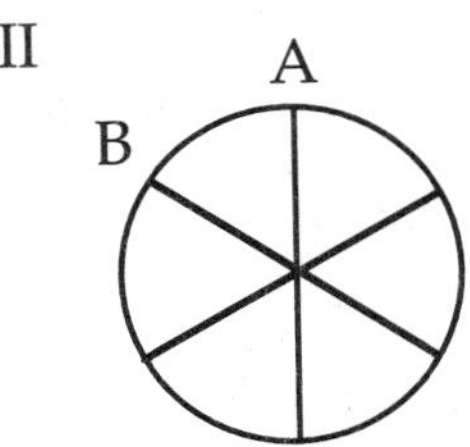

To see this more clearly, hold this page up to the light and look at Figure I from behind the page. A is now to the left of B. If you turn the page back, A is to the right of B. Clearly, during this process, the relationship between A and B (their relative position) did not change—only your perspective did. Thus Figure II is not fundamentally different from Figure I.

When you draw your circle, insert spokes. Invariably, circular games involve an even number of people (usually 6 or 8) spaced <u>evenly</u> around a circle. Therefore, a particular element will always be directly opposite another element. Drawing spokes inside the circle clarifies and highlights whether two elements are directly opposite each other, which often is a relevant issue.

---

* Left is taken from the perspective of the reader looking inward toward the center of the circle. In other words, *left* is in the clockwise direction.

Now that we have our circle drawn with spokes inserted, we come to **the decision**: which element(s) do we place on the diagram first.

Always place elements whose positions are fixed relative to one another first.

Recall that with linear ordering games we first place any element whose position is fixed (first, second, last, etc.). Then we place any elements whose positions are fixed relative to one another (e.g., B comes after C). Circular diagrams, however, are not fixed. Hence the first step does not apply, and we start with the second step.

The relative position of elements around a circle can be fixed in either of two major ways. First, two elements can be directly opposite each other. This forms a **base axis**, which separates all the remaining elements to either side of it. **Place the base axis on your diagram first.** For example, if A is directly opposite B, then A and B form a base axis as follows:

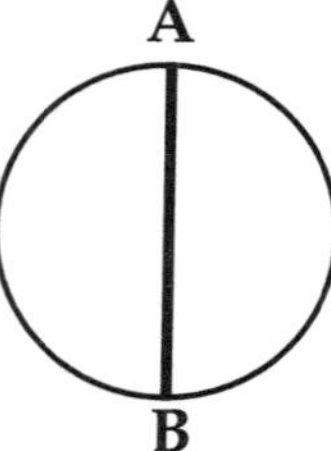

Second, the elements can be immediately next to each other. This forms a **base group**. For example, if B is immediately between A and C, then we have the following base group:

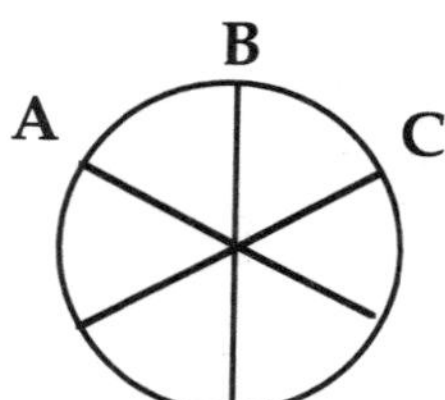

Place the base group on your circle after you have placed the base axis. Place it first if there is no base axis.

Now let's apply these properties and strategies to a circular game of medium difficulty.

Circular Game

Six people—Alice, Bob, Carol, Dave, Emily, Frank—are seated evenly spaced around a circular table according to the following conditions:

Alice does not sit next to Carol.
Bob sits next to Carol or Dave.
Frank sits next to Dave.
If Emily sits next to Frank, then she does not sit next to Carol.

1. Of the following, which one is a possible seating arrangement of the six people?
   (A) Alice, Frank, Dave, Carol, Emily, Bob
   (B) Alice, Bob, Carol, Frank, Dave, Emily
   (C) Alice, Bob, Carol, Emily, Frank, Dave
   (D) Alice, Emily, Frank, Dave, Bob, Carol
   (E) Alice, Dave, Bob, Emily, Carol, Frank

2. If Bob is seated next to Frank, then in which one of the following pairs must the people be seated next to each other?
   (A) Alice and Emily
   (B) Bob and Dave
   (C) Bob and Emily
   (D) Carol and Dave
   (E) Carol and Frank

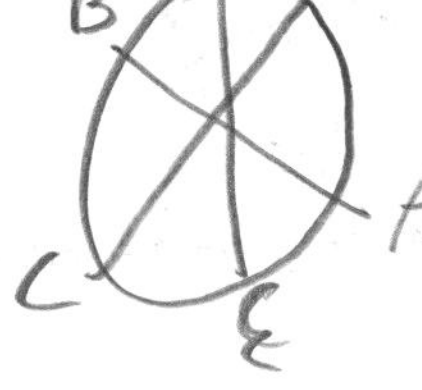

3. If Dave and Carol sit next to each other, then Alice could sit immediately between
   (A) Bob and Carol
   (B) Bob and Frank
   (C) Dave and Emily
   (D) Dave and Frank
   (E) Frank and Emily

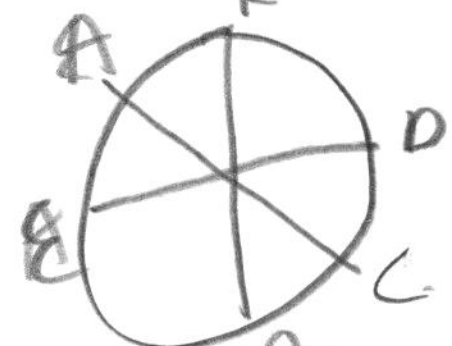

4. If Bob sits next to Carol, then which one of the following is a complete and accurate list of the people who could also sit next to Bob?
   (A) Alice
   (B) Alice, Dave
   (C) Dave, Frank
   (D) Alice, Emily, Frank
   (E) Alice, Dave, Emily, Frank

5. Which of the following must be false if Bob sits next to Dave?
   I. Emily sits next to Frank.
   II. Carol sits directly opposite Bob.
   III. Carol sits immediately between Emily and Bob.

   (A) I only
   (B) III only
   (C) I and II only
   (D) II and III only
   (E) I, II, and III

6. If Alice sits next to Emily, then Bob CANNOT sit immediately between
   (A) Alice and Carol
   (B) Alice and Dave
   (C) Carol and Dave
   (D) Carol and Frank
   (E) Dave and Emily

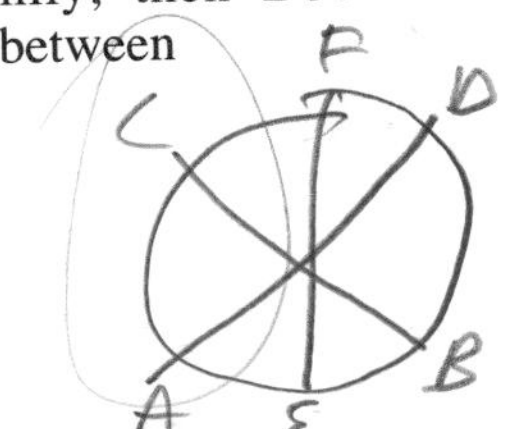

As usual we construct a diagram to aid in answering the questions. First, translate the given conditions into symbols—abbreviating each name with its first letter.

The most concrete condition is *"Frank sits next to Dave"*; it is naturally symbolized as **FD.**

Next, we symbolize the second most concrete condition, *"Bob sits next to Carol or Dave,"* as **BC or BD.** The "or" in this symbol is inclusive. That is, it includes the case in which B sits next to both C and D—in other words, immediately between them. (Unless otherwise stated, the meaning of "or" is inclusive on the LSAT.)

Next, *"Alice does not sit next to Carol"* is symbolized as **~(AC).**

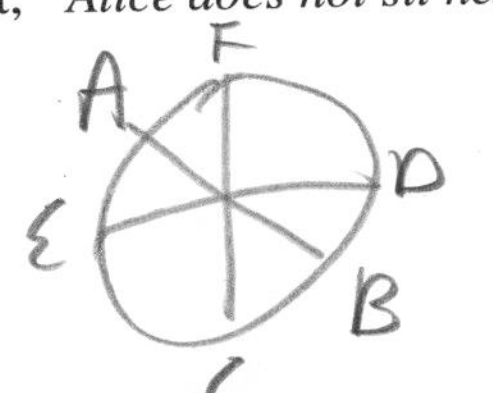

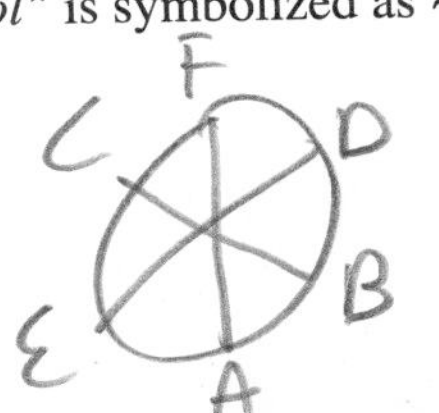

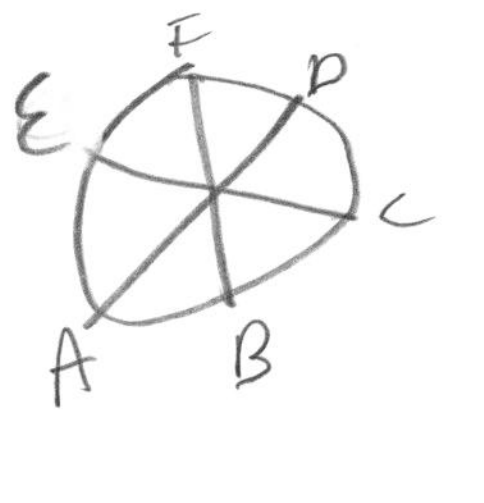

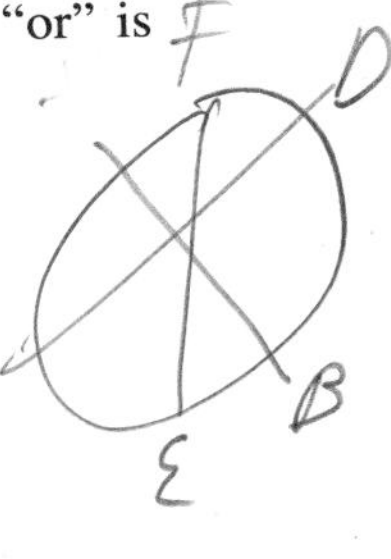

Finally, we come to the last and most complicated condition, *"If Emily sits next to Frank, then she does not sit next to Carol."* An initial symbol for this sentence might be **(EF)—>~(EC)**, where the arrow stands for "if..., then...." However, we can derive a more descriptive symbol as follows: If Emily were to sit next to both Frank and Carol, then she would be seated immediately between them. This is not allowed. Thus the more concise symbol **~(FEC)** is equivalent to our original symbol **(EF)—>~(EC)**.

We now have the following schematic for our conditions:

ABCDEF
FD
BC or BD
~(AC)
~(FEC)

We need, however, a diagram to fill out our scheme. To this end, draw the following circle with spokes inside:

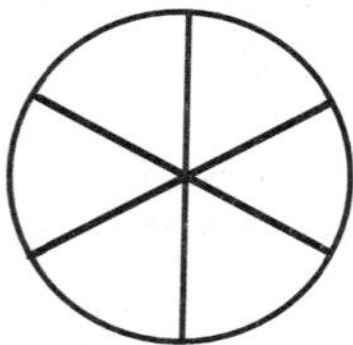

Next, following the strategies developed earlier, we scan the initial conditions for a base axis. There is none. So we look for a base group. The only condition that fixes the relative position of two of the elements is **FD**; it forms our base group.

Since circle diagrams are not fixed, we may initially place **FD** anywhere on the circle. Following convention, however, we put F at the top of the circle, creating the following two possible diagrams:

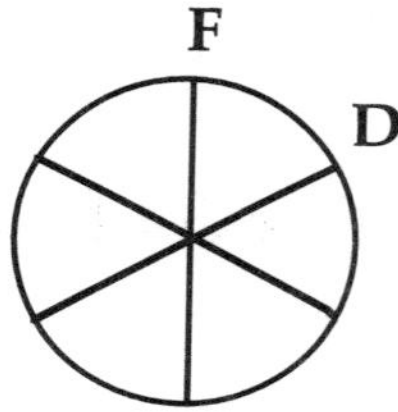

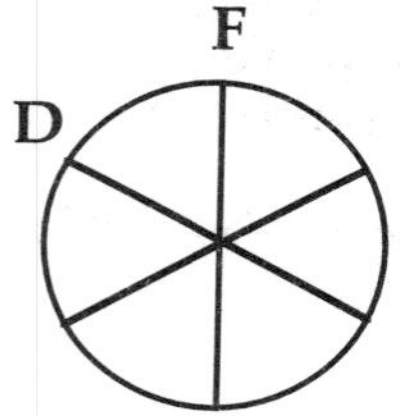

In this problem, there is no mention of the circle's orientation (left or right). We, therefore, need to consider only the first diagram, the other being the mirror image of it.

No other conditions fix the relative positions of the other elements, so our schematic is complete with diagram as follows:

ABCDEF
FD
BC or BD
~(AC)
~(FEC)

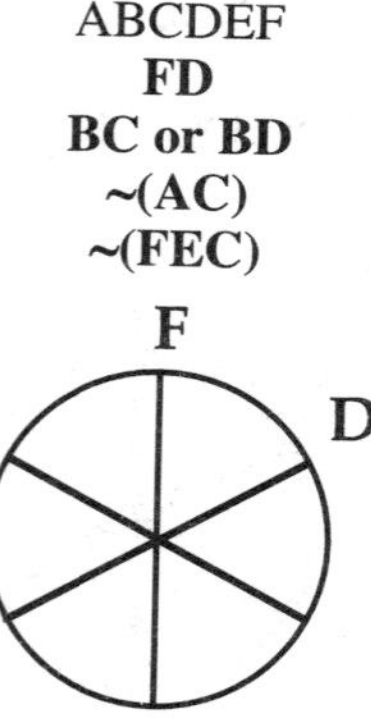

This schematic is self-contained. There is no need to refer to the original problem, which should be avoided whenever possible. Now we'll use this schematic to answer the questions.

1. **Of the following, which one is a possible seating arrangement of the six people?**

   (A) **Alice, Frank, Dave, Carol, Emily, Bob**
   (B) **Alice, Bob, Carol, Frank, Dave, Emily**
   (C) **Alice, Bob, Carol, Emily, Frank, Dave**
   (D) **Alice, Emily, Frank, Dave, Bob, Carol**
   (E) **Alice, Dave, Bob, Emily, Carol, Frank**

This is a straightforward elimination question. We merely take the initial conditions in succession and test them against each answer-choice, eliminating any answer-choices that do not satisfy the conditions. The last remaining answer-choice will be the answer.

Let's start the elimination process with the condition **FD**. All the answer-choices have F next to D except choice (E). This eliminates (E). Next, we use the condition **BC or BD**. Choices (B), (C), and (D) all satisfy this condition; (A) does not. This eliminates (A). Next, using the condition **~(AC)**, we eliminate choice (D), which has A next to C. Note: Since this is a circular ordering, the list A, E, F, D, B, C does not end at C (recall that there is no first or last on a circle). Instead, the sequence returns to A and repeats the cycle. This is shown more clearly by the following "flow chart":

–> A–> E–> F–> D–> B–> C

Finally, choice (C) contradicts the condition **~(FEC)**. This eliminates (C). Hence, by process of elimination, the answer is (B)—the only answer-choice remaining.

2. **If Bob is seated next to Frank, then in which one of the following pairs must the people be seated next to each other?**

   (A) **Alice and Emily**
   (B) **Bob and Dave**
   (C) **Bob and Emily**
   (D) **Carol and Dave**
   (E) **Carol and Frank**

The new condition, *"Bob is seated next to Frank,"* is naturally symbolized as **BF**. Adding this condition to our original diagram gives

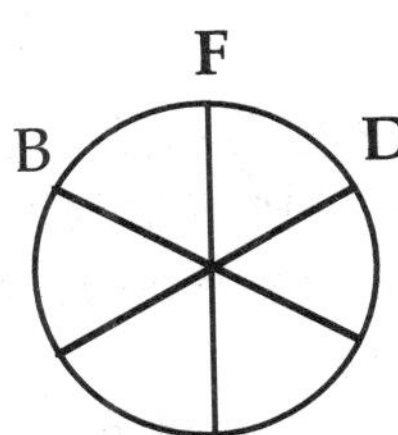

Next, from the condition **BC or BD**, we see that B must be next to C, as it is not next to D in the diagram. Our diagram, therefore, is as follows:

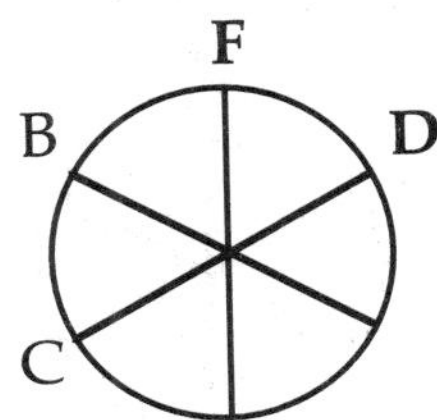

Finally, the condition **~(AC)** forces A next to D (otherwise it would be next to C), which in turn forces E between A and C. Thus our uniquely determined diagram is

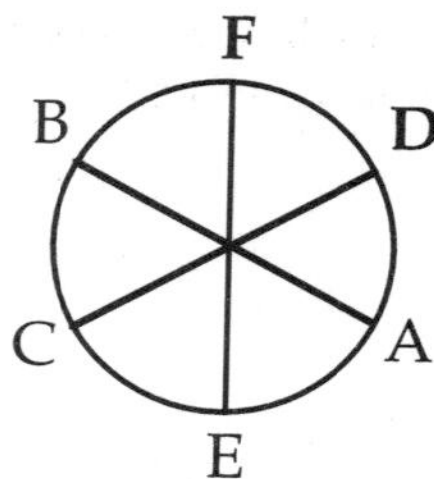

From this diagram, we see that A must sit next to E and therefore the answer is (A).

3. **If Dave and Carol sit next to each other, then Alice could sit immediately between**

   (A) Bob and Carol
   (B) Bob and Frank
   (C) Dave and Emily
   (D) Dave and Frank
   (E) Frank and Emily

Remember that the questions in a game problem are independent of one another. So the condition **BF**, in Question 2, does not apply to this question.

Begin by adding the new condition *"Dave sits next to Carol"*—**DC**—to the original diagram:

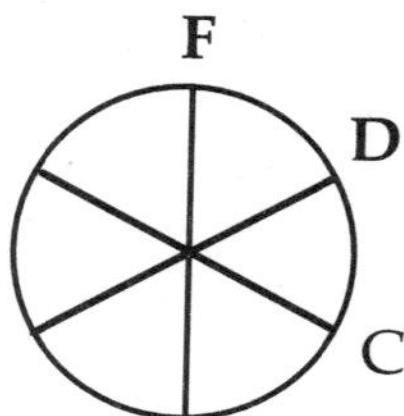

As in Question 2, the second condition, **BC or BD**, forces B next to C, and our diagram becomes

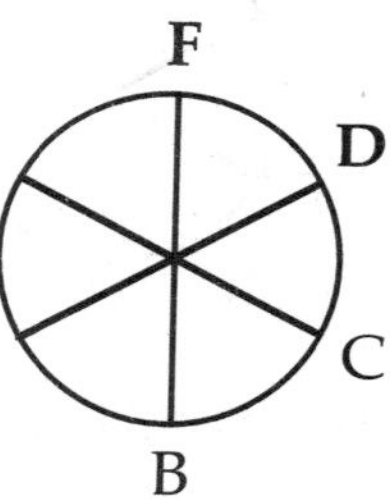

This diagram also satisfies the remaining initial conditions—**~(AC)** and **~(FEC)**. [Why?] Therefore the placement of A and E is arbitrary, and the following two diagrams are possible:

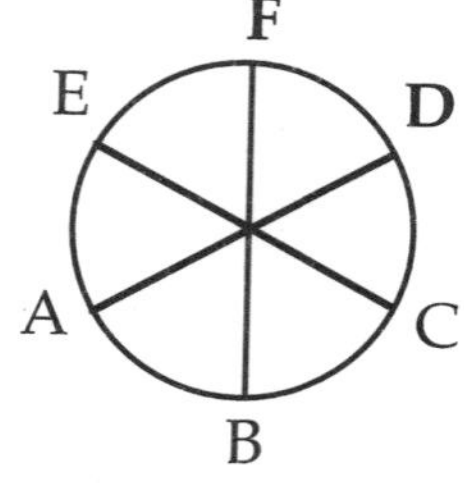

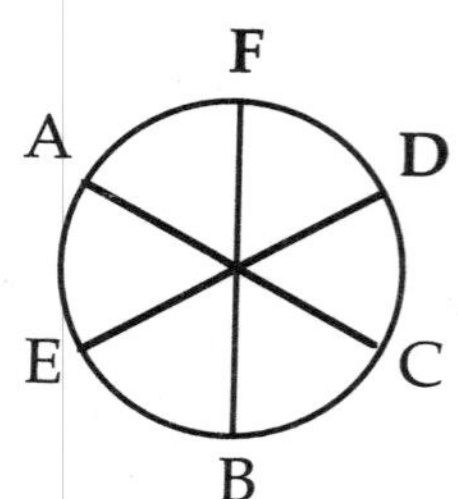

The second diagram satisfies choice (E). The answer, therefore, is (E).

4. **If Bob sits next to Carol, then which one of the following is a complete and accurate list of people who could also sit next to Bob?**

   (A) Alice
   (B) Alice, Dave
   (C) Dave, Frank
   (D) Alice, Emily, Frank
   (E) Alice, Dave, Emily, Frank

This question illustrates that during the test you should not erase previously derived diagrams, for we can use the diagrams derived in solving Questions 2 and 3 to help solve this question. (Note by "a complete and accurate list" the writers of the LSAT mean a list of all possible people, and only those people.)

Referring to the final diagram in Question 2, which has B seated next to C, we see that F *can* be next to B. This eliminates both (A) and (B)—they don't contain F. Next, referring to the final two diagrams in Question 3, we see that both A and E *can* sit next to B. This eliminates (C). Finally, we need to decide between choices (D) and (E). Choice (E) differs from choice (D) only in that it contains D. So we place D next to BC in our original diagram and then check whether this leads to a contradiction of the conditions:

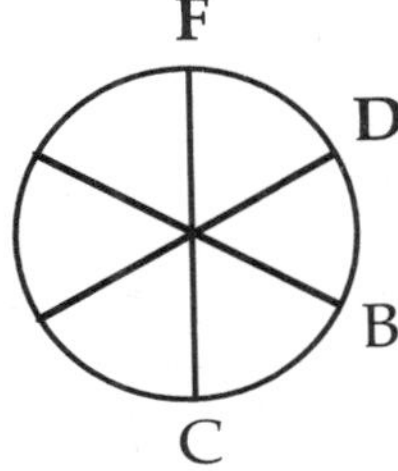

Now if we place A next to F, and E next to C, then all the initial conditions are satisfied by the following diagram:

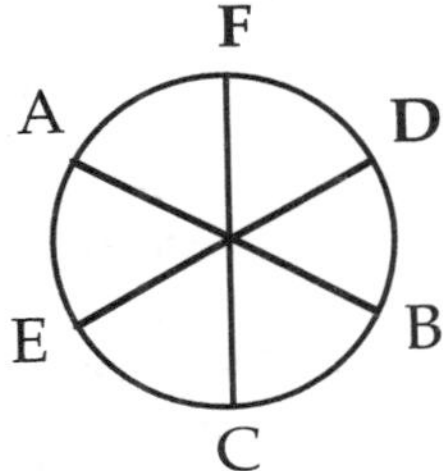

Hence it is possible for D to be next to B, and ADEF is therefore the complete and accurate list of people who can sit next to B. The answer is (E).

5. Which of the following must be false if Bob sits next to Dave?

I. Emily sits next to Frank.
II. Carol sits directly opposite Bob.
III. Carol sits immediately between Emily and Bob.

(A) I only
(B) III only
(C) I and II only
(D) II and III only
(E) I, II, and III

The most efficient way to solve triple-multiple-choice questions is to eliminate answer-choices as you check each sub-statement. Additionally, this method often gives a bonus: you may not need to check the final statement, which typically is the hardest. Even if you're not able to solve the problem, elimination allows you to make an educated guess. (Remember there is no guessing penalty on the LSAT.)

The logic of this question is convoluted because the correct answer will always make a false statement! This question would be much easier if it were worded, "Which of the following is possible?" (See Obfuscation.)

Let's begin our solution by adding the new condition *"Bob sits next to Dave"*—**BD**—to the original diagram:

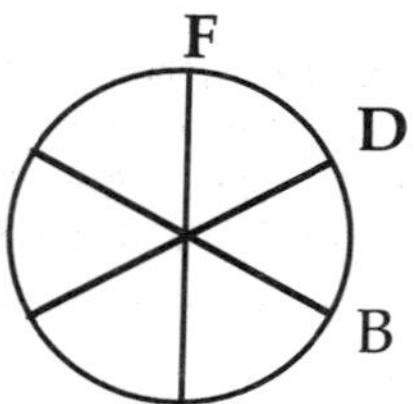

Next, test the first statement "Emily sits next to Frank"—**EF**. To this end, place it on the diagram as follows

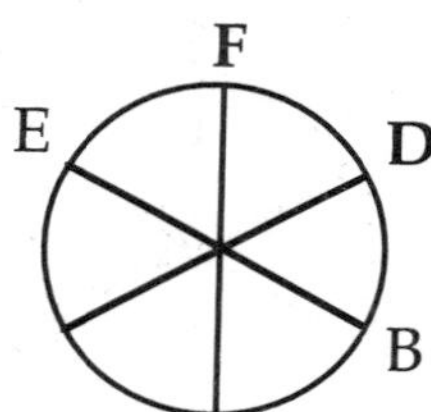

This diagram forces A and C next to each other, which violates the condition **~(AC)**. Hence Statement I is always false and therefore it is a correct choice.[*] This eliminates choices (B) and (D); they don't contain I.

Next, test the second statement "Carol sits directly opposite Bob," **C<—>B,** which forms a base axis. Place it on the original diagram as follows:

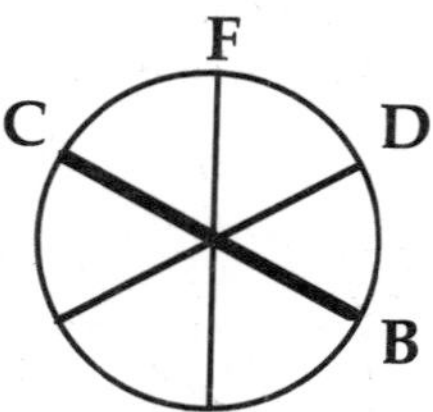

* Note: I used "correct" instead of "true," because in this context "true" would have been perfectly confusing.

Then placing A next to B—otherwise it would be next to C, which violates the condition **~(AC)**—and placing E next to C gives

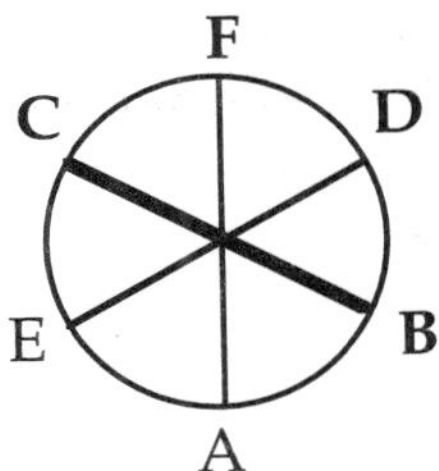

This diagram satisfies all the initial conditions, so it is true. Hence the statement **C<—>B** is not always false. Hence Statement II is incorrect (Whew!). This eliminates both (C) and (E), since they both contain II. By elimination, therefore, the answer is (A), and there is no need to check the third statement.

6. If Alice sits next to Emily, then Bob CANNOT sit immediately between

(A) Alice and Carol
(B) Alice and Dave
(C) Carol and Dave
(D) Carol and Frank
(E) Dave and Emily

This question is hard (or at least long) because there are many places where Alice and Emily may sit. However, the answers and diagrams we derived for previous questions will help here. The final diagram in Question 4 has B immediately between C and D. This eliminates choice (C). Furthermore, the final diagrams in Questions 2 and 3 have B immediately between C and F, and A and C, respectively. This eliminates choices (D) and (A). Now the question is not so daunting: we need only to decide between choices (B) and (E).

Let's test choice (B), first. If Bob sits immediately between Alice and Dave, i.e., **ABD**, then combining this condition with "Alice sits next to Emily," **AE,** generates the base group **EABD**. Adding this to the original diagram gives

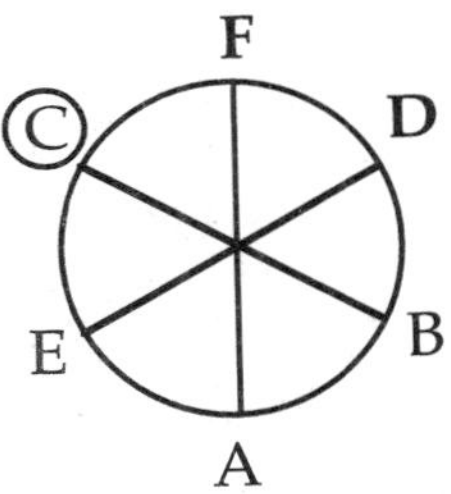

(Note the circle around C indicates that it was forced into that position by the other conditions.)

This diagram satisfies all four of the initial conditions, which eliminates choice (B). Therefore, by the elimination method, we have learned that the answer is (E).

It is, however, instructive to verify that B cannot sit immediately between D and E. To this end, form the symbol **DBEA** and place it on the diagram as follows:

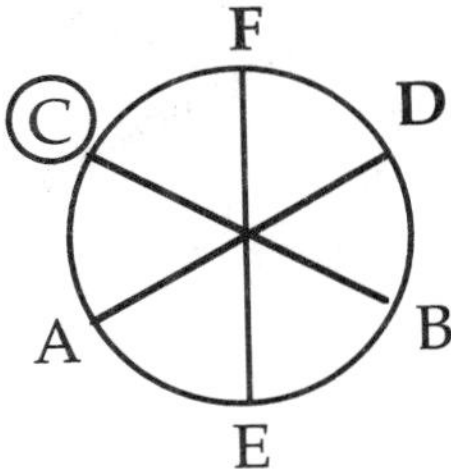

This diagram clearly violates the condition **~(AC)**.

Points to Remember

1. Circular games are, in general, harder than linear games.
2. Circular diagrams—unlike linear diagrams—are not fixed. That is, circular diagrams do not have a first, second, . . ., or last position. (But there is a left and right.)
3. If there is no mention of the circle's orientation (e.g., A is to the left of B), then the mirror-image diagram need not be considered. However, if a question asks for the number of distinct orderings, then you <u>must</u> count the mirror-image diagram.
4. Draw the circle with spokes inside.
5. Place the base axis on the diagram first. Then place the base group.
6. Left-right is taken from the perspective of the reader looking inward toward the center of the circle.
7. Counting problems are nearly always hard. Consider this when deciding whether to "skip" a question.

Warm-Up Drills

Drill A

Four people—A, B, C, D—are seated, evenly spaced, around a circular table. For each of the following conditions, count the number of possible orderings of the people around the table.

1. B sits to the immediate left of A.
2. A sits next to B.
3. A sits opposite B.

Drill B

Six people are seated evenly spaced around a circular table. For each of the following pairs of conditions, count the number of possible orderings of the people around the table.

1. A sits directly opposite B.
   C sits to the immediate left of A.
2. A sits opposite B.
   C sits to the immediate left of A.
   If D sits between B and C, then E sits directly opposite D.
3. A sits opposite B.
   C sits to the immediate left of A.
   If D does not sit between B and C, then D sits next to E.

Answers and Solutions to Warm-Up Drills

Drill A

1. **2 orderings.**

   Following convention, place A at the top of the circle and B to the immediate left of A. The following schematic "tree" shows the possible positions of C and D:

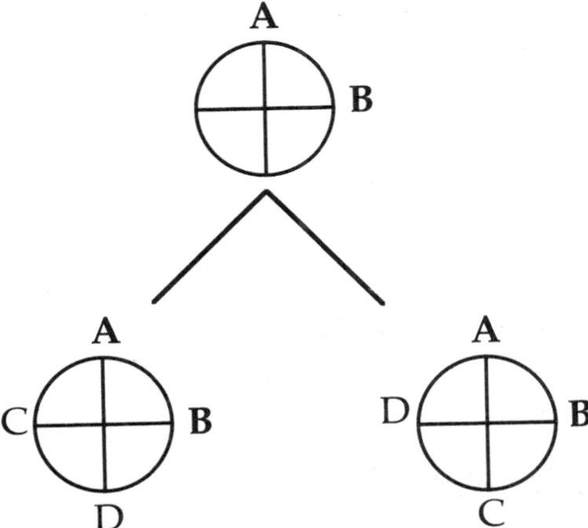

   From the bottom of the diagram, we see that there two possible orderings.

2. **4 orderings.**

   We must now consider two "trees", one with B to the left of A and one with B to the right of A:

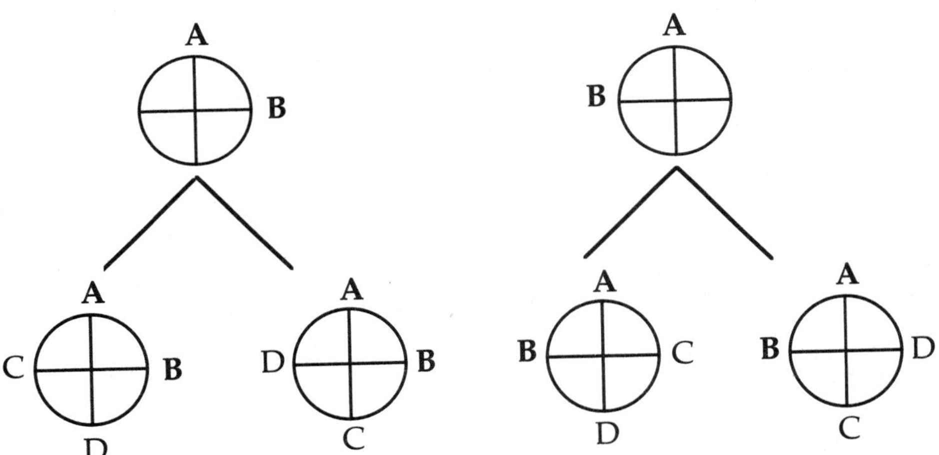

   Counting the number of distinct orderings along the bottom of these "trees", we get 4.

3. **2 orderings.**

   A and B form a base axis that forces C to one side and D to the other. Two distinct orderings are thereby formed as follows:

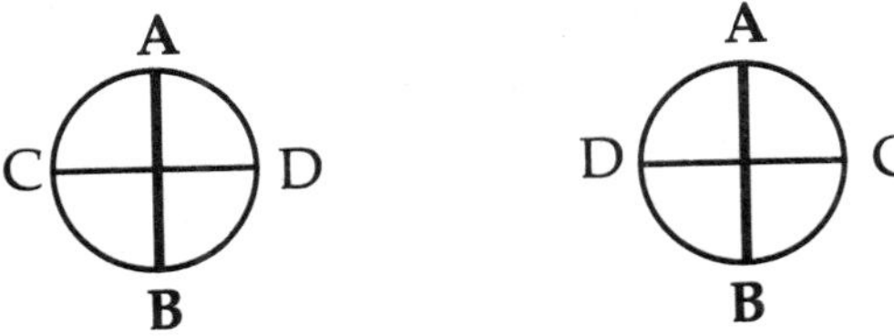

Drill B

1. **6 orderings.**

The initial conditions generate the following diagram, which is numbered consecutively from 1 through 6 solely to facilitate the explanations that follow.

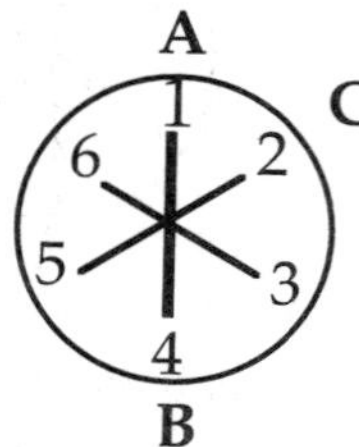

Next, placing D in position 3 generates the following two possible diagrams:

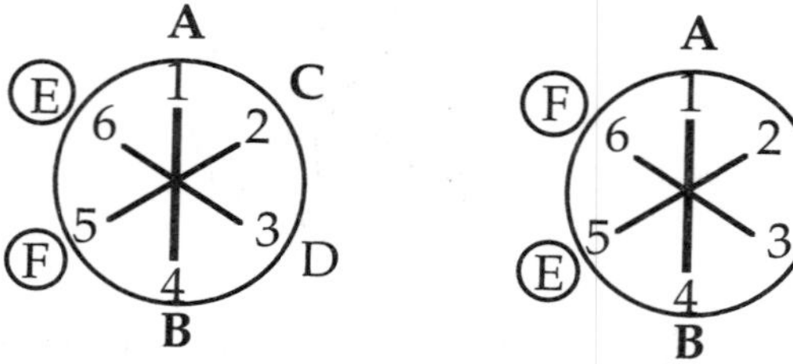

Finally, placing D in positions 5 and 6 will likewise generate two orderings each. So there is a total of 6 possible orderings.

2. **5 orderings.**

From the first two conditions, we get the same diagram as in Problem 1:

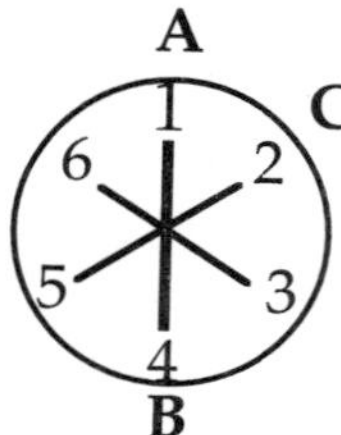

Next, if D occupies position 3, then the condition *"if D sits between B and C, then E sits directly opposite D"* forces F between E and B. Thus our diagram is as follows:

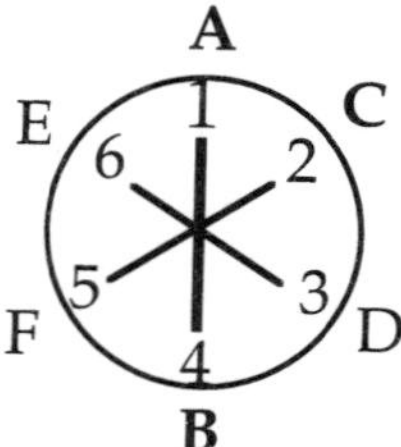

This diagram represents one ordering. But if D is in position 5 or 6, then the third condition does not apply. We get, in these cases, the same number of orderings as in Problem 1—four. So five distinct orderings are possible.

3. **4 orderings.**

Start with the same base diagram as in Problems 1 and 2:

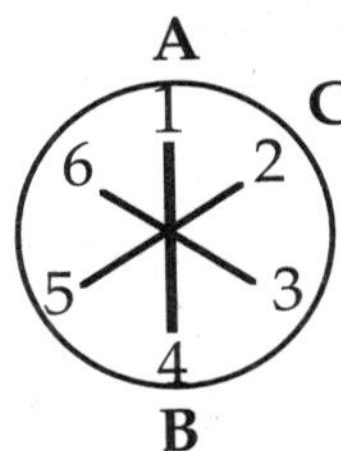

Now if D is in position 6, then the third condition forces E into position 5. This in turn forces F into position 3. Our uniquely determined diagram is now as follows:

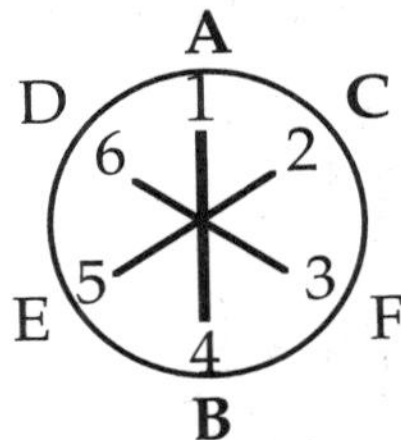

This diagram represents one distinct ordering. Next, if we place D in position 5, we likewise get one distinct ordering. Finally, if we place D in position 3, we get two more distinct orderings (as in Problem 1). This gives a total of four distinct orderings.

Mentor Exercise

Directions: The following group of questions is based on a set of conditions. Choose the response that most accurately and completely answers each question. Hints, insights, and the answers are provided in the right-hand column.

Questions 1–6

Eight people—Adam, Bob, Carrie, Dan, Elaine, Fred, Greg, Hans—are seated around a square table. There are two people to a side, and each person sits directly opposite another.

Bob sits directly opposite Hans.

Adam sits immediately between Greg and Fred.

Although this game involves a square, all the properties derived for circles still hold. The condition *"Bob sits directly opposite Hans"* is naturally symbolized as **B<—>H**, and the condition *"Adam sits immediately between Greg and Fred"* can be symbolized as **GAF** (The flip-flop symbol will not be explicitly written, just remember that G and F can be interchanged.) The diagram will consist of a square:

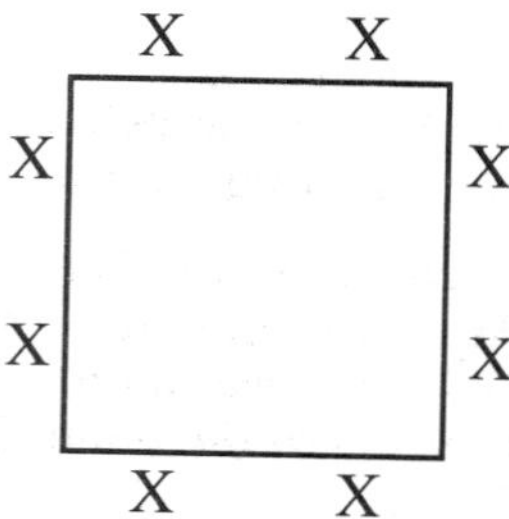

The condition **B<—>H** forms the base axis. Since the properties of circular diagrams hold for square diagrams, we can place the base axis anywhere on the diagram. Place it at the top as follows:

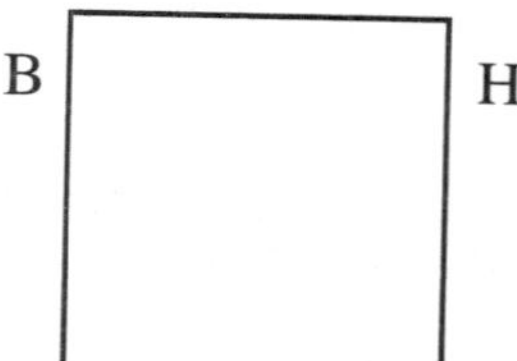

The base group **GAF** cannot be placed on the diagram at this time. Since there is no mention of orientation of the square, we don't have to consider the diagram's mirror image, i.e., the diagram obtained by interchanging B and H (See, however, Questions 4 and 5).

1. **If Elaine does not sit next to Bob, which one of the following must be true?**
   - (A) **Adam or Greg must sit next to Hans.**
   - (B) **Greg must sit directly opposite Elaine.**
   - (C) **Either Carrie or Dan must sit next to Bob.**
   - (D) **Adam must sit next to Hans.**
   - (E) **Fred must sit next to Bob.**

1. There are two possible positions for the condition **GAF**:

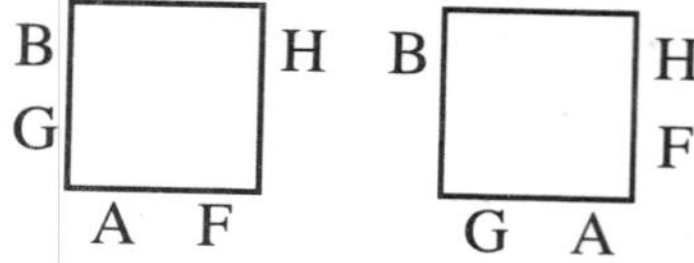

Note the flip-flop of G and F is not needed in this problem. Use these two diagrams to deduce that the answer is (C).

2. **If Dan sits directly across from Adam, and Elaine cannot sit next to Bob, then which of the following people could sit next to Bob?**

I. Dan
II. Carrie
III. Fred

(A) I only
(B) II only
(C) III only
(D) I and II only
(E) I and III only

2. There are two possible places for D:

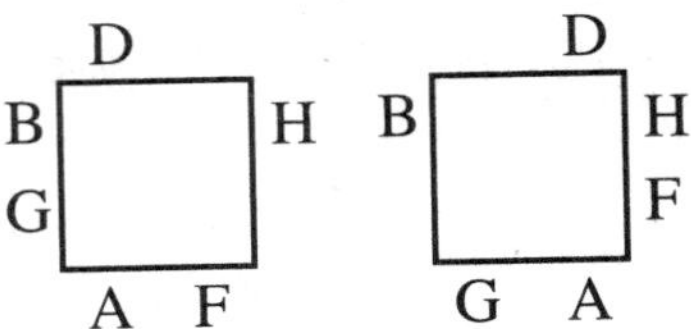

We reject the second diagram since it forces E next to B, violating the supplementary condition **~(EB)**.

Be careful: The flip-flop of G and F is needed for this question.

The answer is (E).

3. **If Carrie does not sit next to Bob, which one of the following must be false?**

(A) Hans sits next to Fred.
(B) Adam sits opposite Carrie.
(C) Greg sits next to Bob.
(D) Dan sits to the immediate right of Hans.
(E) Hans sits between and next to Dan and Fred.

3. If Hans sits between and next to Dan and Fred, then we get the following diagram:

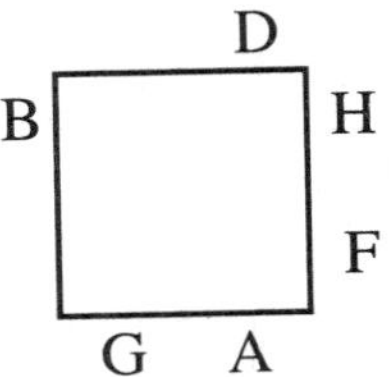

But this diagram forces C next to B, violating the supplementary condition **~(CB)**.

The answer is (E).

4. **If Greg sits to the immediate left of Adam, then which one of the following is possible?**

(A) Adam sits next to Bob.
(B) Hans sits next to Bob.
(C) Adam sits next to Hans.
(D) Fred sits next to Bob.
(E) Bob sits directly opposite Carrie.

4. **Caution:** Since this question applies an orientation to the square, you <u>must</u> consider the mirror image diagram:

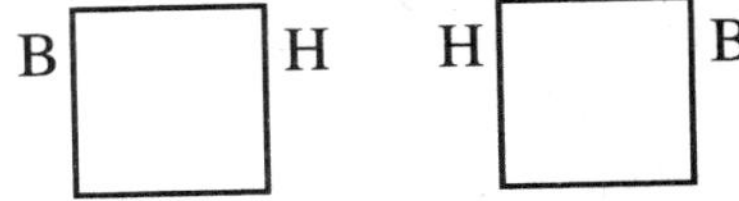

The answer is (D).

5. If Dan sits next to Elaine who sits next to Hans, what is the maximum number of distinct arrangements of the eight people around the square?

(A) 2
(B) 4
(C) 6
(D) 8
(E) 10

5. **Caution:** Although there is no mention of orientation in this question, you still must consider the mirror image diagram, since it is still a distinct order.

The answer is (D).

6. If Greg sits directly opposite Dan, which one of the following is complete and accurate list of the people any one of whom could sit next to Bob?

(A) Greg
(B) Greg, Fred, Dan
(C) Greg, Fred, Elaine, Carrie
(D) Greg, Fred, Dan, Carrie, Elaine
(E) Greg, Fred, Dan, Carrie, Adam

6. There are four possible positions for D:

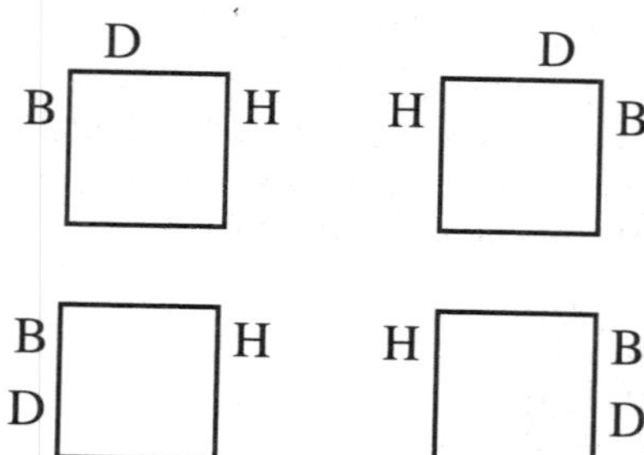

Use these diagrams to deduce that the answer is (D).

Exercise

Directions: The following group of questions is based on a set of conditions. Choose the response that most accurately and completely answers each question.

Four couples—the Potters, the Regans, the Stewarts, the Wilsons—are seated evenly spaced about a circular table.

The Regans do not sit next to the Stewarts.
The Stewarts sit next to each other.
Mr. Potter sits directly opposite Mr. Wilson.

1. Which of the following are possible?

   I. Mrs. Regan sits next to Mr. Potter.
   II. Mrs. Stewart sits next to Mr. Potter.
   III. Mrs. Potter sits between and next to Mr. Regan and Mrs. Wilson.

   (A) I only
   (B) II only
   (C) III only
   (D) I and II only
   (E) I and III only

2. If Mr. Regan sits midway between Mr. Potter and Mr. Wilson, then which of the following persons could sit directly across the table from Mr. Regan?

   (A) Mrs. Regan
   (B) Mrs. Potter
   (C) Mrs. Stewart
   (D) Mr. Wilson
   (E) Mrs. Wilson

3. If Mrs. Potter sits to the left of Mr. Stewart, then which one of the following is a complete and accurate list of the people any one of whom could sit next to Mr. Potter?

   (A) Mrs. Potter, Mrs. Regan
   (B) Mrs. Potter, Mr. Regan, Mrs. Wilson, Mrs. Stewart
   (C) Mrs. Regan, Mrs. Potter, Mr. Regan, Mrs. Wilson
   (D) Mrs. Regan, Mrs. Potter, Mr. Regan, Mrs. Wilson, Mrs. Stewart
   (E) Mrs. Regan, Mrs. Potter, Mr. Regan, Mrs. Wilson, Mrs. Stewart, Mr. Wilson

4. If Mr. Potter is between and next to Mr. Stewart and Mrs. Wilson, then how many different seating arrangements of the eight people are possible?

   (A) 1
   (B) 2
   (C) 3
   (D) 4
   (E) 5

The following game appeared on a recent LSAT.

Questions 5–10

A square parking lot has exactly eight lights numbered 1 through 8 situated along its perimeter as diagrammed below.

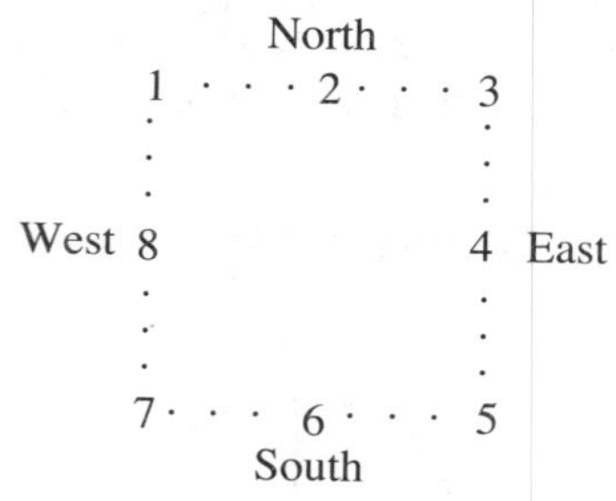

The lot must always be illuminated in such a way that the following specifications are met:

At least one of any three consecutively numbered lights is off.
Light 8 is on.
Neither light 2 nor light 7 is on when light 1 is on.
At least one of the three lights on each side is on.
If any side has exactly one of its three lights on, then that light is its center light.
Two of the lights on the north side are on.

5. Which one of the following could be a complete and accurate list of lights that are on together?

(A) 1, 3, 5, 7
(B) 2, 4, 6, 8
(C) 2, 3, 5, 6, 8
(D) 3, 4, 6, 7, 8
(E) 1, 2, 4, 5, 6, 8

6. Which one of the following lights must be on?

(A) light 2
(B) light 3
(C) light 4
(D) light 5
(E) light 6

7. If light 1 is off, which one of the following is a light that must also be off?

(A) light 3
(B) light 4
(C) light 5
(D) light 6
(E) light 7

8. Which one of the following statements must be true?

(A) If light 2 is on, then light 6 is off.
(B) If light 3 is on, then light 2 is on.
(C) If light 4 is on, then light 3 is off.
(D) If light 5 is off, then light 4 is on.
(E) If light 6 is off, then light 1 is on.

9. If light 5 is on, which one of the following could be true?

(A) Light 1 is off and light 6 is off.
(B) Light 1 is on and light 7 is on.
(C) Light 2 is off and light 4 is on.
(D) Light 2 is off and light 6 is off.
(E) Light 6 is on and light 7 is on.

10. If light 4 is on, each of the following statements must be true EXCEPT:

(A) Light 1 is on.
(B) Light 2 is on.
(C) Light 5 is off.
(D) Light 6 is on.
(E) Light 7 is off.

Answers and Solutions to Exercise

This is a moderately hard game. Let's use the first letter of a name to denote the name, with bold letters denoting men and bold, shadow letters denoting women.

The most concrete condition is *"Mr. Potter sits directly opposite Mr. Wilson"*; it is naturally symbolized as **P<—>W**, where the arrow means "sits directly opposite." This forms a base axis. The next most concrete condition is *"the Stewarts sit next to each other"*; it is naturally symbolized as **S𝕊**. This forms a base group. Finally, the least concrete condition *"the Regans do not sit next to the Stewarts"* can be symbolized as **~(Rℝ/S𝕊)**.*

Now we must decide the order in which to place the conditions on the circle. Following the guidelines derived earlier, place the base axis first:

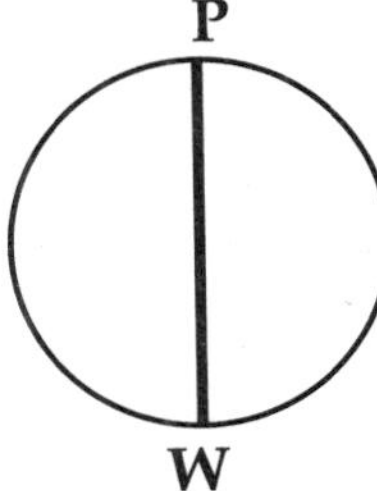

This axis separates the other elements to either side of it.

Next, we place the base group **S𝕊**. However, unlike the base axis, **P<—>W**, the position of this base group is not fixed—it may "float" about the circle. Furthermore, since there is no mention of the circle's orientation (that is, left or right), we place the Stewarts on only one side of the axis. Placing them on the other side of the axis will only generate a mirror-image diagram. (See, however, Questions 3 and 4.) Let's use brackets to indicate that the Stewarts sit <u>somewhere</u> on the right side of the circle:

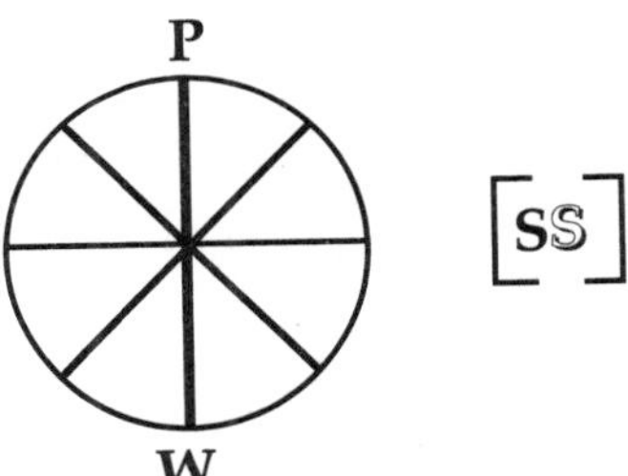

Finally, the fact that the Regans do not sit next to the Stewarts forces the Regans to the other side of the circle, since on the right side of the base axis there are only three spaces between **P** and **W**, two of which are already taken by the Stewarts. The Regans, too, can "float" about their side of the circle. Furthermore, the Regans, unlike the Stewarts, do not necessarily sit next to each other—an important distinction for the questions that follow. We denote this in the diagram by writing **R** above ℝ as follows:

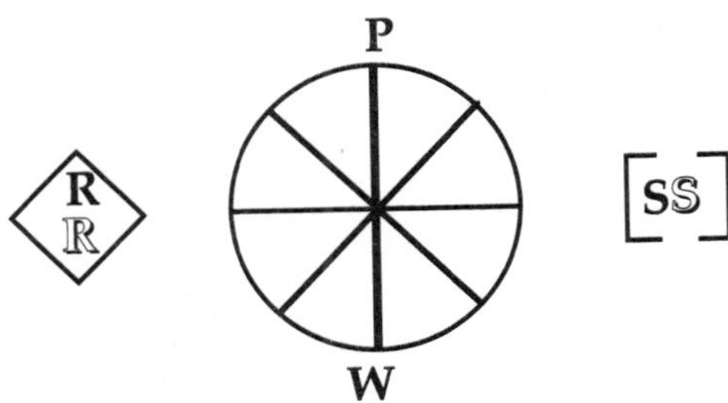

* Note: This is the best symbol that I could create, others such as ~(**RS**)/~(**R𝕊**)/~(**ℝS**)/~(**ℝ𝕊**) being too long and unwieldy. You may prefer a different symbol. Whatever symbol you choose is fine so long as it is short and functional.

Note the elements ℙ and 𝕎 are independent because there are no direct conditions on them. **Remember independent elements can be placed in more positions than dependent elements. Think of independent elements as "wild cards".**

Our schematic with diagram is now compete:

P ℙ R ℝ S 𝕊 W 𝕎 (ℙ and 𝕎 are "wild")

P<—>W

S𝕊

~(Rℝ/S𝕊)

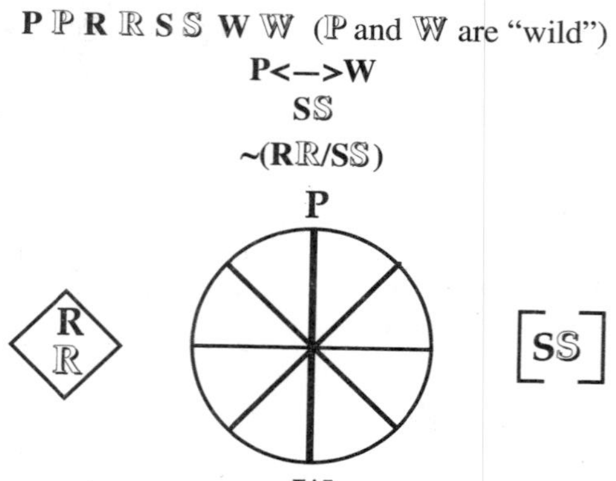

1. First check sub-question I. Placing Mrs. Regan, ℝ next to Mr. Potter, **P**, and next to her husband, **R**, gives the following diagram

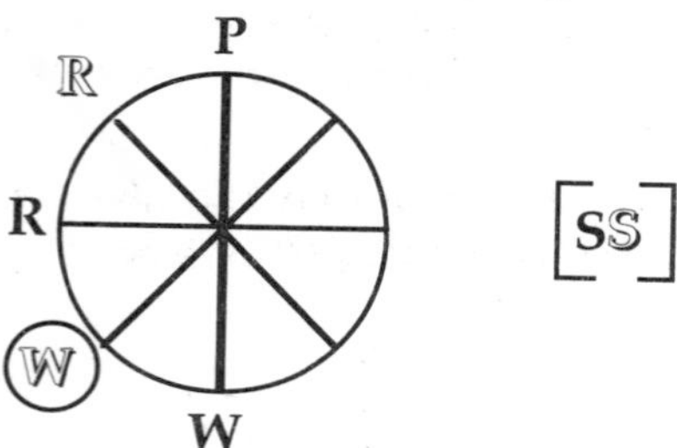

Now, place **S** next to **P** and next to his wife:

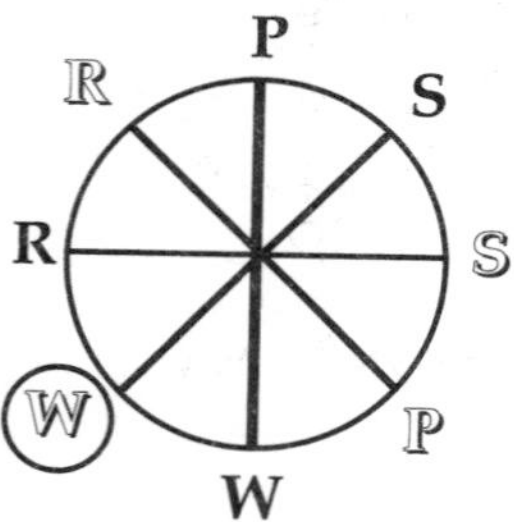

This diagram does not violate any of the initial conditions. Therefore, sub-question I is possible. This eliminates choices (B) and (C) since they do not contain I.

Next, to check sub-question II, place 𝕊 next to **P**. Then place **R** between and next to **P** and 𝕎. This gives the following diagram:

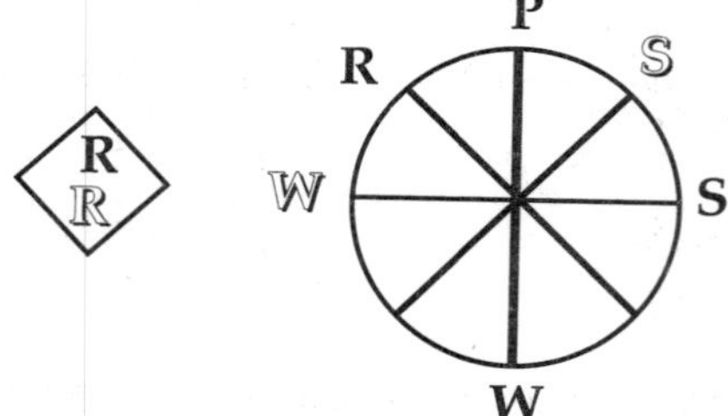

This diagram forces ℝ and ℙ to the left and right of **W**, respectively:

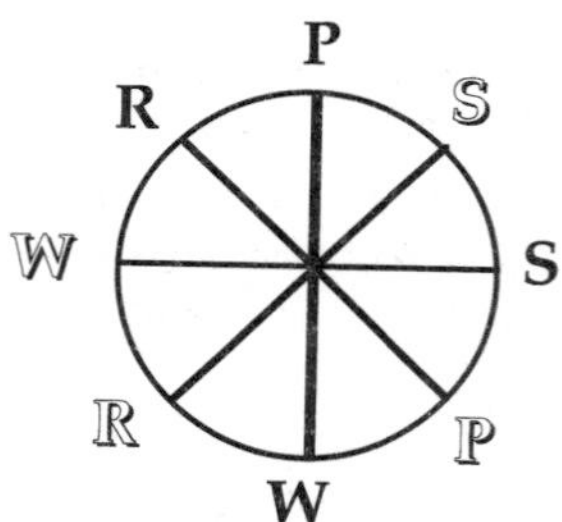

This final diagram does not violate any of the initial conditions. Therefore, sub-question II is possible, which eliminates (A) and (E) since they do not contain II. Hence, by process of elimination, the answer is (D). There is no need to check sub-question III.

2. The key to the solution of this problem is the condition **S𝕊**. Although the Stewarts may 'float' about their side of the table, they must always be next to each other—forcing one of them to sit midway between **P** and **W**. This means that one of the Stewarts will sit directly across the table from **R**. The following is one of many possible diagrams that do not violate any of the initial conditions:

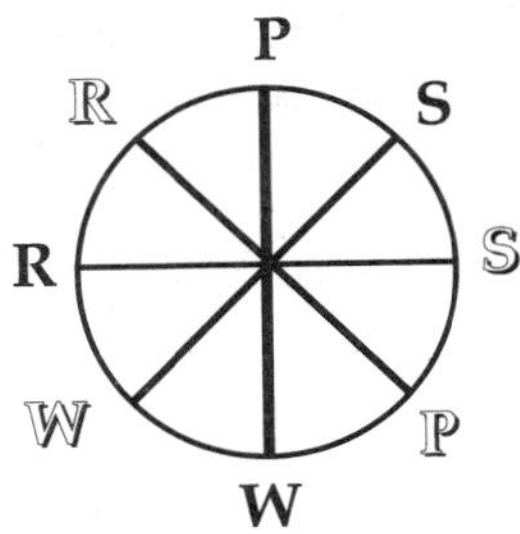

The answer, therefore, is (C).

3. The new condition "Mrs. Potter sits to the left of Mr. Stewart" suggests the following diagrams:

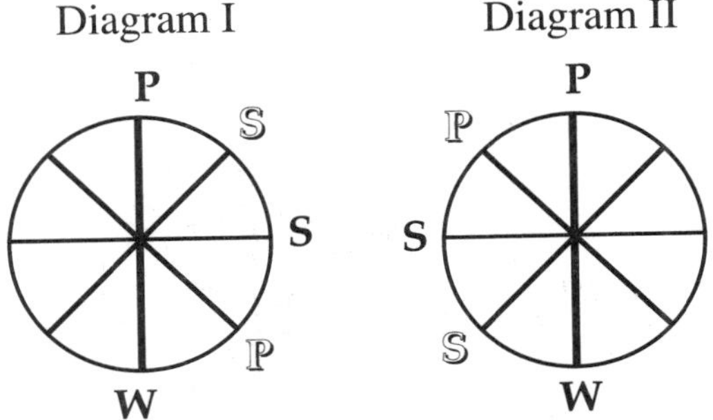

Since the new condition applies an orientation to the circle (ℙ <u>left</u> of S), we must consider both diagrams. Diagram II may not be the mirror image of Diagram I. In fact, it is not.

> Advanced Concepts
>
> If a diagram is the mirror image of another, then spinning the diagram 180 degrees about a base axis will create the mirror image diagram:
>
> 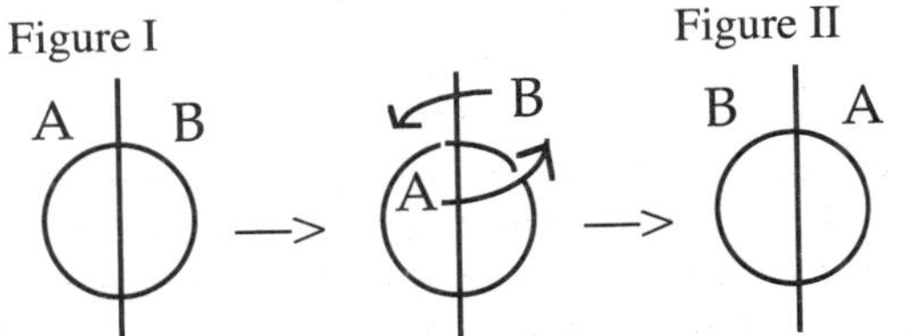
>
>
> But if you spin Diagram I 180 degrees about the vertical axis **P<—>W**, then ℙ will be in the position of 𝕊 (not ℙ) in Diagram II. The two diagrams, therefore, are not mirror images of each other.

Now, clearly in Diagram I besides 𝕊 any one of ℝ, **R**, or 𝕎 could sit next to **P**. Similarly in Diagram II besides ℙ any one of ℝ, **R**, or 𝕎 could sit next to **P**:

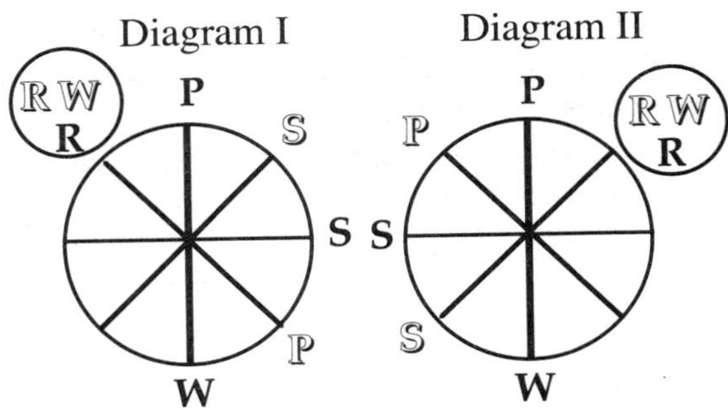

From these two diagrams, we see that any one of ℝ, ℙ, **R**, 𝕎, or 𝕊 could sit next to **P**. The answer, therefore, is (D).

4. Counting problems, such as this one, are nearly always hard. Counting may have been one of man's first thought processes; nevertheless, counting possibilities is deceptively hard. Keep this in mind when deciding whether to skip a particular question.

This problem has the added subtlety that the mirror image of the diagram must be considered even though there is no mention of the circle's orientation.

Let's start by adding the new condition **SP**𝕎 to the original diagram as follows:

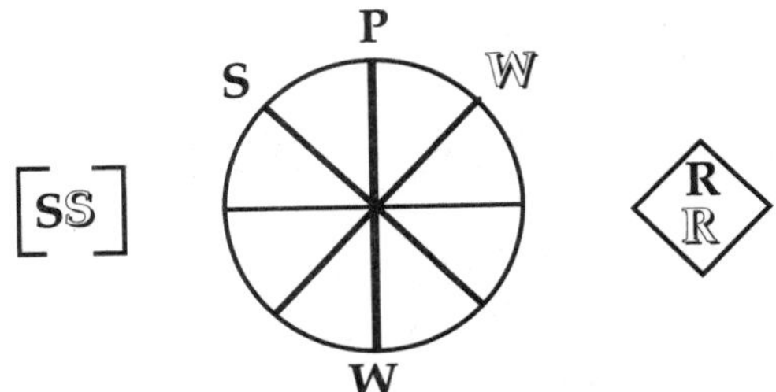

Next, the condition **S**𝕊 gives

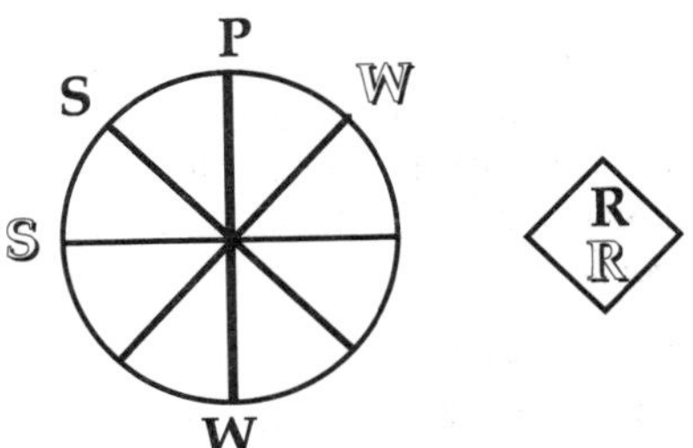

Now ℙ must be between 𝕊 and **W** because both **R** and ℝ are on the right. This suggests the following two valid diagrams—one for each of the two possible positions of **R**.

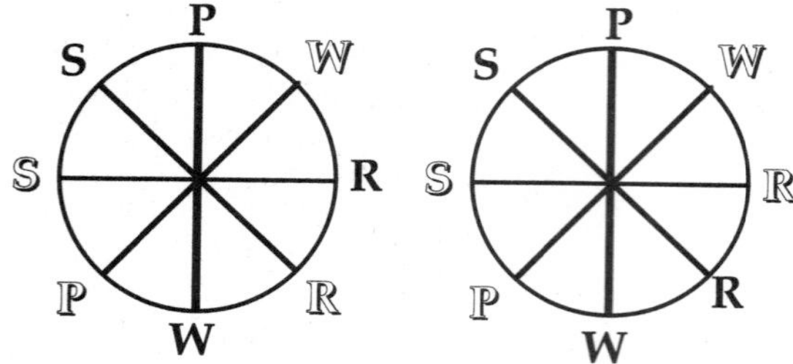

The mirror images of each of these two diagrams, however, must also be considered distinct orderings of the people around the table. Hence there are four possible seating arrangements of the eight people, and the answer is (D).

Note: Earlier it was stated that if a circular diagram does not have an orientation (left or right), then its mirror image need not be considered. This question, nevertheless, does not violate that rule. Although the mirror-image diagram will generate the same answer to any *relational* question, it is still a distinct ordering and therefore must be counted.

Questions 3 and 4 illustrate some of the subtleties that make circular ordering games, in general, harder than linear ordering games.

Questions 5–10

Adding the condition *"light 8 is on"* to the diagram gives

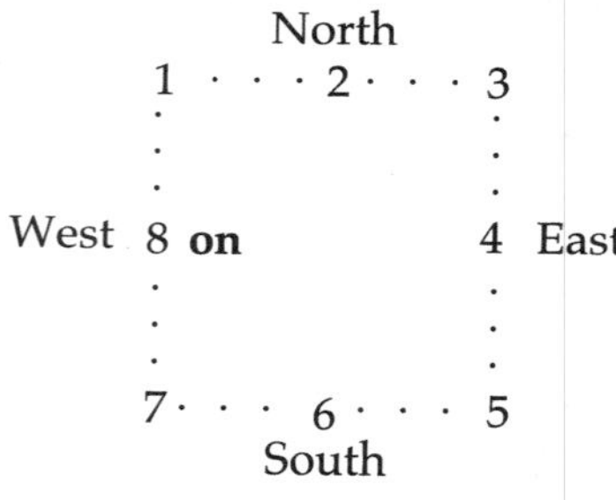

5.
(A) No. This violates the condition *"Neither light 2 nor light 7 is on when light 1 is on."*
(B) No. This violates the condition *"Two of the lights on the north side are on."*
(C) Yes. Placing the information on the diagram yields

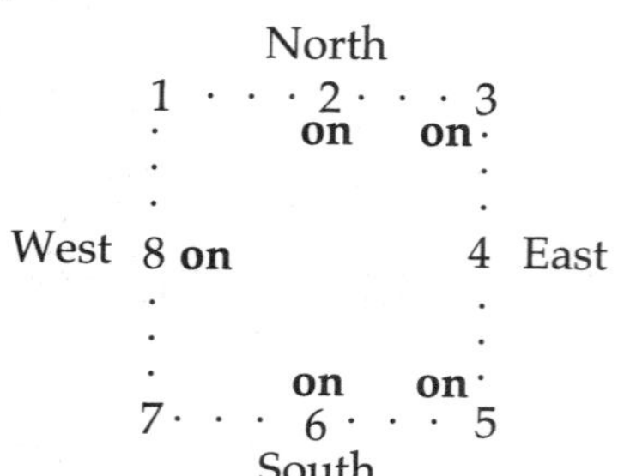

Since this is to be a complete list of the lights that could be on, the remaining lights must be off:

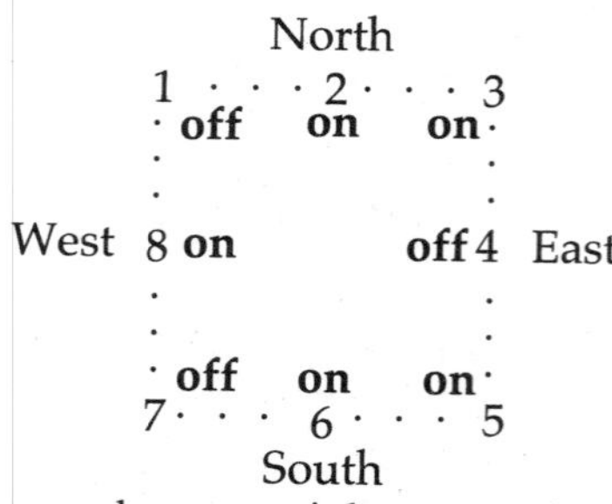

This diagram does not violate any of the conditions: There are not three consecutively numbered lights on. Light 8 is on. Light 1 is off and therefore the condition *"Neither light 2 nor light 7

is on when light 1 is on" does not apply. Each side has a light on. The west side has exactly one light on and it is the center light. Two lights on the north side, 2 and 3, are on.
(D) No. Just as in choice (B), this violates the condition *"Two of the lights on the north side are on."*
(E) No. This violates the condition *"At least one of any three consecutively numbered lights is off."*

6.
(A) No. The following diagram has light 2 off and does not violate any of the conditions:

```
            North
       1 . . . 2 . . . 3
       . on   off   on .
       .                .
West   8 on          off 4  East
       .                .
       . off   on    on .
       7 . . . 6 . . . 5
            South
```

(B) Yes. Suppose light 3 is off. Then from the condition *"Two of the lights on the north side are on,"* we know that lights 1 and 2 must be on. However, this contradicts the condition *"Neither light 2 nor light 7 is on when light 1 is on."* Hence, light 3 must be on.
(C) No. The diagram for choice (A) also shows that light 4 need not be on.
(D) No. The following diagram has light 5 off and does not violate any of the conditions:

```
            North
       1 . . . 2 . . . 3
       . on   off   on .
       .                .
West   8 on           on 4  East
       .                .
       . off   on   off .
       7 . . . 6 . . . 5
            South
```

(E) No. The following diagram has light 6 off and does not violate any of the conditions:

```
            North
       1 . . . 2 . . . 3
       . off   on    on .
       .                .
West   8 on          off 4  East
       .                .
       . on   off    on .
       7 . . . 6 . . . 5
            South
```

7.
(A) No. The following diagram has light 3 on and does not violate any of the conditions:

```
            North
       1 . . . 2 . . . 3
       . off   on    on .
       .                .
West   8 on          off 4  East
       .                .
       . off   on    on .
       7 . . . 6 . . . 5
            South
```

(B) Yes. Suppose light 4 is on. If light 1 is off, then from the condition *"Two of the lights on the north side are on"* we know that lights 2 and 3 must be on. This, however, has three consecutively numbered lights on—2, 3, and 4—contradicting the condition *"At least one of any three consecutively numbered lights is off."* Hence, light 4 must be off.
(C) No. The diagram for choice (A) has light 5 on.
(D) No. The diagram for choice (A) has light 6 on.
(E) No. The following diagram has light 7 on and does not violate any of the conditions:

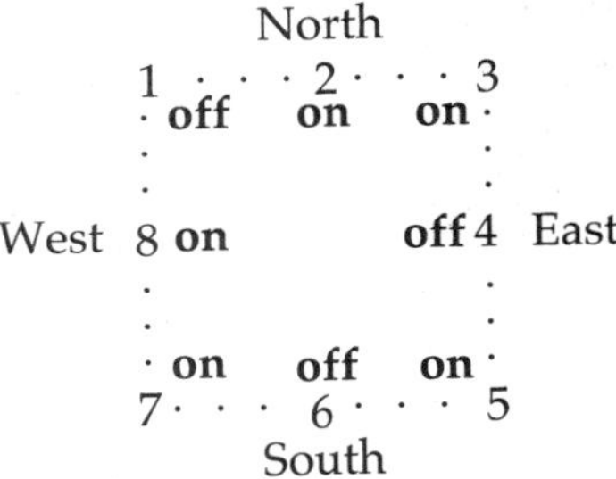

8.
(A) No. The following diagram has lights 2 and 6 on and does not violate any of the conditions:

```
            North
       1 . . . 2 . . . 3
       . off   on    on .
       .                .
West   8 on          off 4  East
       .                .
       . off   on    on .
       7 . . . 6 . . . 5
            South
```

(B) No. The following diagram has light 3 on and light 2 off, and does not violate any of the conditions:

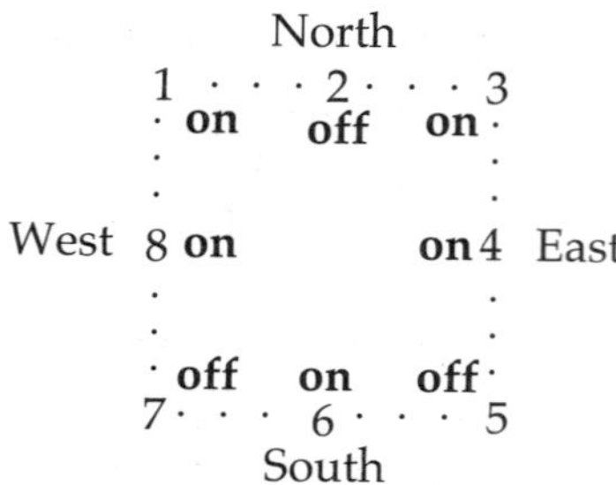

(C) No. The diagram for choice (B) has lights 4 and 3 on.

(D) Yes. Suppose light 5 is off. If light 4 is also off, then light 3 must be on since *"At least one of the three lights on each side is on."* However, light 3 is not the middle light, which contradicts the condition *"If any side has exactly one of its three lights on, then that light is its center light."*

(E) No. The following diagram has lights 6 and 1 off and does not violate any of the conditions:

```
              North
       1 . . . 2 . . . 3
       . off   on   on .
West   8 on          off 4   East
       . on    off  on .
       7 . . . 6 . . . 5
              South
```

9.

(A) Yes. Suppose lights 1 and 6 are off:

```
              North
       1 . . . 2 . . . 3
       . off
West   8 on              4   East
               off  on .
       7 . . . 6 . . . 5
              South
```

Since two lights on the north side must be on, lights 2 and 3 must be on:

```
              North
       1 . . . 2 . . . 3
       . off   on   on .
West   8 on              4   East
               off  on .
       7 . . . 6 . . . 5
              South
```

Since three consecutively numbered lights cannot be on, light 4 must be off:

```
              North
       1 . . . 2 . . . 3
       . off   on   on .
West   8 on          off 4   East
               off  on .
       7 . . . 6 . . . 5
              South
```

Finally, light 7 must be on—otherwise on the south side only light 5 would be on, which would violate the condition *"If any side has exactly one of its three lights on, then that light is its center light."* This yields the following unique diagram, which does not violate any of the conditions:

```
              North
       1 . . . 2 . . . 3
       . off   on   on .
West   8 on          off 4   East
       . on    off  on .
       7 . . . 6 . . . 5
              South
```

Thus, lights 1 and 6 can both be off.

(B) No. This violates the condition *"Neither light 2 nor light 7 is on when light 1 is on."*

(C) No. If light 2 is off, then from the condition *"Two of the lights on the north side are on"* lights 1 and 3 must be on. However, this scenario has three consecutively numbered lights on—3, 4, and 5—violating the condition *"At least one of any three consecutively numbered lights is off."*

(D) No. Since light 2 is off, the condition *"Two of the lights on the north side are on"* forces lights 1 and 3 to be on:

```
              North
       1 . . . 2 . . . 3
       . on    off  on .
West   8 on              4   East
               off  on .
       7 . . . 6 . . . 5
              South
```

This in turn forces light 4 to be off—otherwise three consecutively numbered lights would be on: 3, 4, and 5.

```
             North
      1 . . . 2 . . . 3
      . on   off   on .
      .               .
West  8 on          off 4  East
      .               .
      .      off   on .
      7 . . . 6 . . . 5
             South
```

Also, light 7 must be off since light 1 and light 7 cannot both be on :

```
             North
      1 . . . 2 . . . 3
      . on   off   on .
      .               .
West  8 on          off 4  East
      .               .
      . off  off   on .
      7 . . . 6 . . . 5
             South
```

However, the south side of this diagram violates the condition *"If any side has exactly one of its three lights on, then that light is its center light."*
(E) No. This scenario has three consecutively numbered lights on—5, 6, and 7.

10.
(A) No. Suppose light 1 is off. Then from the condition *"Two of the lights on the north side are on,"* lights 2 and 3 must be on. However, this scenario has three consecutively numbered lights on—2, 3, and 4.
(B) Yes. Suppose light 2 is off. Then from the condition *"Two of the lights on the north side are on,"* lights 1 and 3 must be on:

```
             North
      1 . . . 2 . . . 3
      . on   off   on .
      .               .
West  8 on           on 4  East
      .               .
      .               .
      7 . . . 6 . . . 5
             South
```

Since three consecutively numbered lights cannot be on, light 5 must be off:

```
             North
      1 . . . 2 . . . 3
      . on   off   on .
      .               .
West  8 on           on 4  East
      .               .
      .           off .
      7 . . . 6 . . . 5
             South
```

Further, since light 1 is on, light 7 must be off:

```
             North
      1 . . . 2 . . . 3
      . on   off   on .
      .               .
West  8 on           on 4  East
      .               .
      . off       off .
      7 . . . 6 . . . 5
             South
```

Finally, since *"At least one of the three lights on each side is on,"* light 6 is on:

```
             North
      1 . . . 2 . . . 3
      . on   off   on .
      .               .
West  8 on           on 4  East
      .               .
      . off   on  off .
      7 . . . 6 . . . 5
             South
```

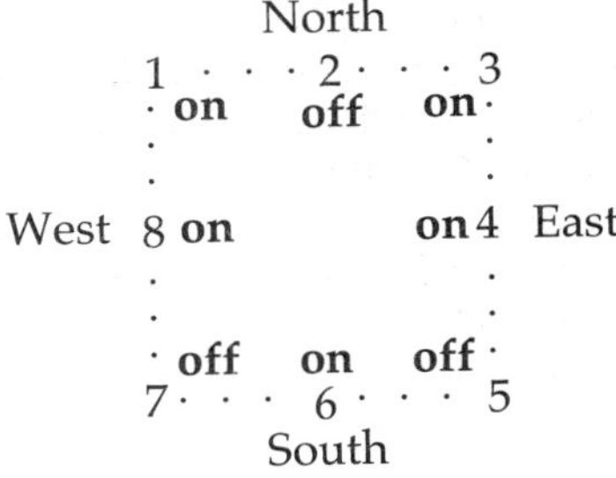

This diagram satisfies all the conditions. Hence, light 2 need not be on.
(C) No. Suppose light 5 is on. Since three consecutively numbered lights cannot be on, light 3 must be off:

```
             North
      1 . . . 2 . . . 3
      .           off .
      .               .
West  8 on           on 4  East
      .               .
      .            on .
      7 . . . 6 . . . 5
             South
```

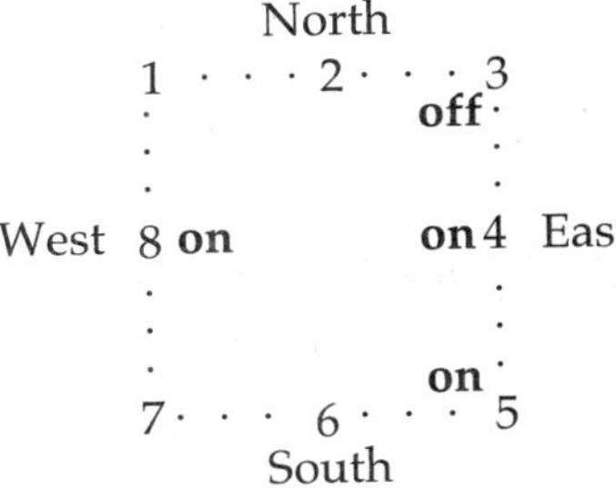

Now, since two lights on the north side must be on, lights 1 and 2 must be on. However, this violates the condition *"Neither light 2 nor light 7 is on when light 1 is on."*
(D) No. Suppose light 6 is off:

```
             North
      1 . . . 2 . . . 3
      .               .
      .               .
West  8 on           on 4  East
      .               .
      .      off      .
      7 . . . 6 . . . 5
             South
```

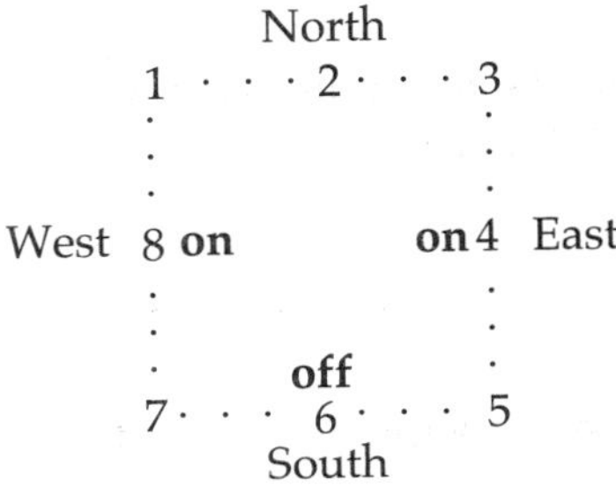

CASE I: If light 1 is off, then from the condition *"Two of the lights on the north side are on"* lights 2 and 3 must be on. However, this scenario has three consecutively numbered lights on—2, 3, and 4.

CASE II: If light 1 is on, then light 7 must be off since *"neither light 2 nor light 7 is on when light 1 is on."*

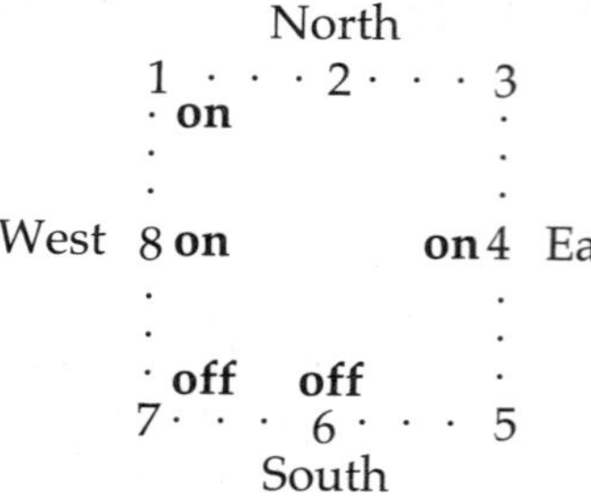

Since *"At least one of the three lights on each side is on,"* light 5 must be on. However, this scenario has light 5 as the only light on the south side on, which violates the condition *"If any side has exactly one of its three lights on, then that light is its center light."*

(E) No. Suppose light 7 is on:

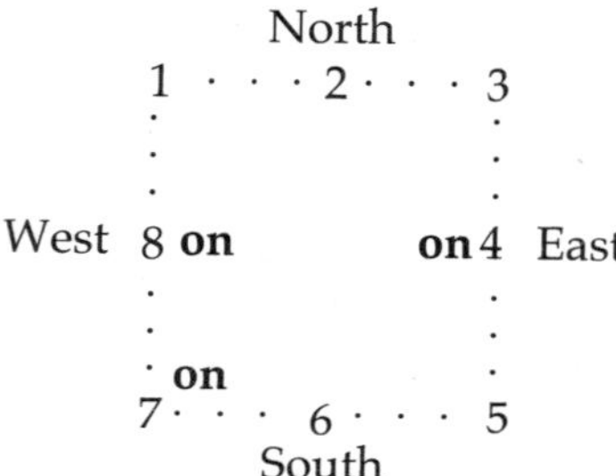

Since *"neither light 2 nor light 7 is on when light 1 is on,"* light 1 must be off:

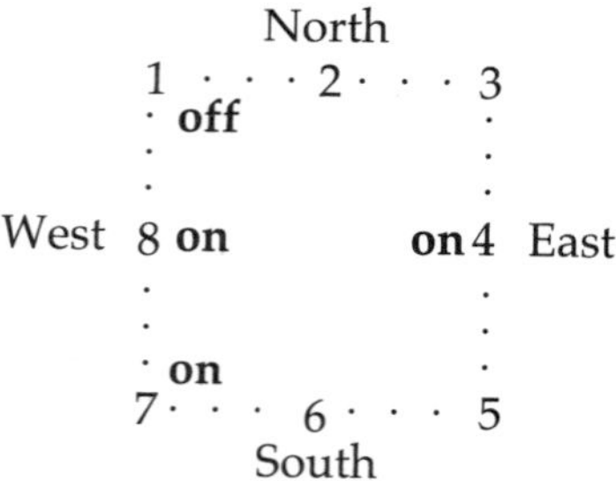

This diagram in turn forces lights 2 and 3 to be on since *"Two of the lights on the north side are on"*:

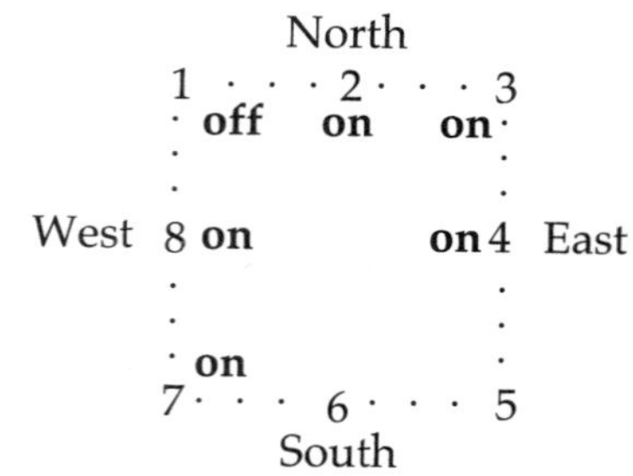

However, this diagram has three consecutively numbered lights on—2, 3, and 4.

Generating Formulas

The previous linear ordering games we studied were static and finite. We were given a fixed number of elements and were asked questions about their possible orderings. Generating formulas, however, tend to be dynamic, in the sense that a basic sequence is given that is used to "generate" other sequences by repeated applications of the formulas. Because the formulas can be applied indefinitely, the sequences often have no end—though typically we are interested in only the beginning of the sequence.

Example:

A particular computer code uses only the letters A, B, C, and D. A "word" is formed in the code according to the following rules:

ABC is the basic word from which all other words are constructed.
D must appear in a word more than once, if at all.
Interchanging the first and last letters in a word creates a new word.
Adding a pair of Ds to the end of a word creates another word.

Notice that the third and fourth conditions are permissive. That is, they *could be* applied but don't have to be.

With permissive conditions, the contrapositive rule of logic does not apply.

The second condition, on the other hand, is mandatory: if D occurs in a word, it *must* occur at least once more.

With mandatory conditions, the contrapositive does apply.

There are only two basic types of questions to these games:

I. **Those that ask you to derive a new sequence from a basic sentence.** In the game above, for example, you may be given the word ABC and then asked to derive a new word by applying the fourth and third rules, in that order.

2. **Those that ask you to "discover" from where a sequence was derived.** In the game above, for example, you may be asked "From which word was the word DBCDA derived?"

The latter type of question tends to be more difficult since there are many paths you can retrace, only one of which will lead to the correct answer.

Because working backwards is often difficult, look for opportunities to reverse the direction by using the contrapositive. But apply the contrapositive only to *mandatory* conditions.

Generating-formula games are one of the few types of games for which it is not advisable to draw a diagram. In fact, typically you cannot draw a diagram. Nevertheless, you may want to symbolize the "rules" for easy reference.

Generating Formulas

In a secret code that uses only the letters A, B, C, and D, a word is formed by applying the following rules:

Rule 1: A B C D is the base word.
Rule 2: If C immediately follows B, then C can be moved to the front of the word.
Rule 3: One letter of the same type can be added immediately after an A, a B, or a C.

1. Which one of the following is not a code word?

   (A) A B C D
   (B) D A B C
   (C) C A B D
   (D) A A B B C C D
   (E) C C C A B D

2. Which of the following letters can start a word?

   I. A
   II. B
   III. C

   (A) I only
   (B) II only
   (C) III only
   (D) I and II only
   (E) I and III only

3. The word C A A B C C D can be formed from the base word by applying the rules in which one of the following orders?

   (A) 22333
   (B) 23232
   (C) 32233
   (D) 3223
   (E) 3233

4. If a fourth rule is added to the other three rules which states that whenever B or D ends a word the sequence obtained by dropping either B or D is still a word, then which of the following would be true?

   I. Some words could end with A.
   II. Some words could start with C and end with C.
   III. A C D would be a word.

   (A) I only
   (B) II only
   (C) I and II only
   (D) I and III only
   (E) I, II, and III

5. If a fourth rule is added to the other three rules which states that a word is created whenever the reversed sequence of a word is added to the end of the word itself, then which one of the following is NOT a word?

   (A) A B C D D C B A
   (B) A B B C C D
   (C) C A B C D D C B A C
   (D) C A B D D B A C
   (E) C B C D D C B A

Notice that Rules 2 and 3 are permissive because they *can* be applied but need not be. No diagram can be drawn, nor are there any readily derived conditions, so we turn to the questions.

1. Which one of the following is not a code word?

(A) A B C D
(B) D A B C
(C) C A B D
(D) A A B B C C D
(E) C C C A B D

Let's use elimination on this question. A B C D is the base word. So (A) is a word—eliminate (A). Applying Rule 2 to the base word gives C A B D. So (C) is a word—eliminate. Applying Rule 3 to the base word *three* times gives A A B B C C D. So (D) is a word—eliminate. Finally, applying Rule 2 to the base word gives C A B D; then applying Rule 3 to C *twice* gives C C C A B D. So (E) is a word--eliminate. Hence, by process of elimination, the answer is (B).

2. Which of the following letters can start a word?

I. A
II. B
III. C

(A) I only
(B) II only
(C) III only
(D) I and II only
(E) I and III only

A can start a word since it starts the base word. This eliminates choices (B) and (C) since they don't contain I. C can start a word since C A B D is formed from the base word by using Rule 2. This eliminates (A) and (D) since they don't contain III. Hence the answer is (E), and there is no need to check Statement II.

3. The word C A A B C C D can be formed from the base word by applying the rules in which one of the following orders?

(A) 22333
(B) 23232
(C) 32233
(D) 3223
(E) 3233

This question is hard, because we don't know to which letter(s) in the base word to apply the rules. Furthermore, there is more than one way to generate the word—but, of course, only one of those ways is listed as an answer-choice. We can, however, narrow the number of answer-choices by analyzing the word C A A B C C D. Notice that C occurs three times and A two times. So Rule 3 must have been applied three times, twice to C and once to A. This eliminates choices (B) and (D) since neither has three 3's. Next, turning to choice (A), we apply Rule 2 to the base word giving C A B D. Now Rule 2 cannot be applied to this word again, since C is not immediately after B. This eliminates (A). Next, choice (C) seems at first glance to be plausible. It begins the same way as does choice (E). But notice in choice (C) that Rule 2 is applied twice in a row. A little fiddling shows that if this is done, then two C's in a row would come at the beginning of the word. So eliminate (C). Hence, by process of elimination, the answer is (E). As a matter of test taking strategy this would be sufficient analysis of the question. However, it is instructive to verify that the answer is (E). To that end, apply Rule 3 to C in the base word A B C D which gives A B C C D. Next, apply Rule 2 which gives C A B C D. Finally, apply Rule 3 to A and then to C which gives C A A B C C D.

4. If a fourth rule is added to the other three rules which states that whenever B or D ends a word the sequence obtained by dropping either B or D is still a word, then which of the following would be true?

I. **Some words could end with A.**
II. **Some words could start with C and end with C.**
III. **A C D would be a word.**

(A) I only
(B) II only
(C) I and II only
(D) I and III only
(E) I, II, and III

Start with the base word A B C D. Applying the new rule gives A B C. Then applying Rule 2 gives C A B. Finally, applying the new rule again gives CA. Hence some words could end with A. So I is true. This eliminates choice (B). Next, starting again with the base word A B C D, apply Rule 3 to C which gives A B C C D. Then apply Rule 2 which gives C A B C D. Finally, apply the new rule which gives C A B C. So some words could start with C and end with C. This eliminates choices (A) and (D). Unfortunately, we have to check the third condition. From the base word all the other words must be derived. Now in the base word, D must be dropped from the end before B can be dropped. Thus A C D cannot be formed. This eliminates choice (E), and therefore the answer is (C).

5. **If a fourth rule is added to the other three rules which states that a word is created whenever the reversed sequence of a word is added to the end of the word itself, then which one of the following is NOT a word?**

   (A) A B C D D C B A
   (B) A B B C C D
   (C) C A B C D D C B A C
   (D) C A B D D B A C
   (E) C B C D D C B A

This problem can be solved either by deriving the four words offered, or by finding the word that violates one or more of the rules. We shall solve it both ways.

Choice (A) is a word because it can be derived by adding the reversed sequence of the base word to the base word itself. So eliminate (A). Choice (B) is word because it can be derived by applying Rule 3, first to B, then to C. So eliminate (B). (Notice that this new rule is also permissive, so it need not be applied for choice (B) to be a word.) Choice (C) is a word because it can be derived by applying Rule 3 to the base word which gives A B C C D. Then applying Rule 2 gives C A B C D. Finally applying the new rule gives C A B C D D C B A C. So eliminate (C). Finally, choice (D) is a word because it can be derived by applying Rule 2 to the base word which gives C A B D. Then applying the new rule gives C A B D D B A C. So eliminate (D). Thus, by process of elimination, the answer is (E).

Turning to the other method, we now show that (E) violates one of the rules. The only way that A can end a word is if the reversed sequence of a word is added to the word itself.* But D C B A is not the reversed sequence of C B C D, which isn't even a word.

Although the latter method was faster than deriving the four words, it can be deceptively hard to spot the choice that violates one or more of the rules.

Points to Remember

1. With permissive conditions, the contrapositive rule of logic does *not* apply.
2. With mandatory conditions, the contrapositive *does* apply.
3. There are only two basic types of questions to these games:
   I. Those that ask you to derive a new sequence from a basic sentence.
   II. Those that ask you to "discover" from where a sequence was derived.
4. Generating-formula games are one of the few types of games for which it is not advisable to draw a diagram. Nevertheless, you may want to symbolize the "rules" for easy reference.

* Recall that supplementary conditions apply only to the questions in which they are introduced. Hence the rule introduced in Question 4 no longer applies.

There will be no mentor exercise for this section.

Exercise

Directions: The following group of questions is based on a set of conditions. Choose the response that most accurately and completely answers each question.

Questions 1-4

In the game of Sense, a word is formed by combining the letters G, H, I, J, K:

G cannot be the first or last letter in a word.
I and J cannot be next to each other.
If J occurs in a word, then it occurs an odd number of times.
H cannot begin a word unless K ends the word.

1. Which one of the following is a word in the game of Sense?

(A) H J I K
(B) G
(C) I G J K H
(D) J H K J K
(E) H I K I

2. In the word □ I K J, which of the following could be placed in the box to make a word?

I. H
II. I
III. J

(A) I only
(B) II only
(C) III only
(D) I and II only
(E) II and III only

3. Which one of the following is NOT a word but could become a word by adding one or more letters to its right end?

(A) G
(B) I J
(C) J
(D) H J J G
(E) H J G K

4. Of the following strings of letters, which can be made into words by adding a J and then reordering the letters?

I. G H J I J
II. I J
III. H K G

(A) I only
(B) II only
(C) I and II only
(D) I and III only
(E) I, II, and III

Answers and Solutions to Exercise

We will not use a diagram to solve this game; however, we will symbolize the conditions for easy reference and to better understand them. The condition *"G cannot be the first or last letter in a word"* can be symbolized as **G ≠ First/Last.** The condition *"I and J cannot be next to each other"* is naturally symbolized as **~(IJ)**. The condition *"If J occurs in a word, then it occurs an odd number of times"* can be symbolized as **J—>(J=odd#)**. Finally, the condition *"H cannot begin a word unless K ends the word"* can be symbolized as **(H=First)—>(K=Last)**. Note that all the conditions in this game are mandatory, so we may safely apply the contrapositive to any of them. Summarizing the conditions yields the following schematic:

G ≠ First/Last
~(IJ)
J—>(J=odd#)
(H=First)—>(K=Last)

1. (A) is not a word because it violates the condition **~(IJ)**. (B) is not a word because it violates the condition **G ≠ First/Last**. If there is only one element in a word, then it both begins and ends the word. (C) is a word: G does not begin or end it; I is not next to J; J appears only once, which is an odd number of times; and the condition **(H=First)—>(K=last)** does not apply since H is not first. The answer is (C).

2. Start with H. Now, **H I K J** is not a word because H is first and K is not last. This eliminates (A) and (D). Next, place I in the box: **I I K J**. This sequences of letters satisfies all the conditions, so it is a word. This eliminates (C). Unfortunately, we have to check Statement III. Placing J in the box gives **J I K J**. This, however, is not a word since J appears an even number of times, which violates the condition **J—>(J=odd#).** The answer is (B).

3. **G** cannot be made into a word by adding letters to its right end because G can never be the first letter of a word. This eliminates (A). Next **I J** cannot be made into a word by adding letters to its right end because I can never be next to J in a word. Next, **H J J G** is not a word because H is first but K is not last; additionally, J appears twice. But if we add J and K, in that order, then there will be an odd number of J_S and K will be the last letter, which makes **H J J G J K** a word. The answer is (D).

Don't make the mistake of choosing (C) or (E); both are already words.* Remember we are looking for a string of letters that is NOT a word but can be made into one by adding one or more letters to its right end.

4. **G H J I J** can be made into a word by first adding another J, which yields three J_S (an odd number). Then moving I to the left of G. Next, **I J** cannot be made into a word by adding another J because that would result in two J_S (an even number). Finally, **H K G** can be made into a word: First, add J to the right of G. Then flip-flop H and K, which yields **K H G J**. The answer is (D).

---

* **J** is a word because it appears an odd number of times (once) and none of the other conditions are violated.

Paths and Flow Charts

Although flow charts and paths are not, strictly speaking, ordering games, they have many of the properties found in ordering games.* Thus it is natural to analyze them here.

Flow charts and paths tend to be highly determinative. Once the chart has been constructed, the questions typically can be answered with little additional thought—often all the answers can be discerned by merely reading the chart.

The catch is that the chart may not be easy to derive. Because this type of game typically has many conditions, the chart can easily get out of control. Charting is an art. However, there are some guidelines that help:

1. **Look for a condition that starts the "flow" or that contains a lot of information.**
2. **Look for an element that occurs in many conditions.**
3. **Keep the chart flexible; it will probably have to evolve with the changing conditions.**

Before we start, we need to address some of the hazards and symbols common to these games. Because flow charts and paths involve a "flowing" of information, the *if-then* symbol, **—>**, is the workhorse for these games. Because the information can often "flow" in both directions, the symbol "**<—>**" also comes into play. A slash through a symbol indicates that information cannot flow in that direction. For example: A/>B means information cannot flow from A to B.

As you work through these games be alert to any opportunity to apply the contrapositive rule of logic. Often negative conditions can be expressed more clearly by rewording them in the contrapositive. For example, the statement

"if it is not sunny, then Biff is not going to the beach"

can be reworded more directly as

"if Biff is going to the beach, then it is sunny."

It is not necessary that both parts of the *if-then* statement be negative for this technique to be effective. For example, the statement *"if Linda is hired, then Roland is not"* can be recast as *"if Roland is hired, then Linda is not."* Although in this case the contrapositive statement is no simpler than the original, it may, and often does, open up connections to other conditions.

We need to review two common fallacies associated with the contrapositive. From the statement "if A, then B" we can conclude, using the contrapositive, "if not B, then not A." It would be fallacious, however, to conclude either *"if not A, then not B"* or *"if B, then A."* Also note that *some* means "at least one and perhaps all."

---

* In fact, as we saw with sequential ordering, many games can be solved more easily and more efficiently using flow charts.

Until this point, our discussion has been out of chronological order: we have discussed how to solve flow and path games without discussing how to identify them. Path games are easy to identify; typically they involve the actual movement of an element or of information. Some examples are

- Four cities are connected by six roads.
- A memo can be passed from Sara to Helen, but not from Sara to John.
- If a litigant filed his case in federal court and lost, then he may appeal to the 4th District Court and from there to the Supreme Court.

Flow charts are harder to identify than paths. In fact, they can be quite cryptic. However, a game with many *if-then* conditions is often a tip-off to a flow-chart game. Unfortunately, the *if-then* thought is often embedded in other equivalent structures. For example, the sentence "All A's are B's" can be reworded as "If x is an A, then x is a B." For a more subtle example take the sentence "Linda and Sara are not both hired"; it can be recast as "if Linda is hired, then Sara is not" (or "if Sara is hired, then Linda is not").

The following drill will help you identify embedded *if-then* statements.

If-then Drill

Directions: Translate each of the following conditions into an equivalent *if-then* statement. Answers and explanations are on page 137.

Condition	*If-then* form
1. No A is a B.	
2. Alice will go to the party only if Bobby goes.	
3. Anyone who is not an A cannot be a B.	
4. Only A's are B's.	
5. Of two light switches A and B, A and B cannot both be on.	
6. Of two light switches A and B: A is off, when B is off; A is on, when B is on.	

As you analyze a flow chart, look for "loops" that connect groups of elements. An example will illustrate:

Flow Chart

Six debutantes—Alison, Bridgette, Courtney, Dominique, Emily, Francine—meet at a party. During the time they have been at the party some girls have come to like certain other girls.

Amiable Alison likes every girl at the party.
Aloof, yet popular Bridgette likes no one at the party, but everyone likes her.
Courtney likes only two girls, one of whom is Dominique.
Dominique likes three girls, none of whom are Courtney or Francine.
Emily and Francine each like only one girl.

1. Of the following girls, who likes Emily?

   I. Alison
   II. Dominique
   III. Francine

   (A) I only
   (B) II only
   (C) III only
   (D) I and II only
   (E) I and III only

2. A "click" is a group of two or more girls who like one another. How many clicks are formed amongst the six girls?

   (A) 0
   (B) 1
   (C) 2
   (D) 3
   (E) 4

3. How many girls at the party like at least one girl whose feelings are not reciprocal?

   (A) 2
   (B) 3
   (C) 4
   (D) 5
   (E) 6

Alison likes every girl, so we start the "flow" with her:

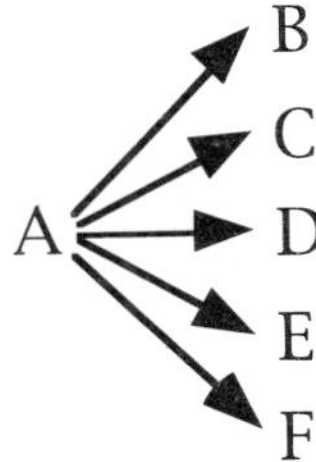

Next, every girl likes Bridgette, but she does not like any of them. So we end the "flow" with Bridgette. (Note how the diagram evolves.)

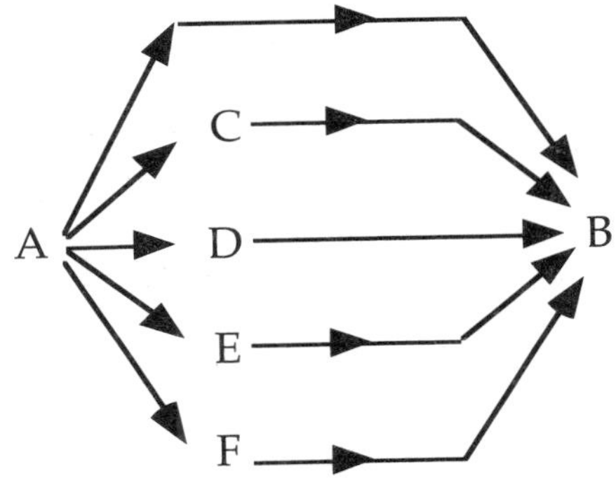

Next, since Dominique likes three girls, two of whom are neither Courtney nor Francine, she must like both Alison and Emily, in addition to Bridgette. Adding this result plus the third condition, "*Courtney likes Dominique*," to the diagram gives

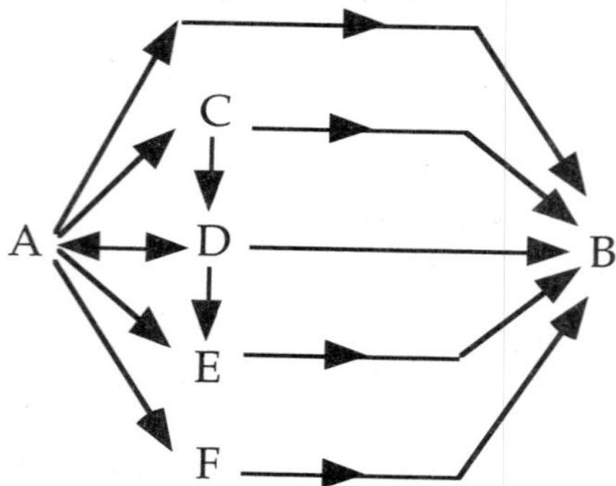

Finally, since Emily and Francine each like only one girl and everyone likes Bridgette, Emily and Francine each must like Bridgette only. So there is nothing else to add to the diagram.

Note A,C,D forms a "loop", because from A the arrows can be followed all the way around the "loop" back to A. But A,D,E does not form a loop, because from A you cannot get back to A, whether you go first to D, or first to E.

1. **Of the following girls, who likes Emily?**

   I. Alison
   II. Dominique
   III. Francine

   (A) I only
   (B) II only
   (C) III only
   (D) I and II only
   (E) I and III only

In the chart, only arrows from A and D point to E. So only Alison and Dominique like Emily. The answer is (D).

2. **A "click" is a group of two or more girls who like one another. How many clicks are formed amongst the six girls?**

   (A) 0
   (B) 1
   (C) 2
   (D) 3
   (E) 4

There is only one. In the chart, a two-way arrow connects A and D, so they form a click. The loop A,C,D does not form a click because it's not two-way: A likes C, but that feeling is not reciprocal. The answer is (B).

3. **How many girls at the party like at least one girl whose feelings are not reciprocal?**

   (A) 2
   (B) 3
   (C) 4
   (D) 5
   (E) 6

In the chart, there are 5 arrows pointing to B, so 5 girls like B. There are no arrows emanating from B, so none of those feelings are reciprocal. The answer is (D).

Flow-chart games can bring to the fore some subtle issues, as the following difficult game illustrates.

Circuit

Six lights—J, K, L, M, N, O—are connected in a circuit. Each light can be either on or off.

If K is on, L is off.
J and N cannot both be on.
M is off if and only if either J or N is on.
If O is on, N is on; if O is off, N is off.

1. How many lights in the circuit must be on?

(A) 0
(B) 1
(C) 2
(D) 3
(E) 4

2. If J is on, which one of the following could be a complete and accurate list of the other lights that are on as well?

(A) K and O
(B) L and N
(C) L and O
(D) M, N, and K
(E) L

To keep the notation simple, let the letter itself stand for *"the light is on,"* and place a tilde before the letter to indicate that the light is off. The condition *"If K is on, L is off"* is naturally symbolized as **K—>~L.** The condition *"J and N cannot both be on"* means that if one is on the other must be off: **N—>~J.*** The condition *"M is off if and only if either J or N is on"* is naturally symbolized as **~M<—>(J or N)**. Finally, the condition *"If O is on, N is on; if O is off, N is off"* means that O is on if and only if N is on: **O<—>N.**

Now we come to the crucial decision—with which condition should we start our chart? Following the guidelines on page 131, look for the element that occurs in the greatest number of conditions; it is N. Of the three conditions that contain N, the condition **O<—>N** is the most restrictive, so we start the flow with it:

O<—>N

Next, adding the condition **N—>~J** gives

O<—>N—>~J

Then, adding the condition **~M<—>(J or N)** gives

O<—>N—>~J
↓
~M<—>(J or N)

Finally, the condition **K—>~L** is independent of the other conditions, so the flow chart consists of two distinct parts:

O<—>N—>~J
↓
~M<—>(J or N)

K—>~L

We will use only this chart to answer the following questions.

1. How many lights in the circuit must be on?

* J—>~N would also suffice, but we don't need both.

(A) 0
(B) 1
(C) 2
(D) 3
(E) 4

Since this is a counting problem, we anticipate that it will be hard. It won't disappoint us.

From the bottom chart, we see that both K and L can be off. (The condition **K—>~L** states only that if K is on then L is off. It says nothing about the case when K is off, so both K and L *could be* off.) Furthermore, since the bottom chart is independent of the top chart, the status of K and L (whether on or off) does not affect the other lights. Next, from the top chart if both O and N are on, then both J and M must be off. Thus it is possible for only two lights, O and N, to be on, which eliminates (D) and (E). Next, we check the alternative circumstance where both O and N are off. From the top chart, we see that if M is also off, then J must be on. While if M is on, J can not be on. Combining these cases (M *on* or *off*), we see that one and only one of M, J, and N must be on. Hence it is possible for only one element to be on, which eliminates (C). Finally, we check whether all the lights could be off. Again, the top chart shows that this is not possible: if M is off, then either N or J must be on, which eliminates (A)—at least one light must be on. The answer, therefore, is (B).

2. If J is on, which one of the following could be a complete and accurate list of the other lights that are on as well?

(A) K and O
(B) L and N
(C) L and O
(D) M, N, and K
(E) L

Notice that (A), (B), (C), and (D) all contain either N or O, but not both. However, the condition **O<—>N** states that they are always on at the same time. This eliminates (A) through (D).

Points to Remember

1. When constructing a flow chart, use the following guidelines:
   (a) Look for a condition that starts the flow.
   (b) Look for an element that occurs in many conditions.
   (c) Keep the chart flexible.

2. Be aware of the fallacies associated with the contrapositive:

   From A—>B you can conclude

   ~B—>~A;

   but you <u>cannot</u> conclude either

   ~A—>~B, or B—>A.

3. *Some* means "at least one and perhaps <u>all</u>."

4. The following statements contain embedded *if-then* statements.

Statement	***If-then* form**
All A's are B's.	If x is an A, then x is a B.
A and B are not both C's.	If A is a C, then B is not.
No A is a B.	If A, then not B.
Only A's are B's.	If B, then A.

Solutions to *If-then* Drill

Condition	*If-then form*
1. No A is a B.	If A, then not B.

2. Alice will go to the party only if Bobby goes.	If Alice goes, then Bobby goes.

Explanation: This common structure causes students much confusion. It states only that if Alice is at the party, then Bobby must also be at the party. (Note, this condition is not reciprocal; the statement "if Bobby is at the party, then Alice is also" is not necessarily true.)

3. Anyone who is not an A cannot be a B.	If not A, then not B.

Explanation: The contrapositive further simplifies this to "if B, then A."

4. Only As are Bs.	If B, then A.

5. Of two light switches A and B, A and B cannot both be on.	If A is on, then B is not.

Explanation: "If B is on, then A is not" will also suffice, but it is not necessary to state both—one is the contrapositive of the other.

6. Of two light switches A and B: A is off, when B is off; A is on, when B is on.	A is off if and only if B is off.

Explanation: "A is on if and only if B is on" will also suffice, but again it is not necessary to state both.

Mentor Exercise

Directions: The following group of questions is based on a set of conditions. Choose the response that most accurately and completely answers each question. Hints, insights, partial solutions, and the answers are provided in the right-hand column.

Questions 1–6

Six people—Albert, Ben, Carrie, Darlene, Emily, and Fred—are competing in a gymnastics event. Two of them compete on the horse, two compete in the vault, and two compete on the parallel bars.

Ben competes on the horse if and only if Carrie competes in the vault.
If Darlene does not compete on the parallel bars, then Fred competes in the vault.
If Emily competes in the vault, then Fred does not.

This is a rather hard game. Its underlying structure is actually simple, but there's lots of information to wade through. We start by symbolizing the conditions. We'll use an equal sign to indicate that a person competes in a particular event. The first condition, *"Ben competes on the horse if and only if Carrie competes in the vault,"* can be symbolized as **(B=H)<—>(C=V)**. The second condition, *"If Darlene does not compete on the parallel bars, then Fred competes in the vault,"* can be symbolized as **(D≠P)—>(F=V)**. This in turn can be recast, using the contrapositive, as **(F≠V)—>(D=P)**. Finally, the condition *"If Emily competes in the vault, then Fred does not"* can be symbolized as **(E=V)—>(F≠V)**. This gives the following schematic:

(B=H)<—>(C=V)
(F≠V)—>(D=P)
(E=V)—>(F≠V)

To start the flow chart, look for the element that occurs in the greatest number of conditions; it is F. So build the chart around it. Start with the third condition:

(E=V)—>(F≠V)

Next, add the second condition:

(E=V)—>(F≠V)—>(D=P)

Finally, the condition **(B=H)<—>(C=V)** cannot be added to the chart, so it forms an independent flow chart:

(E=V)—>(F≠V)—>(D=P)

(B=H)<—>(C=V)

Note that A is "wild" since it is not contained in the diagram.

1. **If Ben competes on the horse, then which one of the following can be true?**

   (A) Both Emily and Albert compete in the vault.
   (B) Emily competes on the horse and Darlene competes in the vault.
   (C) Darlene does not compete on the parallel bars and Albert competes in the vault.
   (D) Albert competes on the parallel bars and Carrie competes in the vault.
   (E) Albert competes on the horse and Darlene does not compete on the parallel bars.

1. Since Ben competes on the horse, we know from the bottom half of the chart that Carrie competes in the vault. Furthermore, if Darlene does not compete on the parallel bars, then applying the contrapositive to the top part of the chart, we see that Fred also competes in the vault. This fills both slots for the vault, so no one else can compete in that event. These restrictions are sufficient to eliminate choices (A), (B), (C), and (E).

The answer is (D).

2. **If Darlene does not compete on the parallel bars, then which one of the following cannot be true?**

   (A) Ben competes on the horse.
   (B) Fred competes in the vault.
   (C) Albert competes on the parallel bars.
   (D) Emily competes in the vault.
   (E) Both Ben and Fred compete in the vault.

2.

Hint!

Apply the contrapositive to the top half of the diagram.

The answer is (D).

3. **If Ben and Carrie compete in the same event, then which one of the following can be true?**

   I. Albert competes on the horse.
   II. Emily competes in the vault.
   III. Darlene does not compete on the parallel bars.

   (A) I only
   (B) II only
   (C) III only
   (D) I and III only
   (E) I, II, and III

3. From the condition **(B=H)<—>(C=V)**, we know that Ben and Carrie must both compete on the parallel bars. (Why?) As to I, since Albert is an independent element, we intuitively expect that he could compete on the horse, but you should verify this. As to II, if Emily competes in the vault, then from the diagram Darlene must compete on the parallel bars. This, however, puts three people in the parallel bar event, contradicting the condition that there are two people in each event. As to III, if Darlene does not compete on the parallel bars, then applying the contrapositive to the top diagram shows that Fred must compete in the vault, and Emily cannot compete in the vault. Now it's easy to work out a schedule with these restrictions.

The answer is (D).

4. Suppose the condition "If Carrie does not compete in the vault, then Emily does" is added to the given conditions. Which one of the following cannot be true if Emily and Darlene do not compete in the same event?

(A) Ben does not compete on the horse and Darlene does.
(B) Fred competes on the horse.
(C) Ben does not compete on the horse and Darlene competes on the parallel bars.
(D) Albert competes on the parallel bars.
(E) Emily competes in the vault.

4. This question is difficult because there are six different ways to assign different events to Carrie and Emily. Additionally, the string of inferences needed to answer the question is quite long.

To begin, add the new condition **(C≠V)—>(E=V)** to the diagram:

(C≠V)—>(E=V)—>(F≠V)—>(D=P)

(B=H)<—>(C=V)

Now assume that Ben does not compete on the horse and Darlene does, choice (A). Then use the above diagram to derive a contradiction—namely that Darlene also competes on the parallel bars.

The answer is (A).

5. If Darlene competes in the vault, then how many different people could possibly compete on the horse?

(A) 2
(B) 3
(C) 4
(D) 5
(E) 6

5. Applying the contrapositive, along with the new condition *"Darlene competes in the vault"* to the original diagram, shows that Fred competes in the vault and Emily does not. Now Ben cannot compete on the horse. (Why?) From these conditions you should be able to work out three valid schedules.

The answer is (B).

6. Suppose the condition "if Fred does not compete in the vault, then Emily does" is added to the original conditions. Of the following, which one cannot be true?

(A) Ben competes on the horse and Albert competes in the vault.
(B) Ben competes on the horse and Emily competes in the vault.
(C) Darlene competes on the parallel bars.
(D) Albert competes on the parallel bars.
(E) Fred competes on the parallel bars and Albert competes on the horse.

6. This question is hard, or at least long, because it actually contains five questions. The new condition changes the diagram only slightly:

(E=V)<—>(F≠V)—>(D=P)

(B=H)<—>(C=V)

Start with (A). If Ben competes on the horse, then from the bottom half of the new diagram Carrie must compete on the vault along with Albert. Turning to the top diagram, clearly Emily cannot compete in the vault, since that would put three people—Emily, Albert, and Carrie—in one event. But if Emily does not compete on the vault, then again from the top diagram and the contrapositive Fred must compete in the vault, which leads to the same contradiction.

The answer is (A).

Exercise

Directions: The following group of questions is based on a set of conditions. Choose the response that most accurately and completely answers each question.

Questions 1–5

Seven small towns—H, I, J, K, L, M, N—are serviced by three roads—Routes 1, 2, and 3.

Route 1 ends at N and L, and passes through M only.
Route 2 starts at H. Then passes through L and I, and ends back at H.
Route 3 ends at N and K, and passes through J only.

Two towns are directly connected if a person can drive from one of the towns to the other without passing through any other town.

1. Of the following towns, which one has the greatest number of direct connections?

   (A) H
   (B) N
   (C) J
   (D) K
   (E) L

2. Which one of the following towns has the fewest number of connections, direct or otherwise, with the other towns?

   (A) H
   (B) K
   (C) N
   (D) L
   (E) I

3. If a new road were built directly connecting I and J, and if all the direct connections between the towns were of equal distance, then in which one of the following pairs of towns is neither town on the shortest route connecting L and K?

   (A) J, H
   (B) H, I
   (C) I, J
   (D) N, I
   (E) M, N

4. If a new road were built directly connecting H and K, then the maximum number of paths connecting L to J, which do not pass through any town more than once, would be

   (A) 1
   (B) 2
   (C) 3
   (D) 4
   (E) 5

5. If two new roads were built directly connecting L to J and K to H, then which one of the following is NOT a complete and accurate list of the towns through which a person could pass on a single trip from L to H?

   (A) I
   (B) J, K
   (C) M, N, J, K
   (D) No town
   (E) M, N, K

Questions 6–7

Six lights—J, K, L, M, N, and O—are connected in a circuit. Each light can be either on or off.

If K is on, N is on.
J and N cannot both be on.
If O is on, N is on; if O is off, N is off.

6. If K is on, which one of the following must be true?

(A) L is on.
(B) L is off.
(C) J is off.
(D) M is on.
(E) N is off.

7. If J is on, what is the maximum number of lights that can be off?

(A) 1
(B) 2
(C) 3
(D) 4
(E) 5

The next three games appeared on recent LSATs.

Questions 8–9

Eight benches—J, K, L, T, U, X, Y, and Z—are arranged along the perimeter of a park as shown below:

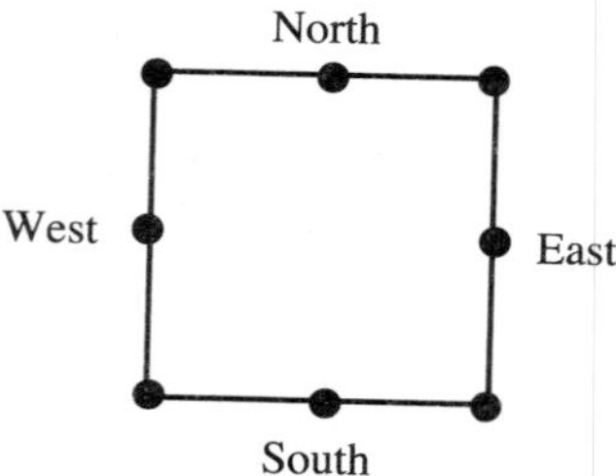

The following is true:

J, K, and L are green; T and U are red; X, Y, and Z are pink.
The green benches stand next to one another along the park's perimeter.
The pink benches stand next to one another along the park's perimeter.
No green bench stands next to a pink bench.
The bench on the southeast corner is T.
J stands at the center of the park's north side.
If T stands next to X, then T does not also stand next to L.

8. For which one of the following benches are there two and no more than two locations either one of which could be the location the bench occupies?

(A) K
(B) T
(C) X
(D) Y
(E) Z

9. If Z is directly north of Y, which one of the following statements must be true?

(A) J is directly west of K.
(B) K is directly east of U.
(C) U is directly north of X.
(D) X is directly south of J.
(E) Z is directly south of J.

Questions 10–11

Six people—Julio, Kevin, May, Norma, Olivia, and Tamio—participate in a track meet. Two of them enter the marathon, two enter the relay, and two enter the sprint.

Each participant enters only one event.
If Kevin enters the marathon, then both Julio and May enter the relay, and if both Julio and May enter the relay, then Kevin enters the marathon.
If Norma does not enter the sprint, then Tamio enters the relay.
If Olivia enters the relay, then Julio does not enter the relay.
Olivia and Tamio do not both enter the relay.

10. If Kevin enters the marathon, then which one of the following cannot be true?

(A) Julio enters the relay and Norma enters the sprint.
(B) Olivia enters the marathon and Norma enters the sprint.
(C) Tamio enters the marathon and Olivia enters the sprint.
(D) Tamio enters the relay and Olivia enters the sprint.
(E) Tamio enters the marathon and May enters the relay.

11. If both Kevin and Olivia enter the relay, then which one of the following must be true?

(A) Julio and Tamio enter the marathon.
(B) May enters the marathon.
(C) May enters the sprint.
(D) Tamio enters the sprint.
(E) Norma enters the sprint.

Questions 12–13

A lake contains exactly five islands—J, K, L, M, O—which are unconnected by bridges. Contractors will build a network of bridges that satisfies the following specifications:

Each bridge directly connects exactly two islands with each other, and no two bridges intersect.
No more than one bridge directly connects any two islands.
No island has more than three bridges that directly connect it with other islands.
J, K, and L are each directly connected by bridge with one or both of M and O.
J is directly connected by bridge with exactly two islands.
K is directly connected by bridge with exactly one island.
A bridge directly connects J with O, and a bridge directly connects M with O.

12. If a bridge directly connects K with O, then which one of the following could be true?

(A) No bridge directly connects L with M.
(B) A bridge directly connects J with L.
(C) A bridge directly connects L with O.
(D) There are exactly three bridges directly connecting L with other islands.
(E) There are exactly two bridges directly connecting O with other islands.

13. If no island that is directly connected by bridge with M is also directly connected by bridge with O, then there must be a bridge directly connecting

(A) J with L
(B) J with M
(C) K with O
(D) L with M
(E) L with O

Questions 14–17

There are five employees—G, H, I, J, and K—in an office. Rumors spread through the office according to the following rules.

Rumors can pass from G to H, but not vice versa.
Rumors can pass from G to I, but not vice versa.
Rumors can pass from G to J, but not vice versa.
Rumors can pass in either direction between H and I.
Rumors can pass from H to J, but not vice versa.
Rumors can pass from J to I, but not vice versa.
Rumors can pass in either direction between J and K.

A direct path from one person to another is called a segment.

14. A rumor begun by I that reaches K will be known by all the following employees EXCEPT:

(A) I
(B) G
(C) K
(D) H
(E) J

15. If all segments have the same length and if rumors always follow the shortest path, then the longest path any rumor follows in the system is the path from

(A) H to J
(B) J to K
(C) H to G
(D) I to J
(E) I to K

16. Which of the following is a complete and accurate list of the people to whom a rumor can be spread along exactly one segment from H?

(A) I
(B) J
(C) I, J
(D) I, J, K
(E) I, J, G

17. If a two-way segment from K to G is added to the rumor mill, which of the following segments would have to be added to the system so that each person could spread a rumor directly to at least two other people and receive a rumor directly from at least two other people?

(A) I to J
(B) H to G
(C) K to H
(D) I to G
(E) J to H

Questions 18–19

A Hollywood production company is hiring six people—John, Kent, Mary, Nora, Olivia, and Tom. Two of them are hired as editors, two as gaffers, and two as actors.

Each person is hired for only one job.
If Kent is hired as an editor, then both John and Mary are hired as gaffers, and if both John and Mary hired as gaffers, then Kent is hired as an editor.
If Nora is not hired as an actor, then Tom is hired as a gaffer.

18. If Kent is hired as an editor, then which one of the following cannot be true?

(A) Nora and Tom are hired as actors.
(B) Olivia is hired as an actor, and Tom as an editor.
(C) Olivia and Nora are hired as actors.
(D) Tom is hired as a gaffer and Olivia is hired as an actor.
(E) Neither John nor Mary are hired as editors.

19. If both Kent and Olivia are hired as gaffers, then which one of the following must be true?

(A) Nora is hired as an editor.
(B) Tom is hired as an actor.
(C) John is hired as an actor.
(D) John and Tom are hired as editors.
(E) Nora is hired as an actor.

Answers and Solutions to Exercise

Questions 1–5

Diagramming makes this a fairly easy game. Start by placing the seven towns in a circle:*

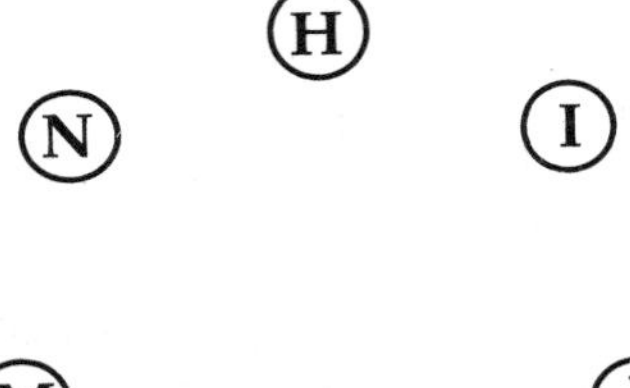

Next, add Route 1 to the diagram:

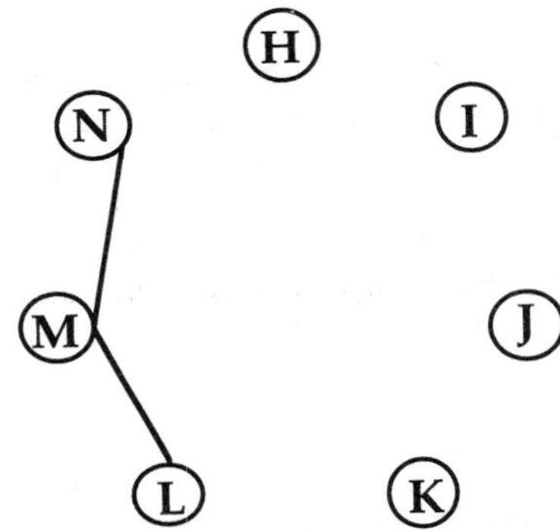

Then, add Route 2:

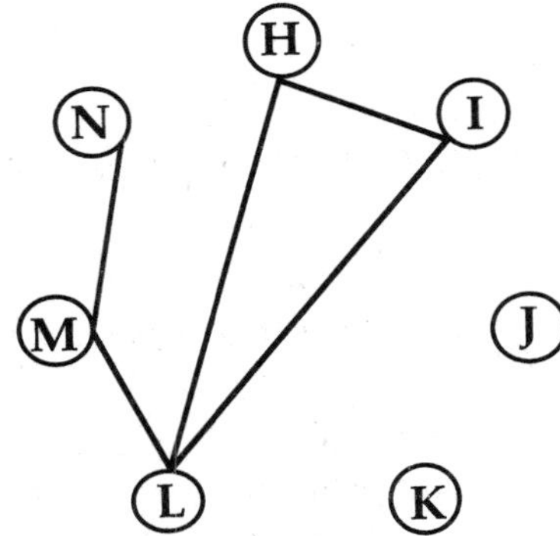

Finally, add Route 3:

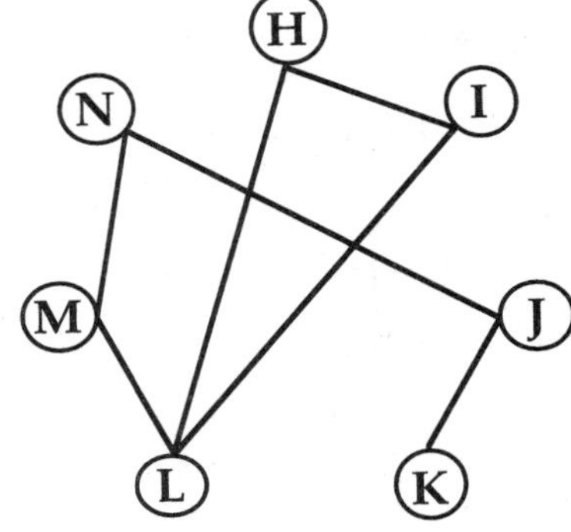

1. From the chart, there are three roads going to L, and no other town has more than two roads going to it. Hence the answer is (E).

2. Again from the chart, there is only one road going to K, and every other town has at least two roads going to it. So K has the fewest number of connections. The answer is (B).

3. Adding the new road to the chart gives

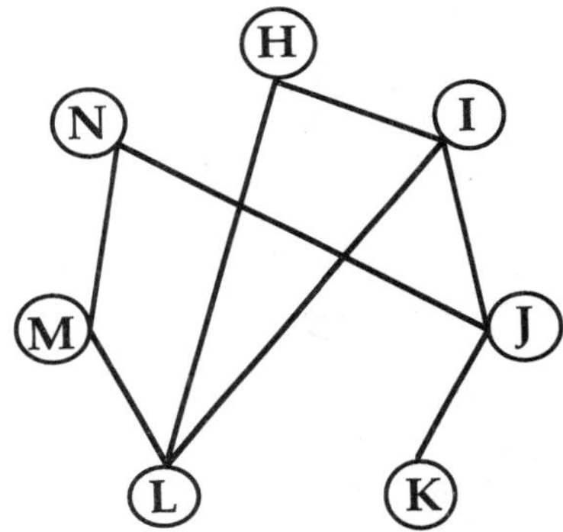

Now the shortest route from L to K passes through I and J:

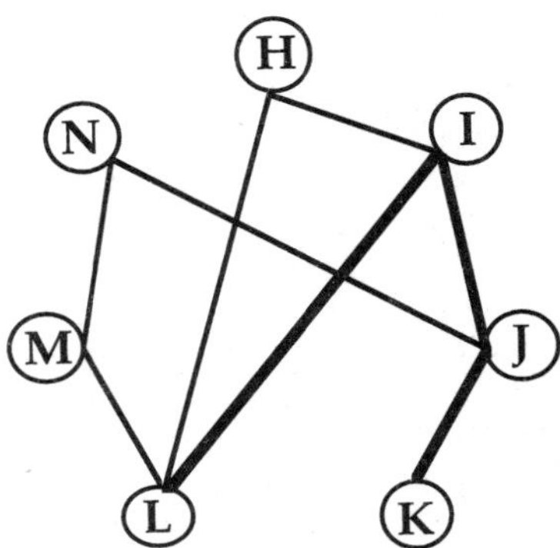

Clearly, in this diagram, neither M nor N is on the shortest path from L to K. The answer is (E).

---

* This is not the most efficient way to arrange the towns, but it is the most natural.

4. Adding the new road to the original diagram yields

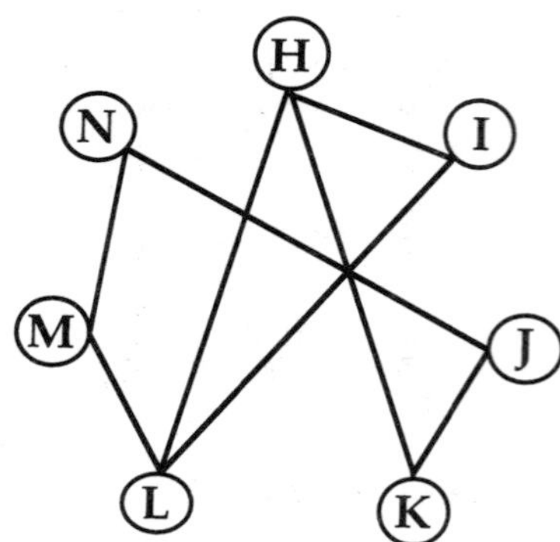

The following three charts display the only three possible paths from L to J:

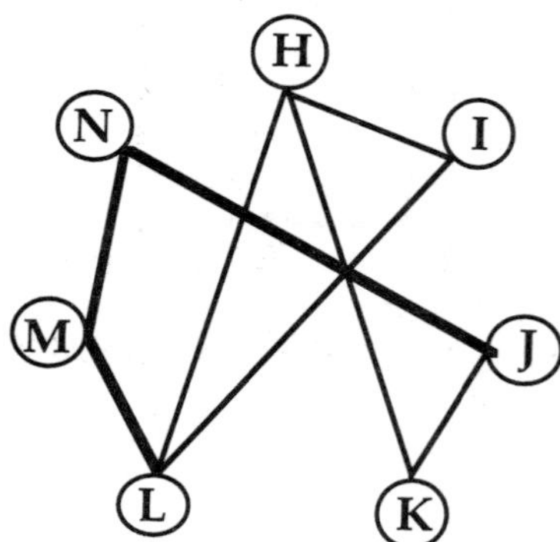

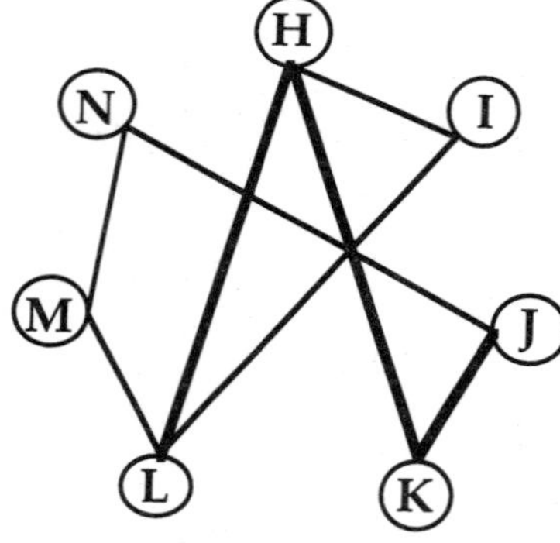

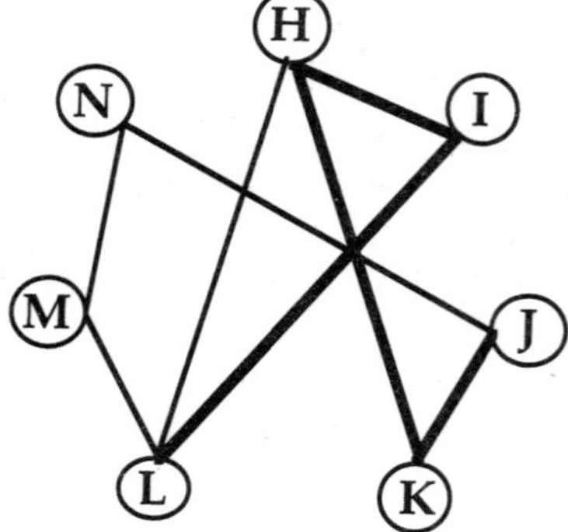

Hence the answer is (C).

5. Adding the new roads to the chart gives

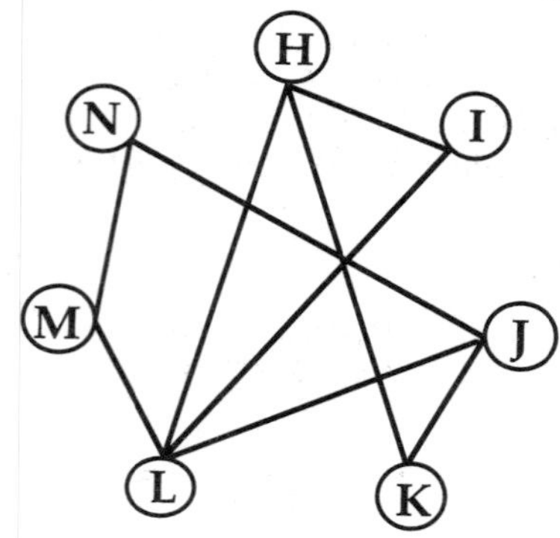

The route in choice (E) directly connects either M or N to K, but in the chart there is no road directly connecting M or N to K. Hence this is impossible, and the answer is (E).

Questions 6–7

Let the letter itself stand for *"the light is on,"* and place a tilde before the letter to indicate that the light is off. We begin the chart with the condition *"If O is on, N is on; if O is off, N is off,"* which means that O is on if and only if N is on:

O<—>N

Next, the condition *"J and N cannot both be on"* means that if one is on the other must be off: **N—>~J.** Adding this to the diagram yields

O<—>N—>~J

Finally, adding the condition *"If K is on, N is on,"* **K—>N**, to the chart gives

O<—>N—>~J

↑

K

6. In the diagram, a sequence of arrows "flows" from K to N to ~J. Hence, J must be off. The answer is (C).

7. The fact that J is on prompts us to apply the contrapositive to the diagram:

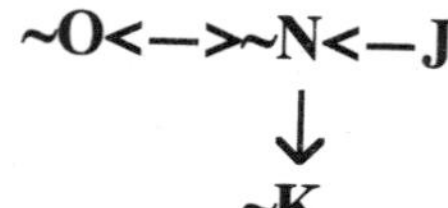

This shows that at least 3 lights must be off. Now, no conditions apply to either L or M. So their status—whether on or off—is independent of the other lights. Hence, both could be off. This gives a maximum of 5 lights off. The answer is (E).

Questions 8–9

The condition *"If T stands next to X, then T does not also stand next to L"* can be symbolized as **TX–>~(TL)**. Summarizing the remaining conditions yields the following diagram:

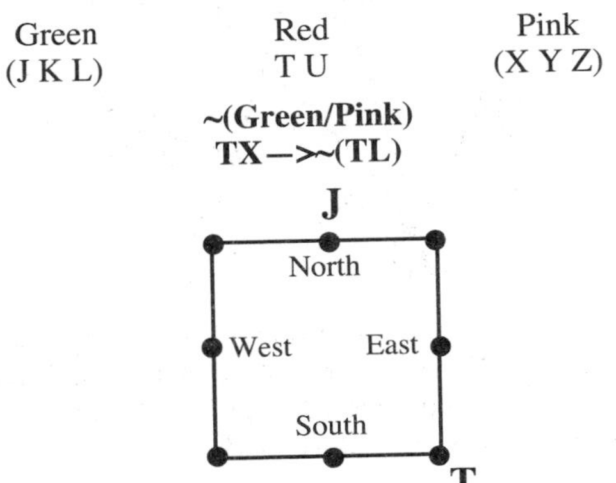

The parentheses around the green and the pink benches remind us that these benches form groups.

Since the green benches cannot be next to the pink benches, the red benches—T and U—must separate them. Now, the pink benches form a group of three, so they must be located on the west and south borders where there is sufficient room. This in turn forces U into the northwest corner of the park, separating the pink benches from the green benches.

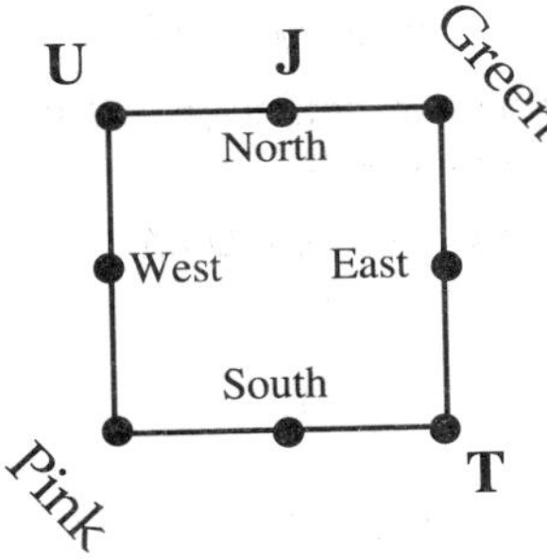

8. Since K is green, we see from the diagram it must be either the middle bench on the east side or the bench on the northeast corner. The answer is (A).

9. Placing the condition *"Z is directly north of Y"* on the diagram yields

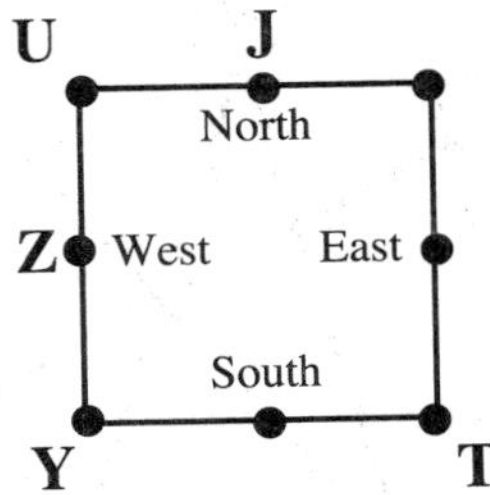

This forces X between Y and T:

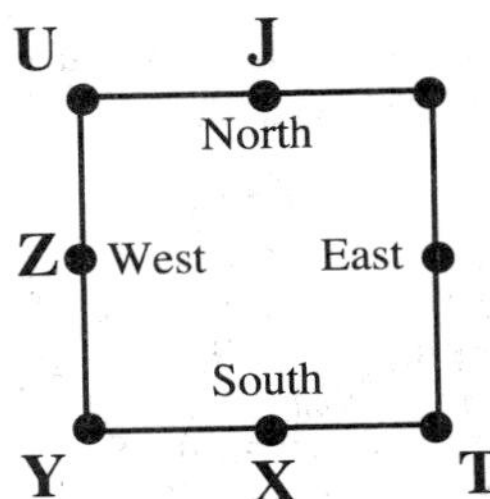

This diagram clearly shows X is directly south of J. The answer is (D).

Questions 10–11

The condition *"If Kevin enters the marathon, then both Julio and May enter the relay, and if both Julio and May enter the relay, then Kevin enters the marathon"* means that Kevin enters the marathon if and only if both Julio and May enter the relay. This can be symbolized as

(K=Ma)<—>(J & M=R)

The condition *"Olivia and Tamio do not both enter the relay"* means that if Olivia enters the relay, then Tamio does not. This in turn can be symbolized as

(O=R)—>(T≠R)*

The remaining conditions can be symbolized in like manner, which yields the following schematic:

(K=Ma)<—>(J & M=R)
(O=R)—>(T≠R)
(N≠S)—>(T=R)
(O=R)—>(J≠R)

10. If Kevin enters the marathon, then from **(K=Ma)<—>(J & M=R)** we know that both Julio and May enter the relay. Look at choice (D); it has Tamio in the relay. This puts three people—Julio, May, and Tamio—in the relay, violating the fact that only two people enter each event. The answer is (D).

11. Since Kevin and Olivia fill the two relay entries, no one else enters the relay. Consider the condition **(N≠S)—>(T=R)** and take the contrapositive to obtain **(T≠R)—>(N=S)**. Now, since Tamio cannot enter the relay, Norma enters the sprint. The answer is (E).

---

* The condition (T=R)—>(O≠R) would also work, but we don't need both.

Questions 12–13

At first glance, this problem appears daunting. However, a diagram will greatly simplify it. Place the condition *"A bridge directly connects J with O, and a bridge directly connects M with O"* on a diagram:

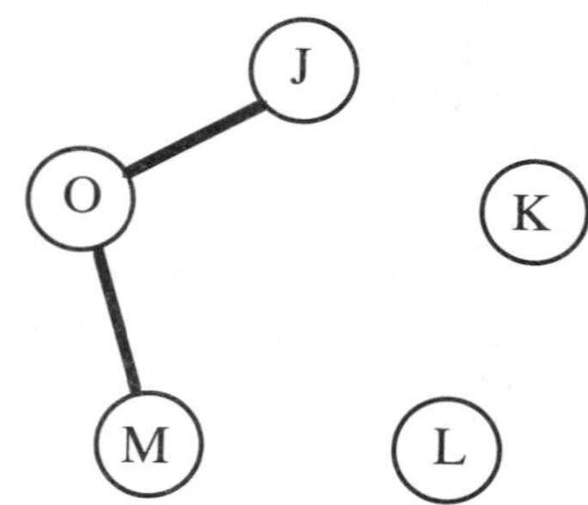

12. Add the condition *"a bridge directly connects K with O"* to the diagram:

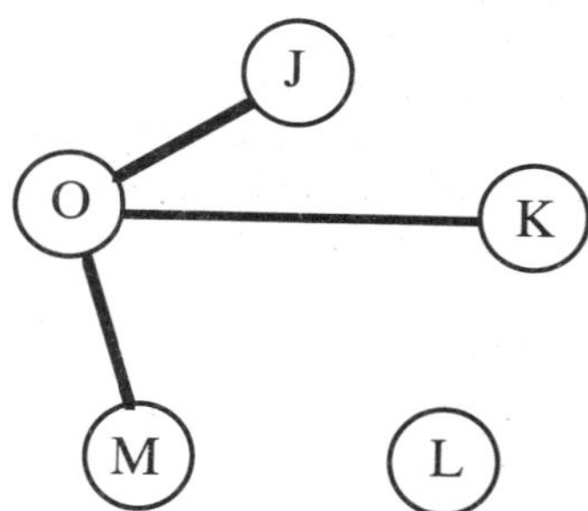

The condition *"J, K, and L are each directly connected by bridge with one or both of M and O"* tells us that L must be directly connected to either M or O. However, L cannot be directly connected to O since O is already directly connected to three other islands. Hence, L must be directly connected to M:

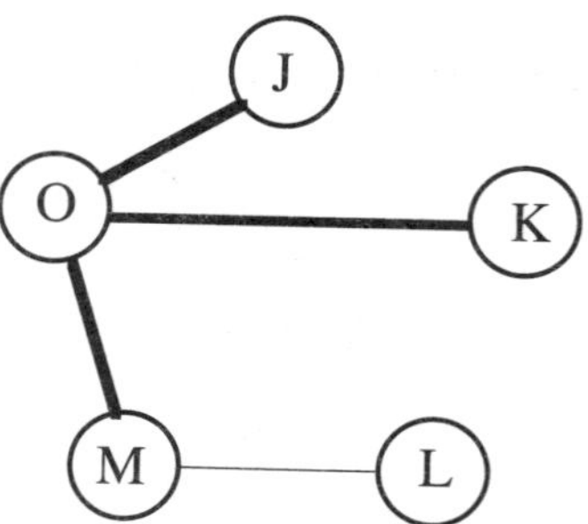

This diagram eliminates choice (A). Turning to choice (B), suppose a bridge directly connects J with L:

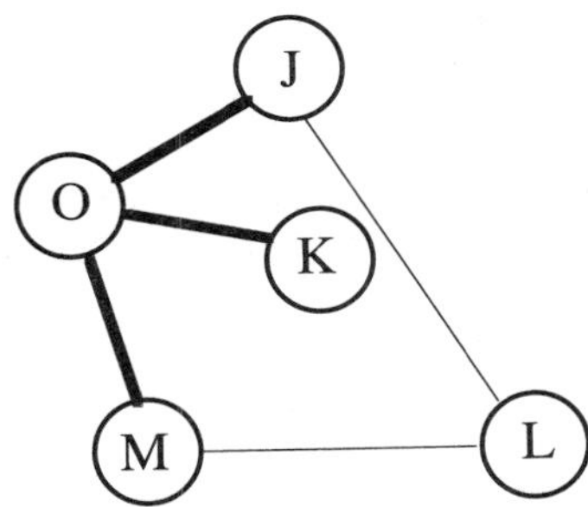

This diagram directly connects J, K, and L with M or O; J with exactly two islands; K with exactly one island; J with O; and M with O. Hence, J *could be* directly connected with L. The answer is (B).

13. J cannot be directly connected to M since J is directly connected to O (see original diagram)—otherwise it would violate the premise of this question. Further, J cannot be directly connected to K since K is directly connected to exactly one other island, M or O. Therefore, as J must be directly connected to exactly two other islands, it must be directly connected to L. The answer is (A).

Questions 14–17

The first three conditions yield the following diagram:

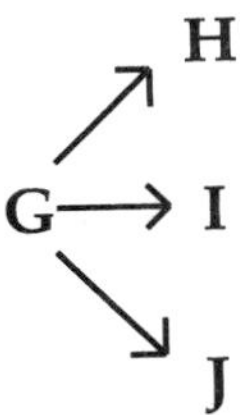

Adding the fourth condition yields

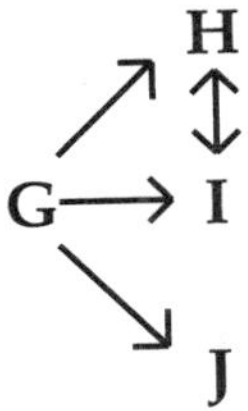

Adding the fifth condition yields

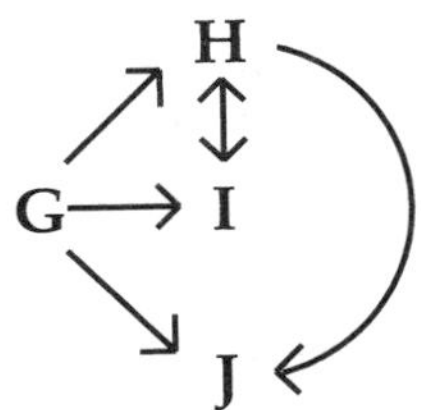

Adding the sixth condition yields

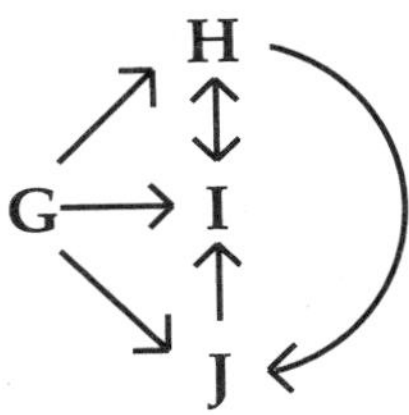

Finally, adding the last condition yields

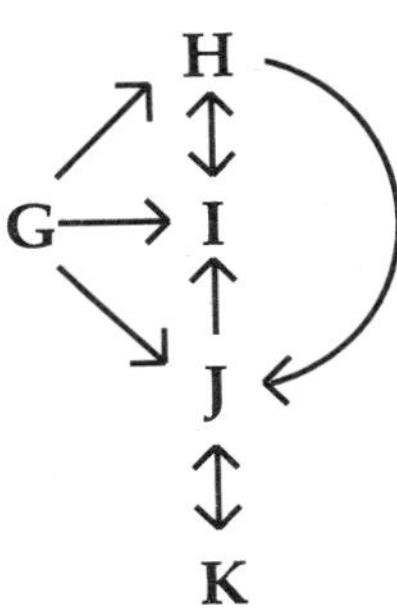

14. The rumor can pass from I to H, and from H to J, and from J to K. This scenario has the rumor passing from I to K without passing through G. The answer is choice (B). The following diagram illustrates the path from I to K:

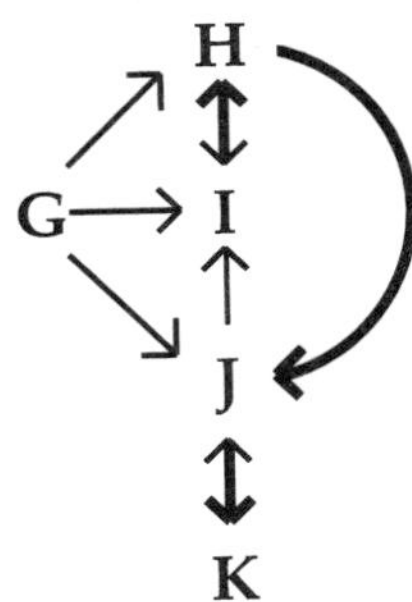

15. Begin with choice (A). The original diagram shows that a rumor can spread directly from H to J, so this is unlikely to be the longest path. Turning to choice (B), the diagram shows that a rumor can also spread directly from J to K. Since there cannot be two answers, this

eliminates both (A) and (B). Turning to choice (C), the diagram clearly shows that no rumor can spread from H to G, eliminate. Turning to choice (D), the diagram shows that a rumor originating at I can spread directly only to H and then from H to J. This rumor consists of 2 segments. Finally, the path taken in choice (E) includes the path in choice (D) plus one additional segment from J to K. Hence, the answer is (E).

16. The original diagram shows arrows leading directly from H to I and to J, and only to these two. Hence, the answer is (C).

As to the other choices, both (A) and (B) are incomplete since we just showed that there are direct paths leading from H to both I and J. Choice (D) is inaccurate since a rumor cannot pass from H to K without passing through J. Hence, a rumor needs at least two segments to reach K from H. Finally, choice (E) is inaccurate: No arrow points from H (nor from any other person) to G. Hence, no rumors can pass from H (nor from any other person) to G.

17. Adding the new condition to the diagram yields

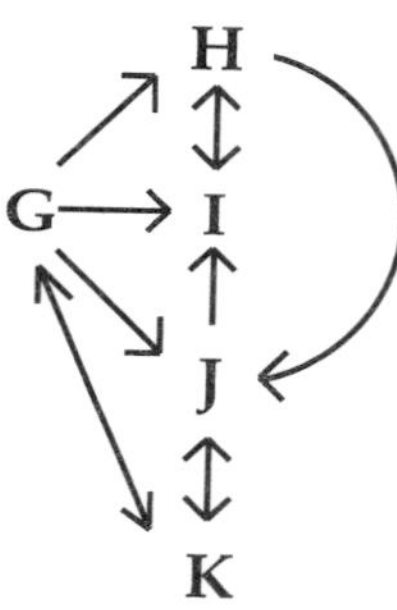

Now, look at choice (D). If there were a segment from I to G, then I could spread rumors to both H and G and could receive rumors from both H and G. Further, H could spread rumors to both I and J and could receive rumors from both G and I. J could spread rumors to both I and K and could receive rumors from both G and K. K could spread rumors to both G and J and could receive rumors from both G and J. Finally, G could spread rumors to both I and K and could receive rumors from both I and K. The answer is choice (D).

Questions 18–19

The condition *"If Kent is hired as an editor, then both John and Mary are hired as gaffers, and if both John and Mary hired as gaffers, then Kent is hired as an editor"* means that Kent is hired as a editor if and only if both John and Mary are hired as gaffers. This can be symbolized as

(K=E)<—>(J & M=G)

The condition *"If Nora is not hired as an actor, then Tom is hired as a gaffer."* can be symbolized as

(N≠A)—>(T=G)

18. If Kent is hired as an editor, then from **(K=E)<—>(J & M=G)** we know that both John and Mary are hired as gaffers. Look at choice (D); it has Tom hired as a gaffer. This forces three people—John, Mary, and Tom—to be gaffers, violating the fact that only two people are hired for each position. The answer is (D).

19. Since Kent and Olivia fill the two gaffer positions, no one else is hired as a gaffer. Consider the condition **(N≠A)—>(T=G)** and take the contrapositive to obtain

(T≠G)—>(N=A)

Now, since Tom cannot be hired as a gaffer (those two positions are already filled by Kent and Olivia), Nora is hired as an actor. The answer is (E).

Grouping Games

We have thoroughly studied various ways to order elements. In this chapter, we'll study various ways to group elements. We got a taste of the tasks involved in grouping elements when we studied hybrid games, which both order and group items.

Because grouping games partition elements into sets, the number of elements is often an issue. As mentioned before, counting can be challenging. This tends to make grouping games more difficult than ordering games.

Pay close attention to the maximum or minimum number of elements in a group; this is often the heart of the game.

Grouping games can be classified as those that partition the elements into 2 groups, and those that partition the elements into 3 or more groups. The former are sometimes called selection games because they "select" elements from a pool, dividing the pool into two groups: those selected and those not selected. The example on the next page will illustrate.

Selection Game

The starting line-up for the Olympic basketball "Dream Team" is chosen from the following two groups:

Group A
Johnson, Drexler, Bird,
Ewing

Group B
Laettner, Robinson, Jordan,
Malone, Pippen

The following requirements must be meet:

Two players are chosen from Group A, and three from Group B.
Jordan starts only if Bird starts.
Drexler and Bird do not both start.
If Jordan starts, then Malone does not.
Exactly 3 of the four fast-break specialists—Johnson, Bird, Jordan, Pippen—must be chosen.

1. If Jordan starts, which of the following must also start?
   (A) Malone or Johnson
   (B) Drexler or Laettner
   (C) Drexler or Johnson
   (D) Johnson or Pippen
   (E) Malone or Robinson

2. All of the following pairs of players can start together EXCEPT
   (A) Ewing and Drexler
   (B) Jordan and Johnson
   (C) Robinson and Johnson
   (D) Johnson and Bird
   (E) Pippen and Malone

3. If the condition "Bird starts only if Pippen doesn't" is added to the other conditions, then which of the following must be false?
   (A) Johnson starts with Bird
   (B) Laettner starts with Malone
   (C) Laettner starts with Bird
   (D) Jordan starts with Robinson
   (E) Jordan starts with Bird

4. If Malone starts, which one of the following is a complete and accurate list of the players from Group A any one of whom could also start?
   (A) Johnson
   (B) Johnson, Drexler
   (C) Johnson, Bird
   (D) Johnson, Drexler, Bird
   (E) Johnson, Ewing, Bird

5. Which one of the following players must start?
   (A) Pippen
   (B) Johnson
   (C) Jordan
   (D) Malone
   (E) Bird

This problem is rather convoluted because not only are there direct conditions on the players, such as *"Drexler and Bird do not both start,"* but there are also constraining numerical conditions, such as *"exactly three fast-break specialists must be chosen."*

It is best to solve this problem without a diagram; however, we will still symbolize the conditions for clarity and easy reference. The condition *"Jordan starts only if Bird starts"* implies only that if Jordan is starting then Bird must be starting as well. So we symbolize it as **Jordan—>Bird**. The condition *"Drexler and Bird do not both start"* means that if one starts then the other does not. So we symbolize it as **Drexler—>~Bird**.* Students often misinterpret this condition to mean that neither of them starts. To state that neither starts, put *both* at the beginning of the sentence: *Both* Drexler and Bird do not start.

---

* **Bird—>~Drexler** would also suffice, but we don't need both.

The condition *"if Jordan starts, then Malone does not"* is naturally symbolized as **Jordan—>~Malone**. It tells us that if J starts then M does not, but tells us nothing when M does not start. Such a condition, where the two parts of an *if-then* statement do not similarly affect each other, is called a nonreciprocal condition. On the other hand, a condition such as Jordan<—>~Malone affects J and M equally. In this case, we are told that if J starts then M does not as before, but we are told additionally that if M does not start then J does. It is important to keep the distinction between reciprocal and nonreciprocal relations clear; a common mistake is to interpret a nonreciprocal relation as reciprocal (see Unwarranted Assumptions, page 26). The remaining conditions cannot be easily written in symbol form, but we will paraphrase them in the schematic:

Jordan—>Bird
Drexler—>~Bird
Jordan—>~Malone
2 from Group A   3 from Group B
fast-break specialists: Johnson, Bird, Jordan, Pippen
3 fast-break specialists
Ewing, Laettner, Robinson are "wild"

Note: Ewing, Laettner, and Robinson are independent because there are no conditions that refer directly to them. We now turn to the questions.

1. **If Jordan starts, which of the following must also start?**

   (A) Malone or Johnson
   (B) Drexler or Laettner
   (C) Drexler or Johnson
   (D) Johnson or Pippen
   (E) Malone or Robinson

From the condition **Jordan—>Bird**, we know that if Jordan starts, then Bird must start as well. Now both Jordan and Bird are fast-break specialists, and three of the four fast-break specialists must start. So at least one of the remaining fast-break specialists—Johnson or Pippen—must also start. The answer is (D).

2. **All of the following pairs of players can start together EXCEPT:**

   (A) Ewing and Drexler
   (B) Jordan and Johnson
   (C) Robinson and Johnson
   (D) Johnson and Bird
   (E) Pippen and Malone

We shall use the method of indirect proof to solve this problem: That is, assume that a particular answer-choice is true. Then check whether it leads to a contradiction or an impossible situation. If so, it is the answer; if not, then select another answer-choice and repeat the process until a contradiction is found.

Begin with choice (A). Both Ewing and Drexler are from Group A, so the remaining 3 starters must be chosen from Group B. Additionally, they must all be fast-break specialists since neither E nor D is—there are exactly 3 fast-break specialists. But Jordan and Pippen are the only fast-break specialists in Group B. So the third fast-break specialist cannot be chosen. The answer therefore is (A). This type of question can be time consuming because you may have to check all the answer-choices—save these questions for last.

3. **If the condition "Bird starts only if Pippen doesn't" is added to the other conditions, then which one of the following must be false?**

 (A) **Johnson starts with Bird**
 (B) **Laettner starts with Malone**
 (C) **Laettner starts with Bird**
 (D) **Jordan starts with Robinson**
 (E) **Jordan starts with Bird**

This problem is both long and hard. Again, we use an indirect proof. Start with (A). Both Johnson and Bird are from Group A, and both are fast-break specialists. So the remaining 3 starters must be chosen from Group B, one of which must be a fast-break specialist. Now if Jordan, Robinson, and Laettner are chosen, there will be three fast-break specialists and none of the initial conditions will be violated. So (A) is not necessarily false; eliminate it. Next, we check (B). Both Laettner and Malone are from Group B, and neither is a fast-break specialist. So the three remaining starters must all be fast-break specialists, and two of them must be from Group A—Johnson and Bird. This leaves only Jordan and Pippen to choose from. Jordan cannot be chosen because Malone has already been chosen (**Jordan—>~Malone**), and from the new condition Pippen cannot be chosen because Bird has already been chosen. Hence the answer is (B).

4. **If Malone starts, which one of the following is a complete and accurate list of the players from Group A any one of whom could also start?**

 (A) **Johnson**
 (B) **Johnson, Drexler**
 (C) **Johnson, Bird**
 (D) **Johnson, Drexler, Bird**
 (E) **Johnson, Ewing, Bird**

Jordan *cannot* start with Malone according to the condition **Jordan—>~Malone**. To play three fast-break specialists, therefore, Johnson, Bird, and Pippen are all *required* to start. Since both Johnson and Bird are from Group A and exactly two players from that group start, these two players comprise the complete list of starters from Group A when Malone also starts. The answer is (C).

5. **Which one of the following players must start?**

 (A) **Pippen**
 (B) **Johnson**
 (C) **Jordan**
 (D) **Malone**
 (E) **Bird**

Suppose Bird does not start. Then the 3 fast-break specialists must be Johnson, Jordan, and Pippen. But if Jordan starts, then from the initial conditions Bird must also start. Hence Bird must always start. The answer is (E).

Grouping by Threes

Three committees are formed from eight people—F, G, H, I, J, K, L, M. Two of the committees have three members, and one of the committees has only two members.

G serves with M.
L serves with only one other person.
F does not serve with M.

1. Which one of the following is a committee?

(A) M, L, I
(B) G, F, M
(C) G, L
(D) G, H, I
(E) K, G, M

2. If F cannot serve with K, and K cannot serve with M, which one of the following must be false?

(A) F serves with L.
(B) F serves with J.
(C) L serves with H.
(D) H serves with I.
(E) I serves with M.

3. If H serves with K, which one of the following cannot be true?

(A) F serves with K.
(B) J serves with F.
(C) I serves with M.
(D) F serves with L.
(E) J serves with L.

4. If K, J, and I serve on different committees, which one of the following must be true?

(A) K serves with G.
(B) I serves on a committee of two.
(C) J serves on a committee of two.
(D) H serves with F.
(E) J serves with F.

5. Which one of the following conditions is inconsistent with the given conditions?

(A) K serves on a committee of three.
(B) M serves with H.
(C) M, H, and I serve together.
(D) F does not serve with G.
(E) H serves with L.

We start by symbolizing the conditions. The condition *"G serves with M"* is naturally symbolized as **G = M**. The condition *"F does not serve with M"* is symbolized as **F ≠ M**. The condition *"L serves with only one other person"* means that L is on the committee of two; we symbolize it as **L = 2**. The diagram will consist of three compartmentalized boxes. This gives the following schematic:

F G H I J K L M (H, I, J, K "wild")
G = M
F ≠ M
L = 2

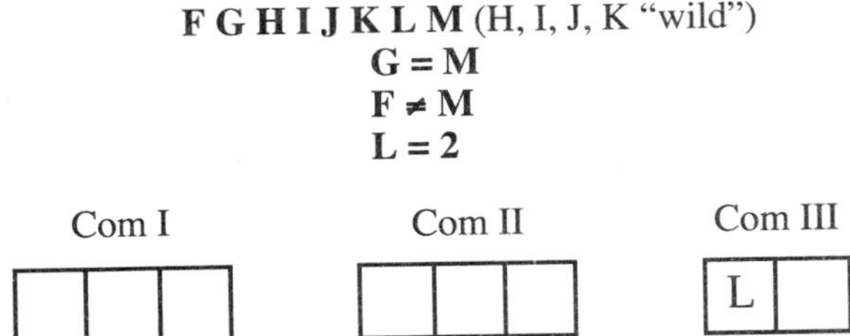

Before turning to the questions, two readily derived conditions should be noted. First, since G serves with M, and F does not serve with M, F cannot serve with G. Second, since L serves on the two-person committee, L cannot serve with G or M (otherwise L would be on a three-person committee).

1. **Which one of the following is a committee?**

   (A) M, L, I
   (B) G, F, M
   (C) G, L
   (D) G, H, I
   (E) K, G, M

(A) is not a committee since L must serve on a committee of two. (B) is not a committee since F cannot serve with G. Neither (C) nor (D) is a committee since G and M must serve together. Hence, by process of elimination, the answer is (E).

2. **If F cannot serve with K, and K cannot serve with M, which one of the following must be false?**

   (A) F serves with L.
   (B) F serves with J.
   (C) L serves with H.
   (D) H serves with I.
   (E) I serves with M.

We shall use an indirect proof. Start with (A). If F serves with L, then G and M could serve on Committee I, K on Committee II, and the remaining people could serve at random without violating any initial condition. So F could serve with L. This eliminates (A). Next, test (B). If F serves with J on Committee I, then G and M would have to serve on Committee II. And the remaining people could be placed as follows:

Com I	Com II	Com III
F J H	G M I	L K

This diagram does not violate any initial condition, so F could serve with J. This eliminates (B). Next, test (C). There are two possible places for the pair G and M, Committee I and Committee II. If G and M serve on Committee I, then F would have to serve on Committee II:

Com I	Com II	Com III
G M _	F _ _	L H

Clearly this diagram leaves no room for K since K cannot serve with either M or F. The case with the pair G and M serving on Committee II leads to a similar result. Hence L cannot serve with H. The answer is (C).

3. **If H serves with K, which one of the following cannot be true?**

   (A) F serves with K.
   (B) J serves with F.
   (C) I serves with M.
   (D) F serves with L.
   (E) J serves with L.

If H serves with K on Committee I, then G and M must serve on Committee II. (Why?) This gives the following diagram:

Com I	Com II	Com III
H K _	G M _	L _

(The diagram with H and K on Committee II is not presented because it generates the same results.) Again we apply an indirect proof. Start with (A). If F serves with K, then from the above diagram F must serve on Committee I. And we can place I and J on Committees II and III, respectively:

This diagram does not violate any initial condition, so F could serve with K. This eliminates (A). Next, test (B). J and F cannot serve on Committee I, since from the above diagram H and K are already there. Likewise, J and F cannot serve on Committees II and III. Hence the answer is (B).

4. If K, J, and I serve on different committees, which one of the following must be true?

(A) K serves with G.
(B) I serves on a committee of two.
(C) J serves on a committee of two
(D) H serves with F.
(E) J serves with F.

We shall construct counter-examples for four of the answer-choices; the one for which we cannot construct a counter-example will be the answer. Start with (A). Suppose K serves on Committee I and G serves on Committee II. Then from the condition **G = M**, we know that M must also serve on Committee II. And the remaining people can be placed without violating any initial condition as follows:

Com I	Com II	Com III
K H F	J G M	L I

This diagram is a counter-example not only to (A) but to (C) and (E) as well. This eliminates (A), (C), and (E). Next, test choice (B). Suppose that I serves on Committee I, with G and M. Then the remaining people can be grouped as follows:

Com I	Com II	Com III
I G M	F H J	L K

This diagram does not violate any initial condition, so it is a counter-example to (B). Hence, by process of elimination, the answer is (D).

5. Which one of the following conditions is inconsistent with the given conditions?

(A) K serves on a committee of three.
(B) M serves with H.
(C) M, H, and I serve together.
(D) F does not serve with G.
(E) H serves with L.

The first counter-example in Question 4 shows that K can serve on a three-person committee. This eliminates (A). Next, turning to choice (B), suppose M serves with H on Committee I. This forces G to also serve on Committee I. Now place F on Committee III and the remaining people as follows:

Com I	Com II	Com III
M H G	J K I	L F

This diagram does not violate any initial condition, so "M serves with H" is consistent with the initial conditions. This eliminates (B). Next, turning to choice (C), suppose M, H, and I serve together on Committee I. But since M must serve with G, there would then be four people on Committee I. The same result occurs when M, H, and G are on Committee II. Hence (C) is inconsistent with the initial conditions, and the answer is (C).

Points to Remember

1. Pay close attention to the maximum or minimum number of elements in a group, for this is often the heart of the game.

2. Grouping games are classified as those that divide the elements into two sets—Selection games—and those that divide the elements into three or more sets.

3. A reciprocal condition affects both elements equally.

4. Don't interpret a nonreciprocal condition as reciprocal.

5. The method of indirect proof is used often with grouping games.

Warm-Up Drill

1. How many groups can be formed from A, B, C?

2. In how many ways can two elements be selected from A, B, C, and D?

3. In how many ways can a group of four be chosen from the sets {A, B, C} and {D, E, F}, given that two elements must be selected from each set, and A can be selected only if D is selected?

4. In how many ways can 3 elements be selected from the sets {A, B} and {C, D, E} if some elements must be selected from {A, B}, and C and D cannot both be selected?

5. How many groups of 3 can be selected from U, V, W, X, Y, Z given that

   V is not selected unless Z is selected.
   Y and W cannot both be selected.
   U is selected only if V is not.
   Either V or Y, but not both, is selected.

Answers and Solutions to Warm-up Drill

1. **7 groups.**
   A; B; C
   AB; AC; BC
   ABC

2. **6 ways.**
   AB; AC; AD
   BC; BD
   CD

3. **7 ways.**

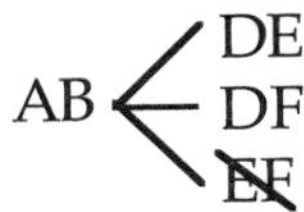

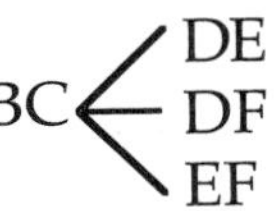

4. **7 ways.**
   If A is chosen, then either CE or DE may be added: ACE ADE

   If B is chosen, then either CE or DE may be added: BCE BDE

   If both A and B are chosen, then C, D, or E may be added: ABC ABD ABE

5. **5 groups.**
   The condition *"V is not selected unless Z is selected"* is equivalent to *"if V is selected, then Z is selected."* The condition *"Y and W cannot both be selected"* is equivalent to *"if Y is selected, then W is not."* The condition *"U is selected only if V is not"* is equivalent to *"if U is selected, then V is not."*

   Now suppose V is selected. Then Z must be selected and neither U nor Y can be selected. Combining the pair VZ with the remaining elements—W and X—gives the following two groups: VZW and VZX.

   Next, suppose Y is selected. Then V cannot be selected, nor can W. Combining Y with the remaining elements—U, X, and Z—gives the following three groups: YUX, YUZ, and YXZ. Hence a total of five groups is possible.

There will be no more mentor exercises for the games.

Exercise

The first three games are taken from recent LSATs.

Questions 1–6

Seven buildings are located in an urban development.

Three of the buildings are residential; the other four are commercial.
Each of the residential buildings is made of either brick or wood.
Each of the commercial buildings is made of either wood, concrete, brick, or steel.
All of the residential buildings and all of the brick buildings have fire escapes, but no other buildings do.
Exactly four of the buildings have fire escapes.

1. Which of the following must be true?

   I. At least one of the buildings is made of wood.
   II. At least one of the buildings is made of steel.
   III. At least one of the buildings is made of brick.

   (A) I only
   (B) II only
   (C) III only
   (D) I and II only
   (E) I and III only

2. If exactly two of the commercial buildings are made of concrete, then which one of the following must be true?

   (A) At least one of the commercial buildings is made of wood.
   (B) Exactly two buildings are made of wood.
   (C) Exactly one of the commercial buildings is made of steel.
   (D) No commercial building is made of wood.
   (E) At most one building is made of steel.

3. If there is at least one wooden building, one concrete building, one brick building, and one steel building, then which one of the following must be false?

   (A) Exactly four buildings are made of brick.
   (B) Exactly three buildings are made of wood.
   (C) Exactly two buildings are made of wood and exactly two buildings are made of steel.
   (D) Exactly two buildings are made of steel and exactly two buildings are made of concrete.
   (E) Exactly two buildings are made of wood and exactly two buildings are made of brick.

4. If there are exactly three brick buildings and one steel building, then any of the following can be true EXCEPT:

   (A) there is exactly one wooden building
   (B) there are no wooden buildings
   (C) there are exactly three wooden buildings
   (D) there are no concrete buildings
   (E) there are exactly two concrete buildings

5. If exactly half of the buildings with fire escapes are wooden, then which one of the following must be false?

   (A) There are more wooden buildings than brick buildings.
   (B) There are more steel buildings than wooden buildings.
   (C) There are exactly three wooden buildings.
   (D) There are exactly three brick buildings.
   (E) The number of steel buildings is equal to the number of concrete buildings.

6. If as many as possible of the buildings with fire escapes are wooden, then which of the following must be true?

   I. There are exactly three wooden buildings.
   II. There is exactly one brick building.
   III. There are fewer concrete buildings than wooden buildings.

   (A) I only
   (B) II only
   (C) I and III only
   (D) II and III only
   (E) I, II, and III

Questions 7–8

A hobbyist is stocking her aquarium with exactly three fish of different types and with exactly two species of plants. The only fish under consideration are a G, an H, a J, a K, and an L, and the only kinds of plants under consideration are of the species W, X, Y, and Z. She will observe the following conditions:

If she selects the G, she can select neither the H nor a Y.
She cannot select the H unless she selects the K.
She cannot select the J unless she selects a W.
If she selects the K, she must select an X.

7. If the hobbyist selects the H, which one of the following must also be true?

(A) She selects at least one W.
(B) She selects at least one X.
(C) She selects the J, but no Y's.
(D) She selects the K, but no X's.
(E) She selects at least one X, but no Y's.

8. If the hobbyist selects a Y, which one of the following must be the group of fish she selects?

(A) G, H, K
(B) H, J, K
(C) H, J, L
(D) H, K, L
(E) J, K, L

Questions 9–10

Petworld has exactly fourteen animals (three gerbils, three hamsters, three lizards, five snakes) that are kept in four separate cages (W, X, Y, Z) according to the following conditions:

Each cage contains exactly two, four, or six animals.
Any cage containing a gerbil also contains at least one hamster; any cage containing a hamster also contains at least one gerbil.
Any cage containing a lizard also contains at least one snake; any cage containing a snake also contains at least one lizard.
Neither cage Y nor cage Z contains a gerbil.
Neither cage W nor cage X contains a lizard.

9. At most, how many snakes can occupy cage Y at any one time?

(A) one
(B) two
(C) three
(D) four
(E) five

10. If there are exactly two hamsters in cage W and the number of gerbils in cage X is equal to the number of snakes in cage Y, then the number of snakes in cage Z must be exactly

(A) one
(B) two
(C) three
(D) four
(E) five

Questions 11–14

A group of four items is selected from seven items—G, H, I, J, K, L, and M—according to the following rules:

Either G or I must be selected.
Either H or K must be selected.
Neither K nor I can be selected with H.
Neither L nor G can be selected unless the other is also selected.

11. Which of the following groups is an acceptable selection of the items?

(A) G, I, L, M
(B) I, K, M, H
(C) G, K, I, M
(D) G, L, J, M
(E) I, G, K, L

12. Which of the following groups of items cannot be among the items selected?

(A) H, J
(B) H, J, M
(C) L, K, I
(D) G, H, M
(E) L, H, J

13. If I and M are selected, which of the following items must also be selected?

(A) G, L
(B) J, H
(C) H
(D) K, J
(E) L

14. There would be only one possible way to select the four items if which of the following restrictions were added to the original set of conditions?

(A) If I is selected, then G is selected.
(B) Both I and G are selected.
(C) If J is selected, then M is selected.
(D) Either L or M is selected.
(E) If I is selected, then K is selected.

Questions 15–18

Six items—U, V, W, X, Y, Z—are being separated into 3 groups—Group 1, Group 2, Group 3—according to the following conditions:

The number of items in Group 1 is less than or equal to the number of items in Group 2.
The number of items in Group 2 is less than or equal to the number of items in Group 3.
V and W cannot be in the same group.
X can be in Group 3 only if Y is in Group 3.

15. Which one of the following is an acceptable grouping of the six items?

	Group 1	Group 2	Group 3
(A)	UV	WXY	Z
(B)	X	Y	VZUW
(C)	V	YW	XUZ
(D)	V	Z	XYUW
(E)	UW	YZ	XV

16. If Group 1 contains only the item Y, which of the following must be true?

(A) Group 3 contains four items.
(B) Group 2 contains the same number of items as Group 3.
(C) V is in Group 3.
(D) Group 2 contains three items.
(E) X is in Group 2.

17. If W and Y are in the same group and V is in Group 3, then which of the following must be false?

(A) W and Y are in Group 2.
(B) U is the only item in Group 1.
(C) X is the only item in Group 1.
(D) U is in Group 3.
(E) Group 3 contains 2 items.

18. If Group 2 contains only one item which is neither W nor V, which of the following must be true?

(A) Group 1 contains only V or only W.
(B) Group 3 contains W.
(C) Group 1 contains both U and V.
(D) Group 2 contains Z.
(E) Group 1 contains only W.

Answers and Solutions to Exercise

Questions 1–6

This is a moderately hard game. To solve it, we'll use the following schematic:

3 Res B or W	4 (Res, B) = Fx	4 Com B, W, C, or S

[Where Fx stands for fire escape, and the condition **(Res, B) = Fx** means that all residential and all brick buildings have fire escapes.] The key to this problem is the condition **(Res, B) = Fx**.

1. Statement I is false. All three residential buildings could be brick and one commercial building could also be brick to give four buildings with fire escapes. This eliminates (A), (D), and (E). Statement II is false. With the same scenario as in Statement I, the three remaining commercial buildings could all be concrete. This eliminates (B). Hence, we have learned that the answer is (C), without having to check Statement III. But let's verify that it's true.

The greatest number of wooden buildings with fire escapes is obtained when all three residential buildings are wooden. Now in order to have a fourth building with a fire escape, one of the commercial buildings must be brick.

2. Now we use a diagram consisting of two boxes, one for the residential buildings and one for the commercial buildings. Place the two concrete buildings as follows:

3 Res	4 Com C C

Next, attempt to construct a counter-example for each answer-choice. The one for which this cannot be done will be the answer. Start with (A). Suppose all three residential buildings are wood:

3 Res W W W	4 Com C C

Now in order to have four buildings with fire escapes, one of the commercial buildings must be brick and one more could be steel:

3 Res W W W	4 Com B C C S

This diagram is a counterexample for (A) and (B). Furthermore, replacing S with a W gives a counterexample to (C) and (D). Hence, by process of elimination, the answer is (E). But again it is instructive to verify this. To that end, assume two of the buildings are steel:

3 Res	4 Com C C S S

Now only the three remaining residential buildings have fire escapes, but there must be four buildings with fire escapes. Hence, it is impossible to have more than one steel building.

3. Our work at the end of Question 2 shows that the answer is (D).

Notice that we did not use the supplemental condition. Typically, this indicates that something was overlooked. Sometimes, as in this case, the supplementary condition is introduced just to obfuscate.

4. If there are no wooden buildings, then the three residential buildings must all be brick. Now we need a fourth building that has a fire escape. But all the remaining commercial buildings are either steel or concrete, none of which can have a fire escape. Hence the answer is (B). Notice that we needed only the first part of the supplementary condition.

5. All brick buildings have fire escapes. Now if three of the buildings are brick, choice (D), then there must be three wooden buildings with fire escapes—since half of the buildings with fire escapes are wooden. This gives a total of six buildings with fire escapes. But this violates the condition that exactly four buildings have fire escapes. The answer is (D).

6. In order to have as many of the wooden buildings with fire escapes as possible, all three residential buildings must be wooden.

3 Res W W W	4 Com

Now in order to have four buildings with fire escapes, exactly one of the commercial buildings must be brick:

3 Res W W W	4 Com B

This shows that Statement II is true, which eliminates (A) and (C). Next, three concrete commercial buildings can be added to this diagram without violating any given condition:

3 Res W W W	4 Com B C C C

This diagram has the same number of wooden as concrete buildings. Hence Statement III is false. This eliminates (D) and (E). So without having to check Statement I, we have learned the answer is (B).

Questions 7–8

The first and last conditions are naturally symbolized as follows:

1. **G—>(~H & ~Y)**
2. **K—>X**

The second and third conditions are rather complicated structures. Remember, the statement A unless B translates as ~B—>A. So the condition *"She cannot select the H unless she selects the K"* translates as ~K—>~H. Likewise, the third condition translates as ~W—>~J. The contrapositive simplifies these conditions to*

3. **H—>K**
4. **J—>W**

The transitive property combines the second and third conditions into

5. **H—>K—>X**

Summarizing what we have developed gives

Fish (3)	**Plants (2)**
G, H, J, K, L	W, X, Y, Z

G—>(~H & ~Y)
H—>K—>X
J—>W

7. If H is selected, then the condition **H—>K—>X** shows that X is also selected. The answer is (B).

8. Begin with choice (A). If she selects G, then the condition **G—>(~H & ~Y)** indicates she did not select Y. This, however, contradicts the premise that she selected Y—eliminate choice (A). As to choice (B), since she selects an H, the condition **H—>K—>X** shows she also selects an X. Further, since she selects a J, the condition **J—>W** shows she also selects a W. This has her selecting three plants—Y, X, and W, which violates the condition that she selects exactly two plants—eliminate choice (B). A similar analysis eliminates choices (C) and (E). Thus, by process of elimination, the answer is (D).

* Note: Two negatives make a positive, so symbol statements such as ~~H were simplified to H.

Questions 9–10

The condition *"Any cage containing a gerbil also contains at least one hamster"* can be symbolized as **G—>H**. The condition *"any cage containing a hamster also contains at least one gerbil"* can be symbolized as **H—>G**. Combining these two conditions gives **G<—>H**. In other words, a cage contains a gerbil if and only if it contains a hamster. The condition *"Neither cage Y nor cage Z contains a gerbil"* can be symbolized as **G ≠ Y, Z.** Symbolizing the other conditions in like manner yields

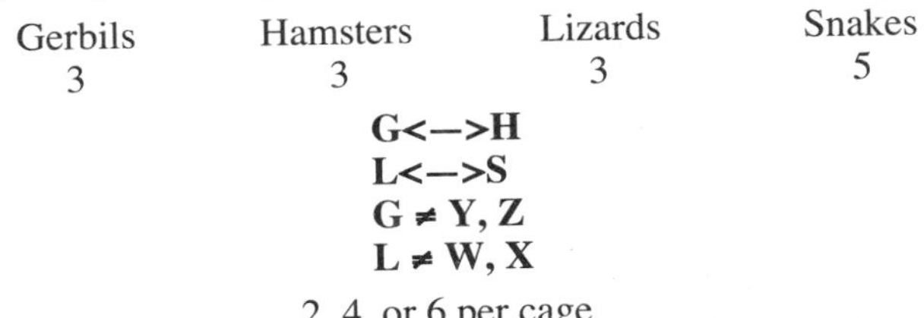

Gerbils	Hamsters	Lizards	Snakes
3	3	3	5

G<—>H
L<—>S
G ≠ Y, Z
L ≠ W, X
2, 4, or 6 per cage

A few properties should be noted before turning to the questions: Since lizards and snakes are always together and lizards cannot be in cages W and X, snakes also cannot be in cages W and X. Similarly, hamsters cannot be in cages Y and Z.

9. For questions that ask you to maximize a situation, begin with the highest number. Then the next highest, and so on. The first choice for which a valid diagram can be constructed will be the answer. So we begin with five snakes in cage Y:

W	X	Y	Z
		SSSSS	

The condition **L<—>S** forces an L into cage Y, which fills up cage Y and forces the other L's into cage Z—as they cannot be in cages W or X:

W	X	Y	Z
		SSSSSL	LL

Now, every cage containing a lizard must also contain a snake. So cage Z must contain a snake. This is impossible, however, since all five snakes have already been placed in cage Y. This eliminates choice (E).

Turning to choice (D), place four snakes in cage Y, along with two lizards:

W	X	Y	Z
		SSSSLL	

This forces the other snake and lizard into cage Z:

W	X	Y	Z
		SSSSLL	SL

The remaining animals can be placed as follows:

W	X	Y	Z
GGHH	GH	SSSSLL	SL

This diagram satisfies every condition. Hence, four snakes can occupy cage Y. The answer is (D).

10. Begin with two hamsters in cage W:

W	X	Y	Z
HH			

The condition **G<—>H** forces a gerbil into cage W. Further, the condition **2, 4, or 6 per cage** forces another gerbil into cage W:

W	X	Y	Z
HHGG			

Since gerbils cannot be in cages Y or Z, the remaining hamster and gerbil must be in cage X:

W	X	Y	Z
HHGG	HG		

If *"the number of gerbils in cage X is equal to the number of snakes in cage Y,"* then there is one snake in cage Y. Hence, the 4 remaining snakes must be in cage Z:

W	X	Y	Z
HHGG	HG	S	SSSS

The answer is (D)

Questions 11–14

The condition *"Neither K nor I can be selected with H"* can be symbolized as

H—>~K
H—>~I

The condition *"Neither L nor G can be selected unless the other is also selected"* simply means that if either L or G is selected then both must be selected:

L<—>G

Symbolizing the remaining conditions yields the following schematic:

G or I
H or K
H—>~K
H—>~I
L<—>G

11. Choices (A) and (D) violate the condition **H or K**. Choice (B) violates the condition **H—>~K**. Choice (C) violates the condition **L<—>G**. Hence, by process of elimination, the answer is (E).

12. Begin with (A). Selecting both H and J will satisfy all the conditions, eliminate (A). Turning to choice (B), since H is selected, I cannot be selected (**H—>~I**). Hence, from the condition **G or I**, we must select G. Now, from the condition **L<—>G**, we must select L. This scenario has five items being selected, violating the fact that only four items are selected. The answer is (B).

13. Since I is selected, the condition **H—>~I**† prevents H from being selected. Hence, the condition **H or K** forces K to be selected. Now, neither G nor L can be selected since they must be selected together, which would yield a group of five. This leaves only J to be selected. The answer is (D).

14. Begin with choice (A). If I is actually selected, then the four items selected would be fully determined. But choice (A) does not require that I be selected. Suppose G is selected.* Then L must be selected since G and L must be selected together. Now, we can satisfy all the conditions by selecting either H and M or H and J. Hence, the items selected are not fully determined, eliminate choice (A). Turning to choice (B), from the condition **L<—>G**, we know L must be selected. Now, since I has been selected, H cannot be selected (**H—>~I**). Hence, from the condition **H or K**, we know K must be selected. Thus, the four items are uniquely determined—I, G, L, K. The answer is choice (B).

† Taking the contrapositive of **H—>~I** yields I—>~H.

Questions 15–18

15.
(A) No. This violates the condition "The number of items in Group 2 is less than or equal to the number of items in Group 3."
(B) No. This violates the condition "V and W cannot be in the same group."
(C) No. This violates the condition "X can be in Group 3 only if Y is in Group 3."
(D) Yes. The four conditions are satisfied:

(1) Group 1 has the same number of items as Group 2.
(2) Group 2 has fewer items than Group 3.
(3) V and W are in different groups.
(4) Y is with X in Group 3.

(E) No. This violates the condition "X can be in Group 3 only if Y is in Group 3."

16. X cannot be in Group 1 since "Group 1 contains only the item Y." Suppose X is in Group 3. Then Y must also be in Group 3 since "X can be in Group 3 only if Y is in Group 3." But this violates the fact that Y is in Group 1. Since we have shown that X cannot be in either Group 1 or Group 3, it must be in Group 2. The answer is (E).

17.
(A) No. The following grouping satisfies all the conditions and has W and Y in Group 2:

Group 1	Group 2	Group 3
X	WY	UVZ

(B) Yes. Place U and V on a diagram:

Group 1	Group 2	Group 3
U		V

Since "V and W cannot be in the same group," W must be in Group 2. Further, since "W and Y

* Remember either G or I must be selected.

are in the same group," Y must also be in Group 2:

Group 1	Group 2	Group 3
U	WY	V

Now, since "the number of items in Group 2 is less than or equal to the number of items in Group 3," the remaining items must be in Group 3:

Group 1	Group 2	Group 3
U	WY	VXZ

However, this diagram violates the condition "X can be in Group 3 only if Y is in Group 3."

(C) No. The following grouping satisfies all the conditions and has X as the only item in Group 1:

Group 1	Group 2	Group 3
X	WY	UVZ

(D) No. The following grouping satisfies all the conditions and has U in Group 3:

Group 1	Group 2	Group 3
WY	XZ	VU

(E) No. The following grouping satisfies all the conditions and has 2 items in Group 3:

Group 1	Group 2	Group 3
WY	XZ	VU

18. Since Group 2 contains only one item, Group 1 must contain only one item: "The number of items in Group 1 is less than or equal to the number of items in Group 2." Now, Group 3 cannot contain both V and W since "V and W cannot be in the same group." Hence, either V or W must be in Group 1 as neither can be in Group 2. The answer is (A).

Assignment Games

We have discussed various ways to order elements—**ordering games**, and various ways to group elements—**grouping games**. Now we will discuss various ways to assign characteristics to elements—these are **assignment games**. Assignment games will wind up our discussion of the three major types of games. They tend to be the hardest games, so it's wise to save them for last.

Assignment games match a characteristic with an element of the game. For example, you may be asked to assign a schedule: Bob works only Monday, Tuesday, or Friday. Or you may be told that a person is either a Democrat or a Republican.

Because the characteristics are typically assigned to groups of elements, assignment games can look very similar to grouping games. Additionally, in grouping games the groups are often identified by their characteristics. However, in assignment games you pair each element with one or more characteristics, whereas in grouping games you partition the elements into two or more groups.

It is important to identify the type of game you are dealing with because different methods are needed to solve each type. The following examples illustrate the distinction between these two kinds of games. The first, from the grouping games chapter, is the Olympic Dream Team game. The second is an assignment game.

Example: ***(Grouping game)***

The starting line-up for the Olympic basketball "Dream Team" is chosen from the following two groups:

Group A	**Group B**
Johnson, Drexler, Bird, Ewing	Laettner, Robinson, Jordan, Malone, Pippen

The following requirements must be meet:

Two players are chosen from Group A, and three from Group B.
Jordan starts only if Bird starts.
Drexler and Bird do not both start.
If Jordan starts, then Malone does not.
Exactly 3 of the four fast-break specialists—Johnson, Bird, Jordan, Pippen—must be chosen.

In this game the goal is to select the starting line-up, thereby dividing the elements into two groups: those selected, and those not. Notice how the goal in the following game differs:

Example: ***(Assignment game)***

There are eight players on a particular basketball team—A, B, C, D, F, G, H, I. Three are guards, three are forwards, and two are centers. Each player is either a free agent or not a free agent.

All of the guards are free agents.
A and C are forwards; F and H are not forwards.
Only one forward is a free agent.

In this game the team has already been selected; now the goal is to assign a position (characteristic) to each player and decide whether he is a free agent (characteristic). Notice that conditions, such as *"All of the guards are free agents,"* apply to groups of individuals; this makes the game at first glance appear to be a grouping game.

Many assignment games can be solved very efficiently by using a elimination grid. An example will illustrate this method of diagramming.

Elimination Grid

Dean Peterson, Head of the Math Department at Peabody Polytech, is making the fall teaching schedule. Besides himself there are four other professors—Warren, Novak, Dornan, and Emerson. Their availability is subject to the following constraints.

Warren cannot teach on Monday or Thursday.
Dornan cannot teach on Wednesday.
Emerson cannot teach on Monday or Friday.
Associate Professor Novak can teach at any time.
Dean Peterson cannot teach evening classes.
Warren can teach only evening classes.
Dean Peterson cannot teach on Wednesday if Novak teaches on Thursday, and Novak teaches on Thursday if Dean Peterson cannot teach on Wednesday.
At any given time there are always three classes being taught.

1. At which one of the following times can Warren, Dornan, and Emerson all be teaching?
   (A) Monday morning
   (B) Friday evening
   (C) Tuesday evening
   (D) Friday morning
   (E) Wednesday morning

2. For which day will the dean have to hire a part-time teacher?
   (A) Monday
   (B) Tuesday
   (C) Wednesday
   (D) Thursday
   (E) Friday

3. Which one of the following must be false?
   (A) Dornan does not work on Tuesday.
   (B) Emerson does not work on Tuesday morning.
   (C) Peterson works on Tuesday.
   (D) Novak works every day of the week except Wednesday.
   (E) Dornan works every day of the week except Wednesday.

4. If Novak does not work on Thursday, then which one of the following must be true?
   (A) Peterson works Tuesday morning.
   (B) Dornan works Tuesday morning.
   (C) Emerson works Tuesday.
   (D) Peterson works on Wednesday.
   (E) Warren works Tuesday morning.

We indicate that a teacher does not work at a particular time by placing an X on the elimination grid. Placing the two conditions *"Warren cannot teach on Monday or Thursday"* and *"Warren can teach only evening classes"* on the grid gives

		M	T	W	TH	F	
Warren		X	X	X	X	X	a.m.
		X			X		p.m.
Dornan							a.m.
							p.m.
Novak							a.m.
							p.m.
Emerson							a.m.
							p.m.
Peterson							a.m.
							p.m.

Placing the remaining conditions in like manner gives

		M	T	W	TH	F	
Warren		X	X	X	X	X	a.m.
		X			X		p.m.
Dornan				X			a.m.
				X			p.m.
Novak							a.m.
							p.m.
Emerson		X				X	a.m.
		X				X	p.m.
Peterson							a.m.
		X	X	X	X	X	p.m.

To answer the following questions, we will refer only to the grid, not the original problem.

1. **At which one of the following times can Warren, Dornan, and Emerson all be teaching?**

   (A) Monday morning
   (B) Friday evening
   (C) Tuesday evening
   (D) Friday morning
   (E) Wednesday morning

The grid clearly shows that all three can work on Tuesday night. The answer is (C).

2. For which day will the dean have to hire a part-time teacher?

- **(A) Monday**
- **(B) Tuesday**
- **(C) Wednesday**
- **(D) Thursday**
- **(E) Friday**

Dornan and Novak are the only people who can work Monday evenings, and three classes are always in session, so extra help will be needed for Monday evenings. The answer is (A).

3. Which one of the following must be false?

- **(A) Dornan does not work on Tuesday.**
- **(B) Emerson does not work on Tuesday morning.**
- **(C) Peterson works on Tuesday.**
- **(D) Novak works every day of the week except Wednesday.**
- **(E) Dornan works every day of the week except Wednesday.**

The condition *"Dean Peterson cannot teach on Wednesday if Novak teaches on Thursday, and Novak teaches on Thursday if Dean Peterson cannot teach on Wednesday"* can be symbolized as **(P≠W)<—>(N=TH)**. Now, if Novak works every day of the week, except Wednesday, then in particular he works Thursday. So from the condition **(P≠W)<—>(N=TH)**, we know that Dean Peterson cannot work on Wednesday. But from the grid this leaves only Novak and Emerson to teach the three Wednesday morning classes. Hence the answer is (D).

4. If Novak does not work on Thursday, then which one of the following must be true?

- **(A) Peterson works Tuesday morning.**
- **(B) Dornan works Tuesday morning.**
- **(C) Emerson works on Tuesday.**
- **(D) Peterson works on Wednesday.**
- **(E) Warren works on Tuesday morning.**

If you remember to think of an *if-and-only-if* statement as an equality, then this will be an easy problem. Negating both sides of the condition

(P≠W)<—>(N=TH)

gives

(P=W)<—>(N≠TH).

This tells us that Dean Peterson must work on Wednesday if Novak does not work on Thursday. The answer, therefore, is (D).

Caution: Not all scheduling games lend themselves to an elimination grid. It's sweet when this method can be applied because the answers typically can be read directly from the grid with little thought. Only one-third of the assignment games, however, can be solved this way. Most often the game will require a more functional diagram, and you will need to spend more time tinkering with it.

When you first read an assignment game, you need to quickly decide whether or not to use an elimination grid. You may decide to use a grid. Then spend three minutes trying to set it up, only to realize you have taken the wrong path and have wasted three minutes. Unfortunately, exact criteria cannot be given for when to use an elimination grid. But this much can be said: if only two options (characteristics) are available to the elements—yes/no, on/off, etc.—then an elimination grid is probably indicated.

In the next game, which is considerably harder, more than two options are available to each element. It is, therefore, a game of multiple-choice.

Multiple-Choice Game

There are four partners in a particular law firm. Each partner is an expert in at least one of three fields: criminal law, worker's compensation, and patent law. These are the only areas of law that the partners of the firm practice.

D and F both practice in at least one of the same fields.
D practices in worker's compensation and patent law.
F practices in only two fields.
D and E do not practice in the same field.
F and H do not practice in the same field.

1. Which one of the following must be false?

(A) F practices in exactly two fields.
(B) H practices in exactly one field.
(C) E practices in more than one field.
(D) E practices in only one field.
(E) D practices in exactly two fields.

2. The people in which one of the following pairs could practice in exactly the same fields?

(A) D and H
(B) E and F
(C) D and E
(D) E and H
(E) H and F

3. If the combination of fields in which F practices is different from any of the combinations in which her colleagues practice, then which one of the following must be true?

(A) H does not practice patent law.
(B) F does not practice patent law.
(C) H does not practice worker's compensation.
(D) F practices criminal law.
(E) F and H practice in the same fields.

4. If a new partner who practices in exactly two fields joins the firm, then he cannot practice in all of the fields that the combination

(A) D and F do
(B) E and H do
(C) E and F do
(D) D and H do
(E) F and H do

In this game, the goal is to assign one or more characteristics (fields of practice) to each element (partner). Hence it is a multiple-choice game, and therefore an elimination grid is unwarranted.

The diagram for this game will consist of four compartments, one for each of the partners D, E, F, and H:

D	E	F	H

Let the letters C, W, and P stand for "practices in criminal law," "practices in worker's comp.," and "practices in patent law," in that order. Placing the condition *"D practices in worker's comp. and patent law"* on the diagram gives

D	E	F	H
W&P			

Next, the condition *"D and E do not practice in the same field"* means that E practices only criminal law, and D practices only worker's comp. and patent law—otherwise they would practice in some of the same fields. Adding this to the diagram yields

D	E	F	H
W&P	C		
2	1		

Next, the condition *"D and F both practice in at least one of the same fields"* means that F must practice in either worker's comp. or patent law, or both. Adding this to the diagram along with the condition *"F practices in only two fields"* gives

D	E	F	H
W&P	C	W or P	
2	1	2	

Finally, the condition *"H and F do not practice in the same field"* means that if F practices worker's comp., then H does not; and if F practices patent law, then H does not. In other words, ~W or ~P. In the diagram, we use an arrow to indicate this conditional relationship between F and H as follows:*

D	E	F	H
W&P	C	W or P →	~Wor~P
2	1	2	1

This diagram is a bit more restrictive than the situation warrants: F could practice criminal law. A more precise diagram would be

D	E	F	H
W&P	C	WorPorC →	~Wor~Por~C
2	1	2	1

However, the previous diagram is sufficient for answering the questions that follow.

1. Which one of the following must be false?

(A) F practices in exactly two fields.
(B) H practices in exactly one field.
(C) E practices in more than one field.
(D) E practices in only one field.
(E) D practices in exactly two fields.

The diagram clearly shows that (A), (B), (D), and (E) are true and that (C) is false. Thus the answer is (C).

2. The people in which one of the following pairs could practice in exactly the same fields?

(A) D and H
(B) E and F
(C) D and E
(D) E and H
(E) H and F

From the diagram, we see that D and H cannot practice in exactly the same fields because D practices in two fields, whereas H practices in only one. This dismisses (A). A similar analysis dismisses choices (B), (C), and (E). As a matter of test taking strategy this would be sufficient to mark the answer (D), but it is instructive to work out a possible assignment. You should verify that the following diagram is consistent with all the initial conditions:

D	E	F	H
W&P	C	W&P	C
2	1	2	1

---

* Note because F practices in two fields, and H and F do not practice in the same fields, H can practice in only one field.

3. **If the combination of fields in which F practices is different from any of the combinations in which her colleagues practice, then which one of the following must be true?**
   (A) H does not practice patent law.
   (B) F does not practice patent law.
   (C) H does not practice worker's compensation.
   (D) F practices criminal law.
   (E) F and H practice in the same fields.

From the diagram, we know that F must practice either worker's comp. or patent law; but because of the new condition, she cannot practice both—otherwise she would practice in the same fields as D. So F must practice criminal law, and the answer is (D).

4. **If a new partner who practices in exactly two fields joins the firm, then he cannot practice in all of the fields that the combination**

   (A) D and F do
   (B) E and H do
   (C) E and F do
   (D) D and H do
   (E) F and H do

Again from the diagram, we see that F and H practice in mutually exclusive fields. Furthermore, F practices in two fields and H practices in one field, so between them they practice in all three fields. But we are told that the new partner practices in only two fields. Hence he cannot practice in as many fields as do F and H combined. The answer is (E).

You probably have noticed that once the diagram has been constructed, assignment games are somewhat manageable. However, the diagram may not be easy to construct, and it may require considerable inspiration to figure out what kind of diagram to use. As you work the exercises in this section, you will develop more intuition in this regard.

Points to Remember

1. Assignment games tend to be the hardest, so save them for last.

2. Assignment games pair each element with one or more characteristics, whereas grouping games partition the elements into two or more groups.

3. It is important that you identify whether you are dealing with an assignment game or a grouping game because different methods are used to solve each type of game.

4. Elimination grids are very effective when they can be applied, which is about one-third of the time.

5. Exact criteria cannot be given for when to use an elimination grid. But if only two options (characteristics) are available to the elements—yes/no, on/off, etc.—then an elimination grid is probably indicated.

Exercise

Directions: The following group of questions is based on a set of conditions. Choose the response that most accurately and completely answers each question.

Questions 1–6

The Mom & Pop liquor store employs five cashiers—Adams, Bates, Cox, Drake, and Edwards—each of whom works alone on exactly one day, Monday through Friday.

Adams works only Mondays or Wednesdays.
Bates will not work Wednesdays or Fridays.
Drake and Edwards work on consecutive days.

1. Which one of the following is a possible work schedule?

(A) Edwards, Bates, Adams, Drake, Cox
(B) Bates, Adams, Cox, Edwards, Drake
(C) Edwards, Drake, Adams, Cox, Bates
(D) Adams, Bates, Edwards, Cox, Drake
(E) Drake, Edwards, Adams, Bates, Cox

2. If Cox works on Tuesday, then all of the following statements must be true EXCEPT:

(A) Bates works on Monday.
(B) Adams works on Wednesday.
(C) Drake could work on Thursday.
(D) Edwards could work on Friday.
(E) Drake could work on Wednesday.

3. Which one of the following CANNOT be true?

(A) Cox works on Thursday.
(B) Edwards works on Monday.
(C) Adams and Bates work on consecutive days.
(D) Drake and Edwards work on consecutive days.
(E) Cox works on Monday.

4. If Bates works Thursday, which one of the following must be true?

(A) Adams works Wednesday.
(B) Drake works Tuesday.
(C) Cox works Friday.
(D) Edwards works Wednesday.
(E) Adams works Monday.

5. If Adams and Bates CANNOT work on consecutive days, then which one of the following must be false?

(A) Cox works Tuesday.
(B) Edwards works Monday.
(C) Drake works Tuesday.
(D) Edwards works Wednesday.
(E) Adams works Monday.

6. If Bates CANNOT work either immediately before or after Edwards, then which one of the following must be false?

(A) Edwards works on Monday.
(B) Edwards works on Tuesday.
(C) Edwards works on Wednesday.
(D) Edwards works on Thursday.
(E) Edwards works on Friday.

The following games are taken from recent LSATs.

Questions 7–10

A street cleaning crew works only Monday to Friday, and only during the day. It takes the crew an entire morning or an entire afternoon to clean a street. During one week the crew cleaned exactly eight streets—First, Second, Third, Fourth, Fifth, Sixth, Seventh, and Eighth streets. The following is known about the crew's schedule for the week:

The crew cleaned no street on Friday morning.
The crew cleaned no street on Wednesday afternoon.
It cleaned Fourth Street on Tuesday morning.
It cleaned Seventh Street on Thursday morning.
It cleaned Fourth Street before Sixth Street and after Eighth Street.
It cleaned Second, Fifth, and Eighth streets on afternoons.

7. If the crew cleaned Second Street earlier in the week than Seventh Street, then it must have cleaned which one of the following streets on Tuesday afternoon?

(A) First Street
(B) Second Street
(C) Third Street
(D) Fifth Street
(E) Eighth Street

8. If the crew cleaned Sixth Street on a morning and cleaned Second Street before Seventh Street, then what is the maximum number of streets whose cleaning times cannot be determined?

(A) 1
(B) 2
(C) 3
(D) 4
(E) 5

9. What is the maximum possible number of streets any one of which could be the one the crew cleaned on Friday afternoon?

(A) 1
(B) 2
(C) 3
(D) 4
(E) 5

10. If the crew cleaned First Street earlier in the week than Third Street, then which one of the following statements must be false?

(A) The crew cleaned First Street on Tuesday afternoon.
(B) The crew cleaned Second Street on Thursday afternoon.
(C) The crew cleaned Third Street on Wednesday morning.
(D) The crew cleaned Fifth Street on Thursday afternoon.
(E) The crew cleaned Sixth Street on Friday afternoon.

Questions 11–12

A store sells shirts only in small, medium, and large sizes, and only in red, yellow, and blue colors. Casey buys exactly three shirts from the store.

A shirt type consists of both a size and a color.
Casey does not buy two shirts of the same type.
Casey does not buy both a small shirt and a large shirt.
No small red shirts are available.
No large blue shirts are available.

11. If Casey buys a small blue shirt, which one of the following must be false?

(A) Casey buys two blue shirts.
(B) Casey buys two red shirts.
(C) Casey buys two yellow shirts.
(D) Casey buys two small shirts.
(E) Casey buys two medium shirts.

12. If Casey buys exactly one medium shirt and does not buy two shirts of the same color, then she cannot buy which one of the following?

(A) a medium red shirt
(B) a medium yellow shirt
(C) a medium blue shirt
(D) a large red shirt
(E) a large yellow shirt

Answers and Solutions to Exercise

Questions 1–6

This is a scheduling game of medium difficulty. We shall use an elimination grid to solve it. To indicate that a person does not work on a particular day, place an **X** on the grid. To indicate that a person does work on a particular day, place a **W** on the grid. Placing the conditions on the grid yields

	M	T	W	TH	F
Adams		**X**		**X**	**X**
Bates			**X**		**X**
Cox					
Drake					
Edwards					

1. (A) and (D) are not possible work schedules since Drake and Edwards must work on consecutive days. (B) is not a possible work schedule since Adams must work on Monday or Wednesday. (C) is not a possible work schedule since Bates will not work on Friday. Hence, by process of elimination, the answer is (E).

2. Adding the new condition to the grid (and recalling only one person works each day) yields

	M	T	W	TH	F
Adams		**X**		**X**	**X**
Bates		**X**	**X**		**X**
Cox	**X**	**W**	**X**	**X**	**X**
Drake		**X**			
Edwards		**X**			

Clearly, from the grid, either Drake or Edwards must work Friday. Further, since Drake and Edwards work on consecutive days, they must work Thursday and Friday. So Drake cannot work Wednesday. The answer is (E).

3. Begin with (A). Add *"Cox works on Thursday"* to the grid:

	M	T	W	TH	F
Adams		X		X	X
Bates			X	X	X
Cox	X	X	X	W	X
Drake				X	
Edwards				X	

Now, the condition *"Drake and Edwards work on consecutive days"* generates two grids—one with Drake and Edwards working on Monday and Tuesday (not necessarily in that order) and one with Drake and Edwards working on Tuesday and Wednesday (not necessarily in that order):

Diagram 1

	M	T	W	TH	F
Adams	X	X		X	X
Bates	X	X	X	X	X
Cox	X	X	X	W	X
Drake	W	X	X	X	X
Edwards	X	W	X	X	X

Diagram II

	M	T	W	TH	F
Adams		X	X	X	X
Bates		X	X	X	X
Cox	X	X	X	W	X
Drake	X	W	X	X	X
Edwards	X	X	W	X	X

Clearly, Diagram I leaves no day for Bates to work. And Diagram II forces Adams and Bates to work together on Monday, violating the condition that only one employee works at a time. Hence, Cox cannot work on Thursday. The answer is (A).

4. Adding the condition *"Bates works Thursday"* yields

	M	T	W	TH	F
Adams		X		X	X
Bates	X	X	X	W	X
Cox				X	
Drake				X	
Edwards				X	

Since Drake and Edwards must work on consecutive days, neither can work on Friday. This leaves only Cox to work on Friday. The answer is (C).

5. Begin with (A). Place Cox on the grid:

	M	T	W	TH	F
Adams		X		X	X
Bates		X	X		X
Cox	X	W	X	X	X
Drake		X			
Edwards		X			

Now, Drake and Edwards could work on Thursday and Friday:

	M	T	W	TH	F
Adams		X		X	X
Bates		X	X	X	X
Cox	X	W	X	X	X
Drake	X	X	X	W	X
Edwards	X	X	X	X	W

Clearly, this diagram forces Bates to work on Monday and Adams to work on Wednesday:

	M	T	W	TH	F
Adams	X	X	W	X	X
Bates	W	X	X	X	X
Cox	X	W	X	X	X
Drake	X	X	X	W	X
Edwards	X	X	X	X	W

This diagram satisfies all the initial conditions and Adams and Bates are not working on consecutive days. This eliminates (A).

Turning to (B), place Edwards on the grid:

	M	T	W	TH	F
Adams	**X**	**X**		**X**	**X**
Bates	**X**		**X**		**X**
Cox	**X**				
Drake	**X**				
Edwards	**W**	**X**	**X**	**X**	**X**

Since Drake and Edwards must work on consecutive days, we know that Drake must work Tuesday:

	M	T	W	TH	F
Adams	**X**	**X**		**X**	**X**
Bates	**X**	**X**	**X**		**X**
Cox	**X**	**X**			
Drake	**X**	**W**	**X**	**X**	**X**
Edwards	**W**	**X**	**X**	**X**	**X**

Clearly, this diagram forces Adams to work on Wednesday and Bates to work on Thursday. However, this violates the supplemental condition *"Adams and Bates CANNOT work on consecutive days."* The answer is (B).

6. Before starting, you should scan the answer-choices for one that eliminates many positions for Bates. Now, if Edwards works Wednesday, then Bates cannot work either Tuesday or Thursday. So we begin with Edwards working Wednesday:

	M	T	W	TH	F
Adams		**X**	**X**	**X**	**X**
Bates			**X**		**X**
Cox			**X**		
Drake			**X**		
Edwards	**X**	**X**	**W**	**X**	**X**

Again, this prevents Bates from working either Tuesday or Thursday:

	M	T	W	TH	F
Adams		X	X	X	X
Bates		X	X	X	X
Cox			X		
Drake			X		
Edwards	X	X	W	X	X

Clearly, this diagram does not leave room for both Adams and Bates since they cannot work the same day. The answer is (C).

Questions 7–10

This is a hard assignment (schedule) game, mainly because it is quite long and contains a labyrinth of information. However, a well-chosen diagram will greatly simplify it.

We symbolize only the last two conditions. The condition *"It cleaned Fourth Street before Sixth Street and after Eighth Street"* can be symbolized as **8th—>4th—>6th**. The condition *"It cleaned Second, Fifth, and Eighth streets on afternoons"* can be symbolized as **2d, 5th, 8th = afternoon**. Place an **X** on the diagram to indicate that a street is not cleaned at a particular time. The first two conditions state that no street is cleaned on either Wednesday afternoon or Friday morning:

	M	T	W	TH	F
a.m.					X
p.m.			X		

Next, use a street's number (1st, 2nd, etc.) to indicate it is cleaned at a particular time. (Note: although the problem does not state it, you are to assume that each street is cleaned only once a week.) The third and fourth conditions say that Fourth Street and Seventh Street were cleaned on Tuesday and Thursday mornings, respectively:

	M	T	W	TH	F
a.m.		4		7	X
p.m.			X		

Now, from the condition **8th—>4th—>6th** and the fact that Fourth Street was cleaned on Tuesday, we see that Eighth Street was cleaned on Monday. Combining this with the condition **2d, 5th, 8th = afternoon** shows that Eighth Street was cleaned on Monday afternoon:

	M	T	W	TH	F
a.m.		4		7	X
p.m.	8		X		

7. From the diagram and the condition **2d, 5th, 8th = afternoon**, we see that the crew must have cleaned Second Street on Tuesday afternoon:

	M	T	W	TH	F
a.m.		4		7	**X**
p.m.	8	**2**	**X**		

The answer is (B).

8. The new condition, *"the crew cleaned Sixth Street on a morning,"* and the condition **8th—>4th—>6th** force Sixth Street to have been cleaned on Wednesday morning:

	M	T	W	TH	F
a.m.		4	**6**	7	**X**
p.m.	8		**X**		

Next, the new condition, *"[the crew] cleaned Second Street before Seventh Street"* and the condition **2d, 5th, 8th = afternoon** force Second Street to have been cleaned on Tuesday afternoon:

	M	T	W	TH	F
a.m.		4	**6**	7	**X**
p.m.	8	**2**	**X**		

This chart leaves undetermined the cleaning times of only three streets—First, Third, and Fifth. The answer is (C).

9. The original diagram

	M	T	W	TH	F
a.m.		4		7	**X**
p.m.	8		**X**		

shows that the cleaning times of only 4th, 7th, and 8th streets are determined. Combining this with the condition **2d, 5th, 8th = afternoon** shows that all the remaining streets could have been cleaned on Friday afternoon. The answer is (E).

10. Suppose the crew cleaned First Street on Tuesday afternoon, choice (A). Then since Second and Fifth streets must be cleaned in the afternoon (**2d, 5th, 8th = afternoon**), we see from the original diagram that they must be cleaned on Thursday and Friday afternoons:

	M	T	W	TH	F
a.m.		4		7	**X**
p.m.	8	**1**	**X**		

2nd/5th

The new condition, *"the crew cleaned First Street earlier in the week than Third Street,"* forces Third Street to be cleaned on Wednesday morning. Further, the condition **8th—>4th—>6th** forces Sixth Street to also be cleaned on Wednesday morning. But only one street at a time can be cleaned. The answer is (A).

Questions 11–12

Be careful not to interpret the condition *"Casey does not buy both a small shirt and a large shirt"* to mean that she buys neither a small shirt nor a large shirt.* We symbolize the condition as **~(S&L)**. The condition *"No small red shirts are available"* can be symbolized as **~(SR)**. The remaining conditions are symbolized in like manner:

~(same type)
~(S&L)
~(SR)
~(LB)

11. We shall attempt to construct a diagram for each answer-choice. The one for which this cannot be done will be the answer. Begin with (A). Suppose Casey buys two blue shirts, one of which is small:

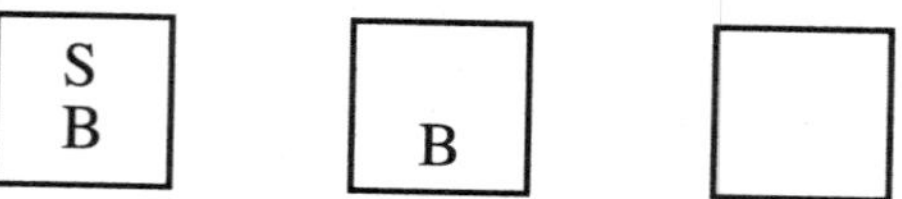

If the other blue shirt is a medium and the third shirt is a medium yellow, the diagram becomes

S B	M B	M Y

This diagram does not have two shirts of the same type, does not have both a small and a large shirt, does not have a small red shirt, and does not have a large blue shirt. Hence, it satisfies every condition. This eliminates (A). Turning to choice (B), if Casey buys two red shirts, the diagram becomes

S B	R	R

Now, neither red shirt can be small, **~(SR)**. Further, neither red shirt can be large since Casey does not buy both small and large shirts, **~(S&L)**. Hence, both red shirts must be mediums. However, this violates the fact that she does not buy two shirts of the same type. Therefore, she cannot buy two red shirts. The answer is (B).

* To give the sentence that meaning rewrite it as "Casey does not buy a small shirt nor a large shirt."

12. The condition *"[she] does not buy two shirts of the same color"* means she buys one shirt of each color. Begin with (A). Suppose Casey buys a medium red shirt:

M R	B	Y

Then the remaining shirts could be a small blue and a small yellow:

M R	S B	S Y

This diagram satisfies every condition. Hence, she can buy a medium red shirt—eliminate (A).

As to (B), if she buys a medium yellow shirt, the diagram becomes

M Y	R	B

Since she does not buy both small and large shirts, the two remaining shirts must be both small or both large:

Diagram I

M Y	S R	S B

Diagram II

M Y	L R	L B

Diagram I violates the condition ~**(SR)**, and Diagram II violates the condition ~**(LB)**. Hence, she cannot buy a medium yellow shirt. The answer is (B).

LSAT GAME SECTION

Give yourself 35 minutes to complete this LSAT section. It is important that you time yourself so that you can find your optimum working pace, and so that you will know what to expect when you take the test.

Note, you will not be allowed any scratch paper during the actual LSAT; all your work must be done on the test booklet. To accustom yourself to writing in a confined space, you should write all your scratch work in the book.

LSAT SECTION

Time—35 minutes
24 Questions

Directions: Each group of questions in this section is based on a set of conditions. In answering some of the questions, it may be useful to draw a rough diagram. Choose the response that most accurately and completely answers each question and blacken the corresponding space on your answer sheet.

Questions 1–5

The Mammoth Corporation has just completed hiring nine new workers: Brandt, Calva, Duvall, Eberle, Fu, Garcia, Haga, Irving, and Jessup.

Fu and Irving were hired on the same day as each other, and no one else was hired that day.
Calva and Garcia were hired on the same day as each other, and no one else was hired that day.
On each of the other days of hiring, exactly one worker was hired.
Eberle was hired before Brandt.
Haga was hired before Duvall.
Duvall was hired after Irving but before Eberle.
Garcia was hired after both Jessup and Brandt.
Brandt was hired before Jessup.

1. Who were the last two workers to be hired?

(A) Eberle and Jessup
(B) Brandt and Garcia
(C) Brandt and Calva
(D) Garcia and Calva
(E) Jessup and Brandt

2. Who was hired on the fourth day of hiring?

(A) Eberle
(B) Brandt
(C) Irving
(D) Garcia
(E) Jessup

3. Exactly how many workers were hired before Jessup?

(A) 6
(B) 5
(C) 4
(D) 3
(E) 2

4. Which one of the following must be true?

(A) Duvall was the first worker to be hired.
(B) Haga was the first worker to be hired.
(C) Fu and Irving were the first two workers to be hired.
(D) Haga and Fu were the first two workers to be hired.
(E) Either Haga was the first worker to be hired or Fu and Irving were the first two workers to be hired.

5. If Eberle was hired on a Monday, what is the earliest day on which Garcia could have been hired?

(A) Monday
(B) Tuesday
(C) Wednesday
(D) Thursday
(E) Friday

GO ON TO THE NEXT PAGE.

Questions 6–12

An apartment building has five floors. Each floor has either one or two apartments. There are exactly eight apartments in the building. The residents of the building are J, K, L, M, N, O, P, and Q, who each live in a different apartment.

J lives on a floor with two apartments.
K lives on the floor directly above P.
The second floor is made up of only one apartment.
M and N live on the same floor.
O does not live on the same floor as Q.
L lives in the only apartment on her floor.
Q does not live on the first or second floor.

6. Which one of the following must be true?

(A) Q lives on the third floor.
(B) Q lives on the fifth floor.
(C) L does not live on the fourth floor.
(D) N does not live on the second floor.
(E) J lives on the first floor.

7. Which one of the following CANNOT be true?

(A) K lives on the second floor.
(B) M lives on the first floor.
(C) N lives on the fourth floor.
(D) O lives on the third floor.
(E) P lives on the fifth floor.

8. If J lives on the fourth floor and K lives on the fifth floor, which one of the following can be true?

(A) O lives on the first floor.
(B) Q lives on the fourth floor.
(C) N lives on the fifth floor.
(D) L lives on the fourth floor.
(E) P lives on the third floor.

9. If O lives on the second floor, which one of the following CANNOT be true?

(A) K lives on the fourth floor.
(B) K lives on the fifth floor.
(C) L lives on the first floor.
(D) L lives on the third floor.
(E) L lives on the fourth floor.

10. If M lives on the fourth floor, which one of the following must be false?

(A) O lives on the fifth floor.
(B) J lives on the first floor.
(C) L lives on the second floor.
(D) Q lives on the third floor.
(E) P lives on the first floor.

11. Which one of the following must be true?

(A) If J lives on the fourth floor, then Q does not live on the fifth floor.
(B) If O lives on the second floor, then L does not live on the fourth floor.
(C) If N lives on the fourth floor, then K does not live on the second floor.
(D) If K lives on the third floor, then O does not live on the fifth floor.
(E) If P lives on the fourth floor, then M does not live on the third floor.

12. If O lives on the fourth floor and P lives on the second floor, which one of the following must be true?

(A) L lives on the first floor.
(B) M lives on the third floor.
(C) Q lives on the third floor.
(D) N lives on the fifth floor.
(E) Q lives on the fifth floor.

GO ON TO THE NEXT PAGE.

Questions 13–17

Hannah spends 14 days, exclusive of travel time, in a total of six cities.

Each city she visits is in one of three countries—X, Y, or Z.
Each of the three countries has many cities.
Hannah visits at least one city in each of the three countries.
She spends at least two days in each city she visits.
She spends only whole days in any city.

13. If Hannah spends exactly eight days in the cities of country X, then which one of the following CANNOT be true?

    (A) She visits exactly two cities in country X.
    (B) She visits exactly two cities in country Y.
    (C) She visits exactly two cities in country Z.
    (D) She visits more cities in country Y than in country Z.
    (E) She visits more cities in country Z than in country Y.

14. If Hannah visits an equal number of cities in each of the countries, what is the greatest total number of days she can spend visiting cities in country X?

    (A) 3
    (B) 4
    (C) 5
    (D) 6
    (E) 7

15. If Hannah spends three days in the cities of country Y and seven days in the cities of country Z, then which one of the following must be false?

    (A) She visits more cities in country X than in country Y.
    (B) She visits exactly two cities in country X.
    (C) She visits more cities in country Z than in country X.
    (D) She visits exactly two cities in country Z.
    (E) She visits exactly three cities in country Z.

16. If the city of Nomo is in country X, and if Hannah spends as many days as possible in Nomo and as few days as possible in each of the other cities that she visits, then which one of the following must be true?

    (A) Hannah cannot visit any other cities in country X.
    (B) Hannah can visit four cities in country Y.
    (C) Hannah can spend six days in Nomo.
    (D) Hannah cannot spend more than four days in country Z.
    (E) Hannah can visit, at most, a total of four cities in countries Y and Z.

17. If Hannah visits a combined total of four cities in countries X and Y, what is the greatest total number of days she can spend visiting cities in country Y?

    (A) 6
    (B) 7
    (C) 8
    (D) 9
    (E) 10

GO ON TO THE NEXT PAGE.

Questions 18–24

Exactly six dogs—P, Q, R, S, T, and U—are entered in a dog show. The judge of the show awards exactly four ribbons, one for each of first, second, third, and fourth places, to four of the dogs. The information that follows is all that is available about the six dogs:

Each dog is either a greyhound or a labrador, but not both.
Two of the six dogs are female and four are male.
The judge awards ribbons to both female dogs, exactly one of which is a labrador.
Exactly one labrador wins a ribbon.
Dogs P and R place ahead of dog S, and dog S places ahead of dogs Q and T.
Dogs P and R are greyhounds.
Dogs S and U are labradors.

18. Which one of the following is a complete and accurate list of the dogs that can be greyhounds?

 (A) P, Q
 (B) P, R
 (C) P, Q, R
 (D) P, R, T
 (E) P, Q, R, T

19. Which one of the following statements CANNOT be true?

 (A) A female greyhound wins the second place ribbon.
 (B) A female labrador wins the second place ribbon.
 (C) A female labrador wins the third place ribbon.
 (D) A male greyhound wins the fourth place ribbon.
 (E) A female greyhound wins the fourth place ribbon.

20. Which one of the following dogs must be male?

 (A) dog P
 (B) dog R
 (C) dog S
 (D) dog T
 (E) dog U

21. Which one of the following statements can be false?

 (A) Dog P places ahead of dog R.
 (B) Dog P places ahead of dog T.
 (C) Dog R places ahead of dog U.
 (D) Dog R places ahead of dog T.
 (E) Dog S places ahead of dog U.

22. If dog Q is female, which one of the following statements can be false?

 (A) Dog P is male.
 (B) Dog R is male.
 (C) Dog Q wins the fourth place ribbon.
 (D) Dog Q is a greyhound.
 (E) Dog T is a greyhound.

23. If dog T wins the fourth place ribbon, then which one of the following statements must be true?

 (A) Dog P is male.
 (B) Dog Q is male.
 (C) Dog T is male.
 (D) Dog Q is a labrador.
 (E) Dog T is a labrador.

24. Which one of the following statements could be true?

 (A) Dog P does not win a ribbon.
 (B) Dog R does not win a ribbon.
 (C) Dog S does not win a ribbon.
 (D) Dog T wins a ribbon.
 (E) Dog U wins a ribbon.

S T O P

IF YOU FINISH BEFORE TIME IS CALLED, YOU MAY CHECK YOUR WORK ON THIS SECTION ONLY. DO NOT WORK ON ANY OTHER SECTION IN THE TEST.

ANSWERS AND SOLUTIONS TO LSAT SECTION

Answers to Questions

1. D
2. A
3. A
4. E
5. D
6. D
7. E
8. A
9. E
10. C
11. B
12. C
13. A
14. D
15. D
16. B
17. C
18. E
19. B
20. E
21. A
22. E
23. B
24. D

Questions 1–5

This is a rather easy linear ordering game. Following the strategies developed earlier, we let the first letter of each name stand for the name and then symbolize the conditions. *"Fu and Irving were hired on the same day as each other, and no one else was hired that day"* is naturally symbolized as **F = I**. We'll use an arrow to indicate that a person was hired before another. The condition *"Duvall was hired after Irving but before Eberle"* can be symbolized as **I—>D—>E**. The remaining conditions can be symbolized in like manner, giving the following schematic:

1. **F = I**
2. **C = G**
3. *
4. **E—>B**
5. **H—>D**
6. **I—>D—>E**
7. **J—>G**
8. **B—>G**
9. **B—>J**

(Note: The * reminds us of the condition *"On each of the other days of hiring, exactly one worker was hired,"* which could not be readily symbolized.) Since the game has no fixed elements (such as "E was hired first"), we'll use a flow chart to solve it. Condition 6 contains the most information, so build the chart around it:

I—>D—>E

Adding Conditions 1 and 5 gives

H ↘
[I/F] —>D—>E

(Note: The rectangle around I and F indicates that they were hired on the same day.)

Adding Conditions 4 and 9 gives

H ↘
[I/F] —>D—>E—>B—>J

Finally, adding Conditions 2 and 7 gives (Note: Condition 8 is superfluous.)

```
H ↘
[I] –>D–>E–>B–>J–>[G]
[F]               [C]
```

This diagram is quite determinative: from it we'll be able to read off the answers to all the questions.

1. Clearly from the diagram, both Garcia and Calva were hired on the last day. The answer is (D).

2. Again from the diagram, we see that Irving and Fu could have been hired on the first day, Haga could have been hired on the second day (or vice versa, since they are not connected by a sequence of arrows), and Duvall must have been hired on the third day. Hence Eberle was hired on the fourth day. The answer is (A).

3. Again, we merely read off the answer from the diagram. Checking the diagram, we see that six people are to the left of Jessup. Therefore, six people were hired before Jessup. The answer is (A).

4. In the diagram, Haga is in a different row than Fu and Irving, so we cannot determine whether Haga was hired first or Fu and Irving were hired first. The answer is (E).

5. If Eberle was hired on Monday, then from the chart we see that Brandt was hired at the earliest on Tuesday, Jessup on Wednesday, and both Garcia and Calva on Thursday. The answer is (D).

Questions 6–12

This is a hybrid (ordering/grouping) game of medium difficulty. As before, we construct a diagram to help answer the questions. The condition *"J lives on a floor with two apartments"* can be symbolized as **J= 2 apts**. The condition *"K lives on the floor directly above P"* is naturally symbolized as **K/P**. The condition *"The second floor is made up of only one apartment"* can be symbolized as **2d = alone**. The condition *"M and N live on the same floor"* is naturally symbolized as **M = N**. The condition *"O does not live on the same floor as Q"* is naturally symbolized as **O ≠ Q**. The condition *"L lives in the only apartment on her floor"* can be symbolized as **L = alone**. Finally, the condition *"Q does not live on the first or second floor"* is naturally symbolized as **Q ≠ 1st, 2d**. This gives the following schematic:

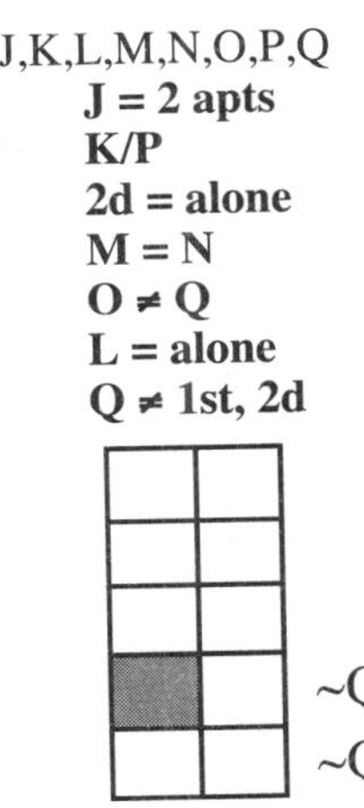

6. From the condition **M = N**, we know that M and N live on the same floor. But there is only one apartment on the second floor, **2d = alone**. Therefore, N cannot live on the second floor. The answer is (D).

7. From the condition **K/P**, we know that P must live directly below K and thus cannot possibly live on the top floor. The answer is (E).

8. Adding the supplementary conditions to the diagram gives

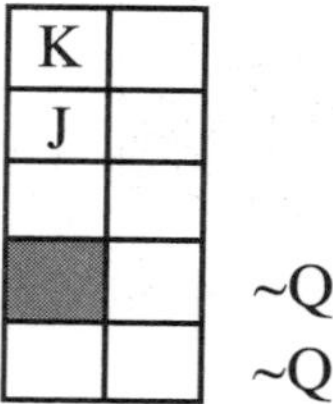

~Q
~Q

From the condition **K/P**, we know that P must live on the fourth floor:

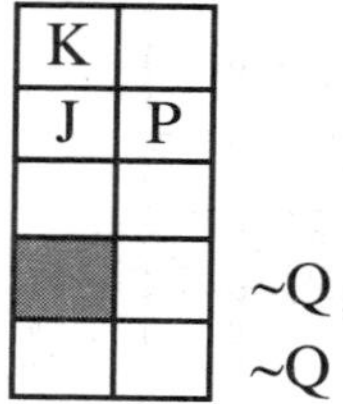

~Q
~Q

Now we try to construct a valid diagram for each of the answer-choices, starting with (A). Placing O on the bottom floor gives

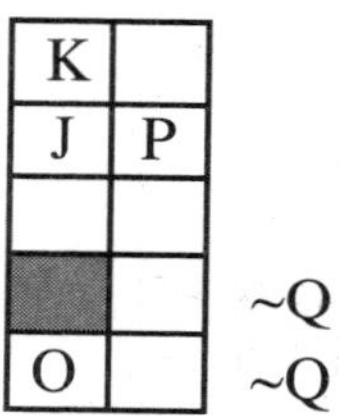

~Q
~Q

From the condition **M = N**, we see that both M and N must live on the 3d floor:

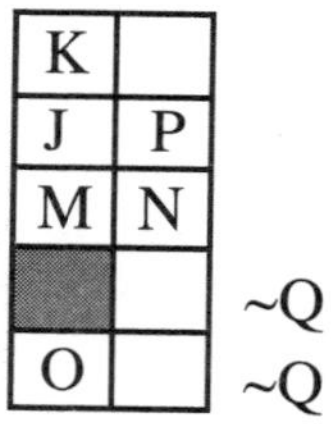

K		
J	P	
M	N	
		~Q
O		~Q

Now from the condition **L = alone**, we know that L must live on the second floor:

K		
J	P	
M	N	
	L	
O		~Q

Finally, the condition **O ≠ Q** forces Q to the top floor:

K	Q
J	P
M	N
▓	L
O	▓

This diagram satisfies all the original and supplementary conditions, so O *can* live on the first floor. The answer is (A).

9. Add the new condition *"O lives on the second floor"* to the diagram:

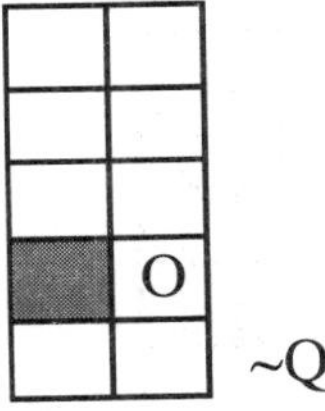

Now we attack the answer-choices, attempting to construct a diagram for each one. The answer-choice for which a valid diagram cannot be constructed will be the answer. Start with choice (E). Place L on the 4th floor:

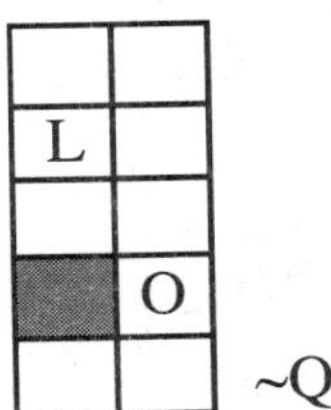

Now the condition **K/P** must be placed on either the 3d and 4th floors, or the 4th and 5th floors. This generates two diagrams:

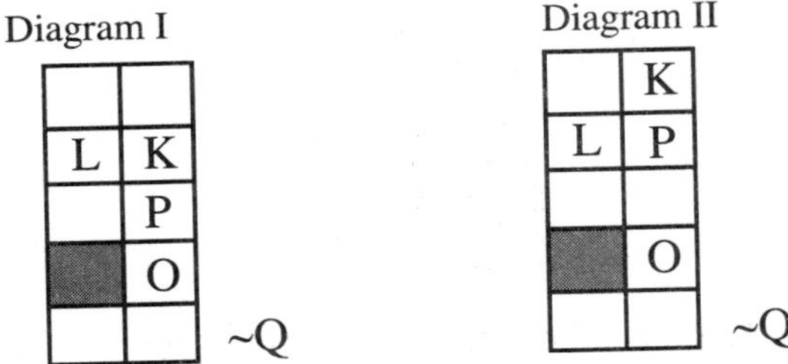

In either diagram, L is on a floor with two apartments, violating the condition **L = alone**. Hence the answer is (E).

Note: We presented the answer directly, instead of applying an indirect proof, because we knew the answer is (E)! These types of problems can be very time consuming; so when you come to them on the test, first scan the answer-choices to see whether you can intuitively pick out the answer (or at least spot a likely candidate). If this fails, then come back to the problem later, if you have time, and apply an indirect proof.

10. The new condition *"M lives on the fourth floor"* plus the condition **M = N** gives

M	N	
		~Q
		~Q

We'll apply an indirect proof. Start with choice (A); place O on the fifth floor:

O		
M	N	
		~Q
		~Q

Next, place J on the top floor and the condition **K/P** on the 2d and 3d floors:

O	J	
M	N	
	K	
	P	
		~Q

Finally, place Q on the 3d floor, and place L by itself on the bottom floor:

O	J
M	N
Q	K
	P
L	

This diagram does not violate any initial condition. Hence O *can* live on the top floor, which eliminates choice (A). Turning to (B), place J on the first floor:

M	N	
		~Q
J		~Q

Next, place the condition **K/P** on the 2d and 3d floors, which forces L to the top floor (**L = alone**):

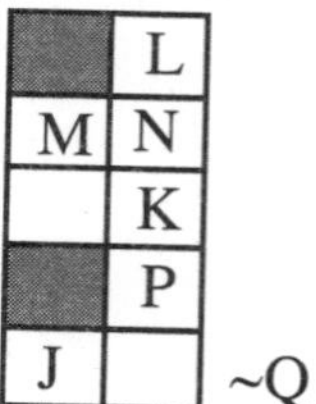

Finally, place O and Q on the 1st and 3d floors, respectively:

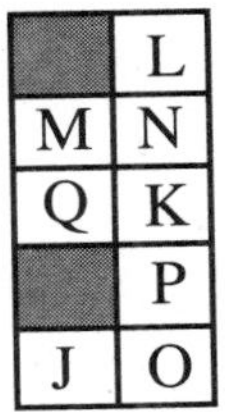

This diagram does not violate any initial condition. Hence J *can* live on the 1st floor, which eliminates choice (B). Turning to (C), place L on the 2d floor:

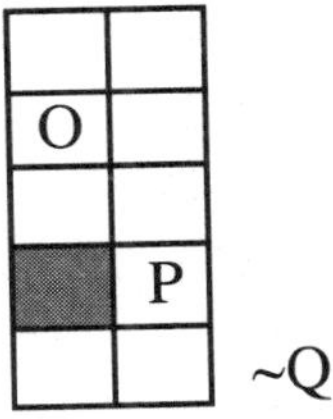

Clearly, this diagram does not allow for the placement of the condition **K/P**. Hence L cannot live on the second floor, and the answer is (C).

11. This question is long because it actually contains five distinct questions. During the test you should save such a question for last. However, if you were alert, you may have noticed that there is a shortcut to this particular question: Notice that answer-choice (B) is merely a rewording of Question 9 and its answer. In Question 9, we learned that if O lives on the second floor, then L cannot live on the fourth floor. This is exactly what choice (B) says. Hence the answer is (B). **Remember, it is not uncommon for the LSAT writers to repeat a question in a different form.**

12. Add the new conditions to the diagram:

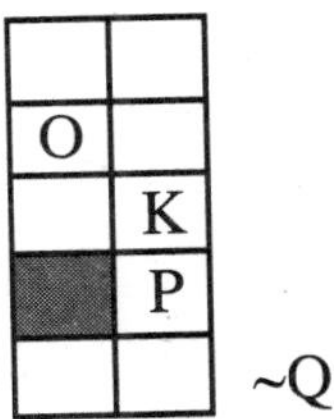

Next, add the condition **K/P**:

O |
--|--
  | K
  | P

~Q

Now the condition **M = N** can be placed on either the bottom or the top floor. We construct separate diagrams for each case:

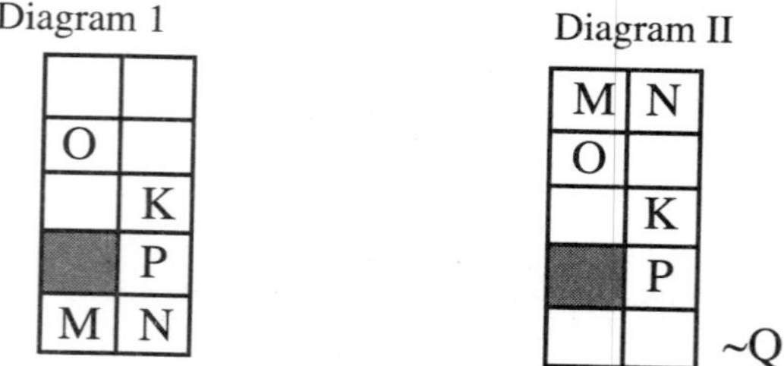

Next, since L must be alone, she must be on top floor in Diagram 1, and on the bottom floor in Diagram 2:

Diagram 1

■	L
O	
	K
■	P
M	N

Diagram II

M	N
O	
	K
■	P
■	L

Clearly in both diagrams, the condition **O ≠ Q** forces Q onto the 3d floor. Hence the answer is (C).

Questions 13–17

Although a diagram is not needed to solve this game efficiently, we will draw one to help keep track of the information. It will consist of three rectangles, representing the three countries:

14 days
6 cities
Visits at least 1 city in each country
Spends at least 2 days in each city

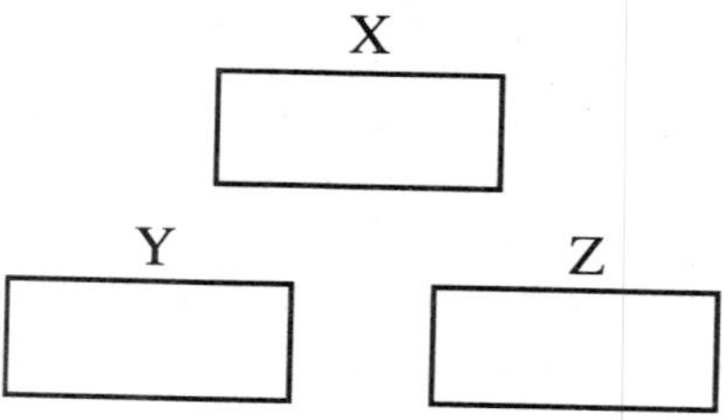

13. Since Hannah spends 8 days out of a total of 14 visiting the cities of country X, she must spend the remaining 6 days in the cities of countries Y and Z. Further, since she must spend at least 2 days in each city, she can visit at most a total of 3 cities in countries Y and Z. Now if she visits only 2 cities in country X, then she will have visited a total of only 5 cities, which contradicts the fact that she visits 6 cities. Hence the answer is (A).

14. To visit an equal number of cities in each country, she must visit 2 cities in each country:

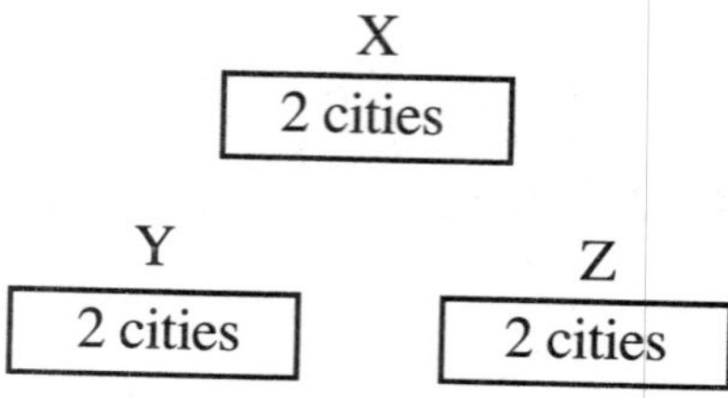

To spend the *greatest* number of days in country X, she must spend the *least* number of days possible in countries Y and Z. Since she must spend at least 2 days in each city, she must spend 4 days in country Y and 4 days in country Z:

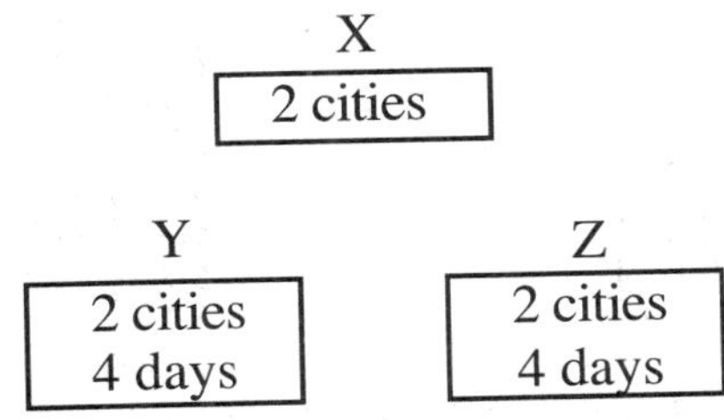

This puts her in country X for 14 – 8 = 6 days. Hence the answer is (D).

15. First, since Hannah spends a total of 10 days visiting cities in countries Y and Z, we know she must spend 4 days in country X (14 – 10 = 4) and can visit a maximum of two cities. Additionally, since she spends 3 days in country Y and must spend at least 2 days in each city, we know that she visits only one city in country Y.

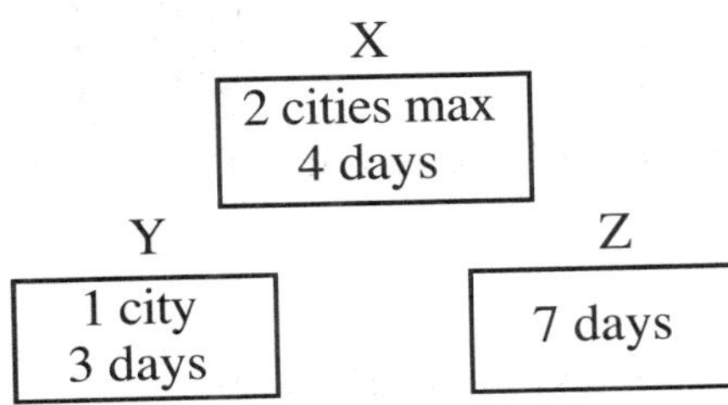

So if she visits 2 cities in country Z, she will have visited at most 5 cities (1 + 2 + 2 = 5). But this contradicts the fact that she visits a total of 6 cities. Hence, the answer is (D).

16. To maximize her time in Nomo, Hannah must spend a minimum of two days in each of the other 5 cities she visits, for a total of 10 days outside Nomo. Hence, the most time she can spend in Nomo is four days. This eliminates (C). Now, the other 5 cities could all be in countries Y and Z, which eliminates (E). On the other hand, up to 3 cities could be in country X (and the remaining cities in countries Y and Z), which eliminates (A). If it happens that three of the five cities besides Nomo are located in country Z, Hannah will spend more than four days in that country, eliminating choice (D). This leaves choice (B) as the answer.

Let's check that Hannah can indeed visit four cities in country Y: She visits Nomo in country X for four days. Then if she visits 4 cities in country Y for eight days and 1 city in country Z for two days, she fulfills all the conditions for her trip. So indeed statement (B) must be true.

Note the unusual and subtle wording of this question: it asks which one of 5 *possibilities* must be true. To say that a *possibility* must be true is to claim that under some circumstances (but not necessarily all) the object of that possibility can be true. For example, to say "it must be true that John can run a four minute mile" is to say that "John ran this particular mile in four minutes can be true." The key point is that the statement may be true but doesn't have to be. The possibility must exist, but it need not be realized in every instance. So, in choice (B), the statement "Hannah can visit four cities in Y" must be true because there is a valid scenario in which she does visit four such cities—even though there are other scenarios as well.

17. To spend the greatest number of days in the cities of country Y, Hannah must visit only one city in country X and for only 2 days. So she visits three cities in country Y. Now since she visits a total of six cities, she must visit two cities in country Z for a total of at least 4 days. Hence she spends a total of 6 days (2 + 4) outside country Y. Thus she can spend at most 8 days (14 – 6) in the cities of country Y. The answer is (C).

Questions 18–24

This game is difficult because it contains reams of information and the conditions are rather subtle. The game requires you to order, group, and assign elements, though it is mainly an assignment game. You are asked to assign characteristics (male, female; labrador, greyhound) to the elements (dogs).

The condition "*Dogs P and R place ahead of dog S, and dog S places ahead of dogs Q and T*" can be symbolized as [P/R] → S → [Q/T]. This diagram will form the core of the schematic. Although symbolizing the remaining conditions will clutter up the schematic, we will do so for consistency and for easy reference. During the test, it would probably be best to work just with the above diagram and make a mental note of the other conditions. Symbolizing the other conditions gives the following schematic:

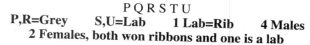

PQRSTU

P,R=Grey S,U=Lab 1 Lab=Rib 4 Males

2 Females, both won ribbons and one is a lab

[P/R] → S → [Q/T]

A few readily derived properties should be noted before turning to the questions. First, from the condition [P/R] → S → [Q/T] and the fact that four ribbons were awarded, we can conclude that P, R, and S all received ribbons. We note this in the schematic with a balloon around P, R, and S:

PQRSTU

P,R=Grey S,U=Lab 1 Lab=Rib 4 Males

2 Females, both won ribbons and one is a lab

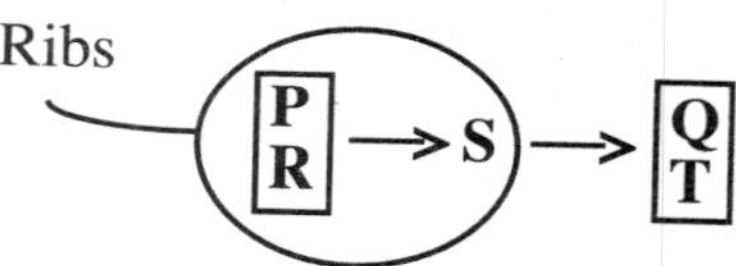

Now since S won a ribbon and only one labrador won a ribbon, we can conclude that U did not win a ribbon and therefore must have placed either fifth or sixth. This also implies that either Q or T (but not both) won a ribbon. (Why?)

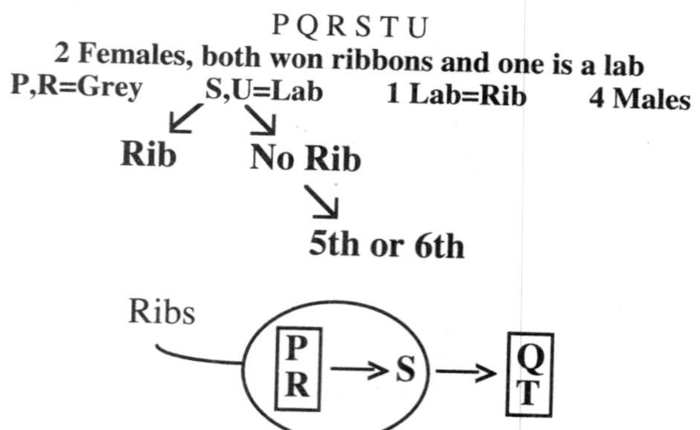

Although this diagram took a bit of work to construct, it will greatly simplify the following problems.

18. Since U finished either 5th or 6th, we see from the condition Ribs (P R —> S) —> Q T that Q or T (but not both) placed fourth. Now suppose Q placed fourth. Then since S is the only labrador to win a ribbon, Q must be a greyhound. Now if we assume that T placed fourth, the same analysis shows that it must be a greyhound. Hence both Q and T can be greyhounds and of course P and R are greyhounds (we were given that). The answer is (E).

19. Earlier, we derived that S is the only labrador awarded a ribbon. Now from the condition Ribs (P R —> S) —> Q T, we see that S did not place second. Hence no labrador placed second. The answer is (B). (Note the fact that the labrador is female was not used.)

20. Since both females received ribbons and U did not, U must be male. The answer is (E).

21. We'll use elimination. From the condition Ribs (P R —> S) —> Q T, we see that both P and R placed ahead of T. Hence both choices (B) and (D) are necessarily true—eliminate. Next, since U placed either 5th or 6th, both R and S placed ahead of U. Hence both choices (C) and (E) are necessarily true—eliminate. Therefore, by process of elimination, the answer is (A).

22. Again, we use elimination. First, we show that S is female: S is a labrador and S wins a ribbon. Only one labrador wins a ribbon, and we are given that a female labrador wins a ribbon. Therefore, S is female. Now if Q is female, then all other dogs <u>must</u> be male. (Remember: 4 males and 2 females) This eliminates both (A) and (B).

Next, since Q is female, she won a ribbon. Now from the condition Ribs (P R —> S) —> Q T, we see that she placed 4th. This eliminates (C).

Finally, because we know Q wins a ribbon and only one lab, S, wins a ribbon, Q must be a greyhound. This eliminates (D). Thus, by process of elimination, the answer is (E).

23. Since dog T placed fourth, the condition Ribs (P R —> S) —> Q T becomes

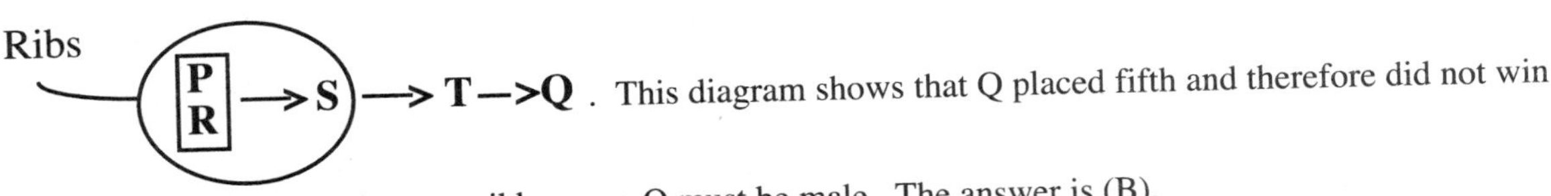

This diagram shows that Q placed fifth and therefore did not win a ribbon. But both females won ribbons, so Q must be male. The answer is (B).

24. This question is a freebie. Question 23 has T in fourth place and therefore winning a ribbon. Hence the answer is (D).

Part Two

ARGUMENTS

ARGUMENTS

- **INTRODUCTION**
- **OBFUSCATION**
  - True but Irrelevant
  - Same Language
  - Overstatement/Understatement
  - False Claim
- **LOGIC I**
  - Conclusions
  - Premises
    1. Suppressed Premises
    2. Counter-Premises
- **LOGIC II (Diagramming)**
  - If..., then...
  - Affirming the Conclusion Fallacy
  - Denying the Premise Fallacy
  - Transitive Property
  - DeMorgan's Laws
  - A unless B
  - Game-like Arguments
- **INDUCTIVE REASONING**
  - Generalization
  - Analogy
  - Causal Reasoning
  - All Things Being Equal
  - Percentage vs. Absolute Number
- **COMMON FALLACIES**
  1. Contradiction
  2. Equivocation
  3. Circular Reasoning
  4. Shifting the Burden of Proof
  5. Unwarranted Assumptions
  6. True but Irrelevant
  7. Appeal to Authority
  8. Personal Attack
- **LSAT SECTIONS**
  - Arguments I
  - Arguments II

Introduction

The arguments (logical reasoning) form the only part of the test that is similar to what a lawyer does. After all, a lawyer argues his client's case before the court or criticizes the argument of his opponent. Nevertheless, you will not be asked to analyze any legal arguments on the LSAT. The arguments come from disparate sources—including sociology, philosophy, science, and even popular culture. The richest source, however, is the Op/Ed page of newspapers.

An argument, as used on the LSAT, is a presentation of facts and opinions in order to support a position. In common jargon, an argument means a heated debate between two people. While the LSAT will offer a few of these arguments, most will be formal presentations of positions.

There are two argument sections; together they comprise one-half of the test. Each section is 35 minutes long and contains roughly 24 questions. This section is not as highly "timed" as the games, so it is reasonable to set as your goal the completion of the entire section. Unlike with games, determining the level of difficulty of an argument is itself difficult, so just start with the first question and then work through the section.

Many arguments will be fallacious. And many correct answers will be false! This often causes students much consternation; they feel that the correct answer should be *true*. But the arguments are intended to test your ability to think logically. Now logic is the study of the relationships between statements, not of the truth of those statements. Being overly concerned with finding the truth can be ruinous to your LSAT score.

Many books recommend reading the question before reading the argument. This method, however, does not work for me; I find it distracting and exhausting. Remember the test is highly "timed", and it is three and one-half hours long. Reading the questions twice can use up precious time and tax your concentration. It seems as though many books recommend this method because it gives the readers a feeling that they are getting the "scoop" on how to beat the test. Nevertheless, you may want to experiment—it may work for *you*.

We will analyze the arguments from four different perspectives. First, we will study how the answer-choices are constructed to obscure the correct answer. The LSAT writers rely heavily on obfuscation in this section. Next, we will study the structure of an argument—the premises, conclusions, counter-premises, etc. Although the questions are designed so that they can be answered without reference to formal logic, some knowledge of the foundations of logic will give you a definite advantage. Then, we will study how to diagram certain arguments. Many of these arguments look like mini-games, and solving them requires techniques similar to those used to solve the games. Finally, we will classify the major types of reasoning used in arguments and their associated fallacies.

Obfuscation

Unlike the games, arguments are inherently easy. In most arguments, the writer is trying to convince you of the validity of her position, so she has a vested interest in presenting the point as clearly as possible. Of course, the point may be complex or subtle or both. Nevertheless, she wants to express it clearly and simply. To obscure this underlying simplicity, the writers of the LSAT cannot change the wording of the statement much because that would leave it vague and poorly written. Their only option, therefore, is to camouflage the answer-choices.

Creating a good but incorrect answer-choice is much harder than developing the correct answer. For this reason, usually only one attractive wrong answer-choice is presented. This is called the "2 out of 5" rule. That is, only two of the five answer-choices will have any real merit. Hence, even if you don't fully understand an argument, you probably can still eliminate the three fluff choices, thereby greatly increasing your odds of answering the question correctly.

Every wrong answer fails to satisfy the conditions of either the argument or the question. Try as the writers of the LSAT may to obscure this fact, it is generally easy to spot the deficiency. Better yet, once you become familiar with the four obfuscating tactics used with the arguments, you can turn them to your advantage: they will flag the wrong answer-choices.

In the arguments section, the four obfuscating tactics used to make wrong answers appear correct are

Making a statement that is true, but irrelevant.

This tactic attracts the test-taker because one expects the answer to be true.* This is the most common obfuscating ploy.

Repeating the same language used in the statement.

This tactic attracts the test-taker because it relates directly to the argument and therefore "sounds" right.

Overstating or understating the point made in the argument.

This tactic attracts the test-taker because it is in part correct. The second-best answer-choice is often created by using this ploy.

Falsely claiming something not supported by the argument.

This tactic attracts the test-taker because it is often couched in authoritative language.

Clearly there is much overlap in these categories. Furthermore, the writers of the LSAT are not loath to use these tactics in various combinations. It is not necessary, however, that you learn all the combinations that can be used; your intuition that you are being manipulated will be sufficient. Also, don't get carried away with identifying the obfuscating tactics used in a particular problem. You need only to develop some awareness of them so that you don't waste time on the fluff answer-choices. Knowledge of the obfuscating tactics directs you to the 2-out-of-5 choices that have any real merit.

---

* Remember, a correct answer on the LSAT need not be true; it must merely be supported by the argument.

Notice how these tactics are combined to obscure the answers in the following arguments—both taken from recent LSATs.

Example 1:

A linguist recently argued that all human languages must have a common origin because some concepts are universal; that is, they appear in all languages. For example, all languages are capable of describing lightness and darkness.

Which one of the following, if true, would most seriously weaken the argument?

(A) The Bernese language does not contain basic nouns like *automobile* and *airplane*.
(B) No one linguist could possibly speak all known languages.
(C) All speakers regardless of their languages are confronted with similar stimuli like lightness and darkness.
(D) The similarity between human language and dolphin language has not been attributed to a common origin.
(E) Some languages include concepts of which speakers of other languages are not even aware.

Choice (A) uses a false claim ploy. We have no way of knowing whether the Bernese language contains words for automobile or airplane (it probably does not); regardless, automobiles and airplanes are not universal terms.

Choice (B) is true but irrelevant, not to mention silly.

Choice (D) is irrelevant [unlike with choice (B), we have no way of knowing whether it is true or false]. Notice how this answer-choice is baited with terms, *common origin* and *human language,* that use the same language as in the argument.

Choice (E) overstates the claim. The author says only that some, not all, concepts are universal. This is the only incorrect choice with any merit.

Finally, choice (C) is the correct answer because if all people are subject to similar stimuli, then one would expect that they would all create words for those stimuli.

Example 2:

The free press is one of the fundamental parts of a democratic society, since it acts both to disseminate information and to express dissent. If a democracy is to remain viable, its press must remain free.

Which one of the following conclusions can most logically be drawn from the passage above?

(A) If a society has a free press, it is a democracy.
(B) Only a free press acts to disseminate information and to express dissent.
(C) A democratic society can place no restrictions on the expression of dissent.
(D) If a society does not have a free press, it does not have a viable democracy.
(E) A democracy that is not viable does not have a free press.

This problem is hard because the second-best answer-choice is nearly as good as the answer. Choice (A) overstates the argument. The author implies merely that a free press is necessary for democracy, not sufficient. Choice (B) uses the same language used in the argument to overstate the second clause. Choice (C) is second-best; it slightly overstates the argument. It is conceivable that the author considers a press with certain restrictions to still be free; for example, restrictions against slander and libel. Choice (D) is the answer since it necessarily follows from the argument. You may have noticed that it is the contrapositive of the conclusion found at the end of the argument. (We will discuss the use of formal logic to solve arguments later.) Finally, choice (E) makes a false claim. A society may have a free press yet fail to be a democracy. For example, historically the U.S. has had a free press. Yet many people would claim that it did not become a true democracy until the right to vote was granted to women and blacks. Notice that choice (E) is merely a rewording of choice (A).

Points to Remember

1. "2 out of 5" rule: Only two of the five answer-choices will have any real merit.

2. The four obfuscating tactics are

    1. Making a statement that is true but irrelevant.
    2. Repeating the same language used in the statement.
    3. Overstating or understating the point made in the argument.
    4. Falsely claiming something not supported by the argument.

Logic I

Although in theory the questions on the LSAT are designed to be answered without any reference to formal logic, the test is essentially a logic test. Some knowledge of the fundamentals of logic, therefore, will give you a definite advantage. Armed with this knowledge, you should quickly notice that the arguments are fundamentally easy and that most of them fall into a few basic categories. In this section, we will study the logical structure of arguments. In Logic II, we will symbolize and diagram arguments in much the same way as we did with games.

Conclusions

Most argument questions hinge, either directly or indirectly, on determining the conclusion of the argument. The conclusion is the main idea of the argument. It is what the writer tries to persuade the reader to believe. Most often the conclusion comes at the end of the argument. The writer organizes the facts and his opinions so that they build up to the conclusion. Sometimes, however, the conclusion will come at the beginning of an argument; rarely does it come in the middle; and occasionally, for rhetorical effect, the conclusion is not even stated.

> **Example:**
> The police are the armed guardians of the social order. The blacks are the chief domestic victims of the American social order. A conflict of interest exists, therefore, between the blacks and the police.—Eldridge Cleaver, *Soul on Ice*

Here the first two sentences anticipate or set up the conclusion. By changing the grammar slightly, the conclusion can be placed at the beginning of the argument and still sound natural:

> A conflict of interest exists between the blacks and the police because the police are the armed guardians of the social order and the blacks are the chief domestic victims of the American social order.

The conclusion can also be forced into the middle:

> The police are the armed guardians of the social order. So a conflict of interest exists between the blacks and the police because the blacks are the chief domestic victims of the American social order.

It is generally awkward, as in the previous paragraph, to place the conclusion in the middle of the argument because then it cannot be fully anticipated by what comes before nor fully explained by what comes after. On the rare occasion when a conclusion comes in the middle of an argument, most often either the material that comes after it or the material that comes before it is not essential.

In summary:
To find the conclusion, check the last sentence of the argument. If that is not the conclusion, check the first sentence. Rarely does the conclusion come in the middle of an argument.

When determining the meaning of a conclusion, be careful not to read any more into it than what the author states. In the section on obfuscation, we talked about incorrect answer-choices that overstate or understate a claim. Although arguments are not worded as precisely as games, you still need to read them with more care than you would use in your everyday reading.

For example, many people will interpret the sentence "Every Republican is not a conservative" to mean that some Republicans are not conservative.* The writers of the LSAT do not use grammar (logic) that loosely. On the LSAT, the above sentence would mean what it literally states—that no Republican is a conservative.

As with games, read the words and sentences of an argument precisely, and use their literal **meaning.**

To illustrate further, consider the meaning of *some* in the sentence "Some of Mary's friends went to the party." It would be unwarranted, based on this statement, to assume that some of Mary's friends did not go to the party. Although it may seem deceiving to say that *some* of Mary's friends went to the party when in fact *all* of them did, it is nonetheless technically consistent with the meaning of *some*.

***Some* means "at least one and perhaps all."**

As mentioned before, the conclusion usually comes at the end of an argument, sometimes at the beginning, and rarely in the middle. Writers use certain words to indicate that the conclusion is about to be stated. Following is a list of the most common conclusion indicators:

CONCLUSION INDICATORS

hence	**therefore**
so	**accordingly**
thus	**consequently**
follows that	**shows that**
conclude that	**implies**
as a result	**means that**

These conclusion flags are very helpful, but you must use them cautiously because many of these words have other functions.

Example:

All devout Muslims abstain from alcohol. Steve is a devout Muslim. Thus, he abstains from alcohol.

In this example, "thus" anticipates the conclusion that necessarily follows from the first two sentences. Notice the different function of *thus* in the following argument.

Example:

The problem is simple when the solution is thus stated.

In this example, *thus* means "in that manner."

Most often the conclusion of an argument is put in the form of a statement (as with every example we have considered so far). Sometimes, however, the conclusion is given as a command or obligation.

Example:

All things considered, you ought to vote.

Here, the author implies that you are obliged to vote.

Example:

Son, unless you go to college, you will not make a success of yourself. No Carnegie has ever been a failure. So you will go to college.

Here the conclusion is given as an imperative command.

---

* To give the sentence that meaning, reword it as "Not every Republican is a conservative".

The conclusion can even be put in the form of a question. This rhetorical technique is quite effective in convincing people that a certain position is correct. We are more likely to believe something if we feel that we concluded it on our own, or at least if we feel that we were not told to believe it. A conclusion put in question form can have this result.

Example:

The Nanuuts believe that they should not take from Nature anything She cannot replenish during their lifetime. This assures that future generations can enjoy the same riches of Nature that they have. At the current rate of destruction, the rain forests will disappear during our lifetime. Do we have an obligation to future generations to prevent this result?

Here the author trusts that the power of her argument will persuade the reader to answer the question affirmatively.

Taking this rhetorical technique one step further, the writer may build up to the conclusion but leave it unstated. This allows the reader to make up his own mind. If the build-up is done skillfully, the reader will be more likely to agree with the author, without feeling manipulated.

Example:

He who is without sin should cast the first stone. There is no one here who does not have a skeleton in his closet.

The unstated but obvious conclusion here is that none of the people has the right to cast the first stone.

When determining the conclusion's scope be careful not to read any more or less into it than the author states. LSAT writers often create wrong answer-choices by slightly overstating or understating the author's claim. Certain words limit the scope of a statement. These words are called quantifiers—pay close attention to them. Following is a list of the most important quantifiers:

Quantifiers

all	**except**	**likely**
some	**most**	**many**
only	**could**	**no**
never	**always**	**everywhere**
probably	**must**	**alone**

Example:

Whether the world is Euclidean or non-Euclidean is still an open question. However, if a star's position is predicted based on non-Euclidean geometry, then when a telescope is pointed to where the star should be it will be there. Whereas, if the star's position is predicted based on Euclidean geometry, then when a telescope is pointed to where the star should be it won't be there. This strongly indicates that the world is non-Euclidean.

Which one of the following best expresses the main idea of the passage?

(A) The world may or may not be Euclidean.
(B) The world is probably non-Euclidean.
(C) The world is non-Euclidean.
(D) The world is Euclidean.
(E) The world is neither Euclidean nor non-Euclidean.

Choice (A) understates the main idea. Although the opening to the passage states that we don't know whether the world is non-Euclidean, the author goes on to give evidence that it is non-Euclidean.

Choice (C) overstates the main idea. The author doesn't say that the world is non-Euclidean, just that evidence strongly indicates that it is.

In choice (B), the word "probably" properly limits the scope of the main idea, namely, that the world is probably non-Euclidean, but we can't yet state so definitively. The answer is (B).

Example:

An oligarchy is a government run by a small, conservative faction. Often, oligarchies consist of families such as the Royal Family in Saudi Arabia. Like the Royal Family in Saudi Arabia, no one person in an oligarchy has the power to make a particular investment. Therefore, risky investments are never made by oligarchies.

The conclusion of the argument is valid if which one of the following is assumed?

(A) Not all oligarchies are run by families.
(B) The Royal Family in Saudi Arabia has never made a risky investment.
(C) Conservative governments rarely make risky investments.
(D) Only liberal governments make risky investments.
(E) Only individuals make risky investments.

If risky investments are never made by oligarchies because no one person has the power to make a particular investment, then it must be the case that only individuals make risky investments. The answer is (E).

Warm-Up Drill I

Directions: Find, then underline, the conclusion to each of the following arguments. If an argument does not state the conclusion, complete it with the most natural conclusion. Answers and solutions begin on page 231.

1. When a man is tired of London, he is tired of life; for there is in London all that life can afford.—Samuel Johnson

2. Some psychiatrists claim that watching violent movies dissipates aggression. Does watching pornography dissipate one's libido?

3. By the age of 10 months, purebred golden retrievers display certain instinctive behaviors. Because this 11-month-old golden retriever does not display these instinctive behaviors, it is not a purebred.

4. Most people would agree that it is immoral to lie. But if a kidnapper accosts you on the street and asks which way his escaped victim went, would it be immoral to point in the opposite direction?

5. Beware, for I am fearless, and therefore, powerful.—Mary Shelley, *Frankenstein*

6. The continuous stream of violent death depicted on television has so jaded society that murder is no longer shocking. It's hardly surprising, then, that violent crime so permeates modern society.

7. Where all other circumstances are equal, wages are generally higher in new than in old trades. When a projector attempts to establish a new manufacture, he must at first entice his workmen from other employments by higher wages than they can either earn in their old trades, or than the nature of his work would otherwise require, and a considerable time must pass away before he can venture to reduce them to the common level.—Adam Smith, *The Wealth of Nations*

8. Existentialists believe that our identity is continually evolving, that we are born into this world without an identity and do not begin to develop one until the act of retrospection. So one's identity is always trailing oneself like the wake of a boat. As one goes through life, the wake becomes wider and wider defining him more and more precisely.

9. In time I began to recognize that all of these smaller complaints about rigidity, emotional suffocation, the tortured logic of the law were part of a more fundamental phenomenon in the law itself. Law is at war with ambiguity, with uncertainty. In the courtroom, the adversary system—plaintiff against defendant—guarantees that someone will always win, someone loses. No matter if justice is evenly with each side, no matter if the issues are indefinite and obscure, the rule of law will be declared.—Scott Turow, *One L*

10. Either God controls all of man's behavior or God does not control any of man's behavior. God must not control man's behavior since there is so much evil in the world.

11. The more deeply I understand the central role of caring in my own life, the more I realize it to be central to the human condition.—Milton Mayeroff, *On Caring*

Premises

Once you've found the conclusion, most often everything else in the argument will be either premises or "noise." The premises provide evidence for the conclusion; they form the foundation or infrastructure upon which the conclusion depends. To determine whether a statement is a premise, ask yourself whether it supports the conclusion. If so, it's a premise. Earlier we saw that writers use certain words to flag conclusions; likewise writers use certain words to flag premises. Following is a partial list of the most common premise indicators:

PREMISE INDICATORS

because
since
if
as
suppose
assume
for
is evidence that
in that
owing to
inasmuch as
may be derived from

Premise indicators are very helpful. As with conclusion indicators, though, you must use them cautiously because they have other functions. For example, *since* can indicate a premise, or it can merely indicate time.

Example:

Since the incumbent's views are out of step with public opinion, he probably will not be reelected.

Here "since" is used to flag the premise that the incumbent's positions are unpopular. Contrast this use of "since" with the following example.

Example:

Since the incumbent was elected to office, he has spent less and less time with his family.

In this case, "since" merely expresses a passage of time. The statement as a whole expresses an observation, rather than an argument.

SUPPRESSED PREMISES

Most arguments depend on one or more unstated premises. Sometimes this indicates a weakness in the argument, an oversight by the writer. More often, however, certain premises are left tacit because they are too numerous, or the writer assumes that his audience is aware of the assumptions, or he wants the audience to fill in the premise themselves and therefore be more likely to believe the conclusion.

Example:

Conclusion: I knew he did it.
Premise: Only a guilty person would accept immunity from prosecution.

The suppressed premise is that he did, in fact, accept immunity. The speaker assumes that his audience is aware of this fact or at least is willing to believe it, so to state it would be redundant and ponderous. If the unstated premise were false (that is, he did not accept immunity), the argument would not technically be a lie; but it would be very deceptive. The unscrupulous writer may use this ploy if he thinks that he can get away with it. That is, his argument has the intended effect and the false premise, though implicit, is hard to find or is ambiguous. Politicians are not at all above using this tactic.

Example:

Politician: A hawk should not be elected President because this country has seen too many wars.

The argument has two tacit premises—one obvious, the other subtle. Clearly, the politician has labeled his opponent a hawk, and he hopes the audience will accept that label. Furthermore, although he does not state it explicitly, the argument rests on the assumption that a hawk is likely to start a war. He hopes the audience will fill in that premise, thereby tainting his opponent as a warmonger.

A common question on the LSAT asks you to find the suppressed premise of an argument. Finding the suppressed premise, or assumption, of an argument can be difficult. However, on the LSAT you have an advantage—the suppressed premise is listed as one of the five answer-choices. To test whether an answer-choice is a suppressed premise, ask yourself whether it would make the argument more plausible. If so, then it is very likely a suppressed premise.

Example:

American attitudes tend to be rather insular, but there is much we can learn from other countries. In Japan, for example, workers set aside some time each day to exercise, and many corporations provide elaborate exercise facilities for their employees. Few American corporations have such exercise programs. Studies have shown that the Japanese worker is more productive than the American worker. Thus it must be concluded that the productivity of American workers will lag behind their Japanese counterparts, until mandatory exercise programs are introduced.

The conclusion of the argument is valid if which one of the following is assumed?

(A) Even if exercise programs do not increase productivity, they will improve the American worker's health.
(B) The productivity of all workers can be increased by exercise.
(C) Exercise is an essential factor in the Japanese worker's superior productivity.
(D) American workers can adapt to the longer Japanese work week.
(E) American corporations don't have the funds to build elaborate exercise facilities.

The unstated essence of the argument is that exercise is an integral part of productivity and that Japanese workers are more productive than American workers because they exercise more. The answer is (C).

Example: (This example is taken from a recent LSAT.)

J. J. Thomson, the discoverer of the electron and a recipient of the Nobel Prize in physics, trained many physicists, among them seven Nobel Prize winners, 32 fellows of the Royal Society of London, and 83 professors of physics. This shows that the skills needed for creative research can be taught and learned.

Which one of the following is an assumption on which the argument depends?

(A) J. J. Thomson was an internationally known physicist, and scientists came from all over the world to work with him.
(B) All the scientists trained by J. J. Thomson were renowned for their creative scientific research.
(C) At least one of the eminent scientists trained by J. J. Thomson was not a creative researcher before coming to study with him.
(D) Creative research in physics requires research habits not necessary for creative research in other fields.
(E) Scientists who go on to be the most successful researchers often receive their scientific education in classes taught by renowned research scientists.

If the physicists trained by J. J. Thomson were creative researchers before studying under him, then clearly the argument would be specious. On the other hand, if none of the physicists were creative researchers before studying under Thomson, then the argument would be strong. However, the argument does not require this strong of a statement in order to be valid. All it needs is one person whose research skills profited from the tutelage of Thomson. The answer is (C).

Many students have problems with this type of question. They read through the answer-choices and find no significant statements. They may pause at (C) but reject it—thinking that the argument would be deceptive if only one person out of 122 profited from the tutelage of Thomson. However, the missing premise doesn't have to make the argument good, just valid.

Example: (Suppressed false premise.)

The petrochemical industry claims that chemical waste dumps pose no threat to people living near them. If this is true, then why do they locate the plants in sparsely populated regions? By not locating the chemical dumps in densely populated areas the petrochemical industry tacitly admits that these chemicals are potentially dangerous to the people living nearby.

Which of the following, if true, would most weaken the author's argument?

(A) Funding through the environmental Super Fund to clean up poorly run waste dumps is reserved for rural areas only.
(B) Until chemical dumps are proven 100% safe, it would be imprudent to locate them were they could potentially do the most harm.
(C) Locating the dumps in sparsely populated areas is less expensive and involves less government red tape.
(D) The potential for chemicals to leach into the water table has in the past been underestimated.
(E) People in cities are more likely to sue the industry if their health is harmed by the dumps.

The suppressed *false* premise of the argument is that, all things being equal, there is no reason to prefer locating the sites in sparsely populated areas. To weaken the argument, we need to show it is not true that all things are equal. In other words, there are advantages other than safety in locating the sites in sparsely populated areas. Choice (C) gives two possible advantages—cost and ease. Hence (C) is the answer.

The following example has a hidden true premise.

Example: (Suppressed true premise.)

The news media is often accused of being willing to do anything for ratings. However, recent action by a television network indicates that the news media is sometimes guided by moral principle. This network had discovered through polling voters on the east coast that the Republican candidate for President had garnered enough votes to ensure victory before the polls closed on the west coast. However, the network withheld this information until the polls on the west coast closed so that the information would not affect the outcome of key congressional races.

Which one of the following most strengthens the argument?

(A) The network had endorsed the Republican candidate for President.
(B) The network expected its ratings to increase if it predicted the winner of the presidential race, and to decrease if did not predict the winner.
(C) A rival network did predict a winner of the presidential race before the polls on the west coast closed.
(D) The network believed that it would receive higher ratings by not predicting the winner of the presidential race.
(E) The network feared that predicting the winner of the presidential race could so anger Congress that it might enact legislation preventing all future polling outside of voting centers.

The suppressed premise in this argument is that the network hurt itself by not predicting the winner of the presidential race, or at least did not help itself. To strengthen the argument, we need to show that this assumption is true. Choice (B) implies that this is the case by stating that the network expected to lose ratings if it did not predict a winner. Hence the answer is (B).

Warm-Up Drill II

Directions: For each of the following arguments, identify the suppressed premise and state whether it is a reasonable assumption for the author to make. Answers and solutions are on page 232.

1. Sacramento is the capital of California; thus it is located northeast of San Francisco.
2. I read it in a book, so it must be true.
3. Any government action that intrudes on the right of privacy is unconstitutional. Therefore, requiring government employees to take a drug test is unconstitutional.
4. After studying assiduously for three months, Sean retook the SAT and increased his score by more than four hundred points. Therefore, the Educational Testing Service canceled his score.
5. When explorers arrived in the Americas in the 1500's A.D., they observed the natives hunting with bronze tipped arrows. Archaeological evidence shows that bronze was not smelted in the Americas until the 1200's A.D. Therefore, native Americans must have begun hunting with arrows sometime between 1200 and 1500 A.D.
6. Fiction is truer than history, because it goes beyond the evidence.—E. M. Forster
7. In Knox's theory of military strategy, all decisions about troop deployment must be made by a committee of generals. If, however, his model of command were in effect during World War II, then daring and successful operations—such as Patton's unilateral decision to land paratroopers behind enemy lines during the Battle of the Bulge—would not have been ordered.
8. In recent years many talented and dedicated teachers have left the public school system for the private sector because the public school system's salary scale is not sufficient for a family to maintain a quality standard of living. To lure these dedicated teachers back to the public schools, we must immediately raise the pay scale to a level comparable to that of the private sector, and thereby save our schools.

COUNTER-PREMISES

When presenting a position, you obviously don't want to argue against yourself. However, it is often effective to concede certain minor points that weaken your argument. This shows that you are open-minded and that your ideas are well considered. It also disarms potential arguments against your position. For instance, in arguing for a strong, aggressive police department, you may concede that in the past the police have at times acted too aggressively. Of course, you will then need to state more convincing reasons to support your position.

Example:

I submit that the strikers should accept the management's offer. Admittedly, it is less than what was demanded. But it does resolve the main grievance—inadequate health care. Furthermore, an independent study shows that a wage increase greater than 5% would leave the company unable to compete against Japan and Germany, forcing it into bankruptcy.

The conclusion, "the strikers should accept the management's offer," is stated in the first sentence. Then "Admittedly" introduces a concession; namely, that the offer was less than what was demanded. This weakens the speaker's case, but it addresses a potential criticism of his position before it can be made. The last two sentences of the argument present more compelling reasons to accept the offer and form the gist of the argument.

Following are some of the most common counter-premise indicators:

COUNTER-PREMISE INDICATORS

but	**despite**
admittedly	**except**
even though	**nonetheless**
nevertheless	**although**
however	**in spite of the fact**

As you may have anticipated, the LSAT writers sometimes use counter-premises to bait wrong answer-choices. Answer-choices that refer to counter-premises are very tempting because they refer directly to the passage and they are *in part* true. But you must ask yourself "Is this the main point that the author is trying to make?" It may merely be a minor concession.

In the following argument, taken from a recent LSAT, notice how the counter-premise is used as bait.

Example:

Nature constantly adjusts the atmospheric carbon level. An increase in the level causes the atmosphere to hold more heat, which causes more water to evaporate from the oceans, which causes increased rain. Rain washes some carbon from the air into the oceans, where it eventually becomes part of the seabed. A decrease in atmospheric carbon causes the atmosphere to hold less heat, which causes decreased evaporation from the oceans, which causes less rain, and thus less carbon is washed into the oceans. Yet some environmentalists worry that burning fossil fuels may raise atmospheric carbon to a dangerous level. It is true that a sustained increase would threaten human life. But the environmentalists should relax—nature will continually adjust the carbon level.

Which one of the following, if true, would most weaken the argument in the passage?

(A) Plant life cannot survive without atmospheric carbon.
(B) It is not clear that breathing excess carbon in the atmosphere will have a negative effect on human life.
(C) Carbon is part of the chemical "blanket" that keeps the Earth warm enough to sustain human life.
(D) Breathing by animals releases almost 30 times as much carbon as does the burning of fossil fuels.
(E) The natural adjustment process, which occurs over millions of years, allows wide fluctuations in the carbon level in the short term.

The counter-premise in this argument is the sentence "It is true that a sustained increase [in atmospheric carbon] would threaten human life." By making this concession, the author shows that he is aware of the alternatives and the potential seriousness of situation; it also provides a hedge against potential criticism that the situation is too important to risk following his advice.

The question asks us to weaken the argument. As mentioned before, to weaken an argument typically you attack a premise (either expressed or suppressed) of the argument. Now someone who did not fully understand the author's main point might mistake the counter-premise for a premise. Look at answer-choice (B); it directly attacks the counter-premise by implying that it may not be true. The LSAT writers offer (B) as bait. They know that some people will fall for it because it attacks a statement in the argument, as should the answer. The best answer, however, will attack the main premise.

One possibility the author did not account for is that the natural adjustment process may require many years and that in the short run dangerous levels of carbon could accumulate. This directly attacks the main premise of the argument, "Nature *constantly* adjusts the atmospheric carbon level." Hence the answer is (E).

It is often clarifying to outline an argument's logical structure. An outline can make clear the argumentative strategy the author is using. The above argument has the following structure:

Main Premise
Explanation of Main Premise
Secondary Premise
Counter-Premise
Conclusion

The first sentence introduces the main premise that nature constantly adjusts the atmospheric carbon level. The next three sentences explain that premise. Then in the fifth sentence, the secondary premise is introduced that environmentalists are concerned that burning fossil fuels may increase atmospheric carbon to dangerous levels. Then the penultimate (next to last) sentence introduces the counter-premise that an increase in the carbon level would be a threat to human life. This measures the conclusion that environmentalists should relax because nature will adjust the carbon level.

The next example is also taken from a recent LSAT.

Example:

How do the airlines expect to prevent commercial plane crashes? Studies have shown that pilot error contributes to two-thirds of all such crashes. To address this problem, the airlines have upgraded their training programs by increasing the hours of classroom instruction and emphasizing communication skills in the cockpit. But it is unrealistic to expect such measures to compensate for pilots' lack of actual flying time. Therefore, the airlines should rethink their training approach to reducing commercial crashes.

Which one of the following is an assumption upon which the argument depends?

(A) Training programs can eliminate pilot errors.
(B) Commercial pilots routinely undergo additional training throughout their careers.
(C) The number of airline crashes will decrease if pilot training programs focus on increasing actual flying time.
(D) Lack of actual flying time is an important contributor to pilot error in commercial plane crashes.
(E) Communication skills are not important to pilot training programs.

The sentence "To address this problem . . . cockpit" is the counter-premise because it shows that the airlines are doing something about the problem. However, the author goes on to imply that it is not enough, that no training program can be a substitute for actual flying time. Notice that choice (A) baits the reader because it refers to the counter-premise. If the counter-premise stood alone, (A) would not be a bad answer (though it would still overstate the case). However, in the sentence, "But it is . . . time," the author states that training programs are not only insufficient but only marginally effective.

This argument is difficult because the second-best answer-choice is almost as good as the best one. Choices (B) and (E) can be quickly dismissed. Choice (C), though probably true, slightly overstates the author's claim. The author implied only that actual flying time is essential; he made no claim that it would actually decrease the number of crashes. Furthermore, he did not imply that airlines should focus on actual flying time, only that it plays an essential part in reducing the number of pilot errors. Hence, by process of elimination, the answer is (D).

Points to Remember

1. Most argument questions hinge on determining the conclusion of the argument.

2. To find the conclusion, check the final sentence of the argument. If the last sentence is not the conclusion, check the first sentence. Rarely does the conclusion come in the middle of the argument.

3. *Some* means "at least one and perhaps all."

4. Some of the most common conclusion flags are

hence	**therefore**	**conclude that**
so	**accordingly**	**as a result**
thus	**consequently**	**implies**
follows that	**shows that**	**means that**

5. Premises provide evidence for the conclusion; they form the foundation or infrastructure upon which the conclusion depends. To determine whether a statement is a premise, ask yourself whether it supports the conclusion. If so, it's a premise.

6. The following is a partial list of the most common premise indicators:

because	**suppose**	**in that**
since	**assume**	**owing to**
if	**for**	**inasmuch as**
as	**is evidence that**	**may be derived from**

7. To test whether an answer-choice is a suppressed premise, ask yourself whether it would make the argument more plausible. If so, then it is very likely a suppressed premise.

8. A common argument question asks you to either strengthen or weaken an argument. Typically, these questions pivot on suppressed premises: to strengthen an argument, show that a suppressed premise is true; to weaken an argument, show that a suppressed premise is false.

9. A counter-premise is a concession to a minor point that weakens your argument.

10. The following are some of the most common counter-premise indicators.

but	**however**	**although**
admittedly	**despite**	**regardless**
even though	**except**	**notwithstanding**
nevertheless	**nonetheless**	**in spite of the fact**

Exercise

Directions: The questions in this section are based on the reasoning contained in brief statements or passages. For some questions, more than one of the choices could conceivably answer the question. However, you are to choose the best answer; that is, the response that most accurately and completely answers the question. You should not make assumptions that are by common sense standards implausible, superfluous, or incompatible with the passage.

1. Two prestigious fine art schools are located in New England, Central and Northeast. Talented vocal students attend each school. At Central, voice students are required to take voice lessons twice each week and to practice their singing at least one hour each day. At Northeast, voice students are required to take voice lessons only once per week, and they are required to practice only three times each week. The voice students from both schools were recently tested on a variety of vocal techniques, including breath control. Voice students at Central were able to hold a single note for 60 seconds, which was 15 seconds longer than the Northeast voice students. Thus, one must conclude that Northeast voice students will improve their breath control only if they increase their voice lessons to twice per week and their practice to one hour each day.

   The paragraph assumes which one of the following?

   (A) All students would be able to hold a note for 60 seconds if they take frequent voice lessons and practice their singing at least one hour per day.
   (B) All students can have the same quality singing voices if they take voice lessons and practice one hour per day.
   (C) Students with better breath control appreciate music more.
   (D) Taking voice lessons twice per week and practicing one hour each day are essential factors in the ability of Central voice students to hold notes longer than the Northeast voice students.
   (E) If students practice singing regularly, they will prefer voice to other forms of musical expression.

2. Gasoline-powered boat engines manufactured in the a North American country prior to 1990 contribute significantly to the pollution found in the world's oceans. In 1990, however, the government imposed stricter pollution controls on gasoline engines manufactured for boats, and beginning in 1995, the government imposed a program of inspections for pre-1990 boat engines with increasingly rigorous pollution standards. As the older boat engines fail to pass inspection, boat owners are increasingly retiring their old engines in favor of newer, less-polluting boat engines. As a result, the amount of pollution these older boat engines emit into the world's oceans will steadily decrease over the next ten years.

   Which one of the following statements, if true, most seriously undermines the argument?

   (A) Water from the various oceans cannot be accurately divided among nations because ocean currents travel thousands of miles and cross numerous national boundary lines.
   (B) Even as they become older, boat engines manufactured after 1990 will never pollute as much as boat engines manufactured prior to 1990.
   (C) When boat owners retire their older boat engines in favor of newer ones, the older engines are frequently sent overseas to countries with less stringent pollution standards, where they are in high demand.
   (D) The government's pollution control standards for boat engines are increasingly stricter up until 1998; then they level off.
   (E) If demand for new fishing and pleasure boats increases significantly every year, then pollution of the world's oceans will continue to increase, regardless of the fact that older boat engines are being retired.

3. Plants that exhibit certain leaf diseases tend to measure extremely high in the amount of zinc in their leaf and stem tissue. Botanists have discovered that phosphorus of the type typically used in a phosphorus-high fertilizer reacts with the zinc in such a way as to prevent treated plants from exhibiting the leaf diseases. Thus, plants can be cured from these leaf diseases by the use of a fertilizer high in phosphorus.

   The passage's conclusion is based upon which one of the following premises?

   (A) Plants with certain leaf diseases contain the same high level of zinc in their leaf and stem tissue.
   (B) Zinc is the cause and not merely an effect of the leaf diseases.
   (C) Treating the plants with a fertilizer high in phosphorus will have no negative effect on the plants.
   (D) The amount of phosphorus-high fertilizer which should be used depends upon the size and location of the plants.
   (E) Normal plant tissue does not contain zinc.

4. A prestigious golf association hosts a special tournament every year over the Labor Day weekend. It accepts into the tournament only those golfers who pay the entry fee by June 1 and who have won a major tournament during the previous calendar year. Fred Smith, a successful professional golfer for many years, paid the entry fee by June 1 to be in the Labor Day tournament. The golf association accepted Smith to play in the tournament.

   Which one of the following conclusions flows logically from the paragraph?

   (A) Smith won a major golf tournament the previous calendar year.
   (B) Smith has played in the Labor Day tournament in previous years.
   (C) Smith is well know for his professional golfing career.
   (D) The golf association asked Smith to enter the tournament.
   (D) Television coverage of the Labor Day tournament will focus on Smith's participation.

5. Explorers of the northern regions in the early 1700s observed the natives playing an instrument similar to the mandolin. The instrument was strung with horse hair. Horses were not introduced into the New World until the 1500s. Thus, we can conclude that natives developed the instrument sometime between the introduction of horses to the New World and the time of the explorers in the early 1700s.

   Which one of the following assumptions is critical to the passage's conclusion?

   (A) Natives used the mandolin-like instrument in all their religious events.
   (B) Using horse hair in the mandolin-like instrument was one of the natives' earliest uses of horse hair.
   (C) This instrument was used by natives throughout North America.
   (D) Since it was first developed, the instrument was made with horse hair.
   (E) Explorers in the 1700s were the first to document natives' use of horse hair.

6. The math professor's goals for classroom honesty and accurate student assessment were founded upon his belief that the fear of punishment and corresponding loss of privileges would make students think twice or even three times before cheating on exams, thus virtually eliminating cheating in his classroom. In order for this atmosphere to prevail, the students had to believe that the consequences for cheating were severe and that the professor had the means to discover cheaters and enforce the punishment against them.

   If the statements contained in the preceding passage are true, which one of the following can be properly inferred?

   (A) A student would only be deterred from cheating if he knew he would be discovered and punished.
   (B) A student will not cheat on an exam if he feels he is well prepared for the exam.
   (C) A student who cheats on an exam believes that he will not be able to pass the exam without cheating.
   (D) If the professor wants to achieve his goals, he should make his students aware of his policy on cheating and the consequences that would befall those who cheat on his exams.
   (E) If the professor wants never to have an incident of cheating in his classroom, his policy on cheating must be stronger than any other professor's policy on cheating.

7. The survival of the publishing industry depends upon the existence of a public who will buy the printed word in the form of newspapers, books and magazines. Over the past several years, however, the advance of electronic media, particularly CD-ROMs, online computer services, and the Internet, has made information available to the public electronically without the need for printed materials. As the availability of electronic media increases and as it is more easily accessible, the public has less need for printed materials.

   Which one of the following statements flows logically from the passage?

   (A) Teachers and libraries must promote the importance of books and other written materials.
   (B) The publishing industry is threatened by the advance of the computer information age.
   (C) Every member of the public has a duty to become informed about the Internet.
   (D) Tabloids will most successfully compete with computers.
   (E) The publishing industry will survive if the educated members of the public continue to purchase written materials.

8. Pharmacists recently conducted a study with respect to the reasons their customers purchased eye drops to soothe eye dryness. Dry eyes were more frequently experienced by customers who wore contact lenses than by customers who did not wear contact lenses. The pharmacists concluded that wearing contact lenses, by itself, can cause contact wearers to have dry eyes.

   Which one of the following statements, if true, most seriously undermines the pharmacists' conclusion?

   (A) An inherited condition can cause both weak eyesight and dry eyes.
   (B) Physical exertion causes dry eyes in many people who wear contact lenses.
   (C) Most people who have dry eyes do not wear contact lenses.
   (D) Most people who wear contact lenses do not have dry eyes.
   (E) Both weak vision and dry eyes cause headaches.

9. One theory of school governance can be pictured as an upside-down triangle. Students, teachers and the faculty/parent committee make up the body of the triangle, but the triangle has no point, that is, it has no school principal. Schools are run by the faculty/parent committee, which makes all significant decisions concerning academic standards, curriculum, discipline, extra-curricular activities, etc. As a result, under this theory, innovative teaching methods and progressive academic programs cannot be implemented.

   The argument depends upon which one of the following assumptions?

   (A) Innovative teaching methods and progressive academic programs are usually implemented by individual private schools, not by public school systems.
   (B) Only principals will try new methods and programs.
   (C) A person acting by himself is more likely to direct that new methods be tried than if he is acting as part of a committee.
   (D) All school principals achieved their positions by taking academic risks.
   (E) All innovative teaching methods and progressive academic programs encompass some risk.

10. The Agricultural Board of a western European country determines when and under what conditions new food-producing plants and seeds can be sold to the public. As a result, the Agricultural Board plays an important part in improving agricultural production in western Europe. Individual farmers and farm research centers are involved in the time-consuming task of discovering and testing new varieties of fruits and vegetables. But the Agricultural Board is responsible for verifying the qualities of the new products and for approving their sale and distribution to the public. New plants and seeds are not available to improve agricultural production until after they have been approved by the Agricultural Board.

    The passage implies which one of the following statements?

    (A) The Agricultural Board requires that new varieties of fruits and vegetables be regulated.
    (B) Before new varieties of fruits and vegetables are made available to the public, they do not improve agricultural production.
    (C) Researchers who develop new varieties of fruits and vegetables are responsible for the long period of time before such products are released to the public, not the Agricultural Board.
    (D) The Agricultural Board should work more closely with farm research centers to guarantee the quality of new fruit and vegetable varieties.
    (E) If the discovery of a new variety of apple has progressed from the research center to the public, it will improve agricultural production.

11. It has been suggested that with the continued advance of technology, robots will be able to replace skilled craftsmen who currently assemble and test sophisticated manufactured goods, such as musical instruments. This suggestion is based on the belief that the assembly and testing of musical instruments consists of learning a series of techniques and processes, which can be programmed automatically without any understanding of how the various parts are supposed to work together to produce a high quality musical instrument. If this were the case, then robots could be programmed to follow the techniques and processes, and craftsmen would not be needed to assemble and test the instruments. But to do their jobs, skilled craftsmen must also understand the principles of sound production, together with the nuances of tone quality and the other criteria of a high quality musical instrument. Therefore, the idea that robots will replace people in the production of musical instruments is seriously flawed.

    Which one of the following selections, if true, would most seriously weaken the author's conclusion that robots will not replace skilled craftsmen in the production of musical instruments?

    (A) Not as many musical instruments are being produced today, so the industry cannot afford to pay skilled craftsmen.
    (B) Musical instruments are not produced individually any more, but are mass produced in factories.
    (C) Robots can be programmed to understand the principles of sound production, the nuances of tone quality and the other criteria of a high quality musical instrument.
    (D) Robots can accomplish mundane assembly tasks much more cost-effectively than skilled craftsmen can.
    (E) Skilled craftsmen are responsible for ensuring that musical instruments meet high quality standards.

12. Over the past two decades, a wide gap in pay has arisen between medical professionals who practice in the public health arena as opposed to those who practice privately. As a result, many doctors, nurses and other health professionals employed by public and nonprofit agencies have left their public health jobs in favor of private clinics and hospitals. Public and nonprofit agencies will be able to entice these professionals to return to public health jobs if salaries are made commensurate with those paid in the private sector. The quality of medical care provided by public and nonprofit agencies will thus be improved.

Which one of the following is presumed in the position stated above?

(A) The experience obtained by medical professionals in private clinics and hospitals will be especially important in the public health arena.
(B) How well public and nonprofit health agencies perform depends for the most part upon the experience level of their health professionals.
(C) Unless public and nonprofit health agencies act, the salaries paid to medical professionals in private practice will continue to outpace those paid in the public health arena.
(D) Medical health professionals who moved from the public sector to the private sector would change jobs again.
(E) If the pay disparity between the public and private medical sectors continues to increase, many doctors and nurses will move from private practice to the public health area.

13. Diseases have always plagued the earth's living organisms. Scientists believe that huge numbers of plant and animal diseases have developed and been eradicated naturally over time. This ongoing emergence and disappearance of diseases is ignored by those who blame the widespread incidence of cancer entirely upon man's alteration of naturally occurring substances to, for instance, produce bigger and better food sources. For example, some claim that the use of hormones to increase meat production heightens the risk of cancer in people who eat meat. People who hold this view need to accept the fact that even if cancer was not such a prevalent disease, another disease would have arisen naturally to take its place.

Which one of the following identifies a flaw in the passage's reasoning?

(A) The writer wrongly assumes that the use of hormones in meat production never has an effect upon people who eat meat.
(B) The writer ignores the fact that scientists are developing cures for some types of cancer.
(C) The writer does not consider the fact that a number of diseases have not yet been discovered.
(D) While the writer identifies a group that believes cancer is caused by man's interference with natural forms of food production, he does not identify or recognize scientists who disagree with this contention.
(E) The author does not acknowledge that man's alteration of naturally occurring substances might trigger the emergence of new diseases.

14. Based upon studies conducted over the last two decades that show head injuries can be reduced if children wear bicycle helmets, some jurisdictions have passed laws requiring that children under the age of 12 wear helmets when they ride their bicycles. A surprising result has been observed, however. Even though a large number of children do wear bicycle helmets, more head injuries than expected are continuing to occur. And this is the result even though the studies have shown that wearing a helmet reduces the incidence of head injuries.

    Which one of the following statements, if true, might suitably explain the unexpected finding?

    (A) A large number of parents are not making their children wear bicycle helmets.
    (B) More children are riding bicycles now than before bicycle helmets were introduced.
    (C) Because bicycle helmets are quite expensive, many parents don't buy them for their children.
    (D) Bicycle helmets were not designed to prevent all head injuries, so it is not surprising that head injuries still occur.
    (E) Bicycle helmets do not work properly if they are not properly secured with the chin strap, and many children and their parents do not secure the chin strap properly.

15. Donna: For the most part, medical researchers agree that someone who regularly consumes large amounts of alcohol will probably have serious health problems.

    Steve: Heavy drinking does not adversely impact one's health. My great uncle drank heavily for years and seemed in perfect health. In fact, he lived to be 87 years old.

    Which one of the following is a major flaw in Steve's argument?

    (A) Steve's argument uses only one example to attempt to refute a probable, not a foregone, result.
    (B) Steve cites an example that medical researchers did not study.
    (C) Steve's argument implies that there can be no correlation between heavy drinking and poor health.
    (D) Steve's argument fails to acknowledge the possibility that his great uncle may not have been in good health after all.
    (E) Steve doesn't indicate how long ago his great uncle lived so that different medical treatments can be taken into account.

16. Government take-over of foreign private industry in developing countries is generally regarded as an example by which the profits and benefits of a foreign enterprise can be redirected to improve the lot of native populations. The government's take-over of a large foreign mining operation in a fledgling African country a few years ago is a poor example of this principle, however. The government ousted the corporation in name, but the management team and workforce, most of whom were foreign, remained to operate the facility and were given a large pay increase. Profits from the operation were thus severely reduced. As a result, native projects did not receive large profits from the operation, nor were natives hired to replace foreign workers.

    Which one of the following describes the type of argument used in the passage?

    (A) The author supplies an example that supports the general principle.
    (B) The author compares and contrasts two divergent examples of the same principle.
    (C) The author weakens the argument by supplying evidence which undermines the argument.
    (D) The author disproves the argument with one compelling example.
    (E) The author explains why all general principles have flaws.

17. Edward Grieg: Your gallery is biased against my paintings. I have submitted twenty canvases in the last three years and you have not accepted any of them for display. You are punishing me because I won the Western Art award three years ago and your manager thought the award should have gone to his artist son.

Gallery owner: You are wrong! Our acceptance standards and display policies do not discriminate against you. Our staff covers the painters' names, so the review board does not know who the artist is when it determines which pieces of art will be accepted for display and sale. The review board would not know which paintings you submitted.

Which one of the following assumptions does the gallery owner make in his reply?

(A) The gallery manager holds no bad feelings about Edward Grieg winning the Western Art award over his artist son.
(B) Many artists submit their work to galleries without having any pieces accepted for display.
(C) The review board cannot recognize Edward Grieg's paintings without seeing his name on the canvases.
(D) The gallery accepts only nature studies, and Edward Grieg's paintings frequently portray people and interior settings.
(E) The review board has tended to favor oil paintings over the last several years and Edward Grieg more typically paints water colors.

18. Scientists have studied the effects of electromagnetic fields associated with high voltage power lines upon people whose homes are located within 300 yards of the lines. They have compared the growth rate of children who live near the lines with the growth rate of children who live elsewhere. Because they found no significant differences in the growth rates in the two study areas, they have concluded that electromagnetic fields are harmless.

Which one of the following, if true, would most seriously jeopardize the scientists' conclusion?

(A) The scientists did not consider other possible impacts upon growth rates.
(B) In studying people who lived near high voltage power lines, the scientists did not consider what type of housing those people lived in.
(C) The growth rates of children have changed considerably since the 1920s.
(D) People who live near electromagnetic fields suffer health problems that are not reflected in the growth rates of their children.
(E) As children get older, their activities tend to occur away from home more often.

19. Scientists used to think that pepper plants had the ability to produce an unlimited number of peppers. So long as the plant was properly fertilized and pollinated, and temperature, water and sunlight controlled, they believed pepper plants would continue to produce indefinitely. However, scientists have now learned that a pepper plant will not produce more than 200 peppers in its lifetime. If a pepper plant goes dormant due to a deficiency of light or water, for example, when reinvigorated, it will start producing peppers where it left off. But a normal pepper plant will produce no more than 200 peppers.

Assume the information in the passage is true, and assume that a pepper plant has been discovered that has produced 225 peppers and is still producing. If so, the still-producing pepper plant CANNOT fit which one of the following categories?

(A) An abnormal pepper plant flourishing under ideal temperature, humidity, water and light conditions.
(B) A normal pepper plant that went into a dormancy stage and then was revived.
(C) An abnormal pepper plant grown organically.
(D) A normal pepper plant grown from the seed of an abnormal pepper plant.
(E) A abnormal pepper plant grown in the lab without soil.

20. In the last decade, the use of bicycle helmets has increased tremendously, particularly among young children. Although bicycle helmets appear to be as sturdy and safe as football helmets, they are exempt from the safety standards the government has imposed upon the manufacture of football helmets. As a result, a child involved in a bicycle accident is more likely to suffer a serious head injury than is a child injured in a football game.

The argument depends upon which one of the following assumptions:

(A) Youngsters ride their bicycles less carefully when they wear helmets.
(B) The government has mandated a set of safety standards for manufacturers of bicycle helmets.
(C) Children are more likely to be injured riding their bicycles than playing football.
(D) More children ride bicycles than play football.
(E) Bicycle helmets are less likely to meet the government's helmet safety standards than are football helmets, which are subject to the safety standards.

21. The first African slaves were brought to the Americas in the early 1600s, where their labor was used primarily for agricultural and household purposes. The institution of slavery in the New World presupposes not only the existence of slaves and owners, but also a system of laws in place which recognized and protected the practice of slavery. However, laws were not enacted, for example, declaring slaves the personal property of their owners and imposing punishments upon those who aided slaves in escape, until many years later.

    If the sentences in the passage above are true, then they support which one of the following statements?

    (A) Arguing that laws needed to be enacted recognizing and protecting the institution of slavery before the practice of slavery could have existed in the New World is to ignore historical fact.
    (B) Prior to 1700, some of the Europeans who came to the New World enslaved native Indian populations.
    (C) Slavery was practiced in many parts of the world before Africans were first brought to the New World as slaves.
    (D) The prior existence of a supportive legal system is needed before an institutional practice can develop.
    (E) One of the reasons slavery developed in the New World was the tremendous need for manual labor.

22. It is certain that at least as many migratory birds fly through Hilden every fall as fly through Paluska.

    The conclusion above follows logically from which one of the following statements?

    (A) Paluska's average snowfall exceeds Hilden's by eight inches.
    (B) Residents of Paluska have been warned not to use bird feeders this fall to avoid spreading a disease diagnosed in dead birds found at a few feeders in Paluska.
    (C) Hilden is the county in which Paluska is located.
    (D) More natural predators have been reported in Hilden than in Paluska.
    (E) Hilden's population exceeds Paluska's population by 25,000.

23. The football coach at a midwestern college noticed that some of his players were frequently late to morning football practices and seemed somewhat lethargic after they did arrive. He directed his assistant coach to look into the matter. The assistant coach reported back that most of the late and less active players belonged to fraternities on campus which were renowned for their frequent and late-night parties. The head coach then prohibited all of his football players from being members of fraternities. He reported that this would ensure that his players would get to practice on time and that they would have more productive practice sessions.

    The head coach's reasoning is not sound because he fails to establish which one of the following:

    (A) He fails to establish a system to monitor his players' fraternity membership and to impose penalties for those who do not follow his new rule.
    (B) He fails to establish that his players are physically big and strong enough to be successful football players.
    (C) He fails to establish that his new policy will ensure that at least some of his football players will go to bed at a more reasonable hour.
    (D) He fails to establish that his best football players did not belong to fraternities anyway.
    (E) He fails to establish that the success of the fraternity system will not suffer if the football players are precluded from becoming members.

24. Steve Cooper, senior sales officer, has trained many top salespeople in this company, including 14 who have become the top salespersons in their regions and 3 who have won the top salesperson award. Although there is an art to selling, Mr. Cooper's success at training top salespeople shows that the skills required to become a top salesperson can be both taught and learned.

    The argument depends on which one of the following assumptions?

    (A) Mr. Cooper does not teach the hard-sell method. Nor does he teach the I'll-be-your-pal method. Instead, he stresses the professional-client relationship.
    (B) More than 50% of the people trained by Mr. Cooper went on to become successful salespeople.
    (C) One of the successful salespeople who trained under Mr. Cooper was not an accomplished salesperson before learning the Cooper Method.
    (D) There is a large and expanding industry dedicated to training salespeople.
    (E) There is no one method with which to approach sales; a method that works for one person may not for another person.

25. To be accepted as a member at the Brown Country Club, one must have a net worth of over ten million dollars and must not have any connections to the entertainment industry. Robert Chase, the publishing magnate, has a net worth of 5 billion dollars and has been accepted as a member at the Brown Country Club.

    Given the statements above, which one of the following conclusions must be true?

    (A) Chase's membership was preapproved.
    (B) Chase does not know anyone who has connections to the entertainment industry.
    (C) Chase's ex-business partner is a major concert promoter, has a net worth of 100 million dollars, and is a member of the Brown Country Club.
    (D) Chase's brother, who has also petitioned for membership at Brown, has a net worth of 10 billion dollars and considers it beneath his dignity to associate with anyone in the entertainment industry. Hence, his petition will be accepted.
    (E) Chase has not financed any Hollywood movies.

26. Kirkland's theory of corporate structure can be represented by a truncated pyramid. There are workers, middle management, and executive management, but no head of the corporation. Instead, all major decisions are made by committee. As a consequence, in Kirkland's structure, risky, cutting-edge technologies cannot be developed.

    Which one of the following is an assumption on which the argument depends?

    (A) Cutting-edge technologies are typically developed by entrepreneurs, not by big corporations.
    (B) Only single individuals will make risky decisions.
    (C) An individual is more likely to take a gamble on his own than in a group.
    (D) All heads of corporations reached their positions by taking risks.
    (E) All cutting-edge technologies involve some risk.

Solutions to Warm-Up Drill I

1. When a man is tired of London, he is tired of life; for there is in London all that life can afford.—Samuel Johnson

2. The conclusion is not stated, but the arguer implies that watching violent movies does *not* dissipate aggression.

3. By the age of 10 months, purebred golden retrievers display certain instinctive behaviors. Because this 11 month-old golden retriever does not display these instinctive behaviors, it is not a purebred.

4. No conclusion is stated. But the author implies that to lie is not always immoral.

5. Beware, for I am fearless, and therefore, powerful.—Mary Shelley, *Frankenstein*

6. The implied conclusion is that violence depicted on television contributes to society's high rate of violence.

7. Where all other circumstances are equal, wages are generally higher in new than in old trades. When a projector attempts to establish a new manufacture, he must at first entice his workmen from other employments by higher wages than they can either earn in their old trades, or than the nature of his work would otherwise require, and a considerable time must pass away before he can venture to reduce them to the common level.—Adam Smith, *The Wealth of Nations*

8. Existentialists believe that our identity is continually evolving, that we are born into this world without an identity and do not begin to develop one until the act of retrospection. So one's identity is always trailing oneself like the wake of a boat. As one goes through life, the wake becomes wider and wider defining him more and more precisely.

9. In time I began to recognize that all of these smaller complaints about rigidity, emotional suffocation, the tortured logic of the law were part of a more fundamental phenomenon in the law itself. Law is at war with ambiguity, with uncertainty. In the courtroom, the adversary system—plaintiff against defendant—guarantees that someone will always win, someone loses. No matter if justice is evenly with each side, no matter if the issues are indefinite and obscure, the rule of law will be declared.—Scott Turow, *One L*

10. Either God controls all of man's behavior or God does not control any of man's behavior. God must not control man's behavior since there is so much evil in the world.

11. The more deeply I understand the central role of caring in my own life, the more I realize it to be central to the human condition.—Milton Mayeroff, *On Caring*

Solutions to Warm-Up Drill II

1. The suppressed premise is that the capital of California is located northeast of San Francisco. This is a reasonable assumption because it is true!

2. The suppressed premise is that only the truth is published. Clearly this is not a reasonable assumption.

3. The suppressed premise is that being forced to take a drug test is an invasion of privacy. This is a reasonable assumption.

4. ETS's suppressed premise is that extremely high score improvements indicate cheating. This is arguably a reasonable assumption, but it is not consistent with the tradition of assuming one innocent until proven otherwise. (By the way, this is a true story. Sean sued ETS and the courts ordered them to release his score.)

5. The suppressed premise is that hunting with arrows did not begin until the arrows were tipped with bronze. This seems to be a questionable assumption.

6. The suppressed premise is that what goes beyond the evidence is truer that what does not. This is a questionable assumption; arguably just the opposite is the case.

7. The suppressed premise is that only decisions made by a single individual can be daring. This assumption has some truth to it, but it's a bit extreme.

8. The suppressed premise is that comparable pay would be sufficient to entice the teachers to change their careers again. This is probably a reasonable assumption since the teachers were described as dedicated.

Answers and Solutions to Exercise

1. D	7. B	13. E	19. B	25. E
2. C	8. A	14. E	20. E	26. B
3. B	9. B	15. A	21. A	
4. A	10. B	16. C	22. C	
5. D	11. C	17. C	23. C	
6. D	12. D	18. D	24. C	

1. The implied premise of the first question is that Central voice students have better breath control than Northeast voice students because the Central students take more frequent voice lessons and are required to practice more often. Further, it is assumed that more lessons and practice are indispensable factors to this result. (D) is the correct answer.

Selection (A) is the second best answer. The conclusion in the first question states that Northeast students "*will improve their breath control* only if *they increase*" their lessons and practice. Put another way, more frequent voice lessons and practice are required for greater breath control. Selection (A) says that all students who take frequent lessons and practice often would have good breath control, but (A) does not imply that such a schedule of lessons and practice are necessary.

2. Typically, to weaken an argument, one of its premises must be shown to be false or flawed. The argument implies that when boat owners buy new engines for their boats, their old engines will be discarded or destroyed. Selection (C) contradicts this assumption by explaining that old boat engines are in high demand in countries with less rigorous pollution standards and that old engines are often sent overseas to satisfy that demand. Thus these old engines may still be in use. Selection (C) is the right answer.

3. In this question, the premise has been suppressed. If the high level of zinc found in diseased plants is merely a symptom of the diseases, and zinc does not actually cause the diseases, then the fact that a fertilizer high in phosphorus causes plants not to exhibit the diseases, is irrelevant. So the question is based upon the assumption set forth in Selection (B).

4. The golf association requires two conditions to be met before a golfer will be admitted into the Labor Day tournament. First, the golfer must pay the entry fee by June 1. Second, the golfer must have won a major tournament during the previous calendar year. Since Smith was accepted to play in the Labor Day tournament, he must have won a major tournament the previous year. Selection (A) is correct.

5. Natives could have initially developed their mandolin-like instrument with strings made from something other than horse hair, perhaps tree bark. In order for the conclusion in the argument to be valid, we must assume that the instrument was first developed with horse hair. Selection (D) is the assumption upon which the conclusion is based.

6. A conclusion for this argument is requested. In order to accurately assess his students on exams, the professor desires to eliminate cheating from his classroom. He believes that a tough policy on cheating will deter students from cheating. Therefore, he is more likely to reach his goal if he announces his policy on cheating and makes it known that he will track down cheaters and punish them. The answer is (D).

7. The first sentence is critical to this question: publishers depend upon people who buy books and other printed materials. If the advance of the computer information age eliminates the need for printed information, then the publishing industry is threatened by the public's wide-spread use of computers and the Internet. The correct answer is (B).

8. This argument does not consider that an outside factor may cause some people to have both poor vision and dry eyes. Selection (A) provides an outside factor for both conditions. It is the correct answer.

Selection (D) is tempting, but don't be misled. Even if most people who wear contact lenses do not have dry eyes, this does not weaken the argument because it is based on the incidence of dry eyes between people who wear contact lenses and those who do not. Secondly, the author does not argue that wearing contact lenses *must* cause dry eyes, only that it *can* cause dry eyes.

9. The link that allows the conclusion to be drawn in this problem is the assumption that only principals will try new methods and programs. Under this theory of governance by committee, new methods and programs cannot be implemented. Thus, the theory assumes that only individuals will try new ideas. Selection (B) is the correct answer.

Selection (C) is a close second. It is supported by the argument, but it understates the breadth of the implied premise. The question states that in this theory of school governance, new methods and programs cannot be implemented, not that they are less likely to be implemented.

10. This question is fairly simple; students should not agonize over it. Clearly, before a new variety of fruit or vegetable can improve agricultural production, it must be made available to the public. Selection (B) is the correct answer.

Answers such as (B) often cause students much difficulty. Students may hesitate to mark such a clear and simple answer because they believe they must have missed something. Sometimes they have. But sometimes the simple answer is the correct answer. Caution: Students should attempt to distinguish the simple answer from the simplistic answer. While the simple answer may more often be the correct answer over a complex answer, rarely is the simplistic answer correct.

Don't be misled by answer (C). Even though the argument supports (C), the question asks for a statement that is inferred from the passage. Thus, the answer must go beyond what is divulged in the passage.

11. Remember that in order to weaken or undermine an argument, one of the premises of the argument must be disproved. The implied premise of this passage is that robots cannot be programmed to understand the principles of sound production and the other criteria of a quality musical instrument, and thus they will not replace skilled craftsmen.

(A) No. Whether or not the industry can afford to pay skilled craftsmen is irrelevant to the question of whether robots could be programmed to perform the craftsmen's work at the same skill level.

(B) No. This selection is also irrelevant to the argument, which considers whether robots can perform the skilled work of craftsmen.

(C) Yes. The implied premise of the argument is that robots cannot understand the workings of musical instruments or how to produce a high quality musical instrument. If robots can be programmed with these understandings, the author's conclusion would be seriously undermined.

(D) No. This statement is true, but the tasks in issue are not mundane assembly tasks. Rather, they involve the more sophisticated understandings and nuances of musical instruments.

(E) No. This statement does not weaken the argument. Instead, it reinforces it.

12. Don't ponder too long over this question. The answer is fairly simple. The question presumes that medical professionals who left their jobs in the public health sector for higher paying private jobs would return to the public health sector if salaries go up enough. (D) is the correct choice.

Students often assume the LSAT will contain only difficult questions because it has the reputation of being a difficult test. But the LSAT contains questions with a wide range of difficulty levels, from easy to very difficult. Students are often bewildered when they read a fairly easy question and find an obvious answer in the selections available. They believe they might have missed something, and often try to make the question more difficult than it is. When one of the selections seems too self-evident, then perhaps it is. However, because the LSAT questions do vary tremendously by difficulty level, perhaps the obvious answer to a simple question is correct.

If a question bothers you for this reason, don't become obsessed with discovering what you have missed in the question. Perhaps you haven't missed anything and the obvious answer is the correct choice. If you carefully read back through the question and selections and don't find anything you missed the first time, select your answer and go on with the next LSAT question. You might want to mark that question somehow in the margin so that you can come back to it if you have time after you complete the exam.

13. The author seems to consider the emergence of new diseases as entirely independent of man's use of technological advances. However, the implementation of scientific advances might impact the "ongoing emergence and disappearance of diseases." Therefore, the flaw in the writer's reasoning stems from his refusal to consider the possible impact of man's alteration of naturally occurring substances upon the emergence of new diseases. The correct answer is (E).

Selection (A) is tempting. However, the author disagrees with those who argue that man's conduct is "entirely" responsible for the high incidence of cancer. Thus, he implies that man's actions might have some role in the prevalence of cancer. There is nothing in the passage to indicate whether or not (B) is true, even though it is common knowledge that scientists are continually conducting cancer research. The LSAT test is designed so that outside knowledge is not needed to answer the questions. Rather, the questions should be answered solely on the basis of what is stated or implied in the passage. Inadvertently, the LSAT authors might include a question that can be more readily answered with outside knowledge, but they make every effort to avoid that situation. With respect to (C), whether or not diseases have been discovered or not is irrelevant to the passage, and (D) is similarly irrelevant.

14. Before looking at the possible answers, take a few seconds to think about what might be causing the unexpected result. What could explain the continuing incidence of head injuries? Perhaps children's bicycle helmets were not designed properly or perhaps children are not using the helmets properly.

Now look at the possible selections. (A) and (C) are not correct because they are possible explanations for why children do not wear helmets. The passage asks why injuries still occur in children who do wear helmets. (B) is irrelevant; it does not explain why head injuries occur in children who wear bicycle helmets. The passage implies that bicycle helmets reduce the total incidence of head injuries, not that they eliminate all head injuries. Selection (D) contradicts this implication because it states that the same injuries occur that bicycle helmets help prevent. Selection (E) remains, and it is the correct selection. It also fits an explanation we thought of before reviewing the LSAT selections.

15. Selection (A) is correct. Donna's argument does not state that people who drink heavily will necessarily have serious health problems, only that they will probably have serious health problems. Providing only one example to attempt to disprove a probable result is a serious flaw.

We do not know whether medical researchers considered the case of Steve's great uncle, so (B) is not correct. Steve's argument does not imply that there is no correlation between drinking and health. He is unequivocal that there is no correlation. Therefore, (C) is not correct. Steve's great uncle clearly didn't have any serious health problems because he appeared to be in good health and he lived to be 87, so selection (D) cannot be correct. Finally, (E) is irrelevant to the arguments presented. What type medical treatments were used is irrelevant to whether or not Steve's great uncle was affected by his heavy drinking.

16. (A) is not the correct answer. The example does not support the general principle—that government take-over of foreign business benefits native populations.

(B) is not correct, because the author presents only one example of the principle, not two divergent examples.

(C) is the correct selection. The author challenges the general principle by identifying a situation in which the native population did not benefit by government's take-over of a foreign business.

(D) is not correct. The author didn't completely disprove the argument; he only provided one example that didn't follow the general principle.

(E) is not correct. In the passage, the author points out why this principle is not borne out by every situation, but he does not argue that all general principles have flaws.

17.

(A) No. The gallery owner's argument attempts to directly refute this charge; it is not an assumption in his argument.

(B) No. The gallery owner's argument is based on the quality and style of Grieg's paintings, not the number of pieces of artwork Grieg or any other artist submits.

(C) Yes. The gallery owner states that the artists' names are covered so the review board could not know who the artists are. He or she assumes that the members of the review board will not be able to recognize Grieg's paintings if his name is not disclosed. But the review board could recognize Grieg's paintings based on his style, medium, subject matter, and other things.

(D) No. We have no information as to the type of artwork displayed in the gallery.

(E) No. Again, we have no information as to what type of art the review board has favored in the gallery in recent years.

18.

(A) No. The study is concerned only with the effects of electromagnetic fields. Determining what other factors might impact children's growth rates would be irrelevant to determining the effects of electromagnetic fields.

(B) No. Since the growth rate for both groups of children was the same, it does not appear that the type of housing was important in determining the effects of exposure to electromagnetic fields.

(C) No. The growth rate of children in the 1920s is insignificant to the purpose of this study—to determine whether proximity to electromagnetic fields has any harmful effects.

(D) Yes. The scientists assume that the only negative effect from living near electromagnetic fields would be a lower growth rate in children. Perhaps adults and children who live near the lines suffer from other ailments. These would not be reflected in a study of children's growth rates and thus, this statement, if true, would seriously jeopardize the scientists' conclusion.

(E) No. Children's growth rates were the same, so how much time children who lived near the power lines spent at home would appear to be irrelevant.

19. The question asks us to find the category that COULD NOT APPLY to the plant. So if the passage could describe the high-bearing pepper plant, then it is <u>not</u> the correct choice.

(A) No. If the pepper plant has already produced 225 peppers and is still producing, it is not a normal pepper plant. So the high-bearing plant could be an abnormal pepper grown under ideal conditions.

(B) Yes. The high producing plant cannot be a normal pepper plant, even one that went into a dormancy stage and then was revived. The passage tells us that normal plants cannot produce more than 200 peppers, even those that go through a dormancy period. We know that the plant will "start producing peppers where it left off" and produce no more than 200 peppers.

(C) No. We know from the passage that no normal pepper plant can produce more than 200 peppers. If the plant is abnormal in any way, it cannot be a normal plant. So the high-bearing plant could be an abnormal plant grown organically.

(D) No. This plant was grown from the seed of an abnormal plant, so it could have produced the abnormal results reported.

(E) No. Again, we know that a plant that produces more than 200 peppers is abnormal. Therefore, the high-bearing plant could be an abnormal plant grown in the lab without soil.

20.

(A) No. Nothing in the argument suggests that the incidence of accidents has gone up with the increased use of bicycle helmets.

(B) No. In fact, the argument states just the opposite—that bicycle helmets are exempt from the safety standards the government requires for football helmets.

(C) No. This argument concerns the incidence of <u>head</u> injuries in children who ride bicycles contrasted with children who play football. This selection encompasses all types of injuries, not merely head injuries. We have no information about the incidence of other types of injuries sustained in these activities, i.e., broken bones, sprained ankles, etc.

(D) No. Again, the author provides no information as to how many children play football and ride bicycles. And the conclusion in the passage deals with the probability of head injuries in children who participate in both activities, not the number of children who participate in these activities.

(E) Yes. The argument implies that because bicycle helmets are exempt from the government safety standards for football helmets, children will more likely be injured in bicycle accidents. However, bicycle helmets might be exempt from the standards because the government believes bicycle helmets already meet the safety standards applicable to football helmets. We don't know the reason bicycle helmets are not covered by the standards. The implication in this argument is that bicycle helmets are not as safe as football helmets, and therefore, they are less likely to meet the football helmet safety standards.

21.

(A) Yes. According to the passage, the practice of slavery began much sooner than laws were enacted to protect its practice. Thus, to argue that laws needed to be in place *first* is to ignore historical fact.

(B) No. The passage is concerned with the importation of African slaves and when laws were first enacted concerning slavery. We don't know the timing of slavery laws relative to when Europeans enslaved native Indian populations, so this statement is not supported by the passage.

(C) No. Whether or not slavery was practiced elsewhere prior to the importation of African slaves is irrelevant to the question—which statement is <u>supported</u> by the passage with respect to the <u>institution of slavery in the New World</u>?

(D) No. This statement is directly contradicted by the passage. The facts set forth in the passage prove just the opposite—that slavery was practiced long before a supportive legal system developed.

(E) No. Again, this statement is irrelevant to the question. The reasons slavery developed in the New World are not significant to the timing of a legal system supportive of slavery.

22.
(A) No. We are not given any information as to how average snowfall might impact migratory bird flight patterns.

(B) No. We don't know whether migratory birds are susceptible to the disease or if they might in fact be carriers of the disease. If they are carriers of the disease, then the fact that the disease has been diagnosed in Paluska would not necessarily affect the levels of migratory birds flying through either Hilden or Paluska.

(C) Yes. If Paluska is a town in Hilden County, then birds that fly through Paluska are also flying through Hilden County. So at least as many birds fly through Hilden as fly through Paluska. The following diagram might be helpful in conceptualizing this problem.

(D) No. Knowing that more natural predators have been reported in Hilden does not verify that there actually are more predators in Hilden. Furthermore, we don't know the sizes of Hilden and Paluska. If Paluska is very small and Hilden is very large, the fact that more predators have been sighted in Hilden would not be significant to this passage.

(E) No. Again, while population density might impact migratory bird patterns, we don't know how big Paluska and Hilden are. If Hilden's area exceeds Paluska's area significantly, the fact that Hilden has a bigger population might not affect the numbers of migratory birds that fly through each place.

23.
(A) No. This answer deals with enforcement of the new policy, not whether the new policy is likely to change the unwanted behavior in the first place.

(B) No. This answer is irrelevant to the issue—behavior the coach wishes to change.

(C) Yes. The coach assumes that if his players do not belong to fraternities, they will not have other distractions at night to keep them from getting a reasonable night's sleep. Many other reasons may keep the players up late at night—non-fraternity parties, library research, part time jobs, etc.

(D) No. We know from the passage that only <u>some</u> of the football players were late and lethargic at practice and that <u>many</u> of these later players were fraternity members. Perhaps his best players were fraternity members who showed up to practice on time, but we cannot tell this from the passage.

(E) No. This answer is also irrelevant to the issue. The impact of the coach's rule upon the fraternity system is unimportant in this scenario.

24. If the salespeople trained by Mr. Cooper were successful before studying under him, then clearly the argument would be specious. On the other hand, if none of the salespeople were successful before studying under him, then the argument would be strong. However, the argument does not require this strong of a statement in order to be valid. All it needs is one person who profited from the tutelage of Mr. Cooper. The answer is (C).

Many students have problems with this type of question. They read through the answer-choices and find no significant statements. They may pause at (C) but reject it—thinking that the argument would be deceptive if only one person out of 17 profited from the tutelage of Mr. Cooper. However, the missing premise doesn't have to make the argument good, just valid.

25. The argument states that two criteria must be met before the Brown Country Club will accept a person:

I. He or she must have a net worth of over ten million dollars.
II. He or she must not have any connections to the entertainment industry.

Since the Chase was accepted as a member, he must not have any connections to the entertainment industry and therefore could not have financed a Hollywood movie. The answer is (E).

26. The link that allows the conclusion to be drawn is the assumption that <u>only</u> individuals make risky decisions. The answer is (B).

Both (A) and (C) are close second-best choices (a double-detractor pair). Both are supported by the passage, but each understates the scope of the suppressed premise. The argument states that in Kirkland's model of corporate structure cutting-edge technologies <u>cannot</u> be developed, not that they are less likely to be developed.

Logic II
(Diagramming)

We thoroughly covered diagramming in the game section. Diagramming is also useful with arguments. However, the diagrams won't be as elaborate as those used with games. In fact, in these cases, the term "diagramming " is somewhat of a misnomer. Rarely will we actually draw a diagram; instead we will symbolize the arguments, much as we did the conditions of the games.

Diagramming is very helpful with arguments that ask you to select the statement that is most similar in structure to the original. The first step with these arguments is to decide whether the original statement is valid. If it is, the answer must be valid as well. If it is invalid, then the answer must be invalid. Some common questions for these types of arguments are

- The logical structure of the argument above is most similar to which one of the following?
- Which one of the following arguments contains a flaw that is most similar to one in the argument above?

Typically these arguments use some variation of an *if-then* statement, often the contrapositive. Before we begin diagramming, we need to review some of the logical connectives that were introduced earlier and discuss in more detail those connectives only briefly covered.

As stated in the introduction to this section, most logical-structure arguments are based on some variation of an *if-then* statement. However, the *if-then* statement is often embedded in other equivalent structures. We already studied embedded *if-then* statements in the chapter on flow charts. Still, we need to further develop the ability to recognize these structures.

If-Then

A—>B

By now you should be well aware that if the premise of an *if-then* statement is true then the conclusion must be true as well. This is the defining characteristic of a conditional statement; it can be illustrated as follows:

A—>B
A
∴ **B** (where the symbol ∴ means "therefore")

This diagram displays the *if-then* statement "A—>B," the affirmed premise "A," and the necessary conclusion "B." Such a diagram can be very helpful in showing the logical structure of an argument.

Example: ***(If-then)***

If Jane does not study for the LSAT, then she will not score well. Jane, in fact, did not study for the LSAT; therefore she scored poorly on the test.

When symbolizing games, we let a letter stand for an element. When symbolizing arguments, however, we may let a letter stand for an element, a phrase, a clause, or even an entire sentence. The clause *"Jane does not study for the LSAT"* can be symbolized as ~S, and the clause *"she will not score well"* can be symbolized as ~W. Substituting these symbols into the argument yields the following diagram:

~S—>~W
~S
∴ **~W**

This diagram shows that the argument has a valid *if-then* structure. A conditional statement is presented, ~S—>~W; its premise affirmed, ~S; and then the conclusion that necessarily follows, ~W, is stated.

Most of the arguments that you will have to diagram are more complex than this one—but not much more. In fact, once you master diagramming, you will find these arguments rather routine.

At first, many students get hopelessly lost with logical-structure arguments because they develop tunnel vision—analyzing the meaning of each word. For these arguments, you should step back and take a bird's-eye view. Diagramming brings out the superstructure and the underlying simplicity of these arguments.

EMBEDDED *IF-THEN* STATEMENTS

Usually, logical reasoning arguments involve an *if-then* statement. Unfortunately, the *if-then* thought is often embedded in other equivalent structures. In this section, we study how to spot these structures.

Example: ***(Embedded If-then)***

John and Ken cannot both go to the party.

At first glance, this sentence does not appear to contain an *if-then* statement. But it essentially says: *"if John goes to the party, then Ken does not."* Note, the statement "if Ken goes to the party, then John does not" expresses the same thing. So we don't need to state both.

Example: ***(Embedded If-then)***

Danielle will be accepted to law school only if she does well on the LSAT.

Given this statement, we know that *if* Danielle is accepted to law school, *then* she must have done well on the LSAT. Note: Students often wrongly interpret this statement to mean *"if Danielle does well on the LSAT, then she will be accepted to law school."* There is no such guarantee. The only guarantee is that if she does not do well on the LSAT, then she will not be accepted to law school.

"A only if B" is logically equivalent to "if A, then B."

Embedded If-Then Drill

Directions: Each of the following sentences contains an embedded *if-then* statement. Translate each sentence into an equivalent *if-then* form. Solutions are on page 255.

Sentence	*If-Then* Form
1. Only if John is allowed to go will Ken go.	
2. Give a talented teacher academic freedom, and she will excel.	
3. No Montague is a Rothschild.	
4. Anyone who is not a Montague cannot be a Rothschild.	
5. All Montagues are Rothschilds.	
6. Only Montagues are Rothschilds.	
7. A Montague will not attend a party hosted by a Rothschild.	
8. Men and women cannot understand one another.	
9. There is no God but Allah.	
10. None but the worthy are saved.	
11. For a Montague to attend a party it is necessary for a Rothschild to attend.	

Affirming the Conclusion Fallacy

A—>B
B
∴ A

Remember that an *if-then* statement, **A—>B**, tells us only two things:

(1) If A is true, then B is true as well.
(2) If B is false, then A is false as well (contrapositive).

If, however, we know the conclusion is true, the *if-then* statement tells us *nothing* about the premise. And if we know that the premise is false (we will consider this next), then the *if-then* statement tells us *nothing* about the conclusion.

Example: ***(Affirming the Conclusion Fallacy)***

If he is innocent, then when we hold him under water for sixty seconds he will not drown. Since he did not die when we dunked him in the water, he must be innocent.

The logical structure of the argument above is most similar to which one of the following?

(A) To insure that the remaining wetlands survive, they must be protected by the government. This particular wetland is being neglected. Therefore, it will soon perish.
(B) There were nuts in that pie I just ate. There had to be, because when I eat nuts I break out in hives, and I just noticed a blemish on my hand.
(C) The president will be reelected unless a third candidate enters the race. A third candidate has entered the race, so the president will not be reelected.
(D) Every time Melinda has submitted her book for publication it has been rejected. So she should not bother with another rewrite.
(E) When the government loses the power to tax one area of the economy, it just taxes another. The Supreme Court just overturned the sales tax, so we can expect an increase in the income tax.

To symbolize this argument, let the clause "*he is innocent*" be denoted by I, and let the clause "*when we hold him under water for sixty seconds he will not drown*" be denoted by ~D. Then the argument can be symbolized as

I—>~D
~D
∴ **I**

Notice that this argument is fallacious: the conclusion "*he is innocent*" is also a premise of the argument. Hence the argument is circular—it proves what was already assumed. The argument affirms the conclusion then invalidly uses it to deduce the premise. The answer will likewise be fallacious.

We start with answer-choice (A). The sentence

"To insure that the remaining wetlands survive, they must be protected by the government"

contains an embedded *if-then* statement:

"If the remaining wetlands are to survive, then they must be protected by the government."

This can be symbolized as S—>P. Next, the sentence "*This particular wetland is being neglected*" can be symbolized as ~P. Finally, the sentence "*It will soon perish*" can be symbolized as ~S. Using these symbols to translate the argument gives the following diagram:

S—>P
~P
∴ **~S**

The diagram clearly shows that this argument does not have the same structure as the given argument. In fact, it is a valid argument by contraposition.

Turning to (B), we reword the statement

"when I eat nuts, I break out in hives"

as

"If I eat nuts, then I break out in hives."

This in turn can be symbolized as N—>H.

Next, we interpret the clause "*there is a blemish on my hand*" to mean "*hives*," which we symbolize as H. Substituting these symbols into the argument yields the following diagram:

N—>H
H
∴ N

The diagram clearly shows that this argument has the same structure as the given argument. The answer, therefore, is (B).

Denying the Premise Fallacy

A—>B
~A
∴ ~B

This fallacy is not tested as often on the LSAT as the affirming-the-conclusion fallacy because it is usually easy to detect. The fallacy of denying the premise occurs when an *if-then* statement is presented, its premise denied, and then its conclusion wrongly negated.

Example: ***(Denying the Premise Fallacy)***

The senator will be reelected only if he opposes the new tax bill. But he was defeated. So he must have supported the new tax bill.

The sentence *"The senator will be reelected only if he opposes the new tax bill"* contains an embedded *if-then* statement: *"If the senator is reelected, then he opposes the new tax bill."** This in turn can be symbolized as

R—>~T

The sentence *"But the senator was defeated"* can be reworded as *"He was not reelected,"* which in turn can be symbolized as

~R

Finally, the sentence *"He must have supported the new tax bill"* can be symbolized as

T

Using these symbols the argument can be diagrammed as follows:

R—>~T
~R
∴ T

[Note: Two negatives make a positive, so the conclusion ~(~T) was reduced to T.] This diagram clearly shows that the argument is committing the fallacy of denying the premise. An *if-then* statement is made; its premise is negated; then its conclusion is negated.

---

* Remember: "A only if B" is equivalent to "If A, then B."

Transitive Property

A—>B
B—>C
∴ A—>C

These arguments are rarely difficult, provided you step back and take a bird's-eye view. It may be helpful to view this structure as an inequality in mathematics. For example, $5 > 4$ and $4 > 3$, so $5 > 3$.

Notice that the conclusion in the transitive property is also an *if-then* statement. So we don't know that C is true unless we know that A is true. However, if we add the premise "A is true" to the diagram, then we can conclude that C is true:

A—>B
B—>C
A
∴ C

As you may have anticipated, the contrapositive can be generalized to the transitive property:

A—>B
B—>C
~C
∴ ~A

Example: ***(Transitive Property)***

If you work hard, you will be successful in America. If you are successful in America, you can lead a life of leisure. So if you work hard in America, you can live a life of leisure.

Let W stand for *"you work hard,"* S stand for *"you will be successful in America,"* and L stand for *"you can lead a life of leisure."* Now the first sentence translates as W—>S, the second sentence as S—>L, and the conclusion as W—>L. Combining these symbol statements yields the following diagram:

W—>S
S—>L
∴ W—>L

The diagram clearly displays the transitive property.

DeMorgan's Laws

~(A & B) = ~A or ~B
~(A or B) = ~A & ~B

If you have taken a course in logic, you are probably familiar with these formulas. Their validity is intuitively clear: The conjunction **A&B** is false when either, or both, of its parts are false. This is precisely what **~A or ~B** says. And the disjunction **A or B** is false only when both A and B are false, which is precisely what **~A and ~B** says.

You will rarely get an argument whose main structure is based on these rules—they are too mechanical. Nevertheless, DeMorgan's laws often help simplify, clarify, or transform parts of an argument. They are also useful with games.

Example: ***(DeMorgan's Law)***

It's not the case that the senator will be both reelected and not acquitted of campaign fraud.

Let R stand for *"the senator will be reelected,"* and let A stand for *"acquitted of campaign fraud."* Using these symbol statements to translate the argument yields

~(R & ~A)

which by the first of DeMorgan's laws is equivalent to

~R or ~(~A)

This in turn can be reduced to

~R or A

This final diagram tells us that the senator either will not be reelected or will be acquitted, or both.

Example: ***(DeMorgan's Law)***

It is not the case that either Bill or Jane is going to the party.

This argument can be diagrammed as ~(B or J), which by the second of DeMorgan's laws simplifies to (~B and ~J). This diagram tells us that neither of them is going to the party.

A unless B

~B—>A

"A unless B" is a rather complex structure. Though surprisingly we use it with little thought or confusion in our day-to-day speech.

To see that "A unless B" is equivalent to "~B—>A," consider the following situation:

Biff is at the beach unless it is raining.

Given this statement, we know that if it is not raining, then Biff is at the beach. Now if we symbolize "Biff is at the beach" as B, and "it is raining" as R, then the statement can be diagrammed as

~R—>B

Example: ***(A unless B)***

Melinda can become a lawyer unless she does poorly on the LSAT or does not get a scholarship.

Which one of the following statements cannot be validly drawn from the above statements?

(A) Melinda is lawyer. So she must have both done well on the LSAT and gotten a scholarship.
(B) Melinda is a lawyer and she did well on the LSAT. So she must have gotten a scholarship.
(C) Melinda did poorly on the LSAT. So she will not become a lawyer.
(D) If Melinda does not become a lawyer, then she did poorly on the LSAT or could not get a scholarship.
(E) If Melinda does poorly on the LSAT and does not get a scholarship, then she will not become a lawyer.

This argument says that two things stand in Melinda's way—performing poorly on the LSAT and not getting a scholarship. That is, if Melinda does well on the LSAT and gets a scholarship, then she *can* become a lawyer.

Since Melinda is a lawyer in choice (A), she must have overcome the two obstacles—the LSAT and the scholarship. Hence (A) is valid. This eliminates (A). Next, (B) essentially expresses the same thought as (A). This eliminates (B). Next, (C) says that Melinda didn't meet one of the two criteria, so she won't become a lawyer. Hence (C) is valid. This eliminates (C). You should notice that the conclusion in (D) is too strong. Melinda may do well on the LSAT *and* get a scholarship yet decide not to become a lawyer. The answer, therefore, is (D).

Advanced Concepts

Example: ***(A unless B)***

Any person who scores poorly on the LSAT will not get into Law School unless he bribes the admissions officers or has a relative on the board of regents.

Based on the above statements, all of the following statements can be made EXCEPT.

(A) If a person who did poorly on the LSAT has neither the money to bribe the admissions officers nor a relative on the board of regents, then he will not get into law school.

(B) If a person did poorly on the LSAT, is in law school, and does not have a relative on the board of regents, then he must have bribed the admissions officers.

(C) If a person does not take the LSAT but has a relative on the board of regents, then he will get into law school.

(D) If a person is in law school and does not have relatives on the board of regents nor has ever committed bribery, then he must have done well on the LSAT.

(E) If a person did poorly on the LSAT, is in law school, and did not bribe anyone, then he must have a relative on the board of regents.

Let's start by symbolizing the argument. Symbolize the phrase "will get into law school" as S.* Next, symbolize the phrase "he bribes an admission officer" as B. Finally, symbolize the phrase "has a relative on the board of regents" as R. Substituting the symbols into the argument, we get the following diagram:

~(B or R)<—>~S

which simplifies to

(B or R)<—>S

(Note: We'll add the phrase "any person who scored poorly on the LSAT" to the diagram later.)

We now use this diagram to analyze each of the answer-choices. As for choice (A), from ~S we can conclude, by applying the contrapositive to the diagram, ~(B or R). From DeMorgan's laws, we know that this is equivalent to ~B & ~R. This is the premise of (A). That is, (A) is a valid argument by contraposition. This eliminates (A).

Since choice (B) affirms S, we know from the diagram that B or R must be true. But choice (B) denies R. So from the meaning of "or," we know that B must be true. This is the conclusion of choice (B). Hence choice (B) is a valid deduction. This eliminates choice (B).

For simplicity we did not diagram the entire argument. But for choice (C), we need to complete the diagram. The premise of the argument is "any person who scores poorly on the LSAT." This clause can be reworded as "If a person does poorly on the LSAT," which can be symbolized as P. Affixing this to the original diagram gives

P—>[(B or R)<—>S].

Recall that if the premise of an *if-then* statement is true then the conclusion must be true as well. But if the premise is false, then we cannot determine whether the conclusion is true or false. Now (C) negates the premise, ~P. So its conclusion—that a person will get into law school, S—is a non sequitur. Hence (C) is the answer.

* Note that we dropped the "not" from the original phrase.

Game-Like Arguments

Although they do not occur frequently, game-like arguments are common enough to warrant study. Game-like arguments are symbolized just like logical structure arguments, but in these cases you will be asked to draw a conclusion.

Example: ***(Game)***

No one will be admitted to Yale Law School unless he or she studies hard for the LSAT. No one studied hard for the LSAT unless he or she was not a graduate from Tri-State University.

Which one of the following conclusions necessarily follows from the above statements?

(A) No graduate of Tri-State University was admitted to Yale Law School.
(B) Some graduates of Tri-State University were admitted to Yale Law School.
(C) All graduates of Tri-State University studied hard for the LSAT.
(D) Only graduates of Tri-State University did well on the LSAT.
(E) Only college graduates did well on the LSAT.

We begin by symbolizing the statements. "*No one will be admitted to Yale Law School unless he or she studies hard for the LSAT*" can be symbolized as

~SH—>~Y,

where SH stands for "*he or she studies hard for the LSAT,*" and Y stands for "*admitted to Yale Law School.*"

The second condition appears confusing at first but is actually straightforward once we get around the obfuscating tactics. "*No one studied hard for the LSAT unless he or she was not a graduate from Tri-State University*" can be symbolized as

~(~G)—>~SH,

where G indicates "*a graduate of Tri-State University.*" Recalling that two negatives make a positive, we simplify this to

G—>~SH

Using the transitive property to combine this with the first premise, **~SH—>~Y**, yields

G—>~Y

In other words, if a person graduated from Tri-State University, he or she was not admitted to Yale. The answer is (A).

Points to Remember

1. The first step in analyzing a logical-structure argument is to decide whether the original statement is valid. If it is, then the answer must be valid as well. If it is invalid, then the answer must be invalid.

2. Look for embedded *if-then* statements.

3. An *if-then* statement, A—>B, tells us only two things: (1) If A is true, then B is true as well. (2) If B is false, then A is false as well (contrapositive).

4. Affirming the conclusion fallacy:

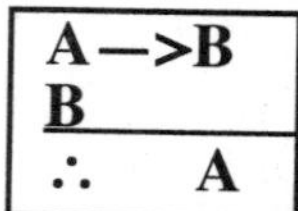

5. Denying the premise fallacy:

A—>B
~A
∴ ~B

6. Transitive property:

A—>B
B—>C
∴ A—>C

7. DeMorgan's Laws:

~(A & B) = ~A or ~B
~(A or B) = ~A & ~B

8. A unless B:

~B—>A

Exercise

Directions: The questions in this section are based on the reasoning contained in brief statements or passages. For some questions, more than one of the choices could conceivably answer the question. However, you are to choose the best answer; that is, the response that most accurately and completely answers the question. You should not make assumptions that are by common sense standards implausible, superfluous, or incompatible with the passage.

1. When a region is in a drought, the water level of rivers and streams is seriously reduced. When water levels are down, food is also scarce for wildlife. Therefore, if food is not scarce for wildlife, then the region is not in a drought.

   In which one of the following selections does the reasoning most closely follow the reasoning in the above passage?

   (A) If the dirty clothes hamper is full, the sock drawer is empty, and if the sock drawer is empty, the dirty clothes hamper is full, so if the sock drawer is not empty, the clothes hamper is not full.

   (B) If the temperature falls below freezing, the petunias will die, and if the petunias die, they will not flower any more, so if the petunias still produce flowers, the temperature is not below freezing.

   (C) If raccoons bear live young, they must be mammals, so if they are amphibians, they must lay eggs to reproduce, if they reproduce at all.

   (D) If you want to fix an omelet, you will have to use six eggs, and you will have no eggs left for pancakes, so if you make the omelet, you won't be able to fix pancakes.

   (E) If earth scientists are correct, global temperatures are warming, and if the earth's temperature increases, ocean levels will rise, so if ocean levels rise, earth scientists were correct.

2. Magazine commentary: If the major television networks acted responsibly, they would commit their most talented writers, directors and actors to create quality programs suitable for family viewing during "prime time" viewing hours each weekday evening. Instead, television programming is full of sex, violence, and adult situations and language. In fact, the most-watched programs are a situation comedy full of degrading and sexual humor and a police show with frequent violence and adult language. At present, only a few networks carry quality programs that are suitable for family viewing.

   If you assume that the statements in the commentary are true, then which one of the following statements must also be true?

   (A) Children are being exposed to adult situations and language at a younger age.

   (B) Networks that carry programs unsuitable for family viewing are only concerned with the bottom line financially and do not act responsibly toward their viewing public.

   (C) Only a minority of families watch programs carried on public television stations.

   (D) Advertisers must put pressure on the major networks to carry more programs suitable for family viewing.

   (E) Most of the major networks are not meeting their responsibility to bring the public high quality programs suitable for family viewing.

3. Some folks who live in the hills belong to the Hatfield clan; others belong to the McCoy clan.
No Hatfields can farm.
All McCoys can farm.
Therefore, McCoys are not Hatfields.
Everyone who is not a Hatfield is a horseback rider.

Assume that each one of the above statements is true. Which of the following must be true if it is also true that no Hatfields ride horses.

(A) The only people who can farm are horseback-riding McCoys.
(B) Anyone who does not belong to the McCoy clan belongs to the Hatfield clan.
(C) All horseback riders can farm.
(D) All horseback riders must be McCoys.
(E) All McCoys are horseback riders.

4. If you make good grades in high school, you will get into a good college. If you get into a good college, you will find a good job. So, if you make good grades in high school, you will find a good job.

Which one of the following selections most closely follows the reasoning in the passage?

(A) If you brush your teeth twice every day, you will keep your teeth clean. If you keep your teeth clean, you will not get cavities. So, if you brush your teeth twice every day, you will have low dental bills.
(B) If you vacuum your room on Fridays, it will stay clean. If your room stays clean, you can invite your friends over. So, if you invite your friends over, your room will stay clean.
(C) If you plant your garden in healthy soil, your vegetable plants will grow well. If your vegetable plants grow well, you will have a high vegetable yield. So, if you plant your garden in healthy soil, you will have a high vegetable yield.
(D) If you invest in the stock market, you are optimistic that the market will go up. If you have a good attitude about things in general, then you are optimistic that the market will go up. So, if you invest in the market, you have a good attitude about things in general.
(E) If you study hard for the math exam, you will make an A on the exam. If you study hard for the math exam, you will not get enough sleep. So if you make an A on the math exam, you will not get enough sleep.

5. If the dog is a collie, it will shed its downy undercoat only in the spring. The dog shed in the spring, so it must be a collie.

Which one of the following selections demonstrates the same reasoning presented in the passage?

(A) In the winter time in the mountains, it frequently snows. Three inches of snow fell last night, so it must be winter.
(B) When the wind sweeps down from the mountains, a cold front will follow right behind. Right now the winds are gusting up to 40 mph, so a cold front must be on its way.
(C) The crystal paperweights in Sharon's paperweight collection are always dusted very carefully. The red paperweight is not handled carefully when dusted, so it must not be a crystal paperweight.
(D) One more hard frost would kill the tomato plants. But a week later, the tomato plants were still alive. Therefore, a hard frost must not have occurred within the last week.
(E) One must be very coordinated like Franklin to be a good drummer. However, Franklin's inability to read music will prevent him from being a good drummer.

6. The art jury will select either Fillmore's or Clivestone's sculptures, but not both, for the midwest art show to be held next spring. If Fillmore's sculptures are chosen, then the show will contain bronze works. If Clivestone's sculptures are selected, the show will contain sculptures made from stainless steel.

Assuming the statements in the passage are true, which one of the following statements must also be true?

(A) The art show might contain no bronze or stainless steel sculptures.
(B) If the art show contains bronze sculptures, then it is certain that Fillmore's sculptures were chosen for the show.
(C) The art show will certainly contain either bronze or stainless steel sculptures, and the art show will most certainly not contain both types of sculptures.
(D) If the art show contains stainless steel sculptures, it is possible, but not certain, that Clivestone's sculptures were selected by the jury for the show.
(E) If the art show contains neither bronze nor stainless steel sculptures, it is certain that neither Fillmore's nor Clivestone's sculptures were selected for the show.

7. Senator Janice White is quietly lobbying to become chairman of one of the Senate's most prestigious committees. However, that post currently belongs to Senator Dan Smith. If Senator Smith already has twenty senators committed to his continued chairmanship of the committee, then Senator White will consider another committee. If Senator Smith does not have that much support lined up yet, then Senator White will study Senator Smith's past committee voting record for inconsistent and unpopular votes. If Senator White finds that Smith's voting record is out of favor with today's voter and publicizes it, then her chances of capturing the chairmanship would be increased, and she would publicly announce her interest in the chairmanship. If Senator Smith's committee voting record is in keeping with current public sentiment and contains no inconsistencies, then Senator White will focus her attention on another committee chairmanship.

Based upon the information provided in the passage, which one of the following statements must be false?

(A) Senator Smith has lined up only five votes, and Senator White drops her interest in the committee chairmanship.
(B) A number of inconsistencies are found in Senator Smith's voting record, and Senator White publicly announces her interest in the committee chairmanship.
(C) Several of Senator Smith's past committee votes would find disfavor with today's voting public, and Senator White does not pursue the committee chairmanship.
(D) Senator Smith's past committee voting record contains nothing that would increase Senator White's chances of obtaining the chairmanship, and Senator White publicly announces her interest in being named chairman.
(E) Senator Smith already has the support of thirty of his fellow senators, and Senator White focuses her interest on another committee.

8. People who do well in the sled pull competition have tremendous upper body strength. Caleb has tremendous upper body strength. Therefore, Caleb performed well in the sled pull competition.

Which one of the following contains the same reasoning that is presented in the passage?

(A) People who are anemic cannot donate blood. Mary donates blood regularly. Therefore, she must not be anemic.
(B) People who swim competitively are thin and muscular. Ben is thin and muscular Therefore, Ben is a competitive swimmer.
(C) People who volunteer at the trauma center must handle being on their feet all day. Casey is a frequent volunteer at the trauma center. Therefore, he must handle being on his feet all day.
(D) People who are overly sensitive to the cold cannot work at the Arctic substation. John is overly sensitive to the cold. Therefore John cannot work at the Arctic substation.
(E) People who have ulcers cannot eat spicy hot food. Kevin has recurrent ulcers. Therefore Kevin is on a bland diet.

9. If the City Parks Department receives the same allocation in next year's municipal budget, it is expected to raise admission fees to the indoor recreation center by fifty cents. If the City Parks Department announces a higher admission fee increase, then its budget allocation for next year must have been reduced.

Which of the following selections expresses a reasoning pattern most similar to the pattern expressed in the passage?

(A) If the mountains continue to receive snow at the rate experienced for the past two weeks, ski areas would have a record snow base this winter. Instead, snow fall diminished, and ski areas have a normal ski base this winter.

(B) If urban neighborhoods wish to reduce crime in their neighborhoods, they should implement neighborhood crime watch programs. If neighborhoods experience higher burglary and theft rates, it must mean that they have not have implemented crime watch programs.

(C) If the price of raw plastic pellets remains the same, companies that manufacture molded plastic parts such as fishing bobbers can be expected to keep their wholesale prices at last year's levels. Thus, if these wholesalers raise their prices on fishing bobbers, it will be because raw material costs increased.

(D) If major league baseball teams wish to increase attendance at home games, they should not increase their ticket prices. If they do increase ticket prices, they should be expected to provide better seating and concessions at the stadiums.

(E) If television networks want to broadcast quality programming, they should recruit programs with good writers and actors. Thus, if the networks recruit poorly written and poorly acted programs, it is likely their television viewership will decline.

10. A movie publicist accompanied a new movie release with the following endorsement: This movie is a must-see for men and women who are in or want to have a committed relationship in the Nineties. While the leading actor in the movie has unrefined edges, he eventually becomes sensitive and caring. The leading actress begins to understand and appreciate her lover's uniquely male characteristics without booting him out the door. If you are a true Nineties man or woman—self-reliant, yet perceptive and caring—you must see this movie!

If the publicist's claims about the movie are true, which one of the following is also true?

(A) Men and women who are perceptive and caring are also self-reliant.

(B) A man who has seen the movie but is still not perceptive and caring misrepresents himself as a true Nineties man.

(C) People who go to the movie described in the passage are more sensitive than people who go to action thriller movies.

(D) No other movie recognizes true Nineties men and women.

(E) Most everyone would recognize the type of man or woman who would go to see the movie described in the passage.

11. A manufacturer can only recoup its retooling costs for redesigning a product if it sells enough of the product to its distributors to pass its break-even point. Unless retail companies believe the product will sell well, however, they will not buy enough of the product from distributors to enable the manufacturer to recoup its costs. Manufacturers are more likely to retool products if the products have scored favorably in market studies or if large advance orders for the redesigned products have come in before the retooling process is started, or both.

Of the following selections, which one can be appropriately inferred from the above passage?

(A) If a manufacturer receives large advance orders for the redesigned product from its distributors, it will recoup its retooling costs.

(B) Retail companies that stock products based on favorable market studies will sell a lot of products.

(C) A manufacturer that has recouped its retooling costs has sold enough of the redesigned product to pass its break-even point.

(D) A manufacturer that did not get many advance orders for a redesigned product did not make a profit.

(E) A manufacturer that had enough sales of a redesigned product to pass its break-even point by a wide margin did not make a profit on its sale of the product.

12. If a person studies four hours a day for the LSAT, he will score in the top 10 percent. Every student at Harvard School of Law scored in the top 10 percent. Thus, Sarah who is studying at Harvard School of Law must have studied at least four hours a day.

The reasoning in the argument above is flawed because it

(A) fails to consider that many students at Harvard studied more than four hours a day.
(B) fails to consider that studies have shown that studying one subject more than three hours a day can be counterproductive.
(C) fails to consider that studying less than four hours a day may be sufficient for some people to score in the top 10 percent.
(D) fails to consider that people who studied less than three hours a day did not get into Harvard.
(E) fails to consider that an additional eight hours a week of studying is an impossible burden for most college students.

13. To avoid economic collapse, Russia must increase its GNP by 20%. However, due to the structure of its economy, if the 20% threshold is reached, then a 40% increase in GNP is achievable.

Assuming that the above statements are true, which one of the following must also be true?

(A) If ethnic strife continues in Russia, then a 20% increase in GNP will be unattainable.
(B) If a 40% increase in Russia's GNP is impossible, its economy will collapse.
(C) If Russia's GNP increases by 40%, its economy will not collapse.
(D) If the 20% threshold is reached, then a 40% increase in GNP is achievable and a 60% increase is probable.
(E) If Russia's economy collapses, then it will not have increased its GNP by 40%.

14. If the rebels truly want a political settlement, they will stop shelling the Capitol. They did stop shelling the Capitol. Hence, the rebels sincerely want peace.

Which one of the following uses reasoning that is most similar to that used in the above argument?

(A) There's a cat in this house. There must be, because I'm allergic to cats; and I just sneezed.
(B) In order for a bill to pass, it must be supported by the President. The Crime Bill is not being supported by the President. Therefore, it will not pass.
(C) The flood of refugees will continue unless the U.N. sends in peace keepers. The U.N. has announced that peace-keeping troops will not be sent, so the flood of refugees will continue.
(D) Every time the United States attempts to mediate between two warring parties, it becomes the target of both. So the same will occur with the civil war in Girunda.
(E) If you want dessert, you must eat your vegetables. You did not eat your vegetables, so there will be no dessert for you.

15. If Joan was growing marijuana plants in her home, she would not allow police investigators to search her home without a warrant. As a result, allowing the police to search her home without a warrant shows that Joan does not grow marijuana plants in her home.

Which one of the following contains an argument logically most similar to the argument presented in the passage?

(A) If Justin were playing golf at the city golf course, he would not be home until dinner. Therefore, the fact that he gets home by mid-afternoon shows that he is not playing golf at the city course.
(B) If Paul were stingy, he would not buy Dorian a birthday present. Therefore, Paul's buying Francis a birthday present shows that he is stingy.
(C) If Jason were over 30, he would not want to listen to rap music. Therefore, the fact that Jason does not like to listen to rap music shows that he is over 30.
(D) If Sandra were a good seamstress, she would not buy cheap fabric. Therefore, the fact that Sandra is not a good seamstress shows that she bought cheap fabric.
(E) If Kevin were hungry, he would not skip breakfast. Therefore, the fact that Kevin is hungry shows that he did not skip breakfast.

16. Students at Lincoln High School will boycott graduation ceremonies unless the administration allows the band director to keep his teaching position rather than forcing him to retire at the end of the school year. If the band director continues to teach at the high school, however, then the administration will have to eliminate one of the new coaching positions it planned for next year. So, the new coaching position will be eliminated.

The conclusion stated in the passage above is properly drawn if which one of the following assumptions is made?

(A) Students will drop out of the band program.
(B) The administration will insist that the high school band director retire.
(C) The students will not boycott graduation ceremonies.
(D) The administration has the authority to allow the band director to keep his teaching position.
(E) The high school students will not drop their threat to boycott graduation ceremonies if other student benefits are offered.

17. A lawyer who does not return phone calls from her clients cannot be a skillful, experienced lawyer. I feel comfortable with the skill and experience of my attorney because she returns all of my phone calls, even when she is busy.

Which of the following selections presents a reasoning pattern most similar to the flawed pattern presented in the passage?

(A) Anyone who plays on a baseball team has had to make sacrifices for the good of the team. Ted is used to making sacrifices, so he might play on a baseball team.
(B) Anyone who is opposed to the city bond issue has not received the city's information packet on the issue. Sandy says she will vote against the city bond issue, so she hasn't received the city information packet.
(C) No one who likes science fiction movies will miss seeing the second release of the Star Wars trilogy in movie theaters. Jimmy loves the Star Wars movies, but he did not see the second movie of the trilogy when it was released recently.
(D) A school-age child who spends three afternoons a week at gymnastics practice does not have a proper balance between school work and gymnastics. Tom spends only one afternoon per week at gymnastics practice, so he has a proper balance between school and gymnastics.
(E) A person who is jumpy and impatient will not work well with animals. Janice is impatient, so she would not be a good animal trainer.

18. Rebecca: When I went hiking in the mountains the other day, every bird that scolded me was a Steller's Jay, and every Steller's Jay I saw scolded me.

Which one of the following statements can be inferred from Rebecca's observations?

(A) The only jays that Rebecca saw while hiking were Steller's Jays.
(B) There were no Gray Jays in the area where Rebecca hiked.
(C) While she was hiking, no Gray Jays scolded Rebecca.
(D) All the jays that Rebecca saw scolded her.
(E) Rebecca did not see any Gray Jays while she was hiking.

Solutions to Embedded If-Then Drill

	Sentence	*If-Then* Form
1.	Only if John is allowed to go will Ken go.	If Ken goes, then John is allowed to go.
2.	Give a talented teacher academic freedom, and she will excel.	If a talented teacher is given academic freedom, she will excel.
3.	No Montague is a Rothschild.	If Montague, then not Rothschild.
4.	Anyone who is not a Montague cannot be a Rothschild.	If not a Montague, then not Rothschild.
5.	All Montagues are Rothschilds.	If Montague, then Rothschild.
6.	Only Montagues are Rothschilds.	If Rothschild, then Montague.
7.	A Montague will not attend a party hosted by a Rothschild.	If a Rothschild hosts a party, then a Montague will not attend.
8.	Men and women cannot understand each other.	If Pat is a man, then he can't understand women. If Pat is a woman, then she can't understand men.
9.	There is no God but Allah.	If G is God, then G is Allah.
10.	None but the worthy are saved.	If X is saved, then X is worthy.
11.	For a Montague to attend a party it is necessary for a Rothschild to attend.	If a Montague attends a party, then a Rothschild attends.

Answers and Solutions to Exercise

1.	B	7.	D	13.	B
2.	E	8.	B	14.	A
3.	E	9.	C	15.	A
4.	C	10.	B	16.	C
5.	A	11.	C	17.	D
6.	D	12.	C	18.	C

1. The statement, "When a region is in a drought, the water level of rivers and streams is seriously reduced," can be pictured as:

D—>WR

The statement, "When water levels are down, food is also scarce for wildlife," can be pictured as:

WR—>FS

The statement "if food is not scarce for wildlife, then the region is not in a drought" can be pictured as:

~FS—>~D

The diagram for the entire passage looks like this:

D—>WR
WR—>FS
~FS—>~D

The diagram shows the argument to be a valid application of the transitive and contrapositive properties.

Take a minute to diagram the five possible answers. In choice (B), the statement, "If the temperature falls below freezing, the petunias will die" can be pictured as:

F—>PD

The clause "if the petunias die, they will not flower any more" can be pictured as:

PD—>NF

Finally, the clause "if the petunias still produce flowers, the temperature is not below freezing" can be pictured as:

~NF—>~F

If you diagram the entire petunia passage, it looks like this:

F—>PD
PD—>NF
~NF—>~F

The diagram follows the same sequence as the diagram for the passage. Thus the argument in selection (B) is also a valid application of the transitive and contrapositive properties. The answer is selection (B).

2.
(A) No. The commentator argues that the networks are not acting responsibly. While the author could perhaps place some of the blame on the viewing audience, he does not.
(B) No. The commentator does not tell us why the networks don't broadcast more family programs, so this statement does not follow from the passage.
(C) No. Again, we do not know from the passage anything about the programming on public television stations or what the viewership is for those stations.
(D) No. The commentator is concerned that the networks are not acting responsibly; he does not elicit help from television advertisers in this passage.
(E) **Yes.** The commentator states that if networks acted responsibly, they would broadcast more family programming. The passage strongly implies that the networks are not currently meeting their responsibility to the viewing public.

Selection (E) is an application of the contrapositive. The commentator's argument can be diagrammed as follows:

R—>~SVL

R stands for "If the major television networks acted responsibly," and **~SVL** stands for "they would commit their most talented writers, directors and actors to create quality programs suitable for family viewing during "prime time" viewing hours each weekday evening." The next statement in the passage negates both sides of this diagram, changing the **R** to **~R** and **~SVL** to **SVL**. "Instead, television programming is full of sex, violence, and adult situations and language." The diagram would look like the following:

~R—>SVL

Selection (E) also applies the contrapositive to the author's initial conclusion. The networks are not acting responsibly, so "prime time" television is still full of sex, adult language and violence. **~R—>SVL**. Thus, (E) follows from the commentator's position. Most major networks are not meeting their responsibility to provide high quality programs suitable for family viewing.

3. This problem looks rather complicated at first glance. But only the last two statements of the passage are necessary to solve the problem. The statement, *"Therefore, McCoys are not Hatfields"* contains an embedded if-then statement. *"If a person belongs to the McCoy clan, they he does not belong to the Hatfield clan."* This statement can be diagrammed as follows:

M—>~H

The next statement, "Everyone who is not a Hatfield is a horseback rider" also contains an embedded if-then statement: "If a person is not a Hatfield, then he is a horseback rider." This can be diagrammed as:

~H—>R

If you use the transitive property to combine these two diagrams, the following diagram results:

M—>R

This diagram is translated to read that if a person belongs to the McCoy clan, then he is a horseback rider. This is the same as saying that all McCoys are horseback riders. Thus, selection (E) is the correct answer.

4. This passage applies the transitive property, just like the preceding passage did. *"If you make good grades in high school, you will get into a good college"* can be diagrammed as:

GG—>GC

The next statement, "If you get into a good college, you will find a good job," can be diagrammed as follows:

GC—>GJ

Finally, if you combine these two statements using the transitive property, your diagram will look like the following:

GG—>GJ

The author concludes that good grades in high school will result in a good job.

Quickly diagram out the statements contained in each of the five possible answers. Notice that selection (C) also makes use of the transitive property. The first statement, *"If you plant your garden in healthy soil, your vegetable plants will grow well,"* can be diagrammed as follows:

HS—>PG

The next statement, "If your vegetable plants grow well, you will have a high vegetable yield," looks like the following:

PG—>HY

If you combine these two statements using the transitive property, your conclusion will be: "If *you plant your garden in healthy soil, you will have a high vegetable yield"* and your diagram will look like:

HS—>HY

This is the same reasoning followed in the passage. As a result, selection (C) is correct. The other selections do not follow the same reasoning presented in the passage.

5. This question presents an example of faulty reasoning. "If the dog is a collie, it will shed its downy undercoat only in the spring" can be pictured as

C—>S

The next clause, *"The dog shed in the spring,"* can be pictured as

S

The conclusion of the passage, *"so it must be a collie,"* can be pictured as

∴ C

The entire passage can be diagrammed as follows:

C—>S
S____
∴ C

This diagram shows that the argument mistakenly affirms the conclusion. One of the selections makes the same mistake. Briefly diagram the answer selections to see which argument mistakenly affirms the conclusion the same way the collie example does.

In selection (A), the first sentence, "In the winter time in the mountains, it frequently snows," can be pictured as

W—>S

The next clause, *"Three inches of snow fell last night,"* can be diagrammed as follows:

S

Finally, the conclusion, *"so it must be winter,"* can be diagrammed as follows:

∴ W

The entire argument in diagram form is pictured as

W—>S
S____
∴ W

The argument in selection (A) presents the same diagram as the argument in the passage. Both commit the fallacy of affirming the conclusion. Selection (A) is the correct answer.

6. The passage indicates that the sculptures of Fillmore or Clivestone will be selected for the art show, but not both. The diagram would look like (**F—>B) or (C—>SS)**. Each of the selections can be considered against this diagram.

Selection (A) states that the show will not contain bronze or stainless steel sculptures. It is obviously false because the passage says that one or the other type sculptures will be selected for the show. Selection (B) is flawed because the conclusion is used to affirm the premise. Instead of **F—>B**, selection (B) concludes **B—>F**. But we don't know if the reverse is true. Bronze sculptures by another artist might have been selected for the show. The first part of selection (C) is correct because we know that either Fillmore's or Clivestone's works will be selected for the show. But we do not have enough information to know whether the second part of (C) is true. As with (B), perhaps other artists will be featured whose work includes bronze or stainless steel sculptures. Selection (E) sounds true, but it contradicts the passage. The author tells us that one or the other will be selected. So (E) is not correct.

Selection (D) is the best answer. Since Clivestone's sculptures might be chosen over Fillmore's, it is certainly possible that the show would contain his stainless steel sculptures. (D) begins by affirming the conclusion to the diagram **C—>SS**. But unlike the flawed selection (B), (D) does not rule out other possibilities. In fact, selection (D) is perhaps too weak to be untrue. It states that the stainless steel sculptures in the show might be Clivestone's sculptures. This is true.

7. The question asks which one of the selections is false based upon the information provided in the passage below. Selection (A) might be true because Senator Smith's voting record might be unchallengeable. The scenario in selection (B) could certainly happen. If Senator Smith hasn't lined up enough support, and if his voting record isn't perfect, Senator White will challenge him for the chairmanship. Selection (C) does not consider the amount of support behind Senator Smith. If twenty-five senators are already lined up behind him, then his voting record is irrelevant. Selection (E) is correct because if Senator Smith has the support of thirty senators, Senator White will not challenge him.

Selection (D) is the correct answer. It is inconsistent with the passage that Senator White would strive for the chairmanship if Senator Smith's voting record is good. The passage indicates that "*If Senator White finds that Smith's voting record is out of favor with today's voter and publicizes it, then her chances of capturing the chairmanship would be increased.*" This can diagrammed as follows:

BV—>I

If you apply the contrapositive to this statement, your diagram will look like this:

~I—>~BV

The next sentence in the passage, "If Senator Smith's committee voting record is in keeping with current public sentiment and contains no inconsistencies, then Senator White will focus her attention on another committee chairmanship," can be reworded to say that "If Senator Smith has a good committee voting record, then Senator White will not seek the chairmanship." This can be diagrammed as follows:

~BV—>~CH

If you use the transitive property to combine this with the statement **~I—>~BV**, your diagram will look like the following:

~I—>~CH

In selection (D), the clause "Senator Smith's past committee voting record contains nothing that would increase Senator White's chances of obtaining the chairmanship" — **~I** — affirms the premise of the last diagram. Hence, we conclude that Senator White does not seek the chairmanship — **~CH**. But Selection (D) negates this conclusion. It states that despite Senator Smith's good voting record, Senator White publicly announces her interest in being named chairman — **CH**. Thus, the statement in Selection (D) is false and is the correct answer.

8. The error in this passage is that it affirms the conclusion. The first sentence, "*People who do well in the sled pull competition have tremendous upper body strength,*" is represented by the following:

SP—>UBS

The next sentence, "*Caleb has tremendous upper body strength,*" affirms the conclusion. But the last sentence, "*Therefore, Caleb performed well in the sled pull competition,*" invalidly affirms the premise that leads to the conclusion. This fallacy is diagrammed below.

SP—>UBS
UBS
∴ **SP**

This diagram clearly displays the fallacy in affirming the conclusion.

In selection (B), the same fallacy exists. It can be demonstrated by diagramming the sentences in selection (B). "People who swim competitively are thin and muscular. Ben is thin and muscular. Therefore, Ben is a competitive swimmer."

SC—>TM
TM
∴ **SC**

Diagramming one of the other answer choices shows why the flaw exists in both the passage and selection (B). For example, take selection (D). "*People who are overly sensitive to the cold cannot work at the Arctic substation*" can be diagrammed as:

OS—>~AS

The last part of selection (D), "John is overly sensitive to the cold. Therefore John cannot work at the Arctic substation," adds to the diagram as follows:

OS—>~AS
<u>OS</u>
∴ **~AS**

In selection (D), the premise and conclusion are merely repeated in the last two sentences. In contrast, in the last part of the passage and in selection (B), the conclusion is used to affirm the premise. By diagramming these two different selections, the fallacy in the passage and in selection (B) becomes clear.

9. Diagramming this problem helps to simplify it. The sentence, "If the City Parks Department receives the same allocation in next year's municipal budget, it is expected to raise admission fees to the indoor recreation center by fifty cents," can be diagrammed as:

SA—>50¢

SA stands for "receives the same allocation in next year's municipal budget" and **50¢** stands for "raise admission fees to the indoor recreation center by fifty cents." The next sentence, "*If the City Parks Department announces a higher admission fee increase, then its budget allocation for next year must have been reduced,*" can be diagrammed as:

~50¢—>~SA

This diagram can be recognized as the contrapositive. Thus, in finding the answer to this problem, you should look for an "if, then" statement and its contrapositive. In selection (C), the sentence, "*If the price of raw plastic pellets remains the same, companies that manufacture molded plastic parts such as fishing tackles and other plastic fishing bobbers can be expected to keep their wholesale prices at last year's levels,*" can be diagrammed as follows:

P$—>W$

P$** stands for "the price of raw plastic pellets remains the same" and **W$ stands for "keep their wholesale prices at last year's levels." The sentence, "*Thus, if these wholesalers raise their prices on fishing bobbers, it will be because raw material costs increased.*" can be diagrammed as follows:

~W$—>~P$

This is the contrapositive of **P$—>W$**. The reasoning is the same as that expressed in the passage. The answer is selection (C).

10. The passage contains an embedded *if-then* statement. If you go to the movie, then you must be a true Nineties man or woman and have the three qualities listed—self-reliance, perceptiveness and a caring disposition. The selections should be considered with this *if-then* statement in mind.

(A) No. The passage states that if you are a Nineties man or woman and see the movie, you are self-reliant, perceptive and caring. But nothing in the passage makes these three characteristics interdependent upon each other.
(B) **Yes**. Again, as the passage recites, if you see the movie, you are a true Nineties man or woman—self-reliant, perceptive and caring. If a man sees the movie but he doesn't have all three characteristics, then he is not a true Nineties man and he misrepresents himself by going to the movie with that in mind.
(C) No. The passage doesn't tell us anything about the type of people who go see action thriller movies.
(D) No. The passage doesn't tell us anything about what claims have been made about other movies.
(E) No. The passage doesn't tell us how to make this determination.

11. The first sentence is all that is needed to determine the answer to this question. "A manufacturer <u>can only</u> recoup its retooling costs for redesigning a product if it sells enough of the product to its distributors to pass its break-even point." We can conclude from this statement that if a manufacturer has recouped its retooling costs on a product, it had enough sales to pass its break-even point. This can be symbolized as **RC—>BEP**. **RC** stands for "recoup costs" and **BEP** stands for "break-even point." Selection (C) affirms this hypothesis. It states that a manufacturer that has recouped its retooling costs, or **RC**, has sold enough product to pass its break-even point, **BEP**.

Selection (A) is not correct because we are not told how many orders it will take for the manufacturer to recoup its retooling costs. Selection (B) is irrelevant to the issue. Selection (D) is not correct because again, we are not told how many orders were necessary for the manufacturer to pass its break-even point. Maybe its retooling costs for the particular product were not high and not many sales would be needed to reach the break-even point. We aren't given enough information in (D) to know if it can be correctly inferred from the passage. Finally, (E) would appear to be contradictory and thus not properly inferred from the passage.

12. Begin by symbolizing the argument. The sentence "If a person studies four hours a day for the LSAT, he will score in the top 10 percent" can be symbolized as

4hrs—>10%

The sentence "Every student at Harvard School of Law scored in the top 10 percent" can be reworded as an if-then statement: "If a person is a student at Harvard School of Law, then he scored in the top 10 percent." This in turn can be symbolized as

H—>10%,

where H stands for *"a student at Harvard School of Law."* Now, the phrase *"Sarah who is studying at Harvard School of Law"* affirms the premise in the conditional **H—>10%**. Hence, we know she scored in the top 10%. This affirms the conclusion in the conditional **4hrs—>10%**. Up to here the argument is valid. But it then commits the fallacy of affirming the conclusion by stating than she must have studied 4 hours a day. This ignores the possibility that Sarah may be gifted and hence studying only two hours a day may have been sufficient for her. The answer is (C).

13. Diagramming will show this seemingly difficult problem to be simply an application of the contrapositive. The sentence *"To avoid economic collapse, Russia must increase its GNP by 20%"* can be reworded as *"if Russia does not increase its GNP by 20%, its economy will collapse."* This in turn can be symbolized as

~20% —>Collapse

Next, symbolize the clause *"if the 20% threshold is reached, then a 40% increase is achievable"* as

20% —>40%

Applying the contrapositive to this statement yields

~40% —>~20%

Using the transitive property to combine this with the first symbol statement yields

~40% —>Collapse

In other words, if a 40% increase in GNP is unattainable, the economy will collapse. This is precisely what choice (B) states. The answer is (B).

14. Let T stand for *"the rebels truly want a political settlement,"* and let S stand for *"they will stop shelling the Capitol."* Now the argument can be symbolized as

T—>S
S
∴ **T**

This diagram clearly shows that the argument is committing the fallacy of affirming the conclusion. The answer will commit the same fallacy.

Begin with choice (A). The clause *"I'm allergic to cats"* contains an embedded *if-then* statement: *"If there is a cat around, I start sneezing."* This in turn can be symbolized as **C—>Sn**, where C stands for *"there is a cat around,"* and Sn stands for *"I start sneezing."* Substituting these symbols into the argument yields

C—>Sn
Sn
∴ **C**

The diagram shows that this argument has the same structure as the original argument. The answer is (A).

15. In order to find the solution to this question, you should diagram the arguments presented in the passage and in the answer selections. The first clause, *"If Joan were growing marijuana plants in her home,"* can be symbolized as **MP**. The second clause, *"she would not allow police investigators to search her home without a warrant,"* can be symbolized as **~S**. The entire argument can be diagrammed as follows:

M—>~S
S
∴ **~MP**

This diagram shows that the argument is a valid application of the contrapositive.

Diagram each of the answer selections. For instance, selection (C) can be diagrammed as follows, where **>30** represents *"If Jason were over 30,"* and **~RM** represents *"he would not want to listen to rap music."* Diagramming the entire selection would look like this:

>30—>~RM
RM
∴ **>30**

As can be seen from the diagram, it does not correspond to the logic in the passage. Now, let's diagram selection (A). The first clause, *"If Justin were playing golf at the city golf course,"* can be represented as **G**, and the second clause, *"he would* *not be home until dinner,"* can be represented as **~H**. The rest of the argument can be represented as follows:

G—>~H
H
∴ **~G**

As you can see, the logic is the same in selection (A) as it is in the passage. It is a valid application of the contrapositive. You should also diagram the remaining selections to see how their logic patterns differ from the logic presented in the passage.

16. Remember, "A unless B" is the equivalent of ~B—>A. The first sentence in the passage can be depicted as

~BD—>BG

where **BD** stands for "the administration allows the band director to keep his teaching position" and **BG** stands for "Students at Lincoln High School will boycott graduation ceremonies." The second sentence contains an implied if-then statement. It can be stated as follows: "If the administration allows the band director to keep his teaching position, then it will have to eliminate one of the new coaching positions." This can be depicted as

BD—>EC

Of course, **EC** stands for *"it will have to eliminate one of the new coaching positions."* As presented, the two diagrammed statements cannot be connected. However, let's suppose the high school students do not boycott graduation ceremonies, which is selection (C). If we apply the contrapositive to the first diagram, **~BD—>BG**, the statement becomes

~BG—>BD

Then we can use the transitive property to combine **~BG—>BD** with **BD—>EC** to yield the following diagram:

~BG—>EC

That is, if the students don't boycott graduation ceremonies, then a new coaching position will be eliminated. Thus, the correct assumption is that the students will not boycott graduation ceremonies. The answer is selection (C).

17. The first part of the passage contains an implied if-then statement. It can be restated as, "If a lawyer does not return phone calls from her clients, then she cannot be a skillful, experienced lawyer." This can be pictured as

~PC—>~SE

Part of the next sentence in the passage, *"she returns all of my phone calls,"* negates the premise in the "if-then" statement. From this, the author concludes that her lawyer is skillful and experienced. This can be summarized as follows:

~PC—>~SE
PC
∴ **SE**

Remember that an *if-then* statement tells us only two things: First, it tells us that if the premise is true, then the conclusion is also true. Second, if the conclusion is false, then we know that the premise is also false. (This is the contrapositive.).

Thus, the diagram presents an *if-then* statement, and then denies the premise of the statement. Thus, we cannot say anything about the conclusion, not based upon what we know generally about *if-then* statements. If the conclusion were denied, then we would know the premise is false. But if the premise is false, we can go no further. We do not know the effect of a false premise upon the conclusion. This passage is an example of the fallacy of denying the premise.

Look at the structure of the answer selections. Selection (D) contains an implied if-then statement as follows: "If a school-age child spends three afternoons a week at gymnastics practice, then he does not have a proper balance between school work and gymnastics." This can be depicted as

3G—>~B

The next part of (D) negates the premise because it states that Tom does not spend three afternoons at gymnastics practice; he only spends one afternoon there. But the argument erroneously concludes that denying the premise also denies the conclusion. Denying that Tom does not have a proper balance (or concluding that Tom does have a proper balance between school work and gymnastics) does not necessarily follow from denying the premise. Thus, selection (D) presents the same erroneous reasoning presented in the passage and it is the correct answer.

18. The passage contains an embedded if-then statement. "Every bird that scolded me was a Steller's Jay" can be transformed into: If the bird scolded me, then it was a Steller's Jay. This can be diagrammed as

BS—>SJ

Keep this diagram in mind as you consider the answer selections.

(A). No. The passage indicates that every bird that scolded Rebecca was a Steller's Jay. Stating it another way, a bird scolded Rebecca if and only if it was a Steller's Jay. The passage doesn't preclude the possibility that Rebecca saw other types of jays that didn't scold her.
(B) No. Remember the diagram above, **BS—>SJ**. Gray Jays are not in the equation, but the equation indicates that if Rebecca saw any Gray Jays, they didn't scold her.
(C) **Yes**. Review the diagram again, **BS—>SJ**. If a particular bird scolded Rebecca, then it must have been a Steller's Jay, not a Gray Jay. Let's apply the contrapositive to the diagram:

~SJ—>~BS

A Gray Jay is not a Steller Jay. The hypothesis of the *if-then* contrapositive statement, **~SJ—>~BS**, is thus supported. As a result, the conclusion **~BS**, must follow. No Gray Jays scolded Rebecca.
(D) No. Unless all the jays Rebecca saw were Steller's Jays (which we do not know), this statement does not follow. This statement is not supported by the diagram, which is limited to Steller Jays.
(E) No. Again, consider the diagram, **BS—>SJ**. It does not exclude Gray Jays, but it does not allow them to scold Rebecca. So again, Rebecca could have seen Gray Jays, but they didn't scold her as she hiked.

Inductive Reasoning

In Logic II, we studied deductive arguments. However, the bulk of arguments on the LSAT are *inductive*. In this section we will classify and study the major types of inductive arguments.

An argument is deductive if its conclusion *necessarily* follows from its premises—otherwise it is inductive. In an inductive argument, the author presents the premises as evidence or reasons for the conclusion. The validity of the conclusion depends on how compelling the premises are. Unlike deductive arguments, the conclusion of an inductive argument is never certain. The *truth* of the conclusion can range from highly likely to highly unlikely. In reasonable arguments, the conclusion is likely. In fallacious arguments, it is improbable.

We will study both reasonable and fallacious arguments. Further, we will classify the three major types of inductive reasoning—generalization, analogy, and causal—and their associated fallacies.

Generalization

Generalization and analogy, which we consider in the next section, are the main tools by which we accumulate knowledge and analyze our world. Many people define *generalization* as "inductive reasoning." In colloquial speech, the phrase "to generalize" carries a negative connotation. To argue by generalization, however, is neither inherently good nor bad. The relative validity of a generalization depends on both the context of the argument and the likelihood that its conclusion is true. Polling organizations make predictions by generalizing information from a small sample of the population, which hopefully represents the general population. The soundness of their predictions (arguments) depends on how representative the sample is and on its size. Clearly, the less comprehensive a conclusion is the more likely it is to be true.

Example:

During the late seventies when Japan was rapidly expanding its share of the American auto market, GM surveyed owners of GM cars and asked them whether they would be more willing to buy a large, powerful car or a small, economical car. Seventy percent of those who responded said that they would prefer a large car. On the basis of this survey, GM decided to continue building large cars. Yet during the '80s, GM lost even more of the market to the Japanese.

Which one of the following, if it were determined to be true, would best explain this discrepancy.

(A) Only 10 percent of those who were polled replied.
(B) Ford which conducted a similar survey with similar results continued to build large cars and also lost more of their market to the Japanese.
(C) The surveyed owners who preferred big cars also preferred big homes.
(D) GM determined that it would be more profitable to make big cars.
(E) Eighty percent of the owners who wanted big cars and only 40 percent of the owners who wanted small cars replied to the survey.

The argument generalizes *from* the survey *to* the general car-buying population, so the reliability of the projection depends on how representative the sample is. At first glance, choice (A) seems rather good, because 10 percent does not seem large enough. However, political opinion polls are typically based on only .001 percent of the population. More importantly, we don't know what percentage of GM car owners received the survey. Choice (B) simply states that Ford made the same mistake that GM did. Choice (C) is irrelevant. Choice (D), rather than explaining the discrepancy, gives even more reason for GM to continue making large cars. Finally, choice (E) points out that part of the survey did not represent the entire public, so (E) is the answer.

Analogy

To argue by analogy is to claim that because two things are similar in some respects, they will be similar in others. Medical experimentation on animals is predicated on such reasoning. The argument goes like this: the metabolism of pigs, for example, is similar to that of humans, and high doses of saccharine cause cancer in pigs. Therefore, high doses of saccharine probably cause cancer in humans.

Clearly, the greater the similarity between the two things being compared, the stronger the argument will be. Also, the less ambitious the conclusion, the stronger the argument will be. The argument above would be strengthened by changing "probably" to "may." It can be weakened by pointing out the dissimilarities between pigs and people.

The following words usually indicate that an analogy is being drawn:

ANALOGY INDICATORS

like
similar
too
as with
likewise
also
compared to
just as . . . so too . . .

Often, however, a writer will use an analogy without flagging it with any of the above words.

Example:

Just as the fishing line becomes too taut, so too the trials and tribulations of life in the city can become so stressful that one's mind can snap.

Which one of the following most closely parallels the reasoning used in the argument above?

(A) Just as the bow may be drawn too taut, so too may one's life be wasted pursuing self-gratification.
(B) Just as a gambler's fortunes change unpredictably, so too do one's career opportunities come unexpectedly.
(C) Just as a plant can be killed by over watering it, so too can drinking too much water lead to lethargy.
(D) Just as the engine may race too quickly, so too may life in the fast lane lead to an early death.
(E) Just as an actor may become stressed before a performance, so too may dwelling on the negative cause depression.

The argument compares the tautness in a fishing line to the stress of city life; it then concludes that the mind can snap just as a fishing line can. So we are looking for an answer-choice that compares two things and draws a conclusion based on their similarity. Notice that we are looking for an argument that uses similar reasoning, but not necessarily similar concepts. In fact, an answer-choice that mentions either tautness or stress will probably be a same-language trap.

Choice (A) uses the same-language trap—notice "too taut." The analogy between a taut bow and self-gratification is weak, if existent. Choice (B) offers a good analogy but no conclusion. Choice (C) offers both a good analogy and a conclusion; however, the conclusion, "leads to lethargy," understates the scope of what the analogy implies. Choice (D) offers a strong analogy and a conclusion with the same scope found in the original: "the engine blows, the person dies"; "the line snaps, the mind snaps." This is probably the best answer, but still we should check every choice. The last choice, (E), uses language from the original, "stressful," to make its weak analogy more tempting. The *best* answer, therefore, is (D).

Causal Reasoning

Of the three types of inductive reasoning we will discuss, causal reasoning is both the weakest and the most prone to fallacy. Nevertheless, it is a useful and common method of thought.

To argue by causation is to claim that one thing causes another. A causal argument can be either weak or strong depending on the context. For example, to claim that you won the lottery because you saw a shooting star the night before is clearly fallacious. However, most people believe that smoking causes cancer because cancer often strikes those with a history of cigarette use. Although the connection between smoking and cancer is virtually certain, as with all inductive arguments it can never be 100 percent certain. Cigarette companies have claimed that there may be a genetic predisposition in some people to both develop cancer and crave nicotine. Although this claim is highly improbable, it is conceivable.

There are two common fallacies associated with causal reasoning:

1. **Confusing <u>Correlation</u> with <u>Causation</u>.**

   To claim that A caused B merely because A occurred immediately before B is clearly questionable. It may be only coincidental that they occurred together, or something else may have caused them to occur together. For example, the fact that insomnia and lack of appetite often occur together does not mean that one necessarily causes the other. They may both be symptoms of an underlying condition.

2. **Confusing Necessary Conditions with Sufficient Conditions.**

   A is necessary for B means "B cannot occur without A." *A is sufficient for B* means "A causes B to occur, but B can still occur without A." For example, a small tax base is sufficient to cause a budget deficit, but excessive spending can cause a deficit even with a large tax base. A common fallacy is to assume that a necessary condition is sufficient to cause a situation. For example, to win a modern war it is necessary to have modern, high-tech equipment, but it is not sufficient, as Iraq discovered in the Persian Gulf War.

Example: (This example is taken from a recent LSAT.)

The mind and the immune system have been shown to be intimately linked, and scientists are consistently finding that doing good deeds benefits one's immune system. The bone marrow and spleen, which produce the white blood cells needed to fight infection, are both connected by neural pathways to the brain. Recent research has shown that the activity of these white blood cells is stimulated by beneficial chemicals produced by the brain as a result of magnanimous behavior.

The statements above, if true, support the view that

(A) good deeds must be based on unselfish motives
(B) lack of magnanimity is the cause of most serious illnesses
(C) magnanimous behavior can be regulated by the presence or absence of certain chemicals in the brain
(D) magnanimity is beneficial to one's own interests
(E) the number of white blood cells will increase radically if behavior is consistently magnanimous

The gist of the argument is that being magnanimous makes you feel good, both mentally and physically. In other words, it is to your benefit to be kind and friendly. The answer is (D).

The other choices can be quickly dismissed. (A) is not supported by the passage. (B) commits the fallacy of denying the premise. The premise of the argument is *"when you behave magnanimously"* and the conclusion is *"you are less likely to get ill."* (B) negates the premise: *"lack of magnanimity."* Then invalidly concludes that illness will result. (C) has the wrong direction. It is magnanimous behavior that causes certain chemicals to be released; it is not chemicals that cause certain magnanimous impulses. Finally, (E) grossly overstates the argument. Beware of extreme words. (E) would be a much better choice if "radically" were dropped, though it would still be off the mark. The argument presents evidence only that the activity of white blood cells is stimulated by magnanimous behavior, not that their number increases.

All Things Being Equal

This rather amorphous category is the source of many LSAT questions. Usually, two situations are given that appear similar in all important aspects. From these two apparently similar situations, a conclusion will be drawn that may be surprising or contradictory. Your task in these problems is to show or speculate that there is a critical dissimilarity between the two situations (i.e., *Not All Things Are Equal*). The following example is a classic all-things-being-equal question.

Example: (This example is taken from a recent LSAT.)

If the public library shared by the adjacent towns of Redville and Glenwood were relocated from the library's current, overcrowded building in central Redville to a larger, available building in central Glenwood, the library would then be within walking distance of a larger number of library users. That is because there are many more people living in central Glenwood than in central Redville, and people generally will walk to the library only if it is located close to their homes.

Which one of the following, if true, most strengthens the argument?

(A) The public library was located between Glenwood and Redville before being moved to its current location in central Redville.
(B) The area covered by central Glenwood is approximately the same size as that covered by central Redville.
(C) The building that is available in Glenwood is smaller than an alternative building that is available in Redville.
(D) Many of the people who use the public library do not live in either Glenwood or Redville.
(E) The distance that people currently walk to get to the library is farther than what is generally considered walking distance.

This question hinges on the population densities of the two cities. Suppose Glenwood's population is twice Redville's but that the area of Glenwood is 10 times as large as the area of Redville. Then the population density of Glenwood would be one-fifth that of Redville. Hence, fewer people in Glenwood would be within walking distance of the library. The figure below illustrates the situation:

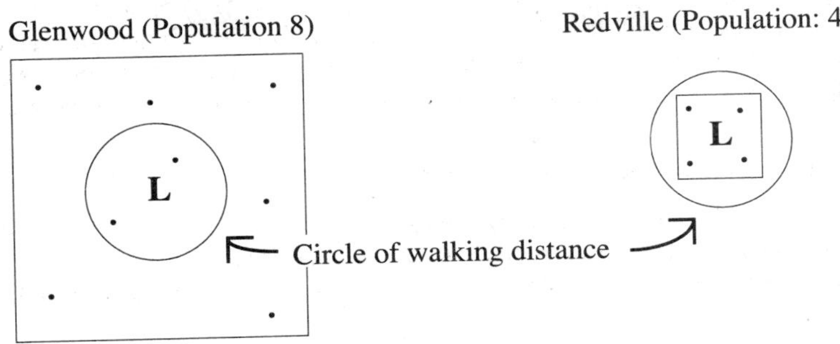

However, if the areas covered by Glenwood and Redville are roughly the same, then the population density of Glenwood would be greater than that of Redville. Hence, there would probably be more people within walking distance of the library in Glenwood than in Redville. The answer is (B).

CONTROLLED EXPERIMENTS

When applying a theory to a test group, one must also form a control group subject to identical conditions except for the one variable being tested. Only in this way can one be reasonably confident that the variable being tested was the cause of any observed difference in the test group.

Example: (This example is taken from a recent LSAT.)

A large group of hyperactive children whose regular diets included food containing large amounts of additives was observed by researchers trained to assess the presence or absence of behavior problems. The children were then placed on a low-additive diet for several weeks, after which they were observed again. Originally nearly 60 percent of the children exhibited behavior problems; after the change in diet, only 30 percent did so. On the basis of these data, it can be concluded that food additives can contribute to behavior problems in hyperactive children.

The evidence cited fails to establish the conclusion because

(A) there is no evidence that the reduction in behavior problems was proportionate to the reduction in food-additive intake

(B) there is no way to know what changes would have occurred without the change of diet, since only children who changed to a low-additive diet were studied

(C) exactly how many children exhibited behavior problems after the change in diet cannot be determined, since the size of the group studied is not precisely given

(D) there is no evidence that the behavior of some of the children was unaffected by additives

(E) the evidence is consistent with the claim that some children exhibit more frequent behavior problems after being on the low-additive diet than they had exhibited when first observed

In order for the conclusion to reasonably follow, we need to know what would have happened had the diet not been changed. Perhaps the same decrease in behavior problems would have occurred even if the diet was not changed. In other words, we need a control group with which to compare the results of the test group. The answer is (B).

Percentage vs. Absolute Number

We are prone to assume that if something occurs with a high percentage then there must be a large amount of it. The writers of the LSAT like to capitalize on this tendency. The following example will illustrate.

Example: (This example is taken from a recent LSAT.)

Nutritionists have recommended that people eat more fiber. Advertisements for a new fiber-supplement pill state only that it contains "44 percent fiber."

The advertising claim is misleading in its selection of information on which to focus if which one of the following is true?

(A) There are other products on the market that are advertised as providing fiber as a dietary supplement.
(B) Nutritionists base their recommendation on medical findings that dietary fiber protects against some kinds of cancer.
(C) It is possible to become addicted to some kinds of advertised pills, such as sleeping pills and painkillers.
(D) The label of the advertised product recommends taking 3 pills every day.
(E) The recommended daily intake of fiber is 20 to 30 grams, and the pill contains one-third gram.

Although a pill with 44 percent fiber sounds good, the more important issue is "How much of the fiber we need each day does the 44 percent represent?" If we need 100 grams of fiber daily and the pill though almost half fiber contains only one gram of fiber, then we would have to take 100 pills a day to get our daily intake. In this case, the fact that the pill is 44 percent fiber is insignificant, and it is therefore misleading for the advertisement to focus on the percentage of fiber instead of the absolute amount. The answer is (E).

Example: (This example is taken from a recent LSAT.)

The number of North American children who are obese—that is, who have more body fat than do 85 percent of North American children their age—is steadily increasing, according to four major studies conducted over the past 15 years.

If the finding reported above is correct, it can be properly concluded that

(A) when four major studies all produce similar results, those studies must be accurate
(B) North American children have been progressively less physically active over the past 15 years
(C) the number of North American children who are not obese increased over the past 15 years
(D) over the past 15 years, the number of North American children who are underweight has declined
(E) the incidence of obesity in North American children tends to increase as the children grow older

Notice that the percentage of children who are obese is by definition always 15 percent: Obese children are those "who have more body fat than do 85 percent of ... children their age." So if the absolute number of obese children increases, there must be a proportionate increase in the absolute number of children who are not obese. Otherwise, the 15 percent figure would change. For example, suppose in a particular population of 100 people, 15 are obese and 85 are not obese. Then the rate of obesity would be 15 percent. If 20 years later there are 200 people in the population, then for the obesity rate to remain 15 percent there would have to be 15 *more* obese people and 85 *more* non-obese people. The answer is (C).

Most people who miss this question assume that the general population is not increasing. In this case, as the absolute number of obese children increases, the absolute number of non-obese children must decrease. But then, of course, the 15 percent figure would increase.

Points to Remember

1. An argument is inductive if its conclusion does not necessarily follow from its premises—otherwise it is deductive. Most LSAT arguments are inductive.

2. The three major types of inductive reasoning are
    - Generalization
    - Analogy
    - Causal
        a. Confusing Correlation with Causation
        b. Confusing Necessary Conditions with Sufficient Conditions

3. A controlled experiment needs both a test group and a control group.

Exercise

Exercises 11-18 are actual LSAT problems taken from recent tests.

<u>Directions:</u> The questions in this section are based on the reasoning contained in brief statements or passages. For some questions, more than one of the choices could conceivably answer the question. However, you are to choose the <u>best</u> answer; that is, the response that most accurately and completely answers the question. You should not make assumptions that are by common sense standards implausible, superfluous, or incompatible with the passage.

1. An author writing a book about birth order advertised in his local paper for people who were first born. Fifty people consented to be interviewed and assessed for certain personality traits. As the writer suspected, the interview results and personality assessments showed that first-borns were more goal-oriented and serious-minded than random samples of the general public. These findings support the conclusion that people are affected by their birth order.

   Which one of the following selections, if true, points out the most critical weakness in the method used by the author to investigate birth order characteristics?

   (A) Last born children are typically more laid-back and calm than their older siblings.
   (B) The interviews and assessments were performed by an outside firm, not by the author.
   (C) People who saw the newspaper ad were not more likely to be first born than the number of first-born people in the population in general.
   (D) The author's subsequent contact with people who were middle children or last born tended to reinforce his initial impression of the character traits of people who were not first born.
   (E) People who are not goal-oriented and serious-minded were not as likely to respond to the author's newspaper ad nor were they as likely to agree to participate in the study.

2. Heavy snow fall in the Sierra Nevada Mountains is usually preceded by subzero temperatures in northwestern Canada. When snow fall is high in Canada's northwestern provinces, the same storm typically produces heavy snows in the Sierra Nevadas. Therefore, subzero temperatures cause winter snow storms to rebuild as they move down from Canada to the Sierra Nevadas.

   Which selection contains the same type flaw as that contained in the passage above?

   (A) Professional golfers tend to have lean builds. Therefore, professional golfers typically have healthy eating habits.
   (B) People tend to write larger when they use wide-ruled notebook paper than when they use narrow-ruled paper. Therefore, people write more neatly on the wide-ruled paper.
   (C) Students who participate in debate in high school often end up as trial lawyers. Therefore, participating in high school debate must somehow influence students to attend law school.
   (D) During the hottest part of the day, song birds do not visit unshaded feeders. Therefore, song birds must visit the feeders before dawn.
   (E) The kind of shows on Broadway can impact the type of shows premiered during new television seasons. Therefore, if the new Broadway shows feature aliens as characters in their productions, then the new television shows will also feature alien characters.

3. The Blane County District Attorney claims that her senior assistant, Tom Feather, is the best criminal prosecutor in Blane County. Inexplicably, a much lower percentage of the criminal defendants Mr. Feather prosecutes are convicted of serious crimes than criminal defendants tried by other prosecutors.

   Which one of the following selections goes farthest in crediting both the district attorney's confidence in Mr. Feather and Mr. Feather's low conviction rate?

   (A) Since the Blane County District Attorney appointed Mr. Feather as her senior assistant, her judgment would be questioned if she didn't claim that Mr. Feather is the best.
   (B) The district attorney followed established procedure in promoting Mr. Feather to senior assistant from among the ranks of assistant district attorneys.
   (C) Several years ago, Mr. Feather was involved in training attorneys new to the district attorney's office, and he trained a number of the assistant district attorneys currently on the staff.
   (D) In the district attorney's office, the weakest, most difficult cases are usually assigned to Mr. Feather.
   (E) Mr. Feather's conviction record is much better than the conviction record of the previous senior assistant district attorney.

4. Ten years after graduation, men and women who had participated in the Thompson High School basketball program were surveyed with regard to their individual playing records for their teams. Some of the results of the survey were curious. Seventy-five percent of those responding reported that they had started for their respective boys' or girls' teams, when the actual number of boys and girls who had started for their teams was only 50%.

   Which one of the following provides the most helpful explanation for the apparent contradiction in these survey results?

   (A) A very small number of those responding were incorrect in reporting that they held starting positions.
   (B) A disproportionately high number of players who started for their teams responded to the survey.
   (C) Not all starting players responded to the survey.
   (D) Almost all men and women who played basketball for Thompson High School ten years earlier responded to the survey.
   (E) Not all good basketball players started for their teams; some good players were deliberately held out to play later in the game.

5. Magazine ad: Men and women who run competitively learn that at least two of their human capabilities—physical stamina and breath control—can be stretched to higher and higher levels. The vigorous conditioning runners undergo is critical to their performance. Proper conditioning can also stretch another human capability—our minds. If you rigorously condition your mind, it can also attain higher and higher levels. Stretch and stimulate your mind! Join your local Puzzlemaster Club.

   This magazine ad uses which one of the following strategies in its approach?

   (A) The ad relies on the results of experiments to suggest that joining a Puzzlemaster Club will have the effect of improving mental abilities.
   (B) The ad ridicules people who don't join a Puzzlemaster Club by suggesting that they don't want to improve their minds.
   (C) The ad explains why becoming a member of a Puzzlemaster Club will stretch and stimulate your mind.
   (D) The ad supports or justifies its goal, i.e., that people join a Puzzlemaster Club, by carefully documenting the benefits of competitive running.
   (E) The ad implies that because physical stamina, breath control and the mind are all human capabilities, our minds can be stretched to higher levels just as stamina and breath control can be stretched.

6. Participants at a continuing legal education seminar were asked to evaluate the seminar schedule, location and topic selection to determine whether changes would increase attendance at next year's seminar. A majority of the evaluations recommended that the seminar schedule be changed so that the sessions would be held from 8:00 a.m. to 4:00 p.m. instead of the current 9:00 a.m. to 5:00 p.m. schedule. Based upon the results of the evaluations, the sponsors of the seminar decided to change to an earlier schedule for next year's program.

   Which of the following selections, if true, would most prove the sponsors right in their decision to change to an earlier schedule next year?

   (A) Approximately 85% of the people who received evaluation forms completed their forms and handed them in.
   (B) Other seminar sponsors have made changes in their programs based on comments they have received in evaluation forms.
   (C) About the same percentage of people attending the seminar wanted the earlier schedule as those who returned their evaluation forms.
   (D) An earlier seminar schedule would make commuting easier for the participants.
   (E) A significantly larger percentage of people who preferred the earlier schedule returned their evaluation forms than people who preferred the 9:00 a.m. to 5:00 p.m. schedule.

7. Psychologists have studied the impact a person's attitude has on his ability to accomplish tasks. In one study, a group of college students was outfitted with contraptions designed to administer soothing heat pulses to the students' neck and shoulder muscles. The students were told that the pulses would enhance their performance of in-class assignments. Only half of these contraptions worked, but neither the students nor the psychologists were told which students would actually receive these pulses. This component of the experiment is often frustrated, however, because ______________

   Which one of the following selections, if it is true, completes the sentence most appropriately?

   (A) frequently the faces of the students who actually receive the pulses become a little flushed.
   (B) students who believe they are receiving the warm pulses do better on their class assignments.
   (C) students who participate in the studies are volunteers who must be told that some of them will not receive the heat pulses.
   (D) many students will not complete the experiment if the sessions last too long.
   (E) many of the participating students suffer from tension headaches which readily respond to the heat pulses.

8. In a suburban community in the Southeast, neighborhood security guards have their residents' permission to call local police if anyone is observed entering the home of a resident who is out of town. When residents leave town, they report their departure and return dates to the neighborhood security office. If guards observe someone entering the home of a resident who is out of town, they will immediately call the police. The residential burglary rate for that community has decreased since the implementation of this reporting procedure.

   If it is true that the burglary rate has decreased in this community since the reporting procedure was implemented, then which of the following would be most important to know to make sure the conclusion is valid?

   (A) Are residents who report their travel plans to the security office also taking other precautions to protect their homes while they are away?
   (B) How many other communities utilize this reporting procedure with their neighborhood security offices?
   (C) Will residents be harassed by security guards or the police if they return home early from their travels?
   (D) Is this community similar to other guarded suburban communities in the Southeast?
   (E) Are homes in this community sometimes burglarized even when residents are in town?

9. The number of citations issued to convenience stores for selling tobacco products to minors has dramatically decreased in recent years. Between the years 1985-1990, a total of 5,511 citations were issued to convenience stores for this infraction. For the period 1990-1995, however, only 3,189 citations were issued. These statistics prove that local enforcement agencies have seriously neglected their inspection and surveillance of tobacco sales practices since 1990.

   Which one of the following does the author assume in reaching his conclusion?

   (A) Monitoring and enforcement of tobacco violations became more lax due to a change in the political climate in Washington, D.C.
   (B) The decrease in the number of citations was not due to a reduction in the number of tobacco sales actually made to minors.
   (C) Authorities focused more on enforcing the ban on liquor sales to minors than the ban on the sale of tobacco products to minors.
   (D) Local enforcement agencies suffered from a reduction in personnel during the period 1990-1995.
   (E) For several years prior to 1985, in excess of 1,500 citations per year were issued in connection with tobacco sales to minors.

10. County building inspectors report that almost fifty percent of the homes they inspect are equipped with gauges that monitor carbon monoxide levels. Fifteen years ago, only twenty-five percent of inspected homes were equipped with these gauges. However, even though more homes are now monitored for poisonous carbon monoxide fumes, the total number of homes with confirmed dangerous fume levels is no higher now than it was fifteen years ago because a large proportion of gauges produce false readings.

    Which one of the following assumptions must be made in order for the author to be correct in drawing the conclusion stated in the passage?

    (A) Thirty percent of the residential carbon monoxide gauges have been installed within the last fifteen years.
    (B) The number of confirmed dangerous fume readings per year in homes with carbon monoxide gauges has increased in recent years.
    (C) Not all carbon monoxide gauges report false carbon monoxide fume levels.
    (D) The percentage of malfunctioning carbon monoxide gauges has increased in the last fifteen years.
    (E) Properly functioning gauges do not, in themselves, decrease the risk that dangerous carbon monoxide fumes will enter people's homes.

11. That the policy of nuclear deterrence has worked thus far is unquestionable. Since the end of the Second World War, the very fact that there were nuclear armaments in existence has kept major powers from using nuclear weapons, for fear of starting a worldwide nuclear exchange that would make the land of the power initiating it uninhabitable. The proof is that a third world war between superpowers has not happened.

    Which one of the following, if true, indicates a flaw in the argument?

    (A) Maintaining a high level of nuclear armaments represents a significant drain on a country's economy.
    (B) From what has happened in the past, it is impossible to infer with certainty what will happen in the future, so an accident could still trigger a third world war between superpowers.
    (C) Continuing to produce nuclear weapons beyond the minimum needed for deterrence increases the likelihood of a nuclear accident.
    (D) The major powers have engaged in many smaller-scale military operations since the end of the Second World War, while refraining from a nuclear confrontation.
    (E) It cannot be known whether it was nuclear deterrence that worked, or some other factor, such as a recognition of the economic value of remaining at peace.

12. The translator of poetry must realize that word-for-word equivalents do not exist across languages, any more than piano sounds exist in the violin. The violin can, however, play recognizably the same music as the piano, but only if the violinist is guided by the nature and possibilities of the violin as well as by the original compositions.

    As applied to the act of translating poetry from one language into another, the analogy above can best be understood as saying that

    (A) poetry cannot be effectively translated because, unlike music, it is composed of words with specific meanings
    (B) some languages are inherently more musical and more suitable to poetic composition than others
    (C) the translator should be primarily concerned with reproducing the rhythms and sound patterns of the original, not with transcribing its meaning exactly
    (D) the translator must observe the spirit of the original and also the qualities of expression that characterize the language into which the original is translated
    (E) poetry is easier to translate if it focuses on philosophical insights or natural descriptions rather than on subjective impressions

13. Most of the ultraviolet radiation reaching the Earth's atmosphere from the Sun is absorbed by the layer of stratospheric ozone and never reaches the Earth's surface. Between 1969 and 1986, the layer of stratospheric ozone over North America thinned, decreasing by about 3 percent. Yet, the average level of ultraviolet radiation measured at research stations across North America decreased over the same period.

    Which one of the following, if true, best reconciles the apparently discrepant facts described above?

    (A) Ultraviolet radiation increases the risk of skin cancer and cataracts; the incidence of skin cancer and cataracts increased substantially between 1969 and 1986.
    (B) Between 1969 and 1986, the layer of stratospheric ozone over Brazil thinned, and the average level of ultraviolet radiation reaching the Earth's surface in Brazil increased.
    (C) Manufactured chlorine chemicals thin the layer of stratospheric ozone.
    (D) Ozone pollution, which absorbs ultraviolet radiation, increased dramatically between 1969 and 1986.
    (E) Thinning of the layer of stratospheric ozone varies from one part of the world to another and from year to year.

14. In an attempt to counter complaints that a certain pesticide is potentially hazardous to humans if absorbed into edible plants, the pesticide manufacturer has advertised that "ounce for ounce, the active ingredient in this pesticide is less toxic than the active ingredient in mouthwash."

    Which one of the following, if true, indicates a weakness in the manufacturer's argument?

    (A) The ounce-for-ounce toxicity of the active ingredient in mouthwash is less than that of most products meant for external use by humans, such as nail polish or other cosmetics.
    (B) The quantity of toxins humans ingest by consuming plants treated with the pesticide is, on average, much higher than the quantity of toxins humans ingest by using mouthwash.
    (C) The container in which the pesticide is packaged clearly identifies the toxic ingredients and carries warnings about their potential danger to humans.
    (D) On average, the toxins present in the pesticide take longer than the toxins present in mouthwash to reach harmful levels in the human body.
    (E) Since the government began to regulate the pesticide industry over ten years ago, there has been a growing awareness of the dangers of toxins used in pesticides.

15. In 1990 major engine repairs were performed on 10 percent of the cars that had been built by the National Motor Company in the 1970s and that were still registered. However, the corresponding figure for the cars that the National Motor Company had manufactured in the 1960s was only five percent.

    Which one of the following, if true, most helps to explain the discrepancy?

    (A) Government motor vehicle regulations generally require all cars, whether old or new, to be inspected for emission levels prior to registration.
    (B) Owners of new cars tend to drive their cars more carefully than do owners of old cars.
    (C) The older a car is, the more likely it is to be discarded for scrap rather than repaired when major engine work is needed to keep the car in operation.
    (D) The cars that the National Motor Company built in the 1970s incorporated simplified engine designs that made the engines less complicated than those of earlier models.
    (E) Many of the repairs that were performed on the cars that the National Motor Company built in the 1960s could have been avoided if periodic routine maintenance had been performed.

16. The great medieval universities had no administrators, yet they endured for centuries. Our university has a huge administrative staff, and we are in serious financial difficulties. Therefore, we should abolish the positions and salaries of the administrators to ensure the longevity of the university.

Which one of the following arguments contains flawed reasoning that most closely parallels the flawed reasoning in the argument above?

(A) No airplane had jet engines before 1940, yet airplanes had been flying since 1903. Therefore, jet engines are not necessary for the operation of airplanes.
(B) The novelist's stories began to be accepted for publication soon after she started using a computer to write them. You have been having trouble getting your stories accepted for publication, and you do not use a computer. To make sure your stories are accepted for publication, then, you should write them with the aid of a computer.
(C) After doctors began using antibiotics, the number of infections among patients dropped drastically. Now, however, resistant strains of bacteria cannot be controlled by standard antibiotics. Therefore, new methods of control are needed.
(D) A bicycle should not be ridden without a helmet. Since a good helmet can save the rider's life, a helmet should be considered the most important piece of bicycling equipment.
(E) The great cities of the ancient world were mostly built along waterways. Archaeologists searching for the remains of such cities should therefore try to determine where major rivers used to run.

Questions 17–18

A distemper virus has caused two-thirds of the seal population in the North Sea to die since May 1988. The explanation for the deaths cannot rest here, however. There must be a reason the normally latent virus could prevail so suddenly: clearly the severe pollution of the North Sea waters must have weakened the immune system of the seals so that they could no longer withstand the virus.

17. The argument concerning the immune system of the seals presupposes which one of the following?

(A) There has been a gradual decline in the seal population of the North Sea during the past two centuries.
(B) No further sources of pollution have been added since May 1988 to the already existing sources of pollution in the North Sea.
(C) There was no sudden mutation in the distemper virus which would have allowed the virus successfully to attack healthy North Sea seals by May 1988.
(D) Pollution in the North Sea is no greater than pollution in the Mediterranean Sea, off the coast of North America, or in the Sea of Japan.
(E) Some species that provide food for the seals have nearly become extinct as a result of the pollution.

18. Which one of the following, if true, most strongly supports the explanation given in the argument?

(A) At various times during the last ten years, several species of shellfish and seabirds in the North Sea have experienced unprecedentedly steep drops in population.
(B) By reducing pollution at its source, Northern Europe and Scandinavia have been taking the lead in preventing pollution from reaching the waters of the North Sea.
(C) For many years, fish for human consumption have been taken from the waters of the North Sea.
(D) There are two species of seal found throughout the North Sea area, the common seal and the gray seal.
(E) The distemper caused by the virus was a disease that was new to the population of North Sea seals in May 1988, and so the seals' immune systems were unprepared to counter it.

Answers and Solutions to Exercise

1.	**E**	**7.**	**A**	**13.**	**D**
2.	**C**	**8.**	**A**	**14.**	**B**
3.	**D**	**9.**	**B**	**15.**	**C**
4.	**B**	**10.**	**D**	**16.**	**B**
5.	**E**	**11.**	**E**	**17.**	**C**
6.	**C**	**12.**	**D**	**18.**	**A**

1. The argument generalizes from a small sample to the population as a whole. If the sample is shown not to be representative of the general population, then the author's conclusion is weakened. If goal-oriented and serious-minded people were more likely to respond to the author's newspaper ad and agree to be studied, then this shows that the sample was not representative of the general population. Selection (E) points out this weakness and is the correct answer. If first-born people who were not serious-minded and goal-oriented simply didn't respond to the newspaper ad, then the sample studied by the author was not representative of first-borns in the general population. Rather, his sample consisted heavily of first-borns who had those two personality traits, and thus his conclusion would be seriously flawed.

Selection (C) is tempting. Although it goes to the core of the question, that is, how representative is the study sample of the general public, it actually strengthens the writer's argument. Selection (C) suggests that the newspaper ad was exposed to the general public as opposed to a more limited audience.

2. The author of this passage uses a false correlation in his argument. He assumes that subzero temperatures lead to heavy snow storms in the Sierra Nevada Mountains. The author doesn't recognize that some other weather condition might lead to both the subzero temperatures and the heavy snow storms. As you look over the answer selections, it appears that selection (C) makes the same mistake. In (C), it is assumed that participation in high school debate must influence students to attend law school. Instead, perhaps a student's interest in public affairs or some other subject *causes* her to take high school debate classes *and* go to law school. The argument doesn't contemplate another possible cause. Thus, selection (C) is the correct answer. The other selections also contain flaws, but they do not pattern the same defect contained in the passage.

3. This question wants to be an "all things being equal" question. But in finding the best answer to this question, we are asked to pick an explanation for why not all things are equal. For only if things are not equal can both seemingly contradictory statements in the passage be supported. If cases are randomly assigned in the district attorney's office, then Mr. Feather's low conviction rate discredits the district attorney's claim. However, if Mr. Feather is assigned the cases that are the most difficult to prove, then it is reasonable that his conviction rate will be lower than the conviction rates of other prosecutors in the office. Perhaps a less skillful prosecutor would have an even lower conviction rate if given the weakest cases to take to trial. Selection (D) is the correct answer.

Selection (A) is the second best answer because it provides an explanation for the district attorney's claim. Obviously, the district attorney will want her staff and the public to think that she has chosen the best person for the job of first assistant district attorney. She might exaggerate Mr. Feather's capabilities to bolster her own image. But the answer doesn't explain why even if Mr. Feather is quite talented, he has such a low conviction record.

Selection (B) doesn't really explain either of the positions in the passage. Explaining that Mr. Feather was promoted from within the ranks doesn't support the district attorney's claim about Mr. Feather's prosecuting abilities or explain why Mr. Feather has such a low conviction record.

Neither does selection (C) explain why the district attorney touts Mr. Feather as the best. Selection (C) also does not explain Mr. Feather's poor conviction record.

Selection (E) just compares Mr. Feather's record with that of his predecessor. It doesn't support the claims contained in the passage.

4. If all of the men and women who had played basketball for Thompson High School ten years earlier had responded to the survey, then the results would indeed contradict the facts. However, if a disproportionately higher number of starting players responded to the survey, then the apparent contradiction can be easily explained. If only four people responded to the survey and three of them were in fact starting players, then 75% of those responding were starters. This would explain the apparent contradiction. The answer is Selection (B).

Selection (A) does not explain the contradiction; in fact, it seems to support the contradiction because it states that people reported their starting positions correctly. If instead Selection (A) had indicated that people's faulty memories accounted for inaccurate responses, then it would help explain the contradiction.

Selection (C) is too vaguely worded to be of much help. Perhaps only two starting players failed to respond while all the other starting players responded to the survey. This might help explain the contradiction if a larger percentage of non-starters failed to respond.

If Selection (D) were true, then it would not help resolve the contradiction. Rather, it would make the contradiction more inexplicable, particularly if we assume that the people who responded were correct in their responses.

Finally, Selection (E) might help explain the contradiction if good players who played later in the game were confused about whether they were classified as starters or not. But this answer is not the best answer. Selection (B) is by far the best answer.

5. The advertisement draws an analogy between muscles and brains, and it concludes that since exercise improves the performance of one's muscles it will also improve the performance of one's brain. The answer is (E).

6. The argument presumes that the comments in the evaluation forms are representative of all the people who attended the seminar. So the reliability of the preferences expressed in the evaluation forms depends upon how representative they are of all seminar participants. If the evaluation comments were representative of all participants, then reliance upon them would be warranted in determining the schedule for next year.

Upon first glance, selection (A) looks correct. But a close reading of selection (A) suggests there might be a problem with how many people actually received the evaluation forms. If the evaluation forms were handed out only at every other table, then the comments might be representative of only half of the participants. Selections (B) and (D) are irrelevant to the argument here. Selection (E) weakens the reliability of the results rather than strengthens them because it appears that a rather small number of people would have a big impact on the results. Selection (C) is correct because it strengthens the connection between the sample and the general population. It states that the percentage results would be the same for the sample who returned evaluation forms and for all people who attended the seminar.

7. One of the purposes of these studies, of course, is to find out whether or not students who think they are receiving the soothing heat pulses do better on their assignments than they would otherwise. If the psychologists knew ahead of time which students were receiving the pulses, they might subconsciously evaluate the students' assignments based on the results they anticipated. Only if both students and psychologists are shielded from knowing who is receiving the pulses can the students' assignments be graded and the results fairly tallied and analyzed. Selection (A) states that often students who receive the heat pulses become flushed in the face. This condition would be observable by both students and psychologists and would definitely frustrate one of the purposes of the experiment. Thus (A) is the correct answer. The other answer selections do not indicate how either students or psychologists would learn which students were actually receiving the heat pulses. Selection (C) is tempting, but it does not suggest that students know which of them will actually receive the pulses and which will not.

8. This passage is an example of an argument that generalizes from the purported success the reporting program has had in reducing burglary rates. In order for the conclusion to be valid, it must be based upon all other things being the same. If some other factor is instrumental in reducing the burglary rate, then concluding that the reporting program is responsible for the reduced crime rate would be weakened. Look at selection (A). If people who travel take additional precautions, for instance, if they installed motion detector lights on the outside of their homes, then perhaps increased lighting is responsible for lowering the burglary rate rather than the new travel reporting procedure.

The other selections are irrelevant to determining what caused the lower burglary rate in the community under study. What happens in other communities doesn't impact results in the subject community. Selection (C) is a tempting choice because the answer might suggest that the security guards and police are observant and taking action as a result of the reporting procedure. But (C) does not suggest a reason that might weaken the validity of the conclusion. Selection (A) does, and it is the correct answer.

9. Based on the conclusion of the passage, the author believes that convenience stores continued to sell tobacco products to minors but that they just weren't caught as often during the years 1990-1995. He places the blame for this at the feet of local enforcement agencies. Thus, selection (B) is assumed in the author's conclusion and is the correct selection. The author assumes that the number of tobacco sales to minors did not decrease. However, if in fact the number of tobacco sales to minors decreased from 1990-1995, then the author's conclusion is flawed. But that isn't the question here. Rather, the question asks about the assumptions the author has made in reaching his conclusion, valid or not. This question points out the importance of reading the specific question asked about the test passage.

Selections (A), (C) and (D) would perhaps explain why fewer citations were issued during 1990- 1995. But they are not assumptions the author has necessarily made in reaching his conclusion. The basic underpinning of the author's conclusion is his belief or assumption that convenience stores continued to sell tobacco products to minors at the same levels sold during the preceding five year period. Selection (E) is irrelevant to the conclusion because it has no bearing on why the number of citations decreased during 1990-1995.

10. If the percentage of malfunctioning carbon monoxide gauges is the same now as it was fifteen years ago, then the number of homes with confirmed dangerous fume levels would be twice as high today as it was then because there are twice as many gauges in homes now (50% is twice as high as 25%). But if the percentage of defective gauges has increased within the last fifteen years, then the number of confirmed dangerous readings would decrease, perhaps even to the numbers experienced fifteen years ago. But this would occur only if the proportion of defective gauges increased dramatically within the last fifteen years. Thus, selection (D) is the correct answer.

Since the assumption is based on the proportion of gauges that accurately read fume levels, selection (A) is irrelevant. Selection (B) is inconsistent with the author's conclusion. Selection (C) does not provide us with any information as to how many gauges are flawed. This statement would be true if even one gauge works properly. Selection (E) might be true, but it has no bearing on the author's conclusion and the assumptions upon which it is based.

11. The argument commits the fallacy of false correlation. The argument assumes the fear of the destructive effects of nuclear war has prevented a nuclear exchange. It does not take into account that other factors may have affected events, such as the economic value of remaining at peace. The answer is (E).

12. This argument contains two counter-premise indicators—"however" and "but." The author opens the argument implying that the violin cannot play the "same" music as the piano. Then the counter-premise indicator "however" introduces a qualification of this claim; namely that the violin can play recognizably the same music. "But" introduces a further qualification: the violinist should be *"guided by the nature and possibilities of the violin as well as by the original composition."* This is the key to the question. By analogy the translator of poetry should be guided by (observe) the nature (spirit) of the original as well as the nature (qualities) of the language into which the original is translated. Hence the answer is (D). Note that (D) paraphrases the last clause of the argument.

(A) may be true but is irrelevant; it's also baited with same language from the passage—"music."

(B) is not stated in or implied by the passage.

(C) is second-best. The clause *"[the translator should] not [be concerned] with transcribing its meaning exactly"* is supported by the argument's opening, *"The translator of poetry must realize that word-for-word equivalents do not exist across languages."* But the author does not state that the translation should be *"primarily concerned with reproducing the rhythms and sound patterns of the original."* Note the subtle use of the same language ploy: the analogy is to the translation of the meanings of words, not their sound patterns or rhythm—i.e., musical qualities.

(E) sounds like an English professor wrote it. Most often such pretentious answer-choices can be summarily dismissed.

13. All-things-being-equal, one would expect the amount of ultraviolet radiation reaching the Earth's surface to increase as the ozone layer decreased in the upper atmosphere. So we are looking for something that might offset the decrease in ozone in the upper atmosphere. Look at choice (D). It states that as ozone decreased in the upper atmosphere it increased dramatically in the lower atmosphere. Thus, overall there would be more ozone in the atmosphere and therefore more ultraviolet light would be absorbed before reaching the Earth's surface. The answer is (D).

The first part of choice (A) is irrelevant. The second part rather than reconciling the discrepant facts would add another discrepant fact: If the amount of cancer causing ultraviolet light reaching the Earth decreased, the incidence of cancer should also decrease, not increase.

Choice (B) is irrelevant since the passage is about what happened in North America, not Brazil. Even if it were relevant, it would strengthen, not reconcile, the apparently discrepant facts.

Choice (C) explains why the ozone is being depleted in the upper atmosphere, but this does not reconcile the discrepancy.

Choice (E) offers another explanation for why the ozone in the upper atmosphere is being depleted, but again this does not reconcile the discrepancy.

14. This is a percent vs. absolute number (quantity) problem. Although the *percentage* of toxic ingredients in the pesticide and mouthwash may be the same, the *quantity* of mouthwash ingested is much less—after all the mouthwash is spit out. The answer is (B).

15. The answer is (C). All things being equal, one would expect the older the car, the more likely it would need major repairs. However, perhaps the older cars are considered classics and are therefore driven on only special occasions. Or perhaps when the older cars break down, their owners opt for new cars, which is what choice (C) says.

16. The passage presents a false causal argument. It implies that medieval universities endured for centuries because they had no administrators, but gives no evidence for this cause and effect relationship. There may have been other factors that caused the universities' longevity. Choice (B) presents a similar false causal argument, implying the use of a computer caused the novelist's stories to be accepted for publication. The answer is (B).

As to the remaining choices, (A) is neither invalid nor a causation argument. (C) is a *valid* argument. (D) is a reasonable argument, though a bit strong. Finally, (E) is not an invalid argument.

<u>Questions 17–18</u>

17.
(A) No. This does not relate to the fact that the seal population has suffered a severe decline in population since 1988.
(B) No. Adding more sources of pollution would strengthen the argument.
(C) Yes. This is an all-things-being-equal argument. If all other factors are the same, then it must be the pollution that caused the seals to become more susceptible to the virus. So for the argument to be valid, it must assume that the virus has not increased in virulence.
(D) No. This has no affect on the argument. If we knew that the seal population also decreased dramatically in these areas, then it would support the argument. On the other hand, if we knew that the seal population did not change in these areas, then it would weaken the argument.
(E) No. Although one can theorize that lack of food caused the seals to become malnourished, in turn weakening their immune systems, the argument does not presume any particular mechanism by which the pollution affected the seals. There are many other scenarios (some more direct) which could explain how the pollution weakened the seals' immune system.

18.
(A) Yes. Since presumably the distemper virus that affects seals would not affect such disparate animals as shellfish and seabirds, it is likely that another agent caused all three populations to decrease—pollution.
(B) No. This would weaken the argument. If pollution is being reduced, then pollution is less likely now to be the cause of the weakening of the seals' immune system than in the past.
(C) No. We don't know how this has affected the immune system of humans. If humans are becoming more susceptible to similar viruses, then it would support the argument. However, if humans are not becoming more susceptible to similar viruses, then it would weaken the argument.
(D) No. This is irrelevant. The passage is about the general population of seals. We don't need to know the distribution of the various species.
(E) No. This would weaken the argument. If the seals' immune system were unprepared for the new strain of virus, then the spread of the virus probably would have occurred even without the pollution.

Common Fallacies

In this chapter, we will study the most common fallacies you are asked to identify on the LSAT. The LSAT will not ask you to identify these fallacies by name, but you will be required to identify the thought process behind each. A common question of this type asks *"Which one of the following contains the same flawed logic as contained in the passage?"*

Contradiction

Contradiction is the most glaring type of fallacy. It is committed when two opposing statements are simultaneously asserted. For example, saying "it is raining *and* it is not raining" is a contradiction. If the contradictions on the LSAT were this basic, the test would be significantly easier. Typically, however, the arguer obscures the contradiction to the point that the argument can be quite compelling. Take, for instance, the following argument: "We cannot know anything, because we intuitively realize that our thoughts are unreliable." This argument has an air of reasonableness to it. But "intuitively realize" means "to know." Thus the arguer is in essence saying that we *know* that we don't know anything. This is self-contradictory.

Example:

In the game of basketball, scoring a three-point shot is a skill that only those with a soft shooting touch can develop. Wilt Chamberlain, however, was a great player, so even though he did not have a soft shooting touch he would have excelled at scoring three point shots.

Which one of the following contains a flaw that most closely parallels the flaw contained in the passage?

(A) Eighty percent of the freshmen at Berkeley go on to get a bachelor's degree. David is a freshman at Berkeley, so he will probably complete his studies and receive a bachelor's degree.

(B) If the police don't act immediately to quell the disturbance, it will escalate into a riot. However, since the police are understaffed, there will be a riot.

(C) The meek shall inherit the earth. Susie received an inheritance from her grandfather, so she must be meek.

(D) During the Vietnam War, the powerful had to serve along with the poor. However, Stevens' father was a federal judge, so Stevens was able to get a draft deferment.

(E) All dolphins are mammals and all mammals breathe air. Therefore, all mammals that breathe air are dolphins.

The argument clearly contradicts itself. So look for an answer-choice that contradicts itself in like manner. Choice (A) is not self-contradictory. In fact, it's a fairly sound argument—eliminate it. Choice (B), on the other hand, is not a very sound argument. The police, though understaffed, may realize the seriousness of the situation and rearrange their priorities. Nevertheless, (B) does not contain a contradiction—eliminate it. Choice (C), though questionable, does not contain a contradiction—eliminate it. Choice (D), however, does contain a contradiction. It begins by stating that both the powerful and the poor had to serve in Vietnam and ends by stating that some powerful people—namely, Stevens—did not have to serve. This is a contradiction, so (D) is probably the answer. Choice (E), like the original argument, is invalid but does not contain a contradiction—eliminate it. The answer is (D).

Equivocation

Equivocation is the use of a word in more than one sense during an argument. It is often done intentionally.

Example:

Individual rights must be championed by the government. It is right for one to believe in God. So government should promote the belief in God.

In this argument, *right* is used ambiguously. In the phrase "individual rights" it is used in the sense of a privilege, whereas in the second sentence *right* is used to mean correct or moral. The questionable conclusion is possible only if the arguer is allowed to play with the meaning of the critical word *right*.

Example:

Judy: Traditionally, Republican administrations have supported free trade. But the President must veto the North American Free Trade Act because it will drain away American jobs to Mexico and lead to wholesale exploitation of the Mexican workers by international conglomerates.

Tina: I disagree. Exploitation of workers is the essence of any economic system just like the exploitation of natural resources.

Judy and Tina will not be able to settle their argument unless they

(A) explain their opinions in more detail
(B) ask an expert on international trade to decide who is correct
(C) decide whose conclusion is true but irrelevant
(D) decide whose conclusion is based on a questionable premise
(E) define a critical word

Clearly, Judy and Tina are working with different definitions of the word *exploitation*. Judy is using the meaning that most people attribute to exploitation—abuse. We can't tell the exact meaning Tina intends, but for her exploitation must have a positive, or at least neutral, connotation, otherwise she would be unlikely to defend it as essential. Their argument will be fruitless until they agree on a definition for *exploitation*. Hence the answer is (E).

Circular Reasoning

Circular reasoning involves assuming as a premise that which you are trying to prove. Intuitively, it may seem that no one would fall for such an argument. However, the conclusion may appear to state something additional, or the argument may be so long that the reader may forget that the conclusion was stated as a premise.

Example:

The death penalty is appropriate for traitors because it is right to execute those who betray their own country and thereby risk the lives of millions.

This argument is circular because "right" means essentially the same thing as "appropriate." In effect, the writer is saying that the death penalty is appropriate because it is appropriate.

Example:

Democracy is the best form of government yet created. Therefore, we must be vigilant in its defense; that is, we must be prepared to defend the right to freedom. Because this right is fundamental to any progressive form of government, it is clear that democracy is better than any other form of government.

Which one of the following illustrates the same flawed reasoning as found in the passage?

(A) I never get a headache when I eat only Chinese food, nor when I drink only wine. But when I eat Chinese food and drink wine, I get a headache. So the combination of the two must be the cause of my headaches.

(B) The two times I have gone to that restaurant something bad has happened. The first time the waiter dropped a glass and it shattered all over the table. And after the second time I went there, I got sick. So why should I go there again—something bad will just happen again.

(C) I would much rather live a life dedicated to helping my fellow man than one dedicated to gaining material possessions and seeing my fellow man as a competitor. At the end of each day, the satisfaction of having helped people is infinitely greater than the satisfaction of having achieved something material.

(D) I'm obsessed with volleyball; that's why I play it constantly. I train seven days a week, and I enter every tournament. Since I'm always playing it, I must be obsessed with it.

(E) In my academic studies, I have repeatedly changed majors. I decide to major in each new subject that I'm introduced to. Just as a bee lights from one flower to the next, tasting the nectar of each, I jump from one subject to the next getting just a taste of each.

The argument in the passage is circular (and filled with non-sequiturs). It is incumbent on the writer to give evidence or support for the conclusion. In this argument, though, the writer first states that democracy is the best government, the rest is merely "noise," until he restates the conclusion.

Choice (A) is a reasonably valid causation argument—eliminate. (B) argues by generalization. Although it is of questionable validity, it is not circular because the conclusion, "it will happen again," is not stated, nor is it implicit in the premises—eliminate. (C) is not circular because the conclusion is mentioned only once—eliminate. (D) begins by stating, "I'm obsessed with volleyball." It does not, however, provide compelling evidence for that claim: training seven days a week, rather than indicating obsession, may be required for, say, members of the Olympic Volleyball Team. Furthermore, the argument repeats the conclusion at the end. So it is circular in the same manner as the original. Hence (D) is our answer.

Shifting the Burden of Proof

As mentioned before, it is incumbent upon the writer to provide evidence or support for her position. To imply that a position is true merely because no one has disproved it is to shift the burden of proof to others.

Example:

Since no one has been able to prove God's existence, there must not be a God.

There are two major weaknesses in this argument. First, the fact that God's existence has yet to be proven does not preclude any future proof of existence. Second, if there is a God, one would expect that his existence is independent of any proof by man.

Reasoning by shifting the burden of proof is not always fallacious. In fact, our legal system is predicated on this method of thought. The defendant is *assumed* innocent until proven guilty. This assumption shifts the onus of proof to the state. Science can also validly use this method of thought to better understand the world—so long as it is not used to claim "truth." Consider the following argument: "The multitude of theories about our world have failed to codify and predict its behavior as well as Einstein's theory of relativity. Therefore our world is probably 'Einsteinian.'" This argument is strong so long as it is qualified with "probably"—otherwise it is fallacious: someone may yet create a better theory of our world.

Example:

Astronomers have created a mathematical model for determining whether life exists outside our solar system. It is based on the assumption that life as we know it can exist only on a planet such as our own, and that our sun, which has nine planets circling it, is the kind of star commonly found throughout the universe. Hence it is projected that there are billions of planets with conditions similar to our own. So astronomers have concluded that it is highly probable, if not virtually certain, that life exists outside our solar system. Yet there has never been detected so much as one planet beyond our solar system. Hence life exists only on planet Earth.

Which one of the following would most weaken the above argument?

(A) Thousands of responsible people, people with reputations in the community to protect, have claimed to have seen UFOs. Statistically, it is virtually impossible for this many people to be mistaken or to be lying.
(B) Recently it has been discovered that Mars has water, and its equatorial region has temperatures in the same range as that of northern Europe. So there may be life on Mars.
(C) Only one percent of the stars in the universe are like our sun.
(D) The technology needed to detect planets outside our solar system has not yet been developed.
(E) Even if all the elements for life as we know it are present, the probability that life would spontaneously generate is infinitesimal.

This argument implies that since no planet has been discovered outside our solar system, none exist and therefore no life exists elsewhere in the universe. Hence the burden of proof is shifted from the arguer to the astronomers.

Although choice (A) weakens the argument, it has a flaw: the UFOs may not be life forms. Choice (B) is irrelevant. Although the argument states that the only life in the universe is on Earth, it is essentially about the possibility of life beyond our solar system. Choice (C) also weakens the argument. However, one percent of billions is still a significant number, and it is not clear whether one percent should be considered "common." Since an LSAT answer must be indisputable, there is probably a better answer-choice. The underlying premise of the argument is that since no other planets have been detected, no others exist. Choice (D) attacks this premise directly by stating that no planets outside our solar system have been discovered because we don't yet have the ability to detect them. This is probably the best answer, but we must check all the choices. Choice (E) strengthens the argument by implying that even if there were other planets it would be extremely unlikely that they would contain life. The answer, therefore, is (D).

At this time, I would like to discuss the relative difficulty of the problems we have been studying. You may feel that the arguments have been fairly easy. However, they have the same level of difficulty as those on the LSAT (many have been actual LSAT arguments). When arguments are classified by the method of reasoning used, their underlying simplicity becomes apparent. Better yet, the arguments compose fifty percent of the test; and with sufficient study, everyone can master them.

Unwarranted Assumptions

We talked about unwarranted assumptions in connection with analyzing a problem. Now we will discuss it as a method of fallacious thought. The *fallacy of unwarranted assumption* is committed when the conclusion of an argument is based on a premise (implicit or explicit) that is false or unwarranted. An assumption is unwarranted when it is false—these premises are usually suppressed or vaguely written. An assumption is also unwarranted when it is true but does not apply in the given context—these premises are usually explicit. The varieties of unwarranted assumptions are too numerous to classify, but a few examples should give you the basic idea.

Example: ***(False Dichotomy)***

Either restrictions must be placed on freedom of speech or certain subversive elements in society will use it to destroy this country. Since to allow the latter to occur is unconscionable, we must restrict freedom of speech.

The conclusion above is unsound because

(A) subversives do not in fact want to destroy the country
(B) the author places too much importance on the freedom of speech
(C) the author fails to consider an accommodation between the two alternatives
(D) the meaning of "freedom of speech" has not been defined
(E) subversives are a true threat to our way of life

The arguer offers two options: either restrict freedom of speech, or lose the country. He hopes the reader will assume that these are the only options available. This is unwarranted. He does not state how the so-called "subversive elements" would destroy the country, nor for that matter why they would want to destroy it. There may be a third option that the author did not mention; namely, that society may be able to tolerate the "subversives"; it may even be improved by the diversity of opinion they offer. The answer is (C).

Example:

To score in the ninetieth percentile on the LSAT, one must study hard. If one studies four hours a day for one month, she will score in the ninetieth percentile. Hence, if a person scored in the top ten percent on the LSAT, then she must have studied at least four hours a day for one month.

Which one of the following most accurately describes the weakness in the above argument?

(A) The argument fails to take into account that not all test-prep books recommend studying four hours a day for one month.
(B) The argument does not consider that excessive studying can be counterproductive.
(C) The argument does not consider that some people may be able to score in the ninetieth percentile though they studied less than four hours a day for one month.
(D) The argument fails to distinguish between how much people should study and how much they can study.
(E) The author fails to realize that the ninetieth percentile and the top ten percent do not mean the same thing.

You may have noticed that this argument uses the converse of the fallacy *"Confusing Necessary Conditions with Sufficient Conditions"* mentioned earlier. In other words, it assumes that something which is sufficient is also necessary. In the given argument, this is fallacious because some people may still score in the ninetieth percentile, though they studied less than four hours a day for one month. Therefore the answer is (C).

Example:

Of course Steve supports government sponsorship of the arts. He's an artist.

Which one of the following uses reasoning that is most similar to the above argument?

(A) Of course if a person lies to me, I will never trust that person again.
(B) Conservatives in the past have prevented ratification of any nuclear arms limitation treaties with the Soviet Union (or Russia), so they will prevent the ratification of the current treaty.
(C) Mr. Sullivan is the police commissioner, so it stands to reason that he would support the NRA's position on gun control.
(D) Following her conscience, Congresswoman Martinez voted against the death penalty, in spite of the fact that she knew it would doom her chances for reelection.
(E) You're in no position to criticize me for avoiding paying my fair share of taxes. You don't even pay your employees a fair wage.

This argument is fallacious—and unfair—because it assumes that all artists support government sponsorship of the arts. Some artists, however, may have reasons for not supporting government sponsorship of the arts. For example, they may believe that government involvement stifles artistic expression. Or they may reject government involvement on purely philosophical grounds. The argument suggests a person's profession taints his opinion. Choice (C) does the same thing, so it is the answer.

True But Irrelevant

We have thoroughly discussed the use of irrelevance as an obfuscating tactic with answer-choices. Now we will analyze its use as a method of fallacious thought. The tactic is quite simple: the arguer bases a conclusion on information that is true but not germane to the issue.

Example:

This pain relief product can be bought over the counter or in a stronger form with a prescription. But according to this pamphlet, for the prescription strength product to be effective it must be taken at the immediate onset of pain, it must be taken every four hours thereafter, and it cannot be taken with any dairy products. So it actually doesn't matter whether you use the prescription strength or the over-the-counter strength product.

Which one of the following best identifies the flaw in the above argument?

(A) The fact that many people could not live a full life without the prescription strength product cannot be ignored.
(B) It cannot be concluded that just because the prescription strength product has certain guidelines and restrictions on its use that it is not more effective.
(C) It does not consider that complications may arise from the prescription strength product.
(D) It fails to consider that other products may be more effective in relieving pain.
(E) It is unreasonable to assume that the over-the-counter strength product does not have similar restrictions and guidelines for its use.

It is unreasonable to reject the effectiveness of a product merely because it has modest requirements for use. All medications have directions and restrictions. Hence the answer is (B). Don't make the mistake of choosing (A). Although it is a good rebuttal, it does not address the flaw in the argument. Interestingly, it too is true but irrelevant.

Appeal to Authority

To appeal to authority is to cite an expert's opinion as support for one's own opinion. This method of thought is not necessarily fallacious. Clearly, the reasonableness of the argument depends on the "expertise" of the person being cited and whether he or she is an expert in a field relevant to the argument. Appealing to a doctor's authority on a medical issue, for example, would be reasonable; but if the issue is about dermatology and the doctor is an orthopedist, then the argument would be questionable.

Example:

The legalization of drugs is advocated by no less respectable people than William F. Buckley and federal judge Edmund J. Reinholt. These people would not propose a social policy that is likely to be harmful. So there is little risk in experimenting with a one-year legalization of drugs.

In presenting her position the author does which one of the following?

(A) Argues from the specific to the general.
(B) Attacks the motives of her opponents.
(C) Uses the positions of noted social commentators to support her position.
(D) Argues in a circular manner.
(E) Claims that her position is correct because others cannot disprove it.

The only evidence that the author gives to support her position is that respected people agree with her. She is appealing to the authority of others. Thus, the answer is (C).

Personal Attack

In a personal attack (ad hominem), a person's character is challenged instead of her opinions.

Example:

Politician: How can we trust my opponent to be true to the voters? He isn't true to his wife!

This argument is weak because it attacks the opponent's character, not his positions. Some people may consider fidelity a prerequisite for public office. History, however, shows no correlation between fidelity and great political leadership.

Example:

A reporter responded with the following to the charge that he resorted to tabloid journalism when he rummaged through and reported on the contents of garbage taken from the home of Henry Kissinger.

"Of all the printed commentary . . . only a few editorial writers thought to express the obvious point that when it comes to invasion of privacy, the man who as National Security Advisor helped to bug the home phones of his own staff members is one of our nation's leading practitioners."—Washington Monthly, October 1975

In defending his actions, the reporter does which one of the following?

(A) Attacks the character of Henry Kissinger.
(B) Claims Henry Kissinger caused the reporter to act as he did.
(C) Claims that "bugging" is not an invasion of privacy.
(D) Appeals to the authority of editorial writers.
(E) Claims that his actions were justified because no one was able to show otherwise.

The reporter justifies his actions by claiming that Kissinger is guilty of wrongdoing. So, instead of addressing the question, he attacks the character of Henry Kissinger. The answer is (A).

Points to Remember

The most common fallacies are

1. Contradiction
2. Equivocation
3. Circular Reasoning
4. Shifting the Burden of Proof
5. Unwarranted Assumptions
6. True but Irrelevant
7. Appeal to Authority
8. Personal Attack

Exercise

Arguments 1–25 in this exercise are actual LSAT problems taken from recent tests. Note, not all problems in this exercise involve fallacies.

Directions: The questions in this section are based on the reasoning contained in brief statements or passages. For some questions, more than one of the choices could conceivably answer the question. However, you are to choose the best answer; that is, the response that most accurately and completely answers the question. You should not make assumptions that are by common sense standards implausible, superfluous, or incompatible with the passage.

1. The senator has long held to the general principle that no true work of art is obscene, and thus that there is no conflict between the need to encourage free artistic expression and the need to protect the sensibilities of the public from obscenity. When well-known works generally viewed as obscene are cited as possible counterexamples, the senator justifies accepting the principle by saying that if these works really are obscene then they cannot be works of art.

   The senator's reasoning contains which one of the following errors?

   (A) It seeks to persuade by emotional rather than intellectual means.
   (B) It contains an implicit contradiction.
   (C) It relies on an assertion of the senator's authority.
   (D) It assumes what it seeks to establish.
   (E) It attempts to justify a position by appeal to an irrelevant consideration.

2. When workers do not find their assignments challenging, they become bored and so achieve less than their abilities would allow. On the other hand, when workers find their assignments too difficult, they give up and so again achieve less than what they are capable of achieving. It is, therefore, clear that no worker's full potential will ever be realized.

   Which one of the following is an error of reasoning contained in the argument?

   (A) mistakenly equating what is actual and what is merely possible
   (B) assuming without warrant that a situation allows only two possibilities
   (C) relying on subjective rather than objective evidence
   (D) confusing the coincidence of two events with a causal relation between the two
   (E) depending on the ambiguous use of a key term

3. The high cost of production is severely limiting which operas are available to the public. These costs necessitate reliance on large corporate sponsors, who in return demand that only the most famous operas be produced. Determining which operas will be produced should rest only with ticket purchasers at the box office, not with large corporate sponsors. If we reduce production budgets so that operas can be supported exclusively by box-office receipts and donations from individuals, then the public will be able to see less famous operas.

   Which one of the following, if true, would weaken the argument?

   (A) A few opera ticket purchasers go to the opera for the sake of going to the opera, not to see specific operatic productions.
   (B) The reduction of opera production budgets would not reduce the desire of large corporate sponsors to support operas.
   (C) Without the support of large corporate sponsors, opera companies could not afford to produce any but the most famous of operas.
   (D) Large corporate sponsors will stop supporting opera productions if they are denied control over which operas will be produced.
   (E) The combination of individual donations and box-office receipts cannot match the amounts of money obtained through sponsorship by large corporations.

4. The 1980s have been characterized as a period of selfish individualism that threatens the cohesion of society. But this characterization is true of any time. Throughout history all human actions have been motivated by selfishness. When the deeper implications are considered, even the simplest "unselfish" acts prove to be instances of selfish concern for the human species.

Which one of the following is a flaw in the argument?

(A) The claim that selfishness has been present throughout history is not actually relevant to the argument.
(B) No statistical evidence is provided to show that humans act selfishly more often than they act unselfishly.
(C) The argument assumes that selfishness is unique to the present age.
(D) The argument mentions only humans and does not consider the behavior of other species.
(E) The argument relies on two different uses of the term "selfish."

5. When machines are invented and technologies are developed, they alter the range of choices open to us. The clock, for example, made possible the synchronization of human affairs, which resulted in an increase in productivity. At the same time that the clock opened up some avenues, it closed others. It has become harder and harder to live except by the clock, so that now people have no choice in the matter at all.

Which one of the following propositions is best illustrated by the example presented in the passage?

(A) New machines and technologies can enslave as well as liberate us.
(B) People should make a concerted effort to free themselves from the clock.
(C) Some new machines and technologies bring no improvement to our lives.
(D) The increase in productivity was not worth our dependence on the clock.
(E) Most new machines and technologies make our lives more synchronized and productive.

6. In Brazil, side-by-side comparisons of Africanized honeybees and the native honeybees have shown that the Africanized bees are far superior honey producers. Therefore, there is no reason to fear that domestic commercial honey production will decline in the United States if local honeybees are displaced by Africanized honeybees.

Each of the following, if true, would weaken the argument EXCEPT:

(A) The honeybees native to Brazil are not of the same variety as those most frequently used in the commercial beekeeping industry in the United States.
(B) Commercial honey production is far more complicated and expensive with Africanized honeybees than it is with the more docile honeybees common in the United States.
(C) If Africanized honeybees replace local honeybees, certain types of ornamental trees will be less effectively pollinated.
(D) In the United States a significant proportion of the commercial honey supply comes from hobby beekeepers, many of whom are likely to abandon beekeeping with the influx of Africanized bees.
(E) The area of Brazil where the comparative study was done is far better suited to the foraging habits of the Africanized honeybees than are most areas of the United States.

7. Some of the most prosperous nations in the world have experienced a pronounced drop in national savings rates—the percentage of after-tax income an average household saves. This trend will undoubtedly continue if the average age of these nations' populations continues to rise, since older people have fewer reasons to save than do younger people.

Which one of the following indicates an error in the reasoning leading to the prediction above?

(A) It fails to specify the many reasons younger people have for saving money, and it fails to identify which of those reasons is the strongest.
(B) It assumes that a negative savings rate—the result of the average household's spending all of its after-tax income as well as some of its existing savings—cannot ever come about in any nation.
(C) It fails to cite statistics showing that the average age of the populations of certain nations is rising.
(D) It only takes into account the comparative number of reasons older and younger people, respectively, have for saving, and not the comparative strength of those reasons.
(E) It uses after-tax income as the base for computing the national savings rate without establishing by argument that after-tax income is a more appropriate base than before-tax income.

8. The current proposal to give college students a broader choice in planning their own courses of study should be abandoned. The students who are supporting the proposal will never be satisfied, no matter what requirements are established. Some of these students have reached their third year without declaring a major. One first-year student has failed to complete four required courses. Several others have indicated a serious indifference to grades and intellectual achievement.

A flaw in the argument is that it does which one of the following?

(A) avoids the issue by focusing on supporters of the proposal
(B) argues circularly by assuming the conclusion is true in stating the premises
(C) fails to define the critical term "satisfied"
(D) distorts the proposal advocated by opponents
(E) uses the term "student" equivocally

9. The public is aware of the possibility of biases in the mass media and distrusts the media as too powerful. The body of information against which the public evaluates the plausibility of each new media report comes, however, from what the public has heard of through the mass media.

If the view above is correct, it provides a reason for accepting which one of the following conclusions?

(A) If there is a pervasive bias in the presentation of news by the mass media, it would be hard for the public to discern that bias.
(B) The mass media tailor their reports to conform to a specific political agenda.
(C) The biases that news media impose on reporting tend not to be conscious distortions but rather part of a sense they share about what is interesting and believable.
(D) News reporters and their public hold largely the same view about what is most important in society, because news reporters come out of that society.
(E) When a news event occurs that contradicts a stereotype formerly incorporated into reporting by the mass media, the public is predisposed to believe reports of the event.

10. Politician: Homelessness is a serious social problem, but further government spending to provide low-income housing is not the cure for homelessness. The most cursory glance at the real-estate section of any major newspaper is enough to show that there is no lack of housing units available to rent. So the frequent claim that people are homeless because of a lack of available housing is wrong.

That homelessness is a serious social problem figures in the argument in which one of the following ways?

(A) It suggests an alternative perspective to the one adopted in the argument.
(B) It sets out a problem the argument is designed to resolve.
(C) It is compatible either with accepting the conclusion or with denying it.
(D) It summarizes a position the argument as a whole is directed toward discrediting.
(E) It is required in order to establish the conclusion.

11. Until he was dismissed amid great controversy, Hastings was considered one of the greatest intelligence agents of all time. It is clear that if his dismissal was justified, then Hastings was either incompetent or else disloyal. Soon after the dismissal, however, it was shown that he had never been incompetent. Thus, one is forced to conclude that Hastings must have been disloyal.

    Which one of the following states an assumption upon which the argument depends?

    (A) Hastings' dismissal was justified.
    (B) Hastings was a high-ranking intelligence officer.
    (C) The dismissal of anyone who was disloyal would be justified.
    (D) Anyone whose dismissal was justified was disloyal.
    (E) If someone was disloyal or incompetent, then his dismissal was justified.

12. The true scientific significance of a group of unusual fossils discovered by the paleontologist Charles Walcott is more likely to be reflected in a recent classification than it was in Walcott's own classification. Walcott was, after all, a prominent member of the scientific establishment. His classifications are thus unlikely to have done anything but confirm what established science had already taken to be true.

    Which one of the following most accurately describes a questionable technique used in the argument?

    (A) It draws conclusions about the merit of a position and about the content of that position from evidence about the position's source.
    (B) It cites two pieces of evidence, each of which is both questionable and unverifiable, and uses this evidence to support its conclusions.
    (C) It bases a conclusion on two premises that contradict each other and minimizes this contradiction by the vagueness of the terms employed.
    (D) It attempts to establish the validity of a claim, which is otherwise unsupported, by denying the truth of the opposite of that claim.
    (E) It analyzes the past on the basis of social and political categories that properly apply only to the present and uses the results of this analysis to support its conclusion.

13. Economist: Some policymakers believe that our country's continued economic growth requires a higher level of personal savings than we currently have. A recent legislative proposal would allow individuals to set up savings accounts in which interest earned would be exempt from taxes until money is withdrawn from the account. Backers of this proposal claim that its implementation would increase the amount of money available for banks to loan at a relatively small cost to the government in lost tax revenues. Yet, when similar tax-incentive programs were tried in the past, virtually all of the money invested through them was diverted from other personal savings, and the overall level of personal savings was unchanged.

    The passage as a whole provides the most support for which one of the following conclusions?

    (A) Backers of the tax-incentive proposal undoubtedly have some motive other than their expressed aim of increasing the amount of money available for banks to loan.
    (B) The proposed tax incentive is unlikely to attract enough additional money into personal savings accounts to make up for the attendant loss in tax revenues.
    (C) A tax-incentive program that resulted in substantial loss of tax revenues would be likely to generate a large increase in personal savings.
    (D) The economy will be in danger unless some alternative to increased personal savings can be found to stimulate growth.
    (E) The government has no effective means of influencing the amount of money that people are willing to put into savings accounts.

14. "Physicalists" expect that ultimately all mental functions will be explainable in neurobiological terms. Achieving this goal requires knowledge of how neurons interact, and a delineation of the psychological faculties to be explained. At present, there is a substantial amount of fundamental knowledge about the basic functions of neurons, and the scope and character of such psychological capacities as visual perception and memory are well understood. Thus, as the physicalists claim, mental functions are bound to receive explanations in neurobiological terms in the near future.

    Which one of the following indicates an error in the reasoning in the passage?

    (A) The conclusion contradicts the claim of the physicalists.
    (B) The passage fails to describe exactly what is currently known about the basic functions of neurons.
    (C) The word "neurobiological" is used as though it had the same meaning as the word "mental."
    (D) The argument does not indicate whether it would be useful to explain mental functions in neurobiological terms.
    (E) The passage does not indicate that any knowledge has been achieved about how neurons interact.

15. It has been claimed that an action is morally good only if it benefits another person and was performed with that intention; whereas an action that harms another person is morally bad either if such harm was intended or if reasonable forethought would have shown that the action was likely to cause harm.

    Which one of the following judgments most closely conforms to the principle cited above?

    (A) Pamela wrote a letter attempting to cause trouble between Edward and his friend; this action of Pamela's was morally bad, even though the letter, in fact, had an effect directly opposite from the one intended.
    (B) In order to secure a promotion, Jeffrey devoted his own time to resolving a backlog of medical benefits claims; Jeffrey's action was morally good since it alone enabled Sara's claim to be processed in time for her to receive much-needed treatment.
    (C) Intending to help her elderly neighbor by clearing his walkway after a storm, Teresa inadvertently left ice on his steps; because of this exposed ice, her neighbor had a bad fall, thus showing that morally good actions can have bad consequences.
    (D) Marilees, asked by a homeless man for food, gave the man her own sandwich; however, because the man tried to talk while he was eating the sandwich, it caused him to choke, and thus Marilees unintentionally performed a morally bad action.
    (E) Jonathan agreed to watch his three-year-old niece while she played but, becoming engrossed in conversation, did not see her run into the street where she was hit by a bicycle; even though he intended no harm, Jonathan's action was morally bad.

16. Although all birds have feathers and all birds have wings, some birds do not fly. For example, penguins and ostriches use their wings to move in a different way from other birds. Penguins use their wings only to swim under water at high speeds. Ostriches use their wings only to run with the wind by lifting them as if they were sails.

Which one of the following is most parallel in its reasoning to the argument above?

(A) Ancient philosophers tried to explain not how the world functions but why it functions. In contrast, most contemporary biologists seek comprehensive theories of how organisms function, but many refuse to speculate about purpose.
(B) Some chairs are used only as decorations, and other chairs are used only to tame lions. Therefore, not all chairs are used for sitting in spite of the fact that all chairs have a seat and some support such as legs.
(C) Some musicians in a symphony orchestra play the violin, and others play the viola, but these are both in the same category of musical instruments, namely string instruments.
(D) All cars have similar drive mechanisms, but some cars derive their power from solar energy, whereas others burn gasoline. Thus, solar-powered cars are less efficient than gasoline-powered ones.
(E) Sailing ships move in a different way from steamships. Both sailing ships and steamships navigate over water, but only sailing ships use sails to move over the surface.

Questions 17–18

Jones: Prehistoric wooden tools found in South America have been dated to 13,000 years ago. Although scientists attribute these tools to peoples whose ancestors first crossed into the Americas from Siberia to Alaska, this cannot be correct. In order to have reached a site so far south, these peoples must have been migrating southward well before 13,000 years ago. However, no such tools dating to before 13,000 years ago have been found anywhere between Alaska and South America.

Smith: Your evidence is inconclusive. Those tools were found in peat bogs, which are rare in the Americas. Wooden tools in soils other than peat bogs usually decompose within only a few years.

17. The point at issue between Jones and Smith is

(A) whether all prehistoric tools that are 13,000 years or older were made of wood
(B) whether the scientists' attribution of tools could be correct in light of Jones's evidence
(C) whether the dating of the wooden tools by the scientists could be correct
(D) how long ago the peoples who crossed into the Americas from Siberia to Alaska first did so
(E) whether Smith's evidence entails that the wooden tools have been dated correctly

18. Smith responds to Jones by

(A) citing several studies that invalidate Jones's conclusion
(B) accusing Jones of distorting the scientists' position
(C) disputing the accuracy of the supporting evidence cited by Jones
(D) showing that Jones's evidence actually supports the denial of Jones's conclusion
(E) challenging an implicit assumption in Jones's argument

Questions 19–20

Saunders: Everyone at last week's neighborhood association meeting agreed that the row of abandoned and vandalized houses on Carlton Street posed a threat to the safety of our neighborhood. Moreover, no one now disputes that getting the houses torn down eliminated that threat. Some people tried to argue that it was unnecessary to demolish what they claimed were basically sound buildings, since the city had established a fund to help people in need of housing buy and rehabilitate such buildings. The overwhelming success of the demolition strategy, however, proves that the majority, who favored demolition, were right and that those who claimed that the problem could and should be solved by rehabilitating the houses were wrong.

19. Which one of the following principles, if established, would determine that demolishing the houses was the right decision or instead would determine that the proposal advocated by the opponents of demolition should have been adopted?

    (A) When what to do about an abandoned neighborhood building is in dispute, the course of action that would result in the most housing for people who need it should be the one adopted unless the building is believed to pose a threat to neighborhood safety.
    (B) When there are two proposals for solving a neighborhood problem, and only one of them would preclude the possibility of trying the other approach if the first proves unsatisfactory, then the approach that does not foreclose the other possibility should be the one adopted.
    (C) If one of two proposals for renovating vacant neighborhood buildings requires government funding whereas the second does not, the second proposal should be the one adopted unless the necessary government funds have already been secured.
    (D) No plan for eliminating a neighborhood problem that requires demolishing basically sound houses should be carried out until all other possible alternatives have been thoroughly investigated.
    (E) No proposal for dealing with a threat to a neighborhood's safety should be adopted merely because a majority of the residents of that neighborhood prefer that proposal to a particular counterproposal.

20. Saunders' reasoning is flawed because it

    (A) relies on fear rather than on argument to persuade the neighborhood association to reject the policy advocated by Saunders' opponents
    (B) fails to establish that there is anyone who could qualify for city funds who would be interested in buying and rehabilitating the houses
    (C) mistakenly equates an absence of vocal public dissent with the presence of universal public support
    (D) offers no evidence that the policy advocated by Saunders' opponents would not have succeeded if it had been given the chance
    (E) does not specify the precise nature of the threat to neighborhood safety supposedly posed by the vandalized houses

21. When old-growth forests are cleared of tall trees, more sunlight reaches the forest floor. This results in a sharp increase in the population of leafy shrubs on which the mule deer depend for food. Yet mule deer herds that inhabit cleared forests are less well-nourished than are herds living in old-growth forests.

    Which one of the following, if true, most helps to resolve the apparent paradox?

    (A) Mule deer have enzyme-rich saliva and specialized digestive organs that enable the deer to digest tough plants inedible to other deer species.
    (B) Mule deer herds that inhabit cleared forests tend to have more females with young offspring and fewer adult males than do other mule deer populations.
    (C) Mule deer populations are spread throughout western North America and inhabit hot, sunny climates as well as cool, wet climates.
    (D) As plants receive more sunlight, they produce higher amounts of tannins, compounds that inhibit digestion of the plants' proteins.
    (E) Insect parasites, such as certain species of ticks, that feed primarily on mule deer often dwell in trees, from which they drop onto passing deer.

22. Genevieve: Increasing costs have led commercial airlines to cut back on airplane maintenance. Also, reductions in public spending have led to air traffic control centers being underfunded and understaffed. For these and other reasons it is becoming quite unsafe to fly, and so one should avoid doing it.

Harold: Your reasoning may be sound, but I can hardly accept your conclusion when you yourself have recently been flying on commercial airlines even more than before.

Which one of the following relies on a questionable technique most similar to that used in Harold's reply to Genevieve?

(A) David says that the new film is not very good, but he has not seen it himself, so I don't accept his opinion.
(B) A long time ago Maria showed me a great way to cook lamb, but for medical reasons she no longer eats red meat, so I'll cook something else for dinner tonight.
(C) Susan has been trying to persuade me to go rock climbing with her, claiming that it's quite safe, but last week she fell and broke her collarbone, so I don't believe her.
(D) Pat has shown me research that proves that eating raw green vegetables is very beneficial and that one should eat them daily, but I don't believe it, since she hardly ever eats raw green vegetables.
(E) Gabriel has all the qualifications we have specified for the job and has much relevant work experience, but I don't believe we should hire him, because when he worked in a similar position before his performance was mediocre.

23. All people residing in the country of Gradara approve of legislation requiring that certain hazardous wastes be disposed of by being burned in modern high-temperature incinerators. However, waste disposal companies planning to build such incinerators encounter fierce resistance to their applications for building permits from the residents of every Gradaran community that those companies propose as an incinerator site.

Which one of the following, if true, most helps to explain the residents' simultaneously holding both of the positions ascribed to them?

(A) High-temperature incineration minimizes the overall risk to the human population of the country from the wastes being disposed of, but it concentrates the remaining risk in a small number of incineration sites.
(B) High-temperature incineration is more expensive than any of the available alternatives would be, and the higher costs would be recovered through higher product prices.
(C) High-temperature incineration will be carried out by private companies rather than by a government agency so that the government will not be required to police itself.
(D) The toxic fumes generated within a high-temperature incinerator can be further treated so that all toxic residues from a properly operating incinerator are solids.
(E) The substantial cost of high-temperature incineration can be partially offset by revenue from sales of electric energy generated as a by-product of incineration.

24. Derek: We must exploit available resources in developing effective anticancer drugs such as the one made from mature Pacific yew trees. Although the yew population might be threatened, the trees should be harvested now, since an effective synthetic version of the yew's anticancer chemical could take years to develop.

Lola: Not only are mature yews very rare, but most are located in areas where logging is prohibited to protect the habitat of the endangered spotted owl. Despite our eagerness to take advantage of a new medical breakthrough, we should wait for a synthetic drug rather than threaten the survival of both the yew and the owl, which could have far-reaching consequences for an entire ecosystem.

Which one of the following is the main point at issue between Lola and Derek?

(A) whether the harvesting of available Pacific yews would have far-reaching environmental repercussions
(B) whether the drugs that are effective against potentially deadly diseases should be based on synthetic rather than naturally occurring chemicals
(C) whether it is justifiable to wait until a synthetic drug can be developed when the capacity for producing the yew-derived drug already exists
(D) the extent of the environmental disaster that would result if both the Pacific yew and the spotted owl were to become extinct
(E) whether environmental considerations should ever have any weight when human lives are at stake

25. Mayor Smith, one of our few government officials with a record of outspoken, informed, and consistent opposition to nuclear power plant construction projects, has now declared herself in favor of building the nuclear power plant at Littletown. If someone with her past antinuclear record now favors building this power plant, then there is good reason to believe that it will be safe and therefore should be built.

The argument is vulnerable to criticism on which one of the following grounds?

(A) It overlooks the possibility that not all those who fail to speak out on issues of nuclear power are necessarily opposed to it.
(B) It assumes without warrant that the qualities enabling a person to be elected to public office confer on that person a grasp of the scientific principles on which technical decisions are based.
(C) It fails to establish that a consistent and outspoken opposition is necessarily an informed opposition.
(D) It leads to the further but unacceptable conclusion that any project favored by Mayor Smith should be sanctioned simply on the basis of her having spoken out in favor of it.
(E) It gives no indication of either the basis of Mayor Smith's former opposition to nuclear power plant construction or the reasons for her support for the Littletown project.

26. Ten years ago, the total share of federal, state, and local taxes was 23 percent of the nation's Gross National Product. Now, that share has decreased to 21 percent.

Which one of the following can be properly inferred from the facts given above?

(A) The total amount of federal, state, and local taxes paid now is less than the amount paid ten years ago.
(B) On average, people now have a better standard of living than they did ten years ago.
(C) The average taxpayer keeps a greater percentage of income for his own use than he did ten years ago.
(D) Federal, state, and local governments have reduced the level of services they offer to constituents.
(E) Inefficiency and fraud have been reduced in government services.

27. Those who prepare a nation's armed forces can learn much from the world of college athletics. In athletic competition, winning teams are generally those whose members are well-trained as individuals and as a team, who are inspired by their coach, and who learn from mistakes made in games they lose. Similarly, a military that is successful needs well-trained soldiers who are confident about their capabilities, with each and every soldier learning from his mistakes in order to constantly improve his abilities.

    Which of the following expresses the most serious weakness in the comparison drawn between athletes and soldiers?

    (A) Coaches of athletic teams are often chosen for their ability to teach young adults, while admirals and generals often lack this capability.
    (B) Not all college athletics are team sports. In sports such as tennis or gymnastics, competitors play as individuals.
    (C) College athletic teams that lose games can review mistakes to improve each member's performance, but soldiers who make significant errors in battle may not survive to learn from their mistakes.
    (D) Even those teams from the wealthiest colleges do not have the resources that a nation can marshal in developing its armed forces.
    (E) Both men and women serve in modern armed forces, but there is no college athletic event in which men and women compete on the same team.

28. In 1970, only 10 percent of vacationers traveled by airplanes to their destination. By 1990, that number had increased to 35 percent. Now, in 1970 the risk of being injured in an airline accident was 1 chance per 300 flights. Due to changes in aircraft design, this risk decreased to 1 chance per 1000 flights by 1990.

    Which of the following can be properly inferred from the passage?

    (A) More vacationers were injured in airplane accidents in 1970 compared to 1990.
    (B) More vacationers were injured in airplane accidents in 1990 compared to 1970.
    (C) More vacationers traveled by car in 1970 than in 1990.
    (D) Vacationers were less likely to be injured in a plane accident in 1970 compared to 1990.
    (E) Vacationers were less likely to be injured in a plane accident in 1990 compared to 1970.

29. *Advertisement*: Do you want to be more energetic, vigorous, and physically fit? Take a daily supplement of Vita-plus, a vitamin combination containing additional proprietary ingredients. Our studies using hundreds of volunteers show that after just one week of taking 2 capsules daily, participants report being more energetic and alert on average than the average level reported by the National Institutes of Health survey of all Americans.

    Which of the following would most strengthen the advertisement's claim that Vita-Plus supplements make one more energetic and alert?

    (A) Those who voluntarily chose to take more than 2 capsules daily reported energy levels even greater than those who took only 2 capsules.
    (B) The volunteers were randomly selected from all those who answered a newspaper advertisement and were willing to pay for the cost of the Vita-Plus capsules.
    (C) At the beginning of the study, the volunteers' reports on alertness showed levels on average no different from the average level reported by the National Institutes of Health.
    (D) Some of the volunteers were given capsules that solely contained cellulose, an inert substance with no vitamins or other health-inducing substances. Those volunteers also reported increased levels of alertness and energy.
    (E) Some of the volunteers were given capsules that solely contained cellulose, an inert substance with no vitamins or other health-inducing substances. Those volunteers reported no increase in alertness or energy.

30. Because of winter storm damage, the cost of a pound of apples at the local supermarket has increased 40 percent while the cost of a pound of oranges has increased 20 percent. Therefore, apples are now more expensive than oranges.

    The argument's reasoning is questionable because the argument fails to rule out the possibility that

    (A) before the storm, apples had increased in price less than oranges
    (B) before the storm, apples had already been more expensive than oranges
    (C) before the storm, oranges were significantly more expensive than apples
    (D) apples will fall back to their normal price more quickly than oranges will
    (E) consumers will reduce their purchases of apples until the price falls to below that of oranges

31. Over the last 20 years, psychologists have studied the effect of television viewing on the subsequent levels of violent behavior by young adults. The researchers studied children between the ages of 10 and 15 and found that those children who viewed an average of 6 hours or more of television daily were over four times as likely to be arrested for violent crimes when they were young adults than those young adults who as children watched less than 2 hours of television daily. Therefore, researchers concluded that television viewing causes increased levels of violent activity in young adults.

    Which of the following would indicate a flaw in the researcher's conclusion?

    (A) The researchers did not establish that those who watched more than six hours of television were watching shows that featured violence.
    (B) The researchers did not establish that those who watched more violent shows were even more likely to be arrested than those who watched less violent shows.
    (C) The researchers did not establish that some other reason, such as parental style, was not a factor for both the differences in television viewing and later arrest levels between the two groups.
    (D) The researchers did not carry out their study long enough to determine if television viewing influences arrest records for those over the age of 40.
    (E) The researchers did not establish that those who were arrested for violent crimes had actually caused serious injury to other people.

32. Here-and-There Import Company has always shown a quarterly loss whenever the value of the dollar falls 7% or more against the yen in the previous fiscal quarter. The company had a loss this quarter. Therefore, the dollar must have fallen at least 7% against the yen last quarter.

    Which of the following exhibits a parallel pattern of reasoning as the argument above?

    (A) Every Fourth of July weekend, the police strictly enforce parking regulations. I just received a parking ticket. Therefore, today must be July 4th.
    (B) Whenever the circus comes to town, schoolchildren become very hard to control. Since little Susie is behaving very properly, the circus must not be in town.
    (C) C & D bakery shows a profit whenever the local factory hires overtime workers. Because the factory has hired overtime workers, C & D bakery will show a profit.
    (D) Whenever it has been sunny, Biff has gone to the beach. Therefore it must be sunny, because Biff has just left for the beach.
    (E) Everybody who is somebody went to the awards banquet. Since Steve did not go to the awards banquet, he must not be anybody.

33. This past holiday weekend, the number of traffic accidents that occurred on a particular stretch of Highway 79 was 25 percent lower than the corresponding number of accidents last year in the same location over the same holiday weekend. This is good evidence that the Highway Patrol's publicity campaign against speeding has resulted in safer driving habits among motorists.

    Which of the following is assumed in reaching the conclusion above?

    (A) Traffic accident rates on the particular stretch of Highway 79 will continue to drop as long as the Highway Patrol's publicity campaign continues.
    (B) The two holiday weekends cover exactly the same calendar dates.
    (C) Highway Patrol cars are patrolling the particular stretch of Highway 79 more frequently.
    (D) The total number of miles driven on the particular stretch of Highway 79 has not decreased 25% or more since last year.
    (E) A reduction in speeding is the only driving habit that has improved since last year.

Answers and Solutions to Exercise

1.	D	8.	A	15.	E	22.	D	29.	E
2.	B	9.	A	16.	B	23.	A	30.	C
3.	C	10.	C	17.	B	24.	C	31.	C
4.	E	11.	A	18.	E	25.	E	32.	D
5.	A	12.	A	19.	B	26.	C	33.	D
6.	C	13.	B	20.	D	27.	C		
7.	D	14.	E	21.	D	28.	E		

1. The opening sentence *"The senator has long held to the general principle that no true work of art is obscene"* is the premise of the senator's argument. It contains an embedded if-then statement: *If it is a work of art, then it is not obscene.* This can be diagrammed as follows:

A—>~O,

where A stands for "it is a work of art" and O stands for "it is obscene." Now, the senator justifies this principle by stating *"if these works really are obscene then they cannot be works of art,"* which can be symbolized as

O—>~A.

Applying the contrapositive to this diagram yields

A—>~O.

Now, we have already established that this is the premise of the argument. Hence the senator's argument is circular—he assumes what he seeks to establish. The answer is (D).

2. This argument commits the fallacy of false dichotomy. It assumes that workers have only two reactions to their work—either it's not challenging or it's too challenging. Clearly, there is a wide range of reactions between those two extremes. The answer is (B).

3. This is a rather straightforward question. The essence of the argument is that if production costs were reduced to the point that operas could be developed without corporate sponsors, then the opera companies would be able and willing to produce less famous operas. Choice (C) directly attacks this claim by stating that without corporate sponsorship only the most famous operas could be produced. This is the antithesis of the argument. The answer is (C).

4. In the phrase "selfish individualism" the word "selfish" is being used with its usual meaning—self-centered. But in the phrase "selfish concern for the human species" it appears to mean unselfish or altruistic. Hence the argument equivocates. The answer is (E).

5. This is a straightforward question. The passage uses the example of the clock to illustrate how new technologies can both liberate us, by increasing productivity and therefore increasing the range of choices, and enslave us, "I have to be there by 1:30 p.m. sharp." The answer is (A).

6. The answer is (C), which commits the true-but-irrelevant fallacy. The passage is about the commercial production of honey, not about pollination, nor for that matter about ornamental trees.

7. It is unwarranted to assume that older people's reasons for saving are as compelling as those of younger people. Older people may have stronger reasons to save. For example, in their youth they may have learned the folly of not saving, or they may be more aware of the need for a retirement fund. The answer is (D).

8. Instead of addressing the issue, the argument commits a personal attack against the students supporting the proposal. The answer is (A).

9. If almost all our information comes from the media, then even if we suspect that a particular report is biased we would have little means of confirming our suspicion. The answer, therefore, is (A).

10. Most LSAT questions are not worded as vaguely as this one is. "Figures in the argument" could mean just about anything. This makes the question difficult. However, the underlying structure of the argument is quite simple. Notice that the argument is fallacious. The author states that newspapers list plenty of apartments for rent; he does not state whether these are low-rent apartments—they probably aren't. So the argument is a non sequitur. Hence the conclusion is independent of the premises of the argument. The answer is (C).

11. The statement *"It is clear that if his dismissal was justified, then Hastings was either incompetent or else disloyal"* can be symbolized as

J—>(I or D)

where J stands for "his dismissal was justified," I stands for "incompetent," and D stands for "disloyal." Now, the statement *"it was shown that he had never been incompetent"*—**~I**—reduces the diagram to

J—>D

This diagram tells us that if we assume that J is true, then, as the argument concludes, D must be true. Hence, the argument assumes that Hastings' dismissal was justified. The answer is (A).

12. The argument unfairly assumes that Walcott's background prevents him from being objective. The answer is (A).

13.
(A) No. This is mere speculation.
(B) Yes. Although the government's loss of tax revenues should be small, the passage states *"similar tax-incentive programs left the overall level of personal savings unchanged."*
(C) No. The passage implies that there would be little or no increase in personal savings. The example in the passage shows that a tax incentive program with a small loss in tax revenues did not increase personal savings, so a tax incentive program with a large loss in tax revenues would probably have a similar result.
(D) No. The claim that the economy will be endangered is too strong. Besides the passage does not argue against increasing personal savings, just that the given tax incentive program will fail to increase savings as similar ones have failed in the past.
(E) No. This claim is too broad. The passage does not imply that the government has no means of influencing the savings rate, just that certain tax incentive programs have no affect on savings rates.

14. Two conditions are introduced as necessary for achieving the goal of explaining mental functions in neurobiological terms:

1) knowledge of how neurons interact

2) a delineation of the faculties

The second is partially fulfilled (visual perception and memory are suggested and others are implied), but the first isn't. The passage states that we know a substantial amount about the basic functions of neurons. However, it does not mention anything about how they interact. Hence the passage does not meet the very conditions it requires for explaining mental functions in neurobiological terms—this is an error in reasoning. The answer is (E).

15. The argument claims that an action is morally good only if it meets *both* of the following criteria:

(1) It benefits another person.
(2) It is performed with that intent.

The argument also claims that an action that harms another person is morally bad if it meets *either one* of the following criteria:

(1) The harm was intended.
(2) Reasonable forethought would have shown that the action was likely to cause harm.

In choice (E), Jonathan should have realized that if he became engrossed in conversation, he would be neglecting his niece. This satisfies the second criteria for a morally bad action. Reasonable forethought would have shown Jonathan the error of his choice. The answer is (E).*

As to the other choices, (A) is second best. The first part of (A), "*Pamela wrote a letter attempting to cause trouble between Edward and his friend,*" certainly satisfies the first criterion for a morally bad action. But the remainder of the sentence doesn't seem to relate to the second criterion.

(B) satisfies the first criterion for a morally good action. However, it fails to meet the second criterion because Jeffrey's action was performed to benefit himself (by helping him secure a promotion), not to help others.

(C) does not meet either criteria for a morally bad action. Teresa left the ice on the steps accidentally. One could argue, however, that a reasonable person would double check her work. Nevertheless, choice (E) satisfies the second criterion for a morally bad action more directly.

(D) satisfies only the second criterion for a morally good action, and it does not satisfy either criteria for a morally bad action.

16.
(A) No. The passage uses an example to illustrate a statement: *"although all birds have feathers and all birds have wings, some birds do not fly."* Choice (A), however, draws a contrast between two approaches.
(B) Yes. The passage uses an example to illustrate a statement: *"although all birds have feathers and all birds have wings, some birds do not fly."*

* Remember: Only one of the statements in an *either-or* construction need be true for the whole structure to be true.

Similarly, choice (B) uses an example to illustrate a statement: *"not all chairs are used for sitting in spite of the fact that all chairs have a seat and some support such as legs."*
(C) No. The passage uses an example to illustrate a statement: *"although all birds have feathers and all birds have wings, some birds do not fly."* Choice (C) does not have an example.
(D) No. The passage uses an example to illustrate a statement: *"although all birds have feathers and all birds have wings, some birds do not fly."* Choice (D) does not have an explicit example.
(E) No. Choice (E) draws a comparison between two ships. However, the passage does not draw a comparison between ostriches and penguins; rather it merely uses each to illustrate a statement: *"although all birds have feathers and all birds have wings, some birds do not fly."*

Questions 17–18

17.
(A) No. Whether prehistoric tools were composed of substances other than wood is not discussed.
(B) Yes. They are arguing over the meaning of the evidence. Jones argues that if the wooden tools found in South America were from peoples who migrated from Alaska then there should be even older wooden tools along the path they took. Perhaps 13,500 year-old wooden tools in Central America and 14,000 year-old wooden tools in North America.

Smith, on the other hand, refutes Jones's claim by pointing out that older wooden tools were not found along the migration route because they quickly decompose except in peat bogs, which are rare along the path.
(C) No. There is no discussion of the accuracy of the dating method used.
(D) No. Although this issue is probably in dispute, we cannot tell from the excerpt. Smith does not state or imply that the people crossed at a particular time; rather he points out a flaw in Jones's interpretation of the evidence.
(E) No. The meaning of the evidence is in dispute, not its accuracy. Ostensibly, they both accept that the tools are 13,000 years old. At issue is whether this precludes the possibility of the tools being from people who migrated from Alaska.

18.
(A) No. Smith does not refute Jones by citing any studies but by questioning Jones's logic.
(B) No. Smith responds only to the Jones's interpretation of the evidence, not to Jones's paraphrase of the scientists' position.
(C) No. The accuracy of the evidence is not in dispute, rather the debate is over the meaning of the evidence.
(D) No. Smith does not claim that Jones's conclusion is wrong, just that the "evidence is inconclusive."
(E) Yes. Jones's assumption is that if people from Siberia were in North America and Central America before 13,000 years ago then they would have left wooden tools which scientists would have found. Smith attacks this assumption by pointing out that the wooden tools may have been left in the area more than 13,000 years ago but quickly decomposed. In other words, the fact that remains of wooden tools are not now in the area does not preclude the possibility that they were in the area more than 13,000 years ago.

Questions 19–20

19.
(A) No. This does not address the conflicting proposals: demolition vs. rehabilitation.
(B) Yes. Suppose the houses are destroyed first. Then it cannot be known whether rehabilitating the houses would have solved the problem. However, suppose the houses are rehabilitated first. Now, if rehabilitation fails to solve the problem, the houses can still be demolished. So rehabilitating the houses first *does not* preclude the possibility of destroying the houses later, whereas destroying the houses first *does* preclude the possibility of rehabilitating the houses later.
(C) No. We do not know whether either proposal requires government funding. Besides, only one of the two proposals advocated renovating the buildings, the other advocated destroying the buildings.
(D) No. This is the second-best choice. It is both too strong and too broad. The passage is about only two proposals: destruction and rehabilitation.
(E) No. The question asks which of two possible decisions is right, not which method should be taken to arrive at a decision.

20.
(A) No. Saunders appeals only to the success of the demolition strategy, not to fear.
(B) No. If fact, this would support Saunders' argument. If no one could qualify for city funds, then it would be unlikely for the houses to be rehabilitated.
(C) No. There is no discussion of vocal dissent nor universal support.
(D) Yes. Saunders claims that the success of the destruction strategy proves that it was right and that the rehabilitation strategy was wrong. He is only half right. Since the destruction of the houses precludes the possibility of trying rehabilitation, we

cannot know whether rehabilitation would have also worked.
(E) No. The nature of the threat is not at issue since the opening sentence of the passage implies that everyone agrees there is a threat. Rather, at issue is how to eliminate the threat.

21.
(A) No. The paradox involves the health of mule deer living in old-growth forests and the health of mule deer living in cleared forests, not between the mule deer and other species of deer.
(B) No. It is conceivable that both female deer and their young offspring are less well nourished than adult males; however, this is speculation.
(C) No. Their natural range is irrelevant. At issue is the difference in their health in cleared forest versus old-growth forests.
(D) Yes. We are looking for an agent that would cause the deer to become less well nourished even as their food supply increases. Choice (D) offers an agent—tannins, which inhibit digestion of food. So even though the deer have more food to eat, they receive less nutrition from the food.
(E) No. This should make the deer better nourished in cleared forest since there are few trees from which the parasites could drop onto the deer.

22.
(A) No. Harold is objecting to the fact that Genevieve apparently does not practice what she preaches. She says one should avoid flying, yet she is flying more than ever before. In this argument, David is not offering advice.
(B) No. Harold is objecting to the fact that Genevieve apparently does not practice what she preaches. She says one should avoid flying, yet she is flying more than ever before. The person in this argument is not offering advice.
(C) No. Harold is objecting to the fact that Genevieve apparently does not practice what she preaches. She says one should avoid flying, yet she is flying more than ever before. In this argument, Susan *does* practice what she preaches—that rock climbing is safe.
(D) Yes. Harold is objecting to the fact that Genevieve apparently does not practice what she preaches. She says one should avoid flying, yet she is flying more than ever before. Similarly, the person in this answer-choice is objecting to the fact that Pat apparently does not practice what she preaches. Pat says raw green vegetables should be eaten daily, yet she hardly ever eats them.
(E) No. Harold is objecting to the fact that Genevieve apparently does not practice what she preaches. She says one should avoid flying, yet she is flying more than ever before. In this argument, Gabriel is not offering advice.

23.
(A) Yes. Incineration may pose the least amount of risk for the greatest number of people, yet concentrate the risk for a few people—those living nearby.
(B) No. This would make the general population less likely to approve of incinerators and does not explain why people object when an incinerator is built nearby.
(C) No. This does not explain why the general population approves of incinerators and the people living near incinerators oppose them.
(D) No. This should help allay the fears of nearby residents, assuming that the solids are potentially less harmful. Hence, it would make them less likely to object to the incinerators.
(E) No. This does not explain why the general population approves of incinerators, and the people living near incinerators oppose them. Evidently, the people living near the incinerators worry that they will be exposed to greater amounts of toxins than people further away.

24.
(A) No. Lola states that harvesting the yew *"could have far-reaching consequences for an entire ecosystem."* Although Derek concedes *"the yew population might be threatened,"* he does not discuss whether this would adversely affect the environment.
(B) No. The dispute is over whether the yew trees should be harvested while a synthetic drug is being developed.
(C) Yes. Derek and Lola have different priorities. Derek believes it is more important to get the drug on the market now than to protect the yew trees, whereas Lola believes it is more important to protect the yew trees and the spotted owl.
(D) No. Lola states that harvesting the yew *"could have far-reaching consequences for an entire ecosystem."* Although Derek concedes *"the yew population might be threatened,"* he does not discuss whether this would adversely affect the environment. This answer-choice is essentially the same as (A).
(E) No. Although Derek apparently gives more weight to saving human life—at least in the short run—and Lola gives more weight to saving the environment, choice (E) is too strong. Notice the absolute words *ever* and *any*.

25.
(A) No. Since she *did* speak out, this choice is irrelevant.
(B) No. The argument does assume that the mayor has a grasp of the scientific issues; however, it is not necessary to assume this is due to the qualities that got her elected to public office.

(C) No. The passage does not even imply that consistent and outspoken opposition is necessarily an informed opposition. The three features of her opposition to nuclear power plants—outspoken, informed, and consistent—are presented as an independent series.
(D) No. Although this is a possible criticism of the argument, there are better and more direct criticisms.
(E) Yes. We do not know her motives. Perhaps she changed her mind after carefully weighing the issues, or perhaps she was paid to change her mind.

26. If the various levels of government collect a smaller share of the GNP through taxes, then the average taxpayer keeps a larger share. The answer is (C).

Be careful of choice (A): it commits an error by failing to distinguish between percentage and amount. While the percentage share of taxes has decreased, the overall amount of tax revenue could have increased if the GNP is larger than it was ten years ago.

The other choices can not be logically inferred from the passage. Each choice offers a possible cause or effect of the tax reduction, but none of these must occur.

27. The passage draws an analogy between armed forces and college athletic teams, and concludes that training methods which work in college sports will be effective in the military as well. There are three training methods listed for a successful sports team:

1) trained as individuals and as team
2) inspired by their coach
3) learn from their mistakes

Reasoning by analogy is not made invalid by minor differences between the two items being compared. Choices (A), (B), (D), and (E) point out such differences but do not detract from the essence of the analogy. However, choice (C) states that it may not be possible for soldiers to learn from their mistakes, a definite distinction between sports and the military, and one that weakens the argument. The answer is (C).

28. This question is straightforward once you focus on the relevant information. If the chance of injury was 1 per 300 flights in 1970 and 1 per 1000 flights in 1990, then vacationers were less likely to be injured in a plane accident in 1990 than in 1970. The answer is (E).

Choices (A) and (B) make the error of comparing numbers of vacationers injured when the passage only gives percentages. Without knowing how many vacationers there were in each year (or at least a ratio), we can not determine which year contained a greater number of injuries. Choice (C) seems to assume that vacationers who did not travel by plane traveled by car instead—a likely but not necessary assumption. Finally, choice (D) is contradicted by the passage.

29. To strengthen a claim that a substance has a certain health effect, we often test the substance against a placebo, an inert substitute. If the substance tested produces results that the placebo does not, we attribute these differences to the action of the substance. In choice (E), some of the volunteers were given cellulose instead of Vita-plus, and these volunteers did not show the same increased energy as those who received Vita-plus. This strengthens the conclusion that Vita-plus increased one's energy. The answer is (E).

Choice (A) suffers from the weakness that those who believe in the efficacy of Vita-plus and take increased doses may convince themselves that it truly has an effect. Choice (B) shows the same weakness: maybe only "true believers" are willing to pay for the cost of the capsules.

As for (C), this choice is required to properly compare the two levels, but it is not sufficient to show Vita-plus caused any differences. Finally, choice (D) weakens the claim by stating that another substance shows the same results as Vita-plus.

30. By concluding that apples are more expensive than oranges because the cost of apples went up a greater percentage, we implicitly assume that oranges were not much more expensive initially. For example, if apples were initially $1 per pound and increased 40% to $1.40 per pound while oranges were originally $2 per pound and increased 20% to $2.40 per pound, apples would not be more expensive. The answer is (C).

As for (A), whatever increase in prices occurred before the storm has no effect on the results after the storm. With (B), if apples were previously more expensive and increased in price a greater percentage than oranges, they would be even more expensive. Finally, choices (D) and (E) have no impact on the current prices of apples and oranges.

31. This argument claims that a causal relationship exists between television viewing and arrest levels of young adults because the two situations are correlated. However, the argument does not rule out the possibility that both of these situations may be caused by a third, independent event. The answer is (C).

The other choices may all be true, but they do not impact the researchers' conclusion.

32. With parallel pattern of reasoning questions, we first identify the structure and validity of the passage, and then consider each answer-choice in turn.

The argument in the passage may be diagrammed as follows:

Dollar drops —> Quarterly loss
Quarterly loss
∴ Dollar dropped

This argument is invalid since it commits the fallacy of affirming the conclusion.

Consider choice (D):

Sunny —> Biff goes to beach
Biff goes to beach
∴ Sunny

The answer is (D).

As for (A), a diagram shows:

4th of July weekend —> Parking enforced
Parking enforced
∴ July 4th

This appears to have the same structure as the original passage, but it is in fact much stronger. While the premise in (A) discusses the 4th of July weekend, the choice concludes the day is July 4th itself.

Choices (B) and (C) exhibit valid reasoning and therefore can not be parallel to the original argument. Finally, it's hard to know exactly what choice (E) is saying.

33. This is a case of All-Things-Being-Equal. In order to attribute the reduction in accidents to the Highway Patrol's Publicity campaign, we must remove the possibility of alternative explanations. Choice (D) removes one such explanation—that the decrease in accidents could have been due to a decrease in driving on the highway. The answer is (D).

LSAT SECTIONS

ARGUMENTS I

ARGUMENTS II

Give yourself 35 minutes to complete each of these LSAT sections. It is important that you time yourself so that you can find your optimum working pace, and so that you will know what to expect when you take the test.

Note, you will not be allowed any scratch paper during the actual LSAT; all your work must be done on the test booklet. To accustom yourself to writing in a confined space, you should write all your scratch work in the book.

Answers and solutions begin on page 321.

ARGUMENTS I

Time—35 minutes
24 Questions

Directions: The questions in this section are based on the reasoning contained in brief statements or passages. For some questions, more than one of the choices could conceivably answer the question. However, you are to choose the best answer; that is, the response that most accurately and completely answers the question. You should not make assumptions that are by common sense standards implausible, superfluous, or incompatible with the passage.

1. Some people believe that witnessing violence in movies will discharge aggressive energy. Does watching someone else eat fill one's own stomach?

   In which one of the following does the reasoning most closely parallel that employed in the passage?

   (A) Some people think appropriating supplies at work for their own personal use is morally wrong. Isn't shoplifting morally wrong?
   (B) Some people think nationalism is defensible. Hasn't nationalism been the excuse for committing abominable crimes?
   (C) Some people think that boxing is fixed just because wrestling usually is. Are the two sports managed by the same sort of people?
   (D) Some people think that economists can control inflation. Can meteorologists make the sun shine?
   (E) Some people think workaholics are compensating for a lack of interpersonal skills. However, aren't most doctors workaholics?

2. Ann: All the campers at Camp Winnehatchee go to Tri-Cities High School.
   Bill: That's not true. Some Tri-Cities students are campers at Camp Lakemont.

   Bill's answer can be best explained on the assumption that he has interpreted Ann's remark to mean that

   (A) most of the campers at Camp Lakemont come from high schools other than Tri-Cities
   (B) most Tri-Cities High School students are campers at Camp Winnehatchee
   (C) some Tri-Cities High School students have withdrawn from Camp Lakemont
   (D) all Tri-Cities High School students attend summer camp
   (E) only campers at Camp Winnehatchee are students at Tri-Cities High School

3. More than a year ago, the city announced that police would crack down on illegally parked cars and that resources would be diverted from writing speeding tickets to ticketing illegally parked cars. But no crackdown has taken place. The police chief claims that resources have had to be diverted from writing speeding tickets to combating the city's staggering drug problem. Yet the police are still writing as many speeding tickets as ever. Therefore, the excuse about resources being tied up in fighting drug-related crime simply is not true.

   The conclusion in the passage depends on the assumption that

   (A) every member of the police force is qualified to work on combating the city's drug problem
   (B) drug-related crime is not as serious a problem for the city as the police chief claims it is
   (C) writing speeding tickets should be as important a priority for the city as combating drug-related crime
   (D) the police could be cracking down on illegally parked cars and combating the drug problem without having to reduce writing speeding tickets
   (E) the police cannot continue writing as many speeding tickets as ever while diverting resources to combating drug-related crime

GO ON TO THE NEXT PAGE.

4. Dried grass clippings mixed into garden soil gradually decompose, providing nutrients for beneficial soil bacteria. This results in better-than-average plant growth. Yet mixing fresh grass clippings into garden soil usually causes poorer-than-average plant growth.

   Which one of the following, if true, most helps to explain the difference in plant growth described above?

   (A) The number of beneficial soil bacteria increases whenever any kind of plant material is mixed into garden soil.
   (B) Nutrients released by dried grass clippings are immediately available to beneficial soil bacteria.
   (C) Some dried grass clippings retain nutrients originally derived from commercial lawn fertilizers, and thus provide additional enrichment to the soil.
   (D) Fresh grass clippings mixed into soil decompose rapidly, generating high levels of heat that kill beneficial soil bacteria.
   (E) When a mix of fresh and dried grass clippings is mixed into garden soil, plant growth often decreases.

5. A gas tax of one cent per gallon would raise one billion dollars per year at current consumption rates. Since a tax of fifty cents per gallon would therefore raise fifty billion dollars per year, it seems a perfect way to deal with the federal budget deficit. This tax would have the additional advantage that the resulting drop in the demand for gasoline would be ecologically sound and would keep our country from being too dependent on foreign oil producers.

   Which one of the following most clearly identifies an error in the author's reasoning?

   (A) The author cites irrelevant data.
   (B) The author relies on incorrect current consumption figures.
   (C) The author makes incompatible assumptions.
   (D) The author mistakes an effect for a cause.
   (E) The author appeals to conscience rather than reason.

6. As symbols of the freedom of the wilderness, bald eagles have the unique capacity to inspire people and foster in them a sympathetic attitude toward the needs of other threatened species. Clearly, without that sympathy and the political will it engenders, the needs of more obscure species will go unmet. The conservation needs of many obscure species can only be met by beginning with the conservation of this symbolic species, the bald eagle.

   Which one of the following is the main point of the passage as a whole?

   (A) Because bald eagles symbolize freedom, conservation efforts should be concentrated on them rather than on other, more obscure species.
   (B) The conservation of bald eagles is the first necessary step in conserving other endangered species.
   (C) Without increased public sympathy for conservation, the needs of many symbolic species will go unmet.
   (D) People's love of the wilderness can be used to engender political support for conservation efforts.
   (E) Other threatened species do not inspire people or foster sympathy as much as do bald eagles.

7. There is no reason why the work of scientists has to be officially confirmed before being published. There is a system in place for the confirmation or disconfirmation of scientific findings, namely, the replication of results by other scientists. Poor scientific work on the part of any one scientist, which can include anything from careless reporting practices to fraud, is not harmful. It will be exposed and rendered harmless when other scientists conduct the experiments and obtain disconfirmatory results.

   Which one of the following, if true, would weaken the argument?

   (A) Scientific experiments can go unchallenged for many years before they are replicated.
   (B) Most scientists work in universities, where their work is submitted to peer review before publication.
   (C) Most scientists are under pressure to make their work accessible to the scrutiny of replication.
   (D) In scientific experiments, careless reporting is more common than fraud.
   (E) Most scientists work as part of a team rather than alone.

GO ON TO THE NEXT PAGE.

8. Alice: Quotas on automobile imports to the United States should be eliminated. Then domestic producers would have to compete directly with Japanese manufacturers and would be forced to produce higher-quality cars. Such competition would be good for consumers.

   David: You fail to realize, Alice, that quotas on automobile imports are pervasive worldwide. Since Germany, Britain, and France have quotas, so should the United States.

   Which one of the following most accurately characterizes David's response to Alice's statement?

   (A) David falsely accuses Alice of contradicting herself.
   (B) David unfairly directs his argument against Alice personally.
   (C) David uncovers a hidden assumption underlying Alice's position.
   (D) David takes a position that is similar to the one Alice has taken.
   (E) David fails to address the reasons Alice cites in favor of her conclusion.

9. Governments have only one response to public criticism of socially necessary services: regulation of the activity of providing those services. But governments inevitably make the activity more expensive by regulating it, and that is particularly troublesome in these times of strained financial resources. However, since public criticism of child-care services has undermined all confidence in such services, and since such services are socially necessary, the government is certain to respond.

   Which one of the following statements can be inferred from the passage?

   (A) The quality of child care will improve.
   (B) The cost of providing child-care services will increase.
   (C) The government will use funding to foster advances in child care.
   (D) If public criticism of policy is strongly voiced, the government is certain to respond.
   (E) If child-care services are not regulated, the cost of providing child care will not increase.

10. Advertisers are often criticized for their unscrupulous manipulation of people's tastes and wants. There is evidence, however, that some advertisers are motivated by moral as well as financial considerations. A particular publication decided to change its image from being a family newspaper to concentrating on sex and violence, thus appealing to different readership. Some advertisers withdrew their advertisements from the publication, and this must have been because they morally disapproved of publishing salacious material.

    Which one of the following, if true, would most strengthen the argument?

    (A) The advertisers switched their advertisements to other family newspapers.
    (B) Some advertisers switched from family newspapers to advertise in the changed publication.
    (C) The advertisers expected their product sales to increase if they stayed with the changed publication, but to decrease if they withdrew.
    (D) People who generally read family newspapers are not likely to buy newspapers that concentrate on sex and violence.
    (E) It was expected that the changed publication would appeal principally to those in a different income group.

11. "If the forest continues to disappear at its present pace, the koala will approach extinction," said the biologist.

    "So all that is needed to save the koala is to stop deforestation," said the politician.

    Which one of the following statements is consistent with the biologist's claim but not with the politician's claim?

    (A) Deforestation continues and the koala becomes extinct.
    (B) Deforestation is stopped and the koala becomes extinct.
    (C) Reforestation begins and the koala survives.
    (D) Deforestation is slowed and the koala survives.
    (E) Deforestation is slowed and the koala approaches extinction.

GO ON TO THE NEXT PAGE.

12. People have long been fascinated by the paranormal. Over the years, numerous researchers have investigated telepathy only to find that conclusive evidence for its existence has persistently evaded them. Despite this, there are still those who believe that there must be "something in it" since some research seems to support the view that telepathy exists. However, it can often be shown that other explanations that do comply with known laws can be given. Therefore, it is premature to conclude that telepathy is an alternative means of communication.

In the passage, the author

(A) supports the conclusion by pointing to the inadequacy of evidence for the opposite view
(B) supports the conclusion by describing particular experiments
(C) supports the conclusion by overgeneralizing from a specific piece of evidence
(D) draws a conclusion that is not supported by the premises
(E) rephrases the conclusion without offering any support for it

13. If retail stores experience a decrease in revenues during this holiday season, then either attitudes toward extravagant gift-giving have changed or prices have risen beyond the level most people can afford. If attitudes have changed, then we all have something to celebrate this season. If prices have risen beyond the level most people can afford, then it must be that salaries have not kept pace with rising prices during the past year.

Assume the premises above to be true. If salaries have kept pace with rising prices during the past year, which one of the following must be true?

(A) Attitudes toward extravagant gift-giving have changed.
(B) Retail stores will not experience a decrease in retail sales during this holiday season.
(C) Prices in retail stores have not risen beyond the level that most people can afford during this holiday season.
(D) Attitudes toward extravagant gift-giving have not changed, and stores will not experience a decrease in revenues during this holiday season.
(E) Either attitudes toward extravagant gift-giving have changed or prices have risen beyond the level that most people can afford during this holiday season.

14. The "suicide wave" that followed the United States stock market crash of October 1929 is more legend than fact. Careful examination of the monthly figures on the causes of death in 1929 show that the number of suicides in October and in November was comparatively low. In only three other months were the monthly figures lower. During the summer months, when the stock market was flourishing, the number of suicides was substantially higher.

Which one of the following, if true, would best challenge the conclusion of the passage?

(A) The suicide rate is influenced by many psychological, interpersonal, and societal factors during any given historical period.
(B) October and November have almost always had relatively high suicide rates, even during the 1920s and 1930s.
(C) The suicide rate in October and November of 1929 was considerably higher than the average for those months during several preceding and following years.
(D) During the years surrounding the stock market crash, suicide rates were typically lower at the beginning of any calendar year than toward the end of that year.
(E) Because of seasonal differences, the number of suicides in October and November of 1929 would not be expected to be the same as those for other months.

GO ON TO THE NEXT PAGE.

15. A well-known sports figure found that combining publicity tours with playing tours led to problems, so she stopped combining the two. She no longer allows bookstore appearances and playing in competition to occur in the same city within the same trip. This week she is traveling to London to play in a major competition, so during her stay in London she will not be making any publicity appearances at any bookstore in London.

Which one of the following most closely parallels the reasoning used in the passage?

(A) Wherever there is an Acme Bugkiller, many wasps are killed. The Z family garden has an Acme Bugkiller, so any wasps remaining in the garden will soon be killed.

(B) The only times that the hospital's emergency room staff attends to relatively less serious emergencies are times when there is no critical emergency to attend to. On Monday night the emergency room staff attended to a series of fairly minor emergencies, so there must not have been any critical emergencies to take care of at the time.

(C) Tomato plants require hot summers to thrive. Farms in the cool summers of country Y probably do not have thriving tomato plants.

(D) Higher grades lead to better job opportunities, and studying leads to higher grades. Therefore, studying will lead to better job opportunities.

(E) Butter knives are not sharp. Q was not murdered with a sharp blade, so suspect X's butter knife may have been the murder weapon.

Questions 16–17

The advanced technology of ski boots and bindings has brought a dramatic drop in the incidence of injuries that occur on the slopes of ski resorts: from 9 injuries per 1,000 skiers in 1950 to 3 in 1980. As a result, the remainder of ski-related injuries, which includes all injuries occurring on the premises of a ski resort but not on the slopes, rose from 10 percent of all ski-related injuries in 1950 to 25 percent in 1980. The incidence of these injuries, including accidents such as falling down steps, increases with the amount of alcohol consumed per skier.

16. Which one of the following can be properly inferred from the passage?

(A) As the number of ski injuries that occur on the slopes decreases, the number of injuries that occur on the premises of ski resorts increases.

(B) The amount of alcohol consumed per skier increased between 1950 and 1980.

(C) The technology of ski boots and bindings affects the incidence of each type of ski-related injury.

(D) If the technology of ski boots and bindings continues to advance, the incidence of ski-related injuries will continue to decline.

(E) Injuries that occurred on the slopes of ski resorts made up a smaller percentage of ski-related injuries in 1980 than in 1950.

17. Which one of the following conflicts with information in the passage?

(A) The number of ski injuries that occurred on the slopes was greater in 1980 than in 1950.

(B) A skier was less likely to be injured on the slopes in 1950 than in 1980.

(C) The reporting of ski injuries became more accurate between 1950 and 1980.

(D) The total number of skiers dropped between 1950 and 1980.

(E) Some ski-related injuries occurred in 1980 to people who were not skiing.

GO ON TO THE NEXT PAGE.

18. Learning how to build a nest plays an important part in the breeding success of birds. For example, Dr. Snow has recorded the success of a number of blackbirds in several successive years. He finds that birds nesting for the first time are less successful in breeding than are older birds, and also less successful than they themselves are a year later. This cannot be a mere matter of size and strength, since blackbirds, like the great majority of birds, are fully grown when they leave the nest. It is difficult to avoid the conclusion that they benefit by their nesting experience.

Which one of the following, if true, would most weaken the argument?

(A) Blackbirds build better nests than other birds.
(B) The capacity of blackbirds to lay viable eggs increases with each successive trial during the first few years of reproduction.
(C) The breeding success of birds nesting for the second time is greater than that of birds nesting for the first time.
(D) Smaller and weaker blackbirds breed just as successfully as bigger and stronger blackbirds.
(E) Up to 25 percent of all birds are killed by predators before they start to nest.

19. How do the airlines expect to prevent commercial plane crashes? Studies have shown that pilot error contributes to two-thirds of all such crashes. To address this problem, the airlines have upgraded their training programs by increasing the hours of classroom instruction and emphasizing communication skills in the cockpit. But it is unrealistic to expect such measures to compensate for pilots lack of actual flying time. Therefore, the airlines should rethink their training approach to reducing commercial crashes.

Which one of the following is an assumption upon which the argument depends?

(A) Training programs can eliminate pilot errors.
(B) Commercial pilots routinely undergo additional training throughout their careers.
(C) The number of airline crashes will decrease if pilot training programs focus on increasing actual flying time.
(D) Lack of actual flying time is an important contributor to pilot error in commercial plane crashes.
(E) Communication skills are not important to pilot training programs.

20. All savings accounts are interest-bearing accounts. The interest from some interest-bearing accounts is tax-free, so there must be some savings accounts that have tax-free interest.

Which one of the following arguments is flawed in a way most similar to the way in which the passage is flawed?

(A) All artists are intellectuals. Some great photographers are artists. Therefore, some great photographers must be intellectuals.
(B) All great photographers are artists. All artists are intellectuals. Therefore, some great photographers must be intellectuals.
(C) All great photographers are artists. Some artists are intellectuals. Therefore, some great photographers are intellectuals.
(D) All great photographers are artists. Some great photographers are intellectuals. Therefore, some artists must be intellectuals.
(E) All great photographers are artists. No artists are intellectuals. Therefore, some great photographers must not be intellectuals.

21. One method of dating the emergence of species is to compare the genetic material of related species. Scientists theorize that the more genetically similar two species are to each other, the more recently they diverged from a common ancestor. After comparing genetic material from giant pandas, red pandas, raccoons, coatis, and all seven bear species, scientists concluded that bears and raccoons diverged 30 to 50 million years ago. They further concluded that red pandas separated from the ancestor of today's raccoons and coatis a few million years later, some 10 million years before giant pandas diverged from the other bears.

Which one of the following can be properly inferred from the passage?

(A) Giant pandas and red pandas are more closely related than scientists originally thought they were.
(B) Scientists now count the giant panda as the eighth species of bear.
(C) It is possible to determine, within a margin of just a few years, the timing of divergence of various species.
(D) Scientists have found that giant pandas are more similar genetically to bears than to raccoons.
(E) There is substantial consensus among scientists that giant pandas and red pandas are equally related to raccoons.

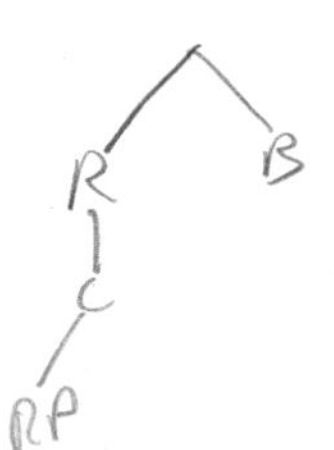

GO ON TO THE NEXT PAGE.

Questions 22–23

Despite improvements in treatment for asthma, the death rate from this disease has doubled during the past decade from its previous rate. Two possible explanations for this increase have been offered. First, the recording of deaths due to asthma has become more widespread and accurate in the past decade than it had been previously. Second, there has been an increase in urban pollution. However, since the rate of deaths due to asthma has increased dramatically even in cities with long-standing, comprehensive medical records and with little or no urban pollution, one must instead conclude that the cause of increased deaths is the use of bronchial inhalers by asthma sufferers to relieve their symptoms.

22. Each of the following, if true, provides support to the argument EXCEPT:
    - (A) Urban populations have doubled in the past decade.
    - (B) Records of asthma deaths are as accurate for the past twenty years as for the past ten years.
    - (C) Evidence suggests that bronchial inhalers make the lungs more sensitive to irritation by airborne pollen.
    - (D) By temporarily relieving the symptoms of asthma, inhalers encourage sufferers to avoid more beneficial measures.
    - (E) Ten years ago bronchial inhalers were not available as an asthma treatment.

23. Which one of the following is an assumption on which the argument depends?
    - (A) Urban pollution has not doubled in the past decade.
    - (B) Doctors and patients generally ignore the role of allergies in asthma.
    - (C) Bronchial inhalers are unsafe, even when used according to the recommended instructions.
    - (D) The use of bronchial inhalers aggravates other diseases that frequently occur among asthma sufferers and that often lead to fatal outcomes even when the asthma itself does not.
    - (E) Increased urban pollution, improved recording of asthma deaths, and the use of bronchial inhalers are the only possible explanations of the increased death rate due to asthma.

24. There is little point in looking to artists for insights into political issues. Most of them hold political views that are less insightful than those of any reasonably well-educated person who is not an artist. Indeed, when taken as a whole, the statements made by artists, including those considered to be great, indicate that artistic talent and political insight are rarely found together.

    Which one of the following can be inferred from the passage?
    - (A) There are no artists who have insights into political issues.
    - (B) A thorough education in art makes a person reasonably well educated.
    - (C) Every reasonably well-educated person who is not an artist has more insight into political issues than any artist.
    - (D) Politicians rarely have any artistic talent.
    - (E) Some artists are no less politically insightful than some reasonably well-educated persons who are not artists.

S T O P

IF YOU FINISH BEFORE TIME IS CALLED, YOU MAY CHECK YOUR WORK ON THIS SECTION ONLY. DO NOT WORK ON ANY OTHER SECTION IN THE TEST.

ARGUMENTS II

Time—35 minutes
25 Questions

Directions: The questions in this section are based on the reasoning contained in brief statements or passages. For some questions, more than one of the choices could conceivably answer the question. However, you are to choose the best answer; that is, the response that most accurately and completely answers the question. You should not make assumptions that are by common sense standards implausible, superfluous, or incompatible with the passage.

1. A major theft from a museum was remarkable in that the pieces stolen clearly had been carefully selected. The criterion for selection, however, clearly had not been greatest estimated market value. It follows that the theft was specifically carried out to suit the taste of some individual collector for whose private collection the pieces were destined.

   The argument tacitly appeals to which one of the following principles?

   (A) Any art theft can, on the evidence of the selection of pieces stolen, be categorized as committed either at the direction of a single known individual or at the direction of a group of known individuals.
   (B) Any art theft committed at the direction of a single individual results in a pattern of works taken and works left alone that defies rational analysis.
   (C) The pattern of works taken and works left alone can sometimes distinguish one type of art theft from another.
   (D) Art thefts committed with no preexisting plan for the disposition of the stolen works do not always involve theft of the most valuable pieces only.
   (E) The pattern of works taken and works left alone in an art theft can be particularly damaging to the integrity of the remaining collection.

2. The teeth of some mammals show "growth rings" that result from the constant depositing of layers of cementum as opaque bands in summer and translucent bands in winter. Cross sections of pigs' teeth found in an excavated Stone Age trash pit revealed bands of remarkably constant width except that the band deposited last, which was invariably translucent, was only about half the normal width.

   The statements above most strongly support the conclusion that the animals died

   (A) in an unusually early winter
   (B) at roughly the same age
   (C) roughly in midwinter
   (D) in a natural catastrophe
   (E) from starvation

3. The United States has never been a great international trader. It found most of its raw materials and customers for finished products within its own borders. The terrible consequences of this situation have become apparent, as this country now owes the largest foreign debt in the world and is a playground for wealthy foreign investors. The moral is clear: a country can no more live without foreign trade than a dog can live by eating its own tail.

   In order to advance her point of view, the author does each of the following EXCEPT

   (A) draw on an analogy
   (B) appeal to historical fact
   (C) identify a cause and an effect
   (D) suggest a cause of the current economic situation
   (E) question the ethical basis of an economic situation

GO ON TO THE NEXT PAGE.

4. Giselle: The government needs to ensure that the public consumes less petroleum. When things cost more, people buy and use less of them. Therefore, the government should raise the sales tax on gasoline, a major petroleum product.

Antoine: The government should not raise the sales tax on gasoline. Such an increase would be unfair to gasoline users. If taxes are to be increased, the increases should be applied in such a way that they spread the burden of providing the government with increased revenues among many people, not just the users of gasoline.

As a rebuttal of Giselle's argument, Antoine's response is ineffective because

(A) he ignores the fact that Giselle does not base her argument for raising the gasoline sales tax on the government's need for increased revenues
(B) he fails to specify how many taxpayers there are who are not gasoline users
(C) his conclusion is based on an assertion regarding unfairness, and unfairness is a very subjective concept
(D) he mistakenly assumes that Giselle wants a sales tax increase only on gasoline
(E) he makes the implausible assumption that the burden of increasing government revenues can be more evenly distributed among the people through other means besides increasing the gasoline sales tax

5. A government agency publishes ratings of airlines, ranking highest the airlines that have the smallest proportion of late flights. The agency's purpose is to establish an objective measure of the relative efficiency of different airlines' personnel in meeting published flight schedules.

Which one of the following, if true, would tend to invalidate use of the ratings for the agency's purpose?

(A) Travelers sometimes have no choice of airlines for a given trip at a given time.
(B) Flights are often made late by bad weather conditions that affect some airlines more than others.
(C) The flight schedules of all airlines allow extra time for flights that go into or out of very busy airports.
(D) Airline personnel are aware that the government agency is monitoring all airline flights for lateness.
(E) Flights are defined as "late" only if they arrive more that fifteen minutes past their scheduled arrival time, and a record is made of how much later than fifteen minutes they are.

6. Although this bottle is labeled “vinegar,” no fizzing occurred when some of the liquid in it was added to powder from this box labeled “baking soda.” But when an acidic liquid such as vinegar is added to baking soda the resulting mixture fizzes, so this bottle clearly has been mislabeled.

A flaw in the reasoning in the argument above is that this argument

(A) ignores the possibility that the bottle contained an acidic liquid other than vinegar
(B) fails to exclude an alternative explanation for the observed effect
(C) depends on the use of the imprecise term “fizz”
(D) does not take into account the fact that scientific principles can be definitively tested only under controlled laboratory conditions
(E) assumes that the fact of a labeling error is proof of an intention to deceive

GO ON TO THE NEXT PAGE.

7. Marine biologists have long thought that variation in the shell color of aquatic snails evolved as protective camouflage against birds and other predators. Brown shells seem to be more frequent when the underlying seafloor is dark-colored and white shells more frequent when the underlying seafloor is light-colored. A new theory has been advanced, however, that claims that shell color is related to physiological stress associated with heat absorption. According to this theory, brown shells will be more prevalent in areas where the wave action of the sea is great and thus heat absorption from the Sun is minimized, whereas white shells will be more numerous in calmer waters, where the snails will absorb more heat from the Sun's rays.

Evidence that would strongly favor the new theory over the traditional theory would be the discovery of a large majority of

(A) dark-shelled snails in a calm inlet with a dark, rocky bottom and many predators
(B) dark-shelled snails in a calm inlet with a white, sandy bottom
(C) light-shelled snails in an inlet with much wave action and a dark, rocky bottom
(D) light-shelled snails in a calm inlet with a dark, rocky bottom and many predators
(E) light-shelled snails in a calm inlet with a white, sandy bottom and many predators

8. Measurements of the extent of amino-acid decomposition in fragments of eggshell found at archaeological sites in such places as southern Africa can be used to obtain accurate dates for sites up to 200,000 years old. Because the decomposition is slower in cool climates, the technique can be used to obtain accurate dates for sites almost a million years old in cooler regions.

The information above provides the most support for which one of the following conclusions?

(A) The oldest archaeological sites are not in southern Africa, but rather in cooler regions of the world.
(B) The amino-acid decomposition that enables eggshells to be used in dating does not take place in other organic matter found at ancient archaeological sites.
(C) If the site being dated has been subject to large unsuspected climatic fluctuations during the time the eggshell has been at the site, application of the technique is less likely to yield accurate results.
(D) After 200,000 years in a cool climate, less than one-fifth of the amino acids in a fragment of eggshell that would provide material for dating with the technique will have decomposed and will thus no longer be suitable for examination by the technique.
(E) Fragments of eggshell are more likely to be found at ancient archaeological sites in warm regions of the world than at such sites in cooler regions.

GO ON TO THE NEXT PAGE.

9. Advertisement: Clark brand-name parts are made for cars manufactured in this country. They satisfy all of our government automotive tests—the toughest such tests in the world. With foreign-made parts, you never know which might be reliable and which are cheap look-alikes that are poorly constructed and liable to cost you hundreds of dollars in repairs. Therefore, be smart and insist on brand-name parts by Clark for your car.

The argument requires the assumption that

(A) Clark parts are available only in this country
(B) foreign-made parts are not suitable for cars manufactured in this country
(C) no foreign-made parts satisfy our government standards
(D) parts that satisfy our government standards are not as poorly constructed as cheap foreign-made parts
(E) if parts are made for cars manufactured in our country, they are not poorly constructed

10. Even if a crime that has been committed by computer is discovered and reported, the odds of being both arrested and convicted greatly favor the criminal.

Each of the following, if true, supports the claim above EXCEPT:

(A) The preparation of computer-fraud cases takes much more time than is required for average fraud cases, and the productivity of prosecutors is evaluated by the number of good cases made.
(B) In most police departments, officers are rotated through different assignments every two or three years, a shorter time than it takes to become proficient as a computer-crime investigator.
(C) The priorities of local police departments, under whose jurisdiction most computer crime falls, are weighted toward visible street crime that communities perceive as threatening.
(D) Computer criminals have rarely been sentenced to serve time in prison, because prisons are overcrowded with violent criminals and drug offenders.
(E) The many police officers who are untrained in computers often inadvertently destroy the physical evidence of computer crime.

11. Every week, the programming office at an FM radio station reviewed unsolicited letters from listeners who were expressing comments on the station's programs. One week, the station received 50 letters with favorable comments about the station's news reporting and music selection and 10 letters with unfavorable comments on the station's new movie review segment of the evening program. Faced with this information, the programming director assumed that if some listeners did not like the movie review segment, then there must be other listeners who did like it. Therefore, he decided to continue the movie review segment of the evening program.

Which one of the following identifies a problem with the programming director's decision process?

(A) He failed to recognize that people are more likely to write letters of criticism than of praise.
(B) He could not properly infer from the fact that some listeners did not like the movie review segment that some others did.
(C) He failed to take into consideration the discrepancy in numbers between favorable and unfavorable letters received.
(D) He failed to take into account the relation existing between the movie review segment and the news.
(E) He did not wait until he received at least 50 letters with unfavorable comments about the movie review segment before making his decision.

GO ON TO THE NEXT PAGE.

12. "Though they soon will, patients should not have a legal right to see their medical records. As a doctor, I see two reasons for this. First, giving them access will be time-wasting because it will significantly reduce the amount of time that medical staff can spend on more important duties, by forcing them to retrieve and return files. Second, if my experience is anything to go by, no patients are going to ask for access to their records anyway."

Which one of the following, if true, establishes that the doctor's second reason does not cancel out the first?

(A) The new law will require that doctors, when seeing a patient in their office, must be ready to produce the patient's records immediately, not just ready to retrieve them.
(B) The task of retrieving and returning files would fall to the lowest-paid member of a doctor's office staff.
(C) Any patients who asked to see their medical records would also insist on having details they did not understand explained to them.
(D) The new law does not rule out that doctors may charge patients for extra expenses incurred specifically in order to comply with the new law.
(E) Some doctors have all along had a policy of allowing their patients access to their medical records, but those doctors' patients took no advantage of this policy.

13. Alia: Hawthorne admits that he has influence with high government officials. He further admits that he sold that influence to an environmental interest group. There can be no justification for this kind of unethical behavior.

Martha: I disagree that he was unethical. The group that retained Hawthorne's services is dedicated to the cause of preventing water pollution. So, in using his influence to benefit this group, Hawthorne also benefited the public.

Alia and Martha disagree on whether

(A) the meaning of ethical behavior has changed over time
(B) the consequences of Hawthorne's behavior can ethically justify that behavior
(C) the standards for judging ethical behavior can be imposed on Hawthorne by another
(D) the meaning of ethical behavior is the same in a public situation as in a private one
(E) the definition of ethical behavior is rooted in philosophy or religion

14. The mayor boasts that the average ambulance turnaround time, the time from summons to delivery of the patient, has been reduced this year for top-priority emergencies. This a serious misrepresentation. This "reduction" was produced simply by redefining "top priority." Such emergencies used to include gunshot wounds and electrocutions, the most time-consuming cases. Now they are limited strictly to heart attacks and strokes.

Which one of the following would strengthen the author's conclusion that it was the redefinition of "top priority" that produced the reduction in turnaround time?

(A) The number of heart attacks and strokes declined this year.
(B) The mayor redefined the city's financial priorities this year.
(C) Experts disagree with the mayor's definition of "top-priority emergency."
(D) Other cities include gunshot wound cases in their category of top-priority emergencies.
(E) One half of all of last year's top-priority emergencies were gunshot wounds and electrocution cases.

GO ON TO THE NEXT PAGE.

15. In a large residential building, there is a rule that no pets are allowed. A group of pet lovers tried to change that rule but failed. The rule-changing procedure outlined in the building's regulations states that only if a group of tenants can obtain the signatures of 10 percent of the tenants on a petition to change a rule will the proposed change be put to a majority vote of all the tenants in the building. It follows that the pet lovers were voted down on their proposal by the majority of the tenants.

The argument depends on which one of the following assumptions?

(A) The pet lovers succeeded in obtaining the signatures of 10 percent of the tenants on their petition.
(B) The signatures of less than 10 percent of the tenants were obtained on the pet lovers' petition.
(C) Ninety percent of the tenants are against changing the rule forbidding pets.
(D) The support of 10 percent of the tenants for a rule change ensures that the rule change will be adopted.
(E) The failure of the pet lovers to obtain the signatures of 10 percent of the tenants on their petition for a rule change ensures that the rule change will be voted down by a majority of the tenants.

16. Nuclear fusion is a process whereby the nuclei of atoms are joined, or "fused," and in which energy is released. One of the by-products of fusion is helium-4 gas. A recent fusion experiment was conducted using "heavy" water contained in a sealed flask. The flask was, in turn, contained in an air-filled chamber designed to eliminate extraneous vibration. After the experiment, a measurable amount of helium-4 gas was found in the air of the chamber. The experimenters cited this evidence in support of their conclusion that fusion had been achieved.

Which one of the following, if true, would cast doubt on the experimenters' conclusion?

(A) Helium-4 was not the only gas found in the experiment chamber.
(B) When fusion is achieved, it normally produces several by-products, including tritium and gamma rays.
(C) The amount of helium-4 found in the chamber's air did not exceed the amount of helium-4 that is found in ordinary air.
(D) Helium-4 gas rapidly breaks down, forming ordinary helium gas after a few hours.
(E) Nuclear fusion reactions are characterized by the release of large amounts of heat.

17. Every photograph, because it involves the light rays that something emits hitting film, must in some obvious sense be true. But because it could always have been made to show things differently than it does, it cannot express the whole truth and, in that sense, is false. Therefore, nothing can ever be definitively proved with a photograph.

Which one of the following is an assumption that would permit the conclusion above to be properly drawn?

(A) Whatever is false in the sense that it cannot express the whole truth cannot furnish definitive proof.
(B) The whole truth cannot be known.
(C) It is not possible to determine the truthfulness of a photograph in any sense.
(D) It is possible to use a photograph as corroborative evidence if there is additional evidence establishing the truth about the scene photographed.
(E) If something is being photographed, then it is possible to prove definitively the truth about it.

GO ON TO THE NEXT PAGE.

Questions 18–19

Some cleaning fluids, synthetic carpets, wall paneling, and other products release toxins, such as formaldehyde and benzene, into the household air supply. This is not a problem in well-ventilated houses, but it is a problem in houses that are so well insulated that they trap toxins as well as heat. Recent tests, however, demonstrate that houseplants remove some household toxins from the air and thereby eliminate their danger. In one test, 20 large plants eliminated formaldehyde from a small, well-insulated house.

18. Assume that a person who lives in a small, well-insulated house that contains toxin-releasing products places houseplants, such as those tested, in the house.

    Which one of the following can be expected as a result?

    (A) There will no longer be any need to ventilate the house.
    (B) The concentration of toxins in the household air supply will remain the same.
    (C) The house will be warm and have a safe air supply.
    (D) If there is formaldehyde in the household air supply, its level will decrease.
    (E) If formaldehyde and benzene are being released into the household air supply, the quantities released of each will decrease.

19. The passage is structured to lead to which one of the following conclusions?

    (A) Houseplants can remove benzene from the air.
    (B) Nonsynthetic products do not release toxins into houses.
    (C) Keeping houseplants is an effective means of trapping heat in a poorly insulated house.
    (D) Keeping houseplants can compensate for some of the negative effects of poor ventilation.
    (E) The air in a well-insulated house with houseplants will contain fewer toxins than the air in a well-ventilated house without houseplants.

20. Normal full-term babies are all born with certain instinctive reflexes that disappear by the age of two months. Because this three-month-old baby exhibits these reflexes, this baby is not a normal full-term baby.

    Which one of the following has a logical structure most like that of the argument above?

    (A) Because carbon dioxide turns limewater milky and this gas is oxygen, it will not turn limewater milky.
    (B) Because no ape can talk and Suzy is an ape, Suzy cannot talk.
    (C) Because humans are social animals and Henry is sociable, Henry is normal.
    (D) Because opossums have abdominal pouches and this animal lacks any such pouch, this animal is not an opossum.
    (E) Because some types of trees shed their leaves annually and this tree has not shed its leaves, it is not normal.

21. Efficiency and redundancy are contradictory characteristics of linguistic systems; however, they can be used together to achieve usefulness and reliability in communication. If a spoken language is completely efficient, then every possible permutation of its basic language sounds can be an understandable word. However, if the human auditory system is an imperfect receptor of sounds, then it is not true that every possible permutation of a spoken language's basic language sounds can be an understandable word.

    If all of the statements above are true, which one of the following must also be true?

    (A) Efficiency causes a spoken language to be useful and redundancy causes it to be reliable.
    (B) Neither efficiency nor redundancy can be completely achieved in spoken language.
    (C) If a spoken language were completely redundant, then it could not be useful.
    (D) If the human auditory system were a perfect receptor of sounds, then every permutation of language sounds would be an understandable word.
    (E) If the human auditory system is an imperfect receptor of sounds, then a spoken language cannot be completely efficient.

GO ON TO THE NEXT PAGE.

22. All intelligent people are nearsighted. I am very nearsighted. So I must be a genius.

    Which one of the following exhibits both of the logical flaws exhibited in the argument above?

    (A) I must be stupid because all intelligent people are nearsighted and I have perfect eyesight.
    (B) All chickens have beaks. This bird has a beak. So this bird must be a chicken.
    (C) All pigs have four legs, but this spider has eight legs. So this spider must be twice as big as any pig.
    (D) John is extremely happy, so he must be extremely tall because all tall people are happy.
    (E) All geniuses are very nearsighted. I must be very nearsighted since I am a genius.

23. An advertisement states:

    Like Danaxil, all headache pills can stop your headache. But when you are in pain, you want relief right away. Danaxil is for you—no headache pill stops pain more quickly.

    Evelyn and Jane are each suffering from a headache. Suppose Evelyn takes Danaxil and Jane takes its leading competitor. Which one of the following can be properly concluded from the claims in the advertisement?

    (A) Evelyn's headache pain will be relieved, but Jane's will not.
    (B) Evelyn's headache pain will be relieved more quickly than Jane's.
    (C) Evelyn's headache will be relieved at least as quickly as Jane's.
    (D) Jane's headache pain will be relieved at the same time as is Evelyn's.
    (E) Jane will be taking Danaxil for relief from headache pain.

Questions 24–25

In opposing the 1970 Clean Air Act, the United States automobile industry argued that meeting the act's standards for automobile emissions was neither economically feasible nor environmentally necessary. However, the catalytic converter, invented in 1967, enabled automakers to meet the 1970 standards efficiently. Currently, automakers are lobbying against the government's attempt to pass legislation that would tighten restrictions on automobile emissions. The automakers contend that these new restrictions would be overly expensive and unnecessary to efforts to curb air pollution. Clearly, the automobile industry's position should not be heeded.

24. Which one of the following most accurately expresses the method used to counter the automakers' current position?

    (A) The automakers' premises are shown to lead to a contradiction.
    (B) Facts are mentioned that show that the automakers are relying on false information.
    (C) A flaw is pointed out in the reasoning used by the automakers to reach their conclusion.
    (D) A comparison is drawn between the automakers' current position and a position they held in the past.
    (E) Evidence is provided that the new emissions legislation is both economically feasible and environmentally necessary.

25. Which one of the following, if true, lends the most support to the automakers' current position?

    (A) The more stringent the legislation restricting emissions becomes, the more difficult it becomes for automakers to provide the required technology economically.
    (B) Emissions-restriction technology can often be engineered so as to avoid reducing the efficiency with which an automobile uses fuel.
    (C) Not every new piece of legislation restricting emissions requires new automotive technology in order for automakers to comply with it.
    (D) The more automobiles there are on the road, the more stringent emission restrictions must be to prevent increased overall air pollution.
    (E) Unless forced to do so by the government, automakers rarely make changes in automotive technology that is not related to profitability.

S T O P

IF YOU FINISH BEFORE TIME IS CALLED, YOU MAY CHECK YOUR WORK ON THIS SECTION ONLY. DO NOT WORK ON ANY OTHER SECTION IN THE TEST.

ARGUMENTS I

Answers and Solutions

1. D
2. E
3. E
4. D
5. C
6. B
7. A
8. E
9. B
10. C
11. B
12. A
13. C
14. C
15. B
16. E
17. B
18. B
19. D
20. C
21. D
22. A
23. E
24. E

1. To answer this question, we need to identify the argument's structure and the author's tone. The argument has two parts. First, a statement is made. Then it is questioned by drawing an extreme analogy. By putting the conclusion in question form, the author hopes you will be more likely to come to the same conclusion she did. It's important to note the sarcasm in the analogy. Obviously, watching someone else eat doesn't fill your own stomach. The author implies it is equally unlikely that watching violent movies will dissipate aggressive energy, or satisfy one's need for violence.

In the argument, the writer throws out a statement and then ridicules it by drawing an extreme analogy. Look at choice (D). It presents a statement: *"Some people think that economists can control inflation."* Then ridicules it with an extreme analogy: *"Can meteorologists make the sun shine?"* Hence the answer is (D).

(B) is somewhat tempting. It does have the same basic structure as the original argument—a statement is offered and then questioned. However, the tone in (B) is not sarcastic. Furthermore, the question *"Hasn't nationalism been the excuse for committing abominable crimes?"* isn't in analogy form.

2. Ann's statement is *"All the campers at Camp Winnehatchee go to Tri-Cities High School."* In other words, if a person camps at Winnehatchee, then he is a student at Tri-Cities High School. Bill has apparently reversed her statement, interpreting it as *"All Tri-Cities High School campers go to Camp Winnehatchee."* In other words, if a camper goes to Tri-Cities High School, then he camps at Winnehatchee. Hence, by noting that some Tri-Cities students camp at Lakemont, Bill thought he had caught Ann in a mistake. The answer is (E).

3. This is a rather straightforward problem. We are asked to find the suppressed premised, or assumption, of the argument. Finding the suppressed premise, of an argument can be difficult. However, on the LSAT you have an advantage—the suppressed premise is listed as one of the five answer-choices. To test whether an answer-choice is a suppressed premise, ask yourself whether it would make the argument more plausible. If so, then it is very likely a suppressed premise.

The argument states that resources have supposedly been diverted from writing speeding tickets to combating the drug problem and yet the same number of speeding tickets are still being written. It then concludes the resources were in fact not diverted to fighting drug-related crime. The link that allows this conclusion to be drawn is the assumption that if resources were diverted to drug enforcement, then fewer speeding tickets would have been written. The answer is (E).

4. Our goal in this problem is to find the agent that causes fresh grass clippings to generate poorer-than-average plant growth. Choice (A) contradicts the implication of the passage. If fresh grass clippings increase beneficial soil bacteria, then plant growth should increase, not decrease. Choice (B) explains why dried grass clippings increase plant growth but does not explain why fresh grass clippings decrease plant growth. A similar analysis shows that choice (C) is incorrect. Choice (D) gives us our agent—heat.

Fresh grass clippings ⇨ Heat ⇨ Fewer beneficial bacteria ⇨ Poorer plant growth

The answer is (D).

5. The author begins, *"A gas tax of one cent per gallon would raise one billion dollars per year."* She then says, *"A tax of fifty cents per gallon would therefore raise fifty billion dollars per year."* This assumes that the tax increase <u>will not decrease</u> the consumption of gasoline. But in the argument's closing lines she says the demand for gasoline <u>will drop</u>. These are contradictory assumptions. The answer is (C).

6. (A) understates the claim made in the argument. It is true that eagles are symbols of freedom; but more importantly, because they are symbols of freedom, they inspire people to help other species.

(B) paraphrases the conclusion at the end of the argument. Hence it is the answer.

(C) makes a subtle, false claim couched in same language disguise. Notice that the author claims only "the needs of more *obscure* species will go unmet," not necessarily that the needs of other *symbolic* species will go unmet. Every word in choice (C) except one is taken directly from the passage.

(D) is probably true but it is irrelevant. Nowhere in the argument is it mentioned or implied that people's love of the wilderness can be tapped.

(E) also understates the claim made in the argument. It merely paraphrases a premise of the argument; namely, "bald eagles have the unique capacity to inspire people and foster in them a sympathetic attitude toward the needs of other threatened species."

7. This question asks us to weaken the argument. Typically, to solve such questions, you need to show that a suppressed premise is not likely to be true. The assumption of the argument is that before shoddy scientific work can do harm it will be exposed by the work of other scientists. Look at choice (A). It directly attacks this assumption by stating that years can pass before the false work is exposed. The answer is (A).

8. In responding to Alice's argument, David commits the *true-but-irrelevant* fallacy. The tactic is quite simple: the arguer bases a conclusion on information that is true but not relevant to the issue. Alice's argument is that quotas on automobile imports should be eliminated because consumers would then benefit from the increased competition amongst manufacturers. David does not address these statements. Instead, he brings up the irrelevant fact that automobile imports are pervasive worldwide. The answer is (E).

9. The argument states that by regulating socially necessary services governments invariably increase their costs. It then says the government is certain to regulate child-care services. Therefore, the costs of providing child-care services will increase. The answer is (B).

It is instructive to analyze this argument using a diagram. The statement *"governments inevitably make [socially necessary services] more expensive by regulating [them]"* can be symbolized as

R—>E,

where R stands for "regulating social services" and E stands for "more expensive." Adding the statement *"government is certain to [regulate child-care services]"* to the diagram yields:

R—>E
R
∴ E

This diagram shows the argument has a valid *if-then* structure.

The other choices are easily dismissed. As to choices (A) and (C), the argument does not imply that government regulation will either increase or decrease the quality of child care. Choice (D) is perhaps second best. It is a paraphrase of the closing lines of the passage. However, the question asks "Which one of the following statements can be <u>inferred</u> from the passage?" Hence, the answer must say <u>more</u> than what is stated in the passage. You should notice that choice (E) commits the fallacy of *denying the premise*. First, the premise: *"If child-care services are regulated"* is denied. Then the conclusion is wrongly negated: *"the cost of providing child care will not increase."* This can be diagrammed as

R—>E
~R
∴ ~E

10. The suppressed premise in this argument is that by emphasizing moral considerations and withdrawing their advertisements the advertisers hurt themselves financially, or at least did not gain by it. To strengthen the argument, we need to show that this assumption is true. Choice (C) implies that this is the case by stating that the advertisers expected to lose sales if they withdrew their advertisements. Hence the answer is (C).

11. Notice that the politician's statement is much stronger than the biologist's. The biologist says merely that if deforestation continues then the koala will approach extinction. This can be diagrammed as

D—>E

where D stands for "deforestation continues" and E stands for "extinction." In other words, ending deforestation is a *necessary* condition for the koala's survival. Now the politician says that if deforestation stops then the koala will not approach extinction. This can be diagrammed as

~D—>~E

This is stronger because it declares that ending deforestation is *sufficient* for the koala to survive. You should notice this as the fallacy of denying the premise. Look at choice (B). It stops deforestation yet the koala still becomes extinct. This is not consistent with the politician's statement since he claimed stopping deforestation would prevent the koala's extinction. But (B) is consistent with the biologist's claim since he said only that if deforestation continued then the koala would become extinct. He said nothing about the case in which deforestation stops—the koala could still become extinct for other reasons. Remember, if the premise of an *if-then* statement is false, then we know nothing about the conclusion. The answer is (B).

12. This is a straightforward question. The author states *"it is premature to conclude that telepathy is an alternative means of communication"* because 1) *"numerous researchers have investigated telepathy only to find that conclusive evidence for its existence has persistently evaded them"* and 2) *"it can often be shown that other explanations that do comply with known laws can be given."* Hence, the author supports the conclusion by pointing to the inadequacy of evidence for the opposite view. The answer is (A).

The other choices are easily ruled out. Choices (B) and (C) are too specific. The author refers to research in general, not to any particular experiments or evidence. Choice (D) makes a false claim. The conclusion is fairly well supported. Choice (E) also make a false claim. The conclusion is mentioned only once—in the closing line.

13. This problem is mostly obfuscation. All we need is the last sentence of the argument. To diagram the last sentence let *"prices have risen beyond the level most people can afford"* be symbolized as R, and let *"it must be that salaries have not kept pace with rising prices during the past year"* be symbolized as ~S. This yields

R—>~S

Now in the question we are told *"salaries have kept pace with rising prices during the past year."* In other words, S. This negates the conclusion in the diagram above, prompting us to apply the contrapositive to the diagram, which yields ~R. In other words, prices have not risen beyond the level that most people can afford. The answer is (C).

14. This is another straightforward question. The more important statistic is the number of suicides in October and November of 1929 compared to other years, not the number of suicides in October and November compared to other months of 1929—there may be seasonal fluctuations. The answer is (C).

15. The essence of the passage is that when she does one activity she will not do the other activity. This can be diagrammed as follows:*

Playing tour —> No publicity tour

* We could also use (Publicity tour —> No playing tour). But we don't need both.

Choice (B) says that when there are critical emergencies to attend to the staff will not attend to less serious emergencies. This can be diagrammed as follows:

Attending to critical emergencies	**—>**	**Not attending to less critical emergencies**

This diagram clearly shows that choice (B) has the same structure as the original argument. The answer is (B).

Questions 16–17

16. Be careful not to read more into this passage than is stated. If the percentage of ski-related injuries that occur off the slopes increased from 10% to 25%, then of course the percentage of injuries that occur on the slopes must have decreased. The answer is (E).

17. If the number of injuries on the slopes dropped from 9 per 1,000 in 1950 to 3 in 1980, then clearly skiers were more likely to be injured on the slopes in 1950 than in 1980. Choice (B) contradicts this. Hence the answer is (B).

Don't make the mistake of choosing (A). The passage states that the *rate* at which injuries occurred on the slopes was less in 1980 than in 1950, not necessarily that the overall *number* of injuries was less. Perhaps many more people took up skiing by 1980 than 1950.

18. Remember, to weaken an argument, typically you must show that a suppressed premise is false. The premise of the argument is that all other things being equal the breeding success of blackbirds increases with experience. To weaken the argument, we need to show that not all things are equal. Choice (B) does this, suggesting that as blackbirds mature they lay more viable eggs. This alone could explain the breeding success of older blackbirds. The answer is (B).

19. This argument is difficult because the second-best answer-choice is almost as good as the best one. Choices (B) and (E) are easily dismissed. Choice (A) is too strong. In the sentence, *"But it is unrealistic to expect such measures to compensate for pilots' lack of actual flying time,"* the author states that training programs are not only insufficient but only marginally effective. Choice (C) is second best. Though it is probably true, it slightly overstates the author's claim. The author implied only that actual flying time is essential; he made no claim that it would actually decrease the number of crashes. Furthermore, he did not imply that airlines should focus on actual flying time, only that it plays an essential part in reducing the number of pilot errors. Hence, by process of elimination, the answer is (D).

20. The argument can be diagrammed as follows:

All S are I
Some I are F
———
Some S are F

where S stands for "savings accounts," I stands for "interest-bearing accounts," and F stands for "tax free." Note the similarity of this argument to the transitive property. If "some" were replaced with "all," the argument would be a valid application of the transitive property. Now choice (C) can be diagrammed as follows:

All GP are A
Some A are I
———
Some GP are I

Where GP stands for "great photographers," A for "artists," and I for "intellectuals." This diagram clearly shows choice (C) has the same structure as the original argument. The answer is (C).

21. The passage says *"the more genetically similar two species are to each other, the more recently they diverged from a common ancestor."* It then states that bears and raccoons diverged from a common ancestor and that giant pandas diverged from bears. So giant pandas are more similar genetically to bears than to raccoons. The answer is (D). A flow chart can illustrate this:

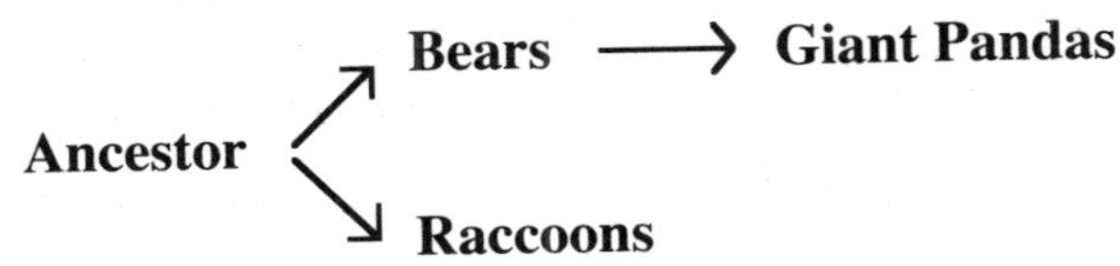

Questions 22–23

22. This is a straightforward question. The passage states that the death rate from asthma has doubled in the past decade, not that the total number of deaths has doubled. So in choice (A) the fact that the population has doubled is irrelevant. The answer is (A).

23. The passage discusses only urban pollution, improved recording of asthma deaths, and the use of bronchial inhalers as factors that might explain the increased death rate. For the argument to be valid, it must assume that these are the only factors. The answer is (E).

24. Choice (A) is too extreme. The argument says that *most* artists are less politically insightful than well-educated non-artists. It does not say that *all* artists are less insightful. Choice (B) is irrelevant. Choice (C) is too extreme. Notice the absolute words "every" and "any." Choice (D) is irrelevant. Finally, choice (E) is the measured response. If most artists are less insightful than other well-educated people, then we expect that some artists are as politically insightful as other well-educated people. Otherwise, the sentence would have read: all artists are less insightful than other well-educated people. Notice that choice (E) says very little and it misses the point of the passage. Nonetheless, it is best of the lot. The answer is (E).

ARGUMENTS II

Answers and Solutions

1. C
2. C
3. E
4. A
5. B
6. B
7. D
8. C —
9. D —
10. D —
11. B —
12. A —
13. B
14. E
15. A
16. C
17. A —
18. D
19. D —
20. D
21. E
22. D —
23. C —
24. D
25. A

1. This is a suppressed premise question. To test whether an answer-choice is a suppressed premise, ask yourself whether it would make the argument more plausible. If so, then it is very likely a suppressed premise. All that we are told about the theft is that the items taken were not selected based on market value. From this the author concludes that the theft was done for a private collector. For the argument to be valid, we must assume that in some cases knowing the pattern of the items stolen can determine the purpose of the theft. The answer, therefore, is (C). Choice (A) is second-best. It uses the overstatement ploy. To make the argument valid, we don't need to know that the purpose of *any* art theft can be identified based on the items stolen, only that *sometimes* this determination can be made. Beware of absolute words.

2. The argument states that opaque bands of cementum are deposited in summer and translucent bands in winter. It then states that the last band was "invariably" translucent and only half the normal width. This implies that the animals died in midwinter. Thus the answer is (C).

As to (A), if the animals died in an early winter, little or no translucent cementum would have been deposited. As to (B), the information in the passage indicates the time of year the animals died, not their age when they died. Finally, choices (D) and (E) are similarly flawed; the passage indicates *when* the animals died, not *how* they died.

3. The argument opens by appealing to a historical fact, *"The United States has never been a great international trader."* This eliminates (B). It then presents a cause, *"It found most of its raw materials . . . within its own borders."* This eliminates (D). Then it presents an effect, *"The terrible consequences of this situation have become apparent, as this country now owes the largest foreign debt in the world . . . ."* This eliminates (C). Finally, the argument closes by drawing an analogy between a country consuming only its own natural resources and a dog eating its own tail. This eliminates (A). Hence, by process of elimination, we have learned the answer is (E).

4. The argument commits the true-but-irrelevant fallacy. In this context, it is often called the *straw-man* fallacy. Instead of addressing Giselle's statement, Antoine sets up a statement that Giselle did not make and then attacks that straw-man. Arguing with someone who employs this tactic can be quite infuriating. Giselle's argument is that taxes should be increased to cut consumption of gasoline, <u>not</u> to raise revenue. Antoine ignores this fact and argues that if the government needs additional revenue (which Giselle does not claim) then the burden should be distributed evenly. The answer is (A).

5. This question asks you to weaken the case for the effectiveness of the airline ratings. Remember, to weaken an argument, typically you need to show that a suppressed premise of the argument is false. In this case, the argument is based on a questionable suppressed premise. If the ranking system is to be *objective*, then there cannot be any adverse conditions beyond the airlines' control that affect some airlines more than others. For instance, some airlines may have a greater proportion of their flights at night, when bad weather is more likely to cause a delay. Hence the answer is (B). Choice (D) is second-best. If airline personnel are aware that they are being monitored, then the personnel from a particular airline may institute special efficiency programs for the duration of the monitoring and thus skew the results. But this is only a conjecture; (B) is much more likely to occur.

6. Another possible explanation for the lack of fizz is that the box labeled *"baking soda"* has been mislabeled. The author does not exclude this possibility from the argument. Hence the answer is (B).

7. This is essentially a suppressed premise question; we are asked to supply a premise (evidence) that would favor the new theory over the traditional theory. The old theory predicts that if there are predators in an area then the shells should have the same color as the seafloor. The new theory, based on heat absorption, predicts that 1) brown shells will be more prevalent in rough waters, and 2) white shells will be more numerous in calm waters. Now we work through the answer-choices, looking for one that contradicts our summary of the old theory and supports our summary of the new theory. Choice (A) has predators, a dark seafloor, and, as the old theory predicts, dark-shelled snails. It thus supports the old theory. Additionally, it has dark shells in calm waters which contradicts the new theory. Eliminate (A). Next, choice (B) contradicts 2) of the new theory. Eliminate (B). Next, choice (C) contradicts 1) of the new theory. Eliminate (C). Next, choice (D) satisfies 2) of the new theory—light-shelled snails in calm waters. It also directly contradicts the old theory, which predicts that with many predators and a dark bottom the shells should be dark. So the answer is probably (D), but it's prudent to check the last choice since we are looking for the **best** answer. Choice (E) satisfies 2) of the new theory, but it also satisfies the old theory, which predicts that with many predators and a light bottom the shells should be light. Eliminate (E). The answer is (D).

8. This is another straightforward, fact-based question. Since the accuracy of the technique depends on temperature, any prolonged change in climate will affect its accuracy. For example, if a particular site now has a cool climate but for most of its past had a tropical climate, then the results from applying the technique would be misleading. The answer is (C).

The other choices are easily dismissed. Choice (A) is not supported by the passage. Climate affects the accuracy of the dating technique, not the age of the site itself. Choice (B) is perhaps second best. Although it is reasonable to assume that some characteristic of eggshells makes them preferable to other organic materials, nothing in the passage implies that the type of amino-acid decomposition found in eggshells is unique. Choice (D) is not supported by the passage. Nothing in the passage indicates the amount of amino acid needed in the eggshell for the technique to be accurate. Finally, choice (E) is not supported by the passage. The passage discusses only the accuracy of the amino-acid method of dating; it does not discuss or imply that fragments of eggshell are more likely to be found in some areas than in others.

9. The needed assumption is that parts manufactured in this country are better constructed, or at least not so poorly constructed, as cheap foreign-made parts. The answer is (D). Note, (B), (C), and (E) are too strong.

10. The passage discusses only the odds of being both arrested and convicted for a computer crime. There is no discussion of sentencing computer criminals. Hence the answer is (D).

All the remaining choices support the claim that computer criminals are unlikely to be both arrested and convicted for their crimes. As to (A), if computer-fraud cases are time consuming, then the courts' limited resources are less likely to be directed toward them. Additionally, if prosecutors are measured by the number of good cases made, then they are unlikely to prosecute marginal cases and therefore the criminals in those cases will go free. As to (B), if the officers are not proficient, then, by definition, they will not catch many computer criminals. As to (C), if police departments give low priority to computer crime, then clearly few computer criminals will be arrested. Finally, as to (E), if a bunch of bunglers are destroying evidence, then few arrested computer criminals will be convicted.

11. Be careful not to read more into this question than is stated. Clearly, it is unwarranted to use the fact that some listeners wrote in expressing disfavor with the movie review segment to conclude that other unspoken listeners favored it. The answer is (B).

12. To begin, look at why the second reason cancels the first. The doctor is concerned first of all that retrieving records will waste time better used for other purposes. But then he seemingly undermines this reason by stating no patients will ask for their records, anyway. If no one asks, no time will be wasted.

The question asks under what condition does the second reason not undermine the first. If time must be spent regardless of a patient's request, that time is certainly wasted. So if the new law requires doctors to have the records immediately at hand, the two reasons given do not cancel. The answer is (A).

13. This is a straightforward question. Alia says there is no justification for selling influence. Martha says there is a justification for selling influence; namely, if its effects benefit society. They disagree on whether the ends justify the means. The answer is (B).

14. This question asks you to strengthen the argument. If there are few, if any, gunshot or electrocution cases in the city, then the author's argument is irrelevant. On the other hand, if there is a significant number of these cases, then the author's argument is strong. Now certainly a situation in which one half of the emergency cases were the result of gunshot wounds or electrocution would be a significant number. Hence the answer is (E).

15. This is a suppressed premise question. The argument states that a rule can be changed only if two criteria are meet: First, 10 percent of the tenants must sign a petition to change the rule. Second, an election must be held in which a majority of the tenants vote in favor of changing the rule. The argument states that the rule was not changed and then concludes that the proposal to change the rule must have been voted down. This presumes that the necessary 10 percent of the people signed the petition. The answer, therefore, is (A).

16. This question asks us to weaken the argument. Recall: To weaken an argument, we typically must attack a premise—either expressed or suppressed—of the argument. Now the underlying premise of any controlled experiment is that there are no outside variables affecting its outcome. Two variables that come immediately to mind are 1) there may be another source for the helium-4, and 2) helium-4 may be naturally occurring in air. Now if the amount of helium-4 in the air after the experiment is the same as before the experiment, then clearly the researchers' claim would be spurious. Hence the answer is (C).

17. The author argues that since a photograph can be deceptive it can never express the whole truth. Therefore, it can never be used to prove something. The assumption needed to connect these two sentences is that if something cannot express the whole truth then it cannot prove anything. The answer, therefore, is (A).

The other choices are easily ruled out. As to (B), the argument does not state that the whole truth cannot be known, merely that it cannot be known *through* a photograph. Choice (C) is similarly flawed. The argument does not state that a photograph cannot express the truth in *any* sense, merely that it cannot express the *whole* truth. (Again, beware of absolute statements.) Choice (D) is a reasonable assumption to make, but it is not relevant to the argument. Finally, choice (E) contradicts the argument.

Questions 18–19

18. This problem asks us to draw a conclusion. Choice (A) overstates the claim made in the passage. The passage states that "houseplants remove *some* household toxins from the air," not all toxins. Choice (B) contradicts what the passage implies would happen. The concentration of toxins in the household air supply should decrease, not remain the same. Choice (C), like (A), overstates the claim made in the passage—"houseplants remove *some* household toxins from the air," not all toxins. Choice (D) is a reasonable conclusion to make since the passage states that "houseplants remove *some* household toxins from the air" and that in one test they even eliminated formaldehyde from a house. Hence the answer is probably (D), but it's prudent to check the last answer-choice. Choice (E) is not supported by the passage. Household plants eliminate certain toxins; nothing in the passage suggests that they prevent the toxins from being released. The answer is (D).

19. Choice (A) is too specific. Besides, the passage discusses formaldehyde more than it does benzene. Choice (B) is not supported by the passage. Choice (C) is not mentioned or implied by the passage. Choice (E) is quite tempting. But it is too strong. Household plants can remove some toxins. However, if the particular toxins are not present in either house, then the plants will not be a factor. Hence, by process of elimination, the answer is (D).

20. This is a straightforward argument by contraposition. The sentence "*Normal full-term babies are all born with certain instinctive reflexes that disappear by the age of two months*" can be reworded as an if-then statement: "*If a baby is normal and full-term, then it will not exhibit certain instinctive reflexes after the age of two months.*" This in turn can be symbolized as follows:

N—>~R

(Where N stands for "normal full-term" and ~R stands for "not having the reflexes.")

Next, the sentence "*because this three-month-old baby exhibits these reflexes, this baby is not a normal full-term baby*" can be reworded as "*If a three-month-old baby still exhibits certain instinctive reflexes, then it is not a normal full-term baby.*" This in turn can be symbolized as follows:

R—>~N

Clearly, this is the contrapositive of the previous diagram, so we are looking for an answer-choice that presents an if-then statement and then forms its contrapositive. Now in choice (D), the phrase "*opossums have abdominal pouches*" contains an embedded if-then statement: "*If an animal is an opossum, then it has an abdominal pouch.*" Which can be symbolized as

O—>P

Choice (D) then states that this animal does not have a pouch and therefore is not an opossum. This can be symbolized as

~P—>~O

Clearly, this is the contrapositive of the previous diagram. Hence the answer is (D).

21. This is a rather challenging question. To solve it, we'll use both the transitive property and the contrapositive. The sentence *"If a spoken language is completely efficient, then every possible permutation of its basic language sounds can be an understandable word"* can be symbolized as

CE—>EPU

where CE stands for "completely efficient," and EPU stands for "every permutation is understandable." Forming the contrapositive of this expression gives

~EPU—>~CE

Next, the sentence *"if the human auditory system is an imperfect receptor of sounds, then it is not true that every possible permutation of a spoken language's basic language sounds can be an understandable word"* can be symbolized as

IR—>~EPU

Now combining this expression with the contrapositive formed above gives

IR—>~EPU—>~CE

Then simplifying using the transitive property gives

IR—>~CE

Writing this express out gives *"If the human auditory system is an imperfect receptor of sounds, then a spoken language cannot be completely efficient."* This is an exact quote of choice (E) and therefore (E) is the answer.

22. This argument commits two errors. First, it takes a necessary condition to be sufficient. The statement "*All intelligent people are nearsighted*" means that for a person to be intelligent he or she must *necessarily* be nearsighted. But being nearsighted is not sufficient to make one intelligent. Second, the argument overstates the claim made in the premise. The premise is about intelligent people in general, not a subgroup of intelligent people—geniuses. Now in choice (D), the statement "*all tall people are happy*" has the same form as "*All intelligent people are nearsighted*"; the statement "*John is extremely happy*" has the same form as "*I am very nearsighted*"; and the statement "*so he must be extremely tall*" has the same form as "*So I must be a genius.*" This shows a one-to-one correspondence between choice (D) and the given argument. Hence the answer is (D).

Choices (A) and (E) are eye-catchers because they mention nearsightedness. Remember the answer to a logical structure (logical flaw) argument will have the same structure as the given argument but will be in a different context.

(B) is second-best. It does commit the fallacy of taking a necessary condition to be sufficient, but it does not overstate the claim.

It's hard to give choice (C) any meaning.

23. Like all good advertising pitches, this one appears to claim more than it actually does. The key to answering this question is the sentence *"Danaxil is for you—no headache pill stops pain more quickly."* In other words, Danaxil is at least as fast as any other headache pill. So Evelyn's headache will be relieved at least as quickly as Jane's. The answer is (C). Choice (B) overstates the case. The advertisement doesn't say that Danaxil stops headache pain more quickly than any other medicine, just that no other medication is faster.

<u>Questions 24–25</u>

24. This is a straightforward question. The author points out that automakers are using the same arguments they used in opposing the 1970 Clean Air Act. The answer is (D).

25. The automakers' position is that the new restrictions are too expensive. So anything that increases costs would support the automakers' position. Look at choice (A). It states that the more stringent the emissions standards become the more expensive the technology becomes. This is precisely the automakers' position. The answer is (A).

Part Three

READING COMPREHENSION

READING COMPREHENSION

- **INTRODUCTION**
  The Source for the Passages
  Passages are Like Arguments

- **READING METHODS**
  Why Speed Reading Doesn't Work
  Why Previewing the Questions Doesn't Work
  Pre-reading the Topic Sentences

- **THE SIX QUESTIONS**
  Main Idea Questions
  Description Questions
  Writing Technique Questions
  Extension Questions
  Application Questions
  Tone Questions

- **PIVOTAL WORDS**

- **THE THREE STEP METHOD**
  1. (Optional) Preview the First Sentences
  2. Note the Six Questions
  3. Circle the Pivotal Words and Annotate

- **LSAT SECTION**

- **EXTRA READING**

Introduction

The reading comprehension portion of the LSAT consists of four passages, each about 500 words long and each with about seven questions. The subject matter of a passage can be almost anything, but the most common themes are politics, history, culture, and science.

Most people find the passages difficult because the subject matter is dry and unfamiliar. Obscure subject matter is chosen so that your reading comprehension will be tested, not your knowledge of a particular subject. Also the more esoteric the subject the more likely everyone taking the test will be on an even playing field. However, because the material must still be accessible to laymen, you won't find any tracts on subtle issues of philosophy or abstract mathematics. In fact, if you read books on current affairs and the Op/Ed page of the newspaper, then the style of writing used in the LSAT passages will be familiar and you probably won't find the reading comprehension section particularly difficult.

The passages use a formal, compact style. They are typically taken from articles in academic journals, but they are rarely reprinted verbatim. Usually the chosen article is heavily edited until it is honed down to the required length. The formal style of the piece is retained but much of the "fluff" is removed. The editing process condenses the article to about one-third its original length. Thus, an LSAT passage contains about three times as much information for its length as does the original article. This is why the passages are similar to the writing on the Op/Ed page of a newspaper. After all, a person writing a piece for the Op/Ed page must express all his ideas in about 500 words, and he must use a formal (grammatical) style to convince people that he is well educated.

In addition to being dry and unfamiliar, LSAT passages often start in the middle of an explanation, so there is no point of reference. Furthermore, the passages are untitled, so you have to hit the ground running.

The passages are not arranged in order of difficulty, so work on the ones that are familiar and interesting to you first.

Passages are like arguments, only longer. So most of what we discussed about arguments still holds for passages, with some minor modifications. The typical reasoning pattern for an argument is *premise, premise, (counter-premise), conclusion.* However, the typical reasoning pattern for a passage is more complex: *premise, conclusion, premise, premise, (counter-premise), restatement of conclusion.* In an argument the premises are typically one sentence long, whereas in a passage the premises are usually a paragraph long.

The same obfuscating tactics are used with passages as with arguments; namely, *same language, overstatement/understatement, true but,* and *false claim.* We will analyze the particular ways these tactics are used with the passages as we come to each situation.

Points to Remember

1. The reading comprehension portion of the LSAT consists of four passages, each about 500 words long and each with about seven questions. The most common themes are politics, history, culture, and science.

2. The passages are not arranged in order of difficulty, so work on the ones that are familiar and interesting to you first.

3. Passages are like arguments, only longer. Most of what works for arguments still holds for passages, with some minor modifications.

Reading Methods

Reading styles are subjective—there is no best method for approaching the passages. There are as many "systems" for reading the passages as there are test-prep books—all "authoritatively" promoting their method, while contradicting some aspect of another. A reading technique that is natural for one person can be awkward and unnatural for another person. However, I find it hard to believe that many of the methods advocated in certain books could help anyone. Be that as it may, I will throw in my own two-cents worth—though not so dogmatically.

Some books recommend speed reading the passages. This is a mistake. Speed reading is designed for ordinary, nontechnical material. Because this material is filled with "fluff," you can skim over the nonessential parts and still get the gist—and often more—of the passage. As mentioned before, however, LSAT passages are dense. Some are actual quoted articles (when the writers of the LSAT find one that is sufficiently compact). Most often, however, they are based on articles that have been condensed to about one-third their original length. During this process no essential information is lost, just the "fluff" is cut. This is why speed reading will not work here—the passages contain too much information. Furthermore, the four passages make up only about two pages, and you have 35 minutes to read them. So the bulk of the time is spent answering the questions, not reading the passages. You should, however, read somewhat faster than you normally do, but not to the point that your comprehension suffers. You will have to experiment to find your optimum pace.

Many books recommend that the questions be read before the passage. This strikes me as a cruel joke. In some of these books it seems that many of the methods, such as this one, are advocated merely to give the reader the feeling that he is getting the "inside stuff" on how to ace the test. But there are two big problems with this method. First, some of the questions are a paragraph long, and reading a question twice can use up precious time. Second, there are usually seven questions per passage, and psychologists have shown that we can hold in our minds a maximum of about three thoughts at any one time (some of us have trouble simply remembering phone numbers). After reading all seven questions, the student will turn to the passage with his mind clouded by half-remembered thoughts. This will at best waste his time and distract him. More likely it will turn the passage into a disjointed mass of information.

However, one technique that you may find helpful is to preview the passage by reading the first sentence of each paragraph. Generally, the topic of a paragraph is contained in the first sentence. Reading the first sentence of each paragraph will give an overview of the passage. The topic sentences act in essence as a summary of the passage. Furthermore, since each passage is only three or four paragraphs long, previewing the topic sentences will not use up an inordinate amount of time. (I don't use this method myself, however. I prefer to see the passage as a completed whole, and to let the passage unveil its main idea to me as I become absorbed in it. I find that when I try to pre-analyze the passage it tends to become disjointed, and I lose my concentration. Nonetheless, as mentioned before, reading methods are subjective, so experiment—this method may work for you.)

Points to Remember

1. Reading styles are subjective—there is no best method for approaching the passages.

2. Don't speed read, or skim, the passage. Instead, read at a faster than usual pace, but not to the point that your comprehension suffers.

3. Don't read the questions before you read the passage.

4. (Optional) Preview the first sentence of each paragraph before you read the passage.

The Six Questions

The key to performing well on the passages is not the particular reading technique you use (so long as it's neither speed reading nor pre-reading the questions). Rather the key is to become completely familiar with the question types—there are only six—so that you can anticipate the questions that *might* be asked as you read the passage and answer those that *are* asked more quickly and efficiently. As you become familiar with the six question types, you will gain an intuitive sense for the places from which questions are likely to be drawn. This will give you the same advantage as that claimed by the "pre-reading-the-questions" technique, without the confusion and waste of time. Note, the order in which the questions are asked roughly corresponds to the order in which the main issues are presented in the passage. Early questions should correspond to information given early in the passage, and so on.

The following passage (taken from a recent LSAT) and accompanying questions illustrate the six question types. Read the passage slowly to get a good understanding of the issues.

There are two major systems of criminal procedure in the modern world—the adversarial and the inquisitorial. The former is associated with common law tradition and the latter with civil law tradition. Both systems were historically preceded by the system of private vengeance in which the victim of a crime fashioned his own remedy and administered it privately, either personally or through an agent. The vengeance system was a system of self-help, the essence of which was captured in the slogan "an eye for an eye, a tooth for a tooth." The modern adversarial system is only one historical step removed from the private vengeance system and still retains some of its characteristic features. Thus, for example, even though the right to institute criminal action has now been extended to all members of society and even though the police department has taken over the pretrial investigative functions on behalf of the prosecution, the adversarial system still leaves the defendant to conduct his own pretrial investigation. The trial is still viewed as a duel between two adversaries, refereed by a judge who, at the beginning of the trial has no knowledge of the investigative background of the case. In the final analysis the adversarial system of criminal procedure symbolizes and regularizes the punitive combat.

By contrast, the inquisitorial system begins historically where the adversarial system stopped its development. It is two historical steps removed from the system of private vengeance. Therefore, from the standpoint of legal anthropology, it is historically superior to the adversarial system. Under the inquisitorial system the public investigator has the duty to investigate not just on behalf of the prosecutor but also on behalf of the defendant. Additionally, the public prosecutor has the duty to present to the court not only evidence that may lead to the conviction of the defendant but also evidence that may lead to his exoneration. This system mandates that both parties permit full pretrial discovery of the evidence in their possession. Finally, in an effort to make the trial less like a duel between two adversaries, the inquisitorial system mandates that the judge take an active part in the conduct of the trial, with a role that is both directive and protective.

Fact-finding is at the heart of the inquisitorial system. This system operates on the philosophical premise that in a criminal case the crucial factor is not the legal rule but the facts of the case and that the goal of the entire procedure is to experimentally recreate for the court the commission of the alleged crime.

MAIN IDEA QUESTIONS

The main idea plays the same role in a passage that the conclusion does in an argument. As with arguments, the main idea of a passage typically comes at the end of a paragraph. With passages, however, it tends to be the last—occasionally the first—sentence of the first paragraph. If it's not there, it will probably be the last sentence of the entire passage. Main idea questions are usually the first questions asked.

Some common main idea questions are

- Which one of the following best expresses the main idea of the passage?
- The primary purpose of the passage is to . . .
- In the passage, the author's primary concern is to discuss . . .

Main idea questions are rarely difficult; after all the author wants to clearly communicate her ideas to you. If, however, after the first reading, you don't have a feel for the main idea, review the first and last sentence of each paragraph; these will give you a quick overview of the passage.

Because main idea questions are relatively easy, the LSAT writers try to obscure the correct answer by surrounding it with close answer-choices ("detractors") that either overstate or understate the author's main point. Answer-choices that stress specifics tend to understate the main idea; choices that go beyond the scope of the passage tend to overstate the main idea.

The answer to a main idea question will summarize the author's argument, yet be neither too specific nor too broad.

In most LSAT passages the author's primary purpose is to persuade the reader to accept her opinion. Occasionally, it is to describe something.

Example: (Refer to passage on page 337.)

The primary purpose of the passage is to

(A) explain why the inquisitorial system is the best system of criminal justice
(B) explain how the adversarial and the inquisitorial systems of criminal justice both evolved from the system of private vengeance
(C) show how the adversarial and inquisitorial systems of criminal justice can both complement and hinder each other's development
(D) show how the adversarial and inquisitorial systems of criminal justice are being combined into a new and better system
(E) analyze two systems of criminal justice and deduce which one is better

The answer to a main idea question will summarize the passage without going beyond it. (A) violates these criteria by *overstating* the scope of the passage. The comparison in the passage is between two specific systems, not between *all* systems. (A) would be a good answer if "best" were replaced with "better." **Beware of extreme words**. (B) violates the criteria by *understating* the scope of the passage. Although the evolution of both the adversarial and the inquisitorial systems is discussed in the passage, it is done to show why one is superior to the other. As to (C) and (D), both can be quickly dismissed since neither is mentioned in the passage. Finally, the passage does two things: it presents two systems of criminal justice and shows why one is better than the other. (E) aptly summarizes this, so it is the best answer.

Following is a mini-passage. These exercises are interspersed among the sections of this chapter and are written to the same specifications as actual LSAT passages, but are one-quarter to one-half the length. Because the mini-passages are shorter and designed to test only one issue, they are more tractable than a full passage.

Application: ***(Mini-passage)***

As Xenophanes recognized as long ago as the sixth century before Christ, whether or not God made man in His own image, it is certain that man makes gods in his. The gods of Greek mythology first appear in the writings of Homer and Hesiod, and, from the character and actions of these picturesque and, for the most part, friendly beings, we get some idea of the men who made them and brought them to Greece.

But ritual is more fundamental than mythology, and the study of Greek ritual during recent years has shown that, beneath the belief or skepticism with which the Olympians were regarded, lay an older magic, with traditional rites for the promotion of fertility by the celebration of the annual cycle of life and death, and the propitiation of unfriendly ghosts, gods or demons. Some such survivals were doubtless widespread, and, prolonged into classical times, probably made the substance of Eleusinian and Orphic mysteries. Against this dark and dangerous background arose Olympic mythology on the one hand and early philosophy and science on the other.

In classical times the need of a creed higher than the Olympian was felt, and Aeschylus, Sophocles and Plato finally evolved from the pleasant but crude polytheism the idea of a single, supreme and righteous Zeus. But the decay of Olympus led to a revival of old and the invasion of new magic cults among the people, while some philosophers were looking to a vision of the uniformity of nature under divine and universal law.

From Sir William Cecil Dampier, *A Shorter History of Science*, ©1957, Meridian Books.

The main idea of the passage is that

(A) Olympic mythology evolved from ancient rituals and gave rise to early philosophy
(B) early moves toward viewing nature as ordered by divine and universal law coincided with monotheistic impulses and the disintegration of classical mythology
(C) early philosophy followed from classical mythology
(D) the practice of science, i.e., empiricism, preceded scientific theory

Most main idea questions are rather easy. This one is not—mainly, because the passage itself is not an easy read. Recall that to find the main idea of a passage, we check the last sentence of the first paragraph; if it's not there, we check the closing of the passage. Reviewing the last sentence of the first paragraph, we see that it hardly presents a statement, let alone the main idea. Turning to the closing line of the passage, however, we find the key to this question. The passage describes a struggle for ascendancy amongst four opposing philosophies: (magic and traditional rites) vs. (Olympic mythology) vs. (monotheism [Zeus]) vs. (early philosophy and science). The closing lines of the passage summarize this and add that Olympic mythology lost out to monotheism (Zeus), while magical cults enjoyed a revival and the germ of universal law was planted. Thus the answer is (B).

As to the other choices, (A) is false. "Olympic mythology [arose] on one hand and early philosophy and science on the other" (closing to paragraph two); thus they initially developed in parallel. (C) is also false. It makes the same type of error as (A). Finally, (D) is not mentioned in the passage.

DESCRIPTION QUESTIONS

Description questions, as with main idea questions, refer to a point made by the author. However, description questions refer to a minor point or to incidental information, not to the author's main point.

Again, these questions take various forms:

- According to the passage . . .
- In line 37, the author mentions . . . for the purpose of . . .
- The passage suggests that which one of the following would . . .

The answer to a description question must refer directly to a statement in the passage, not to something implied by it. However, the correct answer will paraphrase a statement in the passage, not give an exact quote. In fact, exact quotes ("Same language" traps) are often used to bait wrong answers.

Caution: When answering a description question, you must find the point in the passage from which the question is drawn. Don't rely on memory—too many obfuscating tactics are used with these questions.

Not only must the correct answer refer directly to a statement in the passage, it must refer to the relevant statement. The correct answer will be surrounded by wrong choices which refer directly to the passage but don't address the question. These choices can be tempting because they tend to be quite close to the actual answer.

Once you spot the sentence to which the question refers, you still must read a few sentences before and after it, to put the question in context. If a question refers to line 20, the information needed to answer it can occur anywhere from line 15 to 25. Even if you have spotted the answer in line 20, you should still read a couple more lines to make certain you have the proper perspective.

Example: (Refer to passage on page 337.)

According to the passage, the inquisitorial system differs from the adversarial system in that

(A) it does not make the defendant solely responsible for gathering evidence for his case
(B) it does not require the police department to work on behalf of the prosecution
(C) it does not allow the victim the satisfaction of private vengeance
(D) it requires the prosecution to drop a weak case
(E) a defendant who is innocent would prefer to be tried under the inquisitorial system

This is a description question, so the information needed to answer it must be stated in the passage—though not in the same language as in the answer. The needed information is contained in lines 34–36, which state that the public prosecutor has to investigate on behalf of both society and the defendant. Thus, the defendant is not solely responsible for investigating his case. Furthermore, the paragraph's opening implies that this feature is not found in the adversarial system. This illustrates why you must determine the context of the situation before you can safely answer the question. The answer is (A).

The other choices can be easily dismissed. (B) is the second best answer. Lines 17–20 state that in the adversarial system the police assume the work of the prosecution. Then lines 28–30 state that the inquisitorial system begins where the adversarial system stopped; this implies that in both systems the police work for the prosecution. (C) uses a false claim ploy. The passage states that both systems are removed from the system of private vengeance. (D) is probably true, but it is neither stated nor directly implied by the passage. Finally, (E) uses a reference to the passage to make a true but irrelevant statement. People's attitude or preference toward a system is not a part of that system.

Application: ***(Mini-passage)***

If dynamic visual graphics, sound effects, and automatic scorekeeping are the features that account for the popularity of video games, why are parents so worried? All of these features seem quite innocent. But another source of concern is that the games available in arcades have, almost without exception, themes of physical aggression.... There has long been the belief that violent content may teach violent behavior. And yet again our society finds a new medium in which to present that content, and yet again the demand is nearly insatiable. And there is evidence that violent video games breed violent behavior, just as violent television shows do....

The effects of video violence are less simple, however, than they at first appeared. The same group of researchers who found negative effects [from certain video games] have more recently found that two-player aggressive video games, whether cooperative or competitive, reduce the level of aggression in children's play....

It may be that the most harmful aspect of the violent video games is that they are solitary in nature. A two-person aggressive game (video boxing, in this study) seems to provide a cathartic or releasing effect for aggression, while a solitary aggressive game (such as Space Invaders) may stimulate further aggression. Perhaps the effects of television in stimulating aggression will also be found to stem partly from the fact that TV viewing typically involves little social interaction.

From Patricia Marks Greenfield, *Mind and Media: The Effects of Television, Video Games, and Computers*. © 1984 by Harvard University Press.

According to the passage, which of the following would be likely to stimulate violent behavior in a child playing a video game?

I. Watching the computer stage a battle between two opponents
II. Controlling a character in battle against a computer
III. Challenging another player to a battle in a non-cooperative two-person game

(A) II only
(B) III only
(C) I and II only
(D) II and III only

Item I, True: Stimulation would occur. This choice is qualitatively the same as passively watching violence on television. **Item II, True:** Stimulation would also occur. This is another example of solitary aggression (implied by the second sentence of the last paragraph). **Item III, False:** No stimulation would occur. Two-player aggressive games are "cathartic" (again the needed reference is the second sentence of the last paragraph). The answer is (C).

Often you will be asked to define a word or phrase based on its context. For this type of question, again you must look at a few lines before and after the word. Don't assume that because the word is familiar you know the definition requested. Words often have more than one meaning. And the LSAT often asks for a peculiar or technical meaning of a common word. For example, as a noun *champion* means "the winner," but as a verb *champion* means "to be an advocate for someone." You must consider the word's context to get its correct meaning.

On the LSAT the definition of a word will not use as simple a structure as was used above to define *champion*. One common way the LSAT introduces a defining word or phrase is to place it in apposition to the word being defined.

Don't confuse "apposition" with "opposition": they have antithetical [exactly opposite] meanings. Words or phrases in apposition are placed next to each other, and the second word or phrase defines, clarifies, or gives evidence for the first word or phrase. The second word or phrase will be set off from the first by a comma, semicolon, hyphen, or parentheses. (Note: If a comma is not followed by a linking word—such as *and, for, yet*—then the following phrase is probably appositional.)

Example:

The discussions were acrimonious, frequently degenerating into name-calling contests.

After the comma in this sentence, there is no linking word (such as *and, but, because, although*, etc.). Hence the phrase following the comma is in apposition to *acrimonious*—it defines or further clarifies the word. Now acrimonious means bitter, mean-spirited talk, which would aptly describe a name-calling contest.

Application: ***(Mini-passage)***

The technical phenomenon, embracing all the separate techniques, forms a whole.... It is useless to look for differentiations. They do exist, but only secondarily. The common features of the technical phenomenon are so sharply drawn that it is easy to discern that which is the technical phenomenon and that which is not.

... To analyze these common features is tricky, but it is simple to grasp them. Just as there are principles common to things as different as a wireless set and an internal-combustion engine, so the organization of an office and the construction of an aircraft have certain identical features. This identity is the primary mark of that thoroughgoing unity which makes the technical phenomenon a single essence despite the extreme diversity of its appearances.

As a corollary, it is impossible to analyze this or that element out of it—a truth which is today particularly misunderstood. The great tendency of all persons who study techniques is to make distinctions. They distinguish between the different elements of technique, maintaining some and discarding others. They distinguish between technique and the use to which it is put. These distinctions are completely invalid and show only that he who makes them has understood nothing of the technical phenomenon. Its parts are ontologically tied together; in it, use is inseparable from being.

From Jacques Ellul, *The Technological Society*, ©1964 by Alfred A. Knopf, Inc.

The "technical phenomenon" referred to in the opening line can best be defined as

(A) all of the machinery in use today
(B) the abstract idea of the machine
(C) a way of thinking in modern society
(D) what all machines have in common

(A): No, it is clear from the passage that the technical phenomenon is more abstract than that, since it is described in the opening paragraph as uniting all the separate "techniques" (not machines) and as comprising the "features" that such things as an office and an aircraft have in common. (B): No, the passage states that the technical phenomenon is something that includes both techniques and their use (See closing lines of the passage); it is thus broader that just the idea of machinery. **(C): Yes**, this seems to be the best answer; it is broad enough to include both techniques and their uses and abstract enough to go beyond talking only about machines. (D): No, the passage suggests that it is something that techniques have in common and techniques can include airplanes or offices.

WRITING TECHNIQUE QUESTIONS

All coherent writing has a superstructure or blueprint. When writing, we don't just randomly jot down our thoughts; we organize our ideas and present them in a logical manner. For instance, we may present evidence that builds up to a conclusion but intentionally leave the conclusion unstated, or we may present a position and then contrast it with an opposing position, or we may draw an extended analogy.

There is an endless number of writing techniques that authors use to present their ideas, so we cannot classify every method. However, some techniques are very common to the type of explanatory or opinionated writing found in LSAT passages.

A. Compare and contrast two positions.

This technique has a number of variations, but the most common and direct method is to develop two ideas or systems (comparing) and then point out why one is better than the other (contrasting).

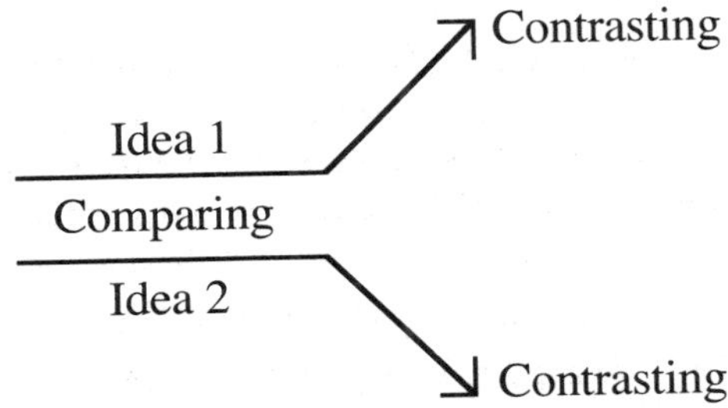

Some common tip-off phrases to this method of analysis are

- By contrast
- Similarly

Some typical questions for these types of passages are

- According to the passage, a central distinction between a woman's presence and a man's presence is:
- In which of the following ways does the author imply that birds and reptiles are similar?

Writing technique questions are similar to main idea questions; except that they ask about how the author presents his ideas, not about the ideas themselves. Generally, you will be given only two writing methods to choose from, but each method will have two or more variations.

Example: (Refer to passage on page 337.)

Which one of the following best describes the organization of the passage?

(A) Two systems of criminal justice are compared and contrasted, and one is deemed to be better than the other.
(B) One system of criminal justice is presented as better than another. Then evidence is offered to support that claim.
(C) Two systems of criminal justice are analyzed, and one specific example is examined in detail.
(D) A set of examples is furnished. Then a conclusion is drawn from them.
(E) The inner workings of the criminal justice system are illustrated by using two systems.

Clearly the author is comparing and contrasting two criminal justice systems. Indeed, the opening to paragraph two makes this explicit. The author uses a mixed form of comparison and contrast. He opens the passage by developing (comparing) both systems and then shifts to developing just the adversarial system. He opens the second paragraph by contrasting the two criminal justice systems and then further develops just the inquisitorial system. Finally, he closes by again contrasting the two systems and implying that the inquisitorial system is superior.

Only two answer-choices, (A) and (B), have any real merit. They say essentially the same thing—though in different order. Notice in the passage that the author does not indicate which system is better until the end of paragraph one, and he does not make that certain until paragraph two. This contradicts the order given by (B). Hence the answer is (A). (Note: In (A) the order is not specified and therefore is harder to attack, whereas in (B) the order is definite and therefore is easier to attack. Remember that a measured response is harder to attack and therefore is more likely to be the answer.)

B. Show cause and effect.

In this technique, the author typically shows how a particular cause leads to a certain result or set of results. It is not uncommon for this method to introduce a sequence of causes and effects. A causes B, which causes C, which causes D, and so on. Hence B is both the effect of A and the cause of C. For a discussion of the fallacies associated with this technique see Causal Reasoning (page 265). The variations on this rhetorical technique can be illustrated by the following schematics:

(C) —> (E)

(C) —> (E), (E), (E)

(C) —> (C/E) —> (C/E) —> (E)

Example: ***(Mini-passage)***

Thirdly, I worry about the private automobile. It is a dirty, noisy, wasteful, and lonely means of travel. It pollutes the air, ruins the safety and sociability of the street, and exercises upon the individual a discipline which takes away far more freedom than it gives him. It causes an enormous amount of land to be unnecessarily abstracted from nature and from plant life and to become devoid of any natural function. It explodes cities, grievously impairs the whole institution of neighborliness, fragmentizes and destroys communities. It has already spelled the end of our cities as real cultural and social communities, and has made impossible the construction of any others in their place. Together with the airplane, it has crowded out other, more civilized and more convenient means of transport, leaving older people, infirm people, poor people and children in a worse situation than they were a hundred years ago. It continues to lend a terrible element of fragility to our civilization, placing us in a situation where our life would break down completely if anything ever interfered with the oil supply.

George F. Kennan

Which of the following best describes the organization of the passage?

(A) A problem is presented and then a possible solution is discussed.
(B) The benefits and demerits of the automobile are compared and contrasted.
(C) A topic is presented and a number of its effects are discussed.
(D) A set of examples is furnished to support a conclusion.

This passage is laden with effects. Kennan introduces the cause, the automobile, in the opening sentence and from there on presents a series of effects—the automobile pollutes, enslaves, and so on. Hence the answer is (C). Note: (D) is the second-best choice; it is disqualified by two flaws. First, in this context, "examples" is not as precise as "effects." Second, the order is wrong: the conclusion, *"I worry about the private automobile"* is presented first and then the examples: it pollutes, it enslaves, etc.

C. State a position and then give supporting evidence.

This technique is common with opinionated passages. Equally common is the reverse order. That is, the supporting evidence is presented and then the position or conclusion is stated. And sometimes the evidence will be structured to build up to a conclusion which is then left unstated. If this is done skillfully the reader will be more likely to arrive at the same conclusion as the author.

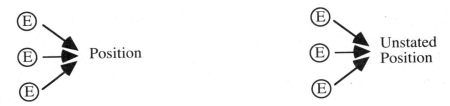

Following are some typical questions for these types of passages:

- According to the author, which of the following is required for one to become proficient with a computer?
- Which of the following does the author cite as evidence that the bald eagle is in danger of becoming extinct?

EXTENSION QUESTIONS

Extension questions are the most common. They require you to go beyond what is stated in the passage, asking you to draw an inference from the passage, to make a conclusion based on the passage, or to identify one of the author's tacit assumptions.

You may be asked to draw a conclusion based on the ideas or facts presented:

- ➢ It can be inferred from the passage that . . .
- ➢ The passage suggests that . . .

Since extension questions require you to go beyond the passage, the correct answer must say *more* than what is said in the passage. Beware of same language traps with these questions: the correct answer will often both paraphrase and extend a statement in the passage, but it will not directly quote it.

> **"Same Language" traps:** For extension questions, any answer-choice that explicitly refers to or repeats a statement in the passage will probably be wrong.

The correct answer to an extension question will not require a quantum leap in thought, but it will add significantly to the ideas presented in the passage.

Example: (Refer to passage on page 337.)

The author views the prosecution's role in the inquisitorial system as being

(A) an advocate for both society and the defendant
(B) solely responsible for starting a trial
(C) a protector of the legal rule
(D) an investigator only
(E) an aggressive but fair investigator

This is an extension question. So the answer will not be explicitly stated in the passage, but it will be strongly supported by it.

The author states that the prosecutor is duty bound to present any evidence that may prove the defendant innocent and that he must disclose all pretrial evidence (i.e., have no tricks up his sleeve). This is the essence of fair play. So the answer is probably (E).

However, we should check all the choices. (A) overstates the case. Although the prosecutor must disclose any evidence that might show the defendant innocent, the prosecutor is still advocating society's case against the defendant—it must merely be measured advocacy. This is the second-best answer. As for (B), although it is implied that in both systems the right to initiate a case is extended to all people through the prosecutor, it is not stated or implied that this is the only way to start a case. Finally, neither (C) nor (D) is mentioned or implied in the passage. The answer, therefore, is (E).

Application: ***(Mini-passage)***

Often, the central problem in any business is that money is needed to make money. The following discusses the sale of equity, which is one response to this problem.

Sale of Capital Stock: a way to obtain capital through the sale of stock to individual investors beyond the scope of one's immediate acquaintances. Periods of high interest rates turn entrepreneurs to this equity market. This involves, of necessity, a dilution of ownership, and many owners are reluctant to take this step for that reason. Whether the owner is wise in declining to use outside equity financing depends upon the firm's long-range prospects. If there is an opportunity for substantial expansion on a continuing basis and if other sources are inadequate, the owner may decide logically to bring in other owners. Owning part of a larger business may be more profitable than owning all of a smaller business.

Small-Business Management, 6th Ed., © 1983 by South-Western Publishing Co.

The passage implies that an owner who chooses not to sell capital stock despite the prospect of continued expansion is

(A) subject to increased regulation
(B) more conservative than is wise under the circumstances
(C) likely to have her ownership of the business diluted
(D) sacrificing security for rapid growth

(A): No. This is not mentioned in the passage. **(B): Yes.** The passage states that *"the owner may decide logically to bring in other owners"*; in other words, the owner would be wise to sell stock in this situation. (C): No. By NOT selling stock, the owner retains full ownership. (D) No. Just the opposite: the owner would be sacrificing a measure of security for growth if she did sell stock.

APPLICATION QUESTIONS

Application questions differ from extension questions only in degree. Extension questions ask you to apply what you have learned from the passage to derive new information about the same subject, whereas application questions go one step further, asking you to apply what you have learned from the passage to a different or hypothetical situation.

The following are common application questions:

- Which one of the following is the most likely source of the passage?
- Which one of the following actions would be most likely to have the same effect as the author's actions?

You may be asked to complete a thought for the author:

- The author would most likely agree with which one of the following statements?
- Which one of the following sentences would the author be most likely to use to complete the last paragraph of the passage?

To answer an application question, take the author's perspective. Ask yourself: what am I arguing for? what might make my argument stronger? what might make it weaker?

Because these questions go well beyond the passage, they tend to be the most difficult. Furthermore, because application questions and extension questions require a deeper understanding of the passage, skimming (or worse yet, speed reading) the passage is ineffective. Skimming may give you the main idea and structure of the passage, but it is unlikely to give you the subtleties of the author's attitude.

Example: (Refer to passage on page 337.)

Based on the information in the passage, it can be inferred that which one of the following would most logically begin a paragraph immediately following the passage?

(A) Because of the inquisitorial system's thoroughness in conducting its pretrial investigation, it can be concluded that a defendant who is innocent would prefer to be tried under the inquisitorial system, whereas a defendant who is guilty would prefer to be tried under the adversarial system.

(B) As the preceding analysis shows, the legal system is in a constant state of flux. For now the inquisitorial system is ascendant, but it will probably be soon replaced by another system.

(C) The accusatorial system begins where the inquisitorial system ends. So it is three steps removed from the system of private vengeance, and therefore historically superior to it.

(D) Because in the inquisitorial system the judge must take an active role in the conduct of the trial, his competency and expertise have become critical.

(E) The criminal justice system has evolved to the point that it no longer seems to be derivative of the system of private vengeance. Modern systems of criminal justice empower all of society with the right to instigate a legal action, and the need for vengeance is satisfied through a surrogate—the public prosecutor.

The author has rather thoroughly presented his position, so the next paragraph would be a natural place for him to summarize it. The passage compares and contrasts two systems of criminal justice, implying that the inquisitorial system is superior. We expect the concluding paragraph to sum up this position. Now all legal theory aside, the system of justice under which an innocent person would choose to be judged would, as a practical matter, pretty much sum up the situation. Hence the answer is (A).

Application: ***(Mini-passage)***

The idea of stuff expresses no more than the experience of coming to a limit at which our senses or our instruments are not fine enough to make out the pattern.

Something of the same kind happens when the scientist investigates any unit or pattern so distinct to the naked eye that it has been considered a separate entity. He finds that the more carefully he observes and describes it, the more he is *also* describing the environment in which it moves and other patterns to which it seems inseparably related. As Teilhard de Chardin has so well expressed it, the isolation of individual, atomic patterns "is merely an intellectual dodge."

...Although the ancient cultures of Asia never attained the rigorously exact physical knowledge of the modern West, they grasped in principle many things which are only now occurring to us. Hinduism and Buddhism are impossible to classify as religions, philosophies, sciences, or even mythologies, or again as amalgamations of all four, because departmentalization is foreign to them even in so basic a form as the separation of the spiritual and the material.... Buddhism ... is not a culture but a critique of culture, an enduring nonviolent revolution, or "loyal opposition," to the culture with which it is involved. This gives these ways of liberation something in common with psychotherapy beyond the interest in changing states of consciousness. For the task of the psychotherapist is to bring about a reconciliation between individual feeling and social norms without, however, sacrificing the integrity of the individual. He tries to help the individual to be himself and to go it alone in the world (of social convention) but not of the world.

From Alan W. Watts, *Psychotherapy East and West*, © 1961 by Pantheon Books, a division of Random House.

What does the passage suggest about the theme of the book from which it is excerpted?

(A) The book attempts to understand psychotherapy in the context of different and changing systems of thought.
(B) The book argues that psychotherapy unites elements of an exact science with elements of eastern philosophy.
(C) The book describes the origins of psychotherapy around the world.
(D) The book compares psychotherapy in the West and in the East.

(A): Yes, this is the most accurate inference from the passage. The passage discusses how the more carefully a scientist views and describes something the more he describes the environment in which it moves, and the passage traces similarities between psychotherapy and Eastern systems of (evolving) thought. (B): No, this is too narrow an interpretation of what the whole book would be doing. (C): No, too vague; the passage is too philosophical to be merely a history. (D): No, also too vague, meant to entrap those of you who relied on the title without thinking through the passage.

TONE QUESTIONS

Tone questions ask you to identify the writer's attitude or perspective. Is the writer's feeling toward the subject positive, negative, or neutral? Does the writer give his own opinion, or does he objectively present the opinions of others?

Before you read the answer-choices, decide whether the writer's tone is positive, negative, or neutral. It is best to do this without referring to the passage.

However, if you did not get a feel for the writer's attitude on the first reading, check the adjectives that he chooses. Adjectives and, to a lesser extent, adverbs express our feelings toward subjects. For instance, if we agree with a person who holds strong feelings about a subject, we may describe his opinions as impassioned. On the other hand, if we disagree with him, we may describe his opinions as excitable, which has the same meaning as "impassioned" but carries a negative connotation.

Example: (Refer to passage on page 337.)

The author's attitude toward the adversarial system can best be described as

(A) encouraged that it is far removed from the system of private vengeance
(B) concerned that it does not allow all members of society to instigate legal action
(C) pleased that it does not require the defendant to conduct his own pretrial investigation
(D) hopeful that it will be replaced by the inquisitorial system
(E) doubtful that it is the best vehicle for justice

The author does not reveal his feelings toward the adversarial system until the end of paragraph one. Clearly the clause "the adversarial system of criminal procedure symbolizes and regularizes the punitive combat" indicates that he has a negative attitude toward the system. This is confirmed in the second paragraph when he states that the inquisitorial system is historically superior to the adversarial system. So he feels that the adversarial system is deficient.

The "two-out-of-five" rule is at work here: only choices (D) and (E) have any real merit. Both are good answers. But which one is better? Intuitively, choice (E) is more likely to be the answer because it is more measured. To decide between two choices attack each: the one that survives is the answer. Now a tone question should be answered from what is directly stated in the passage—not from what it implies. Although the author has reservations toward the adversarial system, at no point does he say that he hopes the inquisitorial system will replace it, he may prefer a third system over both. This eliminates (D); the answer therefore is (E).

The remaining choices are not supported by the passage. (A), using the same language as in the passage, overstates the author's feeling. In lines 12–15, he states that the adversarial system is only *one* step removed from the private vengeance system—not *far* removed. Remember: Be wary of extreme words. (A) would be a better choice if "far" were dropped. (B) makes a false claim. In lines 16–19, the author states that the adversarial system *does* extend the right to initiate legal action to all members of society. Finally, (C) also makes a false claim. In lines 20–21, the author states that the defendant in the adversarial system is still left to conduct his own pretrial investigation.

Application: ***(Mini-passage)***

An elm in our backyard caught the blight this summer and dropped stone dead, leafless, almost overnight. One weekend it was a normal-looking elm, maybe a little bare in spots but nothing alarming, and the next weekend it was gone, passed over, departed, taken....

The dying of a field mouse, at the jaws of an amiable household cat, is a spectacle I have beheld many times. It used to make me wince.... Nature, I thought, was an abomination.

Recently I've done some thinking about that mouse, and I wonder if his dying is necessarily all that different from the passing of our elm. The main difference, if there is one, would be in the matter of pain. I do not believe that an elm tree has pain receptors, and even so, the blight seems to me a relatively painless way to go. But the mouse dangling tail-down from the teeth of a gray cat is something else again, with pain beyond bearing, you'd think, all over his small body. There are now some plausible reasons for thinking it is not like that at all.... At the instant of being trapped and penetrated by teeth, peptide hormones are released by cells in the hypothalamus and the pituitary gland; instantly these substances, called endorphins, are attached to the surfaces of other cells responsible for pain perception; the hormones have the pharmacologic properties of opium; there is no pain. Thus it is that the mouse seems always to dangle so languidly from the jaws, lies there so quietly when dropped, dies of his injuries without a struggle. If a mouse could shrug, he'd shrug....

Pain is useful for avoidance, for getting away when there's time to get away, but when it is end game, and no way back, pain is likely to be turned off, and the mechanisms for this are wonderfully precise and quick. If I had to design an ecosystem in which creatures had to live off each other and in which dying was an indispensable part of living, I could not think of a better way to manage.

From Lewis Thomas, *On Natural Death,* © 1979 by Lewis Thomas.

Which one of the following would best characterize the author's attitude toward the relationship between pain and death?

(A) Dismay at the inherent cruelty of nature
(B) Amusement at the irony of the relationship between pain and death
(C) Admiration for the ways in which animal life functions in the ecosystem
(D) A desire to conduct experiments on animals in order to discover more about the relationship between pain and death

The author's attitude toward the relationship between pain and death evolves through three stages. First, he expresses revulsion at the relationship. This is indicated in the second paragraph by the words *"wince"* and *"abomination."* Then in the third paragraph, he adopts a more analytical attitude and questions his previous judgment. This is indicated by the clause, *"I wonder if his dying is necessarily all that different from the passing of our elm."* And in closing the paragraph, he seems resigned to the fact the relationship is not all that bad. This is indicated by the sentence, *"If a mouse could shrug, he'd shrug."* Finally, in the last paragraph, he comes to express admiration for the relationship between pain and death. This is indicated by the phrase *"wonderfully precise and quick,"* and it is made definite by the closing line, *"If I had to design an ecosystem . . . in which dying was an indispensable part of living, I could not think of a better way to manage."* Thus, the answer is (C).

The other choices are easily ruled out. Choice (A) is perhaps superficially tempting. In the second paragraph the author does express dismay at the ways of nature, but notice that his concerns are in the past tense. He is *now* more understanding, wiser of the ways of nature. As to (B), the author is subtly reverential, never ironical, toward nature. Finally, (D) is not mentioned or alluded to in the passage.

Beware of answer-choices that contain extreme emotions. Remember the passages are taken from academic journals. In the rarefied air of academic circles, strong emotions are considered inappropriate and sophomoric. The writers want to display opinions that are considered and reasonable, not spontaneous and off-the-wall. So if an author's tone is negative, it may be disapproving—not snide. Or if her tone is positive, it may be approving—not ecstatic.

Furthermore, the answers must be indisputable. If the answers were subjective, then the writers of the LSAT would be deluged with letters from angry test takers, complaining that their test-scores are unfair.

To avoid such a difficult position, the writers of the LSAT never allow the correct answer to be either controversial or grammatically questionable.

Let's use these theories to answer the following questions, which are taken from recent LSATs.

Example:

Which one of the following most accurately characterizes the author's attitude with respect to Phillis Wheatley's literary accomplishments?

(A) enthusiastic advocacy
(B) qualified admiration
(C) dispassionate impartiality
(D) detached ambivalence
(E) perfunctory dismissal

Even without reference to the passage, this is not a difficult question to answer.

Scholars may advocate each other's work, but they are unlikely to be enthusiastic advocates. Furthermore, the context stretches the meaning of advocacy—to defend someone else's cause or plight. So (A) is unlikely to be the answer.

(B) is the measured response and therefore is probably the answer.

"Dispassionate impartiality" is a rather odd construction; additionally, it is redundant. It could never be the answer to an LSAT question. This eliminates (C).

"Detached ambivalence" is not as odd as "dispassionate impartiality," but it is unusual. So (D) is unlikely to be the answer.

Remember, scholars want their audience to consider their opinions well thought out, not off-the-wall. But *perfunctory* means "hasty and superficial." So (E) could not be the answer.

Hence, even without the passage we can still find the answer, (B).

Example:

Which one of the following best describes the author's attitude toward scientific techniques?

(A) critical
(B) hostile
(C) idealistic
(D) ironic
(E) neutral

(A) is one of two measured responses offered. Now a scholar may be critical of a particular scientific technique, but only a crackpot would be critical of *all* scientific techniques—eliminate (A).

"Hostile" is far too negative. Scholars consider such emotions juvenile—eliminate (B).

"Idealistic," on the other hand, is too positive; it sounds pollyannaish—eliminate (C).

"Ironic" seems illogical in this context. It's hard to conceive of a person having an ironic attitude toward scientific techniques—eliminate (D).

(E) is the other measured response, and by elimination it is the answer.

Description, extension, and application questions make up about 80% of the reading comprehension questions, main idea questions about 10%, and tone and writing technique questions about 5% each.

Points to Remember

1. The order of the passage questions roughly corresponds to the order in which the issues are presented in the passage.

2. The six questions are

   Main Idea
   Description
   Writing Technique
   Extension
   Application
   Tone

3. The main idea of a passage is usually stated in the last, sometimes the first, sentence of the first paragraph. If it's not there, it will probably be the last sentence of the entire passage.

4. If after the first reading, you don't have a feel for the main idea, review the first and last sentence of each paragraph.

5. The answer to a description question must refer directly to a statement in the passage, not to something implied by it. However, the correct answer will paraphrase a passage statement, not quote it exactly. In fact, exact quotes are used with these questions to bait wrong answers.

6. When answering a description question, you must find the point in the passage from which the question is drawn.

7. If a description question refers to line 20, the information needed to answer it can occur anywhere from line 15 to 25.

8. Some writing techniques commonly used in the LSAT passages are
   A. Compare and contrast two positions.
   B. Show cause and effect.
   C. State a position; then give supporting evidence.

9. For extension questions, any answer-choice that refers explicitly to or repeats a statement in the passage will probably be wrong.

10. Application questions differ from extension questions only in degree. Extension questions ask you to apply what you have learned from the passage to derive new information about the same subject, whereas application questions go one step further, asking you to apply what you have learned from the passage to a different or hypothetical situation.

11. To answer an application question, take the perspective of the author. Ask yourself: what am I arguing for? what might make my argument stronger? what might make it weaker?

12. Because application questions go well beyond the passage, they tend to be the most difficult.

13. For tone questions, decide whether the writer's tone is positive, negative, or neutral before you look at the answer-choices.

14. If you do not have a feel for the writer's attitude after the first reading, check the adjectives that she chooses.

15. Beware of answer-choices that contain extreme emotions. If an author's tone is negative, it may be disapproving—not snide. Or if her tone is positive, it may be approving—not ecstatic.

16. The answers must be indisputable. A correct answer will never be controversial or grammatically questionable.

17. Description, extension, and application questions make up about 80% of the reading comprehension questions, main idea questions about 10%, and tone and writing technique questions about 5% each.

Mentor Exercise

Directions: This passage is followed by a group of questions to be answered based on what is stated or implied in the passage. For some questions, more than one choice could conceivably answer the question. However, choose the best answer; the one that most accurately and completely answers the question. Hints, insights, and answers immediately follow the questions.

From Romania to Germany, from Tallinn to Belgrade, a major historical process—the death of communism—is taking place. The German Democratic Republic no longer exists as a separate state. And the former German Democratic Republic will serve as the first measure of the price a post-Communist society has to pay for entering the normal European orbit. In Yugoslavia we will see whether the federation can survive without communism.

One thing seems common to all these countries: dictatorship has been defeated and freedom has won, yet the victory of freedom has not yet meant the triumph of democracy. Democracy is something more than freedom. Democracy is freedom institutionalized, freedom submitted to the limits of the law, freedom functioning as an object of compromise between the major political forces on the scene.

We have freedom, but we still have not achieved the democratic order. That is why this freedom is so fragile. In the years of democratic opposition to communism, we supposed that the easiest thing would be to introduce changes in the economy. In fact, we thought that the march from a planned economy to a market economy would take place within the framework of the bureaucratic system, and that the market within the Communist state would explode the totalitarian structures. Only then would the time come to build the institutions of a civil society; and only at the end, with the completion of the market economy and the civil society, would the time of great political transformations finally arrive.

The opposite happened. First came the big political change, the great shock, which either broke the monopoly and the principle of Communist Party rule or simply pushed the Communists out of power. Then came the creation of civil society, whose institutions were created in great pain, and which had trouble negotiating the empty space of freedom. Only then, as the third moment of change, the final task was undertaken: that of transforming the totalitarian economy into a normal economy where different forms of ownership and different economic actors will live one next to the other.

Today we are in a typical moment of transition. No one can say where we are headed. The people of the democratic opposition have the feeling that we won. We taste the sweetness of our victory the same way the Communists, only yesterday our prison guards, taste the bitterness of their defeat. Yet, even as we are conscious of our victory, we feel that we are, in a strange way, losing. In Bulgaria the Communists have won the parliamentary elections and will govern the country, without losing their social legitimacy. In Romania the National Salvation Front, largely dominated by people from the old Communist bureaucracy, has won. In other countries democratic institutions seem shaky, and the political horizon is cloudy. The masquerade goes on: dozens of groups and parties are created, each announces similar slogans, each accuses its adversaries of all possible sins, and each declares itself representative of the national interest. Personal disputes are more important than disputes over values. Arguments over values are fiercer than arguments over ideas.

1. The author originally thought that the order of events in the transformation of communist society would be represented by which one of the following?

(A) A great political shock would break the totalitarian monopoly, leaving in its wake a civil society whose task would be to change the state-controlled market into a free economy.
(B) The transformation of the economy would destroy totalitarianism, after which a new and different social and political structure would be born.
(C) First the people would freely elect political representatives who would transform the economy, which would then undermine the totalitarian structure.
(D) The change to a democratic state would necessarily undermine totalitarianism, after which a new economic order would be created.
(E) The people's frustration would build until it spontaneously generated violent revolution, which would sentence society to years of anarchy and regression.

1. This is a description question, so you should locate the point in the passage from which it was drawn. It is the third paragraph. In lines 22–27, the author recalls his expectation that, by introducing the market system, the communist system would topple from within.

Be careful not to choose (A). It chronicles how the events actually occurred, not how they were *anticipated* to occur. (A) is baited with the words "great shock," "monopoly," and "civil society."

The answer is (B).

2. Beginning in the second paragraph, the author describes the complicated relationship between "freedom" and "democracy." In the author's view, which one of the following statements best reflects that relationship?

(A) A country can have freedom without having democracy.
(B) If a country has freedom, it necessarily has democracy.
(C) A country can have democracy without having freedom.
(D) A country can never have democracy if it has freedom.
(E) If a country has democracy, it cannot have freedom.

2. This is an extension question, so the answer must say more than what is said in the passage, without requiring a quantum leap in thought. The needed reference is *"Democracy is something more than freedom"* (lines 13–14). Since freedom can exist without democracy, freedom alone does not insure democracy.

The answer is (A).

3. From the passage, a reader could conclude that which one of the following best describes the author's attitude toward the events that have taken place in communist society?

(A) Relieved that at last the democratic order has surfaced.
(B) Clearly wants to return to the old order.
(C) Disappointed with the nature of the democracy that has emerged.
(D) Confident that a free economy will ultimately provide the basis for a true democracy.
(E) Surprised that communism was toppled through political rather than economic means.

3. This is a tone question. The key to answering this question is found in the closing comments. There the author states *"The masquerade goes on,"* referring to nascent democracies. So he has reservations about the newly emerging democracies.

Watch out!

Watch out for (E). Although it is supported by the passage, it is in a supporting paragraph. The ideas in a concluding paragraph take precedence over those in a supporting paragraph.

The answer is (C).

4. A cynic who has observed political systems in various countries would likely interpret the author's description of the situation at the end of the passage as

(A) evidence that society is still in the throws of the old totalitarian structure.
(B) a distorted description of the new political system.
(C) a necessary political reality that is a prelude to "democracy."
(D) a fair description of many democratic political systems.
(E) evidence of the baseness of people.

4. This is an application question. These are like extension questions, but they go well beyond what is stated in the passage. In this case we are asked to interpret the author's comments from a cynic's perspective. Because application questions go well beyond the passage, they are often difficult, as is this one.

Hint!

A cynic looks at reality from a negative perspective, usually with a sense of dark irony and hopelessness.

Don't make the mistake of choosing (E). Although a cynic is likely to make such a statement, it does not address the subject of the passage—political and economic systems. The passage is not about human nature, at least not directly.

The answer is (D).

5. Which one of the following does the author imply may have contributed to the difficulties involved in creating a new democratic order in eastern Europe?

   I. The people who existed under the totalitarian structure have not had the experience of "negotiating the empty space of freedom."
   II. Mistaking the order in which political, economic, and social restructuring would occur.
   III. Excessive self-interest among the new political activists.

   (A) I only
   (B) II only
   (C) I and III only
   (D) II and III only
   (E) I, II, and III

5. This is an extension question. Statement I is true. In lines 36–38, the author implies that the institutions of the new-born, free society were created in great pain because the people lacked experience. Statement II is true. Expectations that the market mechanisms would explode totalitarianism and usher in a new society were dashed, and having to readjust one's expectations certainly makes a situation more difficult. Finally, statement III is true. It summarizes the thrust of the passage's closing lines.

The answer is (E).

6. By stating "even as we are conscious of our victory, we feel that we are, in a strange way, losing" (lines 49–51) the author means that

   (A) some of the old governments are still unwilling to grant freedom at the individual level.
   (B) some of the new governments are not strong enough to exist as a single federation.
   (C) some of the new democratic governments are electing to retain the old political parties.
   (D) no new parties have been created to fill the vacuum created by the victory of freedom.
   (E) some of the new governments are reverting to communism.

6. This is a hybrid extension and description question. Because it refers to a specific point in the passage, you must read a few sentences before and after it. The answer can be found in lines 52–62.

The answer is (C).

Exercise

Directions: This passage is followed by a group of questions to be answered based on what is stated or implied in the passage. For some questions, more than one choice could conceivably answer the question. However, choose the best answer; the one that most accurately and completely answers the question.

In the United States the per capita costs of schooling have risen almost as fast as the cost of medical treatment. But increased treatment by both doctors and teachers has shown steadily declining results. Medical expenses concentrated on those above forty-five have doubled several times over a period of forty years with a resulting 3 percent increase in the life expectancy of men. The increase in educational expenditures has produced even stranger results; otherwise President Nixon could not have been moved this spring to promise that every child shall soon have the "Right to Read" before leaving school.

In the United States it would take eighty billion dollars per year to provide what educators regard as equal treatment for all in grammar and high school. This is well over twice the $36 billion now being spent. Independent cost projections prepared at HEW and at the University of Florida indicate that by 1974 the comparable figures will be $107 billion as against the $45 billion now projected, and these figures wholly omit the enormous costs of what is called "higher education," for which demand is growing even faster. The United States, which spent nearly eighty billion dollars in 1969 for "defense," including its deployment in Vietnam, is obviously too poor to provide equal schooling. The President's committee for the study of school finance should ask not how to support or how to trim such increasing costs, but how they can be avoided.

Equal obligatory schooling must be recognized as at least economically unfeasible. In Latin America the amount of public money spent on each graduate student is between 350 and 1,500 times the amount spent on the median citizen (that is, the citizen who holds the middle ground between the poorest and the richest). In the United States the discrepancy is smaller, but the discrimination is keener. The richest parents, some 10 percent, can afford private education for their children and help them to benefit from foundation grants. But in addition they obtain ten times the per capita amount of public funds if this is compared with the per capita expenditure made on the children of the 10 percent who are poorest. The principal reasons for this are that rich children stay longer in school, that a year in a university is disproportionately more expensive than a year in high school, and that most private universities depend—at least indirectly—on tax-derived finances.

Obligatory schooling inevitably polarizes a society; it also grades the nations of the world according to an international caste system. Countries are rated like castes whose educational dignity is determined by the average years of schooling of its citizens, a rating which is closely related to per capita gross national product, and much more painful.

1. Which one of the following best expresses the main idea of the passage?

   (A) The educational shortcomings of the United States, in contrast to those of Latin America, are merely the result of poor allocation of available resources.
   (B) Both education and medical care are severely underfunded.
   (C) Defense spending is sapping funds which would be better spent in education.
   (D) Obligatory schooling must be scrapped if the goal of educational equality is to be realized.
   (E) Obligatory education does not and cannot provide equal education.

2. The author most likely would agree with which one of the following solutions to the problems presented by obligatory education?

(A) Education should not be obligatory at all.
(B) Education should not be obligatory for those who cannot afford it.
(C) More money should be diverted to education for the poorest.
(D) Countries should cooperate to establish common minimal educational standards.
(E) Future spending should be capped.

3. According to the passage, education is like health care in all of the following ways EXCEPT:

(A) It has reached a point of diminishing returns, increased spending no longer results in significant improvement.
(B) It has an inappropriate "more is better" philosophy.
(C) It is unfairly distributed between rich and poor.
(D) The amount of money being spent on older students is increasing.
(E) Its cost has increased nearly as fast.

4. Why does the author consider the results from increased educational expenditures to be "even stranger" than those from increased medical expenditures?

(A) The aging of the population should have had an impact only on medical care, not on education.
(B) The "Right to Read" should be a bare minimum, not a Presidential ideal.
(C) Educational spending has shown even poorer results than spending on health care, despite greater increases.
(D) Education has become even more discriminatory than health care.
(E) It inevitably polarizes society.

5. Which one of the following most accurately characterizes the author's attitude with respect to obligatory schooling?

(A) qualified admiration
(B) critical
(C) neutral
(D) ambivalent
(E) resentful

6. By stating "In Latin America the amount of public money spent on each graduate student is between 350 and 1,500 times the amount spent on the median citizen" and "In the United States the discrepancy is smaller" the author implies that

(A) equal education is possible in the United States but not in Latin America.
(B) equal education for all at the graduate level is an unrealistic ideal.
(C) educational spending is more efficient in the United States.
(D) higher education is more expensive than lower education both in Latin America and in the United States, but more so in Latin America.
(E) underfunding of lower education is a world-wide problem.

Answers and Solutions to Exercise

1. The answer to a main idea question will summarize the passage, without going beyond it.

(A) fails to meet these criteria because it makes a false claim. The second sentence of paragraph III implies that the discrepancy in allocation of funds is greater in Latin America. Besides, Latin America is mentioned only in passing, so this is not the main idea.

(B) also makes a false claim. The author implies that increased funding for education is irrelevant, if not counterproductive. In fact, the sentence *"The President's committee for the study of school finance should ask not how to support or how to trim such increasing costs, but how they can be avoided"* implies that he thinks an increase in funding would be counterproductive.

(C) is implied by the sentence *"The United States . . . is obviously too poor to provide equal schooling,"* but the author does not fully develop this idea. Besides, he implies that the problem is not financial.

(D) is the second-best answer-choice. The answer to a main idea question should sum up the passage, not make a conjecture about it. Clearly the author has serious reservations about obligatory schooling, but at no point does he state or imply that it should be scrapped. He may believe that it can be modified, or he may be resigned to the fact that, for other reasons, it is necessary. We don't know.

Finally, (E) aptly summarizes the passage, without going beyond it. The key to seeing this is the opening to paragraph three, *"Equal obligatory schooling must be recognized as at least economically unfeasible."* In other words, regardless of any other failings, it cannot succeed economically and therefore cannot provide equal education.

2. This is an application question. These questions tend to be rather difficult, though this one is not. To answer an application question, put yourself in the author's place. If you were arguing his case, which of the solutions would you advocate?

As to (A), although we rejected the recommendation that obligatory education be eliminated as Question 1's answer, it is the answer to Question 2. The author does not merely imply that obligatory education has some shortcomings; he suggests that it is fundamentally flawed. Again this is made clear by the opening to paragraph three, *"Equal obligatory schooling must be recognized as at least economically unfeasible."* Still, there is a possible misunderstanding here: perhaps the author believes that obligatory education is a noble but unrealistic idea. This possibility, however, is dispelled by the closing paragraph in which he states that obligatory education polarizes society and sets up a caste system. Obviously, such a system, if this is true, should be discarded. The answer is (A).

The other choices can be easily dismissed. (B) is incorrect because nothing in the passage suggests that the author would advocate a solution that would polarize society even more. Indeed, at the end of paragraph three, he suggests that the rich already get more than their fair share.

(C) is incorrect because it contradicts the author. Paragraph two is dedicated to showing that the United States is too poor to provide equal schooling. You can't divert money you don't have.

(D) is incorrect. It reads too much into the last paragraph.

Finally, (E) is the second-best answer-choice. Although the author probably believes that future spending should be restrained or capped, this understates the thrust of his argument. However, he might offer this as a compromise to his opponents.

3. This is a description question, so we must find the place from which it is drawn. It is the first paragraph. The sentence *"But increased treatment by both doctors and teachers has shown steadily declining results"* shows that both have reached a point of diminishing returns. This eliminates (A) and (B). Next, the passage states *"Medical expenses concentrated on those above forty-five have doubled several times"* (first paragraph) and that the demand and costs of higher education are growing faster than the demand and costs of elementary and high school education. This eliminates (D). Next, the opening to the passage states that the costs of education *"have risen almost as fast as the cost of medical treatment."* This eliminates (E). Hence, by process of elimination, the answer is (C). We should, however, verify this. In paragraph three, the author does state that there is a "keen" discrepancy in the funding of education between rich and poor, but a survey of the passage shows that at no point does he mention that this is also the case with health care.

4. This is an extension question. We are asked to interpret a statement by the author. The needed reference is the closing sentence to paragraph one. Remember: extension questions require you to go beyond the passage, so the answer won't be explicitly stated in the reference—we will have to interpret it.

The implication of President Nixon's promise is that despite increased educational funding many children cannot even read when they graduate from school. Hence the answer is (B).

Don't make the mistake of choosing (C). Although at first glance this is a tempting inference, it would be difficult to compare the results of education and medical care directly (how would we do so?). Regardless, the opening line to the passage states that educational costs have risen "almost as fast" as medical costs, not faster.

(A) is incorrect because the passage never mentions the aging of the population. The same is true for (D).

Many students who cannot solve this question choose (E)—don't. It uses as bait language from the passage, *"inevitably polarizes a society."* Note: The phrase "Right to Read" in (B) is not a same language trap; it is merely part of a paraphrase of the passage. The correct answer to an extension question will often both paraphrase and extend a passage statement but will not quote it directly, as in (E).

5. Like most tone questions this one is rather easy. Although choice (A) is a measured response, the author clearly does not admire the obligatory school system. This eliminates (A); it also eliminates (C) and (D). Of the two remaining choices, (B) is the measured response, and it is the answer. Although the author strongly opposes obligatory schooling, "resentful" is too strong and too personal. A scholar would never directly express resentment or envy, even if that is his true feeling.

6. This is another extension question. By stating that the amount of funding spent on graduate students is more than 350 times the amount spent on the average citizen, the author implies that it would be impossible to equalize the funding. Hence the answer is (B).

None of the other choices have any real merit. (A) is incorrect because the import of the passage is that the rich get better schooling and more public funds in the United States and therefore discrimination is "keener" here (lines 38–40).

(C) and (D) are incorrect because they are neither mentioned nor implied by the passage.

(E) is the second-best choice. Although this is implied by the numbers given, it has little to do with the primary purpose of the passage—to show that obligatory education is perhaps not such a good idea.

Pivotal Words

As mentioned before, each passage contains 400 to 600 words and only six to eight questions, so you will not be tested on most of the material in the passage. Your best reading strategy, therefore, is to identify the places from which questions will most likely be drawn and concentrate your attention there.

Pivotal words can help in this regard. Following are the most common pivotal words.

PIVOTAL WORDS

But	**Although**
However	**Yet**
Despite	**Nevertheless**
Nonetheless	**Except**
In contrast	**Even though**

As you may have noticed, these words indicate contrast. Many are also the counter-premise indicators from the argument section. Pivotal words warn that the author is about to either make a U-turn or introduce a counter-premise (concession to a minor counterpoint). However, because passages are much longer than arguments, the author has the space to elaborate on the concession. So with passages, counter-premises tend to be a paragraph, or more, long.

In fact, because the author has more space to elaborate on his ideas, pivotal words are more likely to introduce a new direction than a concession.

The following are two typical outlines for reading passages:

Premise	**Premise**
Conclusion	**Premise**
Premise	**Pivotal Word**
Counter-premise	**Continuation of Pivotal Word**
Restatement of Conclusion	**Conclusion**

Pivotal words mark natural places for questions to be drawn. At a pivotal word, the author changes direction. The LSAT writers form questions at these junctures to test whether you turned with the author or you continued to go straight. Rarely do the LSAT writers let a pivotal word pass without drawing a question from its sentence.

As you read a passage, circle the pivotal words and refer to them when answering the questions.

Let's apply this theory to the passage on criminal justice. For easy reference, the passage is reprinted here in the left-hand column, with explanations in the right-hand column. The pivotal words are marked in bold.

There are two major systems of criminal procedure in the modern world—the adversarial and the inquisitorial. The former is associated with common law tradition and the latter with civil law tradition. Both systems were historically preceded by the system of private vengeance in which the victim of a crime fashioned his own remedy and administered it privately, either personally or through an agent. The vengeance system was a system of self-help, the essence of which was captured in the slogan "an eye for an eye, a tooth for a tooth." The modern adversarial system is only one historical step removed from the private vengeance system and still retains some of its characteristic features. Thus, for example, **even though** the right to institute criminal action has now been extended to all members of society and **even though** the police department has taken over the pretrial investigative functions on behalf of the prosecution, the adversarial system still leaves the defendant to conduct his own pretrial investigation. The trial is still viewed as a duel between two adversaries, refereed by a judge who, at the beginning of the trial has no knowledge of the investigative background of the case. In the final analysis the adversarial system of criminal procedure symbolizes and regularizes the punitive combat.

By contrast, the inquisitorial system begins historically where the adversarial system stopped its development. It is two historical steps removed from the system of private vengeance. Therefore, from the standpoint of legal anthropology, it is historically superior to the adversarial system. Under the inquisitorial system the public investigator has the duty to investigate not just on behalf of the prosecutor **but also** on behalf of the defendant. Additionally, the public prosecutor has the duty to present to the court not only evidence that may lead to the conviction of the defendant **but also** evidence that may lead to his exoneration. This system mandates that both parties permit full pretrial discovery of the evidence in their possession. Finally, in an effort to make the trial less like a duel between two adversaries, the inquisitorial system mandates that the judge take an active part in the conduct of the trial, with a role that is both directive and protective.

Fact-finding is at the heart of the inquisitorial system. This system operates on the philosophical premise that in a criminal case the crucial factor is not the legal rule but the facts of the case and that the goal of the entire procedure is to experimentally recreate for the court the commission of the alleged crime.

Even though—Here "even though" is introducing a concession. In the previous sentence, the author stated that the adversarial system is only one step removed from the private vengeance system. The author uses the two concessions as a hedge against potential criticism that he did not consider that the adversarial system has extended the right to institute criminal action to all members of society and that police departments now perform the pretrial investigation. But the author then states that the adversarial system still leaves the defendant to conduct his own pretrial investigation. This marks a good place from which to draw a question. Many people will misinterpret the two concessions as evidence that the adversarial system is two steps removed from the private vengeance system.

By contrast—In this case the pivotal word is not introducing a concession. Instead it indicates a change in thought: now the author is going to discuss the other criminal justice system. This is a natural place to test whether the student has made the transition and whether he will attribute the properties soon to be introduced to the inquisitorial system, not the adversarial system.

But also—In both places, "but also" indicates neither concession nor change in thought. Instead it is part of the coordinating conjunction "not only . . . but also . . . ." Rather than indicating contrast, it emphasizes the second element of the pair.

Let's see how these pivotal words can help answer the questions in the last section. The first is from the Description Section:

Example:

According to the passage, the inquisitorial system differs from the adversarial system in that

(A) it does not make the defendant solely responsible for gathering evidence for his case
(B) it does not require the police department to work on behalf of the prosecution
(C) it does not allow the victim the satisfaction of private vengeance
(D) it requires the prosecution to drop a weak case
(E) a defendant who is innocent would prefer to be tried under the inquisitorial system

The pivotal phrase "by contrast" flags the second paragraph as the place to begin looking. The pivotal phrase "but also" introduces the answer—namely that the prosecutor must also investigate "on behalf of the defendant." The answer is (A).

The next question is from the Writing Techniques Section:

Example:

Which one of the following best describes the organization of the passage?

(A) Two systems of criminal justice are compared and contrasted, and one is deemed to be better than the other.
(B) One system of criminal justice is presented as better than another. Then evidence is presented to support that claim.
(C) Two systems of criminal justice are analyzed, and one specific example is examined in detail.
(D) A set of examples is presented. Then a conclusion is drawn from them.
(E) The inner workings of the criminal justice system are illustrated by using two systems.

The pivotal phrase "by contrast" gives this question away. The author is comparing and contrasting two criminal justice systems, which the opening pivotal word introduces. Hence the answer is (A).

For our final example, consider the question from the Extension Section:

Example:

The author views the prosecution's role in the inquisitorial system as being

(A) an advocate for both society and the defendant
(B) solely responsible for starting a trial
(C) a protector of the legal rule
(D) an investigator only
(E) an aggressive but fair investigator

The information needed to answer this question is introduced by the pivotal phrase, "but also." There it is stated that the prosecutor must present evidence that may exonerate the defendant; that is, he must act fairly. The answer is (E).

Mentor Exercise

Directions: This passage is followed by a group of questions to be answered based on what is stated or implied in the passage. For some questions, more than one choice could conceivably answer the question. However, choose the best answer; the one that most accurately and completely answers the question. Hints, insights, and answers are given in the right-hand column.

The premise with which the multiculturalists begin is unexceptional: that it is important to recognize and to celebrate the wide range of cultures that exist in the United States. In what sounds like a reflection of traditional American pluralism, the multiculturalists argue that we must recognize difference, that difference is legitimate; in its kindlier versions, multiculturalism represents the discovery on the part of minority groups that they can play a part in molding the larger culture even as they are molded by it. And on the campus multiculturalism, defined more locally as the need to recognize cultural variations among students, has tried with some success to talk about how a racially and ethnically diverse student body can enrich everyone's education.

Phillip Green, a political scientist at Smith and a thoughtful proponent of multiculturalism, notes that for a significant portion of the students the politics of identity is all-consuming. Students he says "are unhappy with the thin gruel of rationalism. They require a therapeutic curriculum to overcome not straightforward racism but ignorant stereotyping."

(1) But multiculturalism's hard-liners, who seem to make up the majority of the movement, damn as racism any attempt to draw the myriad of American groups into a common American culture. For these multiculturalists, differences are absolute, irreducible, intractable—occasions not for understanding but for separation. The multiculturalist, it turns out, is not especially interested in the great American hyphen, in the syncretistic (and therefore naturally tolerant) identities that allow Americans to belong to more than a single culture, to be both particularists and universalists.

The time-honored American mixture of assimilation and traditional allegiance is denounced as a danger to racial and gender authenticity. This is an extraordinary reversal of the traditional liberal commitment to a "truth" that transcends parochialisms. In the new race/class/gender formation, universality is replaced by, among other things, feminist science Nubian numerals (as part of an Afro-centric science), and what Marilyn Frankenstein of the University of Massachusetts-Boston describes as "ethno-mathematics," in which the cultural basis of counting comes to the fore.

There are two critical pivotal words in this passage—(1) **But**, and (2) **however**.

(1) **But**. Until this point, the author did not reveal his feeling toward multiculturalism. He presented an objective, if not positive, view of the movement. However, "**But**" introduced an abrupt change in direction (a U-turn). Before he talked about the "kindlier" multiculturalism—to which he appears to be sympathetic. Now he talks about "hard-line" multiculturalism, which he implies is intolerant and divisive.

The pivotal word "**but**" doesn't just change the direction of the passage, it introduces the main idea: that multiculturalism has become an extreme and self-contradictory movement.

The multiculturalists insist on seeing all perspectives as tainted by the perceiver's particular point of view. Impartial knowledge, they argue, is not possible, because ideas are simply the expression of individual identity, or of the unspoken but inescapable assumptions that are inscribed in a culture or a language. The problem, **(2) however,** with this warmed-over Nietzscheanism is that it threatens to leave no ground for anybody to stand on. So the multiculturalists make a leap, necessary for their own intellectual survival, and proceed to argue that there are some categories, such as race and gender, that do in fact embody an unmistakable knowledge of oppression. Victims are at least epistemologically lucky. Objectivity is a mask for oppression. And so an appalled former 1960s radical complained to me that self-proclaimed witches were teaching classes on witchcraft. "They're not teaching students how to think," she said, "they're telling them what to believe."

(2) **however**. This is the second critical pivotal word. The author opened this paragraph by presenting the multiculturalist's view; now he will criticize their positions.

1. Which one of the following ideas would a multiculturalist NOT believe?

   (A) That we should recognize and celebrate the differences among the many cultures in the United States.
   (B) That we can never know the "truth" because "truth" is always shaped by one's culture.
   (C) That "difference" is more important than "sameness."
   (D) That a school curriculum should be constructed to compensate for institutionalized racism.
   (E) That different cultures should work to assimilate themselves into the mainstream culture so that eventually there will be no excuse for racism.

1. The sentence introduced by the pivotal word "**But**" gives away the answer to this question.

The answer is (E).

2. According to a hard-line multiculturalist, which one of the following groups is most likely to know the "truth" about political reality?

   (A) Educated people who have learned how to see reality from many different perspectives.
   (B) A minority group that has suffered oppression at the hands of the majority.
   (C) High government officials who have privileged access to secret information.
   (D) Minorities who through their education have risen above the socioeconomic position occupied by most members of their ethnic group.
   (E) Political scientists who have thoroughly studied the problem.

2. This is a rather hard extension question.

Hint!

A subjugated minority group has at least the "unmistakable knowledge of oppression" (last paragraph).

Watch out!

Don't make the mistake of choosing (D). Upper class minorities have simply exchanged one tainted point of view for another—and probably a more tainted one since the adopted position does not allow for knowledge of "oppression."

The answer is (B).

3. The author states that in a "kindlier version" of multiculturalism, minorities discover "that they can play a part in molding the larger culture even as they are molded by it." If no new ethnic groups were incorporated into the American culture for many centuries to come, which one of the following would be the most probable outcome of this "kindlier version"?

(A) At some point in the future, there would be only one culture with no observable ethnic differences.
(B) Eventually the dominant culture would overwhelm the minority cultures, who would then lose their ethnic identities.
(C) The multiplicity of ethnic groups would remain but the characteristics of the different ethnic groups would change.
(D) The smaller ethnic groups would remain, and they would retain their ethnic heritage.
(E) The minority cultures would eventually overwhelm the dominant culture, which would then lose its identity.

3. This application question clearly goes well beyond the passage.

If no new ethnic groups were incorporated into the American culture, then the interplay between the larger and smaller groups would continue, with both groups changing, until there would be only one common (and different from any original) group.

The answer is (A).

4. The author speaks about the "politics of identity" that Phillip Green, a political scientist at Smith, notes is all-consuming for many of the students. Considering the subject of the passage, which one of the following best describes what the author means by "the politics of identity"?

(A) The attempt to discover individual identities through political action
(B) The political agenda that aspires to create a new pride of identity for Americans
(C) The current obsession for therapy groups that help individuals discover their inner selves
(D) The trend among minority students to discover their identities in their ethnic groups rather than in their individuality
(E) The increased political activism of minorities on college campuses

4. This is an extension question. You may find the classification of the these problems as "application" or "extension" to be somewhat arbitrary or even disagree with a particular classification. As mentioned before, application and extension questions differ only in degree. Question 3 is clearly an application question; by asking you to make a conjecture about the future, it goes well beyond the passage. How to classify Question 4, however, is not so clear. I classified it as an extension question because it seems to be asking merely for the author's true meaning of the phrase "the politics of identity." That is, it stays within the context of the passage.

Don't be led astray by (B); it uses the word "political" to tempt you. Although it is perhaps a good description, it is not within the context of the passage, which focuses on ethnic politics, not national identities through "roots."

The answer is (D).

5. Which one of the following best describes the attitude of the writer toward the multicultural movement?

(A) Tolerant. It may have some faults, but it is well-meaning overall.
(B) Critical. A formerly admirable movement has been taken over by radical intellectuals.
(C) Disinterested. He seems to be presenting an objective report.
(D) Enthusiastic. The author embraces the multiculturalist movement and is trying to present it in a favorable light.
(E) Ambivalent. He is simultaneously attracted and repulsed by the movement.

5. Like most tone questions this one is rather easy.

To get a feel for the author's attitude, check the adjectives he chooses. The author starts by introducing the "kindlier" version of multiculturalism and describes a proponent of multiculturalism, Phillip Green, as "thoughtful." Then he introduces the "hard liners" who "damn" any attempt at cultural assimilation. He feels that the movement has changed; that it has gone bad.

The answer is (B).

6. "Multiculturalist relativism" is the notion that there is no such thing as impartial or objective knowledge. The author seems to be grounding his criticism of this notion on

(A) the clear evidence that science has indeed discovered "truths" that have been independent of both language and culture.
(B) the conclusion that relativism leaves one with no clear notions of any one thing that is true.
(C) the absurdity of claiming that knowledge of oppression is more valid than knowledge of scientific facts.
(D) the agreement among peoples of all cultures as to certain undeniable truths—e.g., when the sky is clear, day is warmer than night.
(E) the fact that "truth" is not finitely definable and therefore that any discussion of impartial or objective truth is moot.

6. This is an another extension question.

Hint!

The answer can be derived from the pivotal sentence containing "however" (2).

The answer is (B).

Exercise

Directions: This passage is followed by a group of questions to be answered based on what is stated or implied in the passage. For some questions, more than one choice could conceivably answer the question. However, choose the best answer; the one that most accurately and completely answers the question.

According to usage and conventions which are at last being questioned but have by no means been overcome, the social presence of a woman is different in kind from that of a man. A man's presence is dependent upon the promise of power which he embodies. If the promise is large and credible his presence is striking. If it is small or incredible, he is found to have little presence. The promised power may be moral, physical, temperamental, economic, social, sexual—but its object is always exterior to the man. A man's presence suggests what he is capable of doing to you or for you. His presence may be fabricated, in the sense that he pretends to be capable of what he is not. But the pretense is always toward a power which he exercises on others.

By contrast, a woman's presence expresses her own attitude to herself, and defines what can and cannot be done to her. Her presence is manifest in her gestures, voices, opinions, expressions, clothes, chosen surroundings, taste—indeed there is nothing she can do which does not contribute to her presence. Presence for a woman is so intrinsic to her person that men tend to think of it as an almost physical emanation, a kind of heat or smell or aura.

To be born a woman has been to be born, within an allotted and confined space, into the keeping of men. The social presence of women has developed as a result of their ingenuity in living under such tutelage within such a limited space. But this has been at the cost of a woman's self being split into two. A woman must continually watch herself. Whilst she is walking across a room or whilst she is weeping at the death of her father, she can scarcely avoid envisaging herself walking or weeping. From earliest childhood she has been taught and persuaded to survey herself continually.

And so she comes to consider the *surveyor* and the *surveyed* within her as the two constituent yet always distinct elements of her identity as a woman.

She has to survey everything she is and everything she does because how she appears to others, and ultimately how she appears to men, is of crucial importance for what is normally thought of as the success of her life. Her own sense of being in herself is supplanted by a sense of being appreciated as herself by another. Men survey women before treating them. Consequently how a woman appears to a man can determine how she will be treated. To acquire some control over this process, women must contain it and internalize it. That part of a woman's self which is the surveyor treats the part which is the surveyed so as to demonstrate to others how her whole self would like to be treated. And this exemplary treatment of herself by herself constitutes her presence. Every woman's presence regulates what is and is not "permissible" within her presence. Every one of her actions—whatever its direct purpose or motivation—is also read as an indication of how she would like to be treated. If a woman throws a glass on the floor, this is an example of how she treats her own emotion of anger and so of how she would wish to be treated by others. If a man does the same, his action is only read as an expression of his anger. If a woman makes a good joke this is an example of how she treats the joker in herself and accordingly of how she as joker-woman would like to be treated by others. Only a man can make a good joke for its own sake.

1. According to "usage and conventions," appearance is NECESSARILY a part of reality for
   (A) men
   (B) women
   (C) both men and women
   (D) neither men nor women
   (E) men always and women occasionally

2. In analyzing a woman's customary "social presence," the author hopes to
   (A) justify and reinforce it.
   (B) understand and explain it.
   (C) expose and discredit it.
   (D) demonstrate and criticize it.
   (E) sanction and promote it.

3. It can be inferred from the passage that a woman with a Ph.D. in psychology who gives a lecture to a group of students is probably MOST concerned with
   (A) whether her students learn the material.
   (B) what the males in the audience think of her.
   (C) how she comes off as a speaker in psychology.
   (D) finding a husband.
   (E) whether a man challenges her.

4. The passage portrays women as
   (A) victims
   (B) liars
   (C) actresses
   (D) politicians
   (E) ignorant

5. Which one of the following is NOT implied by the passage?
   (A) Women have split personalities.
   (B) Men are not image-conscious.
   (C) Good looks are more important to women than to men.
   (D) A man is defined by what he does, whereas a woman is defined by how she appears.
   (E) A man's presence is extrinsic, whereas a woman's is intrinsic.

6. The primary purpose of the passage is to
   (A) compare and contrast woman's presence and place in society with that of man's.
   (B) discuss a woman's presence and place in society and to contrast it with a man's presence and place.
   (C) illustrate how a woman is oppressed by society.
   (D) explain why men are better than women at telling jokes.
   (E) illustrate how both men and women are hurt by sexism.

Answers and Solutions to Exercise

This passage is filled with pivotal words, some of which are crucial to following the author's train of thought. We will discuss only the critical pivotal words. The first pivotal word, "but" (line 15), introduces a distinction between a man's presence and a woman's: a man's is external, a woman's internal. The second pivotal word, "by contrast," introduces the main idea of the passage. The author opened the passage by defining a man's presence; now she will define a woman's presence. The last pivotal word, "but" (lines 32–33), also introduces a change in thought. Now the author discusses how a woman's presence has split her identity into two parts—the *surveyor* and the *surveyed*. By closing with, *"Only a man can make a good joke for its own sake,"* the author is saying a man can concentrate on the punch line, whereas a woman must concentrate on its delivery.

1. This is a description question. The needed reference is contained in the second paragraph: *"there is nothing [a woman] can do which does not contribute to her presence. Presence for a woman is intrinsic to her person . . ."* If something is intrinsic to you, then it necessarily is part of your reality. Hence the answer is (B).

Note the question refers to "usage and conventions" discussed in the passage, not to any other way of viewing the world—such as your own!

2. Although the author opens the passage with a hint that she doesn't like the customary sex roles (*"conventions which are at last being questioned"*), the rest of the passage is explanatory and analytical. So (C) and (D) are too strong. The answer is (B).

3. This is an application question; we are asked to apply what we have learned from the passage to a hypothetical situation.

The best way to analyze this question is to compare the speaker to a joke-teller. The passage paints a portrait of a woman as most concerned with the image she presents to the world. She is not concerned with the speech or joke, *per se*, rather with how she delivers it. *"Only a man can make a good joke for its own sake."* The answer is (C).

Don't make the mistake of choosing (B). Although men have, in the main, molded her self-image, she has gone beyond that; she now measures herself in the abstract: "how will I come off to the ultimately critical audience?" and not "how will actual audience members see me?"

4. This description question is a bit tricky because the second-best choice is rather good. Women are concerned with the image they present, so they cannot be themselves—they must act their part. Hence the answer is (C).

You may have been tempted by (A). According to the passage, women are thrown into the role of an actress, "into the keeping of men." So, like victims, they are not responsible for their social position. However, nothing in the passage directly suggests that it is wrong for women to be in this position or that women attempt to refuse this role. According to the passage, therefore, women are not, strictly speaking, victims. (*Victim* means "someone not in control of something injurious happening to him or her.")

5. This is an extension question. The passage discusses the fact that a man may fabricate his image (line 13). This suggests that men *are* conscious of their images, but the passage also states that image is not intrinsic to their personalities, as it is for women. The answer is (B).

6. This is a rather hard main idea question because the second-best choice, (A), is quite good.

The passage does open with a discussion of a man's presence. But in paragraph two the pivotal phrase "by contrast" introduces a woman's presence; from there the discussion of a man's presence is only in regard to how it affects a woman's. So a woman's presence is the main idea; contrasting it with a man's presence is secondary. (B) gives the proper emphasis to these two purposes.

The Three Step Method

Now we apply all the methods we have learned to another passage. First let's summarize the reading techniques we have developed and express them in a three-step attack strategy for reading LSAT passages:

THE THREE STEP METHOD

1. **(Optional) Preview the first sentence of each paragraph.**

2. **Read the passage at a faster than usual pace (but not to the point that comprehension suffers). Stay alert to places from which any of the six questions might be drawn:**

   a.) Main Idea
   b.) Description
   c.) Writing Technique
   d.) Extension
   e.) Application
   f.) Tone

3. **Annotate the passage and circle any pivotal words. Then use them as reference points when answering the questions. Following are some common annotation marks (you may want to add to this list):**

   A = **A**uthor's **A**ttitude
   C = **C**omplex point
   ? = **Question?** I don't understand this part (you can bet that this area will be important to *at least* one question)
   SP = **S**ignificant **p**oint
   ! = **Exclamation!** Strong opinion
   W = **W**eak, questionable or unsupported argument or premise

Notice how the three-step process proceeds from the general to the specific. The **first step**, previewing the first sentences, gives you an overview of the passage. This will help you answer main idea questions. The **second step**, reading the passage at a slightly faster than usual pace, brings out the passage's structure (i.e., does the author compare and contrast, show cause and effect, etc.). Further, it will clue you into the author's attitude (positive, negative, objective, indifferent, etc.). Finally, the **third step**, circling pivotal words and annotating, will solidify your understanding of the passage and highlight specific details.

The three step method should be viewed as a dynamic, and not a static, process. The steps often overlap and they are not performed in strict order. Comprehending a passage is an ebb and flow process. Analyzing a passage to understand how it is constructed can be compared to dismantling an engine to understand how it was built—you may stop occasionally and reassemble parts of it to review what you just did; then proceed again to dismantle more. Likewise, when reading a passage, you may first read and annotate a paragraph (disassembling it) and then go back and skim to reassemble it. During this process, comprehension proceeds from the global to the specific. This can be represented by an inverted pyramid:

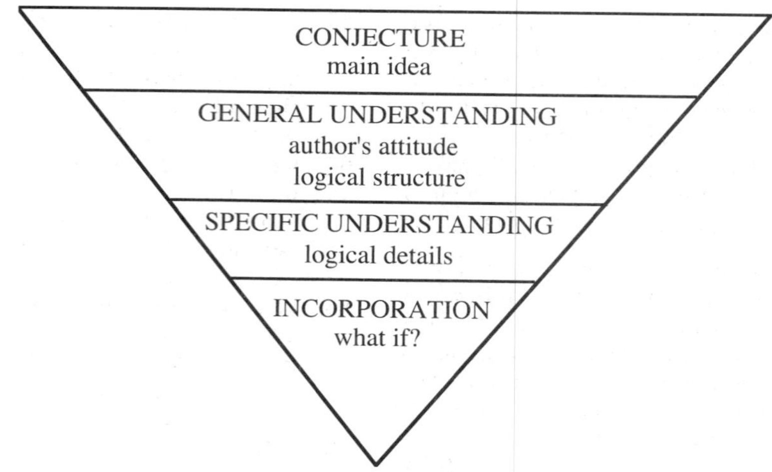

In the conjecture stage, we form a tentative main idea—one which we may have to modify or even reject as we read more deeply into the passage. In the general understanding stage, we develop a feel for the author's tone and discover the schema that she uses to present her ideas. In the specific understanding stage, we fill in the minor gaps in our understanding. Finally, in the incorporation stage, we integrate the ideas presented in the passage into our own thought process. We now understand the ideas sufficiently to defend them, apply them to other situations, or evaluate their validity in a hypothetical situation. Only with complete understanding of the passage can this be done.

Let's apply the three step method to the passage on the next page. Begin by previewing the first sentence of each paragraph:

The sentence *"That placebos can cure everything from dandruff to leprosy is well known"* implies that the passage is about placebos and that they are perhaps cure-alls.

The sentence *"Every drug tested would prove effective if special steps were not taken to neutralize the placebo effect"* gives the first bit of evidence supporting the topic sentence.

The sentence *"Most people feel that the lucky patients in a drug test get the experimental drug because the real drug provides them a chance to be cured"* might be introducing a counter-premise or pivotal point; we won't know until we read the passage.

The sentence *"Placebos regularly cure more than five percent of the patients and would cure considerably more if the doubts associated with the tests were eliminated"* provides more support for the topic sentence.

The sentence *"The actual curing power of placebos probably stems from the faith of the patient in the treatment"* explains why the topic sentence is true.

The sentence *"It may take a while to reach the ten percent level of cure because any newly established program will not have cultivated the word-of-mouth advertising needed to insure its success"* is hard to interpret. This does not help us.

The sentence *"Unfortunately, placebo treatment centers cannot operate as nonprofit businesses"* seems to be off the subject. Again, this does not help us.

In summary, although the last two sentences were not useful, we now have a good idea of what the passage is about: *how* and *why* placebos are effective. We now read the passage—looking for places from which any of the six questions might be drawn, circling the pivotal words, and annotating key points.

Passage begins on the next page. —>

That placebos can cure everything from dandruff to leprosy is well known. They have a long history of use by witch doctors, faith healers, and even modern physicians, all of whom refuse to admit their efficacy. Modern distribution techniques can bring this most potent of medicines to the aid of everyone, not just those lucky enough to receive placebos in a medical testing program.

Every drug tested would prove effective if special steps were not taken to neutralize the placebo effect. This is why drug tests give half the patients the new medication and half a harmless substitute. These tests prove the value of placebos because approximately five percent of the patients taking them are cured even though the placebos are made from substances that have been carefully selected to be useless.

Most people feel that the lucky patients in a drug test get the experimental drug because the real drug provides them a chance to be cured. **(1) Yet** analysis shows that patients getting the placebo may be the lucky ones because they may be cured without risking any adverse effects the new drug may have. Furthermore, the drug may well be found worthless and to have severe side effects. No harmful side effects result from placebos.

Placebos regularly cure more than five percent of the patients and would cure considerably more if the doubts associated with the tests were eliminated. Cures are principally due to the patient's faith, **(2) yet** the patient must have doubts knowing that he may or may not be given the new drug, which itself may or may not prove to be an effective drug. Since he knows the probability of being given the true drug is about fifty percent, the placebo cure rate would be more than doubled by removing these doubts if cures are directly related to faith.

The actual curing power of placebos probably stems from the faith of the patient in the treatment. This suggests that cure rates in the ten percent range could be expected if patients are given placebos under the guise of a proven cure, even when patients know their problems are incurable.

It may take a while to reach the ten percent level of cure because any newly established program will not have cultivated the word-of-mouth advertising needed to insure its success. One person saying "I was told that my problem was beyond medical help, but they cured me," can direct countless people to the treatment with the required degree of faith. Furthermore, when only terminal illnesses are treated, those not cured tell no one of the failure.

Unfortunately, placebo treatment centers cannot operate as nonprofit businesses. The nonprofit idea was ruled out upon learning that the first rule of public medicine is never to give free medicine. Public health services know that medicine not paid for by patients is often not taken or not effective because the recipient feels the medicine is worth just what it cost him. **(3) Even though** the patients would not know they were taking sugar pills, the placebos cost so little that the patients would have no faith in the treatment. Therefore, though it is against higher principles, treatment centers must charge high fees for placebo treatments. This sacrifice of principles, however, is a small price to pay for the greater good of the patients.

The first item is a main idea question:

1. Which one of the following best expresses the main idea of the passage?

(A) Placebo treatment is a proven tool of modern medicine and its expanded use would benefit society's health.
(B) Because modern technology allows for distribution of drugs on a massive scale, the proven efficacy of the placebo is no longer limited to a privileged few.
(C) The curative power of the placebo is so strong that it should replace proven drugs because the patients receiving the placebo will then be cured without risking any adverse side effects.
(D) The price of placebo treatment must be kept artificially high because patients have little faith in inexpensive treatments.
(E) Semi-placebos—drugs that contain only a small amount of the usual dosage—are even more effective curatives than either the placebo or the full-strength drug.

As we found by previewing the topic sentences, the passage is about the efficacy of placebo treatment. Careful reading shows that the passage also promotes expanded use of placebos. Hence the answer is (A).

The other choices can be quickly dismissed. (B) is the second-best choice: the author *does* mention that modern distribution techniques can bring the curative power of placebos to everyone, but he does not fully develop that idea. This answer-choice is tempting because it is contained in the topic paragraph. As to (C), it overstates the author's claim. Although in the third paragraph, the author states that those who receive the placebos may be the lucky ones, this is referring to new, unproven drugs, not to established drugs. As to (D), it, like (B), is mentioned in the passage but is not fully developed. It's tempting because it appears in the last paragraph—a natural place for the conclusion. Finally, (E) is neither mentioned nor implied by the passage.

The second item is an application question.

2. Which one of the following is most analogous to the idea presented in the last paragraph?

(A) Buying a television at a discount house
(B) Making an additional pledge to charity
(C) Choosing the most expensive dishwasher in a manufacturer's line
(D) Waiting until a book comes out in paperback
(E) Contributing one dollar to the Presidential Campaign fund on your tax return

The information needed to answer this question is heralded by the pivotal phrase "Even though" (lines 62–65). The implication of that sentence is "you get what you pay for." This would motivate one to buy the most expensive item in a manufacturer's line. Hence the answer is (C).

The third item is a description question.

3. According to the passage, when testing a new drug medical researchers give half of the subjects the test drug and half a placebo because

(A) proper statistical controls should be observed.
(B) this method reduces the risk of maiming too many subjects if the drug should prove to be harmful.
(C) all drugs which are tested would prove to be effective otherwise.
(D) most drugs would test positively otherwise.
(E) the cost of dispensing drugs to all the patients is prohibitive.

Since this is a description question, you must refer to the passage to answer it. The opening sentence to paragraph two contains the needed information. That sentence states "Every drug would prove effective if special steps were not taken to neutralize the placebo effect." Hence the answer is (C).

Choice (D) illustrates why you must refer directly to the passage to answer a description question: unless you have a remarkable memory, you will be unsure whether the statement was that **all** or that **most** drugs would prove effective.

The fourth item is an extension question.

4. It can be inferred from the passage that the author might

   (A) believe that the benefits of a placebo treatment program that lead patients to believe they were getting a real drug would outweigh the moral issue of lying.
   (B) support legislation outlawing the use of placebos.
   (C) open up a medical clinic that would treat patients exclusively through placebo methods.
   (D) believe that factors other than faith are responsible for the curative power of the placebo.
   (E) believe that placebo treatment centers should be tax-exempt because they are nonprofit businesses.

The answer is (A). One of the first clues to the author's view on this issue is contained in the pivotal clause "yet the patient . . . effective drug" (paragraph four). Later, in paragraph six, the author nearly advocates that the patient should not be told that he or she might be receiving a placebo. Finally, the closing line of the passage cinches it. There, the author implies that certain principles *can be* sacrificed for the greater good of the patients.

The fifth item is a writing technique question.

5. Which one of the following best describes the organization of the material presented in the passage?

   (A) A general proposition is stated; then evidence for its support is given.
   (B) Two types of drug treatment—placebo and non-placebo—are compared and contrasted.
   (C) A result is stated, its cause is explained, and an application is suggested.
   (D) A dilemma is presented and a possible solution is offered.
   (E) A series of examples is presented; then a conclusion is drawn from them.

In the first paragraph the author claims that placebos can cure everything from dandruff to leprosy—this is a result. Then in paragraphs two, three, four, and five, he explains the causes of the result. Finally, he alludes to an application—the placebo treatment centers. The answer is (C).

The sixth item is a tone question.

6. Which one of the following most accurately characterizes the author's attitude toward placebo treatment?

   (A) reserved advocacy
   (B) feigned objectivity
   (C) summary dismissal
   (D) perplexed by its effectiveness
   (E) zealous promotion

This question is a little tricky. Only choices (A) and (B) have any real merit. Although the passage has a detached, third-person style, the author nonetheless *does* present his opinions—namely that placebos work and that their use should be expanded. However, that advocacy is reserved, so the answer is (A).

The other choices can be quickly eliminated:

"Summary dismissal" is not supported by the passage. Besides, a scholar would never summarily dismiss something; he would consider it carefully—or at least give the impression that he has—before rejecting it. This eliminates (C).

Given the human ego, we are unlikely to admit that we don't understand the subject we are writing about. This eliminates (D).

"Zealous promotion" is too strong; "promotion" itself is probably too strong. This eliminates (E).

Points to Remember

1. THE THREE STEP METHOD

    1. (Optional) Preview the first sentence of each paragraph.

    2. Read the passage at a faster than usual pace (but not to the point that comprehension suffers), being alert to places from which any of the six questions might be drawn:

        a.) Main Idea
        b.) Description
        c.) Writing Technique
        d.) Extension
        e.) Application
        f.) Tone

    3. Annotate the passage and circle any pivotal words. Then use these as reference points for answering the questions. Following are some common annotation marks (you may want to add to this list):

        A = **A**uthor's **A**ttitude
        C = **C**omplex point
        ? = Question? I don't understand this part (you can bet that this area will be important to *at least* one question)
        SP = **S**ignificant **p**oint
        ! = Exclamation! Strong opinion
        W = **W**eak, questionable or unsupported argument or premise

Mentor Exercise

Directions: This passage is followed by a group of questions to be answered based on what is stated or implied in the passage. For some questions, more than one choice could conceivably answer the question. However, choose the best answer; the one that most accurately and completely answers the question.

Following the Three Step Method, we preview the first sentence of each paragraph in the passage: (The body of the passage will be presented later.)

The enigmatic opening sentence *"Many readers, I suspect, will take the title of this article [Women, Fire, and Dangerous Things] as suggesting that women, fire, and dangerous things have something in common—say, that women are fiery and dangerous"* does not give us much of a clue to what the passage is about.

The sentence *"The classical view that categories are based on shared properties is not entirely wrong"* is more helpful. It tells us the passage is about categorization and that there are at least two theories about it: the classical view, which has merit, and the modern view, which is apparently superior.

The sentence *"Categorization is not a matter to be taken lightly"* merely confirms the subject of the passage.

Although only one sentence was helpful, previewing did reveal a lot about the passage's subject matter—categorization. Now we read the passage, circling pivotal words, annotating, and noting likely places from which any of the six questions might be drawn. After each paragraph, we will stop to analyze and interpret what the author has presented:

> Many readers, I suspect, will take the title of this article [*Women, Fire, and Dangerous Things*] as suggesting that women, fire, and dangerous things have something in common—say, that women are fiery and dangerous. Most feminists I've mentioned it to have loved the title for that reason, though some have hated it for the same reason. But the chain of inference—from conjunction to categorization to commonality—is the norm. The inference is based on the common idea of what it means to be in the same category: things are categorized together on the basis of what they have in common. The idea that categories are defined by common properties is not only our everyday folk theory of what a category is, it is also the principle technical theory—one that has been with us for more than two thousand years.

In this paragraph, the author introduces the subject matter of the passage—categorization. And the pivotal sentence, introduced by "but," explains the classical theory of categorization, albeit rather obtusely. Namely, like things are placed in the same category.

Now we consider the second paragraph:

> The classical view that categories are based on shared properties is not entirely wrong. We often do categorize things on that basis. But that is only a small part of the story. In recent years it has become clear that categorization is far more complex than that. A new theory of categorization, called *prototype theory*, has emerged. It shows that human categorization is based on principles that extend far beyond those envisioned in the classical theory. One of our goals is to survey the complexities of the way people really categorize. For example, the title of this book was inspired by the Australian aboriginal language Dyirbal, which has a category, *balan*, that actually includes women, fire, and dangerous things. It also includes birds that are *not* dangerous, as well as exceptional animals, such as the platypus, bandicoot, and echidna. This is not simply a matter of categorization by common properties.

In this paragraph, the second pivotal word—but—is crucial. It introduces the main idea of the passage—the prototype theory of categorization. Now everything that is introduced should be attributed to the prototype theory, not to the classical theory. Wrong answer-choices are likely to be baited with just the opposite.

The author states that the prototype theory goes "far beyond" the classical theory. Although he does not tell us what the prototype theory *is*, he does tell us that it *is not* merely categorization by common properties.

Now we turn to the third paragraph:

> Categorization is not a matter to be taken lightly. There is nothing more basic than categorization to our thought, perception, action and speech. Every time we see something as a *kind* of thing, for example, a tree, we are categorizing. Whenever we reason about *kinds* of things—chairs, nations, illnesses, emotions, any kind of thing at all—we are employing categories. Whenever we intentionally perform any *kind* of action, say something as mundane as writing with a pencil, hammering with a hammer, or ironing clothes, we are using categories. The particular action we perform on that occasion is a *kind* of motor activity, that is, it is in a particular category of motor actions. They are never done in exactly the same way, yet despite the differences in particular movements, they are all movements of a kind, and we know how to make movements of that kind. And any time we either produce or understand any utterance of any reasonable length, we are employing dozens if not hundreds of categories: categories of speech sounds, of words, of phrases and clauses, as well as conceptual categories. Without the ability to categorize, we could not function at all, either in the physical world or in our social and intellectual lives.

Though the author does not explicitly state it, this paragraph defines the theory of prototypes. Notice the author likes to use an indirect, even cryptic, method of introducing or switching topics, which makes this a classic LSAT type passage. The LSAT writers have many opportunities here to test whether you are following the author's train of thought.

Now we attack the questions.

1. The author probably chose *Women, Fire, and Dangerous Things* as the title of the article because
   I. he thought that since the Dyirbal placed all three items in the same category, women, fire, and dangerous things necessarily had something in common.
   II. he was hoping to draw attention to the fact that because items have been placed in the same category doesn't mean that they necessarily have anything in common
   III. he wanted to use the Dyirbal classification system as an example of how primitive classifications are not as functional as contemporary Western classification systems.

   (A) I only
   (B) II only
   (C) III only
   (D) II and III only
   (E) I, II, and III

1. This is an extension question. The second paragraph contains the information needed to answer it. There the author states that women, fire, and dangerous things belong to a category called *balan* in an Australian aboriginal language, which is <u>not</u> simply based on common properties. This eliminates Statement I and confirms Statement II.

The answer is (B).

2. According to the author,
   I. categorizing is a fundamental activity of people.
   II. whenever a word refers to a kind of thing, it signifies a category.
   III. one has to be able to categorize in order to function in our culture.

   (A) I only
   (B) II only
   (C) I and II only
   (D) II and III only
   (E) I, II, and III

2. This is a description question, so we must find the points in the passage from which the statements were drawn. Remember, the answer to a description question will not directly quote a statement from the passage, but it will be closely related to one—often a paraphrase. The needed references for Statements I, II, and III are all contained in the closing paragraph.

The answer is (E).

3. Which one of the following facts would most weaken the significance of the author's title?

   (A) The discovery that all the birds and animals classified as *balan* in Dyirbal are female
   (B) The discovery that the male Dyirbal culture considers females to be both fiery and dangerous
   (C) The discovery that all items in the *balan* category are considered female
   (D) The discovery that neither fire nor women are considered dangerous
   (E) The discovery that other cultures have categories similar to the *balan* category

3. This is one of the few questions that does not easily fit into any of the six question types. Nevertheless, our work in the arguments section has prepared us for this type of question. Remember: to weaken an argument, attack one or more of its premises. Now the implication of the title is that *women*, *fire*, and *dangerous things* <u>do not</u> have anything in common. To weaken this implication, the answer should state that all things in the *balan* category <u>have</u> something in common. The answer is (C).

4. If linguistic experts cannot perceive how women, fire, and dangerous things in the category *balan* have at least one thing in common, it follows that

   (A) there probably is something other than shared properties that led to all items in *balan* being placed in that category.
   (B) the anthropologists simply weren't able to perceive what the items had in common.
   (C) the anthropologists might not have been able to see what the items had in common.
   (D) the items do not have anything in common.
   (E) the Australian aboriginal culture is rather mystic.

4. This is an extension question; we are asked to draw a conclusion based on the passage.

The thrust of the passage is that commonality is not the only way to categorize things.

The answer is (A).

5. Which one of the following sentences would best complete the last paragraph of the passage?

   (A) An understanding of how we categorize is central to any understanding of how we think and how we function, and therefore central to an understanding of what makes us human.
   (B) The prototype theory is only the latest in a series of new and improved theories of categorization; undoubtedly even better theories will replace it.
   (C) The prototype theory of categories has not only unified a major branch of linguistics, but it has applications to mathematics and physics as well.
   (D) An understanding of how the prototype theory of categorization evolved from the classical theory is essential to any understanding of how we think and how we function in society.
   (E) To fully understand how modern Australian society functions, we must study how it is influenced by aboriginal culture—most specifically how aborigines organize and classify their surroundings.

5. This is an application question; we are asked to complete a thought for the author.

Most of the third paragraph is introducing the prototype theory of categorization. But in the last sentence the author changes direction somewhat—without any notice, as is typical of his style. Now he is discussing the importance of the ability to categorize. The clause *"Without the ability to categorize, we could not function at all"* indicates that this ability is fundamental to our very being.

Be careful not to choose (D). Although it is probably true, it is too specific: in the final sentence the author is discussing categorization in general.

The answer is (A).

Exercise

Directions: This passage is followed by a group of questions to be answered based on what is stated or implied in the passage. For some questions, more than one choice could conceivably answer the question. However, choose the best answer; the one that most accurately and completely answers the question.

Global strategies to control infectious disease have historically included the erection of barriers to international travel and immigration. Keeping people with infectious diseases outside national borders has reemerged as an important public health policy in the human immunodeficiency virus (HIV) epidemic. Between 29 and 50 countries are reported to have introduced border restrictions on HIV-positive foreigners, usually those planning an extended stay in the country, such as students, workers, or seamen.

Travel restrictions have been established primarily by countries in the western Pacific and Mediterranean regions, where HIV seroprevalence is relatively low. However, the country with the broadest policy of testing and excluding foreigners is the United States. From December 1, 1987, when HIV infection was first classified in the United States as a contagious disease, through September 30, 1989, more than 3 million people seeking permanent residence in this country were tested for HIV antibodies. The U.S. policy has been sharply criticized by national and international organizations as being contrary to public health goals and human-rights principles. Many of these organizations are boycotting international meetings in the United States that are vital for the study of prevention, education, and treatment of HIV infection.

The Immigration and Nationality Act requires the Public Health Service to list "dangerous contagious diseases" for which aliens can be excluded from the United States. By 1987 there were seven designated diseases—five of them sexually transmitted (chancroid, gonorrhea, granuloma inguinale, lymphog-ranuloma venereum, and infectious syphilis) and two nonvenereal (active tuberculosis and infectious leprosy). On June 8, 1987, in response to a Congressional direction in the Helms Amendment, the Public Health Service added HIV infection to the list of dangerous contagious diseases.

A just and efficacious travel and immigration policy would not exclude people because of their serologic status unless they posed a danger to the community through casual transmission. U.S. regulations should list only active tuberculosis as a contagious infectious disease. We support well-funded programs to protect the health of travelers infected with HIV through appropriate immunizations and prophylactic treatment and to reduce behaviors that may transmit infection.

We recognize that treating patients infected with HIV who immigrate to the United States will incur costs for the public sector. It is inequitable, however, to use cost as a reason to exclude people infected with HIV, for there are no similar exclusionary policies for those with other costly chronic diseases, such as heart disease or cancer.

Rather than arbitrarily restrict the movement of a subgroup of infected people, we must dedicate ourselves to the principles of justice, scientific cooperation, and a global response to the HIV pandemic.

1. According to the passage, countries in the western Pacific have

   (A) a very high frequency of HIV-positive immigrants and have a greater reason to be concerned over this issue than other countries.

   (B) opposed efforts on the part of Mediterranean states to establish travel restrictions on HIV-positive residents.

   (C) a low HIV seroprevalence and, in tandem with Mediterranean regions, have established travel restrictions on HIV-positive foreigners.

   (D) continued to obstruct efforts to unify policy concerning immigrant screening.

   (E) joined with the United States in sharing information about HIV-positive individuals.

2. The authors of the passage conclude that

   (A) it is unjust to exclude people based on their serological status without the knowledge that they pose a danger to the public.
   (B) U.S. regulations should require more stringent testing to be implemented at all major border crossings.
   (C) it is the responsibility of the public sector to absorb costs incurred by treatment of immigrants infected with HIV.
   (D) the HIV pandemic is largely overstated and that, based on new epidemiological data, screening immigrants is not indicated.
   (E) only the non-venereal diseases active tuberculosis and infectious leprosy should be listed as dangerous and contagious diseases.

3. It can be inferred from the passage that

   (A) more than 3 million HIV-positive people have sought permanent residence in the United States.
   (B) countries with a low seroprevalence of HIV have a disproportionate and unjustified concern over the spread of AIDS by immigration.
   (C) the United States is more concerned with controlling the number of HIV-positive immigrants than with avoiding criticism from outside its borders.
   (D) current law is meeting the demand for prudent handling of a potentially hazardous international issue.
   (E) actions by countries in the western Pacific and Mediterranean regions to restrict travel are ineffective.

4. Before the Helms Amendment in 1987, seven designated diseases were listed as being cause for denying immigration. We can conclude from the passage that

   (A) the authors agree fully with this policy but disagree with adding HIV to the list.
   (B) the authors believe that sexual diseases are appropriate reasons for denying immigration but not non-venereal diseases.
   (C) the authors disagree with the amendment.
   (D) the authors believe that non-venereal diseases are justifiable reasons for exclusion, but not sexually transmitted diseases.
   (E) the authors believe that no diseases should be cause for denying immigration.

5. In referring to the "costs" incurred by the public (paragraph five), the authors apparently mean

   (A) financial costs.
   (B) costs to the public health.
   (C) costs in manpower.
   (D) costs in international reputation.
   (E) costs in public confidence.

Answers and Solutions to Exercise

Previewing the first sentence of each paragraph shows that the passage is about restricting travel of HIV-positive persons and that the authors feel there should be no restrictions. There are two pivotal words: "however" (line 15), and "Rather than" (line 64), which introduces the concluding paragraph.

1. This is a description question, so we must find the point in the passage from which the question is drawn. It is the opening sentence to paragraph two. There it is stated that countries in the western Pacific and Mediterranean regions have a low incidence of HIV infection and have introduced border restrictions. The answer, therefore, is (C).

2. This is another description question. The answer is (A). This is directly supported by the opening sentence of paragraph four. Note that (A) is a paraphrase of that sentence.

Be careful with (C). Although this is hinted at in paragraph five, it is never directly stated that the public sector is responsible for these costs, only that it would in fact pick up these costs. Remember: A description question must be answered from what is directly stated in the passage, not from what it implies.

3. This is an extension question. Lines 23–24 state *"U.S. policy has been sharply criticized by national and international organizations."* Given that this criticism has not caused the United States to change its policies, it must be more concerned with controlling the number of HIV-positive immigrants than with avoiding criticism. The answer, therefore, is (C).

Don't be tempted by (A); it's a same language trap. Every word in it is taken from the passage. However, the passage states that over 3 million people were tested for HIV antibodies (lines 20–22), not that they were tested "positive" for HIV antibodies.

4. This is another extension question. In paragraph four, the authors state that only active tuberculosis should be listed as a dangerous contagious disease. We expect that they would oppose adding HIV to the list. The answer is (C).

5. Although governments have ostensibly restricted the immigration of HIV-positive persons out of fear that they may spread the disease, the authors apparently are referring to financial costs, not costs to public health. This is indicated in paragraph five, where they describe heart disease and cancer as non-contagious and costly, yet still admissible. The answer, therefore, is (A).

LSAT READING SECTION

Give yourself 35 minutes to complete this LSAT section. It is important that you time yourself so that you can find your optimum working pace, and so that you will know what to expect when you take the test.

Note, you will not be allowed any scratch paper during the actual LSAT; all your work must be done on the test booklet. To accustom yourself to writing in a confined space, you should write all your scratch work in the book.

Answers and solutions begin on page 404.

LSAT SECTION

Time—35 minutes
28 Questions

Directions: Each passage in this section is followed by a group of questions to be answered on the basis of what is stated or implied in the passage. For some questions, more than one of the choices could conceivably answer the question. However, you are to choose the best answer; that is, the response that most accurately and completely answers the question.

There is substantial evidence that by 1926, with the publication of *The Weary Blues*, Langston Hughes had broken with two well-established traditions in African American literature. In *The Weary Blues*, Hughes chose to modify the traditions that decreed that African American literature must promote racial acceptance and integration, and that, in order to do so, it must reflect an understanding and mastery of Western European literary techniques and styles. Necessarily excluded by this decree, linguistically and thematically, was the vast amount of secular folk material in the oral tradition that had been created by Black people in the years of slavery and after. It might be pointed out that even the spirituals or "sorrow songs" of the slaves—as distinct from their secular songs and stories—had been Europeanized to make them acceptable within these African American traditions after the Civil War. In 1862 northern White writers had commented favorably on the unique and provocative melodies of these "sorrow songs" when they first heard them sung by slaves in the Carolina sea islands. But by 1916, ten years before the publication of *The Weary Blues*, Harry T. Burleigh, the Black baritone soloist at New York's ultrafashionable Saint George's Episcopal Church, had published *Jubilee Songs of the United States*, with every spiritual arranged so that a concert singer could sing it "in the manner of an art song." Clearly, the artistic work of Black people could be used to promote racial acceptance and integration only on the condition that it became Europeanized.

Even more than his rebellion against this restrictive tradition in African American art, Hughes's expression of the vibrant folk culture of Black people established his writing as a landmark in the history of African American literature. Most of his folk poems have the distinctive marks of this folk culture's oral tradition: they contain many instances of naming and enumeration, considerable hyperbole and understatement, and a strong infusion of street-talk rhyming. There is a deceptive veil of artlessness in these poems. Hughes prided himself on being an impromptu and impressionistic writer of poetry. His, he insisted, was not an artfully constructed poetry. Yet an analysis of his dramatic monologues and other poems reveals that his poetry was carefully and artfully crafted. In his folk poetry we find features common to all folk literature, such as dramatic ellipsis, narrative compression, rhythmic repetition, and monosyllabic emphasis. The peculiar mixture of irony and humor we find in his writing is a distinguishing feature of his folk poetry. Together, these aspects of Hughes's writing helped to modify the previous restrictions on the techniques and subject matter of Black writers and consequently to broaden the linguistic and thematic range of African American literature.

1. The author mentions which one of the following as an example of the influence of Black folk culture on Hughes's poetry?

   (A) his exploitation of ambiguous and deceptive meanings
   (B) his care and craft in composing poems
   (C) his use of naming and enumeration
   (D) his use of first-person narrative
   (E) his strong religious beliefs

2. The author suggests that the "deceptive veil" (line 41) in Hughes's poetry obscures

   (A) evidence of his use of oral techniques in his poetry
   (B) evidence of his thoughtful deliberation in composing his poems
   (C) his scrupulous concern for representative details in his poetry
   (D) his incorporation of Western European literary techniques in his poetry
   (E) his engagement with social and political issues rather than aesthetic ones

GO ON TO THE NEXT PAGE.

3. With which one of the following statements regarding *Jubilee Songs of the United States* would the author be most likely to agree?

(A) Its publication marked an advance in the intrinsic quality of African American art.
(B) It paved the way for publication of Hughes's *The Weary Blues* by making African American art fashionable.
(C) It was an authentic replication of African American spirituals and "sorrow songs."
(D) It demonstrated the extent to which spirituals were adapted in order to make them more broadly accepted.
(E) It was to the spiritual what Hughes's *The Weary Blues* was to secular songs and stories.

4. The author most probably mentions the reactions of northern White writers to non-Europeanized "sorrow songs" in order to

(A) indicate that modes of expression acceptable in the context of slavery in the South were acceptable only to a small number of White writers in the North after the Civil War
(B) contrast White writers' earlier appreciation of these songs with the growing tendency after the Civil War to regard Europeanized versions of the songs as more acceptable
(C) show that the requirement that such songs be Europeanized was internal to the African American tradition and was unrelated to the literary standards or attitudes of White writers
(D) demonstrate that such songs in their non-Europeanized form were more imaginative than Europeanized versions of the same songs
(E) suggest that White writers benefited more from exposure to African American art forms than Black writers did from exposure to European art forms

5. The passage suggests that the author would be most likely to agree with which one of the following statements about the requirement that Black writers employ Western European literary techniques?

(A) The requirement was imposed more for social than for aesthetic reasons.
(B) The requirement was a relatively unimportant aspect of the African American tradition.
(C) The requirement was the chief reason for Hughes's success as a writer.
(D) The requirement was appropriate for some forms of expression but not for others.
(E) The requirement was never as strong as it may have appeared to be.

6. Which one of the following aspects of Hughes's poetry does the author appear to value most highly?

(A) its novelty compared to other works of African American literature
(B) its subtle understatement compared to that of other kinds of folk literature
(C) its virtuosity in adapting musical forms to language
(D) its expression of the folk culture of Black people
(E) its universality of appeal achieved through the adoption of colloquial expressions

GO ON TO THE NEXT PAGE.

Historians generally agree that, of the great modern innovations, the railroad had the most far-reaching impact on major events in the United States in the nineteenth and early twentieth centuries, particularly on the Industrial Revolution. There is, however, considerable disagreement among cultural historians regarding public attitudes toward the railroad, both at its inception in the 1830s and during the half century between 1880 and 1930, when the national rail system was completed and reached the zenith of its popularity in the United States. In a recent book, John Stilgoe has addressed this issue by arguing that the "romantic-era distrust" of the railroad that he claims was present during the 1830s vanished in the decades after 1880. But the argument he provides in support of this position is unconvincing.

What Stilgoe calls "romantic-era distrust" was in fact the reaction of a minority of writers, artists, and intellectuals who distrusted the railroad not so much for what it was as for what it signified. Thoreau and Hawthorne appreciated, even admired, an improved means of moving things and people from one place to another. What these writers and others were concerned about was not the new machinery as such, but the new kind of economy, social order and culture that it prefigured. In addition, Stilgoe is wrong to imply that the critical attitude of these writers was typical of the period; their distrust was largely a reaction against the prevailing attitude in the 1830s that the railroad was an unqualified improvement.

Stilgoe's assertion that the ambivalence toward the railroad exhibited by writers like Hawthorne and Thoreau disappeared after the 1880s is also misleading. In support of this thesis, Stilgoe has unearthed an impressive volume of material, the work of hitherto unknown illustrators, journalists, and novelists, all devotees of the railroad; but it is not clear what this new material proves except perhaps that the works of popular culture greatly expanded at the time. The volume of the material proves nothing if Stilgoe's point is that the earlier distrust of a minority of intellectuals did not endure beyond the 1880s, and, oddly, much of Stilgoe's other evidence indicates that it did. When he glances at the treatment of railroads by writers like Henry James, Sinclair Lewis, or F. Scott Fitzgerald, what comes through in spite of Stilgoe's analysis is remarkably like Thoreau's feeling of contrariety and ambivalence. (Had he looked at the work of Frank Norris, Eugene O'Neill, or Henry Adams, Stilgoe's case would have been much stronger.) The point is that the sharp contrast between the enthusiastic supporters of the railroad in the 1830s and the minority of intellectual dissenters during that period extended into the 1880s and beyond.

7. The passage provides information to answer all of the following questions EXCEPT:

(A) During what period did the railroad reach the zenith of its popularity in the United States?
(B) How extensive was the impact of the railroad on the Industrial Revolution in the United States, relative to that of other modern innovations?
(C) Who are some of the writers of the 1830s who expressed ambivalence toward the railroad?
(D) In what way could Stilgoe have strengthened his argument regarding intellectuals' attitudes toward the railroad in the years after the 1880s?
(E) What arguments did the writers after the 1880s, as cited by Stilgoe, offer to justify their support for the railroad?

8. According to the author of the passage, Stilgoe uses the phrase "romantic-era distrust" (line 13) to imply that the view he is referring to was

(A) the attitude of a minority of intellectuals toward technological innovation that began after 1830
(B) a commonly held attitude toward the railroad during the 1830s
(C) an ambivalent view of the railroad expressed by many poets and novelists between 1880 and 1930
(D) a critique of social and economic developments during the 1830s by a minority of intellectuals
(E) an attitude toward the railroad that was disseminated by works of popular culture after 1880

GO ON TO THE NEXT PAGE.

9. According to the author, the attitude toward the railroad that was reflected in writings of Henry James, Sinclair Lewis, and F. Scott Fitzgerald was
   (A) influenced by the writings of Frank Norris, Eugene O'Neill, and Henry Adams
   (B) similar to that of the minority of writers who had expressed ambivalence toward the railroad prior to the 1880s
   (C) consistent with the public attitudes toward the railroad that were reflected in works of popular culture after the 1880s
   (D) largely a reaction to the works of writers who had been severely critical of the railroad in the 1830s
   (E) consistent with the prevailing attitude toward the railroad during the 1830s

10. It can be inferred from the passage that the author uses the phrase "works of popular culture" (line 39) primarily to refer to the
   (A) work of a large group of writers that was published between 1880 and 1930 and that in Stilgoe's view was highly critical of the railroad
   (B) work of writers who were heavily influenced by Hawthorne and Thoreau
   (C) large volume of writing produced by Henry Adams, Sinclair Lewis, and Eugene O'Neill
   (D) work of journalists, novelists, and illustrators who were responsible for creating enthusiasm for the railroad during the 1830s
   (E) work of journalists, novelists, and illustrators that was published after 1880 and that has received little attention from scholars other than Stilgoe

11. Which one of the following can be inferred from the passage regarding the work of Frank Norris, Eugene O'Neill, and Henry Adams?
   (A) Their work never achieved broad popular appeal.
   (B) Their ideas were disseminated to a large audience by the popular culture of the early 1800s.
   (C) Their work expressed a more positive attitude toward the railroad than did that of Henry James, Sinclair Lewis, and F. Scott Fitzgerald.
   (D) Although they were primarily novelists, some of their work could be classified as journalism.
   (E) Although they were influenced by Thoreau, their attitude toward the railroad was significantly different from his.

12. It can be inferred from the passage that Stilgoe would be most likely to agree with which one of the following statements regarding the study of cultural history?
   (A) It is impossible to know exactly what period historians are referring to when they use the term "romantic era."
   (B) The writing of intellectuals often anticipates ideas and movements that are later embraced by popular culture.
   (C) Writers who were not popular in their own time tell us little about the age in which they lived.
   (D) The works of popular culture can serve as a reliable indicator of public attitudes toward modern innovations like the railroad.
   (E) The best source of information concerning the impact of an event as large as the Industrial Revolution is the private letters and journals of individuals.

13. The primary purpose of the passage is to
   (A) evaluate one scholar's view of public attitudes toward the railroad in the United States from the early nineteenth to the early twentieth century
   (B) review the treatment of the railroad in American literature of the nineteenth and twentieth centuries
   (C) survey the views of cultural historians regarding the railroad's impact on major events in United States history
   (D) explore the origins of the public support for the railroad that existed after the completion of a national rail system in the United States
   (E) define what historians mean when they refer to the "romantic-era distrust" of the railroad

GO ON TO THE NEXT PAGE.

Three basic adaptive responses—regulatory, acclimatory, and developmental—may occur in organisms as they react to changing environmental conditions. In all three, adjustment of biological features (morphological adjustment) or of their use (functional adjustment) may occur. Regulatory responses involve rapid changes in the organism's use of its physiological apparatus—increasing or decreasing the rates of various processes, for example. Acclimation involves morphological change—thickening of fur or red blood cell proliferation—which alters physiology itself. Such structural changes require more time than regulatory response changes. Regulatory and acclimatory responses are both reversible.

Developmental responses, however, are usually permanent and irreversible; they become fixed in the course of the individual's development in response to environmental conditions at the time the response occurs. One such response occurs in many kinds of water bugs. Most water-bug species inhabiting small lakes and ponds have two generations per year. The first hatches during the spring, reproduces during the summer, then dies. The eggs laid in the summer hatch and develop into adults in late summer. They live over the winter before breeding in early spring. Individuals in the second (overwintering) generation have fully developed wings and leave the water in autumn to overwinter in forests, returning in spring to small bodies of water to lay eggs. Their wings are absolutely necessary for this seasonal dispersal. The summer (early) generation, in contrast, is usually dimorphic—some individuals have normal functional (macropterous) wings; others have much-reduced (micropterous) wings of no use for flight. The summer generation's dimorphism is a compromise strategy, for these individuals usually do not leave the ponds and thus generally have no use for fully developed wings. But small ponds occasionally dry up during the summer, forcing the water bugs to search for new habitats, an eventuality that macropterous individuals are well adapted to meet.

The dimorphism of micropterous and macropterous individuals in the summer generation expresses developmental flexibility; it is not genetically determined. The individual's wing form is environmentally determined by the temperature to which developing eggs are exposed prior to their being laid. Eggs maintained in a warm environment always produce bugs with normal wings, but exposure to cold produces micropterous individuals. Eggs producing the overwintering brood are all formed during the late summer's warm temperatures. Hence, all individuals in the overwintering brood have normal wings. Eggs laid by the overwintering adults in the spring, which develop into the summer generation of adults, are formed in early autumn and early spring. Those eggs formed in autumn are exposed to cold winter temperatures, and thus produce micropterous adults in the summer generation. Those formed during the spring are never exposed to cold temperatures, and thus yield individuals with normal wings. Adult water bugs of the overwintering generation, brought into the laboratory during the cold months and kept warm, produce only macropterous offspring.

14. The primary purpose of the passage is to

(A) illustrate an organism's functional adaptive response to changing environmental conditions

(B) prove that organisms can exhibit three basic adaptive responses to changing environmental conditions

(C) explain the differences in form and function between micropterous and macropterous water bugs and analyze the effect of environmental changes on each

(D) discuss three different types of adaptive responses and provide an example that explains how one of those types of responses works

(E) contrast acclimatory responses with developmental responses and suggest an explanation for the evolutionary purposes of these two responses to changing environmental conditions

15. The passage supplies information to suggest that which one of the following would happen if a pond inhabited by water bugs were to dry up in June?

(A) The number of developmental responses among the water-bug population would decrease.

(B) Both micropterous and macropterous water bugs would show an acclimatory response.

(C) The generation of water bugs to be hatched during the subsequent spring would contain an unusually large number of macropterous individuals.

(D) The dimorphism of the summer generation would enable some individuals to survive.

(E) The dimorphism of the summer generation would be genetically transferred to the next spring generation.

GO ON TO THE NEXT PAGE.

16. It can be inferred from the passage that if the winter months of a particular year were unusually warm, the

(A) eggs formed by water bugs in the autumn would probably produce a higher than usual proportion of macropterous individuals
(B) eggs formed by water bugs in the autumn would probably produce an entire summer generation of water bugs with smaller than normal wings
(C) eggs of the overwintering generation formed in the autumn would not be affected by this temperature change
(D) overwintering generation would not leave the ponds for the forest during the winter
(E) overwintering generation of water bugs would most likely form fewer eggs in the autumn and more in the spring

17. According to the passage, the dimorphic wing structure of the summer generation of water bugs occurs because

(A) the overwintering generation forms two sets of eggs, one exposed to the colder temperatures of winter and one exposed only to the warmer temperatures of spring
(B) the eggs that produce micropterous and macropterous adults are morphologically different
(C) water bugs respond to seasonal changes by making an acclimatory functional adjustment in the wings
(D) water bugs hatching in the spring live out their life spans in ponds and never need to fly
(E) the overwintering generation, which produces eggs developing into the dimorphic generation, spends the winter in the forest and the spring in small ponds

18. It can be inferred from the passage that which one of the following is an example of a regulatory response?

(A) thickening of the plumage of some birds in the autumn
(B) increase in pulse rate during vigorous exercise
(C) gradual darkening of the skin after exposure to sunlight
(D) gradual enlargement of muscles as a result of weight lifting
(E) development of a heavy fat layer in bears before hibernation

19. According to the passage, the generation of water bugs hatching during the summer is likely to

(A) be made up of equal numbers of macropterous and micropterous individuals
(B) lay its eggs during the winter in order to expose them to cold
(C) show a marked inability to fly from one pond to another
(D) exhibit genetically determined differences in wing form from the early spring-hatched generation
(E) contain a much greater proportion of macropterous water bugs than the early spring-hatched generation

20. The author mentions laboratory experiments with adult water bugs (lines 62–65) in order to illustrate which one of the following?

(A) the function of the summer generation's dimorphism
(B) the irreversibility of most developmental adaptive responses in water bugs
(C) the effect of temperature on developing water-bug eggs
(D) the morphological difference between the summer generation and the overwintering generation of water bugs
(E) the functional adjustment of water bugs in response to seasonal temperature variation

21. Which one of the following best describes the organization of the passage?

(A) Biological phenomena are presented, examples of their occurrence are compared and contrasted, and one particular example is illustrated in detail.
(B) A description of related biological phenomena is stated, and two of those phenomena are explained in detail with illustrated examples.
(C) Three related biological phenomena are described, a hypothesis explaining their relationship is presented, and supporting evidence is produced.
(D) Three complementary biological phenomena are explained, their causes are examined, and one of them is described by contrasting its causes with the other two.
(E) A new way of describing biological phenomena is suggested, its applications are presented, and one specific example is examined in detail.

GO ON TO THE NEXT PAGE.

The Constitution of the United States does not explicitly define the extent of the President's authority to involve United States troops in conflicts with other nations in the absence of a declaration of war. Instead, the question of the President's authority in this matter falls in the hazy area of concurrent power, where authority is not expressly allocated to either the President or the Congress. The Constitution gives Congress the basic power to declare war, as well as the authority to raise and support armies and a navy, enact regulations for the control of the military, and provide for the common defense. The President, on the other hand, in addition to being obligated to execute the laws of the land, including commitments negotiated by defense treaties, is named commander in chief of the armed forces and is empowered to appoint envoys and make treaties with the consent of the Senate. Although this allocation of powers does not expressly address the use of armed forces short of a declared war, the spirit of the Constitution at least requires that Congress should be involved in the decision to deploy troops, and in passing the War Powers Resolution of 1973, Congress has at last reclaimed a role in such decisions.

Historically, United States Presidents have not waited for the approval of Congress before involving United States troops in conflicts in which a state of war was not declared. One scholar has identified 199 military engagements that occurred without the consent of Congress, ranging from Jefferson's conflict with the Barbary pirates to Nixon's invasion of Cambodia during the Vietnam conflict, which President Nixon argued was justified because his role as commander in chief allowed him almost unlimited discretion over the deployment of troops. However, the Vietnam conflict, never a declared war, represented a turning point in Congress's tolerance of presidential discretion in the deployment of troops in undeclared wars. Galvanized by the human and monetary cost of those hostilities and showing a new determination to fulfill its proper role, Congress enacted the War Powers Resolution of 1973, a statute designed to ensure that the collective judgment of both Congress and the President would be applied to the involvement of United States troops in foreign conflicts.

The resolution required the President, in the absence of a declaration of war, to consult with Congress "in every possible instance" before introducing forces and to report to Congress within 48 hours after the forces have actually been deployed. Most important, the resolution allows Congress to veto the involvement once it begins, and requires the President, in most cases, to end the involvement within 60 days unless Congress specifically authorizes the military operation to continue. In its final section, by declaring that the resolution is not intended to alter the constitutional authority of either Congress or the President, the resolution asserts that congressional involvement in decisions to use armed force is in accord with the intent and spirit of the Constitution.

22. In the passage, the author is primarily concerned with

(A) showing how the Vietnam conflict led to a new interpretation of the Constitution's provisions for use of the military
(B) arguing that the War Powers Resolution of 1973 is an attempt to reclaim a share of constitutionally concurrent power that had been usurped by the President
(C) outlining the history of the struggle between the President and Congress for control of the military
(D) providing examples of conflicts inherent in the Constitution's approach to a balance of powers
(E) explaining how the War Powers Resolution of 1973 alters the Constitution to eliminate an overlap of authority

23. With regard to the use of United States troops in a foreign conflict without a formal declaration of war by the United States, the author believes that the United States Constitution does which one of the following?

(A) assumes that the President and Congress will agree on whether troops should be used
(B) provides a clear-cut division of authority between the President and Congress in the decision to use troops
(C) assigns a greater role to the Congress than to the President in deciding whether troops should be used
(D) grants final authority to the President to decide whether to use troops
(E) intends that both the President and Congress should be involved in the decision to use troops

24. The passage suggests that each of the following contributed to Congress's enacting the War Powers Resolution of 1973 EXCEPT

(A) a change in the attitude in Congress toward exercising its role in the use of armed forces
(B) the failure of Presidents to uphold commitments specified in defense treaties
(C) Congress's desire to be consulted concerning United States military actions instigated by the President
(D) the amount of money spent on recent conflicts waged without a declaration of war
(E) the number of lives lost in Vietnam

25. It can be inferred from the passage that the War Powers Resolution of 1973 is applicable only in "the absence of a declaration of war" (lines 45–46) because

(A) Congress has enacted other laws that already set out presidential requirements for situations in which war has been declared
(B) by virtue of declaring war, Congress already implicitly participates in the decision to deploy troops
(C) the President generally receives broad public support during wars that have been formally declared by Congress
(D) Congress felt that the President should be allowed unlimited discretion in cases in which war has been declared
(E) the United States Constitution already explicitly defines the reporting and consulting requirements of the President in cases in which war has been declared

26. It can be inferred from the passage that the author believes that the War Powers Resolution of 1973

(A) is not in accord with the explicit roles of the President and Congress as defined in the Constitution
(B) interferes with the role of the President as commander in chief of the armed forces
(C) signals Congress's commitment to fulfill a role intended for it by the Constitution
(D) fails explicitly to address the use of armed forces in the absence of a declaration of war
(E) confirms the role historically assumed by Presidents

27. It can be inferred from the passage that the author would be most likely to agree with which one of the following statements regarding the invasion of Cambodia?

(A) Because it was undertaken without the consent of Congress, it violated the intent and spirit of the Constitution.
(B) Because it galvanized support for the War Powers Resolution, it contributed indirectly to the expansion of presidential authority.
(C) Because it was necessitated by a defense treaty, it required the consent of Congress.
(D) It served as a precedent for a new interpretation of the constitutional limits on the President's authority to deploy troops.
(E) It differed from the actions of past Presidents in deploying United States troops in conflicts without a declaration of war by Congress.

28. According to the provisions of the War Powers Resolution of 1973 as described in the passage, if the President perceives that an international conflict warrants the immediate involvement of United States armed forces, the President is compelled in every instance to

(A) request that Congress consider a formal declaration of war
(B) consult with the leaders of both houses of Congress before deploying armed forces
(C) desist from deploying any troops unless expressly approved by Congress
(D) report to Congress within 48 hours of the deployment of armed forces
(E) withdraw any armed forces deployed in such a conflict within 60 days unless war is declared

S T O P

IF YOU FINISH BEFORE TIME IS CALLED, YOU MAY CHECK YOUR WORK ON THIS SECTION ONLY. DO NOT WORK ON ANY OTHER SECTION IN THE TEST.

EXTRA READING

This section contains four reading passages. Give yourself 35 minutes to complete it. It is important that you time yourself so that you can find your optimum reading pace and so that you will know what to expect when you take the test.

Reading

Time—35 minutes
26 Questions

<u>Directions:</u> Each passage is followed by a group of questions to be answered based on what is <u>stated</u> or <u>implied</u> in the passage. For some questions, more than one choice could conceivably answer the question. However, choose the <u>best</u> answer; the one that most accurately and completely answers the question.

Most students arrive at [college] using "discrete, concrete, and absolute categories to understand people, knowledge, and values." These students live with a *dualistic* view, seeing "the world in polar terms of we-right-good vs. other-wrong-bad." These students cannot acknowledge the existence of more than one point of view toward any issue. There is one "right" way. And because these absolutes are assumed by or imposed on the individual from external authority, they cannot be personally substantiated or authenticated by experience. These students are slaves to the generalizations of their authorities. An eye for an eye! Capital punishment is apt justice for murder. The Bible says so.

Most students break through the dualistic stage to another equally frustrating stage—*multiplicity.* Within this stage, students see a variety of ways to deal with any given topic or problem. However, while these students accept multiple points of view, they are unable to evaluate or justify them. To have an opinion is everyone's right. While students in the dualistic stage are unable to produce evidence to support what they consider to be self-evident absolutes, students in the multiplistic stage are unable to connect instances into coherent generalizations. Every assertion, every point, is valid. In their democracy they are directionless. Capital punishment? What sense is there in answering one murder with another?

The third stage of development finds students living in a world of *relativism.* Knowledge is relative: right and wrong depend on the context. No longer recognizing the validity of each individual idea or action, relativists examine everything to find its place in an overall framework. While the multiplist views the world as unconnected, almost random, the relativist seeks always to place phenomena into coherent larger patterns. Students in this stage view the world analytically. They appreciate authority for its expertise, using it to defend their own generalizations. In addition, they accept or reject ostensible authority *after systematically* evaluating its validity. In this stage, however, students resist decision making. Suffering the ambivalence of finding several consistent and acceptable alternatives, they are almost overwhelmed by diversity and need means for managing it. Capital punishment is appropriate justice—in some instances.

In the final stage students manage diversity through individual *commitment.* Students do not deny relativism. Rather they assert an identity by forming commitments and assuming responsibility for them. They gather personal experience into a coherent framework, abstract principles to guide their actions, and use these principles to discipline and govern their thoughts and actions. The individual has chosen to join a particular community and agrees to live by its tenets. The accused has had the benefit of due process to guard his civil rights, a jury of peers has found him guilty, and the state has the right to end his life. This is a principle my community and I endorse.

1. It can be inferred from the passage that the author would consider which of the following to be good examples of "dualistic thinking"?

    I. People who think "there is a right way and a wrong way to do things"
    II. Teenagers who assume they know more about "the real world" than adults do
    III. People who back our country "right or wrong" when it goes to war

    (A) I only
    (B) II only
    (C) III only
    (D) I and II only
    (E) I and III only

GO ON TO THE NEXT PAGE.

2. Students who are "dualistic" thinkers may not be able to support their beliefs convincingly because

(A) most of their beliefs *cannot* be supported by arguments.
(B) they have accepted their "truths" simply because authorities have said these things are "true."
(C) they half-believe and half-disbelieve just about everything.
(D) their teachers almost always think that "dualistic" thinkers are wrong.
(E) they are enslaved by their authorities.

3. Which one of the following assertions is supported by the passage?

(A) *Committed* thinkers are not very sure of their positions.
(B) *Relativistic* thinkers have learned how to make sense out of the world and have chosen their own positions in it.
(C) *Multiplicity* thinkers have difficulty understanding the relationships between different points of view.
(D) *Dualistic* thinkers have thought out the reasons for taking their positions.
(E) *Dualistic* thinkers fear the power of authority.

4. In paragraph two, the author states that in their "democracy" students in the *multiplicity* stage are directionless. The writer describes *multiplicity* students as being in a "democracy" because

(A) there are so many different kinds of people in a democracy.
(B) in an "ideal" democracy, all people are considered equal; by extension, so are their opinions.
(C) Democrats generally do not have a good sense of direction.
(D) although democracies may grant freedom, they are generally acknowledged to be less efficient than more authoritarian forms of government.
(E) in a democracy the individual, not the state, has ultimate authority over himself.

5. Which one of the following kinds of thinking is NOT described in the passage?

(A) People who assume that there is no right or wrong in any issue
(B) People who make unreasoned commitments and stick by them
(C) People who believe that right or wrong depends on the situation
(D) People who commit themselves to a particular point of view after having considered several alternative concepts
(E) People who think that all behavior can be accounted for by cause and effect relationships

6. If students were asked to write essays on the different *concepts* of tragedy as exemplified by Cordelia and Antigone, and they all responded by showing how each character exemplified a traditional definition of tragedy, we could, according to the passage, hypothesize which one of the following about these students?

(A) The students were locked into the relativist stage.
(B) The students had not advanced beyond the dualist stage.
(C) The students had at least achieved the multiplicity stage.
(D) The students had reached the commitment stage.
(E) We have no indication of which cognitive stage the students were in.

7. Which one of the following best describes the organization of the passage?

(A) Four methods of thought are compared and contrasted.
(B) It is shown how each of four types of thought evolved from each other.
(C) Four methods of thought are presented, and each is shown to complement the other.
(D) The evolution of thought from simplistic and provincial through considered and cosmopolitan is illustrated by four stages.
(E) The evolution of thought through four stages is presented, and each stage is illustrated by how it views capital punishment.

GO ON TO THE NEXT PAGE.

A growing taste for shark steaks and shark-fin soup has for the first time in 400 million years put the scourge of the sea at the wrong end of the food chain. Commercial landings of this toothsome fish have doubled every year since 1986, and shark populations are plunging. It is hardly a case of good riddance. Sharks do for gentler fish what lions do for the wildebeest: they check populations by feeding on the weak. Also, sharks apparently do not get cancer and may therefore harbor clues to the nature of that disease.

Finally, there is the issue of motherhood. Sharks are viviparous. That is, they bear their young alive and swimming (not sealed in eggs) after gestation periods lasting from nine months to two years. Shark mothers generally give birth to litters of from eight to twelve pups and bear only one litter every other year.

This is why sharks have one of the lowest fecundity rates in the ocean. The female cod, for example, spawns annually and lays a few million eggs at a time. If three quarters of the cod were to be fished this year, they could be back in full force in a few years. But if humans took that big of a bite out of the sharks, the population would not recover for 15 years.

So, late this summer, if all goes according to plan, the shark will join the bald eagle and the buffalo on the list of managed species. The federal government will cap the U.S. commercial catch at 5,800 metric tons, about half of the 1989 level, and limit sportsmen to two sharks per boat. Another provision discourages finning, the harvesting of shark fins alone, by limiting the weight of fins to 7 percent of that of all the carcasses.

Finning got under the skin of environmentalists, and the resulting anger helped to mobilize support for the new regulations. Finning itself is a fairly recent innovation. Shark fins contain noodle-like cartilaginous tissues that Chinese chefs have traditionally used to thicken and flavor soup. Over the past few years rising demand in Hong Kong has made the fins as valuable as the rest of the fish. Long strands are prized, so unusually large fins can be worth considerably more to the fisherman than the average price of about $10 a pound.

But can U.S. quotas save shark species that wander the whole Atlantic? The blue shark, for example, migrates into the waters of something like 23 countries. John G. Casey, a biologist with the National Marine Fisheries Service Research Center in Narragansett, R.I., admits that international coordination will eventually be necessary. But he supports U.S. quotas as a first step in mobilizing other nations. Meanwhile the commercial fishermen are not waiting for the new rules to take effect. "There's a pre-quota rush on sharks," Casey says, "and it's going on as we speak."

8. According to the passage, shark populations are at greater risk than cod populations because

(A) sharks are now being eaten more than cod.
(B) the shark reproduction rate is lower than that of the cod.
(C) sharks are quickly becoming fewer in number.
(D) sharks are now as scarce as bald eagles and buffalo.
(E) sharks are scavengers and therefore more susceptible to disease.

9. According to the passage, a decrease in shark populations

I. might cause some fish populations to go unchecked.
II. would hamper cancer research.
III. to one-quarter the current level would take over a decade to recover from.

(A) II only
(B) III only
(C) I and III only
(D) I and II only
(E) I, II, and III

GO ON TO THE NEXT PAGE.

10. If the species *Homo logicus* was determined to be viviparous and to have extremely low fecundity rates on land, we might expect that

(A) *Homo logicus* could overpopulate its niche and should be controlled.
(B) *Homo logicus* might be declared an endangered species.
(C) *Homo logicus* would pose no danger to other species and would itself be in no danger.
(D) *Homo logicus* would soon become extinct.
(E) None of these events would be expected with certainty.

11. Which one of the following best describes the author's attitude toward the efforts to protect shark populations?

(A) strong advocate
(B) impartial observer
(C) opposed
(D) perplexed
(E) resigned to their ineffectiveness

12. It can be inferred from the passage that

I. research efforts on cancer will be hindered if shark populations are threatened.
II. U.S. quotas on shark fishing will have limited effectiveness in protecting certain species.
III. some practices of Chinese chefs have angered environmentalists.

(A) I only
(B) II only
(C) I and II only
(D) II and III only
(E) I, II, and III

13. An irony resulting from the announcement that sharks will be placed on the managed species list is

(A) we will now find out less about cancer, so in effect by saving the sharks, we are hurting ourselves.
(B) sharks are far more dangerous to other fish than we are to them.
(C) more chefs are now using the cartilaginous tissues found in shark fins.
(D) more sharks are being killed now than before the announcement.
(E) man will now protect a creature that he has been the victim of.

GO ON TO THE NEXT PAGE.

"A writer's job is to tell the truth," said Hemingway in 1942. No other writer of our time had so fiercely asserted, so pugnaciously defended or so consistently exemplified the writer's obligation to speak truly. His standard of truth-telling remained, moreover, so high and so rigorous that he was ordinarily unwilling to admit secondary evidence, whether literary evidence or evidence picked up from other sources than his own experience. "I only know what I have seen," was a statement which came often to his lips and pen. What he had personally done, or what he knew unforgettably by having gone through one version of it, was what he was interested in telling about. This is not to say that he refused to invent freely. But he always made it a sacrosanct point to invent in terms of what he actually knew from having been there.

The primary intent of his writing, from first to last, was to seize and project for the reader what he often called "the way it was." This is a characteristically simple phrase for a concept of extraordinary complexity, and Hemingway's conception of its meaning subtly changed several times in the course of his career—always in the direction of greater complexity. At the core of the concept, however, one can invariably discern the operation of three aesthetic instruments: the sense of place, the sense of fact, and the sense of scene.

The first of these, obviously a strong passion with Hemingway, is the sense of place. "Unless you have geography, background," he once told George Antheil, "you have nothing." You have, that is to say, a dramatic vacuum. Few writers have been more place-conscious. Few have so carefully charted out the geographical ground work of their novels while managing to keep background so conspicuously unobtrusive. Few, accordingly, have been able to record more economically and graphically the way it is when you walk through the streets of Paris in search of breakfast at a corner café . . . Or when, at around six o'clock of a Spanish dawn, you watch the bulls running from the corrals at the Puerta Rochapea through the streets of Pamplona towards the bullring.

"When I woke it was the sound of the rocket exploding that announced the release of the bulls from the corrals at the edge of town. Down below the narrow street was empty. All the balconies were crowded with people. Suddenly a crowd came down the street. They were all running, packed close together. They passed along and up the street toward the bullring and behind them came more men running faster, and then some stragglers who were really running. Behind them was a little bare space, and then the bulls, galloping, tossing their heads up and down. It all went out of sight around the corner. One man fell, rolled to the gutter, and lay quiet. But the bulls went right on and did not notice him. They were all running together."

This landscape is as morning-fresh as a design in India ink on clean white paper. First is the bare white street, seen from above, quiet and empty. Then one sees the first packed clot of runners. Behind these are the thinner ranks of those who move faster because they are closer to the bulls. Then the almost comic stragglers, who are "really running." Brilliantly behind these shines the "little bare space," a desperate margin for error. Then the clot of running bulls—closing the design, except of course for the man in the gutter making himself, like the designer's initials, as inconspicuous as possible.

14. According to the author, Hemingway's primary purpose in telling a story was

(A) to construct a well-told story that the reader would thoroughly enjoy.
(B) to construct a story that would reflect truths that were not particular to a specific historical period.
(C) to begin from reality but to allow his imagination to roam from "the way it was" to "the way it might have been."
(D) to report faithfully reality as Hemingway had experienced it.
(E) to go beyond the truth, to "create" reality.

GO ON TO THE NEXT PAGE.

15. From the author's comments and the example of the bulls (paragraph 4), what was the most likely reason for which Hemingway took care to include details of place?
    (A) He felt that geography in some way illuminated other, more important events.
    (B) He thought readers generally did not have enough imagination to visualize the scenes for themselves.
    (C) He had no other recourse since he was avoiding the use of other literary sources.
    (D) He thought that landscapes were more important than characters to convey "the way it was."
    (E) He felt that without background information the readers would be unable to follow the story.

16. One might infer from the passage that Hemingway preferred which one of the following sources for his novels and short stories?
    (A) Stories that he had heard from friends or chance acquaintances
    (B) Stories that he had read about in newspapers or other secondary sources
    (C) Stories that came to him in periods of meditation or in dreams
    (D) Stories that he had lived rather than read about
    (E) Stories adapted from myths

17. It has been suggested that part of Hemingway's genius lies in the way in which he removes himself from his stories in order to let readers experience the stories for themselves. Which of the following elements of the passage support this suggestion?
    I. The comparison of "the designer's initials" to the man who fell and lay in the gutter (lines 55–56) during the running of the bulls
    II. Hemingway's stated intent to project for the reader "the way it was" (line 19)
    III. Hemingway's ability to invent fascinating tales from his own experience

    (A) I only
    (B) II only
    (C) I and II only
    (D) I and III only
    (E) I, II, and III

18. From the passage, one can assume that which of the following statements would best describe Hemingway's attitude toward knowledge?
    (A) One can learn about life only by living it fully.
    (B) A wise person will read widely in order to learn about life.
    (C) Knowledge is a powerful tool that should be reserved only for those who know how to use it.
    (D) Experience is a poor teacher.
    (E) One can never truly "know" anything.

19. The author calls "the way it was" a "characteristically simple phrase for a concept of extraordinary complexity" (lines 19–21) because
    (A) the phrase reflects Hemingway's talent for obscuring ordinary events.
    (B) the relationship between simplicity and complexity reflected the relationship between the style and content of Hemingway's writing.
    (C) Hemingway became increasingly confused about "the way it was" throughout the course of his career.
    (D) Hemingway's obsession for geographic details progressively overshadowed the dramatic element of his stories.
    (E) it typifies how Hemingway understated complex issues.

GO ON TO THE NEXT PAGE.

Imagine that we stand on any ordinary seaside pier, and watch the waves rolling in and striking against the iron columns of the pier. Large waves pay very little attention to the columns—they divide right and left and re-unite after passing each column, much as a regiment of soldiers would if a tree stood in their way; it is almost as though the columns had not been there. But the short waves and ripples find the columns of the pier a much more formidable obstacle. When the short waves impinge on the columns, they are reflected back and spread as new ripples in all directions. To use the technical term, they are "scattered." The obstacle provided by the iron columns hardly affects the long waves at all, but scatters the short ripples.

We have been watching a working model of the way in which sunlight struggles through the earth's atmosphere. Between us on earth and outer space the atmosphere interposes innumerable obstacles in the form of molecules of air, tiny droplets of water, and small particles of dust. They are represented by the columns of the pier.

The waves of the sea represent the sunlight. We know that sunlight is a blend of lights of many colors—as we can prove for ourselves by passing it through a prism, or even through a jug of water, or as Nature demonstrates to us when she passes it through the raindrops of a summer shower and produces a rainbow. We also know that light consists of waves, and that the different colors of light are produced by waves of different lengths, red light by long waves and blue light by short waves. The mixture of waves which constitutes sunlight has to struggle through the obstacles it meets in the atmosphere, just as the mixture of waves at the seaside has to struggle past the columns of the pier. And these obstacles treat the light waves much as the columns of the pier treat the sea-waves. The long waves which constitute red light are hardly affected, but the short waves which constitute blue light are scattered in all directions.

Thus, the different constituents of sunlight are treated in different ways as they struggle through the earth's atmosphere. A wave of blue light may be scattered by a dust particle, and turned out of its course. After a time a second dust particle again turns it out of its course, and so on, until finally it enters our eyes by a path as zigzag as that of a flash of lightning. Consequently, the blue waves of the sunlight enter our eyes from all directions. And that is why the sky looks blue.

20. We know from experience that if we look directly at the sun, we will see red light near the sun. This observation is supported by the passage for which one of the following reasons?

(A) It seems reasonable to assume that red light would surround the sun because the sun is basically a large fireball.
(B) It seems reasonable to assume that the other colors of light would either cancel each other or combine to produce red.
(C) It seems reasonable to assume that red light would not be disturbed by the atmospheric particles and would consequently reach us by a relatively direct path from the sun to our eyes.
(D) It is not supported by the passage. The author does not say what color of light should be near the sun, and he provides no reasons that would allow us to assume that the light would be red.
(E) Gazing directly at the sun forces the eye to focus on the longer red waves.

21. Scientists have observed that shorter wavelength light has more energy than longer wavelength light. From this we can conclude that

(A) red light will exert more energy when it hits the surface of the earth than will blue light.
(B) lightning is caused by the collision of blue light with particles in the air.
(C) red light will travel faster than blue light.
(D) blue light has more energy than red light.
(E) blue light has less energy than red light.

GO ON TO THE NEXT PAGE.

22. A scientist makes new observations and learns that water waves of shorter wavelengths spread in all directions not only because they scatter off piers but also because they interact with previously scattered short water waves. Drawing upon the analogy between water waves and light waves, we might hypothesize which of the following?

(A) Blue light waves act like ripples that other blue light waves meet and scatter from.
(B) Red light waves will be scattered by blue light waves like incoming long water waves are scattered by outgoing ripples.
(C) Red light waves can scatter blue light waves, but blue light waves cannot scatter red.
(D) The analogy between water and light waves cannot be extended to include the way in which short water waves become ripples and scatter one another.
(E) The scattering effect of blue light waves is canceled by that of red.

23. Which one of the following is a reason for assuming that sunlight is constituted of waves of many colors?

(A) The mixture of waves that make up sunlight has to struggle through a variety of obstacles in the atmosphere.
(B) When passing through water in the atmosphere, sunlight is sometimes broken down into an array of colors.
(C) Many different wavelengths of light enter our eyes from all directions.
(D) The mere fact that light waves can be scattered is a reason for assuming that sunlight is constituted of waves of different colors.
(E) When passing through dust in the atmosphere, sunlight is sometimes broken down into an array of colors.

24. From the information presented in the passage, what can we conclude about the color of the sky on a day with a large quantity of dust in the air?

(A) The sky would be even bluer
(B) The sky would be redder
(C) The sky would not change colors
(D) We do not have enough information to determine a change in color
(E) The sky would assume a violet hue

25. We all know that when there is a clear sky, the western sky appears red as the sun sets. From the information presented in the passage, this phenomenon would seem to be explained by which of the following?

I. Light meets more obstacles when passing parallel to the earth's surface than when traveling perpendicular. Consequently, even red light is diffused.
II. The blue light may not make it through the denser pathway of the evening sky, leaving only the long light waves of red.
III. The short red light waves have more energy and are the only waves that can make it through the thick atmosphere of the evening sky.

(A) I only
(B) II only
(C) I and II only
(D) II and III only
(E) I, II, and III

26. Which one of the following does the author seem to imply?

(A) Waves of light and waves of water are identical.
(B) Waves of light have the same physical shape as waves of water.
(C) Waves of light and waves of water do not have very much in common.
(D) Waves of water are only models of waves of light.
(E) There are colors of light waves just as there are colors of water waves.

S T O P

IF YOU FINISH BEFORE TIME IS CALLED, YOU MAY CHECK YOUR WORK ON THIS SECTION ONLY. DO NOT WORK ON ANY OTHER SECTION IN THE TEST.

Answers and Solutions to LSAT Section

Answers to Questions

1. C
2. B
3. D
4. B
5. A
6. D
7. E
8. B
9. B
10. E
11. C
12. D
13. A
14. D
15. D
16. A
17. A
18. B
19. E
20. C
21. A
22. B
23. E
24. B
25. B
26. C
27. A
28. D

Questions 1–6

There are two pivotal words in this passage—"but" (line 22) and "yet" (line 44). Both are crucial to answering the questions.

1. This is a description question, so we must find the point in the passage from which it is drawn. The needed information is contained in lines 36–41. There it is stated that Hughes's poems have the mark of Black folk culture—*"containing many instances of naming and enumeration."* The answer is (C).

The other choices are easily dismissed. Choices (A), (D), and (E) are not mentioned in the passage. Choice (B) is second best. Lines 44–47 state that Hughes used craft and care in composing his poems. However, this was not due to the influence of Black folk culture.

2. This is an extension question. We are asked to interpret the author's remarks. The key phrase for answering this question—"carefully and artfully"—is introduced by the pivotal sentence containing "yet" (lines 44–47). The metaphor "a deceptive veil of artlessness" implies that the poems have an appearance of innocence and spontaneity while in fact they are "carefully and artfully crafted." The answer is (B).

3. This is an application question. By asking us to speculate on what the author might agree with, the question goes well beyond the passage. The information needed to answer it is introduced by the pivotal word "but" (lines 22–31). The key is the sentence *"Clearly, the artistic work of Black people could be used to promote racial acceptance and integration only on the condition that it became Europeanized."* In other words, before spirituals could be accepted, they had to adopt Western European literary styles. The answer is (D).

As to the other choices, the author would disagree with (A). The sentence *"Clearly, the artistic work of Black people could be used to promote racial acceptance and integration only on the condition that it became Europeanized"* implies that one had to "sell out" to get Black spirituals accepted—this is not an advancement. Choice (B) is false. *The Weary Blues* broke from the traditions of African American literature exemplified by *Jubilee Songs of the United States*. The author would disagree with (C). Since *Jubilee Songs of the United States* adopts Western European literary styles, it is not an authentic replication of African American spirituals. Finally, choice (E) is neither mentioned nor implied by the passage.

4. This is another application question: We are asked to interpret the author's intent. The author states that in 1862 northern White writers expressed appreciation of "sorrow songs." However, sixty years later, the fashionable portrayal of these spirituals was in a Europeanized format, presumably because the original versions were not popular nor accepted among White audiences. The answer is (B).

5. This is yet another application question. The key to this question is again the sentence *"Clearly, the artistic work of Black people could be used to promote racial acceptance and integration only on the condition that it became Europeanized."* In other words, the requirement was imposed for social—not artistic—reasons. The answer is (A).

6. This is an application question. Expect many application questions with literary passages since these passages tend to be subjective. This question is hard since the second-best choice—(A)—is rather good. At the time of publication, *The Weary Blues* was novel since it broke from the traditions of African American literature, and the author expresses admiration for this "rebellion." However, the opening to paragraph two shows that the author valued even more highly *"Hughes's expression of the vibrant folk culture of Black people,"* which *"established his writing as a landmark in the history of African American literature."* The answer is (D).

Regarding the other choices. Although "understatement" is mentioned in the passage, it is not elaborated on. This eliminates (B). Choice (C) is superficially tempting. There is a long discussion of "sorrow songs," but this example merely illustrates how Black culture had to be Europeanized to be accepted. The bulk of the passage is about Hughes's poetry. Finally, choice (E) is not supported by the passage. The author states that Hughes's writing helped broaden the linguistic range of African American literature but does not imply that this was due to a universal appeal of Hughes's writings. In fact, because Hughes rebelled against cultural norms, it is likely his writings did not have universal appeal.

Questions 7–13

7. This is a description question. We must find the points in the passage from which each wrong answer-choice is drawn. Choice (A) is mentioned in the passage. Lines 5–11 state the railroad reached its zenith between 1880 and 1930. Eliminate (A). Choice (B) is mentioned in the passage. The opening to the passage states, *"the railroad had the most far-reaching impact on major events . . . particularly on the Industrial Revolution."* Eliminate (B). Choice (C) is mentioned in the passage. The second paragraph states that in the 1830s Thoreau and Hawthorne expressed an appreciation of the railroad's ability to move people and things from one place to another but they also expressed concern about the new kind of economy and culture it forced on the land. In other words, they were ambivalent toward the railroad. Eliminate (C). Choice (D) is mentioned in the passage. In lines 48–51, the author says Stilgoe's argument would have been stronger had he analyzed the work of Frank Norris, Eugene O'Neill, or Henry Adams. Eliminate (D). Hence, by process of elimination, the answer is (E).

8. This is another description question. Since the question refers to line 13, we must read several lines before and after the reference to get the proper perspective. The answer is contained in lines 5–15. There the author mentions *"public attitudes toward the railroad."* That is, the commonly held attitude toward the railroad during the 1830s. The answer is (B).

Regarding the other choices. Choices (A), (C), and (D) are all opinions of the author, not of Stilgoe. Choice (E) is not mentioned in the passage.

9. This is yet another description question. The needed reference is lines 44–48. *"When he glances at the treatment of railroads by writers like Henry James, Sinclair Lewis, or F. Scott Fitzgerald, what comes through in spite of Stilgoe's analysis is remarkably like Thoreau's feeling of contrariety and ambivalence."* In other words, these writers expressed an ambivalence toward the railroad similar to that of writers before 1880. The answer is (B).

As to the other choices, (A), (C), and (D) are not mentioned in the passage. Choice (E) expresses Stilgoe's view, not the author's.

10. This is an extension question. We are asked to draw an inference from the passage. In lines 34–37, the author says that Stilgoe has unearthed a large volume of previously unknown work. But in lines 37–39 he implies that these "works of popular culture" are irrelevant to Stilgoe's argument. In other words, all that Stilgoe has done is expose a large volume of previously unknown work. The answer is (E).

The other choices are easily dismissed. Choice (A) contradicts Stilgoe's assertion that ambivalence toward the railroad disappeared after the 1880s. Choices (B) and (C) are not mentioned in the passage. Finally, choice (D) is false. The material is from the 1880s and after, not the 1830s.

11. This is another extension question. As mentioned in the solution to Question 7, the author implies that the work of these authors supports Stilgoe's assertion that ambivalence toward the railroad ended after 1880 (see lines 48–51). The answer is (C).

12. This is an application question. By asking us to speculate on Stilgoe's view toward the study of cultural history, the question goes well beyond the passage. All of Stilgoe's conclusions concerning public attitudes toward the railroad are based on works of popular culture. So underlying Stilgoe's arguments is the assumption that works of popular culture can reliably measure public opinion. The answer is (D).

13. Like most main idea questions, this one is rather easy. The passage is a critique of Stilgoe's view of public attitudes toward the railroad. This is made explicit by, among other places, the closing of paragraph one (the typical place for the main idea to be stated) and the openings of paragraphs two and three. The answer is (A).

Remember, the answer to a main idea question will summarize the passage without going beyond it. (B) violates these criteria by *overstating* the scope of the passage. The passage does mention many works of literature. But this is done only to illustrate how Stilgoe used literature to support his views, or how the author felt Stilgoe should have used literature. Choice (C) also *overstates* the scope of the passage. The only cultural historian mentioned in the passage is Stilgoe. Choice (D) makes a false claim. Although the origins of intellectuals' opposition to railroads is discussed (their attitude was a reaction against the prevailing opinion that railroads were an unqualified improvement, end of paragraph 2), the origins of public support for the railroads is not discussed. Choice (E) violates the criteria by *understating* the scope of the passage. Defining the "romantic-era distrust" is only a small part of the passage.

Questions 14–21

14. This is a main idea question. The first paragraph introduces three adaptive responses—regulatory, acclimatory, and developmental. Then paragraph two introduces an extended example of a developmental response—wing development in water bugs. The answer is (D).

15. This is an extension question. The information needed to answer it is found in the second half of paragraph two. There it is stated: *"The summer (early) generation, in contrast, is usually dimorphic—some individuals have normal functional (macropterous) wings; others have much-reduced (micropterous) wings of no use for flight. But small ponds occasionally dry up during the summer, forcing the water bugs to search for new habitats, an eventuality that macropterous individuals are well adapted to meet."* So if a pond dries up, the water bugs with normal wings (macropterous) can still survive by flying to another pond. The answer is (D). Note the underlined pivotal words.

16. This is another extension question. Lines 57–60 contain the needed reference: *"Those eggs formed in autumn are exposed to cold winter temperatures, and thus produce micropterous adults in the summer generation."* So if the winter is unusually warm, there should a higher than usual percentage of macropterous individuals. The answer is (A).

17. This is a description question. The needed reference is contained in lines 49–57. There it is stated that the overwintering adults form two sets of eggs, one in early autumn and one in early spring. The passage indicates that *"eggs formed in autumn are exposed to cold winter temperatures, and thus produce micropterous adults"* and that *"[eggs] formed during the spring are never exposed to cold temperatures, and thus yield individuals with normal wings."* This establishes the mechanism for dimorphism and the answer is therefore (A).

18. This is an application question. We are asked to apply what we have learned in the passage to another situation. Lines 6–9 offer the passage's only description of regulatory responses. There it is stated, *"Regulatory responses involve rapid changes in the organism's use of its physiological apparatus."* The key is the word "rapid." The only answer-choice that involves a quick change is (B), and it is the answer.

19. This is a description question. According to the passage (lines 24–30), those water bugs which hatch during the summer have fully developed wings (all are macropterous), unlike the generation laid and hatched during the spring. The answer is (E).

20. This an application question. We are asked to discern the author's intent. The purpose of the last paragraph is to show that the varied wing development of water bugs is determined by environment, not genetics. By showing that changes in temperature affect wing development in water bugs, the author is presenting evidence that wing development is environmentally determined. The answer is (C).

21. This is a writing technique question. Pivotal words *"however"* and *"in contrast"* show that the passage is comparing and contrasting biological phenomena. Paragraphs two and three present a detailed illustration of one particular phenomenon—wing development in water bugs. Thus, the answer is (A).

Questions 22–28

22. The information needed to answer this question is found in the closing lines of paragraph one (the primary place for presenting the main idea). The key is the sentence *"in passing the War Powers Resolution of 1973, Congress has at last reclaimed [from the President] a role in such decisions."* The answer is (B).

The other choices are easily dismissed. (A) is perhaps the second-best choice. According the passage, the Vietnam conflict led Congress to reassert its constitutional role, not reinterpret it. (C) is not supported by the passage. Lines 34–38 state that until the Vietnam War Congress was "tolerant" of presidential discretion in deploying troops. (D) is not mentioned in the passage. Finally, (E) contradicts the passage. By bringing Congress back into the decision-making process, the War Powers Resolution increased, not decreased, the overlap of authority.

23. This is a description question. The needed reference is also found at the end of paragraph one, where it states, *"The spirit of the Constitution at least requires that Congress should be involved in the decision to deploy troops."* In other words, both Congress and the President should be involved in the decision making process. The answer is (E).

24. This again is a description question. We must find the points in the passage from which each wrong answer-choice is drawn. (A) is mentioned in lines 35–37: *"The Vietnam conflict . . . represented a turning point in Congress's tolerance of presidential discretion in the deployment of troops."* (C), (D), and (E) are all mentioned in lines 38–41: *"Galvanized by the human and monetary cost of those hostilities and showing a new determination to fulfill its proper role, Congress enacted the War Powers Resolution of 1973."* Thus, by process of elimination, the answer is (B).

25. This is an extension question. We are asked to draw an inference from the passage. The key to this question is found in lines 8–9: *"The Constitution gives Congress the basic power to declare war."* By declaring war, Congress implicitly authorizes the deployment of troops. The answer is (B).

26. This is an application question. By asking us to complete a thought for the author, it goes well beyond the passage. The needed information is found in lines 39–40. In particular, the phrase *"showing a new determination to fulfill its proper role."* That is, Congress was committed to fulfilling a role intended for it by the Constitution. The answer is (C).

Choice (A) contradicts the passage. The War Powers Resolution reasserted the constitutionally defined roles of the President and Congress. Choice (B) is neither mentioned nor implied by the passage. Choice (D) makes a false claim. The War Powers Resolution applies only in the absence of a declaration of war; once Congress has declared war, the resolution is moot. Choice (E) also makes a false claim. Historically, Presidents deployed troops without consulting Congress. The War Powers Resolution brings Congress back into the decision making process.

27. This is a hard application question because the second-best choice is quite good. The author states, *"The spirit of the Constitution at least requires that Congress should be involved in the decision to deploy troops"* (lines 19–21). Thus, by unilaterally invading Cambodia, the President violated the spirit of the Constitution. The answer is (A).

Choice (B) contradicts the passage. The War Powers Resolution <u>limited</u> presidential authority. Choice (C) is not mentioned in the passage. Choice (D) is a close second-best. The passage does imply that the Vietnam War served as a precedent for reinterpreting the President's authority to deploy troops, and the Cambodian invasion was part of the Vietnam War. Nevertheless, choice (A) is more direct. Finally, choice (E) contradicts the passage. Historically, Presidents have deployed troops without a declaration of war by Congress.

28. This is a description question. The needed information is found in the opening to paragraph three: *"The resolution required the President . . . to report to Congress . . . within 48 hours after the forces have actually been deployed."* The answer is (D).

Neither (A) nor (B) is mentioned in the passage. (C) overstates the restriction in the War Powers Resolution. The Resolution states merely that the President must report to Congress within 48 hours after forces have been deployed. Choice (E) is second best. The passage does state, *"[The Resolution] requires the President, in <u>most</u> cases to end the involvement within 60 days unless Congress specifically authorizes the military operation to continue."* However, the question states in <u>every</u> case, not <u>most</u> cases. Additionally, the War Powers Resolution states that after 60 days Congress must merely authorize the continuation of military action, not declare war.

Answers and Solutions to Extra Reading

Answers to Questions

1.	E	8.	B	15.	A	22.	D
2.	B	9.	C	16.	D	23.	B
3.	C	10.	E	17.	C	24.	D
4.	B	11.	B	18.	A	25.	C
5.	E	12.	B	19.	B	26.	D
6.	B	13.	D	20.	C		
7.	E	14.	D	21.	D		

Questions 1–7

Before we turn to the answers, three pivotal words in the first passage should be noted: "However" (line 18), "however" (line 43), and "Rather" (line 51).

1. This is an extension question. Statement I is true. This is the essential characteristic of dualistic (right/wrong) thinkers (lines 3–8). This eliminates (B) and (C). Statement II is false. Dualistic thinkers grant authority (right thinking) to adults and adult figures. This is clear from the sentence, *"These students are slaves to the generalizations of their authorities."* This eliminates (D). Unfortunately, we have to check Statement III. It is true since Dualistic thinkers believe *their* group is right and the *other* group is wrong. (Again, see lines 3–8.) The answer, therefore, is (E).

2. This is another extension question. Dualistic thinkers probably cannot give cogent arguments for their beliefs since they have adopted them unquestioningly from authority figures; dualistic thinkers do not know (have never thought of) the reasons for which their beliefs are right or wrong. Hence the answer is (B).

3. This is a description question. (A) is false. After carefully thinking through their reasons, committed thinkers are reasonably sure of their position. (B) is also false. Relativistic thinkers make sense of the world, but they have not chosen their position; indeed they cannot even choose a position. (C) is true. Multiplicity thinkers see the world as randomly organized; they can't see the relationships that connect different positions. (See the first pivotal word, "however" [line 18].)

4. This is an extension question. Multiplicity students view all opinions as equally valid. They have yet to learn how to rank opinions (truths)—all votes (thoughts) count equally. The answer is (B).

Note, (C) is offered to humor Republicans. The test-makers sometimes run out of tempting wrong choices. Don't dwell on such humorous nonsense.

5. This is another description question. (A): No, these are the Multiplists. (B): No, Dualists think this way. (C): No, this describes Relativists. Don't confuse (A) and (C). Multiplists acknowledge no right or wrong; whereas Relativists acknowledge a morality, but one that is context dependent. (D): No, Committed thinkers fit this description rather nicely. Hence, by process of elimination, we have learned the answer is (E).

6. This is an application question. Since all the students showed how the characters exemplified the *same* concept of "tragedy," they must be working from a common definition of tragedy (the traditional one). They have accepted "authority's" definition of tragedy and have shown how each character fits it. It never occurred to them that there may be other ways to view a tragedy. Hence they are all dualistic thinkers. The answer is (B).

7. This is a writing technique question. In each paragraph the author shows how a stage of thought evolved from a previous stage—except the dualistic stage, which starts the analysis. Further, the thought process in each stage is illustrated by how it views capital punishment. Hence the answer is (E).

Be careful not to choose (D). Although dualistic thinking certainly is simplistic and provincial, and committed thinking seems to be considered and cosmopolitan, neither of these judgments is stated nor implied by the passage.

Questions 8–13

8. This is a description question. Paragraph 3 contains the information needed to answer it. There it is stated that the cod population can replenish itself in a few years, but the shark population would take 15 years. Hence the answer is (B).

Don't make the mistake of choosing (C). Although it is certainly supported by the passage, it does not state how this relates to cod—they too may be decreasing in number. (C) uses the true-but-irrelevant ploy.

9. This is a description question. Statement I is true. It is supported by the analogy drawn between lions and sharks (lines 7–9). This eliminates (A) and (B). Statement II is false. It is too strong an inference to draw from the information in lines 9–11. If sharks were on the verge of extinction, this "could hamper" research. But given that the author does not claim or imply that sharks are near extinction, "would hamper" is too strong. Besides, the author does not state that sharks are being used in research, just that they may be useful in that regard. This eliminates (D) and (E). Hence, by process of elimination, we have learned the answer is (C).

10. This is an application question; we are asked to apply what we have learned in the passage to a hypothetical situation. A review of the passage shows that only (B) and (E) have any real merit. But sharks have survived for 400 million years with an extremely low fecundity rate. This eliminates (B). Hence the answer is (E).

11. This is a rather easy tone question. The passage has a matter-of-fact or journalistic tone to it. So the answer is (B).

12. This is an extension question. Statement I is incorrect. Like Statement II in Question 9, it overstates the case. Statement II is correct. We know from lines 47–50 that some species of sharks migrate into the waters of over 20 countries. U.S. quotas alone cannot "protect" these sharks, even if the quotas reduce the rate of killing in U.S. waters. Statement III is incorrect. The environmentalists are angry at the finning fishermen who are over-fishing the waters, there is nothing in the passage to suggest that this anger is also directed towards the chefs. The answer is (B).

13. By announcing the impending classification, the federal government ironically encourages fishermen to kill as many sharks as they can before the regulations go into effect—stimulating the opposite of what was intended, i.e., the saving of sharks. The answer is (D).

Questions 14–19

14. This is a description question. (A) is false. The enjoyment of the reader was incidental to Hemingway's primary purpose—truth-telling. (B) is false, though very tempting. The first half of this item "*to construct a story that would reflect truths*" looks very good. The second half, however, spoils it by adding the qualifier "*not particular to a specific historical period.*" Reviewing the passage reveals no indication that Hemingway is trying to create any kind of "general truth." In fact, one can argue that Hemingway's emphasis on developing a strong "sense of place" (lines 27–31), and his belief that when trying to tell the truth "I only know what I have seen" (line 9) support the inference that Hemingway sees truth as subjective, not objective. (C) is also false. The passage gives no indication that Hemingway was interested in the way things "might have been." (D) is true. This is clearly the author's interpretation of Hemingway's purpose. Look at the first few sentences of both the first and the second paragraphs. Notice that this question item emphasizes subjective truth, or the truth "as Hemingway had experienced it."

Strategy: In this question, you have two choices—(B) and (D)—which at first glance seem very close. Let's assume you don't understand exactly why a "close second" is wrong. When confronted with this situation, it's a good idea to take a few seconds and try to get into the *Question-Writer's* mindset. What are you missing that the Question-Writer thinks is an important point in this passage? In this case, the Question-Writer is focusing on the subtle point that Hemingway sees his perspective as "subjective," that certain things, true in some places or to some people, may not be true in other places or to other people. In other words, there is no "objective reality."

If intuition is the only way to distinguish between the two close choices, then you should mark them in your test booklet as *close*, perhaps like this

(B)
(C), to show that you had to choose between
(D)

them, and move on. If you have trouble with later questions on the same passage, you may want to go back, analyze the passage, and determine the real difference between the earlier "close pair." The Question-Writer may be testing the same question from a different angle, in which case time is well spent pondering the issue.

15. This is an extension question. In lines 28–30, Hemingway effectively equates geography with background, and says that without them "you have nothing." In lines 32–34, the author refers to the "geographical groundwork" of Hemingway's novels. Both of these statements imply that details of place set the stage for other, more important events. Hence the answer is (A). Don't try to draw a distinction between "geography," "background," and "landscape." The author uses them interchangeably when referring to details of place. Such latitude with labels is often mimicked by the Question-Writers.

Choice (D) is a close second-best. The author indicates that geography, background, and landscape are quite important to Hemingway. In fact, "first" in the opening to paragraph 3 almost indicates that details of place are the most important aspect of his writing. Looking closely, however, we see that the passage gives no indication of Hemingway's perspective on characters. So no comparison can be made.

16. Hemingway's primary intent was to project for the reader "the way it was," as seen through his eyes. The answer is (D).

17. This is an extension question. Statement I is true. The last line of the passage states that the designer's initials (i.e., the writer's presence) are made as inconspicuous as possible. Statement II is also true. Readers cannot see "the way it was" if they are looking through another medium (the author). Hemingway appears to say, in effect: *"I'm striving to report exactly what happened (and not my opinions about it). The readers must draw their own conclusions."* Statement III is false. In fact, a good case could be made that writing only from personal experience would tend to increase, not decrease, the presence of the writer in his writings. The answer is (C).

18. This is an application question; we are asked to put ourselves in Hemingway's mind. From Hemingway's statement "I only know what I have seen" and from the author's assertion that Hemingway refused to honor secondary sources, we can infer that he believed one can "know" only through experience. Hence the answer is (A).

19. This is an extension question. The answer is (B). There is a great parallel here. *Phrase* (in the passage) corresponds to *style* (in the answer-choice), and *concept* corresponds to *content.*

Questions 20–26

20. This is an extension question. According to the passage, red light would not be significantly deflected and consequently would pass through a relatively direct route from the sun to our eyes. Hence the answer is (C).

21. This is another extension question. Since the passage is a science selection, we should expect a lot of extension questions. (A): No, if anything, blue light would exert more energy. (B): No. We can not infer this. The collision of blue light with particles in the air is the reason for a blue sky, not for lightning. (C): No. Speed of light is not mentioned in the passage. (D): Yes. Blue light has a shorter wavelength, consequently it has more energy than red light.

22. This is an application question since it introduces new information about water waves and asks us to conclude how the behavior of light waves might be similarly affected. Given this information, however, we can justify no conclusion about whether light waves imitate water waves in this new regard. The analogy might hold or it might break down. We don't yet know. (To find out we would have to do an experiment using light.) The answer is (D).

23. (A): No. We do not know anything about a "variety" of obstacles; even if we did, we would have no reason to assume that light is constituted of different colors. **(B): Yes.** See lines 22–27. Rainbows occur because light is constituted of many colors. (C): No. This is a distortion of lines 47–49, and it sounds illogical to boot. (D): No. This gives no reason to assume that light is constituted of many colors. (E): No. Water vapor in the atmosphere causes rainbows, not dust.

24. (A): No. Although dust is mentioned as one of the three important obstacles (lines 18–20), we simply do not have enough information to conclude how dust density would change sky color. (B): No. While this idea may fit with the common lore that a lot of dust in the air creates great, red sunsets, the passage itself gives no basis to any conclusion regarding color change. (C): No. Same reason as in (A) and (B). **(D): Yes**. There is not enough information in the passage to determine a relationship between color change and dust density. The dust may give off a certain color of its own—we can't say for certain.

25. Statement I is true. There are obviously more particles on a horizontal than a vertical path. The glowing red sky is reasonable evidence for some diffusion. Note that Question 24 asks "what can we *conclude*" while this question asks what seems *plausible* (what "would seem to be explained"). So, while we are attempting to make very similar inferences in both questions, what we can do with the data depends, among other things, on the degree of certainty requested. Statement II is true. The path of evening light probably has a greater average density, since it spends more time passing through a zone of thicker atmosphere. It is reasonable to assume this significantly greater density, or the absolute number of particles, might present an obstacle to blue light. Statement III is false. There are two things wrong with this answer: (1) red light waves are not short, relative to blue; (2) we do not know that waves with more energy will more readily pass through obstacles. The passage, in fact, implies just the opposite. The answer is (C).

26. (A): No. Water waves offer only a model for light waves. As a model, they are identical in some ways but not in others. (B): No. This is not implied by the passage. What they have in common is the way they act when they impinge on obstacles. (C): No. Waves of water are used as a model because they have much in common with waves of light. **(D): Yes.** See explanation for (A).

Part Four

THE TESTS

LSAT
TEST I

Section I
Time—35 minutes
25 Questions

Directions: The questions in this section are based on the reasoning contained in brief statements or passages. For some questions, more than one of the choices could conceivably answer the question. However, you are to choose the best answer; that is, the response that most accurately and completely answers the question. You should not make assumptions that are by commonsense standards implausible, superfluous, or incompatible with the passage.

1. Before the printing press, books could be purchased only in expensive manuscript copies. The printing press produced books that were significantly less expensive than the manuscript editions. The public's demand for printed books in the first years after the invention of the printing press was many times greater than demand had been for manuscript copies. This increase demonstrates that there was a dramatic jump in the number of people who learned how to read in the years after publishers first started producing books on the printing press.

   Which one of the following statements, if true, casts doubt on the argument?

   (A) During the first years after the invention of the printing press, letter writing by people who wrote without the assistance of scribes or clerks exhibited a dramatic increase.
   (B) Books produced on the printing press are often found with written comments in the margins in the handwriting of the people who owned the books.
   (C) In the first years after the printing press was invented, printed books were purchased primarily by people who had always bought and read expensive manuscripts but could afford a greater number of printed books for the same money.
   (D) Books that were printed on the printing press in the first years after its invention often circulated among friends in informal reading clubs or libraries.
   (E) The first printed books published after the invention of the printing press would have been useless to illiterate people, since the books had virtually no illustrations.

2. Bevex, an artificial sweetener used only in soft drinks, is carcinogenic for mice, but only when it is consumed in very large quantities. To ingest an amount of Bevex equivalent to the amount fed to the mice in the relevant studies, a person would have to drink 25 cans of Bevex-sweetened soft drinks per day. For that reason, Bevex is in fact safe for people.

   In order for the conclusion that Bevex is safe for people to be properly drawn, which one of the following must be true?

   (A) Cancer from carcinogenic substances develops more slowly in mice than it does in people.
   (B) If all food additives that are currently used in foods were tested, some would be found to be carcinogenic for mice.
   (C) People drink fewer than 25 cans of Bevex-sweetened soda per day.
   (D) People can obtain important health benefits by controlling their weight through the use of artificially sweetened soft drinks.
   (E) Some of the studies done on Bevex were not relevant to the question of whether or not Bevex is carcinogenic for people.

3. Harry: Airlines have made it possible for anyone to travel around the world in much less time than was formerly possible.

   Judith: That is not true. Many flights are too expensive for all but the rich.

   Judith's response shows that she interprets Harry's statement to imply that

   (A) the majority of people are rich
   (B) everyone has an equal right to experience world travel
   (C) world travel is only possible via routes serviced by airlines
   (D) most forms of world travel are not affordable for most people
   (E) anyone can afford to travel long distances by air

GO ON TO THE NEXT PAGE.

4. Nutritionists have recommended that people eat more fiber. Advertisements for a new fiber-supplement pill state only that it contains "44 percent fiber."

The advertising claim is misleading in its selection of information on which to focus if which one of the following is true?

(A) There are other products on the market that are advertised as providing fiber as a dietary supplement.
(B) Nutritionists base their recommendation on medical findings that dietary fiber protects against some kinds of cancer.
(C) It is possible to become addicted to some kinds of advertised pills, such as sleeping pills and painkillers.
(D) The label of the advertised product recommends taking 3 pills every day.
(E) The recommended daily intake of fiber is 20 to 30 grams, and the pill contains one-third gram.

5. Many environmentalists have urged environmental awareness on consumers, saying that if we accept moral responsibility for our effects on the environment, then products that directly or indirectly harm the environment ought to be avoided. Unfortunately it is usually impossible for consumers to assess the environmental impact of a product, and thus impossible for them to consciously restrict their purchases to environmentally benign products. Because of this impossibility there can be no moral duty to choose products in the way these environmentalists urge, since ______.

Which one of the following principles provides the most appropriate completion for the argument?

(A) a moral duty to perform an action is never based solely on the effects the action will have on other people
(B) a person cannot possibly have a moral duty to do what he or she is unable to do
(C) moral considerations should not be the sole determinants of what products are made available to consumers
(D) the morally right action is always the one whose effects produce the least total harm
(E) where a moral duty exists, it supersedes any legal duty and any other kind of duty

6. Advertisement: Anyone who exercises knows from firsthand experience that exercise leads to better performance of such physical organs as the heart and the lungs, as well as to improvement in muscle tone. And since your brain is a physical organ, your actions can improve its performance, too. Act now. Subscribe to *Stimulus*: read the magazine that exercises your brain.

The advertisement employs which one of the following argumentative strategies?

(A) It cites experimental evidence that subscribing to the product being advertised has desirable consequences.
(B) It ridicules people who do not subscribe to *Stimulus* by suggesting that they do not believe that exercise will improve brain capacity.
(C) It explains the process by which the product being advertised brings about the result claimed for its use.
(D) It supports its recommendation by a careful analysis of the concept of exercise.
(E) It implies that brains and muscle are similar in one respect because they are similar in another respect.

GO ON TO THE NEXT PAGE.

Questions 7–8

Coherent solutions for the problem of reducing health-care costs cannot be found within the current piecemeal system of paying these costs. The reason is that this system gives health-care providers and insurers every incentive to shift, wherever possible, the costs of treating illness onto each other or any other party, including the patient. That clearly is the lesson of the various reforms of the 1980s: push in on one part of this pliable spending balloon and an equally expensive bulge pops up elsewhere. For example, when the government health-care insurance program for the poor cut costs by disallowing payments for some visits to physicians, patients with advanced illness later presented themselves at hospital emergency rooms in increased numbers.

7. The argument proceeds by

(A) showing that shifting costs onto the patient contradicts the premise of health-care reimbursement
(B) attributing without justification fraudulent intent to people
(C) employing an analogy to characterize interrelationships
(D) denying the possibility of a solution by disparaging each possible alternative system
(E) demonstrating that cooperation is feasible by citing an instance

8. The argument provides the most support for which one of the following?

(A) Under the conditions in which the current system operates, the overall volume of health-care costs could be shrunk, if at all, only by a comprehensive approach.
(B) Relative to the resources available for health-care funding, the income of the higher-paid health-care professionals is too high.
(C) Health-care costs are expanding to meet additional funds that have been made available for them.
(D) Advances in medical technology have raised the expected standards of medical care but have proved expensive.
(E) Since unfilled hospital beds contribute to overhead charges on each patient's bill, it would be unwise to hold unused hospital capacity in reserve for large-scale emergencies.

9. The commercial news media emphasize exceptional events such as airplane crashes at the expense of those such as automobile accidents, which occur far more frequently and represent a far greater risk to the public. Yet the public tends to interpret the degree of emphasis the news media give to these occurrences as indicating the degree of risk they represent.

If the statements above are true, which one of the following conclusions is most strongly supported by them?

(A) Print media, such as newspapers and magazines, are a better source of information than are broadcast media.
(B) The emphasis given in the commercial news media to major catastrophes is dictated by the public's taste for the extraordinary.
(C) Events over which people feel they have no control are generally perceived as more dangerous than those which people feel they can avert or avoid.
(D) Where commercial news media constitute the dominant source of information, public perception of risk does not reflect actual risk.
(E) A massive outbreak of cholera will be covered more extensively by the news media than will the occurrence of a rarer but less serious disease.

10. A large group of hyperactive children whose regular diets included food containing large amounts of additives was observed by researchers trained to assess the presence or absence of behavior problems. The children were then placed on a low-additive diet for several weeks, after which they were observed again. Originally nearly 60 percent of the children exhibited behavior problems; after the change in diet, only 30 percent did so. On the basis of these data, it can be concluded that food additives can contribute to behavior problems in hyperactive children.

The evidence cited fails to establish the conclusion because

(A) there is no evidence that the reduction in behavior problems was proportionate to the reduction in food-additive intake
(B) there is no way to know what changes would have occurred without the change of diet, since only children who changed to a low-additive diet were studied
(C) exactly how many children exhibited behavior problems after the change in diet cannot be determined, since the size of the group studied is not precisely given
(D) there is no evidence that the behavior of some of the children was unaffected by additives
(E) the evidence is consistent with the claim that some children exhibit more frequent behavior problems after being on the low-additive diet than they had exhibited when first observed

11. In 1990 major engine repairs were performed on 10 percent of the cars that had been built by the National Motor Company in the 1970s and that were still registered. However, the corresponding figure for the cars that the National Motor Company had manufactured in the 1960s was only five percent.

Which one of the following, if true, most helps to explain the discrepancy?

(A) Government motor vehicle regulations generally require all cars, whether old or new, to be inspected for emission levels prior to registration.
(B) Owners of new cars tend to drive their cars more carefully than do owners of old cars.
(C) The older a car is, the more likely it is to be discarded for scrap rather than repaired when major engine work is needed to keep the car in operation.
(D) The cars that the National Motor Company built in the 1970s incorporated simplified engine designs that made the engines less complicated than those of earlier models.
(E) Many of the repairs that were performed on the cars that the National Motor Company built in the 1960s could have been avoided if periodic routine maintenance had been performed.

12. No mathematician today would flatly refuse to accept the results of an enormous computation as an adequate demonstration of the truth of a theorem. In 1976, however, this was not the case. Some mathematicians at that time refused to accept the results of a complex computer demonstration of a very simple mapping theorem. Although some mathematicians still hold a strong belief that a simple theorem ought to have a short, simple proof, in fact, some simple theorems have required enormous proofs.

If all of the statements in the passage are true, which one of the following must also be true?

(A) Today, some mathematicians who believe that a simple theorem ought to have a simple proof would consider accepting the results of an enormous computation as a demonstration of the truth of a theorem.
(B) Some individuals who believe that a simple theorem ought to have a simple proof are not mathematicians.
(C) Today, some individuals who refuse to accept the results of an enormous computation as a demonstration of the truth of a theorem believe that a simple theorem ought to have a simple proof.
(D) Some individuals who do not believe that a simple theorem ought to have a simple proof would not be willing to accept the results of an enormous computation as proof of a complex theorem.
(E) Some nonmathematicians do not believe that a simple theorem ought to have a simple proof.

13. If you climb mountains, you will not live to a ripe old age. But you will be bored unless you climb mountains. Therefore, if you live to a ripe old age, you will have been bored.

Which one of the following most closely parallels the reasoning in the argument above?

(A) If you do not try to swim, you will not learn how to swim. But you will not be safe in boats if you do not learn how to swim. Therefore, you must try to swim.
(B) If you do not play golf, you will not enjoy the weekend. But you will be tired next week unless you relax during the weekend. Therefore, to enjoy the weekend, you will have to relax by playing golf.
(C) If you work for your candidate, you will not improve your guitar playing. But you will neglect your civic duty unless you work for your candidate. Therefore, if you improve your guitar playing, you will have neglected your civic duty.
(D) If you do not train, you will not be a good athlete. But you will become exhausted easily unless you train. Therefore, if you train, you will not have become exhausted easily.
(E) If you spend all of your money, you will not become wealthy. But you will become hungry unless you spend all of your money. Therefore, if you become wealthy, you will not become hungry.

14. Marine biologists had hypothesized that lobsters kept together in lobster traps eat one another in response to hunger. Periodic checking of lobster traps, however, has revealed instances of lobsters sharing traps together for weeks. Eight lobsters even shared one trap together for two months without eating one another. The marine biologists' hypothesis, therefore, is clearly wrong.

The argument against the marine biologists' hypothesis is based on which one of the following assumptions?

(A) Lobsters not caught in lobster traps have been observed eating one another.
(B) Two months is the longest known period during which eight or more lobsters have been trapped together.
(C) It is unusual to find as many as eight lobsters caught together in one single trap.
(D) Members of other marine species sometimes eat their own kind when no other food sources are available.
(E) Any food that the eight lobsters in the trap might have obtained was not enough to ward off hunger.

GO ON TO THE NEXT PAGE.

15. Eight years ago hunting was banned in Greenfield County on the grounds that hunting endangers public safety. Now the deer population in the county is six times what it was before the ban. Deer are invading residential areas, damaging property and causing motor vehicle accidents that result in serious injury to motorists. Since there were never any hunting-related injuries in the county, clearly the ban was not only unnecessary but has created a danger to public safety that would not otherwise exist.

    Which one of the following, if true, provides the strongest additional support for the conclusion above?

    (A) In surrounding counties, where hunting is permitted, the size of the deer population has not increased in the last eight years.
    (B) Motor vehicle accidents involving deer often result in damage to the vehicle, injury to the motorist, or both.
    (C) When deer populations increase beyond optimal size, disease and malnutrition become more widespread among the deer herds.
    (D) In residential areas in the county, many residents provide food and salt for deer.
    (E) Deer can cause extensive damage to ornamental shrubs and trees by chewing on twigs and saplings.

16. Comets do not give off their own light but reflect light from other sources, such as the Sun. Scientists estimate the mass of comets by their brightness: the greater a comet's mass, the more light that comet will reflect. A satellite probe, however, has revealed that the material of which Halley's comet is composed reflects 60 times less light per unit of mass than had been previously thought.

    The statements above, if true, give the most support to which one of the following?

    (A) Some comets are composed of material that reflects 60 times more light per unit of mass than the material of which Halley's comet is composed.
    (B) Previous estimates of the mass of Halley's comet which were based on its brightness were too low.
    (C) The total amount of light reflected from Halley's comet is less than scientists had previously thought.
    (D) The reflective properties of the material of which comets are composed vary considerably from comet to comet.
    (E) Scientists need more information before they can make a good estimate of the mass of Halley's comet.

17. Office manager: I will not order recycled paper for this office. Our letters to clients must make a good impression, so we cannot print them on inferior paper.

    Stationery supplier: Recycled paper is not necessarily inferior. In fact, from the beginning, the finest paper has been made of recycled material. It was only in the 1850s that paper began to be made from wood fiber, and then only because there were no longer enough rags to meet the demand for paper.

    In which one of the following ways does the stationer's response fail to address the office manager's objection to recycled paper?

    (A) It does not recognize that the office manager's prejudice against recycled paper stems from ignorance.
    (B) It uses irrelevant facts to justify a claim about the quality of the disputed product.
    (C) It assumes that the office manager is concerned about environmental issues.
    (D) It presupposes that the office manager understands the basic technology of paper manufacturing.
    (E) It ignores the office manager's legitimate concern about quality.

GO ON TO THE NEXT PAGE.

Questions 18–19

When Alicia Green borrowed a neighbor's car without permission, the police merely gave her a warning. However, when Peter Foster did the same thing, he was charged with automobile theft. Peter came to the attention of the police because the car he was driving was hit by a speeding taxi. Alicia was stopped because the car she was driving had defective taillights. It is true that the car Peter took got damaged and the car Alicia took did not, but since it was the taxi that caused the damage this difference was not due to any difference in the blameworthiness of their behavior. Therefore Alicia should also have been charged with automobile theft.

18. The statement that the car Peter took got damaged and the car Alicia took did not plays which one of the following roles in the argument?

    (A) It presents a reason that directly supports the conclusion.
    (B) It justifies the difference in the actual outcome in the two cases.
    (C) It demonstrates awareness of a fact on which a possible objection might be based.
    (D) It illustrates a general principle on which the argument relies.
    (E) It summarizes a position against which the argument is directed.

19. If all of the claims offered in support of the conclusion are accurate, each of the following could be true EXCEPT:

    (A) The interests of justice would have been better served if the police had released Peter Foster with a warning.
    (B) Alicia Green had never before driven a car belonging to someone else without first securing the owner's permission.
    (C) Peter Foster was hit by the taxi while he was running a red light, whereas Alicia Green drove with extra care to avoid drawing the attention of the police to the car she had taken.
    (D) Alicia Green barely missed hitting a pedestrian when she sped through a red light ten minutes before she was stopped by the police for driving a car that had defective taillights.
    (E) Peter Foster had been cited for speeding twice in the preceding month, whereas Alicia Green had never been cited for a traffic violation.

20. According to sources who can be expected to know, Dr. Maria Esposito is going to run in the mayoral election. But if Dr. Esposito runs, Jerome Krasman will certainly not run against her. Therefore Dr. Esposito will be the only candidate in the election.

    The flawed reasoning in the argument above most closely parallels that in which one of the following?

    (A) According to its management, Brown's Stores will move next year. Without Brown's being present, no new large store can be attracted to the downtown area. Therefore the downtown area will no longer be viable as a shopping district.
    (B) The press release says that the rock group Rollercoaster is playing a concert on Saturday. It won't be playing on Friday if it plays on Saturday. So Saturday will be the only day this week on which Rollercoaster will perform.
    (C) Joshua says the interviewing panel was impressed by Marilyn. But if they were impressed by Marilyn, they probably thought less of Sven. Joshua is probably right, and so Sven will probably not get the job.
    (D) An informant says that Rustimann was involved in the bank robbery. If Rustimann was involved, Jones was certainly not involved. Since these two are the only people who could have been involved, Rustimann is the only person the police need to arrest.
    (E) The review said that this book is the best one for beginners at programming. If this book is the best, that other one can't be as good. So this one is the book we should buy.

GO ON TO THE NEXT PAGE.

21. The initial causes of serious accidents at nuclear power plants have not so far been flaws in the advanced-technology portion of the plants. Rather, the initial causes have been attributed to human error, as when a worker at the Browns Mills reactor in the United States dropped a candle and started a fire, or to flaws in the plumbing, exemplified in a recent incident in Japan. Such everyday events cannot be thought unlikely to occur over the long run.

    Which one of the following is most strongly supported by the statements above?

    (A) Now that nuclear power generation has become a part of everyday life, an ever-increasing yearly incidence of serious accidents at the plants can be expected.
    (B) If nuclear power plants continue in operation, a serious accident at such a plant is not improbable.
    (C) The likelihood of human error at the operating consoles of nuclear power generators cannot be lessened by thoughtful design of dials, switches, and displays.
    (D) The design of nuclear power plants attempts to compensate for possible failures of the materials used in their construction.
    (E) No serious accident will be caused in the future by some flaw in the advanced-technology portion of a nuclear power plant.

22. There is a widespread belief that people can predict impending earthquakes from unusual animal behavior. Skeptics claim that this belief is based on selective coincidence: people whose dogs behaved oddly just before an earthquake will be especially likely to remember that fact. At any given time, the skeptics say, some of the world's dogs will be behaving oddly.

    Clarification of which one of the following issues would be most important to an evaluation of the skeptics' position?

    (A) Which is larger, the number of skeptics or the number of people who believe that animal behavior can foreshadow earthquakes?
    (B) Are there means other than the observation of animal behavior that nonscientists can use to predict earthquakes?
    (C) Are there animals about whose behavior people know too little to be able to distinguish unusual from everyday behavior?
    (D) Are the sorts of behavior supposedly predictive of earthquakes as pronounced in dogs as they are in other animals?
    (E) Is the animal behavior supposedly predictive of earthquakes specific to impending earthquakes or can it be any kind of unusual behavior?

23. Defendants who can afford expensive private defense lawyers have a lower conviction rate than those who rely on court-appointed public defenders. This explains why criminals who commit lucrative crimes like embezzlement or insider trading are more successful at avoiding conviction than are street criminals.

    The explanation offered above would be more persuasive if which one of the following were true?

    (A) Many street crimes, such as drug dealing, are extremely lucrative and those committing them can afford expensive private lawyers.
    (B) Most prosecutors are not competent to handle cases involving highly technical financial evidence and have more success in prosecuting cases of robbery or simple assault.
    (C) The number of criminals convicted of street crimes is far greater than the number of criminals convicted of embezzlement or insider trading.
    (D) The percentage of defendants who actually committed the crimes of which they are accused is no greater for publicly defended than for privately defended defendants.
    (E) Juries, out of sympathy for the victims of crimes, are much more likely to convict defendants accused of violent crimes than they are to convict defendants accused of "victimless" crimes or crimes against property.

GO ON TO THE NEXT PAGE.

24. Many major scientific discoveries of the past were the product of serendipity, the chance discovery of valuable findings that investigators had not purposely sought. Now, however, scientific research tends to be so costly that investigators are heavily dependent on large grants to fund their research. Because such grants require investigators to provide the grant sponsors with clear projections of the outcome of the proposed research, investigators ignore anything that does not directly bear on the funded research. Therefore, under the prevailing circumstances, serendipity can no longer play a role in scientific discovery.

    Which one of the following is an assumption on which the argument depends?

    (A) Only findings that an investigator purposely seeks can directly bear on that investigator's research.
    (B) In the past few scientific investigators attempted to make clear predictions of the outcome of their research.
    (C) Dependence on large grants is preventing investigators from conducting the type of scientific research that those investigators would personally prefer.
    (D) All scientific investigators who provide grant sponsors with clear projections of the outcome of their research receive at least some of the grants for which they apply.
    (E) In general the most valuable scientific discoveries are the product of serendipity.

25. Police statistics have shown that automobile antitheft devices reduce the risk of car theft, but a statistical study of automobile theft by the automobile insurance industry claims that cars equipped with antitheft devices are, paradoxically, more likely to be stolen than cars that are not so equipped.

    Which one of the following, if true, does the most to resolve the apparent paradox?

    (A) Owners of stolen cars almost invariably report the theft immediately to the police but tend to delay notifying their insurance company, in the hope that the vehicle will be recovered.
    (B) Most cars that are stolen are not equipped with antitheft devices, and most cars that are equipped with antitheft devices are not stolen.
    (C) The most common automobile antitheft devices are audible alarms, which typically produce ten false alarms for every actual attempted theft.
    (D) Automobile owners who have particularly theft-prone cars and live in areas of greatest incidence of car theft are those who are most likely to have antitheft devices installed.
    (E) Most automobile thefts are the work of professional thieves against whose efforts antitheft devices offer scant protection.

S T O P

IF YOU FINISH BEFORE TIME IS CALLED, YOU MAY CHECK YOUR WORK ON THIS SECTION ONLY.
DO NOT WORK ON ANY OTHER SECTION IN THE TEST.

SECTION II
Time—35 minutes
24 Questions

Directions: Each group of questions in this section is based on a set of conditions. In answering some of the questions, it may be useful to draw a rough diagram. Choose the response that most accurately and completely answers each question.

Questions 1–7

Seven consecutive time slots for a broadcast, numbered in chronological order 1 through 7, will be filled by six song tapes—G, H, L, O, P, S—and exactly one news tape. Each tape is to be assigned to a different time slot, and no tape is longer than any other tape. The broadcast is subject to the following restrictions:

L must be played immediately before O.
The news tape must be played at some time after L.
There must be exactly two time slots between G and P, regardless of whether G comes before P or whether G comes after P.

1. If G is played second, which one of the following tapes must be played third?

(A) the news
(B) H
(C) L
(D) O
(E) S

2. The news tape can be played in any one of the following time slots EXCEPT the

(A) second
(B) third
(C) fourth
(D) fifth
(E) sixth

3. If H and S are to be scheduled as far from each other as possible, then the first, the second, and the third time slots could be filled, respectively, by

(A) G, H, and L
(B) S, G, and the news
(C) H, G, and L
(D) H, L, and O
(E) L, O, and S

4. If P is played fifth, L must be played

(A) first
(B) second
(C) third
(D) fourth
(E) sixth

5. What is the maximum number of tapes that can separate S from the news?

(A) 1
(B) 2
(C) 3
(D) 4
(E) 5

6. Which one of the following is the latest time slot in which L can be played?

(A) the third
(B) the fourth
(C) the fifth
(D) the sixth
(E) the seventh

7. The time slot in which O must be played is completely determined if G is assigned to which one of the following time slots?

(A) the first
(B) the third
(C) the fourth
(D) the fifth
(E) the sixth

GO ON TO THE NEXT PAGE.

Questions 8-12

Doctor Yamata works only on Mondays, Tuesdays, Wednesdays, Fridays, and Saturdays. She performs four different activities—lecturing, operating, treating patients, and conducting research. Each working day she performs exactly one activity in the morning and exactly one activity in the afternoon. During each week her work schedule must satisfy the following restrictions:

She performs operations on exactly three mornings.
If she operates on Monday, she does not operate on Tuesday.
She lectures in the afternoon on exactly two consecutive calendar days.
She treats patients on exactly one morning and exactly three afternoons.
She conducts research on exactly one morning.
On Saturday she neither lectures nor performs operations.

8. Which one of the following must be a day on which Doctor Yamata lectures?

(A) Monday
(B) Tuesday
(C) Wednesday
(D) Friday
(E) Saturday

9. On Wednesday Doctor Yamata could be scheduled to

(A) conduct research in the morning and operate in the afternoon
(B) lecture in the morning and treat patients in the afternoon
(C) operate in the morning and lecture in the afternoon
(D) operate in the morning and conduct research in the afternoon
(E) treat patients in the morning and treat patients in the afternoon

10. Which one of the following statements must be true?

(A) There is one day on which the doctor treats patients both in the morning and in the afternoon.
(B) The doctor conducts research on one of the days on which she lectures.
(C) The doctor conducts research on one of the days on which she treats patients.
(D) The doctor lectures on one of the days on which she treats patients.
(E) The doctor lectures on one of the days on which she operates.

11. If Doctor Yamata operates on Tuesday, then her schedule for treating patients could be

(A) Monday morning, Monday afternoon, Friday morning, Friday afternoon
(B) Monday morning, Friday afternoon, Saturday morning, Saturday afternoon
(C) Monday afternoon, Wednesday morning, Wednesday afternoon, Saturday afternoon
(D) Wednesday morning, Wednesday afternoon, Friday afternoon, Saturday afternoon
(E) Wednesday afternoon, Friday afternoon, Saturday morning, Saturday afternoon

12. Which one of the following is a pair of days on both of which Doctor Yamata must treat patients?

(A) Monday and Tuesday
(B) Monday and Saturday
(C) Tuesday and Friday
(D) Tuesday and Saturday
(E) Friday and Saturday

GO ON TO THE NEXT PAGE.

Questions 13–18

Each of seven judges voted for or else against granting Datalog Corporation's petition. Each judge is categorized as conservative, moderate, or liberal, and no judge is assigned more than one of those labels. Two judges are conservatives, two are moderates, and three are liberals. The following is known about how the judges voted:

If the two conservatives and at least one liberal voted the same way as each other, then both moderates voted that way.
If the three liberals voted the same way as each other, then no conservative voted that way.
At least two of the judges voted for Datalog, and at least two voted against Datalog.
At least one conservative voted against Datalog.

13. If the two moderates did not vote the same way as each other, then which one of the following could be true?
    (A) No conservative and exactly two liberals voted for Datalog.
    (B) Exactly one conservative and exactly one liberal voted for Datalog.
    (C) Exactly one conservative and all three liberals voted for Datalog.
    (D) Exactly two conservatives and exactly one liberal voted for Datalog.
    (E) Exactly two conservatives and exactly two liberals voted for Datalog.

14. Which one of the following must be true?
    (A) At least one conservative voted for Datalog.
    (B) At least one liberal voted against Datalog.
    (C) At least one liberal voted for Datalog.
    (D) At least one moderate voted against Datalog.
    (E) At least one moderate voted for Datalog.

15. If the three liberals all voted the same way as each other, which one of the following must be true?
    (A) Both moderates voted for Datalog.
    (B) Both moderates voted against Datalog.
    (C) One conservative voted for Datalog and one conservative voted against Datalog.
    (D) One moderate voted for Datalog and one moderate voted against Datalog.
    (E) All three liberals voted for Datalog.

16. If exactly two judges voted against Datalog, then which one of the following must be true?
    (A) Both moderates voted for Datalog.
    (B) Exactly one conservative voted for Datalog.
    (C) No conservative voted for Datalog.
    (D) Exactly two liberals voted for Datalog.
    (E) Exactly three liberals voted for Datalog.

17. Each of the following could be a complete and accurate list of those judges who voted for Datalog EXCEPT
    (A) two liberals
    (B) one conservative, one liberal
    (C) two moderates, three liberals
    (D) one conservative, two moderates, two liberals
    (E) one conservative, two moderates, three liberals

18. If the two conservatives voted the same way as each other, but the liberals did not all vote the same way as each other, then each of the following must be true EXCEPT:
    (A) Both conservatives voted against Datalog.
    (B) Both moderates voted for Datalog.
    (C) At least one liberal voted against Datalog.
    (D) Exactly two liberals voted for Datalog.
    (E) Exactly five of the judges voted against Datalog.

GO ON TO THE NEXT PAGE.

Questions 19–24

An official is assigning five runners—Larry, Ned, Olivia, Patricia, and Sonja—to parallel lanes numbered consecutively 1 through 5. The official will also assign each runner to represent a different charity—F, G, H, J, and K—not necessarily in order of the runner's names as given. The following ordering restrictions apply:

The runner representing K is assigned to lane 4.
Patricia is assigned to the only lane between the lanes of the runners representing F and G.
There are exactly two lanes between Olivia's lane and the lane of the runner representing G.
Sonja is assigned to a higher-numbered lane than the lane to which Ned is assigned.

19. Which one of the following is a possible assignment of runners to lanes by the charity they represent?

	1	2	3	4	5
(A)	F	G	H	K	J
(B)	G	H	J	K	F
(C)	G	K	F	J	H
(D)	H	J	G	K	F
(E)	J	H	F	K	G

20. The lane to which Patricia is assigned must be a lane that is

(A) next to the lane to which Larry is assigned
(B) next to the lane to which Ned is assigned
(C) separated by exactly one lane from the lane to which Ned is assigned
(D) separated by exactly one lane from the lane to which Olivia is assigned
(E) separated by exactly one lane from the lane to which Sonja is assigned

21. If Olivia is assigned to lane 2, which one of the following assignments must be made?

	Charity	Lane
(A)	F	1
(B)	G	5
(C)	H	1
(D)	H	3
(E)	J	5

22. Which one of the following is a complete and accurate list of runners each of whom could be the runner representing F?

(A) Larry, Ned
(B) Patricia, Sonja
(C) Larry, Ned, Olivia
(D) Larry, Ned, Sonja
(E) Ned, Patricia, Sonja

23. If Ned is the runner representing J, then it must be true that

(A) the runner representing G is assigned to lane 1
(B) the runner representing H is assigned to lane 2
(C) Larry is the runner representing K
(D) Olivia is the runner representing F
(E) Patricia is the runner representing H

24. If Larry represents J, which one of the following could be the assignment of runners to lanes?

	1	2	3	4	5
(A)	Larry	Olivia	Ned	Patricia	Sonja
(B)	Larry	Ned	Olivia	Sonja	Patricia
(C)	Larry	Sonja	Patricia	Ned	Olivia
(D)	Ned	Olivia	Larry	Patricia	Sonja
(E)	Ned	Sonja	Olivia	Patricia	Larry

S T O P

IF YOU FINISH BEFORE TIME IS CALLED, YOU MAY CHECK YOUR WORK ON THIS SECTION ONLY.
DO NOT WORK ON ANY OTHER SECTION IN THE TEST.

SECTION III
Time—35 minutes
27 Questions

Directions: Each passage in this section is followed by a group of questions to be answered on the basis of what is stated or implied in the passage. For some of the questions, more than one of the choices could conceivably answer the question. However, you are to choose the best answer; that is, the response that most accurately and completely answers the question.

The labor force is often organized as if workers had no family responsibilities. Preschool-age children need full-time care; children in primary school need care after school and during school vacations. Although day-care services can resolve some scheduling conflicts between home and office, workers cannot always find or afford suitable care. Even when they obtain such care, parents must still cope with emergencies, such as illnesses, that keep children at home. Moreover, children need more than tending; they also need meaningful time with their parents. Conventional full-time workdays, especially when combined with unavoidable household duties, are too inflexible for parents with primary child-care responsibility.

Although a small but increasing number of working men are single parents, those barriers against successful participation in the labor market that are related to primary child-care responsibilities mainly disadvantage women. Even in families where both parents work, cultural pressures are traditionally much greater on mothers than on fathers to bear the primary child-rearing responsibilities.

In reconciling child-rearing responsibilities with participation in the labor market, many working mothers are forced to make compromises. For example, approximately one-third of all working mothers are employed only part-time, even though part-time jobs are dramatically underpaid and often less desirable in comparison to full-time employment. Even though part-time work is usually available only in occupations offering minimal employee responsibility and little opportunity for advancement or self-enrichment, such employment does allow many women the time and flexibility to fulfill their family duties, but only at the expense of the advantages associated with full-time employment.

Moreover, even mothers with full-time employment must compromise opportunities in order to adjust to barriers against parents in the labor market. Many choose jobs entailing little challenge or responsibility or those offering flexible scheduling, often available only in poorly paid positions, while other working mothers, although willing and able to assume as much responsibility as people without children, find that their need to spend regular and predictable time with their children inevitably causes them to lose career opportunities to those without such demands. Thus, women in education are more likely to become teachers than school administrators, whose more conventional full-time work schedules do not correspond to the schedules of school-age children, while female lawyers are more likely to practice law in trusts and estates, where they can control their work schedules, than in litigation, where they cannot. Nonprofessional women are concentrated in secretarial work and department store sales, where their absences can be covered easily by substitutes and where they can enter and leave the work force with little loss, since the jobs offer so little personal gain. Indeed, as long as the labor market remains hostile to parents, and family roles continue to be allocated on the basis of gender, women will be seriously disadvantaged in that labor market.

1. Which one of the following best summarizes the main idea of the passage?

(A) Current trends in the labor force indicate that working parents, especially women, may not always need to choose between occupational and child-care responsibilities.

(B) In order for mothers to have an equal opportunity for advancement in the labor force, traditional family roles have to be reexamined and revised.

(C) Although single parents who work have to balance parental and career demands, single mothers suffer resulting employment disadvantages that single fathers can almost always avoid.

(D) Although child-care responsibilities disadvantage many women in the labor force, professional women (such as teachers and lawyers) are better able to overcome this problem than are nonprofessional women.

(E) Traditional work schedules are too inflexible to accommodate the child-care responsibilities of many parents, a fact that severely disadvantages women in the labor force.

GO ON TO THE NEXT PAGE.

2. Which one of the following statements about part-time work can be inferred from the information presented in the passage?

(A) One-third of all part-time workers are working mothers.
(B) Part-time work generally offers fewer opportunities for advancement to working mothers than to women generally.
(C) Part-time work, in addition to having relatively poor wages, often requires that employees work during holidays, when their children are out of school.
(D) Part-time employment, despite its disadvantages, provides working mothers with an opportunity to address some of the demands of caring for children.
(E) Many mothers with primary child-care responsibility choose part-time jobs in order to better exploit full-time career opportunities after their children are grown.

3. It can be inferred from the passage that the author would be most likely to agree with which one of the following statements about working fathers in two-parent families?

(A) They are equally burdened by the employment disadvantages placed upon all parents—male and female—in the labor market.
(B) They are so absorbed in their jobs that they often do not see the injustice going on around them.
(C) They are shielded by the traditional allocation of family roles from many of the pressures associated with child-rearing responsibilities.
(D) They help compound the inequities in the labor market by keeping women from competing with men for career opportunities.
(E) They are responsible for many of the problems of working mothers because of their insistence on traditional roles in the family.

4. Of the following, which one would the author most likely say is the most troublesome barrier facing working parents with primary child-care responsibility?

(A) the lack of full-time jobs open to women
(B) the inflexibility of work schedules
(C) the low wages of part-time employment
(D) the limited advancement opportunities for nonprofessional employees
(E) the practice of allocating responsibilities in the workplace on the basis of gender

5. The passage suggests that day care is at best a limited solution to the pressures associated with child rearing for all of the following reasons EXCEPT:

(A) Even the best day care available cannot guarantee that children will have meaningful time with their parents.
(B) Some parents cannot afford day-care services.
(C) Working parents sometimes have difficulty finding suitable day care for their children.
(D) Parents who send their children to day care still need to provide care for their children during vacations.
(E) Even children who are in day care may have to stay home when they are sick.

6. According to the passage, many working parents may be forced to make any of the following types of career decisions EXCEPT

(A) declining professional positions for nonprofessional ones, which typically have less conventional work schedules
(B) accepting part-time employment rather than full-time employment
(C) taking jobs with limited responsibility, and thus more limited career opportunities, in order to have a more flexible schedule
(D) pursuing career specializations that allow them to control their work schedules instead of pursuing a more desirable specialization in the same field
(E) limiting the career potential of one parent, often the mother, who assumes greater child-care responsibility

7. Which one of the following statements would most appropriately continue the discussion at the end of the passage?

(A) At the same time, most men will remain better able to enjoy the career and salary opportunities offered by the labor market.
(B) Of course, men who are married to working mothers know of these employment barriers but seem unwilling to do anything about them.
(C) On the other hand, salary levels may become more equitable between men and women even if the other career opportunities remain more accessible to men than to women.
(D) On the contrary, men with primary child-rearing responsibilities will continue to enjoy more advantages in the workplace than their female counterparts.
(E) Thus, institutions in society that favor men over women will continue to widen the gap between the career opportunities available for men and for women.

GO ON TO THE NEXT PAGE.

Critics have long been puzzled by the inner contradictions of major characters in John Webster's tragedies. In his The Duchess of Malfi, for instance, the Duchess is "good" in demonstrating the obvious tenderness and sincerity of her love for Antonio, but "bad" in ignoring the wishes and welfare of her family and in making religion a "cloak" hiding worldly self-indulgence. Bosola is "bad" in serving Ferdinand, "good" in turning the Duchess' thoughts toward heaven and in planning to avenge her murder. The ancient Greek philosopher Aristotle implied that such contradictions are virtually essential to the tragic personality, and yet critics keep coming back to this element of inconsistency as though it were an eccentric feature of Webster's own tragic vision.

The problem is that, as an Elizabethan playwright, Webster has become a prisoner of our critical presuppositions. We have, in recent years, been dazzled by the way the earlier Renaissance and medieval theater, particularly the morality play, illuminates Elizabethan drama. We now understand how the habit of mind that saw the world as a battleground between good and evil produced the morality play. Morality plays allegorized that conflict by presenting characters whose actions were defined as the embodiment of good or evil. This model of reality lived on, overlaid by different conventions, in the more sophisticated Elizabethan works of the following age. Yet Webster seems not to have been as heavily influenced by the morality play's model of reality as were his Elizabethan contemporaries; he was apparently more sensitive to the more morally complicated Italian drama than to these English sources. Consequently, his characters cannot be evaluated according to reductive formulas of good and evil, which is precisely what modern critics have tried to do. They choose what seem to be the most promising of the contradictory values that are dramatized in the play, and treat those values as if they were the only basis for analyzing the moral development of the play's major characters, attributing the inconsistencies in a character's behavior to artistic incompetence on Webster's part. The lack of consistency in Webster's characters can be better understood if we recognize that the ambiguity at the heart of his tragic vision lies not in the external world but in the duality of human nature. Webster establishes tension in his plays by setting up conflicting systems of value that appear immoral only when one value system is viewed exclusively from the perspective of the other. He presents us not only with characters that we condemn intellectually or ethically and at the same time impulsively approve of, but also with judgments we must accept as logically sound and yet find emotionally repulsive. The dilemma is not only dramatic: it is tragic, because the conflict is irreconcilable, and because it is ours as much as that of the characters.

8. The primary purpose of the passage is to

(A) clarify an ambiguous assertion
(B) provide evidence in support of a commonly held view
(C) analyze an unresolved question and propose an answer
(D) offer an alternative to a flawed interpretation
(E) describe and categorize opposing viewpoints

9. The author suggests which one of the following about the dramatic works that most influenced Webster's tragedies?

(A) They were not concerned with dramatizing the conflict between good and evil that was presented in morality plays.
(B) They were not as sophisticated as the Italian sources from which other Elizabethan tragedies were derived.
(C) They have never been adequately understood by critics.
(D) They have only recently been used to illuminate the conventions of Elizabethan drama.
(E) They have been considered by many critics to be the reason for Webster's apparent artistic incompetence.

10. The author's allusion to Aristotle's view of tragedy in lines 10–13 serves which one of the following functions in the passage?

(A) It introduces a commonly held view of Webster's tragedies that the author plans to defend.
(B) It supports the author's suggestion that Webster's conception of tragedy is not idiosyncratic.
(C) It provides an example of an approach to Webster's tragedies that the author criticizes.
(D) It establishes the similarity between classical and modern approaches to tragedy.
(E) It supports the author's assertion that Elizabethan tragedy cannot be fully understood without the help of recent scholarship.

GO ON TO THE NEXT PAGE.

11. It can be inferred from the passage that modern critics' interpretations of Webster's tragedies would be more valid if

    (A) the ambiguity inherent in Webster's tragic vision resulted from the duality of human nature
    (B) Webster's conception of the tragic personality was similar to that of Aristotle
    (C) Webster had been heavily influenced by the morality play
    (D) Elizabethan dramatists had been more sensitive to Italian sources of influence
    (E) the inner conflicts exhibited by Webster's characters were similar to those of modern audiences

12. With which one of the following statements regarding Elizabethan drama would the author be most likely to agree?

    (A) The skill of Elizabethan dramatists has in recent years been overestimated.
    (B) The conventions that shaped Elizabethan drama are best exemplified by Webster's drama.
    (C) Elizabethan drama, for the most part, can be viewed as being heavily influenced by the morality play.
    (D) Only by carefully examining the work of his Elizabethan contemporaries can Webster's achievement as a dramatist be accurately measured.
    (E) Elizabethan drama can best be described as influenced by a composite of Italian and classical sources.

13. It can be inferred from the passage that most modern critics assume which one of the following in their interpretation of Webster's tragedies?

    (A) Webster's plays tended to allegorize the conflict between good and evil more than did those of his contemporaries.
    (B) Webster's plays were derived more from Italian than from English sources.
    (C) The artistic flaws in Webster's tragedies were largely the result of his ignorance of the classical definition of tragedy.
    (D) Webster's tragedies provide no relevant basis for analyzing the moral development of their characters.
    (E) In writing his tragedies, Webster was influenced by the same sources as his contemporaries.

14. The author implies that Webster's conception of tragedy was

    (A) artistically flawed
    (B) highly conventional
    (C) largely derived from the morality play
    (D) somewhat different from the conventional Elizabethan conception of tragedy
    (E) uninfluenced by the classical conception of tragedy

GO ON TO THE NEXT PAGE.

Cultivation of a single crop on a given tract of land leads eventually to decreased yields. One reason for this is that harmful bacterial phytopathogens, organisms parasitic on plant hosts, increase in the soil surrounding plant roots. The problem can be cured by crop rotation, denying the pathogens a suitable host for a period of time. However, even if crops are not rotated, the severity of diseases brought on by such phytopathogens often decreases after a number or years as the microbial population of the soil changes and the soil becomes "suppressive" to those diseases. While there may be many reasons for this phenomenon, it is clear that levels of certain bacteria, such as Pseudomonas fluorescens, a bacterium antagonistic to a number of harmful phytopathogens, are greater in suppressive than in nonsuppressive soil. This suggests that the presence of such bacteria suppresses phytopathogens. There is now considerable experimental support for this view. Wheat yield increases of 27 percent have been obtained in field trials by treatment of wheat seeds with fluorescent pseudomonads. Similar treatment of sugar beets, cotton, and potatoes has had similar results.

These improvements in crop yields through the application of Pseudomonas fluorescens suggest that agriculture could benefit from the use of bacteria genetically altered for specific purposes. For example, a form of phytopathogen altered to remove its harmful properties could be released into the environment in quantities favorable to its competing with and eventually excluding the harmful normal strain. Some experiments suggest that deliberately releasing altered nonpathogenic Pseudomonas syringae could crowd out the nonaltered variety that causes frost damage. Opponents of such research have objected that the deliberate and large-scale release of genetically altered bacteria might have deleterious results. Proponents, on the other hand, argue that this particular strain is altered only by the removal of the gene responsible for the strain's propensity to cause frost damage, thereby rendering it safer than the phytopathogen from which it was derived.

Some proponents have gone further and suggest that genetic alteration techniques could create organisms with totally new combinations of desirable traits not found in nature. For example, genes responsible for production of insecticidal compounds have been transposed from other bacteria into pseudomonads that colonize corn roots. Experiments of this kind are difficult and require great care: such bacteria are developed in highly artificial environments and may not compete well with natural soil bacteria. Nevertheless, proponents contend that the prospects for improved agriculture through such methods seem excellent. These prospects lead many to hope that current efforts to assess the risks of deliberate release of altered microorganisms will successfully answer the concerns of opponents and create a climate in which such research can go forward without undue impediment.

15. Which one of the following best summarizes the main idea of the passage?

(A) Recent field experiments with genetically altered Pseudomonas bacteria have shown that releasing genetically altered bacteria into the environment would not involve any significant danger.

(B) Encouraged by current research, advocates of agricultural use of genetically altered bacteria are optimistic that such use will eventually result in improved agriculture, though opponents remain wary.

(C) Current research indicates that adding genetically altered Pseudomonas syringae bacteria to the soil surrounding crop plant roots will have many beneficial effects, such as the prevention of frost damage in certain crops.

(D) Genetic alteration of a number of harmful phytopathogens has been advocated by many researchers who contend that these techniques will eventually replace such outdated methods as crop rotation.

(E) Genetic alteration of bacteria has been successful in highly artificial laboratory conditions, but opponents of such research have argued that these techniques are unlikely to produce organisms that are able to survive in natural environments.

16. The author discusses naturally occurring Pseudomonas fluorescens bacteria in the first paragraph primarily in order to do which one of the following?

(A) prove that increases in the level of such bacteria in the soil are the sole cause of soil suppressivity

(B) explain why yields increased after wheat fields were sprayed with altered Pseudomonas fluorescens bacteria

(C) detail the chemical processes that such bacteria use to suppress organisms parasitic to crop plants, such as wheat, sugar beets, and potatoes

(D) provide background information to support the argument that research into the agricultural use of genetically altered bacteria would be fruitful

(E) argue that crop rotation is unnecessary, since diseases brought on by phytopathogens diminish in severity and eventually disappear on their own

GO ON TO THE NEXT PAGE.

17. It can be inferred from the author's discussion of Pseudomonas fluorescens bacteria that which one of the following would be true of crops impervious to parasitical organisms?

    (A) Pseudomonas fluorescens bacteria would be absent from the soil surrounding their roots.
    (B) They would crowd out and eventually exclude other crop plants if their growth were not carefully regulated.
    (C) Their yield would not be likely to be improved by adding Pseudomonas fluorescens bacteria to the soil.
    (D) They would mature more quickly than crop plants that were susceptible to parasitical organisms.
    (E) Levels of phytopathogenic bacteria in the soil surrounding their roots would be higher compared with other crop plants.

18. It can be inferred from the passage that crop rotation can increase yields in part because

    (A) moving crop plants around makes them hardier and more resistant to disease
    (B) the number of Pseudomonas fluorescens bacteria in the soil usually increases when crops are rotated
    (C) the roots of many crop plants produce compounds that are antagonistic to phytopathogens harmful to other crop plants
    (D) the presence of phytopathogenic bacteria is responsible for the majority of plant diseases
    (E) phytopathogens typically attack some plant species but find other species to be unsuitable hosts

19. According to the passage, proponents of the use of genetically altered bacteria in agriculture argue that which one of the following is true of the altered bacteria used in the frost-damage experiments?

    (A) The altered bacteria had a genetic constitution differing from that of the normal strain only in that the altered variety had one less gene.
    (B) Although the altered bacteria competed effectively with the nonaltered strain in the laboratory, they were not as viable in natural environments.
    (C) The altered bacteria were much safer and more effective than the naturally occurring Pseudomonas fluorescens bacteria used in earlier experiments.
    (D) The altered bacteria were antagonistic to several types of naturally occurring phytopathogens in the soil surrounding the roots of frost-damaged crops.
    (E) The altered bacteria were released into the environment in numbers sufficient to guarantee the validity of experimental results.

20. Which one of the following, if true, would most seriously weaken the proponents' argument regarding the safety of using altered Pseudomonas syringae bacteria to control frost damage?

    (A) Pseudomonas syringae bacteria are primitive and have a simple genetic constitution.
    (B) The altered bacteria are derived from a strain that is parasitic to plants and can cause damage to crops.
    (C) Current genetic-engineering techniques permit the large-scale commercial production of such bacteria.
    (D) Often genes whose presence is responsible for one harmful characteristic must be present in order to prevent other harmful characteristics.
    (E) The frost-damage experiments with Pseudomonas syringae bacteria indicate that the altered variety would only replace the normal strain if released in sufficient numbers.

GO ON TO THE NEXT PAGE.

In 1887 the Dawes Act legislated wide-scale private ownership of reservation lands in the United States for Native Americans. The act allotted plots of 80 acres to each Native American adult. However, the Native Americans were not granted outright title to their lands. The act defined each grant as a "trust patent," meaning that the Bureau of Indian Affairs (BIA), the governmental agency in charge of administering policy regarding Native Americans, would hold the allotted land in trust for 25 years, during which time the Native American owners could use, but not alienate (sell) the land. After the 25-year period, the Native American allottee would receive a "fee patent" awarding full legal ownership of the land.

Two main reasons were advanced for the restriction on the Native Americans' ability to sell their lands. First, it was claimed that free alienability would lead to immediate transfer of large amounts of former reservation land to non-Native Americans, consequently threatening the traditional way of life on those reservations. A second objection to free alienation was that Native Americans were unaccustomed to, and did not desire, a system of private landownership. Their custom, it was said, favored communal use of land.

However, both of these arguments bear only on the transfer of Native American lands to non-Native Americans; neither offers a reason for prohibiting Native Americans from transferring land among themselves. Selling land to each other would not threaten the Native American culture. Additionally, if communal land use remained preferable to Native Americans after allotment, free alienability would have allowed allottees to sell their lands back to the tribe.

When stated rationales for government policies prove empty, using an interest-group model often provides an explanation. While neither Native Americans nor the potential non-Native American purchasers benefited from the restraint on alienation contained in the Dawes Act, one clearly defined group did benefit: the BIA bureaucrats. It has been convincingly demonstrated that bureaucrats seek to maximize the size of their staffs and their budgets in order to compensate for the lack of other sources of fulfillment, such as power and prestige. Additionally, politicians tend to favor the growth of governmental bureaucracy because such growth provides increased opportunity for the exercise of political patronage. The restraint on alienation vastly increased the amount of work, and hence the budgets, necessary to implement the statute. Until allotment was ended in 1934, granting fee patents and leasing Native American lands were among the principal activities of the United States government. One hypothesis, then, for the temporary restriction on alienation in the Dawes Act is that it reflected a compromise between non-Native Americans favoring immediate alienability so they could purchase land and the BIA bureaucrats who administered the privatization system.

21. Which one of the following best summarizes the main idea of the passage?

(A) United States government policy toward Native Americans has tended to disregard their needs and consider instead the needs of non-Native American purchasers of land.
(B) In order to preserve the unique way of life on Native American reservations, use of Native American lands must be communal rather than individual.
(C) The Dawes Act's restriction on the right of Native Americans to sell their land may have been implemented primarily to serve the interests of politicians and bureaucrats.
(D) The clause restricting free alienability in the Dawes Act greatly expanded United States governmental activity in the area of land administration.
(E) Since passage of the Dawes Act in 1887, Native Americans have not been able to sell or transfer their former reservation land freely.

22. Which one of the following statements concerning the reason for the end of allotment, if true, would provide the most support for the author's view of politicians?

(A) Politicians realized that allotment was damaging the Native American way of life.
(B) Politicians decided that allotment would be more congruent with the Native American custom of communal land use.
(C) Politicians believed that allotment's continuation would not enhance their opportunities to exercise patronage.
(D) Politicians felt that the staff and budgets of the BIA had grown too large.
(E) Politicians were concerned that too much Native American land was falling into the hands of non-Native Americans.

GO ON TO THE NEXT PAGE.

23. Which one of the following best describes the organization of the passage?

(A) The passage of a law is analyzed in detail, the benefits and drawbacks of one of its clauses are studied, and a final assessment of the law is offered.
(B) The history of a law is narrated, the effects of one of its clauses on various populations are studied, and repeal of the law is advocated.
(C) A law is examined, the political and social backgrounds of one of its clauses are characterized, and the permanent effects of the law are studied.
(D) A law is described, the rationale put forward for one of its clauses is outlined and dismissed, and a different rationale for the clause is presented.
(E) The legal status of an ethnic group is examined with respect to issues of landownership and commercial autonomy, and the benefits to rival groups due to that status are explained.

24. The author's attitude toward the reasons advanced for the restriction on alienability in the Dawes Act at the time of its passage can best be described as

(A) completely credulous
(B) partially approving
(C) basically indecisive
(D) mildly questioning
(E) highly skeptical

25. It can be inferred from the passage that which one of the following was true of Native American life immediately before passage of the Dawes Act?

(A) Most Native Americans supported themselves through farming.
(B) Not many Native Americans personally owned the land on which they lived.
(C) The land on which most Native Americans lived had been bought from their tribes.
(D) Few Native Americans had much contact with their non-Native American neighbors.
(E) Few Native Americans were willing to sell their land to non-Native Americans.

26. According to the passage, the type of landownership initially obtainable by Native Americans under the Dawes Act differed from the type of ownership obtainable after a 25-year period in that only the latter allowed

(A) owners of land to farm it
(B) owners of land to sell it
(C) government some control over how owners disposed of land
(D) owners of land to build on it with relatively minor governmental restrictions
(E) government to charge owners a fee for developing their land

27. Which one of the following, if true, would most strengthen the author's argument regarding the true motivation for the passage of the Dawes Act?

(A) The legislators who voted in favor of the Dawes Act owned land adjacent to Native American reservations.
(B) The majority of Native Americans who were granted fee patents did not sell their land back to their tribes.
(C) Native Americans managed to preserve their traditional culture even when they were geographically dispersed.
(D) The legislators who voted in favor of the Dawes Act were heavily influenced by BIA bureaucrats.
(E) Non-Native Americans who purchased the majority of Native American lands consolidated them into larger farm holdings.

S T O P

IF YOU FINISH BEFORE TIME IS CALLED, YOU MAY CHECK YOUR WORK ON THIS SECTION ONLY.
DO NOT WORK ON ANY OTHER SECTION IN THE TEST.

SECTION IV
Time—35 minutes
25 Questions

Directions: The questions in this section are based on the reasoning contained in brief statements or passages. For some questions, more than one of the choices could conceivably answer the question. However, you are to choose the best answer; that is, the response that most accurately and completely answers the question. You should not make assumptions that are by commonsense standards implausible, superfluous, or incompatible with the passage.

1. In 1974 the speed limit on highways in the United States was reduced to 55 miles per hour in order to save fuel. In the first 12 months after the change, the rate of highway fatalities dropped 15 percent, the sharpest one-year drop in history. Over the next 10 years, the fatality rate declined by another 25 percent. It follows that the 1974 reduction in the speed limit saved many lives.

Which one of the following, if true, most strengthens the argument?

(A) The 1974 fuel shortage cut driving sharply for more than a year.
(B) There was no decline in the rate of highway fatalities during the twelfth year following the reduction in the speed limit.
(C) Since 1974 automobile manufacturers have been required by law to install lifesaving equipment, such as seat belts, in all new cars.
(D) The fatality rate in highway accidents involving motorists driving faster than 55 miles per hour is much higher than in highway accidents that do not involve motorists driving at such speeds.
(E) Motorists are more likely to avoid accidents by matching their speed to that of the surrounding highway traffic than by driving at faster or slower speeds.

2. Some legislators refuse to commit public funds for new scientific research if they cannot be assured that the research will contribute to the public welfare. Such a position ignores the lessons of experience. Many important contributions to the public welfare that resulted from scientific research were never predicted as potential outcomes of that research. Suppose that a scientist in the early twentieth century had applied for public funds to study molds: who would have predicted that such research would lead to the discovery of antibiotics—one of the greatest contributions ever made to the public welfare?

Which one of the following most accurately expresses the main point of the argument?

(A) The committal of public funds for new scientific research will ensure that the public welfare will be enhanced.
(B) If it were possible to predict the general outcome of a new scientific research effort, then legislators would not refuse to commit public funds for that effort.
(C) Scientific discoveries that have contributed to the public welfare would have occurred sooner if public funds had been committed to the research that generated those discoveries.
(D) In order to ensure that scientific research is directed toward contributing to the public welfare, legislators must commit public funds to new scientific research.
(E) Lack of guarantees that new scientific research will contribute to the public welfare is not sufficient reason for legislators to refuse to commit public funds to new scientific research.

GO ON TO THE NEXT PAGE.

3. When workers do not find their assignments challenging, they become bored and so achieve less than their abilities would allow. On the other hand, when workers find their assignments too difficult, they give up and so again achieve less than what they are capable of achieving. It is, therefore, clear that no worker's full potential will ever be realized.

Which one of the following is an error of reasoning contained in the argument?

(A) mistakenly equating what is actual and what is merely possible
(B) assuming without warrant that a situation allows only two possibilities
(C) relying on subjective rather than objective evidence
(D) confusing the coincidence of two events with a causal relation between the two
(E) depending on the ambiguous use of a key term

4. Our tomato soup provides good nutrition: for instance, a warm bowl of it contains more units of vitamin C than does a serving of apricots or fresh carrots!

The advertisement is misleading if which one of the following is true?

(A) Few people depend exclusively on apricots and carrots to supply vitamin C to their diets.
(B) A liquid can lose vitamins if it stands in contact with the air for a protracted period of time.
(C) Tomato soup contains important nutrients other than vitamin C.
(D) The amount of vitamin C provided by a serving of the advertised soup is less than the amount furnished by a serving of fresh strawberries.
(E) Apricots and fresh carrots are widely known to be nutritious, but their contribution consists primarily in providing a large amount of vitamin A, not a large amount of vitamin C.

Questions 5–6

The government provides insurance for individuals' bank deposits, but requires the banks to pay the premiums for this insurance. Since it is depositors who primarily benefit from the security this insurance provides, the government should take steps to ensure that depositors who want this security bear the cost of it and thus should make depositors pay the premiums for insuring their own accounts.

5. Which one of the following principles, if established, would do most to justify drawing the conclusion of the argument on the basis of the reasons offered in its support?

(A) The people who stand to benefit from an economic service should always be made to bear the costs of that service.
(B) Any rational system of insurance must base the size of premiums on the degree of risk involved.
(C) Government-backed security for investors, such as bank depositors, should be provided only when it does not reduce incentives for investors to make responsible investments.
(D) The choice of not accepting an offered service should always be available, even if there is no charge for the service.
(E) The government should avoid any actions that might alter the behavior of corporations and individuals in the market.

6. Which one of the following is assumed by the argument?

(A) Banks are not insured by the government against default on the loans the banks make.
(B) Private insurance companies do not have the resources to provide banks or individuals with deposit insurance.
(C) Banks do not always cover the cost of the deposit-insurance premiums by paying depositors lower interest rates on insured deposits than the banks would on uninsured deposits.
(D) The government limits the insurance protection it provides by insuring accounts up to a certain legally defined amount only.
(E) The government does not allow banks to offer some kinds of accounts in which deposits are not insured.

GO ON TO THE NEXT PAGE.

7. When individual students are all treated equally in that they have identical exposure to curriculum material, the rate, quality, and quantity of learning will vary from student to student. If all students are to master a given curriculum, some of them need different types of help than others, as any experienced teacher knows.

If the statements above are both true, which one of the following conclusions can be drawn on the basis of them?

(A) Unequal treatment, in a sense, of individual students is required in order to ensure equality with respect to the educational tasks they master.
(B) The rate and quality of learning, with learning understood as the acquiring of the ability to solve problems within a given curriculum area, depend on the quantity of teaching an individual student receives in any given curriculum.
(C) The more experienced the teacher is, the more the students will learn.
(D) All students should have identical exposure to learn the material being taught in any given curriculum.
(E) Teachers should help each of their students to learn as much as possible.

8. George: Some scientists say that global warming will occur because people are releasing large amounts of carbon dioxide into the atmosphere by burning trees and fossil fuels. We can see, though, that the predicted warming is occurring already. In the middle of last winter, we had a month of springlike weather in our area, and this fall, because of unusually mild temperatures, the leaves on our town's trees were three weeks late in turning color.

Which one of the following would it be most relevant to investigate in evaluating the conclusion of George's argument?

(A) whether carbon dioxide is the only cause of global warming
(B) when leaves on the trees in the town usually change color
(C) what proportion of global emissions of carbon dioxide is due to the burning of trees by humans
(D) whether air pollution is causing some trees in the area to lose their leaves
(E) whether unusually warm weather is occurring elsewhere on the globe more frequently than before

9. Student representative: Our university, in expelling a student who verbally harassed his roommate, has erred by penalizing the student for doing what he surely has a right to do: speak his mind!

Dean of students: But what you're saying is that our university should endorse verbal harassment. Yet surely if we did that, we would threaten the free flow of ideas that is the essence of university life.

Which one of the following is a questionable technique that the dean of students uses in attempting to refute the student representative?

(A) challenging the student representative's knowledge of the process by which the student was expelled
(B) invoking a fallacious distinction between speech and other sorts of behavior
(C) misdescribing the student representative's position, thereby making it easier to challenge
(D) questioning the motives of the student representative rather than offering reasons for the conclusion defended
(E) relying on a position of power to silence the opposing viewpoint with a threat

10. Famous personalities found guilty of many types of crimes in well-publicized trials are increasingly sentenced to the performance of community service, though unknown defendants convicted of similar crimes almost always serve prison sentences. However, the principle of equality before the law rules out using fame and publicity as relevant considerations in the sentencing of convicted criminals.

The statements above, if true, most strongly support which one of the following conclusions?

(A) The principle of equality before the law is rigorously applied in only a few types of criminal trials.
(B) The number of convicted celebrities sentenced to community service should equal the number of convicted unknown defendants sentenced to community service.
(C) The principle of equality before the law can properly be overridden by other principles in some cases.
(D) The sentencing of celebrities to community service instead of prison constitutes a violation of the principle of equality before the law in many cases.
(E) The principle of equality before the law does not allow for leniency in sentencing.

GO ON TO THE NEXT PAGE.

11. Scientific research at a certain university was supported in part by an annual grant from a major foundation. When the university's physics department embarked on weapons-related research, the foundation, which has a purely humanitarian mission, threatened to cancel its grant. The university then promised that none of the foundation's money would be used for the weapons research, whereupon the foundation withdrew its threat, concluding that the weapons research would not benefit from the foundation's grant.

Which one of the following describes a flaw in the reasoning underlying the foundation's conclusion?

(A) It overlooks the possibility that the availability of the foundation's money for humanitarian uses will allow the university to redirect other funds from humanitarian uses to weapons research.
(B) It overlooks the possibility that the physics department's weapons research is not the only one of the university's research activities with other than purely humanitarian purposes.
(C) It overlooks the possibility that the university made its promise specifically in order to induce the foundation to withdraw its threat.
(D) It confuses the intention of not using a sum of money for a particular purpose with the intention of not using that sum of money at all.
(E) It assumes that if the means to achieve an objective are humanitarian in character, then the objective is also humanitarian in character.

12. To suit the needs of corporate clients, advertising agencies have successfully modified a strategy originally developed for political campaigns. This strategy aims to provide clients with free publicity and air time by designing an advertising campaign that is controversial, thus drawing prime-time media coverage and evoking public comment by officials.

The statements above, if true, most seriously undermine which one of the following assertions?

(A) The usefulness of an advertising campaign is based solely on the degree to which the campaign's advertisements persuade their audiences.
(B) Only a small percentage of eligible voters admit to being influenced by advertising campaigns in deciding how to vote.
(C) Campaign managers have transformed political campaigns by making increasing use of strategies borrowed from corporate advertising campaigns.
(D) Corporations are typically more concerned with maintaining public recognition of the corporate name than with enhancing goodwill toward the corporation.
(E) Advertising agencies that specialize in campaigns for corporate clients are not usually chosen for political campaigns.

13. The National Association of Fire Fighters says that 45 percent of homes now have smoke detectors, whereas only 30 percent of homes had them 10 years ago. This makes early detection of house fires no more likely, however, because over half of the domestic smoke detectors are either without batteries or else inoperative for some other reason.

In order for the conclusion above to be properly drawn, which one of the following assumptions would have to be made?

(A) Fifteen percent of domestic smoke detectors were installed less than 10 years ago.
(B) The number of fires per year in homes with smoke detectors has increased.
(C) Not all of the smoke detectors in homes are battery operated.
(D) The proportion of domestic smoke detectors that are inoperative has increased in the past ten years.
(E) Unlike automatic water sprinklers, a properly functioning smoke detector cannot by itself increase fire safety in a home.

GO ON TO THE NEXT PAGE.

14. Advertisement: HomeGlo Paints, Inc., has won the prestigious Golden Paintbrush Award given to the one paint manufacturer in the country that has increased the environmental safety of its product most over the past three years—for HomeGlo Exterior Enamel. The Golden Paintbrush is awarded only on the basis of thorough tests by independent testing laboratories. So when you choose HomeGlo Exterior Enamel, you will know that you have chosen the most environmentally safe brand of paint manufactured in this country today.

The flawed reasoning in the advertisement most closely parallels that in which one of the following?

(A) The ZXC audio system received the overall top ranking for looks, performance, durability, and value in Listeners' Report magazine's ratings of currently produced systems. Therefore, the ZXC must have better sound quality than any other currently produced sound system.
(B) Morning Sunshine breakfast cereal contains, ounce for ounce, more of the nutrients needed for a healthy diet than any other breakfast cereal on the market today. Thus, when you eat Morning Sunshine, you will know you are eating the most nutritious food now on the market.
(C) The number of consumer visits increased more at Countryside Market last year than at any other market in the region. Therefore, Countryside's profits must also have increased more last year than those of any other market in the region.
(D) Jerrold's teachers recognize him as the student who has shown more academic improvement than any other student in the junior class this year. Therefore, if Jerrold and his classmates are ranked according to their current academic performance, Jerrold must hold the highest ranking.
(E) Margaret Durring's short story "The Power Lunch" won three separate awards for best short fiction of the year. Therefore, any of Margaret Durring's earlier stories certainly has enough literary merit to be included in an anthology of the best recent short fiction.

15. The consistency of ice cream is adversely affected by even slight temperature changes in the freezer. To counteract this problem, manufacturers add stabilizers to ice cream. Unfortunately, stabilizers, though inexpensive, adversely affect flavor. Stabilizers are less needed if storage temperatures are very low. However, since energy costs are constantly going up, those costs constitute a strong incentive in favor of relatively high storage temperatures.

Which one of the following can be properly inferred from the passage?

(A) Even slight deviations from the proper consistency for ice cream sharply impair its flavor.
(B) Cost considerations favor sacrificing consistency over sacrificing flavor.
(C) It would not be cost-effective to develop a new device to maintain the constancy of freezer temperatures.
(D) Stabilizers function well only at very low freezer temperatures.
(E) Very low, stable freezer temperatures allow for the best possible consistency and flavor of ice cream.

16. Edwina: True appreciation of Mozart's music demands that you hear it exactly as he intended it to be heard; that is, exactly as he heard it. Since he heard it on eighteenth-century instruments, it follows that so should we.

Alberto: But what makes you think that Mozart ever heard his music played as he had intended it to be played? After all, Mozart was writing at a time when the performer was expected, as a matter of course, not just to interpret but to modify the written score.

Alberto adopts which one of the following strategies in criticizing Edwina's position?

(A) He appeals to an academic authority in order to challenge the factual basis of her conclusion.
(B) He attacks her judgment by suggesting that she does not recognize the importance of the performer's creativity to the audience's appreciation of a musical composition.
(C) He defends a competing view of musical authenticity.
(D) He attacks the logic of her argument by suggesting that the conclusion she draws does not follow from the premises she sets forth.
(E) He offers a reason to believe that one of the premises of her argument is false.

GO ON TO THE NEXT PAGE.

17. Since the introduction of the Impanian National Health scheme, Impanians (or their private insurance companies) have had to pay only for the more unusual and sophisticated medical procedures. When the scheme was introduced, it was hoped that private insurance to pay for these procedures would be available at modest cost, since the insurers would no longer be paying for the bulk of health care costs, as they had done previously. Paradoxically, however, the cost of private health insurance did not decrease but has instead increased dramatically in the years since the scheme's introduction.

Which one of the following, if true, does most to explain the apparently paradoxical outcome?

(A) The National Health scheme has greatly reduced the number of medical claims handled annually by Impania's private insurers, enabling these firms to reduce overhead costs substantially.
(B) Before the National Health scheme was introduced, more than 80 percent of all Impanian medical costs were associated with procedures that are now covered by the scheme.
(C) Impanians who previously were unable to afford regular medical treatment now use the National Health scheme, but the number of Impanians with private health insurance has not increased.
(D) Impanians now buy private medical insurance only at times when they expect that they will need care of kinds not available in the National Health scheme.
(E) The proportion of total expenditures within Impania that is spent on health care has declined since the introduction of the National Health scheme.

18. In clinical trials of new medicines, half of the subjects receive the drug being tested and half receive a physiologically inert substance—a placebo. Trials are designed with the intention that neither subjects nor experimenters will find out which subjects are actually being given the drug being tested. However, this intention is frequently frustrated because_______.

Which one of the following, if true, most appropriately completes the explanation?

(A) often the subjects who receive the drug being tested develop symptoms that the experimenters recognize as side effects of the physiologically active drug
(B) subjects who believe they are receiving the drug being tested often display improvements in their conditions regardless of whether what is administered to them is physiologically active or not
(C) in general, when the trial is intended to establish the experimental drug's safety rather than its effectiveness, all of the subjects are healthy volunteers
(D) when a trial runs a long time, few of the experimenters will work on it from inception to conclusion
(E) the people who are subjects for clinical trials must, by law, be volunteers and must be informed of the possibility that they will receive a placebo

19. It takes 365.25 days for the Earth to make one complete revolution around the Sun. Long-standing convention makes a year 365 days long, with an extra day added every fourth year, and the year is divided into 52 seven-day weeks. But since 52 times 7 is only 364, anniversaries do not fall on the same day of the week each year. Many scheduling problems could be avoided if the last day of each year and an additional day every fourth year belonged to no week, so that January 1 would be a Sunday every year.

The proposal above, once put into effect, would be most likely to result in continued scheduling conflicts for which one of the following groups?

(A) people who have birthdays or other anniversaries on December 30 or 31
(B) employed people whose strict religious observances require that they refrain from working every seventh day
(C) school systems that require students to attend classes a specific number of days each year
(D) employed people who have three-day breaks from work when holidays are celebrated on Mondays or Fridays
(E) people who have to plan events several years before those events occur

GO ON TO THE NEXT PAGE.

20. Graphologists claim that it is possible to detect permanent character traits by examining people's handwriting. For example, a strong cross on the "t" is supposed to denote enthusiasm. Obviously, however, with practice and perseverance people can alter their handwriting to include this feature. So it seems that graphologists must hold that permanent character traits can be changed.

The argument against graphology proceeds by

(A) citing apparently incontestable evidence that leads to absurd consequences when conjoined with the view in question
(B) demonstrating that an apparently controversial and interesting claim is really just a platitude
(C) arguing that a particular technique of analysis can never be effective when the people analyzed know that it is being used
(D) showing that proponents of the view have no theoretical justification for the view
(E) attacking a technique by arguing that what the technique is supposed to detect can be detected quite readily without it

Questions 21–22

Historian: There is no direct evidence that timber was traded between the ancient nations of Poran and Nayal, but the fact that a law setting tariffs on timber imports from Poran was enacted during the third Nayalese dynasty does suggest that during that period a timber trade was conducted.

Critic: Your reasoning is flawed. During its third dynasty, Nayal may well have imported timber from Poran, but certainly on today's statute books there remain many laws regulating activities that were once common but in which people no longer engage.

21. The critic's response to the historian's reasoning does which one of the following?

(A) It implies an analogy between the present and the past.
(B) It identifies a general principle that the historian's reasoning violates.
(C) It distinguishes between what has been established as a certainty and what has been established as a possibility.
(D) It establishes explicit criteria that must be used in evaluating indirect evidence.
(E) It points out the dissimilar roles that law plays in societies that are distinct from one another.

22. The critic's response to the historian is flawed because it

(A) produces evidence that is consistent with there not having been any timber trade between Poran and Nayal during the third Nayalese dynasty
(B) cites current laws without indicating whether the laws cited are relevant to the timber trade
(C) fails to recognize that the historian's conclusion was based on indirect evidence rather than direct evidence
(D) takes no account of the difference between a law's enactment at a particular time and a law's existence as part of a legal code at a particular time
(E) accepts without question the assumption about the purpose of laws that underlies the historian's argument

GO ON TO THE NEXT PAGE.

23. The workers at Bell Manufacturing will shortly go on strike unless the management increases their wages. As Bell's president is well aware, however, in order to increase the workers' wages, Bell would have to sell off some of its subsidiaries. So, some of Bell's subsidiaries will be sold.

The conclusion above is properly drawn if which one of the following is assumed?

(A) Bell Manufacturing will begin to suffer increased losses.
(B) Bell's management will refuse to increase its workers' wages.
(C) The workers at Bell Manufacturing will not be going on strike.
(D) Bell's president has the authority to offer the workers their desired wage increase.
(E) Bell's workers will not accept a package of improved benefits in place of their desired wage increase.

24. One sure way you can tell how quickly a new idea—for example, the idea of "privatization"—is taking hold among the population is to monitor how fast the word or words expressing that particular idea are passing into common usage. Professional opinions of whether or not words can indeed be said to have passed into common usage are available from dictionary editors, who are vitally concerned with this question.

The method described above for determining how quickly a new idea is taking hold relies on which one of the following assumptions?

(A) Dictionary editors are not professionally interested in words that are only rarely used.
(B) Dictionary editors have exact numerical criteria for telling when a word has passed into common usage.
(C) For a new idea to take hold, dictionary editors have to include the relevant word or words in their dictionaries.
(D) As a word passes into common usage, its meaning does not undergo any severe distortions in the process.
(E) Words denoting new ideas tend to be used before the ideas denoted are understood.

25. Because migrant workers are typically not hired by any one employer for longer than a single season, migrant workers can legally be paid less than the minimum hourly wage that the government requires employers to pay all their permanent employees. Yet most migrant workers work long hours each day for eleven or twelve months a year and thus are as much full-time workers as are people hired on a year-round basis. Therefore, the law should require that migrant workers be paid the same minimum hourly wage that other full-time workers must be paid.

The pattern of reasoning displayed above most closely parallels that displayed in which one of the following arguments?

(A) Because day-care facilities are now regulated at the local level, the quality of care available to children in two different cities can differ widely. Since such differences in treatment clearly are unfair, day care should be federally rather than locally regulated.
(B) Because many rural areas have few restrictions on development, housing estates in such areas have been built where no adequate supply of safe drinking water could be ensured. Thus, rural areas should adopt building codes more like those large cities have.
(C) Because some countries regulate gun sales more strictly than do other countries, some people can readily purchase a gun, whereas others cannot. Therefore, all countries should cooperate in developing a uniform international policy regarding gun sales.
(D) Because it is a democratic principle that laws should have the consent of those affected by them, liquor laws should be formulated not by politicians but by club and restaurant owners, since such laws directly affect the profitability of their businesses.
(E) Because food additives are not considered drugs, they have not had to meet the safety standards the government applies to drugs. But food additives can be as dangerous as drugs. Therefore, food additives should also be subject to safety regulations as stringent as those covering drugs.

S T O P

IF YOU FINISH BEFORE TIME IS CALLED, YOU MAY CHECK YOUR WORK ON THIS SECTION ONLY.
DO NOT WORK ON ANY OTHER SECTION IN THE TEST.

Test I

Answers

Section I

1. C
2. C
3. E
4. E
5. B
6. E
7. C
8. A
9. D
10. B
11. C
12. A
13. C
14. E
15. A
16. B
17. B
18. C
19. C
20. B
21. B
22. E
23. D
24. A
25. D

Section II

1. C
2. A
3. C
4. C
5. E
6. C
7. D
8. B
9. C
10. E
11. E
12. E
13. B
14. C
15. E
16. A
17. E
18. B
19. E
20. D
21. B
22. D
23. B
24. A

Section III

1. E
2. D
3. C
4. B
5. D
6. A
7. A
8. D
9. A
10. B
11. C
12. C
13. E
14. D
15. B
16. D
17. C
18. E
19. A
20. D
21. C
22. C
23. D
24. E
25. B
26. B
27. D

Section IV

1. D
2. E
3. B
4. E
5. A
6. C
7. A
8. E
9. C
10. D
11. A
12. A
13. D
14. D
15. E
16. E
17. D
18. A
19. B
20. A
21. A
22. D
23. C
24. D
25. E

Score Conversion Chart

Directions:

1. Use the Scoring Worksheet below to compute your raw score.

2. Use the Score Conversion Chart to convert your raw score into the 120–180 scale.

Scoring Worksheet

1. Enter the number of questions you answered correctly in each section.

	Number Correct
SECTION I	______
SECTION II	______
SECTION III	______
SECTION IV	______

2. Enter the sum here: ______

This is your Raw Score

Conversion Chart

For Converting Raw Score to the 120-180 LSAT Scaled Score

Reported Score	Raw Score Lowest	Raw Score Highest
180	98	101
179	97	97
178	95	96
177	94	94
176	93	93
175	92	92
174	91	91
173	90	90
172	89	89
171	88	88
170	86	87
169	85	85
168	84	84
167	82	83
166	81	81
165	79	80
164	78	78
163	76	77
162	75	75
161	73	74
160	72	72
159	70	71
158	68	69
157	67	67
156	65	66
155	64	64
154	62	63
153	60	61
152	59	59
151	57	58
150	56	56
149	54	55
148	53	53
147	51	52
146	50	50
145	48	49
144	47	47
143	45	46
142	44	44
141	42	43
140	41	41
139	39	40
138	38	38
137	37	37
136	35	35
135	34	34
134	33	33
133	31	32
132	30	30
131	29	29
130	28	28
129	27	27
128	26	26
127	24	25
126	23	23
125	22	22
124	21	21
123	20	20
122	19	19
121	18	18
120	0	17

Test I
Section I
Solutions

1. (A) No. If anything, this statement tends to support the conclusion that literacy rates increased after the invention of the printing press.
(B) No. This is irrelevant.
(C) Yes. This shows that the jump in sales was not due to an increase in literacy. Rather, the same people who bought the manuscript copies simply bought more of the printed books.
(D) No. This is irrelevant.
(E) No. Although this may be true, the argument claims there was a drastic jump in the literacy rate after the printing press was invented.

2. (A) No. This fact would make Bevex more dangerous for humans than the studies on mice indicate.
(B) No. This merely indicates that other products may be unsafe.
(C) Yes. If people do drink more than 25 cans of Bevex-sweetened soft drinks per day, then the tests conducted on mice would be very relevant.
(D) No. This may mitigate some of the negative effects of Bevex-sweetened soft drinks, but it does not make Bevex safe.
(E) No. The passage does not question the relevance of the fact that Bevex is carcinogenic for mice. Rather, it merely implies that people do not ingest enough Bevex for there to be a problem.

3. (A) No. Harry is referring to the technical capabilities of modern air travel, but Judith interpreted him as referring to widespread financial availability of air travel.
(B) No. She has interpreted him as saying that everyone can afford air travel, not that everyone has a right to experience air travel.
(C) No. Harry is referring to the technical capabilities of modern air travel, but Judith interpreted him as referring to widespread financial availability of air travel.
(D) No. Harry is referring to the technical capabilities of modern air travel, but Judith interpreted him as referring to widespread financial availability of air travel.
(E) Yes. Harry is referring to the technical capabilities of modern air travel, but Judith interpreted him as referring to widespread financial availability of air travel.

4. (A) No. The advertisement does not claim that the pill's fiber content is unique.
(B) No. This strengthens the advertisement.
(C) No. This is irrelevant since sleeping pills and painkillers are not fiber-supplement pills.
(D) No. This is not an excessively high number.
(E) Yes. Although a pill with 44 percent fiber sounds good, the more important issue is "How much of the fiber we need each day does the 44 percent represent?" If we need 100 grams of fiber daily and the pill, though almost half fiber, contains only one gram of fiber, then we would have to take 100 pills a day to get our daily intake. In this case, the fact that the pill is 44 percent fiber is insignificant, and it is therefore misleading for the advertisement to focus on the percentage of fiber instead of the absolute amount.

5. (A) No. The passage is about the effects that certain actions have on the environment, not on other people. Besides, the point of the passage is that consumers are unable to know these effects.
(B) Yes. The point of the passage is that consumers cannot know which products truly harm the environment and so are unable to choose to restrict their purchases to environmentally benign products.
(C) No. The passage concerns the morality of the choices consumers make, not the options offered to consumers.
(D) No. There is no discussion of the gradation of harm in the passage. Besides, the point of the passage is that consumers are unable to know these effects.
(E) No. The passage is minimizing the moral duty of consumers.

6. (A) No. The argument is by analogy; no evidence is cited.
(B) No. There is no ridicule or sarcasm in the passage.
(C) No. The advertisement merely draws an analogy between muscles and brains.
(D) No. The advertisement is drawing an analogy between muscles and brains.
(E) Yes. The advertisement draws an analogy between muscles and brains, and it concludes that since exercise improves the performance of one's muscles it will also improve the performance of one's brain.

7. (A) No. This is not mentioned or implied.
(B) No. This is not mentioned or implied.
(C) Yes. The passage is drawing an analogy between a balloon and the health care system: Push in on one area of a balloon and another area will bulge out. Likewise, contain one area of health care costs and another area will expand.
(D) No. This is too strong. The passage does disparage the current system, but it does not claim that a solution is impossible. In fact, the passage implies that a solution may be found by a universal approach.
(E) No. This is not mentioned. The only example mentioned points to the failure of a particular approach.

8. (A) Yes. The purpose of the balloon analogy is to point out that any piecemeal attempt at containing costs is doomed to failure. Therefore, if a solution is possible, it can be found only through a comprehensive approach.
(B) No. The passage is advocating a comprehensive approach to health care reform. It is not discussing or advocating any individual issues.
(C) No. The passage is advocating a comprehensive approach to health care reform. It is not discussing or advocating any individual issues.
(D) No. The passage is advocating a comprehensive approach to health care reform. It is not discussing or advocating any individual issues.
(E) No. The passage is advocating a comprehensive approach to health care reform. It is not discussing or advocating any individual issues.

9. (A) No. In the passage, no distinction is made between the various news media.
(B) No. Although the news media probably do emphasize exceptional events to satisfy the public's taste for the extraordinary, the passage does not indicate why the news media emphasize exceptional events.
(C) No. The passage discusses only the effects of the emphasis the media gives to events, not people's psychological reactions to events.
(D) Yes. The passage says that the public fears most what it sees most. So if the news media gives more coverage to rare air crashes than to common car crashes, then the public will mistakenly believe that air travel is more dangerous.
(E) No. Although this is supported by the passages, it misses the main point of the passage: that excessive coverage of exceptional events <u>distorts</u> public perception of the risk of various activities. In this answer-choice, the coverage would give the public a <u>true</u> perception of the risks involved.

10. (A) No. The evidence fails to even establish that it was the reduction in food-additive intake which caused the reduction in behavior problems, let alone that it caused a proportionate reduction.
(B) Yes. In order for the conclusion to reasonably follow, we need to know what would have happened had the diet not been changed. Perhaps the same decrease in behavior problems would have occurred even if the diet was not changed. In other words, we need a control group with which to compare the results of the test group.
(C) No. In this situation, percentage is more important than absolute number.
(D) No. This is irrelevant.
(E) No. Since the evidence fails to establish anything, this answer-choice is not incorrect. However, there is a more precise answer-choice.

11. (A) No. This is irrelevant. Further, it does not give a reason for the different results between cars of the 1960s and 1970s.
(B) No. This is irrelevant since neither cars from the 1960s nor from the 1970s are new.
(C) Yes. This explains the discrepancy well. Another explanation might be that cars from the sixties are more likely to be considered classics and therefore maintained better and driven less.
(D) No. This is irrelevant.
(E) No. This strengthens the discrepancy since even fewer cars from the 1960s would need major engine repairs.

12. (A) Yes. The first sentence says that all mathematicians today accept enormous computations as adequate proof of some theorems. And the last sentence says some mathematicians long for a simple proof to a simple theorem while nevertheless some theorems require enormous proofs. Combined, these two statements imply that *"Today, some mathematicians who believe that a simple theorem ought to have a simple proof would consider accepting the results of an enormous computation as a demonstration of the truth of a theorem."*
(B) No. This is independent of the passage.
(C) No. The first sentence implies that all mathematicians today accept enormous computations as adequate proof of some theorems.
(D) No. This is <u>not</u> true for mathematicians. It may or may not be true for nonmathematicians.
(E) No. We are told nothing about nonmathematicians.

13. (A) No. The first sentence is naturally symbolized as **C—>~O**, where C stands for *"you climb mountains"* and O stands for *"you will ... live to a ripe old age."* Remembering that A unless B means ~B—>A, the second sentence can be translated as **~C—>B**, where B stands for *"you will be bored."* The last sentence can be symbolized as **O—>B**. Summarizing this work in a diagram yields

C—>~O
~C—>B
∴ O—>B

Now, the first sentence of the answer-choice is naturally symbolized as **~T—>~S**, where ~T stands for *"you do not try to swim"* and ~S stands for *"you will not learn how to swim."* The second sentence can be translated as **~S—>~Sa**, where ~Sa stands for *"you will not be safe in boats."* The last sentence is symbolized as **T**. Summarizing this work in a diagram yields

~T—>~S
~S—>~Sa
∴ T

Clearly, this diagram is not similar in structure to the original diagram. In particular, the conclusion is not a conditional statement.
(B) No. The passage is a valid argument, whereas this answer-choice is not a valid argument.
(C) Yes. The first sentence is naturally symbolized as **C—>~O**, where C stands for *"you climb mountains"* and O stands for *"you will ... live to a ripe old age."* Remembering that A unless B means ~B—>A, the second sentence can be translated as **~C—>B**, where B stands for *"you will be bored."* The last sentence can be symbolized as **O—>B**. Summarizing this work in a diagram yields

C—>~O
~C—>B
______
∴ **O—>B**

Now, the first sentence of the answer-choice is naturally symbolized as **W—>~G**, where W stands for *"you work for your candidate"* and G stands for *"you will ... improve your guitar playing."* The second sentence can be translated as **~W—>N**, where N stands for *"you will neglect your civic duty."* The last sentence can be symbolized as **G—>N**. Summarizing this work in a diagram yields

W—>~G
~W—>N
______
∴ **G—>N**

This diagram is identical in structure to the original diagram.
(D) No. The passage is a valid argument, whereas this answer-choice is not a valid argument.
(E) No. The passage is a valid argument, whereas this answer-choice is not a valid argument.

14. (A) No. The argument is concerned only with trapped lobsters.
(B) No. If this choice were false—i.e., if two months was not the longest known period eight or more lobsters were trapped together—the conclusion would not be weakened.
(C) No. This is irrelevant.
(D) No. This is irrelevant—the argument is only about lobsters.
(E) Yes. Perhaps food drifted into the cage from a current, or perhaps other creatures that the lobsters feed on entered the cage. To be valid, the argument must assume that any food which entered the cage was not sufficient to satisfy the lobsters' hunger.

15. (A) Yes. It is possible that the deer population would have increased dramatically even if hunting had not been banned. That the deer population did not increase in nearby counties which permit hunting provides strong evidence that the ban on hunting caused the dramatic increase in population.
(B) No. The passage already states the accidents result in serious injury.
(C) No. This is irrelevant to the conclusion.
(D) No. This is irrelevant to the conclusion.
(E) No. The passage already states that the deer are damaging property; besides, damaged landscaping is not a danger to public safety.

16. (A) No. We can conclude nothing about any comets other than Halley's comet.
(B) Yes. The passage states that the amount of light reflected by a comet increases as its mass increases. From a measurement of a comet's brightness, its mass is calculated. However, if Halley's comet is less reflective than previously believed, it will take more mass than previously believed to reflect the measured amount of light.
(C) No. The amount of light reflected from the comet is measured from earth and does not change with the probe's finding. However, the comet's mass required to reflect this amount of light will need to be re-estimated.
(D) No. This is independent of the passage.
(E) No. This is independent of the passage. It is a good conclusion, though.

17. (A) No. The supplier understands that the office manager believes recycled paper is of inferior quality—an incorrect belief. However, the supplier fails to inform the manager otherwise.
(B) Yes. The stationery supplier's opening line, *"Recycled paper is not necessarily inferior,"* does address the office manager's objection, but the rest of the passage is just a history lesson on how paper has been manufactured. The office manager needs information about today's recycled paper—in particular, information about the type of recycled paper that is being considered for purchase.
(C) No. This is not necessary for the stationery supplier's argument, which is about the quality of recycled paper.
(D) No. This is not necessary for the stationery supplier's argument, which is about the quality of recycled paper.
(E) No. In fact, the response is addressing the office manager's concern about quality, albeit ineffectively.

18. (A) No. It actually weakens the argument. It's a point someone arguing against the conclusion might bring up.
(B) No. Although it does help justify the difference in the actual outcome of the two cases, the statement is made to counter its potential use against the argument. It is often effective to point out the weak points in your argument before someone else does.
(C) Yes. When presenting an argument it is often effective to concede certain minor points that weaken your argument. This shows that your opinion is well

considered, and it also disarms your opposition before they can make an objection.
(D) No. However, it could be used to illustrate a general principle on which opposition to the argument relies.
(E) No. It does point out a position against which the argument is directed. However, it does not summarize that opposite position.

19. (A) No. This is the point of the passage: that the punishment was not equitable.
(B) No. Since this is independent of what is stated in the passage, whether it is true or false does not affect the truth of the passage.
(C) Yes. The passage states that *"the taxi ... caused the damage"* and asserts that there was no difference in the blameworthiness of Peter and Alicia. However, this would be incorrect if Alicia was driving with extra caution while Peter was driving recklessly.
(D) No. Since this is independent of what is stated in the passage, whether it is true or false does not affect the truth of the passage.
(E) No. Since this is independent of what is stated in the passage, whether it is true or false does not affect the truth of the passage.

20. (A) No. Clearly, the original argument is fallacious. Just because a particular person does not run against Esposito does not imply that other people will not. However, this answer-choice is a reasonable argument.
(B) Yes. The original argument can be diagrammed as follows:

E
E-->~K
∴ Only E

where E stands for "Esposito runs in the election," and ~K stands for "Krasman does not run in the election." Clearly, this argument is fallacious. Just because a particular person does not run against Esposito does not imply that other people will not. Now, the answer-choice can be symbolized as follows:

S
S-->~F
∴ Only S

where S stands for "Saturday concert," and ~F stands for "not on Friday." Clearly, there is a one-to-one correspondence between the two diagrams.
(C) No. Clearly, the original argument is fallacious. Just because a particular person does not run against Esposito does not imply that other people will not. However, this answer-choice is a reasonable argument.
(D) No. This is the second-best choice. The argument has essentially the same structure as the original except for the restriction that there are only two people who could be involved. This makes the argument reasonable. However, the original argument is fallacious. Just because a particular person does not run against Esposito does not imply that other people will not.
(E) No. Clearly, the original argument is fallacious. Just because a particular person does not run against Esposito does not imply that other people will not. However, this answer-choice is a reasonable argument.

21. (A) No. This is too strong. The passage does imply that a serious accident is likely to occur, but it does not imply that there will be an ever-increasing yearly incidence of serious accidents.
(B) Yes. The point of the passage is that it is the people who are flawed, not the technology. Further, since people cannot be rewired, they will inevitably make mistakes. Hence, over time a serious accident is likely to occur.
(C) No. Although the passage implies that the technology is well designed, the clause *"have not so far been"* in the first sentence leaves open the possibility that nuclear power plants may have flaws that have yet to become apparent.
(D) No. The point of the passage is that it's the people that are flawed, not the materials used to construct the plants.
(E) No. The passage does indirectly support this conclusion (though, it is a bit strong). However, this conclusion misses the point of the passage, namely that a serious accident is likely to occur due to human error.

22. (A) No. This is irrelevant.
(B) No. This is irrelevant. The skeptics' position is a critique of using animal behavior to predict earthquakes.
(C) No. This is irrelevant.
(D) No. This is irrelevant.
(E) Yes. This significantly weakens the skeptics' position. If animals exhibit a particular, unusual behavior only before earthquakes, then it is less likely to be a coincidence.

23. (A) No. This argues against the claim that *"criminals who commit lucrative crimes like embezzlement or insider trading are more successful at avoiding conviction than are street criminals."* If many street criminals can afford high-priced attorneys, then according to the passage they too should have a low conviction rate.
(B) No. The passage argues that high-priced attorneys get the embezzlers off, whereas this answer-choice provides an alternative explanation: it

is the incompetence of the prosecutors that get the embezzlers off.
(C) No. The relevant figure is the percentage of criminals convicted of street crimes versus criminals convicted of embezzlement, not the absolute number. There may be many more street criminals than embezzlers.
(D) Yes. The underlying premise of the argument is that the percentage of people in either group who are actually guilty is the same. Perhaps nearly all the people who rely on court-appointed public defenders are actually guilty, but few of the people who hire private lawyers are actually guilty.
(E) No. The passage argues that the lesser quality of public defenders causes the higher conviction rate of their clients. This answer-choice argues that a different factor is responsible—juries' sympathy for the victims of street criminals.

24. (A) Yes. The passage states *"investigators ignore anything that does not directly bear on the funded research."* The passage then concludes *"serendipity can no longer play a role in scientific discovery."* This assumes that serendipitous discoveries can occur only outside the area currently being studied. It is conceivable that a scientist could make a serendipitous discovery in an area of funded research while working on another area of funded research.
(B) No. This is irrelevant.
(C) No. This is irrelevant.
(D) No. This is irrelevant.
(E) No. This is irrelevant.

25. (A) No. This would make the insurance industry statistics show a lower theft rate.
(B) No. The conclusion concerns the difference in rates of car theft in two categories (a percentage), not with absolute numbers.
(C) No. This is irrelevant.
(D) Yes. This resolves the paradox well. If the owners of cars with antitheft devices live in areas with high rates of car theft, then even if the devices help prevent car thefts their cars may still be more likely to be stolen than cars without antitheft devices in areas with little or no car theft. Another possible explanation is that the antitheft devices are more likely to be installed on expensive cars, which are more often the target of thieves.
(E) No. According to the passage, police statistics do show that automobile antitheft devices reduce the risk of car theft.

Test I
Section II
Solutions

Questions 1–7

The conditions can be symbolized as follows:

LO
L—>news
G __ __P

_1_ _2_ _3_ _4_ _5_ _6_ _7_

Note, G and P in the symbol statement **G __ __P** can be interchanged.

1. (A) No. Since G is played second, the condition **G __ __P** forces P into space 5:

1	2	3	4	5	6	7
	G			P		

Now, the condition **LO** cannot be placed in spaces 6 and 7 because that would violate the condition **L—>news**. Hence, the condition **LO** must be placed in spaces 3 and 4:

1	2	3	4	5	6	7
	G	L	O	P		

Thus, L must be in space 3.
(B) No. Since G is played second, the condition **G __ __P** forces P into space 5:

1	2	3	4	5	6	7
	G			P		

Now, the condition **LO** cannot be placed in spaces 6 and 7 because that would violate the condition **L—>news**. Hence, the condition **LO** must be placed in spaces 3 and 4:

1	2	3	4	5	6	7
	G	L	O	P		

Thus, L must be in space 3.
(C) Yes. Since G is played second, the condition **G __ __P** forces P into space 5:

1	2	3	4	5	6	7
	G			P		

Now, the condition **LO** cannot be placed in spaces 6 and 7 because that would violate the condition **L—>news**. Hence, the condition **LO** must be placed in spaces 3 and 4:

1	2	3	4	5	6	7
	G	L	O	P		

Thus, L must be in space 3.
(D) No. Since G is played second, the condition **G __ __ P** forces P into space 5:

1	2	3	4	5	6	7
	G			P		

Now, the condition **LO** cannot be placed in spaces 6 and 7 because that would violate the condition **L—>news**. Hence, the condition **LO** must be placed in spaces 3 and 4:

1	2	3	4	5	6	7
	G	L	O	P		

Thus, L must be in space 3.
(E) No. Since G is played second, the condition **G __ __ P** forces P into space 5:

1	2	3	4	5	6	7
	G			P		

Now, the condition **LO** cannot be placed in spaces 6 and 7 because that would violate the condition **L—>news**. Hence, the condition **LO** must be placed in spaces 3 and 4:

1	2	3	4	5	6	7
	G	L	O	P		

Thus, L must be in space 3.

2. (A) Yes. Place the news in slot 2:

1	2	3	4	5	6	7
	news					

Now, the condition **L—>news** forces L into slot 1:

1	2	3	4	5	6	7
L	news					

However, this diagram leaves no room for the condition **LO**. So the news tape cannot be played second.
(B) No. The following valid diagram has the news in slot 3:

1	2	3	4	5	6	7
L	O	news	G	H	S	P

(C) No. The following valid diagram has the news in slot 4:

1	2	3	4	5	6	7
L	O	P	news	H	G	S

(D) No. The following valid diagram has the news in slot 5:

1	2	3	4	5	6	7
G	L	O	P	news	H	S

(E) No. The following valid diagram has the news in slot 6:

1	2	3	4	5	6	7
H	G	L	O	P	news	S

3. (A) No. H and S can be the first and last tapes played, respectively, as the following valid diagram illustrates:

1	2	3	4	5	6	7
H	G	L	O	P	news	S

(B) No. This violates the condition **L—>news**.
(C) Yes. Placing the information on the diagram yields

1	2	3	4	5	6	7
H	G	L				

The condition **LO** forces O into slot 4, and the condition **G __ __ P** forces P into slot 5:

1	2	3	4	5	6	7
H	G	L	O	P		

To be scheduled as far from H as possible, S must be in slot 7, which forces the news into slot 6:

1	2	3	4	5	6	7
H	G	L	O	P	news	S

This diagram satisfies all the conditions and has H, G, and L in the first, second, and third time slots, respectively.
(D) No. Place the information on the diagram:

1	2	3	4	5	6	7
H	L	O				S

Clearly, there is no room on this diagram to place the condition **G __ __ P.**
(E) No. H and S can be the first and last tapes played, respectively, as the following valid diagram illustrates:

1	2	3	4	5	6	7
H	G	L	O	P	news	S

4. (A) No. Place the new condition:

1	2	3	4	5	6	7
				P		

Then the condition **G __ __ P** forces G into space 2:

1	2	3	4	5	6	7
	G			P		

The condition **LO** must be placed in positions 3 and 4; in spaces 6 and 7 it would violate the condition **L—>news**. This yields

1	2	3	4	5	6	7
	G	L	O	P		

Hence, L must be played third. Note, this question is essentially identical to Question 1. It is not uncommon for the LSAT writers to ask the same question in different forms.

(B) No. Place the new condition:

1	2	3	4	5	6	7
				P		

Then the condition **G __ __ P** forces G into space 2:

1	2	3	4	5	6	7
	G			P		

The condition **LO** must be placed in positions 3 and 4; in spaces 6 and 7 it would violate the condition **L—>news**. This yields

1	2	3	4	5	6	7
	G	L	O	P		

Hence, L must be played third. Note, this question is essentially identical to Question 1. It is not uncommon for the LSAT writers to ask the same question in different forms.

(C) Yes. Place the new condition:

1	2	3	4	5	6	7
				P		

Then the condition **G __ __ P** forces G into space 2:

1	2	3	4	5	6	7
	G			P		

The condition **LO** must be placed in positions 3 and 4; in spaces 6 and 7 it would violate the condition **L—>news**. This yields

1	2	3	4	5	6	7
	G	L	O	P		

Hence, L must be played third. Note, this question is essentially identical to Question 1. It is not uncommon for the LSAT writers to ask the same question in different forms.

(D) No. Place the new condition:

1	2	3	4	5	6	7
				P		

Then the condition **G __ __ P** forces G into space 2:

1	2	3	4	5	6	7
	G			P		

The condition **LO** must be placed in positions 3 and 4; in spaces 6 and 7 it would violate the condition **L—>news**. This yields

1	2	3	4	5	6	7
	G	L	O	P		

Hence, L must be played third. Note, this question is essentially identical to Question 1. It is not uncommon for the LSAT writers to ask the same question in different forms.

(E) No. Place the new condition:

1	2	3	4	5	6	7
				P		

Then the condition **G __ __ P** forces G into space 2:

1	2	3	4	5	6	7
	G			P		

The condition **LO** must be placed in positions 3 and 4; in spaces 6 and 7 it would violate the condition **L—>news**. This yields

1	2	3	4	5	6	7
	G	L	O	P		

Hence, L must be played third. Note, this question is essentially identical to Question 1. It is not uncommon for the LSAT writers to ask the same question in different forms.

5. (A) No. Suppose S is in the first slot and the news is in the last slot:

1	2	3	4	5	6	7
S						news

Next, if G is placed in slot 2, then the condition **G __ __ P** forces P into slot 5:

1	2	3	4	5	6	7
S	G			P		news

The condition **LO** must be placed in slots 3 and 4, which in turn forces H into slot 6:

1	2	3	4	5	6	7
S	G	L	O	P	H	news

This diagram satisfies all the conditions. Hence, a maximum of 5 tapes can separate S from the news.
(B) No. Suppose S is in the first slot and the news is in the last slot:

1	2	3	4	5	6	7
S						news

Next, if G is placed in slot 2, then the condition **G __ __ P** forces P into slot 5:

1	2	3	4	5	6	7
S	G			P		news

The condition **LO** must be placed in slots 3 and 4, which in turn forces H into slot 6:

1	2	3	4	5	6	7
S	G	L	O	P	H	news

This diagram satisfies all the conditions. Hence, a maximum of 5 tapes can separate S from the news.
(C) No. Suppose S is in the first slot and the news is in the last slot:

1	2	3	4	5	6	7
S						news

Next, if G is placed in slot 2, then the condition **G __ __ P** forces P into slot 5:

1	2	3	4	5	6	7
S	G			P		news

The condition **LO** must be placed in slots 3 and 4, which in turn forces H into slot 6:

1	2	3	4	5	6	7
S	G	L	O	P	H	news

This diagram satisfies all the conditions. Hence, a maximum of 5 tapes can separate S from the news.
(D) No. Suppose S is in the first slot and the news is in the last slot:

1	2	3	4	5	6	7
S						news

Next, if G is placed in slot 2, then the condition **G __ __ P** forces P into slot 5:

1	2	3	4	5	6	7
S	G			P		news

The condition **LO** must be placed in slots 3 and 4, which in turn forces H into slot 6:

1	2	3	4	5	6	7
S	G	L	O	P	H	news

This diagram satisfies all the conditions. Hence, a maximum of 5 tapes can separate S from the news.
(E) Yes. Suppose S is in the first slot and the news is in the last slot:

1	2	3	4	5	6	7
S						news

Next, if G is placed in slot 2, then the condition **G __ __ P** forces P into slot 5:

1	2	3	4	5	6	7
S	G			P		news

The condition **LO** must be placed in slots 3 and 4, which in turn forces H into slot 6:

1	2	3	4	5	6	7
S	G	L	O	P	H	news

This diagram satisfies all the conditions. Hence, a maximum of 5 tapes can separate S from the news.

6. (A) No. The following diagram satisfies all the conditions and has L fourth:

1	2	3	4	5	6	7
H	S	G	L	O	news	P

(B) No. The following diagram satisfies all the conditions and has L fifth:

1	2	3	4	5	6	7
G	H	S	P	L	O	news

(C) Yes. Suppose L is played fifth. Then the condition **LO** forces O to be played sixth, and the condition **L—>news** forces the news to be played seventh:

1	2	3	4	5	6	7
				L	O	news

Now, the condition **G __ __ P** can be placed as follows:

1	2	3	4	5	6	7
G			P	L	O	news

This diagram satisfies all the conditions. Hence, L can be played fifth. Furthermore, L cannot be played sixth or seventh because that would violate the conditions **LO** and **L—>news**.
(D) No. From the two conditions **LO** and **L—>news**, we see that L can be scheduled no later than fifth.
(E) No. This violates the condition **LO**.

7. (A) No. The following valid diagrams have O in different time slots:

1	2	3	4	5	6	7
G	L	O	P	news	H	S

1	2	3	4	5	6	7
G	H	S	P	L	O	news

(B) No. The following valid diagrams have O in different time slots:

1	2	3	4	5	6	7
L	O	G	news	H	P	S

1	2	3	4	5	6	7
H	S	G	L	O	P	news

(C) No. The following valid diagrams have O in different time slots:

1	2	3	4	5	6	7
L	O	news	G	H	S	P

1	2	3	4	5	6	7
H	L	O	G	news	S	P

(D) Yes. If G is fifth, then the condition **G __ __ P** forces P into slot 2:

1	2	3	4	5	6	7
	P			G		

The condition **LO** cannot be placed in slots 6 and 7 since that would violate the condition **L—>news**. Hence, **LO** must be placed in slots 3 and 4. Therefore, O can only be played fourth.

(E) No. The following valid diagrams have O in different time slots:

1	2	3	4	5	6	7
L	O	P	news	H	G	S

1	2	3	4	5	6	7
H	S	P	L	O	G	news

Questions 8–12

8. (A) No. The following diagram satisfies all the conditions and does not have Doctor Yamata lecturing on Monday (L = lecturing, O = operating, T = treating patients, R = conducting research):

	M	T	W	F	S
am	O	T	O	O	R
pm	T	L	L	T	T

(B) Yes. Since *"On Saturday she neither lectures nor performs operations,"* she must lecture either Monday and Tuesday or Tuesday and Wednesday (*She lectures in the afternoon on exactly two consecutive calendar days*). In either case, this has her lecturing on Tuesday.

Caution: She cannot lecture both Wednesday and Friday because they are not consecutive calendar days.

(C) No. The following diagram satisfies all the conditions and does not have Doctor Yamata lecturing on Wednesday:

	M	T	W	F	S
am	T	O	O	O	R
pm	L	L	T	T	T

(D) No. The following diagram satisfies all the conditions and does not have Doctor Yamata lecturing on Friday:

	M	T	W	F	S
am	O	T	O	O	R
pm	T	L	L	T	T

(E) No. This violates the condition *"On Saturday she neither lectures nor performs operations."*

9. (A) No. *"She lectures in the afternoon on exactly two consecutive calendar days"* and *"She treats patients on exactly one morning and exactly three afternoons."* Since her workweek is 5 days long, in the afternoon she can only lecture or treat patients.

(B) No. Suppose she lectures in the morning and treats patients in the afternoon on Wednesday:

	M	T	W	F	S
am			L		
pm			T		

Since *"She performs operations on exactly three mornings,"* and does not operate on Saturdays, the diagram becomes

	M	T	W	F	S
am	O	O	L	O	
pm			T		

However, this violates the condition *"If she operates on Monday, she does not operate on Tuesday."*

(C) Yes. The following diagram satisfies all the conditions and has Doctor Yamata operating Wednesday morning and lecturing Wednesday afternoon:

	M	T	W	F	S
am	O	T	O	O	R
pm	T	L	L	T	T

(D) No. *"She lectures in the afternoon on exactly two consecutive calendar days"* and *"She treats patients on exactly ... three afternoons."* Since her workweek is 5 days long, in the afternoon she can only lecture or treat patients.

(E) No. Suppose she treats patients in the morning and in the afternoon on Wednesday:

	M	T	W	F	S
am			T		
pm			T		

Since *"She performs operations on exactly three mornings,"* and does not operate on Saturdays, the diagram becomes

	M	T	W	F	S
am	O	O	T	O	
pm			T		

However, this violates the condition *"If she operates on Monday, she does not operate on Tuesday."*

10. (A) No. The following diagram satisfies all the conditions and does not have her treating patients in both the morning and the afternoon on any day:

	M	T	W	F	S
am	O	T	O	O	R
pm	T	L	L	T	T

(B) No. The following diagram satisfies all the conditions and does not have her conducting research on the same day she lectures:

	M	T	W	F	S
am	O	T	O	O	R
pm	T	L	L	T	T

(C) No. The following diagram satisfies all the conditions and does not have her conducting research on the same day she treats patients:

	M	T	W	F	S
am	R	O	O	O	T
pm	L	L	T	T	T

(D) No. The following diagram satisfies all the conditions and does not have her lecturing on the same day she treats patients:

	M	T	W	F	S
am	R	O	O	O	T
pm	L	L	T	T	T

(E) Yes. *"On Saturday she neither lectures nor performs operations."* Since *"She performs operations on exactly three mornings"* of the remaining four days and *"lectures in the afternoon on exactly two consecutive calendar days,"* she must both operate and lecture on at least one day.

11. (A) No. This violates the condition *"She treats patients on exactly one morning . . ."*

(B) No. This violates the condition *"She treats patients on exactly one morning . . ."*

(C) No. Adding the information to the diagram yields

	M	T	W	F	S
am		O	T		
pm	T		T		T

Clearly, this diagram violates the condition *"She lectures in the afternoon on exactly two consecutive calendar days."*

(D) No. Adding the information to the diagram yields

	M	T	W	F	S
am		O	T		
pm			T	T	T

Adding the conditions *"She performs operations on exactly three mornings"* and *"On Saturday she [does not] perform operations"* yields

	M	T	W	F	S
am	O	O	T	O	
pm			T	T	T

However, this diagram violates the condition, *"If she operates on Monday, she does not operate on Tuesday."*

(E) Yes. Adding the information to the diagram yields

	M	T	W	F	S
am					T
pm			T	T	T

Adding the condition *"She lectures in the afternoon on exactly two consecutive calendar days"* yields

	M	T	W	F	S
am					T
pm	L	L	T	T	T

Now, the remaining schedule must be filled in as follows:

	M	T	W	F	S
am	O	R	O	O	T
pm	L	L	T	T	T

This diagram satisfies all the conditions.

12. (A) No. The following diagram satisfies all the conditions and does not have her treating patients on Monday or Tuesday:

	M	T	W	F	S
am	O	R	O	O	T
pm	L	L	T	T	T

(B) No. The following diagram satisfies all the conditions and does not have her treating patients on Monday:

	M	T	W	F	S
am	R	O	O	O	T
pm	L	L	T	T	T

(C) No. The following diagram satisfies all the conditions and does not have her treating patients on Tuesday:

	M	T	W	F	S
am	R	O	O	O	T
pm	L	L	T	T	T

(D) No. The following diagram satisfies all the conditions and does not have her treating patients on Tuesday:

	M	T	W	F	S
am	R	O	O	O	T
pm	L	L	T	T	T

(E) Yes. Since *"On Saturday she neither lectures nor performs operations,"* she must lecture either Monday and Tuesday or Tuesday and Wednesday (*She lectures in the afternoon on exactly two consecutive calendar days*). She cannot lecture both Wednesday and Friday because they are not consecutive calendar days. Combining this with the condition *"She treats patients on … exactly three afternoons,"* yields the two following diagrams:

Diagram I

	M	T	W	F	S
am					
pm	L	L	T	T	T

Diagram II

	M	T	W	F	S
am					
pm	T	L	L	T	T

Thus, in either case, she treats patients on Friday and Saturday.

Questions 13–18

13. (A) No. This choice has both conservatives and one liberal voting against Datalog. Hence, the hypothesis of Condition 1 is satisfied, and therefore both moderates voted the same way. However, this violates the supplemental condition that *"the two moderates did not vote the same way as each other."*
(B) Yes. This choice has exactly one conservative voting for Datalog. Hence, the other conservative voted against Datalog, which satisfies Condition 4. Again, this choice has exactly one conservative and exactly one liberal voting for Datalog. Hence, the other two liberals voted against Datalog. This gives two people voting for Datalog (one conservative and one liberal) and two people voting against Datalog (two liberals). Hence, Condition 3 is satisfied. Further, Conditions 1 and 2 do not apply. Hence, none of the conditions are violated.

Note, we did not need the supplementary condition *"the two moderates did not vote the same way as each other."* This condition was introduced to make some of the other answer-choices incorrect.
(C) No. This violates Condition 2.
(D) No. Since the moderates split their vote, this violates Condition 1.
(E) No. Since the moderates split their vote, this violates Condition 1.

14. (A) No. If both conservatives voted against Datalog and all three liberals voted for Datalog, then all the conditions are satisfied.
(B) No. If both conservatives voted against Datalog and all three liberals voted for Datalog, then all the conditions are satisfied.
(C) Yes. Suppose all three liberals voted against Datalog. Then from Condition 2, we know that both conservatives voted for Datalog. However, this violates Condition 4. Hence, at least one liberal voted for Datalog.
(D) No. If both conservatives voted against Datalog and all three liberals voted for Datalog, then all the conditions are satisfied. The moderates can cast their votes in any combination.
(E) No. If both conservatives voted against Datalog and all three liberals voted for Datalog, then all the conditions are satisfied. The moderates can cast their votes in any combination.

15. (A) No. In Question 14, we learned that at least one liberal voted for Datalog. So if all three liberals voted the same way, then they must have all voted for Datalog. Now, Condition 2 forces both conservatives to vote against Datalog. This already satisfies all the conditions. Hence, one or both moderates could vote against Datalog.
(B) No. In Question 14, we learned that at least one liberal voted for Datalog. So if all three liberals voted the same way, then they must have all voted for

Datalog. Now, Condition 2 forces both conservatives to vote against Datalog. This already satisfies all the conditions. Hence, one or both moderates could vote for Datalog.
(C) No. In Question 14, we learned that at least one liberal voted for Datalog. So if all three liberals voted the same way, then they must have all voted for Datalog. Now, Condition 2 forces both conservatives to vote against Datalog.
(D) No. In Question 14, we learned that at least one liberal voted for Datalog. So if all three liberals voted the same way, then they must have all voted for Datalog. Now, Condition 2 forces both conservatives to vote against Datalog. This already satisfies all the conditions. Hence, both moderates could vote for Datalog or both moderates could vote against Datalog.
(E) Yes. In Question 14, we learned that at least one liberal voted for Datalog. So if all three liberals voted the same way, then they must have all voted for Datalog.

16. (A) Yes. From Condition 4, we know that at least one conservative voted against Datalog. Suppose one moderate also voted against Datalog—contradicting choice (A). This forces the three liberals to vote for Datalog. So from Condition 2, we know that both conservatives voted against Datalog. However, this violates our assumption that only one conservative and only one moderate voted for Datalog.
(B) No. If exactly two conservatives voted against Datalog and all the other judges voted for Datalog, then all the conditions are satisfied.
(C) No. If exactly one liberal and one conservative voted against Datalog and all the other judges—including one conservative—voted for Datalog, then all the conditions are satisfied.
(D) No. If exactly two conservatives voted against Datalog and all the other judges voted for Datalog, then all the conditions are satisfied.
(E) No. If exactly one liberal and one conservative voted against Datalog and all the other judges voted for Datalog, then all the conditions are satisfied.

17. (A) No. If both conservatives and both moderates vote against Datalog, then exactly two liberals can vote for Datalog.
(B) No. If exactly two liberals and both moderates vote against Datalog, then exactly one conservative and exactly one liberal must vote for Datalog.
(C) No. If only the conservatives vote against Datalog, then exactly two moderates and exactly three liberals must vote for Datalog.
(D) No. If the only judges to vote against Datalog are one conservative and one liberal, then exactly one conservative, two moderates, and two liberals must vote for Datalog.
(E) Yes. Choice (E) has six of the seven judges voting for Datalog. This violates Condition 3, which states "at least *two* [judges] voted against Datalog."

18. (A) No. Condition 4 says at least one conservative voted against Datalog, so if both conservatives voted the same way, both conservatives voted against Datalog.
(B) Yes. Condition 4 says at least one conservative voted against Datalog, so if both conservatives voted the same way, both conservatives voted against Datalog. Additionally, the liberals split their vote, so at least one voted for Datalog and at least one against. Summarizing, the two conservatives and at least one liberal voted against Datalog's petition. Condition 1 then requires that both moderates voted this way. So the moderates cannot vote for Datalog.
(C) No. The liberals split their vote, so at least one voted for Datalog and at least one against.
(D) No. Condition 4 says at least one conservative voted against Datalog, so if both conservatives voted the same way, both conservatives voted against Datalog. Additionally, the liberals split their vote, so at least one voted for Datalog and at least one against. Summarizing, the two conservatives and at least one liberal voted against Datalog's petition. Now, Condition 1 requires that both moderates voted this way. Thus, at least 5 judges voted against Datalog. Further, since *"at least two of the judges voted for Datalog,"* the two remaining judges—liberals—voted for Datalog.
(E) No. Condition 4 says at least one conservative voted against Datalog, so if both conservatives voted the same way, both conservatives voted against Datalog. Additionally, the liberals split their vote, so at least one voted for Datalog and at least one against. Summarizing, the two conservatives and at least one liberal voted against Datalog's petition. Now, Condition 1 requires that both moderates voted this way. Thus, at least 5 judges voted against Datalog. Further, since *"at least two of the judges voted for Datalog,"* no more than 5 judges voted against Datalog. In other words, exactly 5 judges voted against Datalog.

<u>Questions 19–24</u>

19. (A) No. This violates the condition *"Patricia is assigned to the only lane between the lanes of the runners representing F and G,"* indicating exactly one lane between F and G.
(B) No. This violates the condition *"Patricia is assigned to the only lane between the lanes of the runners representing F and G,"* indicating exactly one lane between F and G.
(C) No. This violates the condition *"The runner representing K is assigned to lane 4."*
(D) No. This violates the condition *"There are exactly two lanes between Olivia's lane and the lane of the runner representing G."*
(E) Yes. This problem is best solved by elimination:

Choice (A) violates the condition *"Patricia is assigned to the only lane between the lanes of the runners representing F and G."*
Choice (B) violates the condition *"Patricia is assigned to the only lane between the lanes of the runners representing F and G."*
Choice (C) violates the condition *"The runner representing K is assigned to lane 4."*
Choice (D) violates the condition *"There are exactly two lanes between Olivia's lane and the lane of the runner representing G."*

Hence, by process of elimination, the answer is (E).

20. (A) No. The following assignment satisfies all the conditions and does not have Patricia next to Larry:

1	2	3	4	5
Larry	Olivia	Ned	Patricia	Sonja
H	J	F	K	G

(B) No. The following assignment satisfies all the conditions and does not have Patricia next to Ned:

1	2	3	4	5
Ned	Olivia	Larry	Patricia	Sonja
H	J	F	K	G

(C) No. The following assignment satisfies all the conditions and has Patricia separated from Ned by two lanes:

1	2	3	4	5
Ned	Olivia	Larry	Patricia	Sonja
H	J	F	K	G

(D) Yes. The condition *"Patricia is assigned to the only lane between the lanes of the runners representing F and G"* can be represented as follows:

___	Patricia	___
F		G

Now, *"There are exactly two lanes between Olivia's lane and the lane of the runner representing G."* Adding this to the above diagram generates two diagrams:

Diagram I

___	Patricia	___	___	___	Olivia
F		G	?	?	

Diagram II

Olivia	___	Patricia	___
	F		G

Diagram I is invalid since it assigns people to six different lanes—violating the fact that there are only five lanes. This leaves only Diagram II, which has Patricia separated from Olivia by exactly one lane.

(E) No. The following assignment satisfies all the conditions and has Patricia next to Sonja:

1	2	3	4	5
Ned	Olivia	Larry	Patricia	Sonja
H	J	F	K	G

21. (A) No. The following valid assignment has Olivia in lane 2 and F not in lane 1:

1	2	3	4	5
Ned	Olivia	Larry	Patricia	Sonja
H	J	F	K	G

(B) Yes. Since *"There are exactly two lanes between Olivia's lane and the lane of the runner representing G,"* G must be assigned to Lane 5:

1	2	3	4	5
	Olivia			
				G

(C) No. In the following valid assignment, Olivia is in lane 2 and H is not in lane 1:

1	2	3	4	5
Ned	Olivia	Larry	Patricia	Sonja
H	J	F	K	G

(D) No. In the following valid assignment, Olivia is in lane 2 and H is not in lane 3:

1	2	3	4	5
Ned	Olivia	Larry	Patricia	Sonja
J	H	F	K	G

(E) No. In the following valid assignment, Olivia is in lane 2 and J is not in lane 5:

1	2	3	4	5
Ned	Olivia	Larry	Patricia	Sonja
J	H	F	K	G

22. (A) No. The following valid assignment has Sonja representing F, so she must be included in the list:

1	2	3	4	5
Ned	Patricia	Sonja	Olivia	Larry
G	H	F	K	J

(B) No. The following valid assignment has Larry representing F, so he must be included in the list:

1	2	3	4	5
Ned	Olivia	Larry	Patricia	Sonja
J	H	F	K	G

(C) No. The following valid assignment has Sonja representing F, so she must be included in the list:

1	2	3	4	5
Ned	Patricia	Sonja	Olivia	Larry
G	H	F	K	J

(D) Yes. This problem is best solved by elimination:

The following valid assignment has Sonja representing F, so she must be included in the list:

1	2	3	4	5
Ned	Patricia	Sonja	Olivia	Larry
G	H	F	K	J

This eliminates both (A) and (C)—they don't include Sonja.

Next, the following valid assignment has Larry representing F, so he must be included in the list:

1	2	3	4	5
Ned	Olivia	Larry	Patricia	Sonja
J	H	F	K	G

This eliminates both (B) and (E)—they don't include Larry.

Hence, by process of elimination, the answer is (D).
(E) No. The following valid assignment has Larry representing F, so he must be included in the list:

1	2	3	4	5
Ned	Olivia	Larry	Patricia	Sonja
J	H	F	K	G

23. (A) No. The following valid assignment has the runner representing G assigned to lane 5:

1	2	3	4	5
Ned	Olivia	Larry	Patricia	Sonja
J	H	F	K	G

(B) Yes. This problem is best solved by elimination. The following valid arrangement is a counterexample to choices (A), (C), (D), and (E):

1	2	3	4	5
Ned	Olivia	Larry	Patricia	Sonja
J	H	F	K	G

Hence, by process of elimination, the answer is (B).
(C) No. The following valid assignment has Patricia representing K:

1	2	3	4	5
Ned	Olivia	Larry	Patricia	Sonja
J	H	F	K	G

(D) No. The following valid assignment has Larry representing F:

1	2	3	4	5
Ned	Olivia	Larry	Patricia	Sonja
J	H	F	K	G

(E) No. The following valid assignment has Patricia representing K:

1	2	3	4	5
Ned	Olivia	Larry	Patricia	Sonja
J	H	F	K	G

24. (A) Yes. In the following diagram, all 4 conditions are satisfied:

K is assigned to lane 4.
Patricia is immediately between F and G.
Exactly two lanes separate Olivia from G.
Sonja is assigned a higher-numbered lane than Ned is.

1	2	3	4	5
Larry	Olivia	Ned	Patricia	Sonja
J	H	F	K	G

(B) No. This violates the condition *"Patricia is assigned to the only lane between the lanes of the runners representing F and G."*
(C) No. This violates the condition *"Sonja is assigned to a higher-numbered lane than the lane to which Ned is assigned."*
(D) No. Since Larry represents J and *"The runner representing K is assigned to lane 4,"* the assignment becomes

1	2	3	4	5
Ned	Olivia	Larry	Patricia	Sonja
		J	K	

However, this diagram violates the condition *"Patricia is assigned to the only lane between the lanes of the runners representing F and G."*
(E) No. This violates the condition *"There are exactly two lanes between Olivia's lane and the lane of the runner representing G."*

Test I
Section III
Solutions

Questions 1–7

1. (A) No. Just the opposite: working women typically must choose between occupational and child-care responsibilities. *"Conventional full-time workdays, especially when combined with unavoidable household duties, are too inflexible for parents with primary child-care responsibility."*
(B) No. The passage concludes that *"As long as the labor market remains hostile to parents, and family roles continue to be allocated on the basis of gender, women will be seriously disadvantaged in that labor market."* However, to rectify this situation, the author does not indicate whether he believes that traditional family roles should be changed or that the workplace should be modified.
(C) No. The passage does not state that single fathers can avoid employment disadvantages, just that there are far fewer single fathers than single mothers who are affected by child-care responsibilities.
(D) No. This distinction is not made in the passage.
(E) Yes. This is indicated by the last sentence of the first paragraph and the last sentence of the passage: *"Conventional full-time workdays, especially when combined with unavoidable household duties, are too inflexible for parents with primary child-care responsibility.... Indeed, as long, as the labor market remains hostile to parents, and family roles continue to be allocated on the basis of gender, women will be seriously disadvantaged in that labor market."*

2. (A) No. This is backwards. It is one-third of the working mothers who are part-time workers: *"For example, approximately one-third of all working mothers are employed only part-time, even though part-time jobs are dramatically underpaid and often less desirable in comparison to full-time employment."*
(B) No. This distinction is not made in the passage. It is stated that part-time work offers fewer opportunities for advancement for all employees.
(C) No. Nowhere does the passage state that part-time work often requires employees to work during holidays.
(D) Yes. *"Even though part-time work is usually available only in occupations offering minimal employee responsibility and little opportunity for advancement or self-enrichment, such employment does allow many women the time and flexibility to fulfill their family duties, but only at the expense of the advantages associated with full-time employment."*
(E) No. There is no mention that part-time jobs can be a stepping-stone to better positions. In fact, the passage implies that part-time jobs offer little or no career advancement.

3. (A) No. They are less burdened: *"Although a small but increasing number of working men are single parents, those barriers against successful participation in the labor market that are related to primary child-care responsibilities mainly disadvantage women."*
(B) No. There is no indication in the passage that fathers are absorbed in their jobs or that they are unaware of the injustice going on around them.
(C) Yes. This is directly implied by the second paragraph, in particular the following sentence: *"Even in families where both parents work, cultural pressures are traditionally much greater on mothers than on fathers to bear the primary child-rearing responsibilities."*
(D) No. There is no indication in the passage that working fathers in two-parent families prevent women from competing with men for career opportunities.
(E) No. There is no indication in the passage that working fathers in two-parent families insist on traditional roles in the family.

4. (A) No. Full-time jobs are available to women; however, working women cannot take those jobs because of family responsibilities.
(B) Yes. The third paragraph points out that despite all the negative aspects of part-time employment, working mothers still accept such positions because they do allow *"women the time and flexibility to fulfill their family duties."*
(C) No. The low wages of part-time employment are a bridge (albeit inadequate) not a barrier to working mothers: *"For example, approximately one-third of all working mothers are employed only part-time, even though part-time jobs are dramatically underpaid and often less desirable in comparison to full-time employment. Even though part-time work is usually available only in occupations offering minimal employee responsibility and little opportunity for advancement or self-enrichment, such employment does allow many women the time and flexibility to fulfill their family duties, but only at the expense of the advantages associated with full-time employment."*
(D) No. The barrier to successfully mixing family and career is not the limited advancement opportunities for nonprofessional employees (which presumably exist for both parents and non-parents). Rather, working parents face difficulties because the structure of the workplace forces them to choose between career advancement and family responsibilities.
(E) No. The question refers to working parents in general, not just to working mothers.

5. (A) No. Day care is inadequate because *"children need more than tending; they also need meaningful time with their parents."*

(B) No. *"Although day-care services can resolve some scheduling conflicts between home and office, workers cannot always find or afford suitable care."*

(C) No. *"Although day-care services can resolve some scheduling conflicts between home and office, workers cannot always find or afford suitable care."*

(D) Yes. This problem is best solved by elimination:

Choice (A) is suggested: *"Moreover, children need more than tending; they also need meaningful time with their parents."*

Choice (B) is suggested: *"Although day-care services can resolve some scheduling conflicts between home and office, workers cannot always find or afford suitable care."*

Choice (C) is suggested: *"Although day-care services can resolve some scheduling conflicts between home and office, workers cannot always find or afford suitable care."*

Choice (E) is suggested: *"Even when they obtain such [day] care, parents must still cope with emergencies, such as illnesses, that keep children at home."*

Hence, by process of elimination, the answer is (D).

(E) No. *"Even when they obtain such [day] care, parents must still cope with emergencies, such as illnesses, that keep children at home."*

6. (A) Yes. This problem is best solved by elimination:

Choice (B) is mentioned *"In reconciling child-rearing responsibilities with participation in the labor market, many working mothers are forced to make compromises. For example, approximately one-third of all working mothers are employed only part-time..."*

Choice (C) is mentioned *"In reconciling child-rearing responsibilities with participation in the labor market, many working mothers are forced to make compromises. For example, approximately one-third of all working mothers are employed only part-time,.... Even though part-time work is usually available only in occupations offering minimal employee responsibility and little opportunity for advancement or self-enrichment, such employment does allow many women the time and flexibility to fulfill their family duties,..."*

Choice (D) is mentioned: *"Thus, women in education are more likely to become teachers than school administrators, whose more conventional full-time work schedules do not correspond to the schedules of school-age children,..."*

Choice (E) is mentioned: *"... cultural pressures are traditionally much greater on mothers than on fathers to bear the primary child-rearing responsibilities.... many working mothers are forced to make compromises. For example, approximately one-third of all working mothers are employed only part-time, even though part-time jobs are dramatically underpaid and often less desirable in comparison to full-time employment."*

Hence, by process of elimination, the answer is (A).

(B) No. *"In reconciling child-rearing responsibilities with participation in the labor market, many working mothers are forced to make compromises. For example, approximately one-third of all working mothers are employed only part-time, even though part-time jobs are dramatically underpaid and often less desirable in comparison to full-time employment."*

(C) No. *"In reconciling child-rearing responsibilities with participation in the labor market, many working mothers are forced to make compromises. For example, approximately one-third of all working mothers are employed only part-time, ... Even though part-time work is usually available only in occupations offering minimal employee responsibility and little opportunity for advancement or self-enrichment, such employment does allow many women the time and flexibility to fulfill their family duties, but only at the expense of the advantages associated with full-time employment."*

(D) No. *"Thus, women in education are more likely to become teachers than school administrators, whose more conventional full-time work schedules do not correspond to the schedules of school-age children, while female lawyers are more likely to practice law in trusts and estates, where they can control their work schedules, than in litigation, where they cannot."*

(E) No. *". . . Even in families where both parents work, cultural pressures are traditionally much greater on mothers than on fathers to bear the primary child-rearing responsibilities. In reconciling child-rearing responsibilities with participation in the labor market, many working mothers are forced to make compromises. For example, approximately one-third of all working mothers are employed only part-time, even though part-time jobs are dramatically underpaid and often less desirable in comparison to full-time employment."*

7. (A) Yes. If the status quo remains, since nearly all the child-care responsibilities are placed on women and not men, men will remain better able to enjoy the career and salary opportunities offered by the labor market.

(B) No. The point of the passage is that men have advantages over women in the workplace because they do not carry equally the burden of child-care responsibilities. There is no mention that men are indifferent to this inequity.

(C) No. This contradicts the point of the passage: that men have advantages over women in the workplace

because they do not carry equally the burden of child-care responsibilities.
(D) No. Men who do not have primary child-rearing responsibilities will continue to enjoy more advantages in the workplace than their female counterparts. The passage implies that working fathers with child-care responsibilities suffer the same difficulties as do working mothers.
(E) No. This goes far beyond the scope of the passage. The passage discusses only the institutions that involve work and child care.

Questions 8–14

8. (A) No. The author is criticizing the assertion that John Webster was not a competent playwright.
(B) No. The author is criticizing the commonly held view that John Webster was not a competent playwright.
(C) No. Though the author does offer an explanation for the apparent contradictions in John Webster's characters, he does so not to answer an unresolved question but to counter the assertion that John Webster was not a competent playwright.
(D) Yes. The author is pointing out that those who criticize the works of John Webster fail to recognize the subtle complexity of his tragedies. Hence, the critics incorrectly attribute seeming contradictions in a character's personality to poor writing.
(E) No. The author is describing an opposing viewpoint: that John Webster was not a competent playwright. But he does so to introduce the main idea—that Webster's plays are more complex and subtle than critics realize.

9. (A) Yes. *"Yet Webster seems not to have been as heavily influenced by the morality play's model of reality [a battle between good and evil] as were his Elizabethan contemporaries; he was apparently more sensitive to the more morally complicated Italian drama than to these English sources."*
(B) No. Most Elizabethan tragedies were derived from Renaissance and medieval theater, not from Italian sources.
(C) No. The author states that critics do not understand John Webster's works, but he does not suggest that critics do not understand the works that influenced Webster.
(D) No. It is the Renaissance and medieval theater that have recently been discovered to illuminate Elizabethan drama. But it was Italian drama that influenced Webster.
(E) No. The author implies that the critics of Webster do not realize that the true source for Webster's plays was Italian drama.

10. (A) No. The commonly held view of Webster's plays apparently overlooks Aristotle's view of tragedy. The author introduces Aristotle to support his own, novel interpretation.
(B) Yes. *"The ancient Greek philosopher Aristotle implied that such contradictions [a character that is both good and evil] are virtually essential to the tragic personality, and yet critics keep coming back to this element of inconsistency as though it were an eccentric [odd] feature of Webster's own tragic vision."*
(C) No. The author is suggesting that Webster's tragedies should be viewed from the perspective of the Greek tragedy.
(D) No. The modern (Elizabethan) approach views tragedy as a battle between pure good and pure evil, while the classical (Aristotelian) approach sees internal contradictions and duality of character as the essence of tragedy.
(E) No. The author is criticizing recent scholarship (critics).

11. (A) No. Modern critics fail to see the duality of human nature—that a person can have both good and evil characteristics—as an essential part of Webster's ambiguous characters. The critics see these characters as a flaw in Webster's work, a view the author criticizes.
(B) No. Modern critics' interpretations of Webster's tragedies are invalid precisely because they fail to realize that Webster's conception of the tragic personality is similar to that of Aristotle.
(C) Yes. The point of the passage is that the critics inappropriately view Webster's tragedies from the perspective of a morality play rather than from the perspective of Italian drama. Had Webster been more heavily influenced by morality plays, the critics would be correct in attacking the competency of his work.
(D) No. This would make their interpretations even less valid. The critics mistakenly believe that because Webster was an Elizabethan playwright his main influence was the Renaissance morality play. However, Webster was actually influenced more by Italian drama.
(E) No. In his criticism of modern critics, the author praises Webster for creating dramatic conflict which *"is ours as much as that of the characters."*

12. (A) No. The skill of Elizabethan dramatists is not discussed.
(B) No. Although Webster was an Elizabethan playwright, his work exemplified the conventions that shaped Italian drama, not Elizabethan drama.
(C) Yes. *"Morality plays allegorized that conflict [the battle between good and evil] by presenting characters whose actions were defined as the embodiment of good or evil. This model of reality lived on, overlaid by different conventions, in the more sophisticated Elizabethan works of the following age."*

(D) No. Although Webster was an Elizabethan playwright, his work was based on Italian drama. So studying his Elizabethan contemporaries would probably yield a mistaken view of his accomplishments, which is what the passage implies.
(E) No. It was Webster's work, not Elizabethan drama, that was influenced by a composite of Italian and classical sources: *"Yet Webster seems not to have been as heavily influenced by the morality play's model of reality as were his Elizabethan contemporaries; he was apparently more sensitive to the more morally complicated Italian drama than to these English sources."*

13. (A) No. Webster's contemporaries tended to allegorize the conflict between good and evil. His plays were more complicated and subtle, which most modern critics fail to realize.
(B) No. The point of the passage is that the critics inappropriately view Webster's tragedies from the perspective of a morality play (an English source), rather than from the perspective of Italian drama.
(C) No. The critics fail to realize that Webster's tragedies were based on the classical definition of tragedy.
(D) No. Modern critics assume that Webster's work provides some, albeit a flawed, basis for analyzing the moral development of characters: *"[Modern critics] choose what seem to be the most promising of the contradictory values that are dramatized in [Webster's] play, and treat those values as if they were the only basis for analyzing the moral development of the play's major characters, attributing the inconsistencies in a character's behavior to artistic incompetence on Webster's part."* This is the method that the author criticizes.
(E) Yes. The point of the passage is that the critics inappropriately view Webster's tragedies from the perspective of a morality play (which was the source for his contemporary Elizabethan playwrights), rather than from the perspective of Italian drama.

14. (A) No. The author argues against those who criticize Webster's conception of tragedy.
(B) No. His was unconventional. His contemporaries based their concept of tragedy on the morality play, whereas Webster based his concept of tragedy on Italian or classical drama.
(C) No. His contemporaries based their conception of tragedy on the morality play. He based his conception of tragedy on Italian or classical drama.
(D) Yes. The conventional Elizabethan conception of tragedy was based on the morality play from English medieval theater, whereas Webster's conception of tragedy was based on Italian drama.
(E) No. The passage states that Webster's conception of tragedy was heavily influenced by the classical conception of tragedy, unlike his contemporaries.

Questions 15–20

15. (A) No. The passage implies that field experiments with genetically altered Pseudomonas bacteria have yet to be done. *"These prospects lead many to hope that current efforts to assess the risks of deliberate release of altered microorganisms will successfully answer the concerns of opponents."*
(B) Yes. This is summarized by the final sentences: *"Nevertheless, proponents contend that the prospects for improved agriculture through such methods seem excellent. These prospects lead many to hope that current efforts to assess the risks of deliberate release of altered microorganisms will successfully answer the concerns of opponents and create a climate in which such research can go forward without undue impediment."*
(C) No. Although the passage discusses the use of genetically altered Pseudomonas syringae to prevent frost damaged, it does not discuss using these particular bacteria in the soil surrounding corn plant roots to prevent frost damage. Rather, it discusses modifying bacteria that normally colonize corn roots to prevent insect damage to the plants.
(D) No. This is too narrow. In addition to advocating the genetic alteration of a number of harmful phytopathogens, the researchers also advocate using genetic alteration techniques to *"create organisms with totally new combinations of desirable traits not found in nature."*
(E) No. The opponents of this type of research are more concerned with the possible dangers than with possible failure. Further, the passage implies that the fears of opponents would be lessened if bacteria released into nature were unable to survive.

16. (A) No. The passage implies that Pseudomonas fluorescens bacteria are not the sole cause of soil suppressivity. *"While there may be many reasons for this phenomenon, it is clear that levels of certain bacteria, such as Pseudomonas fluorescens, a bacterium antagonistic to a number of harmful phytopathogens, are greater in suppressive than in nonsuppressive soil."*
(B) No. The rest of the passage points out that genetic engineering can weaken or eliminate certain phytopathogens. The reader needs to know why this is helpful.
(C) No. The passage does not detail any chemical processes.
(D) Yes. The rest of the passage points out that genetic engineering can weaken or eliminate certain phytopathogens. The first paragraph establishes why this is beneficial.
(E) No. The passage does state that diseases brought on by phytopathogens diminish in severity over time. But it does not state that the diseases eventually disappear. Nor does the passage state that crop rotation is unnecessary.

17. (A) No. We do not know whether or not Pseudomonas fluorescens would be present in the soil. We know only that since the crop plants are already impervious to parasitical organisms any Pseudomonas fluorescens present would probably have no beneficial effect on the crops.
(B) No. The Pseudomonas fluorescens bacteria would merely be unnecessary since the crops are impervious to parasitical organisms.
(C) Yes. Pseudomonas fluorescens bacteria are beneficial because they attack parasitical organisms. However, if the crops are already impervious to these parasites, then the bacteria would probably have no beneficial effect on the crops.
(D) No. The discussion suggests that the yield would be greater, but not necessarily quicker.
(E) No. This is independent of the discussion.

18. (A) No. *"Cultivation of a single crop on a given tract of land leads eventually to decreased yields. One reason for this is that harmful bacterial phytopathogens, organisms parasitic on plant hosts, increase in the soil surrounding plant roots. The problem can be cured by crop rotation, denying the pathogens a suitable host for a period of time."*
(B) No. There is no indication in the passage that Pseudomonas fluorescens bacteria increase when crops are rotated. Rather, the passage implies that phytopathogens decrease when crops are rotated: *"Cultivation of a single crop on a given tract of land leads eventually to decreased yields. One reason for this is that harmful bacterial phytopathogens, organisms parasitic on plant hosts, increase in the soil surrounding plant roots. The problem can be cured by crop rotation, denying the pathogens a suitable host for a period of time."*
(C) No. Although the passage discusses experimental crops whose roots produce insecticidal compounds, there is no implication that crop rotation is used to protect other plants from phytopathogens. Rather, the passage implies that crop rotation decreases phytopathogens by *"denying the pathogens a suitable host for a period of time."*
(D) No. We cannot determine from the passage whether phytopathogenic bacteria are responsible for the majority of plant diseases. Besides, even if this is the case, it does not explain why crop rotation can increase yields.
(E) Yes. *"Cultivation of a single crop on a given tract of land leads eventually to decreased yields. One reason for this is that harmful bacterial phytopathogens, organisms parasitic on plant hosts, increase in the soil surrounding plant roots. The problem can be cured by crop rotation, denying the pathogens a suitable host for a period of time."*

19. (A) Yes. *"Proponents, on the other hand, argue that this particular strain is altered only by the removal of the gene responsible for the strain's propensity to cause frost damage, thereby rendering it safer than the phytopathogen from which it was derived."*
(B) No. The passage does not discuss the viability of altered bacteria in natural environments.
(C) No. This is not mentioned in the passage.
(D) No. The passage states only that the altered bacteria were antagonistic to ("crowded out") the unaltered strain of the same bacteria.
(E) No. The passage does not discuss the experimental procedures used to test the bacteria.

20. (A) No. This is irrelevant.
(B) No. The passage indicates that the altered Pseudomonas syringae are derived from the natural strain which does cause damage to crops. Prevention of this damage is the reason for the alteration.
(C) No. This is irrelevant.
(D) Yes. If a gene has dual roles—one harmful and one beneficial—then removing the gene may solve a particular problem but cause even greater problems.
(E) No. This is precisely what the proponents want to occur.

Questions 21–27

21. (A) No. The Dawes Act prohibited the sale of Native American lands to non-Native Americans.
(B) No. *"Selling land to each other would not threaten the Native American culture."*
(C) Yes. This is summarized in the final sentence of the passage: *"One hypothesis, then, for the temporary restriction on alienation in the Dawes Act is that it reflected a compromise between non-Native Americans favoring immediate alienability so they could purchase land and the BIA bureaucrats who administered the privatization system."*
(D) No. This explains *how* the United States governmental activity in the area of land administration expanded but does not explain *why* it expanded. In other words, who benefited from the expansion?
(E) No. This contradicts the passage: *"Until allotment was ended in 1934, granting fee patents and leasing Native American lands were among the principal activities of the United States government."*

22. (A) No. The passage implies that politicians were motivated by their own self-interest.
(B) No. This argues to continue the act.
(C) Yes. Political patronage is presented as a motivating factor behind the act: *"It has been convincingly demonstrated that bureaucrats seek to maximize the size of their staffs and their budgets in order to compensate for the lack of other sources of fulfillment, such as power and prestige. Additionally, politicians tend to favor the growth of governmental bureaucracy because such growth provides increased opportunity for the exercise of political patronage."*

(D) No. This is unlikely since *"It has been convincingly demonstrated that bureaucrats seek to maximize the size of their staffs and their budgets in order to compensate for the lack of other sources of fulfillment, such as power and prestige."*
(E) No. This argues to continue the act since the act initially prohibited selling Native American land to non-Native Americans.

23. (A) No. The passage is concerned with the motivations for the Dawes Act, not with its benefits and drawbacks.
(B) No. The Act was repealed in 1934 long before the passage was written.
(C) No. The permanent effects of the law are not mentioned.
(D) Yes. The first paragraph describes the Dawes Act. The second paragraph puts forward a rationale for one of its clauses: *"Two main reasons were advanced for the restriction on the Native Americans' ability to sell their lands."* The third paragraph dismisses the rationale: *"However, both of these arguments bear only on the transfer of Native American lands to non-Native Americans; neither offers a reason for prohibiting Native Americans from transferring land among themselves."* Finally, the closing paragraph puts forward a different rationale for the clause, namely, the self-interest of bureaucrats: *"While neither Native Americans nor the potential non-Native American purchasers benefited from the restraint on alienation contained in the Dawes Act, one clearly defined group did benefit: the BIA bureaucrats."*
(E) No. The passage implies that only bureaucrats benefited from the passage, and they are not a rival group to the Native Americans.

24. (A) No. Just the opposite. He is incredulous: *"However, both of these arguments bear only on the transfer of Native American lands to non-Native Americans; neither offers a reason for prohibiting Native Americans from transferring land among themselves. Selling land to each other would not threaten the Native American culture. Additionally, if communal land use remained preferable to Native Americans after allotment, free alienability would have allowed allottees to sell their lands back to the tribe."* Finally, the author calls the government's rationale for the restriction on alienability *"empty."*
(B) No. He disapproves of the reasons: *"However, both of these arguments bear only on the transfer of Native American lands to non-Native Americans; neither offers a reason for prohibiting Native Americans from transferring land among themselves. Selling land to each other would not threaten the Native American culture. Additionally, if communal land use remained preferable to Native Americans after allotment, free alienability would have allowed allottees to sell their lands back to the tribe."* Finally, the author calls the government's rationale for the restriction on alienability *"empty."*
(C) No. He clearly discounts the reasons advanced: *"However, both of these arguments bear only on the transfer of Native American lands to non-Native Americans; neither offers a reason for prohibiting Native Americans from transferring land among themselves. Selling land to each other would not threaten the Native American culture. Additionally, if communal land use remained preferable to Native Americans after allotment, free alienability would have allowed allottees to sell their lands back to the tribe."* Finally, the author calls the government's rationale for the restriction on alienability *"empty."*
(D) No. He strongly questions their merit: *"However, both of these arguments bear only on the transfer of Native American lands to non-Native Americans; neither offers a reason for prohibiting Native Americans from transferring land among themselves. Selling land to each other would not threaten the Native American culture. Additionally, if communal land use remained preferable to Native Americans after allotment, free alienability would have allowed allottees to sell their lands back to the tribe."* Finally, the author calls the government's rationale for the restriction on alienability *"empty."*
(E) Yes. This is the thrust of the third paragraph: *"However, both of these arguments bear only on the transfer of Native American lands to non-Native Americans; neither offers a reason for prohibiting Native Americans from transferring land among themselves. Selling land to each other would not threaten the Native American culture. Additionally, if communal land use remained preferable to Native Americans after allotment, free alienability would have allowed allottees to sell their lands back to the tribe."* Finally, the author calls the government's rationale for the restriction on alienability *"empty."*

25. (A) No. There is no mention of farming in the passage.
(B) Yes. The passage states that Native Americans preferred communal use of land and were unfamiliar with the concept of private ownership of land: *"A second objection to free alienation was that Native Americans were unaccustomed to, and did not desire, a system of private landownership."*
(C) No. The Dawes Act legislated wide-scale private ownership of land by Native Americans. So ostensibly Native Americans owned little or no land before the Dawes Act.
(D) No. There is no discussion in the passage of the contact between Native Americans and their non-Native American neighbors.
(E) No. The restriction on the Native Americans' ability to sell their lands was prompted in part by the concern *"that free alienability would lead to immedi-*

ate transfer of large amounts of former reservation land to non-Native Americans, consequently threatening the traditional way of life on those reservations." Although the author rejects this reason, it is not because he disagreed that free alienability would lead to the transfer of large amounts of former reservation land to non-Native Americans.

26. (A) No. There is no mention of farming in the passage.
(B) Yes. *"However, the Native Americans were not granted outright title to their lands. The act defined each grant as a "trust patent," meaning that the Bureau of Indian Affairs (BIA), the governmental agency in charge of administering policy regarding Native Americans, would hold the allotted land in trust for 25 years, during which time the Native American owners could use, but not alienate (sell) the land. After the 25-year period, the Native American allottee would receive a "fee patent" awarding full legal ownership of the land."*
(C) No. For the first 25 years, the government had some control over how owners disposed of land. After 25 years, the owners of the land obtained unrestricted ownership.
(D) No. The only restriction was that owners could not sell their land.
(E) No. There is no mention of this in the passage.

27. (A) No. From the passage, we cannot determine whether this would benefit or hurt the legislators.
(B) No. The passage does not indicate how Native American landowners who had fee patent privileges disposed of their landholdings.
(C) No. This is irrelevant.
(D) Yes. The point of the passage is that the Dawes Act was motivated by the self-interest of bureaucrats: *"While neither Native Americans nor the potential non-Native American purchasers benefited from the restraint on alienation contained in the Dawes Act, one clearly defined group did benefit: the BIA bureaucrats."*
(E) No. There is no mention of farming in the passage.

Test I
Section IV
Solutions

1. (A) No. If fuel shortages caused Americans to drive less, it would be expected that the annual rate of traffic fatalities would decrease. While the argument claims that the reduced speed limit saved lives, this answer-choice indicates an alternative possibility and therefore weakens the argument.
(B) No. This does not explain why traffic fatalities decreased during the first eleven years following the speed limit reduction.
(C) No. This would weaken the argument because the safety equipment, not the reduced speed limit, might be responsible for the decreased rate of fatalities.
(D) Yes. This strongly indicates that the decrease in speed reduced the chance of fatal injuries during automobile accidents. A lower speed limit (presuming some people obey it) should therefore reduce the rate of highway fatalities.
(E) No. This suggests that accidents can be avoided by matching speeds with surrounding traffic—regardless of what the speed is. In this case, a lower speed limit should not affect the number of accidents. Note, although this implies the probability of an accident shouldn't be affected by the speed, conceivably the chance of fatalities if an accident does occur might be affected by the speed. However, there's another answer-choice which directly addresses this issue.

2. (A) No. If no research is carried out, there will be no public benefit. However, if research is funded, we cannot conclude that benefits will definitely result. Perhaps all the research will hit dead-ends, or perhaps it will only contribute to theoretical knowledge without having any practical applications.
(B) No. Nothing in the argument states or implies that legislators would necessarily fund research if its outcome were predictable. The legislator's position is this:

No assurance of contribution —> No funding of research

It is not valid to conclude from this:

Assurance of contribution —> Funding of research

(C) No. Nothing in the passage implies that public funding of research would accelerate the rate of scientific discoveries. Other factors might restrict the rate of scientific discoveries. The point of the passage is that some of the greatest benefits to public welfare resulted from scientific research from which no one anticipated such benefits. Therefore, we cannot expect to have a guarantee of social benefit from any particular scientific research program.

(D) No. The point of the passage is that some of the greatest benefits to public welfare resulted from scientific research from which no one anticipated such benefits. Nothing in the passage indicates that public funds are required to ensure that beneficial research is carried out.
(E) Yes. The point of the passage is that some of the greatest benefits to public welfare resulted from scientific research from which no one anticipated such benefits. Therefore, we cannot expect to have a guarantee of social benefit from any particular scientific research program.

3. (A) No. This argument commits the fallacy of false dichotomy. It assumes that workers have only two reactions to their work—either it's not challenging or it's too challenging. Clearly, there is a wide range of reactions between those two extremes.
(B) Yes. This argument commits the fallacy of false dichotomy. It assumes that workers have only two reactions to their work—either it's not challenging or it's too challenging. Clearly, there is a wide range of reactions between those two extremes.
(C) No. We cannot tell from the passage whether the evidence is subjective or objective.
(D) No. This argument commits the fallacy of false dichotomy. It assumes that workers have only two reactions to their work—either it's not challenging or it's too challenging. Clearly, there is a wide range of reactions between those two extremes.
(E) No. This argument commits the fallacy of false dichotomy. It assumes that workers have only two reactions to their work—either it's not challenging or it's too challenging. Clearly, there is a wide range of reactions between those two extremes.

4. (A) No. This is irrelevant.
(B) No. This is irrelevant so long as the time required for the soup to lose the vitamins is longer than the time required for a typical person to consume the soup.
(C) No. The advertisement says nothing about other nutrients the soup might or might not contain.
(D) No. The advertisement does not compare soup and strawberries.
(E) Yes. If apricots and fresh carrots are known **to** be nutritious, then the advertisement might lead consumers to believe that tomato soup is even *more* nutritious. In fact, the relevant vitamins are different, so it is misleading to compare the soup with apricots and carrots.

Questions 5–6
5. (A) Yes. The point of the passage is that those who benefit from bank deposit insurance should pay for the insurance.
(B) No. The conclusion of the passage is that the people who benefit from bank deposit insurance should pay for the insurance. The principle in this answer-choice does not relate to that situation.
(C) No. There is no discussion of incentives in the passage.
(D) No. The passage is about requiring people to pay for any services they receive. It does not discuss whether or not they should be allowed to choose receiving a service.
(E) No. There is no discussion about altering the behavior of corporations or individuals.

6. (A) No. Only customer deposits are discussed in the passage, not bank loans.
(B) No. This is irrelevant since the passage states that the government provides the insurance.
(C) Yes. The passage states that individuals do not pay for deposit insurance. This assumes that they do not pay indirectly through decreased benefits elsewhere.
(D) No. This is irrelevant since depositors still benefit from insurance protection up to the stated limit.
(E) No. Suppose the government did allow banks to offer some kinds of accounts which were not insured and which did not offer any additional benefits to the depositor (e.g., higher interest rates or lower fees). Then owners of insured deposits would receive the same benefits at no extra cost as owners of uninsured deposits, and the argument's conclusion would still hold.

7. (A) Yes. The point of the passage is that if all students receive the same amount of help then some students will not master the material. Hence, to insure that all students learn the material, some will require different help than others.
(B) No. The passage allows the possibility that a student may receive inferior instruction and still master the material, and that a student may receive superior instruction and still fail to master the material. This is the point of the first sentence of the passage.
(C) No. This is independent of the passage.
(D) No. The point of the passage is that some students need more and different types of exposure than others.
(E) No. This is independent of the passage.

8. (A) No. George's conclusion is that global warming is already occurring. He is not concerned with the causes of global warming.
(B) No. George stated all the relevant information need on this point: the leaves turned color three weeks later into fall than usual.
(C) No. George's conclusion is that global warming is already occurring. He is not concerned with the causes of global warming.
(D) No. George's argument concerns global warming. He does not address issues of pollution.

(E) Yes. The unusually warm weather may only be a local phenomenon. It needs to be determined whether similar changes are occurring elsewhere before the climatic shifts can be considered *global* warming.

9. (A) No. The Dean of students does not mention the process by which the student was expelled.
(B) No. Behavior other than speech is not discussed.
(C) Yes. The statement *"But what you're saying is that our university should endorse verbal harassment"* is a misrepresentation of the student representative's position, which is that the university should neither endorse nor penalize a student for speaking his mind. In other words, for the student representative, freedom of speech is paramount.
(D) No. The Dean does not question why the student holds his position, but rather misinterprets that position.
(E) No. There is no threat made or implied in the Dean of students's argument.

10. (A) No. But the passage does imply that the principle is not applied across the board.
(B) No. While the passage supports the statement that the percentage of convicted celebrities sentenced to community service is greater than the percentage of convicted unknown defendants similarly sentenced, nothing can be deduced about the numbers of either group performing community service. To determine this, we would need the number of celebrities and non-celebrities convicted of each type of crime. It's even possible that a greater number of unknown defendants than celebrities are sentenced to community service.
(C) No. This is too strong. The passage only implies that considerations such as fame and publicity should not override the principle of equality before the law, no additional principles are mentioned.
(D) Yes. This in fact would be a logical conclusion to the argument.
(E) No. The point of the principle is that if there is to be leniency then it should be applied equally to everyone, or not applied at all.

11. (A) Yes. The foundation's grant may allow the university to pay off certain bills, which will free up money for weapons-related research.
(B) No. It is reasonable to assume that it was the first attempt by the university to use the fund for nonhumanitarian scientific research, otherwise the foundation would have probably withdrawn its grant previously.
(C) No. This is too Machiavellian. There's another answer-choice which is more likely.
(D) No. The foundation understands that the university will still use the money, just not for weapons-related research.
(E) No. This is irrelevant.

12. (A) Yes. The point of the passage is that advertising that develops name recognition—even negative recognition—can be effective.
(B) No. The voters may be influenced by advertising campaigns without realizing it or admitting it.
(C) No. The passage states that strategies for corporate advertising have been borrowed from political campaigns, not the other way around.
(D) No. The statements actually support this conclusion since the strategy is concerned with developing name recognition (positive or negative), and it has been applied.
(E) No. This is independent of the statements in the passage.

13. (A) No. Not only is this irrelevant, it is incorrect! Fully one-third of smoke detectors were installed within the last ten years, as they jumped from installations in 30 percent of homes to 45 percent.
(B) No. This is irrelevant. The conclusion concerns the probability of early detection of a house fire, not the total number of such fires.
(C) No. This is irrelevant. The conclusion only concerns the percentage of inoperable smoke detectors, not the reason the detectors are not functioning.
(D) Yes. If the proportion of smoke detectors that are inoperative is the same now as in the past, then the detection of fires would be 50 percent more likely (45 is 50 percent larger than 30). However, if the percentage of inoperable smoke detectors has increased over the last 10 years, then the chance of detecting fires would increase less than 50 percent. In fact, it is possible for so many smoke detectors to have become inoperable that there was no increase in the number of properly functioning detectors.
(E) No. The passage is discussing early detection, not safety per se.

14. (A) No. Over the past three years, HomeGlo paint increased in environmental safety more than any other competitive product. However, the argument invalidly concludes that this means HomeGlo Exterior Enamel is the safest brand of paint on the market. Perhaps HomeGlo was so environmentally toxic three years ago that these improvements did not bring it up to the level of other environmentally benign products. In other words, the argument is flawed because it equates the improvement of a product with its final status. However, this answer-choice does not do this. Instead, it says that because ZXC audio system was rated top in areas such as performance it should have better sound quality than any other system.
(B) No. Over the past three years, HomeGlo paint increased in environmental safety more than any other competitive product. However, the argument invalidly concludes that this means HomeGlo Exterior Enamel is the safest brand of paint on the market. Perhaps HomeGlo was so environmentally toxic three

years ago that these improvements did not bring it up to the level of other environmentally benign products. In other words, the argument is flawed because it equates the improvement of a product with its final status. This answer-choice also presents a flawed argument because it cites evidence comparing Morning Sunshine to other cereals but then concludes that Morning Sunshine is more nutritious than any other type of food. However, this flaw is not logically similar to the original passage.
(C) No. This is the second-best choice. It does have the same structure as the original argument. However, in the original the argument the conclusion stays within the context of the evidence:

the most environmentally improved, therefore the most environmentally safe.

Whereas this answer-choice says

the greatest increase in customers, therefore the greatest profit.

This answer-choice would have been correct if it had said

the greatest increase in customers, therefore the greatest number of customers.

(D) Yes. Over the past three years, HomeGlo paint increased in environmental safety more than any other competitive product. However, the argument invalidly concludes that this means HomeGlo Exterior Enamel is the safest brand of paint on the market. Perhaps HomeGlo was so environmentally toxic three years ago that these improvements did not bring it up to the level of other environmentally benign products. In other words, the argument is flawed because it equates the improvement of a product with its final status. Similarly, suppose Jerrold improved his grades from a D average to a B average and that this was the greatest improvement in his class. However, if anybody in Jerrold's class had an A average, Jerrold would not hold the highest ranking.
(E) No. The original argument is based on the false assumption that something is best if it is most improved. However, this answer-choice concludes that something that is best (Margaret Durring's short story) has predecessors which are also best in their category. Although this is not a valid conclusion, the structure of the argument differs from the original passage.

15. (A) No. According to the passage, it's the stabilizers that affect the flavor of ice cream; we are not told that the ice cream's consistency has a similar effect.
(B) No. The passage states that stabilizers are inexpensive.
(C) No. We don't have enough information to decide. Although an inexpensive method of reducing temperature fluctuations in a freezer would solve the problem of poor ice cream consistency, the passage says nothing about the actual cost of developing a device to achieve this.
(D) No. The stabilizers are used to stabilize the consistency of ice cream at higher temperatures, so apparently they function well enough at those temperatures.
(E) Yes. The passage states that the *"consistency of ice cream is adversely affected by even slight temperature changes,"* so the best consistency will occur with stable temperatures. Further, the passage states *"stabilizers, though inexpensive, adversely affect flavor"* and *"stabilizers are less needed if storage temperatures are very low."* So the best flavor will occur at very low stable temperatures.

16. (A) No. There is no authority mentioned in the passage.
(B) No. This is not mentioned.
(C) No. There is no other view of musical authenticity mentioned in the passage.
(D) No. This is the second-best choice. Alberto is not claiming that Edwina's conclusion does not follow from her premises (we cannot tell from the passage whether he believes this or not). Rather, he is denying that one of her premises is valid—namely, that those who played Mozart's music for Mozart played it exactly as he intended it to be played.
(E) Yes. Edwina's premise is that Mozart's heard his music played exactly as he intended it to sound. Alberto argues that this premise is unwarranted because Mozart knew that whoever played his music would interpret and change it. So in fact, Mozart did not hear his music played exactly as he intended it.

17. (A) No. This strengthens the paradox. If the National Health scheme cuts costs for private insurers, then their rates should decrease.
(B) No. This strengthens the paradox. If 80 percent of medical costs are now covered by the National Health scheme, then the private insurance rates should decrease.
(C) No. This is irrelevant.
(D) Yes. If people buy private insurance only when they expect to need it for unusual medical procedures not covered by the National Health scheme, then presumably fewer people have private health insurance than before the National Health scheme. Furthermore, a greater percentage of those with insurance will have claims (since people expect to require these procedures, perhaps because of a family history or because of the existence of early symptoms). Thus, the costs will be spread over a smaller pool of people while the costs themselves may not decrease as much. The net effect is that insurance premiums would rise.
(E) No. This is irrelevant.

18. (A) Yes. The intent is that neither the subject nor experimenter will know which subjects are actually being given the drug. But if the drug has side effects that the experimenter recognizes, then in some cases the experimenter will know who is taking the actual drug.
(B) No. This in fact helps keep everybody in the dark about who is getting the actual drug and who is getting a placebo.
(C) No. This is independent of the passage.
(D) No. This in fact helps keep everybody in the dark about who is getting the actual drug and who is getting a placebo. The less time a researcher works with a subject, the fewer opportunities she has to discover whether the subject is getting the actual drug or a placebo.
(E) No. There is no discussion in the passage of volunteering or of informing the subjects that they may receive a placebo.

19. (A) No. The birthdays and anniversaries would continue to fall on the same date (December 30 or December 31) although the occasions on December 31, the *"last day of the year,"* would not belong to a week and presumably would not be on a "day" (e.g., Sunday, Monday, etc.).
(B) Yes. Let's consider the first year the new calendar is implemented. January 1 falls on a Sunday and is a day of rest. The year progresses until Saturday, December 30, with the people in this answer-choice having rested every seventh day, on Sunday. The next day, December 31, would be a day of rest; but because it is the last day of the year, it does not belong to a week and would not be labeled Sunday. Seven days later, the next day of rest falls on Saturday. In the second year the day of rest would always be Saturday. In the third year the day of rest would always fall on a Friday. The following calendar illustrates the situation at the end of the first year:

Saturday Dec. 30	**"extra day" Dec. 31**	**Sunday Jan. 1**	**Monday Jan. 2**
6th day	7th day	1st day	2nd day
	day of rest		

•
•
•

Friday Jan. 6	**Saturday Jan. 7**	**Sunday Jan. 8**
6th day	7th day	1st day
	day of rest	

Since their day of rest falls on different days of the week each year, they are likely to have scheduling conflicts.
(C) No. Nothing in this proposal changes the number days in a year. Students could continue to attend school the same number of days each year, though conceivably one or two of those days (e.g., the current February 29) might not belong to a *"day of the week"* (e.g., Monday, Tuesday, etc.).
(D) No. The new calendar would be unlikely to affect these people. Conceivably they might actually have a "four-day" holiday if the last day of the year fell on a weekend during the celebration of a holiday since this day would not count as a Friday, Saturday, Sunday or Monday. However, there is a better answer-choice.
(E) No. The new calendar would have no effect on these people. However, if the event was scheduled on the *"last day of the year,"* December 31, or on the extra leap-day, it would not take place on a "day" (e.g., Sunday, Monday, etc.).

20. (A) Yes. The passage implies that graphologists claim that a strong cross on the "t" denotes the <u>permanent</u> character trait, enthusiasm. The passage then states the strong cross on the "t" can be changed and therefore that the character trait enthusiasm can be changed. However, this directly contradicts the assumption that enthusiasm is a <u>permanent</u> character trait. Hence, the graphologists' claim leads to the absurd consequence that a character trait can be simultaneously permanent and not permanent.
(B) No. The argument does not show that the claim is a platitude (a trite remark).
(C) No. There is no discussion of whether the people being analyzed by the graphologists are aware that they are being analyzed. Rather the argument points out that people can intentionally change *"permanent character traits,"* regardless of their reason for doing so.
(D) No. The passage merely presents one counterexample.
(E) No. The passage is arguing that graphology is invalid, not superfluous.

<u>Questions 21–22</u>

21. (A) Yes. The clause *"certainly on today's statute books there remain many laws regulating activities that were once common but in which people no longer engage"* is drawing an analogy between what is common today and what the critic believes was common in the past.
(B) No. There is no principle stated.
(C) No. Both the historian and the critic consider the tariff law as fact and see the existence of timber trade between Poral and Nayal as only a possibility. Therefore, the critic cannot respond to the historian by pointing out the difference between direct evidence giving certain information and indirect evidence providing only probabilities.
(D) No. There are no criteria mentioned.
(E) No. In fact, the critic is presuming just the opposite: that the role laws played in Nayalese society was similar to their role in contemporary society.

22. (A) No. It is flawed because it does not make a crucial distinction between the existence of statutes and their enactment.
(B) No. The critic is drawing a conclusion about laws in general, not about specific laws.
(C) No. The historian explicitly states that the evidence is indirect, not direct. So it would not be insightful for the critic to point this out.
(D) Yes. The historian states that tariff laws were enacted during the third dynasty. The critic responds that sometimes laws remain on the books long after they cease being relevant, implying that the third-dynasty Nayalese laws were out-of-date. However, since the laws were enacted during the third dynasty, presumably they were relevant then. Thus, the critic's reasoning is flawed.
(E) No. The historian does assume that the purpose of tariff laws is to regulate timber trade. However, there is no need to question this assumption.

23. (A) No. This may or may not be an effect of the actions taken by Bell's president, but it is not an assumption of the argument.
(B) No. Remember, "A unless B" is equivalent to ~B—>A. So we can symbolize the first sentence as

~I—>St,

where **I** denotes *"the management increases [the workers'] wages"* and **St** denotes *"the workers at Bell Manufacturing will shortly go on strike."* The second sentence contains an embedded *if-then* statement: *"If Bell increases the workers' wages, then it will have to sell off some of its subsidiaries."* This in turn can be symbolized as

I—>Se,

where **Se** denotes *"it will have to sell off some of its subsidiaries."* As they stand, the two symbol statements above cannot be connected. Now, this answer-choice affirms the premise of the *if-then* statement **~I—>St**. Hence, we can validly conclude that there will be a strike, **St**. However, this still does allow us to tie in the statement **I—>Se**.
(C) Yes. Remember, "A unless B" is equivalent to ~B—>A. So we can symbolize the first sentence as

~I—>St,

where **I** denotes *"the management increases [the workers'] wages"* and **St** denotes *"the workers at Bell Manufacturing will shortly go on strike."* The second sentence contains an embedded *if-then* statement: *"If Bell increases the workers' wages, then it will have to sell off some of its subsidiaries."* This in turn can be symbolized as

I—>Se,

where **Se** denotes *"it will have to sell off some of its subsidiaries."* As they stand, the two symbol statements above cannot be connected. However, suppose the workers don't go on strike. Then applying the contrapositive to the statement **~I—>St** yields

~St—>I.

Using the transitive property to combine this with the statement **I—>Se** yields

~St—>Se.

In other words, if the workers don't go on strike, then some of Bell's subsidiaries will be sold.
(D) No. This is irrelevant.
(E) No. This is irrelevant.

24. (A) No. This would weaken the argument. To determine how quickly words enter into common use, dictionary editors should have a professional interest and awareness of words that have not yet reached popular usage.
(B) No. The passage refers to "professional opinions," not to any exact criteria.
(C) No. The passage is arguing that dictionaries are a means of measuring how quickly a new idea is accepted, not the arbiters of whether a new idea will be accepted.
(D) Yes. If the meaning of a word has changed to the point that it no longer stands for the concept it originally stood for, then the fact that it is in common use does not mean that the original concept is in common use. For example, the word "bad" when used as slang can mean "good."
(E) No. This would weaken the argument. If a word denoting a new idea is commonly used but typically not understood, then the word's popularity will falsely indicate how quickly the idea it denotes is taking hold.

25. (A) No. The point of the passage is that although migrant workers do not meet the exact criteria for being full-time employees they work as much as full-time employees and therefore should receive some of the same benefits. However, nothing in this answer-choice indicates that locally regulated day-care facilities are essentially the same as some other type of federally regulated facility.
(B) No. The point of the passage is that although migrant workers do not meet the exact criteria for being full-time employees they work as much as full-time employees and therefore should receive some of the same benefits. However, nothing in this answer-choice indicates that the building codes of larger cities are determined by other authorities (e.g., country, state) which also have authority over rural towns.
(C) No. The point of the passage is that although migrant workers do not meet the exact criteria for being full-time employees they work as much as full-time employees and therefore should receive some of the same benefits. However, nothing in this answer-

choice indicates that the different counties have the same reasons for regulating gun sales.

(D) No. The point of the passage is that although migrant workers do not meet the exact criteria for being full-time employees they work as much as full-time employees and therefore should receive some of the same benefits. This answer-choice does not indicate that club and restaurant owners are treated differently from other parties with whom these owners share some essential characteristic.

(E) Yes. The point of the passage is that although migrant workers do not meet the exact criteria for being full-time employees they work as much as full-time employees and therefore should receive some of the same benefits. Similarly, the point of this answer-choice is that although food additives do not meet the exact criteria for being drugs they can be as dangerous as drugs and therefore should be regulated in the same way.

LSAT
TEST II

SECTION I
Time—35 minutes
25 Questions

Directions: The questions in this section are based on the reasoning contained in brief statements or passages. For some questions, more than one of the choices could conceivably answer the question. However, you are to choose the best answer; that is, the response that most accurately and completely answers the question. You should not make assumptions that are by commonsense standards implausible, superfluous, or incompatible with the passage.

1. Of all the surgeons practicing at the city hospital, the chief surgeon has the worst record in terms of the percentage of his patients who die either during or immediately following an operation performed by him. Paradoxically, the hospital's administrators claim that he is the best surgeon currently working at the hospital.

   Which one of the following, if true, goes farthest toward showing that the administrators' claim and the statistic cited might both be correct?

   (A) Since the hospital administrators appoint the chief surgeon, the administrators are strongly motivated to depict the chief surgeon they have chosen as a wise choice.
   (B) In appointing the current chief surgeon, the hospital administrators followed the practice, well established at the city hospital, of promoting one of the surgeons already on staff.
   (C) Some of the younger surgeons on the city hospital's staff received part of their training from the current chief surgeon.
   (D) At the city hospital those operations that inherently entail the greatest risk to the life of the patient are generally performed by the chief surgeon.
   (E) The current chief surgeon has a better record of patients' surviving surgery than did his immediate predecessor.

2. Between 1971 and 1975, the government office that monitors drug companies issued an average of 60 citations a year for serious violations of drug-promotion laws. Between 1976 and 1980, the annual average for issuance of such citations was only 5. This decrease indicates that the government office was, on average, considerably more lax in enforcing drug-promotion laws between 1976 and 1980 than it was between 1971 and 1975.

   The argument assumes which one of the following?

   (A) The decrease in the number of citations was not caused by a decrease in drug companies' violations of drug-promotion laws.
   (B) A change in enforcement of drug-promotion laws did not apply to minor violations.
   (C) The enforcement of drug-promotion laws changed in response to political pressure.
   (D) The government office should not issue more than an average of 5 citations a year to drug companies for serious violations of drug-promotion laws.
   (E) Before 1971 the government office issued more than 60 citations a year to drug companies for serious violations of drug-promotion laws.

GO ON TO THE NEXT PAGE.

3. Sheila: Health experts generally agree that smoking a tobacco product for many years is very likely to be harmful to the smoker's health.

Tim: On the contrary, smoking has no effect on health at all: although my grandfather smoked three cigars a day from the age of fourteen, he died at age ninety-six.

A major weakness of Tim's counterargument is that his counterargument

(A) attempts to refute a probabilistic conclusion by claiming the existence of a single counterexample
(B) challenges expert opinion on the basis of specific information unavailable to experts in the field
(C) describes an individual case that is explicitly discounted as an exception to the experts' conclusion
(D) presupposes that longevity and health status are unrelated to each other in the general population
(E) tacitly assumes that those health experts who are in agreement on this issue arrived at that agreement independently of one another

4. The case of the French Revolution is typically regarded as the best evidence for the claim that societies can reap more benefit than harm from a revolution. But even the French Revolution serves this role poorly, since France at the time of the Revolution had a unique advantage. Despite the Revolution, the same civil servants and functionaries remained in office, carrying on the day-to-day work of government, and thus many of the disruptions that revolutions normally bring were avoided.

Which one of the following most accurately characterizes the argumentative strategy used in the passage?

(A) demonstrating that the claim argued against is internally inconsistent
(B) supporting a particular position on the basis of general principles
(C) opposing a claim by undermining evidence offered in support of that claim
(D) justifying a view through the use of a series of persuasive examples
(E) comparing two positions in order to illustrate their relative strengths and weaknesses

5. A person can develop or outgrow asthma at any age. In children under ten, asthma is twice as likely to develop in boys. Boys are less likely than girls to outgrow asthma, yet by adolescence the percentage of boys with asthma is about the same as the percentage of girls with asthma because a large number of girls develop asthma in early adolescence.

Assuming the truth of the passage, one can conclude from it that the number of adolescent boys with asthma is approximately equal to the number of adolescent girls with asthma, if one also knows that

(A) a tendency toward asthma is often inherited
(B) children who develop asthma before two years of age are unlikely to outgrow it
(C) there are approximately equal numbers of adolescent boys and adolescent girls in the population
(D) the development of asthma in childhood is not closely related to climate or environment
(E) the percentage of adults with asthma is lower than the percentage of adolescents with asthma

6. Harry Trevalga: You and your publication have unfairly discriminated against my poems. I have submitted thirty poems in the last two years and you have not published any of them! It is all because I won the Fenner Poetry Award two years ago and your poetry editor thought she deserved it.

Publisher: Ridiculous! Our editorial policy and practice is perfectly fair, since our poetry editor judges all submissions for publication without ever seeing the names of the poets, and hence cannot possibly have known who wrote your poems.

The publisher makes which one of the following assumptions in replying to Trevalga's charges of unfair discrimination?

(A) The poetry editor does not bear a grudge against Harry Trevalga for his winning the Fenner Poetry Award.
(B) It is not unusual for poets to contribute many poems to the publisher's publication without ever having any accepted for publication.
(C) The poetry editor cannot recognize the poems submitted by Harry Trevalga as his unless Trevalga's name is attached to them.
(D) The poetry editor's decisions on which poems to publish are not based strictly on judgments of intrinsic merit.
(E) Harry Trevalga submitted his poems to the publisher's publication under his pen name.

GO ON TO THE NEXT PAGE.

7. In a study of the effect of radiation from nuclear weapons plants on people living in areas near them, researchers compared death rates in the areas near the plants with death rates in areas that had no such plants. Finding no difference in these rates, the researchers concluded that radiation from the nuclear weapons plants poses no health hazards to people living near them.

   Which one of the following, if true, most seriously weakens the researchers' argument?

   (A) Nuclear power plants were not included in the study.
   (B) The areas studied had similar death rates before and after the nuclear weapons plants were built.
   (C) Exposure to nuclear radiation can cause many serious diseases that do not necessarily result in death.
   (D) Only a small number of areas have nuclear weapons plants.
   (E) The researchers did not study the possible health hazards of radiation on people who were employed at the nuclear weapons plants if those employees did not live in the study areas.

8. It was once believed that cells grown in laboratory tissue cultures were essentially immortal. That is, as long as all of their needs were met, they would continue dividing forever. However, it has been shown that normal cells have a finite reproductive limit. A human liver cell, for example, divides 60 times and then stops. If such a cell divides 30 times and then is put into a deep freeze for months or even years, it "remembers" where it stopped dividing. After thawing, it divides another 30 times—but no more.

   If the information above is accurate, a liver cell in which more than 60 divisions took place in a tissue culture CANNOT be which one of the following?

   (A) an abnormal human liver cell
   (B) a normal human liver cell that had been frozen after its first division and afterward thawed
   (C) a normal cell that came from the liver of an individual of a nonhuman species and had never been frozen
   (D) a normal liver cell that came from an individual of a nonhuman species and had been frozen after its first division and afterward thawed
   (E) an abnormal cell from the liver of an individual of a nonhuman species

9. Complaints that milk bottlers take enormous markups on the bottled milk sold to consumers are most likely to arise when least warranted by the actual spread between the price that bottlers pay for raw milk and the price at which they sell bottled milk. The complaints occur when the bottled-milk price rises, yet these price increases most often merely reflect the rising price of the raw milk that bottlers buy from dairy farmers. When the raw-milk price is rising, the bottlers' markups are actually smallest proportionate to the retail price. When the raw-milk price is falling, however, the markups are greatest.

   If all of the statements above are true, which one of the following must also be true on the basis of them?

   (A) Consumers pay more for bottled milk when raw-milk prices are falling than when these prices are rising.
   (B) Increases in dairy farmers' cost of producing milk are generally not passed on to consumers.
   (C) Milk bottlers take substantially greater markups on bottled milk when its price is low for an extended period than when it is high for an extended period.
   (D) Milk bottlers generally do not respond to a decrease in raw-milk prices by straightaway proportionately lowering the price of the bottled milk they sell.
   (E) Consumers tend to complain more about the price they pay for bottled milk when dairy farmers are earning their smallest profits.

GO ON TO THE NEXT PAGE.

Questions 10–11

If the public library shared by the adjacent towns of Redville and Glenwood were relocated from the library's current, overcrowded building in central Redville to a larger, available building in central Glenwood, the library would then be within walking distance of a larger number of library users. That is because there are many more people living in central Glenwood than in central Redville, and people generally will walk to the library only if it is located close to their homes.

10. Which one of the following, if true, most strengthens the argument?

    (A) The public library was located between Glenwood and Redville before being moved to its current location in central Redville.
    (B) The area covered by central Glenwood is approximately the same size as that covered by central Redville.
    (C) The building that is available in Glenwood is smaller than an alternative building that is available in Redville.
    (D) Many of the people who use the public library do not live in either Glenwood or Redville.
    (E) The distance that people currently walk to get to the library is farther than what is generally considered walking distance.

11. Which one of the following, if true, most seriously weakens the argument?

    (A) Many more people who currently walk to the library live in central Redville than in central Glenwood.
    (B) The number of people living in central Glenwood who would use the library if it were located there is smaller than the number of people living in central Redville who currently use the library.
    (C) The number of people using the public library would continue to increase steadily if the library were moved to Glenwood.
    (D) Most of the people who currently either drive to the library or take public transportation to reach it would continue to do so if the library were moved to central Glenwood.
    (E) Most of the people who currently walk to the library would remain library users if the library were relocated to central Glenwood.

12. Light utility trucks have become popular among consumers who buy them primarily for the trucks' rugged appearance. Yet although these trucks are tough-looking, they are exempt from the government's car-safety standards that dictate minimum roof strength and minimum resistance to impact. Therefore, if involved in a serious high-impact accident, a driver of one of these trucks is more likely to be injured than is a driver of a car that is subject to these government standards.

    The argument depends on the assumption that

    (A) the government has established safety standards for the construction of light utility trucks
    (B) people who buy automobiles solely for their appearance are more likely than other people to drive recklessly
    (C) light utility trucks are more likely than other kinds of vehicles to be involved in accidents that result in injuries
    (D) the trucks' rugged appearance is deceptive in that their engines are not especially powerful
    (E) light utility trucks are less likely to meet the car-safety standards than are cars that are subject to the standards

13. Five years ago, during the first North American outbreak of the cattle disease CXC, the death rate from the disease was 5 percent of all reported cases, whereas today the corresponding figure is over 18 percent. It is clear, therefore, that during these past 5 years, CXC has increased in virulence.

    Which one of the following, if true, most substantially weakens the argument?

    (A) Many recent cattle deaths that have actually been caused by CXC have been mistakenly attributed to another disease that mimics the symptoms of CXC.
    (B) During the first North American outbreak of the disease, many of the deaths reported to have been caused by CXC were actually due to other causes.
    (C) An inoculation program against CXC was recently begun after controlled studies showed inoculation to be 70 percent effective in preventing serious cases of the illness.
    (D) Since the first outbreak, farmers have learned to treat mild cases of CXC and no longer report them to veterinarians or authorities.
    (E) Cattle that have contracted and survived CXC rarely contract the disease a second time.

GO ON TO THE NEXT PAGE.

Questions 14–15

Economist: Some policymakers believe that our country's continued economic growth requires a higher level of personal savings than we currently have. A recent legislative proposal would allow individuals to set up savings accounts in which interest earned would be exempt from taxes until money is withdrawn from the account. Backers of this proposal claim that its implementation would increase the amount of money available for banks to loan at a relatively small cost to the government in lost tax revenues. Yet, when similar tax-incentive programs were tried in the past, virtually all of the money invested through them was diverted from other personal savings, and the overall level of personal savings was unchanged.

14. The passage as a whole provides the most support for which one of the following conclusions?

   (A) Backers of the tax-incentive proposal undoubtedly have some motive other than their expressed aim of increasing the amount of money available for banks to loan.
   (B) The proposed tax incentive is unlikely to attract enough additional money into personal savings accounts to make up for the attendant loss in tax revenues.
   (C) A tax-incentive program that resulted in substantial loss of tax revenues would be likely to generate a large increase in personal savings.
   (D) The economy will be in danger unless some alternative to increased personal savings can be found to stimulate growth.
   (E) The government has no effective means of influencing the amount of money that people are willing to put into savings accounts.

15. The author criticizes the proposed tax-incentive program by

   (A) challenging a premise on which the proposal is based
   (B) pointing out a disagreement among policymakers
   (C) demonstrating that the proposal's implementation is not feasible
   (D) questioning the judgment of the proposal's backers by citing past cases in which they had advocated programs that have proved ineffective
   (E) disputing the assumption that a program to encourage personal savings is needed

16. Although all birds have feathers and all birds have wings, some birds do not fly. For example, penguins and ostriches use their wings to move in a different way from other birds. Penguins use their wings only to swim under water at high speeds. Ostriches use their wings only to run with the wind by lifting them as if they were sails.

   Which one of the following is most parallel in its reasoning to the argument above?

   (A) Ancient philosophers tried to explain not how the world functions but why it functions. In contrast, most contemporary biologists seek comprehensive theories of how organisms function, but many refuse to speculate about purpose.
   (B) Some chairs are used only as decorations, and other chairs are used only to tame lions. Therefore, not all chairs are used for sitting in spite of the fact that all chairs have a seat and some support such as legs.
   (C) Some musicians in a symphony orchestra play the violin, and others play the viola, but these are both in the same category of musical instruments, namely string instruments.
   (D) All cars have similar drive mechanisms, but some cars derive their power from solar energy, whereas others burn gasoline. Thus, solar-powered cars are less efficient than gasoline-powered ones.
   (E) Sailing ships move in a different way from steamships. Both sailing ships and steamships navigate over water, but only sailing ships use sails to move over the surface.

GO ON TO THE NEXT PAGE.

Questions 17–18

Jones: Prehistoric wooden tools found in South America have been dated to 13,000 years ago. Although scientists attribute these tools to peoples whose ancestors first crossed into the Americas from Siberia to Alaska, this cannot be correct. In order to have reached a site so far south, these peoples must have been migrating southward well before 13,000 years ago. However, no such tools dating to before 13,000 years ago have been found anywhere between Alaska and South America.

Smith: Your evidence is inconclusive. Those tools were found in peat bogs, which are rare in the Americas. Wooden tools in soils other than peat bogs usually decompose within only a few years.

17. The point at issue between Jones and Smith is

(A) whether all prehistoric tools that are 13,000 years or older were made of wood
(B) whether the scientists' attribution of tools could be correct in light of Jones's evidence
(C) whether the dating of the wooden tools by the scientists could be correct
(D) how long ago the peoples who crossed into the Americas from Siberia to Alaska first did so
(E) whether Smith's evidence entails that the wooden tools have been dated correctly

18. Smith responds to Jones by

(A) citing several studies that invalidate Jones's conclusion
(B) accusing Jones of distorting the scientists' position
(C) disputing the accuracy of the supporting evidence cited by Jones
(D) showing that Jones's evidence actually supports the denial of Jones's conclusion
(E) challenging an implicit assumption in Jones's argument

19. Editorial: It is clear that if this country's universities were living up to both their moral and their intellectual responsibilities, the best-selling publications in most university bookstores would not be frivolous ones like TV Today and Gossip Review. However, in most university bookstores the only publication that sells better than Gossip Review is TV Today.

If the statements in the editorial are true, which one of the following must also be true on the basis of them?

(A) People who purchase publications that are devoted primarily to gossip or to television programming are intellectually irresponsible.
(B) It is irresponsible for university bookstores to carry publications such as Gossip Review and TV Today.
(C) Most people who purchase publications at university bookstores purchase either TV Today or Gossip Review.
(D) Many people who attend this country's universities fail to live up to both their moral and their intellectual responsibilities.
(E) At least some of this country's universities are not meeting their moral responsibilities or their intellectual responsibilities or both.

GO ON TO THE NEXT PAGE.

Questions 20–21

Saunders: Everyone at last week's neighborhood association meeting agreed that the row of abandoned and vandalized houses on Carlton Street posed a threat to the safety of our neighborhood. Moreover, no one now disputes that getting the houses torn down eliminated that threat. Some people tried to argue that it was unnecessary to demolish what they claimed were basically sound buildings, since the city had established a fund to help people in need of housing buy and rehabilitate such buildings. The overwhelming success of the demolition strategy, however, proves that the majority, who favored demolition, were right and that those who claimed that the problem could and should be solved by rehabilitating the houses were wrong.

20. Which one of the following principles, if established, would determine that demolishing the houses was the right decision or instead would determine that the proposal advocated by the opponents of demolition should have been adopted?

    (A) When what to do about an abandoned neighborhood building is in dispute, the course of action that would result in the most housing for people who need it should be the one adopted unless the building is believed to pose a threat to neighborhood safety.
    (B) When there are two proposals for solving a neighborhood problem, and only one of them would preclude the possibility of trying the other approach if the first proves unsatisfactory, then the approach that does not foreclose the other possibility should be the one adopted.
    (C) If one of two proposals for renovating vacant neighborhood buildings requires government funding whereas the second does not, the second proposal should be the one adopted unless the necessary government funds have already been secured.
    (D) No plan for eliminating a neighborhood problem that requires demolishing basically sound houses should be carried out until all other possible alternatives have been thoroughly investigated.
    (E) No proposal for dealing with a threat to a neighborhood's safety should be adopted merely because a majority of the residents of that neighborhood prefer that proposal to a particular counterproposal.

21. Saunders' reasoning is flawed because it

    (A) relies on fear rather than on argument to persuade the neighborhood association to reject the policy advocated by Saunders' opponents
    (B) fails to establish that there is anyone who could qualify for city funds who would be interested in buying and rehabilitating the houses
    (C) mistakenly equates an absence of vocal public dissent with the presence of universal public support
    (D) offers no evidence that the policy advocated by Saunders' opponents would not have succeeded if it had been given the chance
    (E) does not specify the precise nature of the threat to neighborhood safety supposedly posed by the vandalized houses

---

22. For the writers who first gave feudalism its name, the existence of feudalism presupposed the existence of a noble class. Yet there cannot be a noble class, properly speaking, unless both the titles that indicate superior, noble status and the inheritance of such titles are sanctioned by law. Although feudalism existed in Europe as early as the eighth century, it was not until the twelfth century, when many feudal institutions were in decline, that the hereditary transfer of legally recognized titles of nobility first appeared.

    The statements above, if true, most strongly support which one of the following claims?

    (A) To say that feudalism by definition requires the existence of a nobility is to employ a definition that distorts history.
    (B) Prior to the twelfth century, the institution of European feudalism functioned without the presence of a dominant class.
    (C) The fact that a societal group has a distinct legal status is not in itself sufficient to allow that group to be properly considered a social class.
    (D) The decline of feudalism in Europe was the only cause of the rise of a European nobility.
    (E) The prior existence of feudal institutions is a prerequisite for the emergence of a nobility, as defined in the strictest sense of the term.

GO ON TO THE NEXT PAGE.

23. Mayor Smith, one of our few government officials with a record of outspoken, informed, and consistent opposition to nuclear power plant construction projects, has now declared herself in favor of building the nuclear power plant at Littletown. If someone with her past antinuclear record now favors building this power plant, then there is good reason to believe that it will be safe and therefore should be built.

The argument is vulnerable to criticism on which one of the following grounds?

(A) It overlooks the possibility that not all those who fail to speak out on issues of nuclear power are necessarily opposed to it.
(B) It assumes without warrant that the qualities enabling a person to be elected to public office confer on that person a grasp of the scientific principles on which technical decisions are based.
(C) It fails to establish that a consistent and outspoken opposition is necessarily an informed opposition.
(D) It leads to the further but unacceptable conclusion that any project favored by Mayor Smith should be sanctioned simply on the basis of her having spoken out in favor of it.
(E) It gives no indication of either the basis of Mayor Smith's former opposition to nuclear power plant construction or the reasons for her support for the Littletown project.

24. Advertisement: In today's world, you make a statement about the person you are by the car you own. The message of the SKX Mach-5 is unambiguous: Its owner is Dynamic, Aggressive, and Successful. Shouldn't you own an SKX Mach-5?

If the claims made in the advertisement are true, which one of the following must also be true on the basis of them?

(A) Anyone who is dynamic and aggressive is also successful.
(B) Anyone who is not both dynamic and successful would misrepresent himself or herself by being the owner of an SKX Mach-5.
(C) People who buy the SKX Mach-5 are usually more aggressive than people who buy other cars.
(D) No car other than the SKX Mach-5 announces that its owner is successful.
(E) Almost no one would fail to recognize the kind of person who would choose to own an SKX Mach-5.

25. The great medieval universities had no administrators, yet they endured for centuries. Our university has a huge administrative staff, and we are in serious financial difficulties. Therefore, we should abolish the positions and salaries of the administrators to ensure the longevity of the university.

Which one of the following arguments contains flawed reasoning that most closely parallels the flawed reasoning in the argument above?

(A) No airplane had jet engines before 1940, yet airplanes had been flying since 1903. Therefore, jet engines are not necessary for the operation of airplanes.
(B) The novelist's stories began to be accepted for publication soon after she started using a computer to write them. You have been having trouble getting your stories accepted for publication, and you do not use a computer. To make sure your stories are accepted for publication, then, you should write them with the aid of a computer.
(C) After doctors began using antibiotics, the number of infections among patients dropped drastically. Now, however, resistant strains of bacteria cannot be controlled by standard antibiotics. Therefore, new methods of control are needed.
(D) A bicycle should not be ridden without a helmet. Since a good helmet can save the rider's life, a helmet should be considered the most important piece of bicycling equipment.
(E) The great cities of the ancient world were mostly built along waterways. Archaeologists searching for the remains of such cities should therefore try to determine where major rivers used to run.

S T O P

IF YOU FINISH BEFORE TIME IS CALLED, YOU MAY CHECK YOUR WORK ON THIS SECTION ONLY. DO NOT WORK ON ANY OTHER SECTION IN THE TEST.

SECTION II
Time—35 minutes
24 Questions

Directions: Each group of questions in this section is based on a set of conditions. In answering some of the questions, it may be useful to draw a rough diagram. Choose the response that most accurately and completely answers each question.

Questions 1–5

A gymnastics instructor is planning a weekly schedule, Monday through Friday, of individual coaching sessions for each of six students—H, I, K, O, U, and Z. The instructor will coach exactly one student each day, except for one day when the instructor will coach two students in separate but consecutive sessions. The following restrictions apply:

H's session must take place at some time before Z's session.
I's session is on Thursday.
K's session is always scheduled for the day immediately before or the day immediately after the day for which O's session is scheduled.
Neither Monday nor Wednesday can be a day for which two students are scheduled.

1. Which one of the following is a pair of students whose sessions can both be scheduled for Tuesday, not necessarily in the order given?

(A) H and U
(B) H and Z
(C) K and O
(D) O and U
(E) U and Z

2. If K's session is scheduled for Tuesday, then which one of the following is the earliest day for which Z's session can be scheduled?

(A) Monday
(B) Tuesday
(C) Wednesday
(D) Thursday
(E) Friday

3. Which one of the following must be true?

(A) If U's session is scheduled for Monday, H's session is scheduled for Tuesday.
(B) If U's session is scheduled for Tuesday, O's session is scheduled for Wednesday.
(C) If U's session is scheduled for Wednesday, Z's session is scheduled for Tuesday.
(D) If U's session is scheduled for Thursday, Z's session is scheduled for Friday.
(E) If U's session is scheduled for Friday, Z's session is scheduled for Thursday.

4. Scheduling Z's session for which one of the following days determines the day for which U's session must be scheduled?

(A) Monday
(B) Tuesday
(C) Wednesday
(D) Thursday
(E) Friday

5. If H's session is scheduled as the next session after U's session, which one of the following could be true about H's session and U's session?

(A) U's session is scheduled for Monday, and H's session is scheduled for Tuesday.
(B) U's session is scheduled for Thursday, and H's session is scheduled for Friday.
(C) They are both scheduled for Tuesday.
(D) They are both scheduled for Thursday.
(E) They are both scheduled for Friday.

GO ON TO THE NEXT PAGE.

Questions 6–12

A square parking lot has exactly eight lights numbered 1 through 8 situated along its perimeter as diagrammed below.

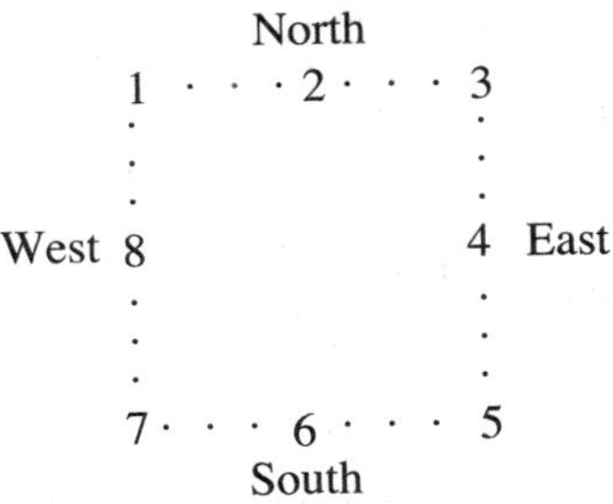

The lot must always be illuminated in such a way that the following specifications are met:

At least one of any three consecutively numbered lights is off.
Light 8 is on.
Neither light 2 nor light 7 is on when light 1 is on.
At least one of the three lights on each side is on.
If any side has exactly one of its three lights on, then that light is its center light.
Two of the lights on the north side are on.

6. Which one of the following could be a complete and accurate list of lights that are on together?

(A) 1, 3, 5, 7
(B) 2, 4, 6, 8
(C) 2, 3, 5, 6, 8
(D) 3, 4, 6, 7, 8
(E) 1, 2, 4, 5, 6, 8

7. Which one of the following lights must be on?

(A) light 2
(B) light 3
(C) light 4
(D) light 5
(E) light 6

8. If light 1 is off, which one of the following is a light that must also be off?

(A) light 3
(B) light 4
(C) light 5
(D) light 6
(E) light 7

9. Which one of the following statements must be true?

(A) If light 2 is on, then light 6 is off.
(B) If light 3 is on, then light 2 is on.
(C) If light 4 is on, then light 3 is off.
(D) If light 5 is off, then light 4 is on.
(E) If light 6 is off, then light 1 is on.

10. If light 5 is on, which one of the following could be true?

(A) Light 1 is off and light 6 is off.
(B) Light 1 is on and light 7 is on.
(C) Light 2 is off and light 4 is on.
(D) Light 2 is off and light 6 is off.
(E) Light 6 is on and light 7 is on.

11. If light 4 is on, each of the following statements must be true EXCEPT:

(A) Light 1 is on.
(B) Light 2 is on.
(C) Light 5 is off.
(D) Light 6 is on.
(E) Light 7 is off.

12. Suppose that it is no longer part of the specifications that two lights on the north side be on. If all of the other original specifications remain the same, and if exactly one light on the north side is on, which one of the following statements could be false?

(A) Light 1 is off.
(B) Light 2 is on.
(C) Light 3 is off.
(D) Light 4 is on.
(E) Light 5 is on.

GO ON TO THE NEXT PAGE.

Questions 13–17

Seven children are to be seated in seven chairs arranged in a row that runs from west to east. All seven children will face north. Four of the children are boys: Frank, Harry, Ivan, and Joel. Three are girls: Ruby, Sylvia, and Thelma. The children are assigned to chairs according to the following conditions:

Exactly one child sits in each chair.
No boy sits next to another boy.
Ivan sits next to and east of the fourth child in the row.
Sylvia sits east of Ivan.
Frank sits next to Ruby.

13. What is the maximum possible number of different pairs of chairs in which Frank and Ruby could sit?

(A) one
(B) two
(C) three
(D) four
(E) five

14. Which one of the following statements must be false?

(A) Both Harry and Joel sit east of Frank.
(B) Both Harry and Ruby sit east of Frank.
(C) Both Harry and Joel sit west of Frank.
(D) Both Harry and Ruby sit west of Frank.
(E) Both Joel and Ruby sit east of Frank.

15. If Thelma sits next to Ivan, and if Frank sits next to Thelma, which one of the following statements could be false?

(A) Both Frank and Ivan sit east of Ruby.
(B) Both Frank and Ruby sit west of Thelma.
(C) Both Frank and Sylvia sit east of Ruby.
(D) Both Frank and Thelma sit west of Sylvia.
(E) Both Frank and Ruby sit west of Joel.

16. If Frank does not sit next to any child who sits next to Ivan, which one of the following statements could be true?

(A) Harry sits west of Frank.
(B) Joel sits west of Ivan.
(C) Ruby sits west of Frank.
(D) Thelma sits west of Frank.
(E) Thelma sits west of Ruby.

17. If Frank sits east of Ruby, which one of the following pairs of children CANNOT sit next to each other?

(A) Frank and Thelma
(B) Harry and Ruby
(C) Harry and Sylvia
(D) Ivan and Ruby
(E) Joel and Ruby

GO ON TO THE NEXT PAGE.

Questions 18–24

The organisms W, X, Y, and Z respond to the antibiotics ferromycin, ganocyclene, and heptocillin in a manner consistent with the following:

Each of the organisms responds to at least one of the antibiotics.
No organism responds to all three antibiotics.
At least two but not all four of the organisms respond to ferromycin.
If W responds to any antibiotic, then X responds to that antibiotic.
If an organism responds to ferromycin, then it responds to ganocyclene.
Y responds to ferromycin.

18. Each of the following can be true EXCEPT:

(A) W responds to heptocillin.
(B) X responds to ganocyclene.
(C) X responds to heptocillin.
(D) Y responds to heptocillin.
(E) Z responds to ganocyclene.

19. Which one of the following could be true?

(A) W, X, and Z all respond to ferromycin.
(B) W, X, and Z all respond to ganocyclene.
(C) W and exactly one other organism respond to ganocyclene.
(D) W responds to more of the antibiotics than X does.
(E) More of the organisms respond to ferromycin than to ganocyclene.

20. Which one of the following could be true?

(A) Exactly one of the organisms responds to ferromycin.
(B) All four of the organisms respond to heptocillin.
(C) At least one of the organisms responds both to ferromycin and to heptocillin.
(D) At least one of the organisms responds neither to ganocyclene nor to heptocillin.
(E) At least one of the organisms responds to ganocyclene but does not respond to ferromycin.

21. If X does not respond to ferromycin, then which one of the following must be true?

(A) W responds to ganocyclene.
(B) X responds to ganocyclene.
(C) X responds to heptocillin.
(D) Z responds to ferromycin.
(E) Z responds to heptocillin.

22. If any of the organisms responds to two of the antibiotics, then which one of the following is true about such an organism?

(A) It must respond to ferromycin.
(B) It must respond to ganocyclene.
(C) It must respond to heptocillin.
(D) It cannot respond to ferromycin.
(E) It cannot respond to ganocyclene.

23. If none of the organisms responds to heptocillin, then which one of the following must be true?

(A) W responds to ferromycin.
(B) X responds to ferromycin.
(C) Z responds to ferromycin.
(D) Exactly three of the organisms respond to ganocyclene.
(E) Exactly four of the organisms respond to ganocyclene.

24. If three of the organisms respond to exactly the same set of antibiotics as each other, and if Z does not respond to ferromycin, then each of the following must be true EXCEPT:

(A) W responds to ferromycin.
(B) X responds to ganocyclene.
(C) Z responds to ganocyclene.
(D) W responds to exactly the same set of antibiotics as Y.
(E) X responds to exactly the same set of antibiotics as Y.

STOP

IF YOU FINISH BEFORE TIME IS CALLED, YOU MAY CHECK YOUR WORK ON THIS SECTION ONLY.
DO NOT WORK ON ANY OTHER SECTION IN THE TEST.

SECTION III
Time—35 minutes
27 Questions

Directions: Each passage in this section is followed by a group of questions to be answered on the basis of what is stated or implied in the passage. For some of the questions, more than one of the choices could conceivably answer the question. However, you are to choose the best answer: that is, the response that most accurately and completely answers the question.

After thirty years of investigation into cell genetics, researchers made startling discoveries in the 1960s and early 1970s which culminated in the development of processes, collectively known as recombinant deoxyribonucleic acid (rDNA) technology, for the active manipulation of a cell's genetic code. The technology has created excitement and controversy because it involves altering DNA—which contains the building blocks of the genetic code.

Using rDNA technology, scientists can transfer a portion of the DNA from one organism to a single living cell of another. The scientist chemically "snips" the DNA chain of the host cell at a predetermined point and attaches another piece of DNA from a donor cell at that place, creating a completely new organism.

Proponents of rDNA research and development claim that it will allow scientists to find cures for disease and to better understand how genetic information controls an organism's development. They also see many other potentially practical benefits, especially in the pharmaceutical industry. Some corporations employing the new technology even claim that by the end of the century all major diseases will be treated with drugs derived from microorganisms created through rDNA technology. Pharmaceutical products already developed, but not yet marketed, indicate that these predictions may be realized.

Proponents also cite nonmedical applications for this technology. Energy production and waste disposal may benefit: genetically altered organisms could convert sewage and other organic material into methane fuel. Agriculture might also take advantage of rDNA technology to produce new varieties of crops that resist foul weather, pests, and the effects of poor soil.

A major concern of the critics of rDNA research is that genetically altered microorganisms might escape from the laboratory. Because these microorganisms are laboratory creations that, in all probability, do not occur in nature. their interaction with the natural world cannot be predicted with certainty. It is possible that they could cause previously unknown perhaps incurable diseases. The effect of genetically altered microorganisms on the world's microbiological predator-prey relationships is another potentially serious problem pointed out by the opponents of rDNA research. Introducing a new species may disrupt or even destroy the existing ecosystem. The collapse of interdependent relationships among species, extrapolated to its extreme, could eventually result in the destruction of humanity.

Opponents of rDNA technology also cite ethical problems with it. For example, it gives scientists the power to instantly cross evolutionary and species boundaries that nature took millennia to establish. The implications of such power would become particularly profound if genetic engineers were to tinker with human genes, a practice that would bring us one step closer to Aldous Huxley's grim vision in Brave New World of a totalitarian society that engineers human beings to fulfill specific roles.

1. In the passage, the author is primarily concerned with doing which one of the following?
   (A) explaining the process and applications of rDNA technology
   (B) advocating continued rDNA research and development
   (C) providing evidence indicating the need for regulation of rDNA research and development
   (D) summarizing the controversy surrounding rDNA research and development
   (E) arguing that the environmental risks of rDNA technology may outweigh its medical benefits

2. According to the passage, which one of the following is an accurate statement about research into the genetic code of cells?
   (A) It led to the development of processes for the manipulation of DNA.
   (B) It was initiated by the discovery of rDNA technology.
   (C) It led to the use of new treatments for major diseases.
   (D) It was universally heralded as a great benefit to humanity.
   (E) It was motivated by a desire to create new organisms.

GO ON TO THE NEXT PAGE.

3. The potential benefits of rDNA technology referred to in the passage include all of the following EXCEPT

(A) new methods of waste treatment
(B) new biological knowledge
(C) enhanced food production
(D) development of less expensive drugs
(E) increased energy production

4. Which one of the following, if true, would most weaken an argument of opponents of rDNA technology?

(A) New safety procedures developed by rDNA researchers make it impossible for genetically altered microorganisms to escape from laboratories.
(B) A genetically altered microorganism accidentally released from a laboratory is successfully contained.
(C) A particular rDNA-engineered microorganism introduced into an ecosystem attracts predators that keep its population down.
(D) Genetically altered organisms designed to process sewage into methane cannot survive outside the waste treatment plant.
(E) A specific hereditary disease that has plagued humankind for generations is successfully eradicated.

5. The author's reference in the last sentence of the passage to a society that engineers human beings to fulfill specific roles serves to

(A) emphasize the potential medical dangers of rDNA technology
(B) advocate research on the use of rDNA technology in human genetics
(C) warn of the possible disasters that could result from upsetting the balance of nature
(D) present Brave New World as an example of a work of fiction that accurately predicted technological developments
(E) illustrate the sociopolitical ramifications of applying genetic engineering to humans

6. Which one of the following, if true, would most strengthen an argument of the opponents of rDNA technology?

(A) Agricultural products developed through rDNA technology are no more attractive to consumers than are traditional crops.
(B) Genetically altered microorganisms have no natural predators but can prey on a wide variety of other microorganisms.
(C) Drugs produced using rDNA technology cost more to manufacture than drugs produced with traditional technologies.
(D) Ecosystems are impermanent systems that are often liable to collapse, and occasionally do so.
(E) Genetically altered microorganisms generally cannot survive for more than a few hours in the natural environment.

GO ON TO THE NEXT PAGE.

Gray marketing, the selling of trademarked products through channels of distribution not authorized by the trademark holder, can involve distribution of goods either within a market region or across market boundaries. Gray marketing within a market region ("channel flow diversion") occurs when manufacturer-authorized distributors sell trademarked goods to unauthorized distributors who then sell the goods to consumers within the same region. For example, quantity discounts from manufacturers may motivate authorized dealers to enter the gray market because they can purchase larger quantities of a product than they themselves intend to stock if they can sell the extra units through gray market channels.

When gray marketing occurs across market boundaries, it is typically in an international setting and may be called "parallel importing." Manufacturers often produce and sell products in more than one country and establish a network of authorized dealers in each country. Parallel importing occurs when trademarked goods intended for one country are diverted from proper channels (channel flow diversion) and then exported to unauthorized distributors in another country.

Trademark owners justifiably argue against gray marketing practices since such practices clearly jeopardize the goodwill established by trademark owners: consumers who purchase trademarked goods in the gray market do not get the same "extended product," which typically includes pre and postsale service. Equally important, authorized distributors may cease to promote the product if it becomes available for much lower prices through unauthorized channels.

Current debate over regulation of gray marketing focuses on three disparate theories in trademark law that have been variously and confusingly applied to parallel importation cases: universality, exhaustion, and territoriality. The theory of universality holds that a trademark is only an indication of the source or origin of the product. This theory does not recognize the goodwill functions of a trademark. When the courts apply this theory, gray marketing practices are allowed to continue because the origin of the product remains the same regardless of the specific route of the product through the channel of distribution. The exhaustion theory holds that a trademark owner relinquishes all rights once a product has been sold. When this theory is applied, gray marketing practices are allowed to continue because the trademark owners' rights cease as soon as their products are sold to a distributor. The theory of territoriality holds that a trademark is effective in the country in which it is registered. Under the theory of territoriality, trademark owners can stop gray marketing practices in the registering countries on products bearing their trademarks. Since only the territoriality theory affords trademark owners any real legal protection against gray marketing practices, I believe it is inevitable as well as desirable that it will come to be consistently applied in gray marketing cases.

7. Which one of the following best expresses the main point of the passage?

(A) Gray marketing is unfair to trademark owners and should be legally controlled.

(B) Gray marketing is practiced in many different forms and places, and legislators should recognize the futility of trying to regulate it.

(C) The mechanisms used to control gray marketing across markets are different from those most effective in controlling gray marketing within markets.

(D) The three trademark law theories that have been applied in gray marketing cases lead to different case outcomes.

(E) Current theories used to interpret trademark laws have resulted in increased gray marketing activity.

8. The function of the passage as a whole is to

(A) criticize the motives and methods of those who practice gray marketing

(B) evaluate the effects of both channel flow diversion and parallel importation

(C) discuss the methods that have been used to regulate gray marketing and evaluate such methods' degrees of success

(D) describe a controversial marketing practice and evaluate several legal views regarding it

(E) discuss situations in which certain marketing practices are common and analyze the economic factors responsible for their development

9. Which one of the following does the author offer as an argument against gray marketing?

(A) Manufacturers find it difficult to monitor the effectiveness of promotional efforts made on behalf of products that are gray marketed.

(B) Gray marketing can discourage product promotion by authorized distributors.

(C) Gray marketing forces manufacturers to accept the low profit margins that result from quantity discounting.

(D) Gray marketing discourages competition among unauthorized dealers.

(E) Quality standards in the manufacture of products likely to be gray marketed may decline.

GO ON TO THE NEXT PAGE.

10. The information in the passage suggests that proponents of the theory of territoriality would probably differ from proponents of the theory of exhaustion on which one of the following issues?

    (A) the right of trademark owners to enforce, in countries in which the trademarks are registered, distribution agreements intended to restrict distribution to authorized channels
    (B) the right of trademark owners to sell trademarked goods only to those distributors who agree to abide by distribution agreements
    (C) the legality of channel flow diversion that occurs in a country other than the one in which a trademark is registered
    (D) the significance consumers attach to a trademark
    (E) the usefulness of trademarks as marketing tools

11. The author discusses the impact of gray marketing on goodwill in order to

    (A) fault trademark owners for their unwillingness to offer a solution to a major consumer complaint against gray marketing
    (B) indicate a way in which manufacturers sustain damage against which they ought to be protected
    (C) highlight one way in which gray marketing across markets is more problematic than gray marketing within a market
    (D) demonstrate that gray marketing does not always benefit the interests of unauthorized distributors
    (E) argue that consumers are unwilling to accept a reduction in price in exchange for elimination of service

12. The author's attitude toward the possibility that the courts will come to exercise consistent control over gray marketing practices can best be characterized as one of

    (A) resigned tolerance
    (B) utter dismay
    (C) reasoned optimism
    (D) unbridled fervor
    (E) cynical indifference

13. It can be inferred from the passage that some channel flow diversion might be eliminated if

    (A) profit margins on authorized distribution of goods were less than those on goods marketed through parallel importing
    (B) manufacturers relieved authorized channels of all responsibility for product promotion
    (C) manufacturers charged all authorized distributors the same unit price for products regardless of quantity purchased
    (D) the postsale service policies of authorized channels were controlled by manufacturers
    (E) manufacturers refused to provide the "extended product" to consumers who purchase goods in the gray market

GO ON TO THE NEXT PAGE.

Any study of autobiographical narratives that appeared under the ostensible authorship of African American writers between 1760 and 1865 inevitably raises concerns about authenticity and interpretation. Should an autobiography whose written composition was literally out of the hands of its narrator be considered as the literary equivalent of those autobiographies that were authored independently by their subjects?

In many cases, the so-called edited narrative of an ex-slave ought to be treated as a ghostwritten account insofar as literary analysis is concerned, especially when it was composed by its editor from "a statement of facts" provided by an African American subject. Blassingame has taken pains to show that the editors of several of the more famous antebellum slave narratives were "noted for their integrity" and thus were unlikely to distort the facts given them by slave narrators. From a literary standpoint, however, it is not the moral integrity of these editors that is at issue but the linguistic, structural, and tonal integrity of the narratives they produced. Even if an editor faithfully reproduced the facts of a narrator's life, it was still the editor who decided what to make of these facts, how they should be emphasized, in what order they ought to be presented, and what was extraneous or germane. Readers of African American autobiography then and now have too readily accepted the presumption of these eighteenth- and nineteenth-century editors that experiential facts recounted orally could be recorded and sorted by an amanuensis-editor, taken out of their original contexts, and then published with editorial prefaces, footnotes, and appended commentary, all without compromising the validity of the narrative as a product of an African American consciousness.

Transcribed narratives in which an editor explicitly delimits his or her role undoubtedly may be regarded as more authentic and reflective of the narrator's thought in action than those edited works that flesh out a statement of facts in ways unaccounted for. Still, it would be naive to accord dictated oral narratives the same status as autobiographies composed and written by the subjects of the stories themselves. This point is illustrated by an analysis of Works Progress Administration interviews with ex-slaves in the 1930s that suggests that narrators often told interviewers what they seemed to want to hear. If it seemed impolitic for former slaves to tell all they knew and thought about the past to interviewers in the 1930s, the same could be said of escaped slaves on the run in the antebellum era. Dictated narratives, therefore, are literary texts whose authenticity is difficult to determine. Analysts should reserve close analytic readings for independently authored texts. Discussion of collaborative texts should take into account the conditions that governed their production.

14. Which one of the following best summarizes the main point of the passage?

    (A) The personal integrity of an autobiography's editor has little relevance to its value as a literary work.
    (B) Autobiographies dictated to editors are less valuable as literature than are autobiographies authored by their subjects.
    (C) The facts that are recorded in an autobiography are less important than the personal impressions of its author.
    (D) The circumstances under which an autobiography was written should affect the way it is interpreted as literature.
    (E) The autobiographies of African Americans written between 1760 and 1865 deserve more careful study than they have so far received.

15. The information in the passage suggests that the role of the "editor" (lines 21-22) is most like that of

    (A) an artist who wishes to invent a unique method of conveying the emotional impact of a scene in a painting
    (B) a worker who must interpret the instructions of an employer
    (C) a critic who must provide evidence to support opinions about a play being reviewed
    (D) an architect who must make the best use of a natural setting in designing a public building
    (E) a historian who must decide how to direct the reenactment of a historical event

16. Which one of the following best describes the author's opinion about applying literary analysis to edited autobiographies?

    (A) The author is adamantly opposed to the application of literary analysis to edited autobiographies.
    (B) The author is skeptical of the value of close analytical reading in the case of edited autobiographies.
    (C) The author believes that literary analysis of the prefaces, footnotes, and commentaries that accompany edited autobiographies would be more useful than an analysis of the text of the autobiographies.
    (D) The author believes that an exclusively literary analysis of edited autobiographies is more valuable than a reading that emphasizes their historical import.
    (E) The author believes that the literary analysis of edited autobiographies would enhance their linguistic, structural, and tonal integrity.

GO ON TO THE NEXT PAGE.

17. The passage supports which one of the following statements about the readers of autobiographies of African Americans that were published between 1760 and 1865?

(A) They were more concerned with the personal details in the autobiographies than with their historical significance.
(B) They were unable to distinguish between ghostwritten and edited autobiographies.
(C) They were less naive about the facts of slave life than are readers today.
(D) They presumed that the editing of the autobiographies did not affect their authenticity.
(E) They had little interest in the moral integrity of the editors of the autobiographies.

18. Which one of the following words, as it is used in the passage, best serves to underscore the author's concerns about the authenticity of the autobiographies discussed?

(A) "ostensible" (line 2)
(B) "integrity" (line 16)
(C) "extraneous" (line 25)
(D) "delimits" (line 36)
(E) "impolitic" (line 46)

19. According to the passage, close analytic reading of an autobiography is appropriate only when the

(A) autobiography has been dictated to an experienced amanuensis-editor
(B) autobiography attempts to reflect the narrator's thought in action
(C) autobiography was authored independently by its subject
(D) moral integrity of the autobiography's editor is well established
(E) editor of the autobiography collaborated closely with its subject in its editing

20. It can be inferred that the discussion in the passage of Blassingame's work primarily serves which one of the following purposes?

(A) It adds an authority's endorsement to the author's view that edited narratives ought to be treated as ghostwritten accounts.
(B) It provides an example of a mistaken emphasis in the study of autobiography.
(C) It presents an account of a new method of literary analysis to be applied to autobiography.
(D) It illustrates the inadequacy of traditional approaches to the analysis of autobiography.
(E) It emphasizes the importance of the relationship between editor and narrator.

GO ON TO THE NEXT PAGE.

A conventional view of nineteenth-century Britain holds that iron manufacturers and textile manufacturers from the north of England became the wealthiest and most powerful people in society after about 1832. According to Marxist historians. these industrialists were the target of the working class in its struggle for power. A new study by Rubinstein, however, suggests that the real wealth lay with the bankers and merchants of London. Rubinstein does not deny that a northern industrial elite existed but argues that it was consistently outnumbered and outdone by a London-based commercial elite. His claims are provocative and deserve consideration.

Rubinstein's claim about the location of wealth comes from his investigation of probate records. These indicate the value of personal property, excluding real property (buildings and land), left by individuals at death. It does seem as if large fortunes were more frequently made in commerce than in industry and, within industry, more frequently from alcohol or tobacco than from textiles or metal. However, such records do not unequivocally make Rubinstein's case. Uncertainties abound about how the probate rules for valuing assets were actually applied. Mills and factories, being real property, were clearly excluded; machinery may also have been, for the same reason. What the valuation conventions were for stock-in-trade (goods for sale) is also uncertain. It is possible that their probate values were much lower than their actual market values; cash or near-cash, such as bank balances or stocks, were, on the other hand, invariably considered at full face value. A further complication is that probate valuations probably took no notice of a business's goodwill (favor with the public) which, since it represents expectations about future profit-making, would today very often be a large fraction of market value. Whether factors like these introduced systematic biases into the probate valuations of individuals with different types of businesses would be worth investigating.

The orthodox view that the wealthiest individuals were the most powerful is also questioned by Rubinstein's study. The problem for this orthodox view is that Rubinstein finds many millionaires who are totally unknown to nineteenth-century historians; the reason for their obscurity could be that they were not powerful. Indeed, Rubinstein dismisses any notion that great wealth had anything to do with entry into the governing elite, as represented by bishops, higher civil servants, and chairmen of manufacturing companies. The only requirements were university attendance and a father with a middle-class income.

Rubinstein, in another study, has begun to buttress his findings about the location of wealth by analyzing income tax returns, which reveal a geographical distribution of middle-class incomes similar to that of wealthy incomes revealed by probate records. But until further confirmatory investigation is done, his claims can only be considered partially convincing.

21. The main idea of the passage is that
    (A) the Marxist interpretation of the relationship between class and power in nineteenth-century Britain is no longer viable
    (B) a simple equation between wealth and power is unlikely to be supported by new data from nineteenth-century British archives
    (C) a recent historical investigation has challenged but not disproved the orthodox view of the distribution of wealth and the relationship of wealth to power in nineteenth-century Britain
    (D) probate records provide the historian with a revealing but incomplete glimpse of the extent and location of wealth in nineteenth-century Britain
    (E) an attempt has been made to confirm the findings of a new historical study of nineteenth-century Britain, but complete confirmation is likely to remain elusive

22. The author of the passage implies that probate records as a source of information about wealth in nineteenth-century Britain are
    (A) self-contradictory and misleading
    (B) ambiguous and outdated
    (C) controversial but readily available
    (D) revealing but difficult to interpret
    (E) widely used by historians but fully understandable only by specialists

23. The author suggests that the total probate valuations of the personal property of individuals holding goods for sale in nineteenth-century Britain may have been
    (A) affected by the valuation conventions for such goods
    (B) less accurate than the valuations for such goods provided by income tax returns
    (C) less, on average, if such goods were tobacco-related than if they were alcohol-related
    (D) greater, on average, than the total probate valuations of those individuals who held bank balances
    (E) dependent on whether such goods were held by industrialists or by merchants or bankers

GO ON TO THE NEXT PAGE.

24. According to the passage, Rubinstein has provided evidence that challenges which one of the following claims about nineteenth-century Britain?

(A) The distribution of great wealth between commerce and industry was not equal.
(B) Large incomes were typically made in alcohol and tobacco rather than in textiles and metal.
(C) A London-based commercial elite can be identified.
(D) An official governing elite can be identified.
(E) There was a necessary relationship between great wealth and power.

25. The author mentions that goodwill was probably excluded from the probate valuation of a business in nineteenth-century Britain most likely in order to

(A) give an example of a business asset about which little was known in the nineteenth century
(B) suggest that the probate valuations of certain businesses may have been significant underestimations of their true market value
(C) make the point that this exclusion probably had an equal impact on the probate valuations of all nineteenth-century British businesses
(D) indicate that expectations about future profit-making is the single most important factor in determining the market value of certain businesses
(E) argue that the twentieth-century method of determining probate valuations of a business may be consistently superior to the nineteenth-century method

26. Which one of the following studies would provide support for Rubinstein's claims?

(A) a study that indicated that many members of the commercial elite in nineteenth-century London had insignificant holdings of real property
(B) a study that indicated that, in the nineteenth century, industrialists from the north of England were in fact a target for working-class people
(C) a study that indicated that, in nineteenth-century Britain, probate values of goods for sale were not as high as probate values of cash assets
(D) a study that indicated that the wealth of nineteenth-century British industrialists did not appear to be significantly greater when the full value of their real property holdings was actually considered
(E) a study that indicated that at least some members of the official governing elite in nineteenth-century Britain owned more real property than had previously been thought to be the case

27. Which one of the following, if true, would cast the most doubt on Rubinstein's argument concerning wealth and the official governing elite in nineteenth-century Britain?

(A) Entry into this elite was more dependent on university attendance than on religious background.
(B) Attendance at a prestigious university was probably more crucial than a certain minimum family income in gaining entry into this elite.
(C) Bishops as a group were somewhat wealthier, at the point of entry into this elite, than were higher civil servants or chairmen of manufacturing companies.
(D) The families of many members of this elite owned few, if any, shares in iron industries and textile industries in the north of England.
(F) The composition of this elite included vice-chancellors, many of whom held office because of their wealth.

STOP

IF YOU FINISH BEFORE TIME IS CALLED, YOU MAY CHECK YOUR WORK ON THIS SECTION ONLY.
DO NOT WORK ON ANY OTHER SECTION IN THE TEST.

SECTION IV
Time—35 minutes
25 Questions

Directions: The questions in this section are based on the reasoning contained in brief statements or passages. For some questions, more than one of the choices could conceivably answer the question. However, you are to choose the best answer; that is, the response that most accurately and completely answers the question. You should not make assumptions that are by commonsense standards implausible, superfluous, or incompatible with the passage.

1. The cafeteria at Acme Company can offer only four main dishes at lunchtime, and the same four choices have been offered for years. Recently mushroom casserole was offered in place of one of the other main dishes for two days, during which more people chose mushroom casserole than any other main dish. Clearly, if the cafeteria wants to please its customers, mushroom casserole should replace one of the regular dishes as a permanent part of the menu.

   The argument is most vulnerable to criticism on the grounds that it fails to consider

   (A) the proportion of Acme Company employees who regularly eat lunch in the company cafeteria
   (B) whether any of the ingredients used in the cafeteria's recipe for mushroom casserole are included in any of the regular main dishes
   (C) a desire for variety as a reason for people's choice of mushroom casserole during the days it was offered
   (D) what foods other than main dishes are regularly offered at lunchtime by the cafeteria
   (E) whether other meals besides lunch are served in the Acme Company cafeteria

2. When old-growth forests are cleared of tall trees, more sunlight reaches the forest floor. This results in a sharp increase in the population of leafy shrubs on which the mule deer depend for food. Yet mule deer herds that inhabit cleared forests are less well-nourished than are herds living in old-growth forests.

   Which one of the following, if true, most helps to resolve the apparent paradox?

   (A) Mule deer have enzyme-rich saliva and specialized digestive organs that enable the deer to digest tough plants inedible to other deer species.
   (B) Mule deer herds that inhabit cleared forests tend to have more females with young offspring and fewer adult males than do other mule deer populations.
   (C) Mule deer populations are spread throughout western North America and inhabit hot, sunny climates as well as cool, wet climates.
   (D) As plants receive more sunlight, they produce higher amounts of tannins, compounds that inhibit digestion of the plants' proteins.
   (E) Insect parasites, such as certain species of ticks, that feed primarily on mule deer often dwell in trees, from which they drop onto passing deer.

GO ON TO THE NEXT PAGE.

3. Genevieve: Increasing costs have led commercial airlines to cut back on airplane maintenance. Also, reductions in public spending have led to air traffic control centers being underfunded and understaffed. For these and other reasons it is becoming quite unsafe to fly, and so one should avoid doing it.

Harold: Your reasoning may be sound, but I can hardly accept your conclusion when you yourself have recently been flying on commercial airlines even more than before.

Which one of the following relies on a questionable technique most similar to that used in Harold's reply to Genevieve?

(A) David says that the new film is not very good, but he has not seen it himself, so I don't accept his opinion.
(B) A long time ago Maria showed me a great way to cook lamb, but for medical reasons she no longer eats red meat, so I'll cook something else for dinner tonight.
(C) Susan has been trying to persuade me to go rock climbing with her, claiming that it's quite safe, but last week she fell and broke her collarbone, so I don't believe her.
(D) Pat has shown me research that proves that eating raw green vegetables is very beneficial and that one should eat them daily, but I don't believe it, since she hardly ever eats raw green vegetables.
(E) Gabriel has all the qualifications we have specified for the job and has much relevant work experience, but I don't believe we should hire him, because when he worked in a similar position before his performance was mediocre.

4. All people residing in the country of Gradara approve of legislation requiring that certain hazardous wastes be disposed of by being burned in modern high-temperature incinerators. However, waste disposal companies planning to build such incinerators encounter fierce resistance to their applications for building permits from the residents of every Gradaran community that those companies propose as an incinerator site.

Which one of the following, if true, most helps to explain the residents' simultaneously holding both of the positions ascribed to them?

(A) High-temperature incineration minimizes the overall risk to the human population of the country from the wastes being disposed of, but it concentrates the remaining risk in a small number of incineration sites.
(B) High-temperature incineration is more expensive than any of the available alternatives would be, and the higher costs would be recovered through higher product prices.
(C) High-temperature incineration will be carried out by private companies rather than by a government agency so that the government will not be required to police itself.
(D) The toxic fumes generated within a high-temperature incinerator can be further treated so that all toxic residues from a properly operating incinerator are solids.
(E) The substantial cost of high-temperature incineration can be partially offset by revenue from sales of electric energy generated as a by-product of incineration.

5. Elena: While I was at the dog show, every dog that growled at me was a white poodle, and every white poodle I saw growled at me.

Which one of the following can be properly inferred from Elena's statement?

(A) The only white dogs that Elena saw at the dog show were poodles.
(B) There were no gray poodles at the dog show.
(C) At the dog show, no gray dogs growled at Elena.
(D) All the white dogs that Elena saw growled at her.
(E) Elena did not see any gray poodles at the dog show.

GO ON TO THE NEXT PAGE.

Questions 6–7

Derek: We must exploit available resources in developing effective anticancer drugs such as the one made from mature Pacific yew trees. Although the yew population might be threatened, the trees should be harvested now, since an effective synthetic version of the yew's anticancer chemical could take years to develop.

Lola: Not only are mature yews very rare, but most are located in areas where logging is prohibited to protect the habitat of the endangered spotted owl. Despite our eagerness to take advantage of a new medical breakthrough, we should wait for a synthetic drug rather than threaten the survival of both the yew and the owl, which could have far-reaching consequences for an entire ecosystem.

6. Which one of the following is the main point at issue between Lola and Derek?

   (A) whether the harvesting of available Pacific yews would have far-reaching environmental repercussions
   (B) whether the drugs that are effective against potentially deadly diseases should be based on synthetic rather than naturally occurring chemicals
   (C) whether it is justifiable to wait until a synthetic drug can be developed when the capacity for producing the yew-derived drug already exists
   (D) the extent of the environmental disaster that would result if both the Pacific yew and the spotted owl were to become extinct
   (E) whether environmental considerations should ever have any weight when human lives are at stake

7. Lola's position most closely conforms to which one of the following principles?

   (A) Unless people's well-being is threatened, there should be no higher priority than preserving endangered plant and animal populations.
   (B) Medical researchers should work with environmentalists to come to an agreement about the fate of the Pacific yew and the spotted owl.
   (C) Environmental concerns should play a role in decisions concerning medical research only if human lives are not at stake.
   (D) Only medical breakthroughs that could save human lives would justify threatening the environment.
   (E) Avoiding actions that threaten an entire ecosystem takes precedence over immediately providing advantage to a restricted group of people.

8. The director of a secondary school where many students were having severe academic problems impaneled a committee to study the matter. The committee reported that these students were having academic problems because they spent large amounts of time on school sports and too little time studying. The director then prohibited all students who were having academic problems from taking part in sports in which they were active. He stated that this would ensure that such students would do well academically.

   The reasoning on which the director bases his statement is not sound because he fails to establish that

   (A) some students who spend time on sports do not have academic problems
   (B) all students who do well academically do so because of time saved by not participating in sports
   (C) at least some of the time the students will save by not participating in sports will be spent on solving their academic problems
   (D) no students who do well academically spend time on sports
   (E) the quality of the school's sports program would not suffer as a result of the ban

9. It can safely be concluded that there are at least as many trees in Seclee as there are in Martown.

   From which one of the following does the conclusion logically follow?

   (A) More trees were planted in Seclee in the past two years than in Martown.
   (B) Seclee is the region within which Martown is located.
   (C) Martown is suffering from an epidemic of tree-virus infection.
   (D) The average annual rainfall for Seclee is greater than the average annual rainfall for Martown.
   (E) The average number of trees cut down annually in Martown is higher than in Seclee.

GO ON TO THE NEXT PAGE.

Questions 10–11

A distemper virus has caused two-thirds of the seal population in the North Sea to die since May 1988. The explanation for the deaths cannot rest here, however. There must be a reason the normally latent virus could prevail so suddenly: clearly the severe pollution of the North Sea waters must have weakened the immune system of the seals so that they could no longer withstand the virus.

10. The argument concerning the immune system of the seals presupposes which one of the following?

    (A) There has been a gradual decline in the seal population of the North Sea during the past two centuries.
    (B) No further sources of pollution have been added since May 1988 to the already existing sources of pollution in the North Sea.
    (C) There was no sudden mutation in the distemper virus which would have allowed the virus successfully to attack healthy North Sea seals by May 1988.
    (D) Pollution in the North Sea is no greater than pollution in the Mediterranean Sea, off the coast of North America, or in the Sea of Japan.
    (E) Some species that provide food for the seals have nearly become extinct as a result of the pollution.

11. Which one of the following, if true, most strongly supports the explanation given in the argument?

    (A) At various times during the last ten years, several species of shellfish and seabirds in the North Sea have experienced unprecedentedly steep drops in population.
    (B) By reducing pollution at its source, Northern Europe and Scandinavia have been taking the lead in preventing pollution from reaching the waters of the North Sea.
    (C) For many years, fish for human consumption have been taken from the waters of the North Sea.
    (D) There are two species of seal found throughout the North Sea area, the common seal and the gray seal.
    (E) The distemper caused by the virus was a disease that was new to the population of North Sea seals in May 1988, and so the seals' immune systems were unprepared to counter it.

12. It is clear that none of the volleyball players at yesterday's office beach party came to work today since everyone who played volleyball at that party got badly sunburned and no one at work today is even slightly sunburned.

    Which one of the following exhibits a pattern of reasoning that most closely parallels that in the argument above?

    (A) Since everyone employed by TRF who was given the opportunity to purchase dental insurance did so and everyone who purchased dental insurance saw a dentist, it is clear that no one who failed to see a dentist is employed by TRF.
    (B) Since no one who was promoted during the past year failed to attend the awards banquet, evidently none of the office managers attended the banquet this year since they were all denied promotion.
    (C) Since the Donnely report was not finished on time, no one in John's group could have been assigned to contribute to that report since everyone in John's group has a reputation for getting assignments in on time.
    (D) Everyone with an office on the second floor works directly for the president and, as a result, no one with a second floor office will take a July vacation because no one who works for the president will be able to take time off during July.
    (E) Since all of the people who are now on the MXM Corporation payroll have been employed in the same job for the past five years, it is clear that no one who frequently changes jobs is likely to be hired by MXM.

GO ON TO THE NEXT PAGE.

Questions 13–14

The dean of computing must be respected by the academic staff and be competent to oversee the use of computers on campus. The only deans whom academics respect are those who hold doctoral degrees, and only someone who really knows about computers can competently oversee the use of computers on campus. Furthermore, the board of trustees has decided that the dean of computing must be selected from among this university's staff. Therefore, the dean of computing must be a professor from this university's computer science department.

13. Which one of the following is an assumption on which the argument depends?

(A) Academics respect only people who hold doctoral degrees.
(B) All of this university's professors have obtained doctoral degrees.
(C) At this university, every professor who holds a doctoral degree in computer science really knows about computers.
(D) All academics who hold doctoral degrees are respected by their academic colleagues.
(E) Among this university's staff members with doctoral degrees, only those in the computer science department really know about computers.

14. Which one of the following statements, if true, would weaken the argument?

(A) There are members of this university's staff who hold doctoral degrees and who are not professors but who really know about computers.
(B) There are members of this university's philosophy department who do not hold doctoral degrees but who really know about computers.
(C) Computer science professors who hold doctoral degrees but who are not members of this university's staff have applied for the position of dean of computing.
(D) Several members of the board of trustees of this university do not hold doctoral degrees.
(E) Some members of the computer science department at this university are not respected by academics in other departments.

Questions 15–16

Consumer advocate: Under the current absence of government standards for food product labeling, manufacturers are misleading or deceiving consumers by their product labeling. For example, a certain brand of juice is labeled "fresh orange juice," yet the product is made from water, concentrate, and flavor enhancers. Since "fresh" as applied to food products is commonly understood to mean pure and unprocessed, labeling that orange juice "fresh" is unquestionably deceptive.

Manufacturer: Using words somewhat differently than they are commonly used is not deceptive. After all, "fresh" can also mean never frozen. We cannot be faulted for failing to comply with standards that have not been officially formulated. When the government sets clear standards pertaining to product labeling, we will certainly comply with them.

15. On the basis of their statements above, the consumer advocate and the manufacturer are committed to disagreeing about the truth of which one of the following statements?

(A) In the absence of government standards, common understanding is the arbiter of deceptive labeling practices.
(B) Truthful labeling practices that reflect common standards of usage can be established by the government.
(C) The term "fresh" when it is applied to food products is commonly understood to mean pure and unprocessed.
(D) Terms that apply to natural foods can be truthfully applied to packaged foods.
(E) Clear government standards for labeling food products will ensure truthful labeling practices.

GO ON TO THE NEXT PAGE.

16. Which one of the following principles, if established, would contribute most to a defense of the manufacturer's position against that of the consumer advocate?

    (A) In the absence of government definitions for terms used in product labeling, common standards of understanding alone should apply.
    (B) Government standards for truthful labeling should always be designed to reflect common standards of understanding.
    (C) People should be free, to the extent that it is legal to do so, to exploit to their advantages the inherent ambiguity and vagueness in language.
    (D) When government standards and common standards for truthful labeling are incompatible with each other, the government standards should always take precedence.
    (E) In their interpretation of language, consumers should never presume that vagueness indicates an attempt to deceive on the part of manufacturers unless those manufacturers would reap large benefits from successful deception.

---

17. Certain items—those with that hard-to-define quality called exclusivity—have the odd property, when they become available for sale, of selling rapidly even though they are extremely expensive. In fact, trying to sell such an item fast by asking too low a price is a serious error, since it calls into question the very thing—exclusivity—that is supposed to be the item's chief appeal. Therefore, given that a price that will prove to be right is virtually impossible for the seller to gauge in advance, the seller should make sure that any error in the initial asking price is in the direction of setting the price too high.

    The argument recommends a certain pricing strategy on the grounds that

    (A) this strategy lacks a counterproductive feature of the rejected alternative
    (B) this strategy has all of the advantages of the rejected alternative, but fewer of its disadvantages
    (C) experience has proven this strategy to be superior, even though the reasons for this superiority elude analysis
    (D) this strategy does not rely on prospective buyers' estimates of value
    (E) the error associated with this strategy, unlike the error associated with the rejected alternative, is likely to go unnoticed

18. In order to control the deer population, a biologist has proposed injecting female deer during breeding season with 10 milligrams of a hormone that would suppress fertility. Critics have charged that the proposal poses health risks to people who might eat the meat of treated deer and thereby ingest unsafe quantities of the hormone. The biologist has responded to these critics by pointing out that humans can ingest up to 10 milligrams of the hormone a day without any adverse effects, and since no one would eat even one entire deer a day, the treatment would be safe.

    The biologist's response to critics of the proposal is based on which one of the following assumptions?

    (A) People would be notified of the time when deer in their area were to be treated with the hormone.
    (B) The hormone that would be injected into the deer is chemically similar to hormones used in human contraceptives.
    (C) Hunting season for deer could be scheduled so that it would not coincide with breeding season.
    (D) The hormone in question does not occur naturally in the female deer that would be injected.
    (E) Most people do not consider deer meat to be part of their daily diet and eat it only on rare occasions.

19. A recent survey conducted in one North American city revealed widespread concern about the problems faced by teenagers today. Seventy percent of the adults surveyed said they would pay higher taxes for drug treatment programs, and 60 percent said they were willing to pay higher taxes to improve the city's schools. Yet in a vote in that same city, a proposition to increase funding for schools by raising taxes failed by a narrow margin to win majority approval.

    Which one of the following factors, if true, would LEAST contribute to an explanation of the discrepancy described above?

    (A) The survey sample was not representative of the voters who voted on the proposition.
    (B) Many of the people who were surveyed did not respond truthfully to all of the questions put to them.
    (C) The proposition was only part of a more expensive community improvement program that voters had to accept or reject in total.
    (D) A proposition for increasing funds for local drug treatment centers also failed to win approval.
    (E) The proposition to raise taxes for schools was couched in terminology that many of the voters found confusing.

GO ON TO THE NEXT PAGE.

Questions 20–21

So-called environmentalists have argued that the proposed Golden Lake Development would interfere with bird-migration patterns. However, the fact that these same people have raised environmental objections to virtually every development proposal brought before the council in recent years indicates that their expressed concern for bird-migration patterns is nothing but a mask for their antidevelopment, antiprogress agenda. Their claim, therefore, should be dismissed without further consideration.

20. Which one of the following questionable argumentative techniques is employed in the passage?

    (A) taking the failure of a given argument to establish its conclusion as the basis for claiming that the view expressed by that conclusion is false
    (B) rejecting the conclusion of an argument on the basis of a claim about the motives of those advancing the argument
    (C) using a few exceptional cases as the basis for a claim about what is true in general
    (D) misrepresenting evidence that supports the position the argument is intended to refute
    (E) assuming that what is true of a group as a whole is necessarily true of each member of that group

21. For the claim that the concern expressed by the so-called environmentalists is not their real concern to be properly drawn on the basis of the evidence cited, which one of the following must be assumed?

    (A) Not every development proposal opposed in recent years by these so-called environmentalists was opposed because they believed it to pose a threat to the environment.
    (B) People whose real agenda is to block development wherever it is proposed always try to disguise their true motives.
    (C) Anyone who opposes unrestricted development is an opponent of progress.
    (D) The council has no reason to object to the proposed Golden Lake Development other than concern about the development's effect on bird-migration patterns.
    (E) When people say that they oppose a development project solely on environmental grounds, their real concern almost always lies elsewhere.

22. Psychologists today recognize childhood as a separate stage of life which can only be understood in its own terms, and they wonder why the Western world took so long to see the folly of regarding children simply as small, inadequately socialized adults. Most psychologists, however, persist in regarding people 70 to 90 years old as though they were 35 year olds who just happen to have white hair and extra leisure time. But old age is as fundamentally different from young adulthood and middle age as childhood is—a fact attested to by the organization of modern social and economic life. Surely it is time, therefore, to acknowledge that serious research into the unique psychology of advanced age has become indispensable.

    Which one of the following principles, if established, would provide the strongest backing for the argument?

    (A) Whenever current psychological practice conflicts with traditional attitudes toward people, those traditional attitudes should be changed to bring them in line with current psychological practice.
    (B) Whenever two groups of people are so related to each other that any member of the second group must previously have been a member of the first, people in the first group should not be regarded simply as deviant members of the second group.
    (C) Whenever most practitioners of a given discipline approach a particular problem in the same way, that uniformity is good evidence that all similar problems should also be approached in that way.
    (D) Whenever a society's economic life is so organized that two distinct times of life are treated as being fundamentally different from one another, each time of life can be understood only in terms of its own distinct psychology.
    (E) Whenever psychologists agree that a single psychology is inadequate for two distinct age groups, they should be prepared to show that there are greater differences between the two age groups than there are between individuals in the same age group.

GO ON TO THE NEXT PAGE.

23. Sabina: The words used in expressing facts affect neither the facts nor the conclusions those facts will support. Moreover, if the words are clearly defined and consistently used, the actual words chosen make no difference to an argument's soundness. Thus, how an argument is expressed can have no bearing on whether it is a good argument.

Emile: Badly chosen words can make even the soundest argument a poor one. After all, many words have social and political connotations that influence people's response to claims expressed in those words, regardless of how carefully and explicitly those words are defined. Since whether people will acknowledge a fact is affected by how the fact is expressed, the conclusions they actually draw are also affected.

The point at issue between Emile and Sabina is whether

(A) defining words in one way rather than another can alter either the facts or the conclusions the facts will justify
(B) a word can be defined without taking into account its social and political connotations
(C) a sound argument in support of a given conclusion is a better argument than any unsound argument for that same conclusion
(D) it would be a good policy to avoid using words that are likely to lead people either to misunderstand the claims being made or to reason badly about those claims
(E) a factor that affects neither the truth of an argument's premises nor the logical relation between its premises and its conclusion can cause an argument to be a bad one

24. Most disposable plastic containers are now labeled with a code number (from 1 to 9) indicating the type or quality of the plastic. Plastics with the lowest code numbers are the easiest for recycling plants to recycle and are thus the most likely to be recycled after use rather than dumped in landfills. Plastics labeled with the highest numbers are only rarely recycled. Consumers can make a significant long-term reduction in the amount of waste that goes unrecycled, therefore by refusing to purchase those products packaged in plastic containers labeled with the highest code numbers.

Which one of the following, if true, most seriously undermines the conclusion above?

(A) The cost of collecting, sorting, and recycling discarded plastics is currently higher than the cost of manufacturing new plastics from virgin materials.
(B) Many consumers are unaware of the codes that are stamped on the plastic containers.
(C) A plastic container almost always has a higher code number after it is recycled than it had before recycling because the recycling process causes a degradation of the quality of the plastic.
(D) Products packaged in plastics with the lowest code numbers are often more expensive than those packaged in the higher-numbered plastics.
(E) Communities that collect all discarded plastic containers for potential recycling later dump in landfills plastics with higher-numbered codes only when it is clear that no recycler will take them.

GO ON TO THE NEXT PAGE.

25. Despite a steady decrease in the average number of hours worked per person per week, the share of the population that reads a daily newspaper has declined greatly in the past 20 years. But the percentage of the population that watches television daily has shown a similarly dramatic increase over the same period. Clearly, increased television viewing has caused a simultaneous decline in newspaper reading.

Which one of the following, if true, would be most damaging to the explanation given above for the decline in newspaper reading?

(A) There has been a dramatic increase over the past 20 years in the percentage of people who tell polltakers that television is their primary source of information about current events.
(B) Of those members of the population who do not watch television, the percentage who read a newspaper every day has also shown a dramatic decrease.
(C) The time people spend with the books and newspapers they read has increased, on average, from 1 to 3 hours per week in the past 20 years.
(D) People who spend large amounts of time each day watching television are less able to process and remember printed information than are those who do not watch television.
(E) A typical television set is on 6 hours a day, down from an average of 6 1/2 hours a day 5 years ago.

S T O P

IF YOU FINISH BEFORE TIME IS CALLED, YOU MAY CHECK YOUR WORK ON THIS SECTION ONLY. DO NOT WORK ON ANY OTHER SECTION IN THE TEST.

Test II

Answers

Section I

1. D
2. A
3. A
4. C
5. C
6. C
7. C
8. B
9. C
10. B
11. B
12. E
13. D
14. B
15. A
16. B
17. B
18. E
19. E
20. B
21. D
22. A
23. E
24. B
25. B

Section II

1. D
2. B
3. D
4. D
5. A
6. C
7. B
8. B
9. D
10. A
11. B
12. E
13. C
14. C
15. E
16. B
17. D
18. D
19. B
20. E
21. D
22. B
23. E
24. C

Section III

1. D
2. A
3. D
4. A
5. E
6. B
7. A
8. D
9. B
10. A
11. B
12. C
13. C
14. D
15. E
16. B
17. D
18. A
19. C
20. B
21. C
22. D
23. A
24. E
25. B
26. D
27. E

Section IV

1. C
2. D
3. D
4. A
5. C
6. C
7. E
8. C
9. B
10. C
11. A
12. D
13. E
14. A
15. A
16. C
17. A
18. D
19. D
20. B
21. A
22. D
23. E
24. C
25. B

Score Conversion Chart

Directions:

1. Use the Scoring Worksheet below to compute your raw score.

2. Use the Score Conversion Chart to convert your raw score into the 120–180 scale.

Scoring Worksheet

1. Enter the number of questions you answered correctly in each section.

	Number Correct
SECTION I	______
SECTION II....................	______
SECTION III	______
SECTION IV	______

2. Enter the sum here: ______

This is your Raw Score

Conversion Chart

For Converting Raw Score to the 120-180 LSAT Scaled Score

Reported Score	Raw Score Lowest	Raw Score Highest
180	99	101
179	98	98
178	97	97
177	96	96
176	95	95
175	94	94
174	93	93
173	92	92
172	91	91
171	90	90
170	89	89
169	87	88
168	86	86
167	84	85
166	83	83
165	81	82
164	80	80
163	78	79
162	76	77
161	74	75
160	73	73
159	71	72
158	69	70
157	67	68
156	66	66
155	64	65
154	62	63
153	60	61
152	59	59
151	57	58
150	55	56
149	53	54
148	52	52
147	50	51
146	48	49
145	46	47
144	45	45
143	43	44
142	41	42
141	40	40
140	38	39
139	37	37
138	35	36
137	34	34
136	32	33
135	31	31
134	31	32
133	28	28
132	27	27
131	26	26
130	25	25
129	24	24
128	23	23
127	22	22
126	21	21
125	20	20
124	19	21
123	20	19
122	17	17
121	__*	__*
120	0	16

* There is no raw score that will produce this scaled score for this form.

Test II
Section I
Solutions

1. (A) No. This is perhaps the second-best answer. The implication of the stated conflict of interest is that the administrators might exaggerate the abilities of the chief surgeon. However, this is speculation. If there were no conflict of interest, it would still be possible that the staff would consider him the best surgeon.
(B) No. How he was appointed does not resolve the discrepancy between the chief surgeon's reputation and his apparently poor record.
(C) No. This does not resolve the discrepancy between chief surgeon's reputation and his apparently poor record, though it does imply that younger surgeons who trained under him might be loyal to him. However, this would have relevance only if these surgeons, not the hospital administrators, claimed the chief surgeon was the hospital's best surgeon.
(D) Yes. This explains the apparent paradox well. If the chief surgeon is assigned the high-risk cases, it's to be expected that he would have a higher number of patients who die. For example, suppose 90 percent of surgery patients at the hospital survive their operations, but only 75 percent of the chief surgeon's patients survive. Clearly, the chief surgeon's survival rate is much lower than the hospital's average. But if the chief surgeon performs only open heart surgery and the national survival rate for these operations is just 50 percent, the chief surgeon's survival rate is impressive.
(E) No. The statements in the passage compare the chief surgeon's current performance to that of the current staff, not to that of the previous staff or previous chief surgeon.

2. (A) Yes. The argument presupposes that the drug companies have not changed their behavior. That is, they committed the same number of violations from '71 through '75 as they did from '76 through '80; but were caught less often from '76 through '80 because of lax enforcement.
(B) No. The argument only discusses *"serious violations of drug-promotion laws."* Besides, this choice uses the argument's conclusion (that enforcement of drug-promotion laws changed) as *its* assumption!
(C) No. This answer-choice is an explanation not an assumption of the argument that the government was lax in enforcing drug-promotion laws. In fact, this choice goes beyond the argument and uses the argument's conclusion as *its* assumption!
(D) No. In fact, the argument presumes the opposite. The author concludes that the government was lax in enforcing drug-promotion laws between 1976 and 1980 because only 5 citations on average were issued each year. To conclude this, the author must assume that more than 5 violations of the laws occurred on average each year.
(E) No. What happened before or after the given time period is irrelevant.

3. (A) Yes. Sheila does not claim that smoking is <u>necessarily</u> harmful to one's health, just that smoking is <u>very likely</u> to be harmful to one's health. Hence, one counterexample is poor evidence against Sheila's claim.
(B) No. We cannot determine whether the experts had information about the cause of death of Tim's grandfather.
(C) No. There is no information in the passage to indicate that the case of Tim's grandfather has been discounted.
(D) No. Tim assumes the opposite. Sheila argues that smoking is unhealthy, and Tim disagrees based on his grandfather's longevity. He assumes that a long life indicates good health.
(E) No. Tim's counterexample is intended to challenge the claim of the experts; it is not concerned with how the experts arrived at their conclusion.

4. (A) No. The author argues that the claim that revolutions can benefit societies is simply incorrect, at no point does he imply that it is self-contradictory.
(B) No. Other than the claim itself, there are no general principles stated in the passage.
(C) Yes. The author attacks the claim that societies in general can reap more benefit than harm from a revolution by showing that the positive effects of the French Revolution were unique and thus cannot generally be expected to occur with other revolutions.
(D) No. There is only one example given, the French Revolution, not a series of examples.
(E) No. The author is not objectively comparing two positions: he is presenting his position.

5. (A) No. The <u>cause</u> of asthma is not the issue here.
(B) No. The conclusion concerns the total number of <u>adolescents</u> of each sex with asthma. It does not directly concern infants with asthma.
(C) Yes. The passage states that *"by adolescence the <u>percentage</u> of boys with asthma is about the same as the <u>percentage</u> of girls with asthma."* So if there are *"approximately equal numbers of adolescent boys and adolescent girls,"* then there should be approximately equal numbers of adolescent boys and adolescent girls with asthma.
(D) No. The issue is the number boys and girls with asthma, not how the asthma develops.
(E) No. This is irrelevant since the passage concerns only adolescents.

6. (A) No. Whether the editor bears a grudge against Mr. Trevalga is irrelevant since the publisher implies

that the editor does not know whose poems she is reviewing.
(B) No. The publisher's argument is based on the method of review, not on the quantity of submissions.
(C) Yes. The publisher states that the editor does not know the names of the authors whose poems she reviews. From this the publisher concludes that the editor does not know whose poems she is reviewing. This assumes that the editor cannot identify the poems of Mr. Trevalga by other means such as their style, handwriting, length, etc.
(D) No. This is not an assumption of the publisher. In fact, it could strengthen Mr. Trevalga's claim since the implication of his claim is that his poems were rejected because of a grudge, not because of their merit.
(E) No. According to the publisher, whether Mr. Trevalga used his real name or a pen name is irrelevant since the editor does not see the names.

7. (A) No. Both the study and the conclusion are about nuclear weapons plants. So nuclear power plants are irrelevant.
(B) No. This would strengthen the researchers' argument. If fact, it is very similar to the evidence they cite.
(C) Yes. Death is not the only negative influence on health. Perhaps the people living near the plants suffer from a host of ailments that are not life threatening but do negatively affect their health.
(D) No. That there is only a small number of plants is irrelevant. Though, the health hazard may appear only occasionally and therefore the small number of plants would represent an insufficient sample. However, there is a much better answer-choice.
(E) No. However, the argument would have been weakened if the researchers had not studied people who both worked at the plants and lived in the study areas since they have the greatest exposure.

8. (A) No. It would be abnormal since a normal human liver cell would *divide "60 times and then stop."*
(B) Yes. The passage is explicit that a normal cell cannot divide more than 60 times regardless of whether it was frozen and afterwards thawed. *"It 'remembers' where it stopped dividing."*
(C) No. Since the cell is normal, it cannot divide indefinitely. However, since it is not a <u>human</u> liver cell it may have a limit of more than 60 divisions—we don't know. This answer choice is essentially the same as choice (D) since the passage implies that it is irrelevant whether the cell has been frozen—*"it divides 60 times and then stops."*
(D) No. Since the cell is normal, it cannot divide indefinitely. However, since it is not a <u>human</u> liver cell it may have a limit of more than 60 divisions—we don't know. This answer choice is essentially the same as choice (C) since the passage implies that it is irrelevant whether the cell has been frozen—*"it divides 60 times and then stops."*
(E) No. All we can say is that it is not a normal human liver cell. Since it divided more than 60 times, it could be an abnormal human cell, an abnormal nonhuman cell, or a normal nonhuman cell.

9. (A) No. Although it is likely that consumers would pay *less* for bottled milk when raw-milk prices are falling, bottlers and retailers could maintain their prices to increase profits. It is unlikely, and certainly not necessary, that consumer prices will *increase*. The passage does state, however, that bottlers' markups rise when raw-milk prices are falling.
(B) No. The passage implies that the costs are passed on to consumers: *"The complaints occur when the bottled-milk price rises, yet these price increases most often merely reflect the rising price of the raw milk that bottlers buy from dairy farmers."*
(C) Yes. The point of the passage is that the markup is proportionally less when the price is high than when the price is low. The following diagram illustrates the situation:

High price: $1.00

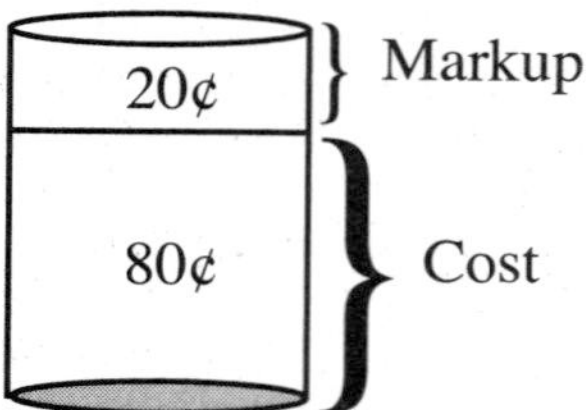

The proportion of the price that is the markup: 20%

Low price: 50¢

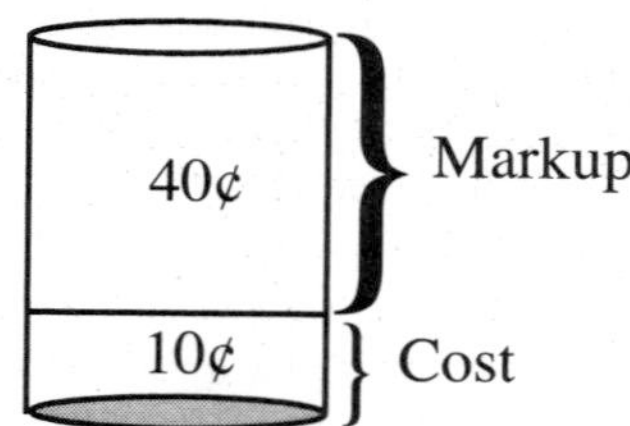

The proportion of the price that is the markup: 80%

(D) No. It is possible that they <u>do</u> respond to a decrease in raw-milk prices by proportionately lowering the price of bottled milk yet <u>do not</u> respond to an increase in raw-milk prices by proportionately raising the price of bottled milk—perhaps retail milk prices rise only half as fast. If so, as the passage indicates,

the bottlers' markups decrease as the price of milk increases.
(E) No. This answer-choice is a bit tricky. The passage does imply that consumers tend to complain more about the price of bottled milk when the bottlers' markup is least. This is the thrust of the first sentence. However, a high markup does not necessarily result in greater profits. A high markup could cause a drop in demand which in turn could cut profits.

Questions 10–11

10. (A) No. To strengthen the argument, we need to show that more people will be able to walk to the library if it is relocated to central Glenwood. The fact that the library was once located between Glenwood and Redville does not address this need.
(B) Yes. This question hinges on the population densities of the cities. Suppose Glenwood's population is twice Redville's but that the area of Glenwood is 10 times as large as the area of Redville. Then the population density of Glenwood would be one-fifth that of Redville. Hence, fewer people in Glenwood would be within walking distance of the library. The figure below illustrates the situation:

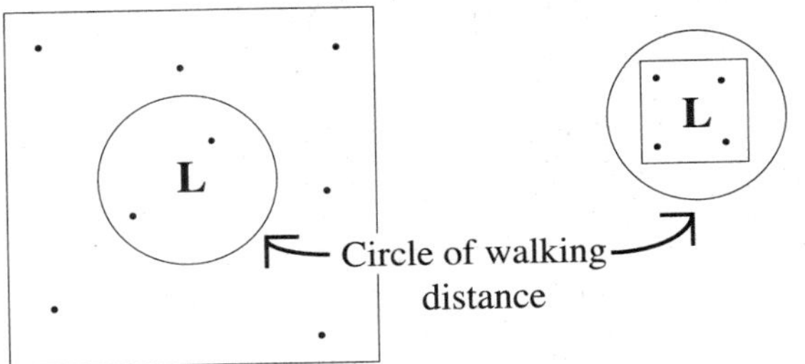

However, if the areas covered by central Glenwood and central Redville are roughly the same, then the population density of Glenwood would be greater than that of Redville. Hence, there would probably be more people within walking distance of the library in Glenwood than in Redville.
(C) No. The argument is predicated on the distance that people must walk to get to the library. The size of the library has no affect on the walking distance.
(D) No. The argument is predicated on the distance that people must walk to get to the library. People living outside both Glenwood and Redville are probably not within walking distance of either site for the library. Perhaps for these people driving distance might be a factor, but not walking distance.
(E) No. If people are walking further than the common walking distance, then for these communities the further distance is "walking distance."

11. (A) No. Since the library is currently in central Redville, it is reasonable to assume it is not within walking distance of people living in central Glenwood.
(B) Yes. That fewer people would use the library in Glenwood implies that fewer library users are actually within walking distance of the library in Glenwood. You might object: There might be more people walking to the library in Glenwood even though overall fewer people use the library. This is a flaw in choice (B); nevertheless, choice (B) does weaken the argument and no other answer-choice does.
(C) No. This would strengthen the argument. That increasing numbers of people would use the library in Glenwood implies that more people are within walking distance of the library in Glenwood. Although the increased use of the library may be from people who commute, this does not weaken the argument.
(D) No. It is irrelevant whether those people who do not walk to the library would continue to use the library in its new location. The argument is concerned with increasing access to those people who walk to the library, not necessarily increasing the overall number of people who use the library.
(E) No. If these people continue to walk to the library's new location, the argument would be greatly strengthened; and if they now commute to the new location, then this answer-choice would be irrelevant.

12. (A) No. In fact, the implication of the argument is that the government has not established safety standards for light utility trucks. Or at least it has not established standards as strict as those for cars.
(B) No. The conclusion of the argument does not state that people who buy light utility trucks for their appearance are more likely to be in serious accidents—just that they are more likely to be injured when in a serious accident.
(C) No. An explicit premise of the argument is *"if involved in a serious high-impact accident."* The argument then concludes *"a driver of one of these trucks is more likely to be injured than is a driver of a car that is subject to these government standards."* So the argument does not need to assume that light utility trucks are more likely than other kinds of vehicles to be involved in accidents that result in injuries.
(D) No. Nothing is stated or implied about the truck engines. However, there is an implication that the truck bodies are not sufficiently strong.
(E) Yes. The argument implies that because these trucks are exempt from the government's car-safety standards people driving them are more likely to be injured in an accident. However, it is conceivable that the government believes it is unnecessary to set standards because all the light utility trucks that have been produced have far exceeded car-safety standards. Hence, for the argument to be valid one must assume that cars are more likely to meet these standards than are light utility trucks.

13. (A) No. This substantially strengthens the argument. If many recent deaths due to CXC have been mistakenly attributed to another disease, then the 18 percent death rate would be even higher.
(B) No. This substantially strengthens the argument. If many of the deaths reported to have been caused by CXC were actually due to other causes, then the 5 percent initial death rate would be lower. Hence, the increase in virulence would be even greater.
(C) No. This choice is irrelevant. The effectiveness of an inoculation program has no bearing on the virulence of a disease. Inoculations are used to prevent infection by a disease. However, once infected, the disease's virulence measures the severity of the sickness. The fact that a disease can often be prevented does not affect its virulence if caught.
(D) Yes. If the mild cases are no longer reported, then the serious cases would be disproportionately represented. For example, suppose of 100 cattle with the disease, 73 have a mild case, 27 have a serious case and 5 will die of the disease. Then the death rate would be 5 percent. Now, if the 77 cattle with mild cases are not considered, then the reported death rate would be approximately 18 percent: $5/27 \approx 18\%$.
(E) No. The passage is about the virulence of the disease, not about an animal's immunity to a second infection.

Questions 14–15

14. (A) No. This is mere speculation.
(B) Yes. Although the government's loss of tax revenues should be small, the passage states *"similar tax-incentive programs left the overall level of personal savings unchanged."*
(C) No. The passage implies that there would be little or no increase in personal savings. The example in the passage shows that a tax incentive program with a small loss in tax revenues did not increase personal savings, so a tax incentive program with a large loss in tax revenues would probably have a similar result.
(D) No. The claim that the economy will be endangered is too strong. Besides, the passage does not argue against increasing personal savings, just that the given tax incentive program will fail to increase savings as similar ones have in the past.
(E) No. This claim is too broad. The passage does not imply that the government has no means of influencing the savings rate, just that certain tax incentive programs have no affect on savings rates.

15. (A) Yes. The premise of the proposed tax-incentive program is that exempting savings accounts from taxes will prompt people to save more. This premise is attacked by showing that when similar programs were tried people just diverted money from other savings accounts into the tax-free account instead of increasing their savings. Thus, the overall savings rate did not increase.
(B) No. There is no discussion about disagreements amongst policymakers.
(C) No. In fact, the past examples imply that the proposal can be implemented, though it will not yield the desired results.
(D) No. The passage questions the proposal, not necessarily the judgment of its backers. Further, the passage does not imply that backers of the current proposal are the same ones who advocated past tax-incentive programs.
(E) No. Though the opening sentence does imply the author may have some reservations about the need of a program to encourage personal savings, she never does directly attack that assumption.

16. (A) No. The passage uses an example to illustrate a statement: *"although all birds have feathers and all birds have wings, some birds do not fly."* Choice (A), however, draws a contrast between two approaches.
(B) Yes. The passage uses an example to illustrate a statement: *"although all birds have feathers and all birds have wings, some birds do not fly."* Similarly, choice (B) uses an example to illustrate a statement: *"not all chairs are used for sitting in despite the fact that all chairs have a seat and some support such as legs."*
(C) No. The passage uses an example to illustrate a statement: *"although all birds have feathers and all birds have wings, some birds do not fly."* Choice (C) does not have an example.
(D) No. The passage uses an example to illustrate a statement: *"although all birds have feathers and all birds have wings, some birds do not fly."* Choice (D) does not have an explicit example.
(E) No. Choice (E) draws a comparison between two ships. However, the passage does not draw a comparison between ostriches and penguins; rather it merely uses each to illustrate a statement: *"although all birds have feathers and all birds have wings, some birds do not fly."*

Questions 17–18

17. (A) No. Whether prehistoric tools were composed of substances other than wood is not discussed.
(B) Yes. They are arguing over the meaning of the evidence. Jones argues that if the wooden tools found in South America were from peoples who migrated from Alaska then there should be even older wooden tools along the path they took. Perhaps 13,500 year old wooden tools in Central America and 14,000 year old wooden tools in North America.

Smith, on the other hand, refutes Jones's claim by pointing out that older wooden tools were not found along the migration route because they quickly decompose except in peat bogs, which are rare along the path.

(C) No. There is no discussion of the accuracy of the dating method used.
(D) No. Although this issue is probably in dispute, we cannot tell from the excerpt. Smith does not state or imply that the people crossed at a particular time; rather he points out a flaw in Jones's interpretation of the evidence.
(E) No. The meaning of the evidence is in dispute, not its accuracy. Ostensibly, they both accept that the tools are 13,000 years old. At issue is whether this precludes the possibility of the tools being from people who migrated from Alaska.

18. (A) No. Smith does not refute Jones by citing any studies but by questioning Jones's logic.
(B) No. Smith responds only to the Jones's interpretation of the evidence, not to Jones's paraphrase of the scientists' position.
(C) No. The accuracy of the evidence is not in dispute, rather the debate is over the meaning of the evidence.
(D) No. Smith does not claim that Jones's conclusion is wrong, just that the "evidence is inconclusive."
(E) Yes. Jones's assumption is that if people from Siberia were in North America and Central America before 13,000 years ago then they would have left wooden tools which scientists would have found. Smith attacks this assumption by pointing out that the wooden tools may have been left in the area more than 13,000 years ago but then quickly decomposed. In other words, the fact that remains of wooden tools are not now in the area does not preclude the possibility that they were in the area more than 13,000 years ago.

19. (A) No. The passage argues that the universities are intellectually irresponsible, not the people who buy the frivolous publications.
(B) No. The passage implies that if the universities were meeting their intellectual responsibilities then students would be interested in more substantive publications than TV Today and Gossip Review.
(C) No. Being the best-selling publication does not necessarily mean that most people buy it. There may be hundreds of publications.
(D) No. The passage argues that the universities, not the students, fail to live up to both their moral and their intellectual responsibilities.
(E) Yes. This is simply an application of the contrapositive. The argument can be diagrammed as follows:

R—>~F

where R stands for *"this country's universities were living up to both their moral and their intellectual responsibilities,"* and ~F stands for *"the best-selling publications in most university bookstores would not be frivolous ones like TV Today and Gossip Review."*

Now, the statement *"in most university bookstores the only publication that sells better than Gossip Review is TV Today"* negates the conclusion of the argument **R—>~F**. This prompts us to take the contrapositive:

R—>~F
F
∴ ~R

That is, universities are not living up to their moral or intellectual responsibilities.

Questions 20–21

20. (A) No. This does not address the conflicting proposals: demolition vs. rehabilitation.
(B) Yes. Suppose the houses are destroyed first. Then it cannot be known whether rehabilitating the houses would have solved the problem. However, suppose the houses are rehabilitated first. Now, if rehabilitation fails to solve the problem, the houses can still be demolished. So rehabilitating the houses first *does not* preclude the possibility of destroying the houses later, whereas destroying the houses first *does* preclude the possibility of rehabilitating the houses later.
(C) No. We do not know whether either proposal requires government funding. Besides, only one of the two proposals advocated renovating the buildings, the other advocated destroying the buildings.
(D) No. This is the second-best choice. It is both too strong and too broad. The passage is about only two proposals: destruction and rehabilitation.
(E) No. The question asks which of two possible decisions is right, not what method should be taken to arrive at a decision.

21. (A) No. Saunders appeals only to the success of the demolition strategy, not to fear.
(B) No. If fact, this would support Saunders' argument. If no one could qualify for city funds, then it would be unlikely for the houses to be rehabilitated.
(C) No. Saunders acknowledges there was dissent—*"some people tried to argue that it was unnecessary to demolish [the buildings]"*—and never claims there was universal support for the chosen strategy, only majority support.
(D) Yes. Saunders claims that the success of the destruction strategy proves that it was right and that the rehabilitation strategy was wrong. He is only half right. Since the destruction of the houses precludes the possibility of trying rehabilitation, we cannot know whether rehabilitation would have also worked.
(E) No. The nature of the threat is not at issue since the opening sentence of the passage implies that everyone agrees there is a threat. Rather, how to eliminate the threat is at issue.

22. (A) Yes. According to the passage, feudalism existed in Europe from the eighth century to the twelfth century, which preceded the existence of a nobility. Hence, to say that feudalism requires the existence of a nobility contradicts history.
(B) No. This is the second-best choice. Choice (A) is better because it refers to the main idea of the passage that feudalism does not presuppose the existence of a noble class. Also choice (B) has a flaw in that we don't know whether "dominant class" is synonymous with "noble class."
(C) No. The opposite, however, is somewhat implied: The noble class was not deemed a social class until its titles were sanctioned by law.
(D) No. The passage implies that there was little or no cause and effect between nobility and feudalism.
(E) No. The passage implies that there was little or no cause and effect between nobility and feudalism.

23. (A) No. Since she *did* speak out, this choice is irrelevant.
(B) No. The argument does assume that the mayor has a grasp of the scientific issues; however, it is not necessary to assume this is due to the qualities that got her elected to public office.
(C) No. The passage does not even imply that consistent and outspoken opposition is necessarily an informed opposition. The three features of her opposition to nuclear power plants—outspoken, informed, and consistent—are presented as an independent series.
(D) No. Although this is a possible criticism of the argument, there are better and more direct criticisms.
(E) Yes. We do not know her motives. Perhaps she changed her mind after carefully weighing the issues, or perhaps she was paid to change her position.

24. (A) No. Dynamic, aggressive, and successful are presented as independent characteristics.
(B) Yes. The statement *"The message of the SKX Mach-5 is unambiguous: Its owner is Dynamic, Aggressive, and Successful"* contains an embedded *if-then* statement: If you own an SKX Mach-5, then you are Dynamic, Aggressive, and Successful. So if you own an SKX Mach-5 and are not both Dynamic and Successful, you would be misrepresenting yourself.
(C) No. The passage does not make any comparisons between people who buy the SKX and people who buy other cars.
(D) No. No other cars are mentioned.
(E) No. This cannot be determined from what is stated in the passage.

25. (A) No. The passage presents a false causal argument. It implies that medieval universities endured for centuries because they had no administrators, but gives no evidence for this cause and effect relationship. The argument in choice (A), however, is neither invalid nor a causation argument.
(B) Yes. The passage presents a false causal argument. It implies that medieval universities endured for centuries because they had no administrators, but gives no evidence for this cause and effect relationship. There may have been other factors that caused the universities' longevity. Choice (B) presents a similar false causal argument, implying the use of a computer caused the novelist's stories to be accepted for publication.
(C) No. Unlike the original passage, this is a *valid* argument.
(D) No. The passage presents a false causal argument. It implies that medieval universities endured for centuries because they had no administrators, but gives no evidence for this cause and effect relationship. Choice (D), however, is not a false causal argument.
(E) No. This is not an invalid argument.

Test II
Section II
Solutions

Questions 1–5

The condition *"H's session must take place at some time before Z's session"* can be symbolized as **H—>Z**. The condition *"K's session is always scheduled for the day immediately before or the day immediately after the day for which O's session is scheduled"* simply means that K and O must be scheduled on consecutive days; it can be symbolized as **KO** (note, the positions of K and O can be interchanged). Symbolizing the remaining conditions yields

H, I, K, O, U, Z
1 day = 2 students
H—>Z
I = Th
KO
M ≠ 2 & W ≠ 2

~2		~2		
M	Tu	W	Th	F
			I	

1. (A) No. Adding H and U to the diagram yields

1	2	1	1	1
M	Tu	W	Th	F
	H		I	
	U			

This diagram shows that there is no room to place the condition **KO**.
(B) No. Adding H and Z to the diagram yields

1	2	1	1	1
M	Tu	W	Th	F
	H		I	
	Z			

This diagram shows that there is no room to place the condition **KO**.
(C) No. K and O must be scheduled on consecutive days.
(D) Yes. The following is one of two scenarios that satisfy all the conditions:

M	Tu	W	Th	F
H	O	K	I	Z
	U			

(E) No. Adding U and Z to the diagram yields

1	2	1	1	1
M	Tu	W	Th	F
	U		I	
	Z			

This diagram shows that there is no room to place the condition **KO**.

2. (A) No. Z's session must be scheduled after H's session, **H—>Z**, and only one student can be scheduled for Monday.
(B) Yes. With K and Z scheduled for Tuesday, we get the following unique ordering:

M	Tu	W	Th	F
H	K	O	I	U
	Z			

(C) No. With K and Z scheduled for Tuesday, we get the following unique ordering:

M	Tu	W	Th	F
H	K	O	I	U
	Z			

(D) No. With K and Z scheduled for Tuesday, we get the following unique ordering:

M	Tu	W	Th	F
H	K	O	I	U
	Z			

(E) No. With K and Z scheduled for Tuesday, we get the following unique ordering:

M	Tu	W	Th	F
H	K	O	I	U
	Z			

3. (A) No. Following is one of several counterexamples:

M	Tu	W	Th	F
U	K	O	I	Z
			H	

(B) No. Following is one of several counterexamples:

M	Tu	W	Th	F
K	U	H	I	Z
	O			

(C) No. Following is one of several counterexamples:

M	Tu	W	Th	F
K	O	U	I	Z
			H	

(D) Yes. Place U on the diagram:

M	Tu	W	Th	F
			I	
			U	

This diagram shows that the condition **KO** must be placed on Monday/Tuesday or Tuesday/Wednesday. Hence, one of the days Monday, Tuesday, or Wednesday is left for H and Z. But since H must be scheduled before Z, Z must be scheduled on Friday.
(E) No. Following is one of several counterexamples:

M	Tu	W	Th	F
K	**O**	**H**	**I**	**U**
				Z

4. (A) No. From the conditions **H—>Z** and $\mathbf{M \neq 2}$, we know that Z cannot be scheduled for Monday.
(B) No. Following are two valid scenarios with U scheduled on different days:

M	Tu	W	Th	F
H	**Z**	**K**	**I**	**U**
			O	

M	Tu	W	Th	F
H	**Z**	**U**	**I**	**K**
			O	

(C) No. Following are two valid scenarios with U scheduled on different days:

M	Tu	W	Th	F
K	**O**	**Z**	**I**	**U**
	H			

M	Tu	W	Th	F
U	**H**	**Z**	**I**	**O**
			K	

(D) Yes. Place Z on the diagram:

M	Tu	W	Th	F
			I	
			Z	

This diagram shows that the condition **KO** must be placed on Monday/Tuesday or Tuesday/Wednesday. Since H must be scheduled before Z, H must be scheduled on Monday or Wednesday, which forces U to be scheduled on Friday.
(E) No. Following are two valid scenarios with U scheduled on different days:

M	Tu	W	Th	F
K	**O**	**U**	**I**	**Z**
			H	

M	Tu	W	Th	F
U	**K**	**O**	**I**	**Z**
			H	

5. (A) Yes. Scheduling U for Monday and H for Tuesday yields the following diagram:

M	Tu	W	Th	F
U	**H**		**I**	

The condition **KO** can be placed on the diagram as follows:

M	Tu	W	Th	F
U	**H**	**O**	**I**	
	K			

Finally, placing Z on Friday yields the following valid scenario:

M	Tu	W	Th	F
U	**H**	**O**	**I**	**Z**
	K			

Note, the supplemental condition *"H's session is scheduled as the next session after U's session"* is not needed for this or any of the other answer-choices. It is not uncommon for the LSAT writers to introduce superfluous conditions.
(B) No. H cannot be scheduled for Friday since H must be scheduled before Z. Note, Z cannot also be scheduled for Friday since there are already two people—I and U—scheduled for Thursday.
(C) No. Place U and H on the diagram:

M	Tu	W	Th	F
	U		**I**	
	H			

This diagram leaves no room to place the condition **KO**.
(D) No. This would schedule three people—I, U, and H—for Thursday. But the setup to the game states that exactly one person is scheduled for each day, except for one day when two people are scheduled.
(E) No. H cannot be scheduled for Friday with U since H must be scheduled before Z.

Questions 6–12

6. (A) No. This violates the condition *"Neither light 2 nor light 7 is on when light 1 is on."*
(B) No. This violates the condition *"Two of the lights on the north side are on."*
(C) Yes. Placing the information on the diagram yields

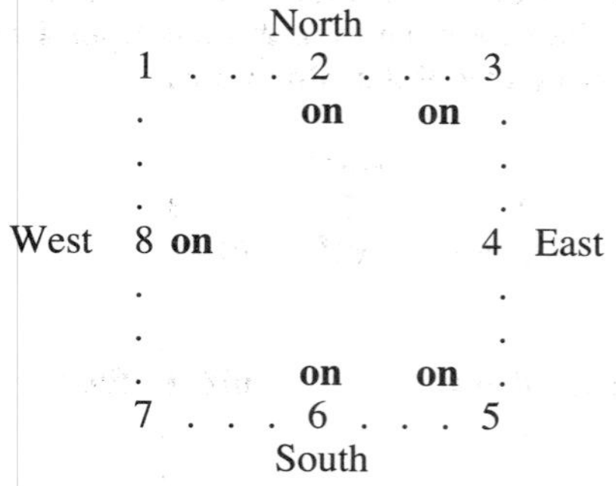

```
                North
        1 . . . . 2 . . . . 3
        .        on     on  .
        .                   .
        .                   .
West    8 on                4   East
        .                   .
        .                   .
        .        on     on  .
        7 . . . . 6 . . . . 5
                South
```

Since this is to be a complete list of the lights that could be on, the remaining lights must be off:

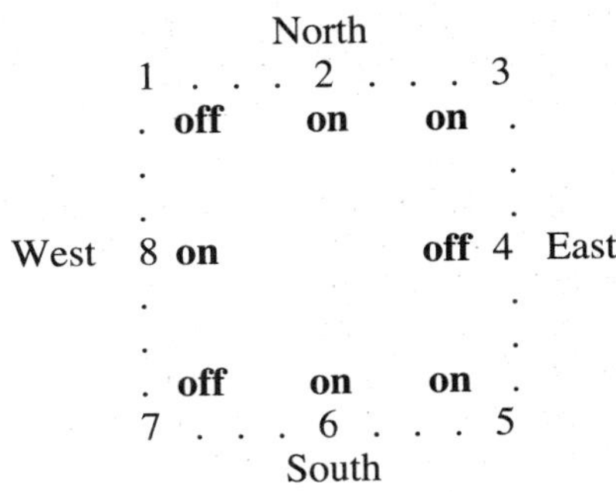

This diagram does not violate any of the conditions: There are not three consecutively numbered lights on. Light 8 is on. Light 1 is off and therefore the condition *"Neither light 2 nor light 7 is on when light 1 is on"* does not apply. Each side has a light on. The west side has exactly one light on and it is the center light. Two lights on the north side, 2 and 3, are on.

(D) No. This violates the condition *"Two of the lights on the north side are on."*

(E) No. This violates the condition *"At least one of any three consecutively numbered lights is off."*

7. (A) No. The following diagram has light 2 off and does not violate any of the conditions:

North
1 . . . 2 . . . 3
. **on** **off** **on** .
West 8 **on** **off** 4 East
. **off** **on** **on** .
7 . . . 6 . . . 5
South

(B) Yes. Suppose light 3 is off. Then from the condition *"Two of the lights on the north side are on,"* we know that lights 1 and 2 must be on. However, this contradicts the condition *"Neither light 2 nor light 7 is on when light 1 is on."* Hence, light 3 must be on.

(C) No. The following diagram has light 4 off and does not violate any of the conditions:

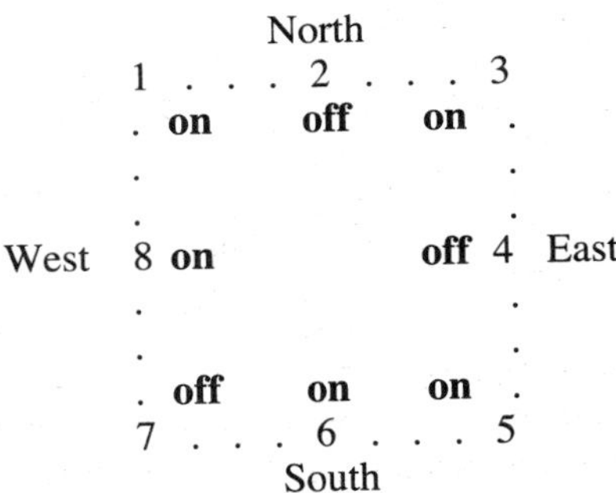

(D) No. The following diagram has light 5 off and does not violate any of the conditions:

North
1 . . . 2 . . . 3
. **on** **off** **on** .
West 8 **on** **on** 4 East
. **off** **on** **off** .
7 . . . 6 . . . 5
South

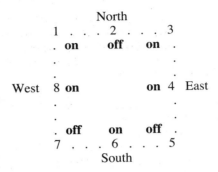

(E) No. The following diagram has light 6 off and does not violate any of the conditions:

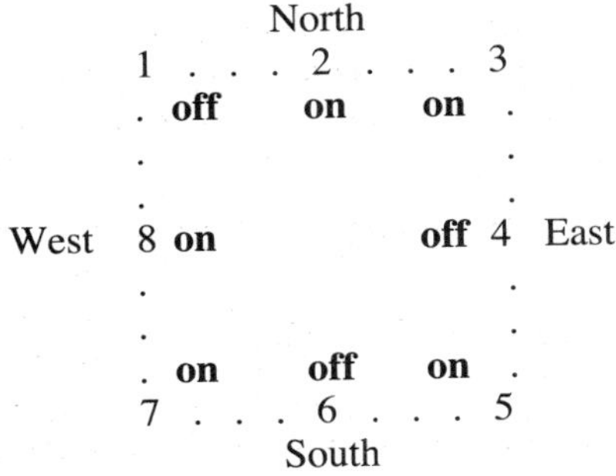

8. (A) No. The following diagram has light 3 on and does not violate any of the conditions:

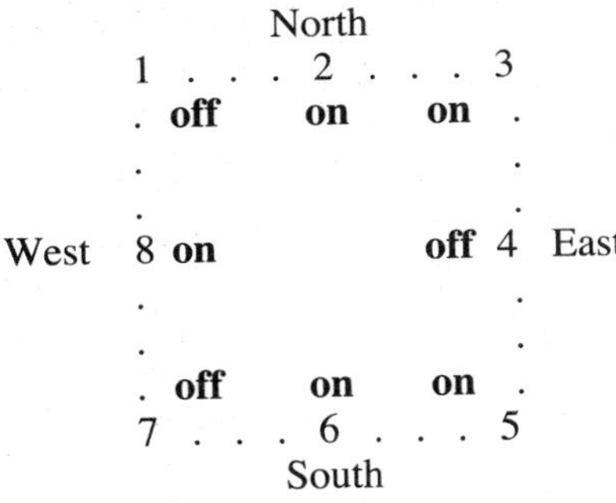

(B) Yes. Suppose light 4 is on. If light 1 is off, then from the condition *"Two of the lights on the north side are on"* we know that lights 2 and 3 must be on. This, however, has three consecutively numbered lights on—2, 3, and 4—contradicting the condition *"At least one of any three consecutively numbered lights is off."* Hence, light 4 must be off.

(C) No. The following diagram has light 5 on and does not violate any of the conditions:

```
              North
        1 . . . 2 . . . 3
        . off   on    on  .
        .                 .
        .                 .
West    8 on          off 4   East
        .                 .
        .                 .
        . off   on    on  .
        7 . . . 6 . . . 5
              South
```

(D) No. The following diagram has light 6 on and does not violate any of the conditions:

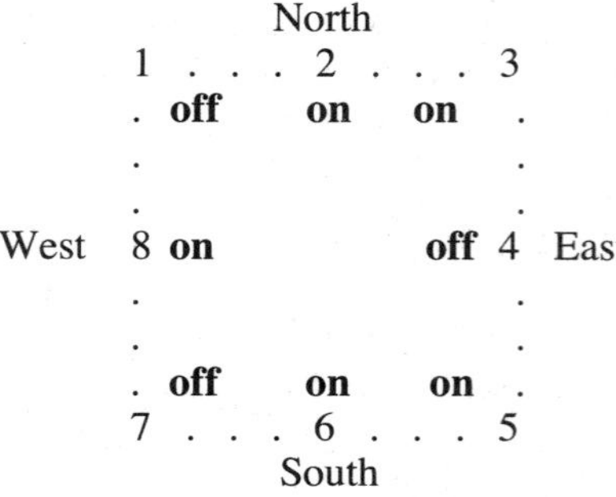

(E) No. The following diagram has light 7 on and does not violate any of the conditions:

```
              North
        1 . . . 2 . . . 3
        . off   on    on  .
        .                 .
        .                 .
West    8 on          off 4   East
        .                 .
        .                 .
        . on    off   on  .
        7 . . . 6 . . . 5
              South
```

9. (A) No. The following diagram has lights 2 and 6 on and does not violate any of the conditions:

```
              North
        1 . . . 2 . . . 3
        . off   on    on  .
        .                 .
        .                 .
West    8 on          off 4   East
        .                 .
        .                 .
        . off   on    on  .
        7 . . . 6 . . . 5
              South
```

(B) No. The following diagram has light 3 on, light 2 off, and does not violate any of the conditions:

```
              North
        1 . . . 2 . . . 3
        . on    off   on  .
        .                 .
        .                 .
West    8 on           on 4   East
        .                 .
        .                 .
        . off   on    off .
        7 . . . 6 . . . 5
              South
```

(C) No. The following diagram has lights 4 and 3 on and does not violate any of the conditions:

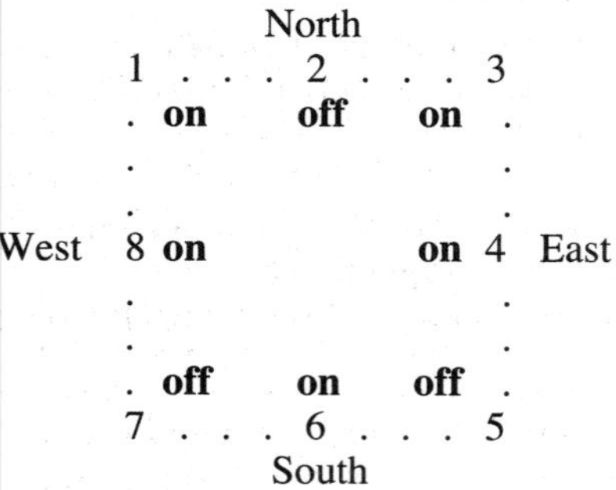

(D) Yes. Suppose light 5 is off. If light 4 is also off, then light 3 must be on since *"At least one of the three lights on each side is on."* However, light 3 is not the middle light, which contradicts the condition *"If any side has exactly one of its three lights on, then that light is its center light."*

(E) No. The following diagram has lights 6 and 1 off and does not violate any of the conditions:

```
              North
        1 . . . 2 . . . 3
        . off   on    on  .
        .                 .
        .                 .
West    8 on          off 4   East
        .                 .
        .                 .
        . on    off   on  .
        7 . . . 6 . . . 5
              South
```

10. (A) Yes. Suppose lights 1 and 6 are off. Since two lights on the north side must be on, lights 2 and 3 must be on:

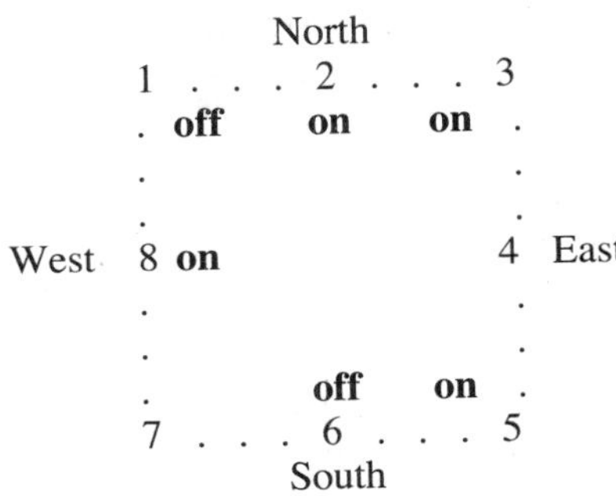

Since three consecutively numbered lights cannot be on, light 4 must be off. Further, light 7 must be on—otherwise on the south side only light 5 would be on, violating the condition *"If any side has exactly one of its three lights on, then that light is its center light."* This yields the following valid diagram:

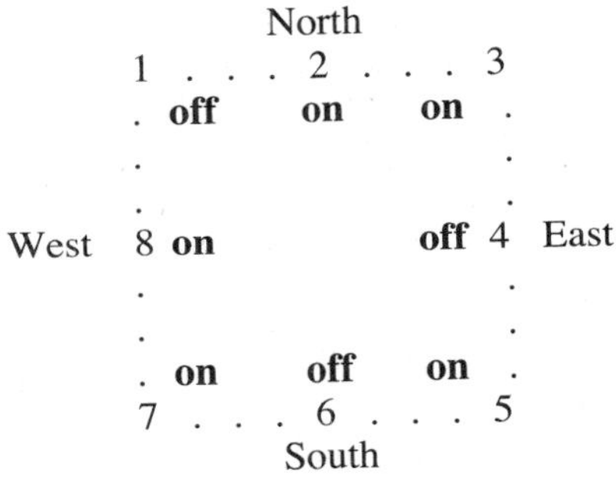

Thus, lights 6 and 1 can both be off.

(B) No. This violates the condition *"Neither light 2 nor light 7 is on when light 1 is on."*

(C) No. If light 2 is off, then from the condition *"Two of the lights on the north side are on"* lights 1 and 3 must be on. However, this scenario has three consecutively numbered lights on—3, 4, and 5—violating the condition *"At least one of any three consecutively numbered lights is off."*

(D) No. Since light 2 is off, the condition *"Two of the lights on the north side are on"* forces lights 1 and 3 to be on. This in turn forces light 4 to be off—otherwise three consecutively numbered lights would be on: 3, 4, and 5:

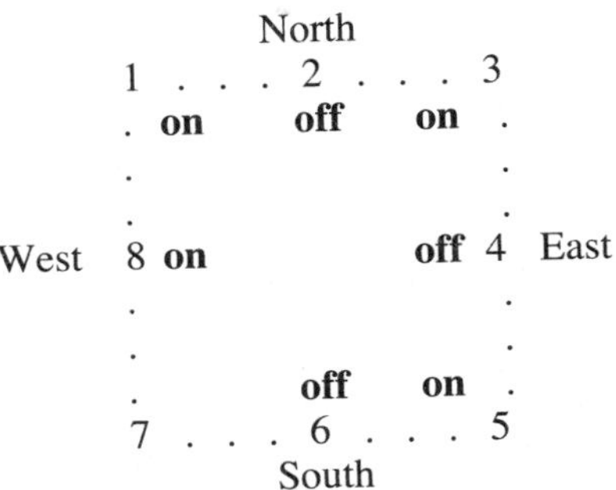

Also, light 7 must be off since light 1 and light 7 cannot both be on :

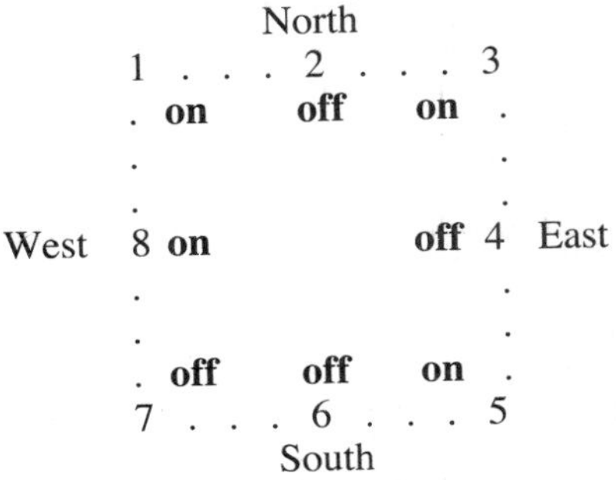

However, the south side of this diagram violates the condition *"If any side has exactly one of its three lights on, then that light is its center light."*

(E) No. This scenario has three consecutively numbered lights on—5, 6, and 7.

11. (A) No. Suppose light 1 is off. Then from the condition *"Two of the lights on the north side are on,"* lights 2 and 3 must be on. However, this scenario has three consecutively numbered lights on—2, 3, and 4.

(B) Yes. Suppose light 2 is off. Then from the condition *"Two of the lights on the north side are on,"* lights 1 and 3 must be on:

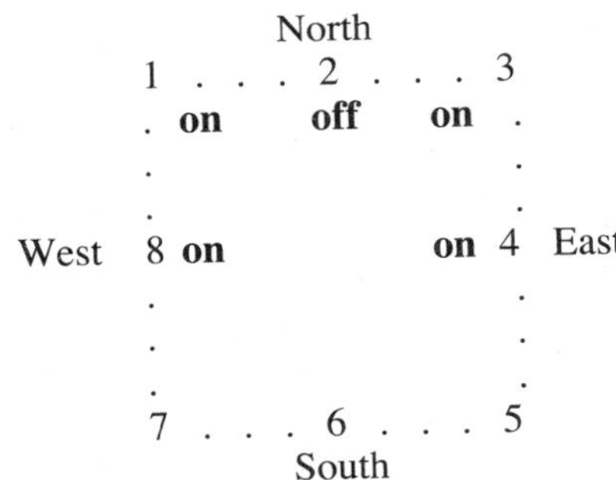

Since three consecutively numbered lights cannot be on, light 5 must be off. Further, since light 1 is on, light 7 must be off. This forces light 6 to be on (At least one of the three lights on each side is on):

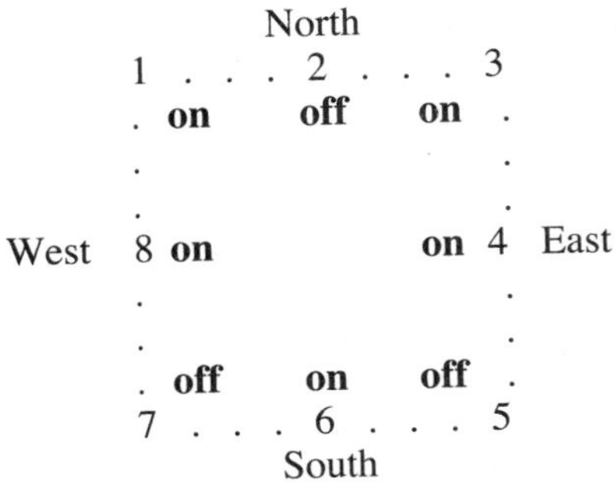

This diagram satisfies every condition. Thus, light 2 need not be on.

(C) No. Suppose light 5 is on. Since three consecutively numbered lights cannot be on, light 3 must be off:

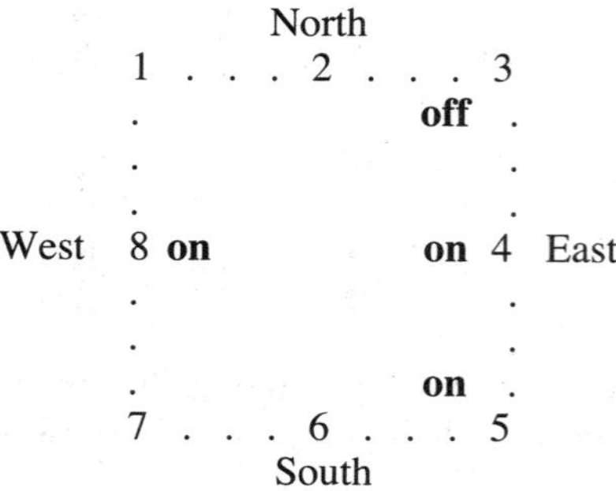

Now, since two lights on the north side must be on, lights 1 and 2 must be on. However, this violates the condition *"Neither light 2 nor light 7 is on when light 1 is on."*

(D) No. Suppose light 6 is off. Now, we consider two cases:

CASE I: If light 1 is off, then the condition *"Two of the lights on the north side are on"* forces lights 2 and 3 to be on. However, this scenario has three consecutively numbered lights on—2, 3, and 4.

CASE II: If light 1 is on, then light 7 must be off since *"neither light 2 nor light 7 is on when light 1 is on."*:

```
              North
         1 . . . 2 . . . 3
         . on            .
         .               .
         .               .
  West   8 on         on 4   East
         .               .
         .               .
         . off   off     .
         7 . . . 6 . . . 5
              South
```

Since *"At least one of the three lights on each side is on,"* light 5 must be on. However, this scenario has light 5 as the only light on the south side on, which violates the condition *"If any side has exactly one of its three lights on, then that light is its center light."*

(E) No. Suppose light 7 is on. Since *"neither light 2 nor light 7 is on when light 1 is on,"* light 1 must be off:

```
              North
         1 . . . 2 . . . 3
         . off           .
         .               .
         .               .
  West   8 on         on 4   East
         .               .
         .               .
         . on            .
         7 . . . 6 . . . 5
              South
```

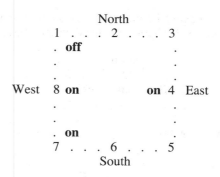

This diagram in turn forces lights 2 and 3 to be on since *"Two of the lights on the north side are on"*:

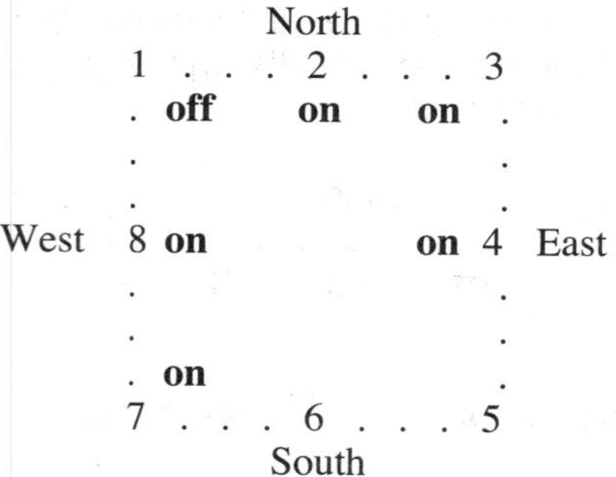

However, this diagram has three consecutively numbered lights on—2, 3, and 4.

12. (A) No. Since only one light on the north side is on, it must be the center light. Hence, light 1 cannot be on.

(B) No. Since only one light on the north side is on, it must be the center light. Hence, light 2 cannot be off.

(C) No. Since only one light on the north side is on, it must be the center light. Hence, light 3 cannot be on.

(D) No. Suppose light 4 is off. Since on the north side only the center light is on, the diagram becomes

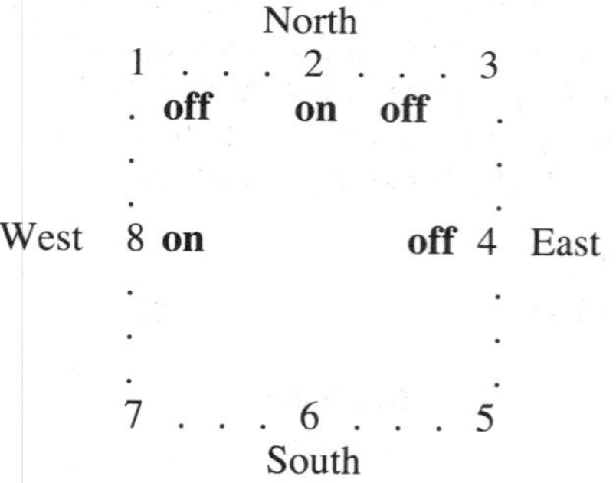

Since *"At least one of the three lights on each side is on,"* light 5 must be on. However, this violates the condition *"If any side has exactly one of its three lights on, then that light is its center light."*

(E) Yes. Suppose light 5 is off. Since on the north side only the center light is on, the diagram becomes

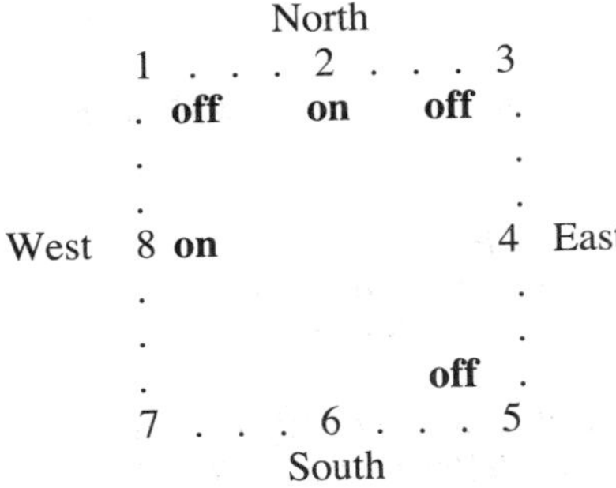

Since *"At least one of the three lights on each side is on,"* light 4 must be on. Finally, light 6 could be on, and light 7 could be off:

North
1 . . . 2 . . . 3
. **off** **on** **off** .
West 8 **on** **on** 4 East
. **off** **on** **off** .
7 . . . 6 . . . 5
South

This diagram satisfies every condition. Thus, light 5 need not be on.

<u>Questions 13–17</u>

The condition *"No boy sits next to another boy"* means that the arrangement will be boy/girl/boy/girl …, which is naturally symbolized as **Boy/Girl**. The condition *"Ivan sits next to and east of the fourth child in the row"* simply means that Ivan is 5th, which can be symbolized as **I = 5th**. The condition *"Sylvia sits east of Ivan"* forces Sylvia into space 6 or 7. However, since the arrangement is boy/girl, Sylvia must be in space 6, **S = 6th**. The final condition, *"Frank sits next Ruby,"* is naturally symbolized as **FR**, where F and R can be flip-flopped.

Boys
FHIJ

Girls
RST

Boy/Girl
I = 5th
S = 6th
FR

1	2	3	4	5	6	7
				I	S	

13. (A) No. As the following diagrams illustrate, Frank and Ruby can sit in chairs 1&2, or 2&3, or 3&4:

1	2	3	4	5	6	7
F	**R**	**H**	**T**	**I**	**S**	**J**

1	2	3	4	5	6	7
H	**R**	**F**	**T**	**I**	**S**	**J**

1	2	3	4	5	6	7
H	**T**	**F**	**R**	**I**	**S**	**J**

(B) No. As the following diagrams illustrate, Frank and Ruby can sit in chairs 1&2, or 2&3, or 3&4:

1	2	3	4	5	6	7
F	**R**	**H**	**T**	**I**	**S**	**J**

1	2	3	4	5	6	7
H	**R**	**F**	**T**	**I**	**S**	**J**

1	2	3	4	5	6	7
H	**T**	**F**	**R**	**I**	**S**	**J**

(C) Yes. As the following diagrams illustrate, Frank and Ruby can sit in chairs 1&2, or 2&3, or 3&4:

1	2	3	4	5	6	7
F	**R**	**H**	**T**	**I**	**S**	**J**

1	2	3	4	5	6	7
H	**R**	**F**	**T**	**I**	**S**	**J**

1	2	3	4	5	6	7
H	**T**	**F**	**R**	**I**	**S**	**J**

(D) No. As the following diagrams illustrate, Frank and Ruby can sit in chairs 1&2, or 2&3, or 3&4:

1	2	3	4	5	6	7
F	**R**	**H**	**T**	**I**	**S**	**J**

1	2	3	4	5	6	7
H	**R**	**F**	**T**	**I**	**S**	**J**

1	2	3	4	5	6	7
H	**T**	**F**	**R**	**I**	**S**	**J**

(E) No. As the following diagrams illustrate, Frank and Ruby can sit in chairs 1&2, or 2&3, or 3&4:

1	2	3	4	5	6	7
F	**R**	**H**	**T**	**I**	**S**	**J**

1	2	3	4	5	6	7
H	**R**	**F**	**T**	**I**	**S**	**J**

1	2	3	4	5	6	7
H	**T**	**F**	**R**	**I**	**S**	**J**

14. (A) No. The following diagram satisfies all the conditions and has both Harry and Joel seated east of Frank:

1	2	3	4	5	6	7
F	**R**	**H**	**T**	**I**	**S**	**J**

(B) No. The following diagram satisfies all the conditions and has both Harry and Ruby seated east of Frank:

1	2	3	4	5	6	7
F	**R**	**H**	**T**	**I**	**S**	**J**

(C) Yes. From Question 13, we know that Frank must sit in chair 1, 2, 3, or 4. Now, since Harry and Joel sit west of Frank, they must sit in chairs 1, 2, or 3. This puts 3 boys in chairs 1 through 4—violating the condition **Boy/Girl**.

(D) No. The following diagram satisfies all the conditions and has both Harry and Ruby seated west of Frank:

1	2	3	4	5	6	7
H	**R**	**F**	**T**	**I**	**S**	**J**

(E) No. The following diagram satisfies all the conditions and has both Joel and Ruby seated east of Frank:

1	2	3	4	5	6	7
F	**R**	**H**	**T**	**I**	**S**	**J**

15. (A) No. Placing Thelma next to Ivan and Frank next to Thelma yields

1	2	3	4	5	6	7
		F	**T**	**I**	**S**	

Since Ruby sits next to Frank, Ruby must sit in space 2:

1	2	3	4	5	6	7
	R	**F**	**T**	**I**	**S**	

(B) No. Placing Thelma next to Ivan and Frank next to Thelma yields

1	2	3	4	5	6	7
		F	**T**	**I**	**S**	

Since Ruby sits next to Frank, Ruby must sit in space 2:

1	2	3	4	5	6	7
	R	**F**	**T**	**I**	**S**	

(C) No. Placing Thelma next to Ivan and Frank next to Thelma yields

1	2	3	4	5	6	7
		F	**T**	**I**	**S**	

Since Ruby sits next to Frank, Ruby must sit in space 2:

1	2	3	4	5	6	7
	R	**F**	**T**	**I**	**S**	

(D) No. Placing Thelma next to Ivan and Frank next to Thelma yields

1	2	3	4	5	6	7
		F	**T**	**I**	**S**	

(E) Yes. Placing Thelma next to Ivan and Frank next to Thelma yields

1	2	3	4	5	6	7
		F	**T**	**I**	**S**	

Since Ruby sits next to Frank, Ruby must sit in space 2:

1	2	3	4	5	6	7
	R	**F**	**T**	**I**	**S**	

Now, suppose Joel sits in space 1. Then Harry would sit in space 7:

1	2	3	4	5	6	7
J	**R**	**F**	**T**	**I**	**S**	**H**

This diagram satisfies all the conditions and has both Frank and Ruby seated <u>east</u> of Joel.

16. (A) No. The condition *"Frank does not sit next to any child who sits next to Ivan"* means that Frank does not sit in spaces 3 or 7. Since the order is boy/girl, Frank must be in space 1:

1	2	3	4	5	6	7
F				**I**	**S**	

(B) Yes. The condition *"Frank does not sit next to any child who sits next to Ivan"* means that Frank does not sit in spaces 3 or 7. Since the order is boy/girl, Frank must be in space 1. This in turn forces Ruby into space 2, **FR**:

1	2	3	4	5	6	7
F	**R**			**I**	**S**	

Now, suppose Joel sits in space 3. Then since the order is boy/girl, Harry and Thelma would be forced into spaces 7 and 4, respectively:

1	2	3	4	5	6	7
F	**R**	**J**	**T**	**I**	**S**	**H**

This diagram satisfies all the conditions and has Joel seated west of Ivan.

(C) No. The condition *"Frank does not sit next to any child who sits next to Ivan"* means that Frank does not sit in spaces 3 or 7. Since the order is boy/girl,

Frank must be in space 1. This in turn forces Ruby into space 2, **FR**:

1	2	3	4	5	6	7
F	**R**			**I**	**S**	

(D) No. The condition *"Frank does not sit next to any child who sits next to Ivan"* means that Frank does not sit in spaces 3 or 7. Since the order is boy/girl, Frank must be in space 1.

1	2	3	4	5	6	7
F				**I**	**S**	

(E) No. The condition *"Frank does not sit next to any child who sits next to Ivan"* means that Frank does not sit in spaces 3 or 7. Since the order is boy/girl, Frank must be in space 1. This in turn forces Ruby into space 2, **FR**:

1	2	3	4	5	6	7
F	**R**			**I**	**S**	

17. (A) No. The following diagram satisfies all the conditions and has Frank seated next to Thelma:

1	2	3	4	5	6	7
J	**R**	**F**	**T**	**I**	**S**	**H**

(B) No. The following diagram satisfies all the conditions and has Harry seated next to Ruby:

1	2	3	4	5	6	7
H	**R**	**F**	**T**	**I**	**S**	**J**

(C) No. The following diagram satisfies all the conditions and has Harry seated next to Sylvia:

1	2	3	4	5	6	7
J	**R**	**F**	**T**	**I**	**S**	**H**

(D) Yes. Since Frank now sits east of Ruby, the condition **FR** becomes **RF**, where R and F cannot be flip-flopped. From our previous work, we know that Frank and Ruby must sit west of Ivan. Hence, Frank will always be seated between Ruby and Ivan. Thus, Ruby and Ivan cannot sit next to each other.
(E) No. The following diagram satisfies all the conditions and has Joel seated next to Ruby:

1	2	3	4	5	6	7
J	**R**	**F**	**T**	**I**	**S**	**H**

Questions 18–24

18. (A) No. The following diagram has W responding to heptocillin and satisfies all the conditions (F = ferromycin, G = ganocyclene, H = heptocillin):

W	X	Y	Z
H	H	F	F
		G	G

(B) No. The following diagram has X responding to ganocyclene and satisfies all the conditions:

W	X	Y	Z
G	G	F	F
		G	G

(C) No. The following diagram has X responding to heptocillin and satisfies all the conditions:

W	X	Y	Z
H	H	F	F
		G	G

(D) Yes. Since "Y responds to ferromycin," the condition "If an organism responds to ferromycin, then it responds to ganocyclene" forces Y to respond to ganocyclene. Now, if Y responds to heptocillin, Y would respond to all three antibiotics, which violates the condition "No organism responds to all three antibiotics."
(E) No. The following diagram has Z responding to ganocyclene and satisfies all the conditions:

W	X	Y	Z
H	H	F	F
		G	G

19. (A) No. Since *"Y responds to ferromycin,"* this choice has 4 organisms responding to ferromycin, which violates the condition *"At least two but not all four of the organisms respond to ferromycin."*
(B) Yes. The following diagram has W, X, and Z all responding to ganocyclene and satisfies all the conditions:

W	X	Y	Z
G	G	F	F
		G	G

(C) No. Since "Y responds to ferromycin," the condition "If an organism responds to ferromycin, then it responds to ganocyclene" forces Y to respond to ganocyclene:

W	X	Y	Z
		F	
		G	

If W responds to ganocyclene, then the condition *"If W responds to any antibiotic, then X responds to that antibiotic"* forces X to also respond to ganocyclene. However, this situation has 3 organisms—W, X, and Y—responding to ganocyclene.
(D) No. This contradicts the condition *"If W responds to any antibiotic, then X responds to that antibiotic."*
(E) No. This contradicts the condition *"If an organism responds to ferromycin, then it responds to ganocyclene."*

20. (A) No. This violates the condition *"At least two but not all four of the organisms respond to ferromycin."*
(B) No. Since *"Y responds to ferromycin,"* the condition *"If an organism responds to ferromycin, then it responds to ganocyclene"* forces Y to respond to ganocyclene. Since this answer-choice has all four organisms responding to heptocillin, Y responds to heptocillin. However, this has Y responding to all three antibiotics, which violates the condition *"No organism responds to all three antibiotics."*
(C) No. Since any organism that responds to ferromycin must also respond to ganocyclene, this answer-choice has at least one organism responding to all three antibiotics. However, this violates the condition *"No organism responds to all three antibiotics."*
(D) No. If an organism responds to neither ganocyclene nor heptocillin, then it must respond to ferromycin (*Each of the organisms responds to at least one of the antibiotics*). But *"If an organism responds to ferromycin, then it responds to ganocyclene."* Thus, every organism must respond to either ganocyclene or heptocillin.
(E) Yes. The following diagram has W responding to only ganocyclene and satisfies all the conditions:

W	X	Y	Z
G	H	F	F
	G	G	G

21. (A) No. The following diagram has W responding to only heptocillin and satisfies all the conditions:

W	X	Y	Z
H	H	F	F
		G	G

(B) No. The following diagram has X responding to only heptocillin and satisfies all the conditions:

W	X	Y	Z
H	H	F	F
		G	G

(C) No. The following diagram has X responding to only ganocyclene and satisfies all the conditions:

W	X	Y	Z
G	G	F	F
		G	G

(D) Yes. From the condition *"At least two but not all four of the organisms respond to ferromycin,"* we know that either W or Z must respond to ferromycin (Y already responds to ferromycin). Suppose W responds to ferromycin. Then from the condition *"If W responds to any antibiotic, then X responds to that antibiotic"* we know that X responds to ferromycin. This, however, contradicts the premise of the question. Hence, Z must respond to ferromycin.
(E) No. The following diagram has Z responding to only ganocyclene and satisfies all the conditions:

W	X	Y	Z
G	G	F	F
		G	G

22. (A) No. The following diagram has X responding to only heptocillin and ganocyclene and satisfies all the conditions:

W	X	Y	Z
H	H	F	F
	G	G	G

(B) Yes. There are 3 different ways of pairing off the antibiotics:

Pair 1	Pair 2	Pair 3
F	G	F
G	H	H

The first two pairs both respond to ganocyclene. Since the third pair responds to ferromycin, it must also respond to ganocyclene (*If an organism responds to ferromycin, then it responds to ganocyclene*). However, this violates the condition *"No organism responds to all three antibiotics."*
(C) No. The following diagram has Y responding to only ferromycin and ganocyclene and satisfies all the conditions:

W	X	Y	Z
H	H	F	F
		G	G

(D) No. The following diagram has Y responding to both ferromycin and ganocyclene and satisfies all the conditions:

W	X	Y	Z
H	H	F	F
		G	G

(E) No. The following diagram has Y responding to both ferromycin and ganocyclene and satisfies all the conditions:

W	X	Y	Z
H	H	F	F
		G	G

23. (A) No. The following diagram has W responding to only ganocyclene and satisfies all the conditions:

W	X	Y	Z
G	G	F	F
		G	G

(B) No. The following diagram has X responding to only ganocyclene and satisfies all the conditions:

W	X	Y	Z
G	G	F	F
		G	G

(C) No. The following diagram has Z responding to only ganocyclene and satisfies all the conditions:

W	X	Y	Z
G	F	F	G
	G	G	

(D) No. Since none of the organisms responds to heptocillin, each organism must respond to either ferromycin or ganocyclene. Now, "If *an organism responds to ferromycin, then it must respond to ganocyclene.*" Hence, all four organisms must respond to ganocyclene.

(E) Yes. Since none of the organisms responds to heptocillin, each organism must respond to either ferromycin or ganocyclene. Now, "If *an organism responds to ferromycin, then it must respond to ganocyclene.*" Hence, in either case an organism must respond to ganocyclene.

24. (A) No. Since *"Y responds to ferromycin,"* the condition *"If an organism responds to ferromycin, then it responds to ganocyclene"* forces Y to respond to ganocyclene. Since *"At least two but not all four of the organisms respond to ferromycin,"* one other organism must respond to ferromycin. Hence, there are always two organisms that respond to both ferromycin and ganocyclene. Now, if three of the organisms are to respond to the same combination of antibiotics, then that combination must be ferromycin and ganocyclene, since there are only four organisms. However, we are given that Z does not respond to ferromycin. Hence, the three organisms that respond to ferromycin and ganocyclene are W, X, and Y. Thus, W must respond to ferromycin.

(B) No. Since *"Y responds to ferromycin,"* the condition *"If an organism responds to ferromycin, then it responds to ganocyclene"* forces Y to respond to ganocyclene. Since *"At least two but not all four of the organisms respond to ferromycin,"* one other organism must respond to ferromycin. Hence, there are always two organisms that respond to both ferromycin and ganocyclene. Now, if three of the organisms are to respond to the same combination of antibiotics, then that combination must be ferromycin and ganocyclene, since there are only four organisms. However, we are given that Z does not respond to ferromycin. Hence, the three organisms that respond to ferromycin and ganocyclene are W, X, and Y. Thus, X must respond to ganocyclene.

(C) Yes. The following diagram has three of the organisms responding to exactly the same set of antibiotics, and it satisfies all the conditions:

W	X	Y	Z
F	F	F	H
G	G	G	

(D) No. Since *"Y responds to ferromycin,"* the condition *"If an organism responds to ferromycin, then it responds to ganocyclene"* forces Y to respond to ganocyclene. Since *"At least two but not all four of the organisms respond to ferromycin,"* one other organism must respond to ferromycin. Hence, there are always two organisms that respond to both ferromycin and ganocyclene. Now, if three of the organisms are to respond to the same combination of antibiotics, then that combination must be ferromycin and ganocyclene, since there are only four organisms. However, we are given that Z does not respond to ferromycin. Hence, the three organisms that respond to ferromycin and ganocyclene are W, X, and Y. Thus, W responds to exactly the same set of antibiotics as Y.

(E) No. Since *"Y responds to ferromycin,"* the condition *"If an organism responds to ferromycin, then it responds to ganocyclene"* forces Y to respond to ganocyclene. Since *"At least two but not all four of the organisms respond to ferromycin,"* one other organism must respond to ferromycin. Hence, there are always two organisms that respond to both ferromycin and ganocyclene. Now, if three of the organisms are to respond to the same combination of antibiotics, then that combination must be ferromycin and ganocyclene, since there are only four organisms. However, we are given that Z does not respond to ferromycin. Hence, the three organisms that respond to ferromycin and ganocyclene are W, X, and Y. Thus, X responds to exactly the same set of antibiotics as Y.

Test II
Section III
Solutions

Questions 1–6

1. (A) No. Although the author does explain some of the processes and applications of rDNA technology, this is done to give context to the controversy over rDNA technology.
(B) No. The passage does not advocate the continuation or cessation of rDNA research and development.
(C) No. The passage has a journalistic style. The author is not advocating any position.
(D) Yes. The passage has a journalistic style. The author is not advocating any position. Rather he is summarizing the controversy surrounding rDNA research and development.
(E) No. The passage has a journalistic style. The author is not advocating any position.

2. (A) Yes. This is the thrust of the opening sentence: *"After thirty years of investigation into cell genetics, researchers made startling discoveries in the 1960s and early 1970s which culminated in the development of processes, collectively known as recombinant deoxyribonucleic acid (rDNA) technology, for the active manipulation of a cell's genetic code."*
(B) No. Just the opposite. Research into the genetic code of cells led to the development of rDNA technology.
(C) No. The passage implies that future treatments for major diseases will result from research into the genetic code of cells, but does not state that this is currently the case.
(D) No. In fact, the passage is presenting opposing positions regarding research into the genetic code of cells.
(E) No. The motivation for research into the genetic code of cells is not discussed in the passage.

3. (A) No. *"Energy production and waste disposal may benefit: genetically altered organisms could convert sewage and other organic material into methane fuel."*
(B) No. *"Proponents of rDNA research and development claim that it will allow scientists to find cures for disease and to better understand how genetic information controls an organism's development."*
(C) No. *"Agriculture might also take advantage of rDNA technology to produce new varieties of crops that resist foul weather, pests, and the effects of poor soil."*
(D) Yes. This question is best answered by elimination:

Choice (A) is mentioned: *"Energy production and waste disposal may benefit: genetically altered organisms could convert sewage and other organic material into methane fuel."*
Choice (B) is mentioned: *"Proponents of rDNA research and development claim that it will allow scientists to find cures for disease and to better understand how genetic information controls an organism's development."*
Choice (C) is mentioned: *"Agriculture might also take advantage of rDNA technology to produce new varieties of crops that resist foul weather, pests, and the effects of poor soil."*
Choice (E) is mentioned: *"Energy production and waste disposal may benefit: genetically altered organisms could convert sewage and other organic material into methane fuel."*

Hence, by process of elimination, the answer is (D). Note: Although the passage does indicate that new drugs may be realized using rDNA technology, nothing indicates these drugs will be less expensive than drugs currently in use.
(E) No. *"Energy production and waste disposal may benefit: genetically altered organisms could convert sewage and other organic material into methane fuel."*

4. (A) Yes. *"A major concern of the critics of rDNA research is that genetically altered microorganisms might escape from the laboratory."* But if it is impossible for genetically altered microorganisms to escape from laboratories, then the opponents' concerns are unwarranted.
(B) No. This strengthens their argument. They expressed concern that genetically altered microorganisms might escape the laboratory—which, in fact, did occur.
(C) No. This somewhat strengthens the opponents' argument since they state that these organisms could alter *"microbiological predator-prey relationships."*
(D) No. Perhaps this weakens the opponents' argument. Since the genetically altered organisms cannot survive outside the waste treatment plant, they cannot interact with the outside world. However, there is a much better answer-choice.
(E) No. This is irrelevant. From the wording of the question, we don't even know that the eradication of the disease was due to rDNA technology.

5. (A) No. It serves to point out the social, not medical, dangers of rDNA technology.
(B) No. It argues against research on the use of rDNA technology in human genetics.
(C) No. It warns against upsetting the balance of society, not nature.
(D) No. It warns that the grim society depicted in Brave New World may result from rDNA technology.
(E) Yes. The point of the last paragraph is that genetic engineering may lead to a totalitarian society

in which human beings are engineered to fulfill specific roles.

6. (A) No. The opponents of rDNA technology warn about its dangers to the environment and society; only the proponents discuss agricultural benefits.
(B) Yes. If genetically altered microorganisms have no natural predators but can prey on a wide variety of other microorganisms, they may cause the extinction of many natural microorganisms and thereby upset the balance of nature.
(C) No. The opponents of rDNA technology warn about its dangers to the environment and society; the proponents discuss pharmaceutical benefits.
(D) No. Although this does somewhat strengthen the opponents' argument—that ecosystems are fragile and can be harmed by the introduction of an unnatural microorganism into the environment—there is a more specific and stronger answer-choice.
(E) No. This tends to weaken the arguments of the opponents of rDNA technology. If genetically altered microorganisms generally cannot survive for more than a few hours in the natural environment, then they are less likely to damage the natural environment.

Questions 7–13

7. (A) Yes. This is expressed in the closing sentence: *"Since only the territoriality theory affords trademark owners any real legal protection against gray marketing practices, I believe it is inevitable as well as desirable that it will come to be consistently applied in gray marketing cases."*
(B) No. In fact, the author states that it should and will be regulated: *"Since only the territoriality theory affords trademark owners any real legal protection against gray marketing practices, I believe it is inevitable as well as desirable that it will come to be consistently applied in gray marketing cases."*
(C) No. This is not mentioned in the passage.
(D) No. This is mentioned, but it is done to support the conclusion, which is summarized in the last sentence: *"Since only the territoriality theory affords trademark owners any real legal protection against gray marketing practices, I believe it is inevitable as well as desirable that it will come to be consistently applied in gray marketing cases."*
(E) No. This is not stated in the passage.

8. (A) No. The author does not criticize the motives of those who practice gray marketing.
(B) No. Although the author does evaluate the effects of both channel flow diversion and parallel importation, it's done to support his conclusion that gray marketing practices should be regulated.
(C) No. The author is concerned more with judging the propriety of the three methods than with evaluating their success.
(D) Yes. Until the last sentence, the passage reads like a textbook describing marketing practices. Only in the closing sentence does the author rather abruptly present his opinion.
(E) No. Although the author does discuss situations in which certain marketing practices are common and analyzes the economic factors responsible for their development, it's done to support his conclusion that gray marketing practices should be regulated.

9. (A) No. This is not mentioned.
(B) Yes. This is stated in the final sentence of the third paragraph: *"Equally important, authorized distributors may cease to promote the product if it becomes available for much lower prices through unauthorized channels."*
(C) No. Although the passage discusses quantity discounting by manufacturers as one possible route for products to enter the gray market, there is no indication that manufacturers are forced to offer such discounts.
(D) No. This is not mentioned.
(E) No. This is not mentioned.

10. (A) Yes. *"The exhaustion theory holds that a trademark owner relinquishes all rights once a product has been sold. When this theory is applied, gray marketing practices are allowed to continue because the trademark owners' rights cease as soon as their products are sold to a distributor. The theory of territoriality holds that a trademark is effective in the country in which it is registered. Under the theory of territoriality, trademark owners can stop gray marketing practices in the registering countries on products bearing their trademarks."*
(B) No. The trademark owners can, of course, sell to whomever they wish. The two legal theories differ on the issue of secondary sales by distributors: whether an authorized distributor is allowed to resell the trademarked product to other distributors not authorized by the product's manufacturer.
(C) No. The proponents of each theory do differ in their interpretation of the legality of channel flow diversion in countries where the trademark is registered: *"The exhaustion theory holds that a trademark owner relinquishes all rights once a product has been sold. When this theory is applied, gray marketing practices are allowed to continue because the trademark owners' rights cease as soon as their products are sold to a distributor. The theory of territoriality holds that a trademark is effective in the country in which it is registered. Under the theory of territoriality, trademark owners can stop gray marketing practices in the registering countries on products bearing their trademarks."* However, no mention is made of trademark protection in countries where the trademark is not registered.

(D) No. This is not at issue.
(E) No. This is not at issue.

11. (A) No. It indicates a way in which manufacturers are damaged by gray marketing.
(B) Yes. *"Trademark owners justifiably argue against gray marketing practices since such practices clearly jeopardize the goodwill established by trademark owners: consumers who purchase trademarked goods in the gray market do not get the same "extended product," which typically includes pre- and postsale service."*
(C) No. The author implies that the impact is across the board.
(D) No. It indicates a way in which manufacturers are damaged by gray marketing.
(E) No. The passage does not indicate whether or not consumers will refuse lower prices to maintain high levels of service.

12. (A) No. The author is encouraging the courts to control gray marketing: *"Since only the territoriality theory affords trademark owners any real legal protection against gray marketing practices, I believe it is inevitable as well as desirable that it will come to be consistently applied in gray marketing cases."*
(B) No. The author is encouraging the courts to control gray marketing: *"Since only the territoriality theory affords trademark owners any real legal protection against gray marketing practices, I believe it is inevitable as well as desirable that it will come to be consistently applied in gray marketing cases."*
(C) Yes. *"Since only the territoriality theory affords trademark owners any real legal protection against gray marketing practices, I believe it is inevitable as well as desirable that it will come to be consistently applied in gray marketing cases."* The underlined words express "reasoned optimism."

Note: The measured or reasoned answer-choice to an author's-attitude question is much more likely to be correct than an emotional or extreme answer-choice, such as "unbridled fervor."
(D) No. The author is encouraging the courts to control gray marketing, but it is a measured promotion: *"Since only the territoriality theory affords trademark owners any real legal protection against gray marketing practices, I believe it is inevitable as well as desirable that it will come to be consistently applied in gray marketing cases."* The underlined words express "measured promotion."
(E) No. The author is encouraging the courts to control gray marketing: *"Since only the territoriality theory affords trademark owners any real legal protection against gray marketing practices, I believe it is inevitable as well as desirable that it will come to be consistently applied in gray marketing cases."*

Note, you should be wary of answer-choices that contain extreme or emotional statements. The reading passages are typically taken from academic journals, and scholars are loath to make extreme or emotional statements. A scholar is unlikely to express "cynical indifference," lest he be viewed as narrow minded.

13. (A) No. In this case, parallel importing would benefit the manufacturers by increasing their profits.
(B) No. The issue of channel flow diversion involves product sales by unauthorized distributors.
(C) Yes. *"For example, quantity discounts from manufacturers may motivate authorized dealers to enter the gray market because they can purchase larger quantities of a product than they themselves intend to stock if they can sell the extra units through gray market channels."*
(D) No. Ostensibly, postsale service policies are already controlled by manufactures.
(E) No. Manufactures are concerned about channel flow in part because they are unable to provide the "extended product" to consumers who purchase goods in the gray market.

Questions 14–20

14. (A) No. The second paragraph notes that even editors known for their moral integrity affected the linguistic, structural, and tonal value of the autobiographies they edited. However, this point is not expanded upon and thus is not the main idea.
(B) No. The passage concludes merely that autobiographies dictated to editors are factually less reliable, not necessarily less valuable.
(C) No. This is not discussed in the passage.
(D) Yes. The passage is primarily concerned with how much credibility should be given to the information in ghostwritten books versus independently authored books. This is summarized in the final two sentences: *"Analysts should reserve close analytic readings for independently authored texts. Discussion of collaborative texts should take into account the conditions that governed their production."*
(E) No. This is not mentioned in the passage.

15. (A) No. The editor does not invent the author's story, but rather portrays and interprets it. Furthermore, there's nothing to indicate that the methods used to accomplish this must be unique.
(B) No. The relationship between an author and an editor is not hierarchical as is the relationship between a worker and an employer. Rather, the editor portrays the author's story using her own skills and interpretation.
(C) No. The passage does not state that the editor promotes opinions which must then be supported.

(D) No. An architect creates a design to fit in a natural setting, but an editor creates an autobiography out of provided facts.
(E) Yes. *"Even if an editor faithfully reproduced the facts of a narrator's life, it was still the editor who decided what to make of these facts, how they should be emphasized, in what order they ought to be presented, and what was extraneous or germane."* In other words, the editor is directing the story.

16. (A) No. This is incorrect for two reasons:
1) "Adamantly opposed" is too strong.
2) The author does not reject all literary analysis of edited autobiographies, just rejects "close analytic readings."

(B) Yes. This is the thrust of the final sentences of the passage: *"Analysts should reserve close analytic readings for independently authored texts. Discussion of collaborative texts should take into account the conditions that governed their production."* Note, the author is actually more than skeptical of the value of close analytical reading in the case of edited autobiographies; he states that it should not be done.
(C) No. Just the opposite: *"Readers of African American autobiography then and now have too readily accepted the presumption of these eighteenth- and nineteenth-century editors that experiential facts recounted orally could be recorded and sorted by an amanuensis-editor, taken out of their original contexts, and then published with editorial prefaces, footnotes, and appended commentary, all without compromising the validity of the narrative as a product of an African American consciousness."*
(D) No. This cannot be determined from the passage.
(E) No. Presumably an analysis of works already written would not affect their integrity. However, the author does believe that the linguistic, structural and moral integrity of autobiographies is enhanced when written directly by their subjects rather than compiled by editors.

17. (A) No. This is not stated in the passage.
(B) No. This is not stated in the passage.
(C) No. This is not stated in the passage.
(D) Yes. *"Readers of African American autobiography then and now have too readily accepted the presumption of these eighteenth- and nineteenth-century editors that experiential facts recounted orally could be recorded and sorted by an amanuensis-editor, taken out of their original contexts, and then published with editorial prefaces, footnotes, and appended commentary, all without compromising the validity of the narrative as a product of an African American consciousness."*
(E) No. This is not stated in the passage.

18. (A) Yes. *Ostensible* means "apparent, but not necessarily true." So the phrase "ostensible authorship" casts doubt on whether stated author wrote the book: perhaps a ghostwriter actually wrote it.
(B) No. The author is concerned with the linguistic integrity of the editors' work, not their moral integrity: *"From a literary standpoint, however, it is not the moral integrity of these editors that is at issue but the linguistic, structural, and tonal integrity of the narratives they produced."*
(C) No. "Extraneous" facts are used by the author to point out why information in inauthentic autobiographies cannot be trusted. However, "Extraneous" facts do not help to determine whether a particular autobiography is authentic.
(D) No. This de-emphasizes the author's concerns. The opening of the third paragraph serves to moderate the author's concerns: he does not reject wholesale the information in transcribed narratives, he just believes that transcribed narratives are not nearly as accurate as actual autobiographies.
(E) No. *Impolitic* means "improper, unwise." Pointing out that the interviewees may have felt that it was impolitic to be candid illustrates why information in inauthentic autobiographies cannot be trusted. However, it does not help to determine whether a particular autobiography is authentic.

19. (A) No. *"Analysts should reserve close analytic readings for independently authored texts."*
(B) No. *"Analysts should reserve close analytic readings for independently authored texts."* The third paragraph differentiates between these texts and transcribed narratives in which an editor tries to capture a narrator's thought in action.
(C) Yes. *"Analysts should reserve close analytic readings for independently authored texts."*
(D) No. This is not stated in the passage.
(E) No. If an editor is involved, then close analytic reading of an autobiography is in-appropriate: *"Analysts should reserve close analytic readings for independently authored texts."*

20. (A) No. Blassingame does not endorse the author's views. In fact, the author criticizes Blassingame's perspective. Hence, it is unlikely that the author would seek Blassingame's endorsement.
(B) Yes. The author is using Blassingame to point out that emphasis should be placed on literary integrity, not moral integrity: *"Blassingame has taken pains to show that the editors of several of the more famous antebellum slave narratives were "noted for their integrity" and thus were unlikely to distort the facts given them by slave narrators. From a literary standpoint, however, it is not the moral integrity of these editors that is at issue but the linguistic,*

structural, and tonal integrity of the narratives they produced."
(C) No. Nothing in the passage indicates that Blassingame's analysis was novel. Indeed, the author is presenting what is a novel analysis.
(D) No. The author is using Blassingame to point out that emphasis should be placed on literary integrity, not moral integrity: *"Blassingame has taken pains to show that the editors of several of the more famous antebellum slave narratives were "noted for their integrity" and thus were unlikely to distort the facts given them by slave narrators. From a literary standpoint, however, it is not the moral integrity of these editors that is at issue but the linguistic, structural, and tonal integrity of the narratives they produced."*
(E) No. The author is using Blassingame to point out that emphasis should be placed on literary integrity, not moral integrity: *"Blassingame has taken pains to show that the editors of several of the more famous antebellum slave narratives were "noted for their integrity" and thus were unlikely to distort the facts given them by slave narrators. From a literary standpoint, however, it is not the moral integrity of these editors that is at issue but the linguistic, structural, and tonal integrity of the narratives they produced."*

Questions 21–27

21. (A) No. Marxism is mentioned only in the first paragraph and is offered only as an alternative theory to the main idea.
(B) No. This is the subject of the third paragraph, but it's too narrow to be the main idea of the entire passage.
(C) Yes. The end of the first paragraph presents the main idea: *"A new study by Rubinstein, however, suggests that the real wealth lay with the bankers and merchants of London. Rubinstein does not deny that a northern industrial elite existed but argues that it was consistently outnumbered and outdone by a London-based commercial elite. His claims are provocative and deserve consideration."*
(D) No. Probate records are discussed extensively in the passage, but this is done to support the main idea.
(E) No. The passage does discuss Rubinstein's attempt to confirm his findings about nineteenth-century Britain, but this is neither the main idea of the passage nor does anything indicate that such confirmation is likely to remain elusive.

22. (A) No. He accepts the accuracy of the probate records, but not without reservations: *"However, such [probate] records do not unequivocally make Rubinstein's case."*
(B) No. Although the author says that probate records *"records do not unequivocally make Rubinstein's case,"* there is no indication that he sees them as outdated.
(C) No. Nothing in the passage indicates how available the probate records are.
(D) Yes. *"However, such [probate] records do not unequivocally make Rubinstein's case. Uncertainties abound about how the probate rules for valuing assets were actually applied.... What the valuation conventions were for stock-in-trade (goods for sale) is also uncertain.... A further complication is that probate valuations probably took no notice of a business's goodwill (favor with the public) which, since it represents expectations about future profit-making, would today very often be a large fraction of market value."*
(E) No. The author implies that it was a novel idea to use probate records as a source of information about wealth in nineteenth-century Britain. Further, he does not state or imply that probate records are fully understandable only by specialists.

23. (A) Yes. *"What the valuation conventions were for stock-in-trade (goods for sale) is also uncertain. It is possible that their probate values were much lower than their actual market values; cash or near-cash, such as bank balances or stocks, were, on the other hand, invariably considered at full face value."*
(B) No. The discussion of income tax returns concerns a second study that was independent of the probate record study but had similar results.
(C) No. This is not stated or implied by the passage.
(D) No. The passage states only that it is possible that goods for sale may have been undervalued, whereas bank balances were always fully valued. However, there is no mention of whether individuals had greater worth in goods or in bank deposits.
(E) No. This is not stated or implied by the passage.

24. (A) No. Rubinstein provides evidence to confirm that the distribution of great wealth between commerce and industry was not equal. However, he claims that there was more wealth in commerce than in industry, contradicting the conventional view that there was more wealth in industry than in commerce.
(B) No. This is Rubinstein's claim: *"Rubinstein's claim about the location of wealth comes from his investigation of probate records.... It does seem as if large fortunes were more frequently made in commerce than in industry and, within industry, more frequently from alcohol or tobacco than from textiles or metal."*
(C) No. Although Rubinstein does identify a London-based commercial elite, there is no indication that this elite was not previously recognized. However, Rubinstein does suggest that this elite was wealthier than previously believed.
(D) No. Rubinstein provides no evidence for this. Presumably the governing elite (*"bishops, higher civil servants, and chairmen of manufacturing companies"*) were previously identified and Rubinstein does not dispute this classification.

(E) Yes. *"A conventional view of nineteenth-century Britain holds that iron manufacturers and textile manufacturers ... became the wealthiest and most powerful people in society after about 1832."* However, *"Rubinstein finds many millionaires who are totally unknown to nineteenth-century historians; the reason for their obscurity could be that they were not powerful. Indeed, Rubinstein dismisses any notion that great wealth had anything to do with entry into the governing elite...."*

25. (A) No. He is using it to suggest that the probate valuations of certain businesses may have significantly underestimated their true market value.
(B) Yes. *"What the valuation conventions were for stock-in-trade (goods for sale) is also uncertain. It is possible that their probate values were much lower than their actual market values; cash or near-cash, such as bank balances or stocks, were, on the other hand, invariably considered at full face value. A further complication is that probate valuations probably took no notice of a business's goodwill (favor with the public) which, since it represents expectations about future profit-making, would today very often be a large fraction of market value."*
(C) No. He is using it to suggest that the probate valuations of certain businesses may have significantly underestimated their true market value.
(D) No. This is too strong. He is merely using it to suggest that the probate valuations of certain businesses may have significantly underestimated their true market value. Although the passage indicates that goodwill is a significant fraction of the market value of today's businesses, it neither indicates that is the most important component nor that the same was true in nineteenth-century Britain.
(E) No. This is too strong. He is merely using it to suggest that the probate valuations of certain businesses may have significantly underestimated their true market value.

26. (A) No. Rubinstein's claim is that the commercial elite in nineteenth-century London had more accumulated wealth than the industrial elite in the North. So this certainly does not help his argument.
(B) No. This simply implies that the working-class also misidentified the greatest source of wealth.
(C) No. The passage implies that industrialists had more goods for sale than commercial businessmen. Thus, the determination of wealth based on probate records would underestimate the value of assets held by industrialists, and Rubinstein's claim that the commercial elite was wealthier than the industrialists would be weakened.
(D) Yes. A weak spot in Rubinstein's argument is that probate records do not include property holdings. So if a study indicated that the wealth of nineteenth-century British industrialists did not appear to be significantly greater when the full value of their real property holdings was considered, Rubinstein's claim that there was more wealth in commerce than in industry would still hold.
(E) No. This is irrelevant to the comparison of wealth between the northern industrialists and the London commercial elite.

27. (A) No. This supports his claim: *"The only requirements were university attendance and a father with a middle-class income."*
(B) No. Rubinstein states that these are the only two criteria for entry into the governing elite. He does not imply that one is more important than the other.
(C) No. This is irrelevant.
(D) No. This is irrelevant.
(E) Yes. Rubinstein claims that there was no connection between great wealth and the governing elite: *"Indeed, Rubinstein dismisses any notion that great wealth had anything to do with entry into the governing elite, as represented by bishops, higher civil servants, and chairmen of manufacturing companies."*

Test II
Section IV
Solutions

1. (A) No. This is irrelevant.
(B) No. This is irrelevant.
(C) Yes. Since the same four dishes have been offered for years, any new item would probably become the most popular—at least for a while.
(D) No. This is irrelevant.
(E) No. This is irrelevant.

2. (A) No. The paradox involves the health of mule deer living in old-growth forests and the health of mule deer living in cleared forests, not between the mule deer and other species of deer.
(B) No. It is conceivable that both female deer and their young offspring are less well nourished than adult males; however, this is speculation.
(C) No. Their natural range is irrelevant. At issue is the difference in their health in cleared forests versus old-growth forests.
(D) Yes. We are looking for an agent that would cause the deer to become less well nourished even as their food supply increases. Choice (D) offers an agent—tannins, which inhibit digestion of food. So even though the deer have more food to eat, they receive less nutrition from the food.
(E) No. This should make the deer <u>better</u> nourished in cleared forests since there are fewer trees from which the parasites could drop onto the deer.

3. (A) No. Harold is objecting to the fact that Genevieve apparently does not practice what she preaches. She says one should avoid flying, yet she is flying more than ever before. In this argument, David is not offering advice.
(B) No. Harold is objecting to the fact that Genevieve apparently does not practice what she preaches. She says one should avoid flying, yet she is flying more than ever before. The person in this argument is not offering advice.
(C) No. Harold is objecting to the fact that Genevieve apparently does not practice what she preaches. She says one should avoid flying, yet she is flying more than ever before. In this argument, Susan *does* practice what she preaches—that rock climbing is safe.
(D) Yes. Harold is objecting to the fact that Genevieve apparently does not practice what she preaches. She says one should avoid flying, yet she is flying more than ever before. Similarly, the person in this answer-choice is objecting to the fact that Pat apparently does not practice what she preaches. Pat says raw green vegetables should be eaten daily, yet she hardly ever eats them.
(E) No. Harold is objecting to the fact that Genevieve apparently does not practice what she preaches. She says one should avoid flying, yet she is flying more than ever before. In this argument, Gabriel is not offering advice.

4. (A) Yes. Incineration may pose the least amount of risk for the greatest number of people, yet concentrate the risk for a few people—those living nearby.
(B) No. This would make the general population less likely to approve of incinerators. Further, it does not explain why people object when an incinerator is built nearby.
(C) No. This does not explain why the general population approves of incinerators yet the people living near incinerators oppose them.
(D) No. This should help allay the fears of nearby residents, assuming that the solids are potentially less harmful. Hence, it would make them less likely to object to the incinerators.
(E) No. This does not explain why the general population approves of incinerators, yet the people living near incinerators oppose them. Evidently, the people living near the incinerators worry they will be exposed to greater amounts of toxins than people further away.

5. (A) No. The passage does tell us that a dog growled at Elena if and only if it was a white poodle. However, this does not preclude the possibility of other white dogs being at the show—they just didn't growl at Elena.
(B) No. The clause *"every dog that growled at me was a white poodle"* contains an embedded *if-then* statement: if a dog growled at me, it was a white poodle. This in turn can be diagrammed as follows:

G—>WP

This diagram allows gray poodles; they just can't growl at Elena.
(C) Yes. The clause *"every dog that growled at me was a white poodle"* contains an embedded *if-then* statement: if a dog growled at me, it was a white poodle. This in turn can be diagrammed as follows:

G—>WP

Now, if a particular dog growled at Elena, it must be a white, not gray, poodle.

It may help to apply the contrapositive to the above diagram: **~WP—>~G**. Now, a gray dog is not a white poodle. Hence, the hypothesis of the *if-then* statement **~WP—>~G** is satisfied. Therefore, the conclusion ~G must follow—that is, no gray dog growled at Elena.
(D) No. The clause *"every dog that growled at me was a white poodle"* contains an embedded *if-then* statement: if a dog growled at me, it was a white poodle. This in turn can be diagrammed as follows:

G—>WP

Now, if a particular dog growled at Elena, it must be a white poodle. Hence, it does not follow that all white dogs growled at Elena unless there were only white poodles at the dog show.
(E) No. The clause *"every dog that growled at me was a white poodle"* contains an embedded *if-then* statement: if a dog growled at me, it was a white poodle. This in turn can be diagrammed as follows:

G—>WP

This diagram allows gray poodles; they just can't growl at Elena.

Questions 6–7

6. (A) No. Lola states that harvesting the yew *"could have far-reaching consequences for an entire ecosystem."* Although Derek concedes *"the yew population might be threatened,"* he does not discuss whether this would adversely affect the environment.
(B) No. The dispute is over whether the yew trees should be harvested while waiting for a synthetic drug to be developed.
(C) Yes. Derek and Lola have different priorities. Derek believes it is more important to get the drug on the market now than to protect the yew trees, whereas Lola believes it is more important to protect the yew trees and the spotted owl.
(D) No. Lola states that harvesting the yew *"could have far-reaching consequences for an entire ecosystem."* Although Derek concedes *"the yew population might be threatened,"* he does not discuss whether this would adversely affect the environment. This answer-choice is essentially the same as choice (A).
(E) No. Although Derek apparently gives more weight to saving human life—at least in the short run—and Lola gives more weight to saving the environment, choice (E) is too strong. Notice the absolute words *ever* and *any*.

7. (A) No. Apparently she would reject the proviso *"unless people's well-being is threatened"* since she does not apply it to the cancer drug derived from the yew trees. Further, the rest of the statement is too strong. Notice the absolute word *no*.
(B) No. There is no discussion of whether medical researchers should work with environmentalists.
(C) No. Apparently Lola believes that environmental concerns should play a role in decisions concerning medical research whether or not human lives are at stake.
(D) No. The cancer drug derived from the yew would save human lives, yet Lola still opposes harvesting the yew because that would threaten the environment.
(E) Yes. Lola believes it is more important to protect the yew trees and the spotted owl than to develop the drug: *"Despite our eagerness to take advantage of a new medical breakthrough, we should wait for a synthetic drug rather than threaten the survival of both the yew and the owl, which could have far-reaching consequences for an entire ecosystem."* This position conforms to a guiding doctrine that *"avoiding actions that threaten an entire ecosystem takes precedence over immediately providing advantage to a restricted group of people."*

8. (A) No. The passage does not say that all students who play sports are having academic problems, merely that many students who play sports are having academic problems.
(B) No. The passage does not say all students who play sports are having academic problems. So possibly there are some students who play sports yet are succeeding academically.
(C) Yes. A major assumption in the director's argument is that the students will apply some of the time they save by not participating in sports to studying. However, conceivably the students will use that time to watch television or hang out on the street corner. In other words, the time they save may not be applied to studying.
(D) No. The passage does not say all students who play sports are having academic problems. So possibly there are some students who play sports yet are succeeding academically.
(E) No. The director's argument does not depend on either the success or the failure of the sports program.

9. (A) No. Initially, there may have been many more trees in Martown than in Seclee. So it may take many years of planting trees in Seclee before their number is greater than in Martown.
(B) Yes. If Martown were entirely within the boundary of Seclee, then there would be at least as many trees in Seclee (probably more) as there are in Martown since every tree in Martown would also be in Seclee. The following diagram may help:

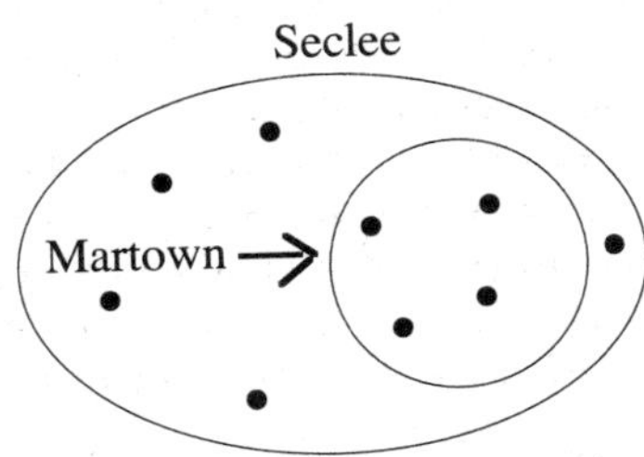

(C) No. We don't know whether the virus caused the trees to die. Even if it did, we still don't know whether this caused the number of trees in Martown to be less than or equal to the number of trees in Seclee unless the virus destroyed all the trees in Martown.
(D) No. We don't know how rainfall affects the proliferation of trees.
(E) No. There may have been many more trees in Martown than in Seclee. So it may take many years of cutting down the trees before their number is fewer in

Martown than in Seclee. Also, new trees may spring up more quickly in Martown than in Seclee.

Questions 10–11

10. (A) No. This does not relate to the fact that seal population has suffered a severe decline since 1988.
(B) No. Adding more sources of pollution would strengthen the argument.
(C) Yes. This is an all-things-being-equal argument. If all other factors are the same, then it must be the pollution that caused the seals to become more susceptible to the virus. So for the argument to be valid, it must assume that the virus has not increased in virulence.
(D) No. This has no affect on the argument. If we knew that the seal population also decreased dramatically in these areas, then it would support the argument. On the other hand, if we knew that the seal population did not change in these areas, then it would weaken the argument.
(E) No. Although one can theorize that lack of food caused the seals to become malnourished, in turn weakening their immune systems, the argument does not presume any particular mechanism by which the pollution affected the seals. There are many other scenarios (some more direct) which could explain how the pollution weakened the seals' immune system.

11. (A) Yes. Since presumably the distemper virus that affects seals would not affect such disparate animals as shellfish and seabirds, it is likely that another agent caused all three populations to decrease—pollution.
(B) No. This would weaken the argument. If pollution is being reduced, then pollution is less likely now to be the cause of the weakening of the seals' immune system than in the past.
(C) No. We don't know how this has affected the immune system of humans. If humans are becoming more susceptible to similar viruses, then it would support the argument. However, if humans are not becoming more susceptible to similar viruses, then it would weaken the argument.
(D) No. This is irrelevant. The passage is about the general population of seals. We don't need to know the distribution of the various species.
(E) No. This would weaken the argument. If the seals' immune system were unprepared for the new strain of virus, then the spread of the virus probably would have occurred even without the pollution.

12. (A) No. *"Everyone who played volleyball at that party got badly sunburned"* can be symbolized as

Vb—>Sb

and *"no one at work today is even slightly sunburned"* is symbolized as

W—>~Sb

The conclusion, *"none of the volleyball players at yesterday's office beach party came to work today"* is symbolized as

Vb—>~W

with the overall structure of the argument being

Vb—>Sb
W—>~Sb
∴ Vb—>~W

Applying the contrapositive to the second statement shows that the argument is a valid application of the transitive property:

Vb—>Sb
Sb—>~W
∴ Vb—>~W

Now, the argument in this answer-choice can be symbolized as:

Employed by TRF and opportunity to purchase —> Purchased dental insurance
Purchased dental insurance —> Saw a dentist
∴ Not seeing a dentist —> Not employed by TRF

This argument is invalid: Perhaps some employees of TRF did not have the opportunity to purchase dental insurance and so did not see a dentist. Note, the argument would be valid if the phrase *"who was given the opportunity to purchase dental insurance"* was removed.
(B) No. *"Everyone who played volleyball at that party got badly sunburned"* can be symbolized as

Vb—>Sb

and *"no one at work today is even slightly sunburned"* is symbolized as

W—>~Sb

The conclusion, *"none of the volleyball players at yesterday's office beach party came to work today"* is symbolized as

Vb—>~W

with the overall structure of the argument being

Vb—>Sb
W—>~Sb
∴ Vb—>~W

Applying the contrapositive to the second statement shows that the argument is a valid application of the transitive property:

Vb—>Sb
Sb—>~W
∴ Vb—>~W

Now, the argument in this answer-choice can be symbolized as:

Promoted —> Attended banquet
Manager —> Not promoted
∴ Manager —> Not attended banquet

This argument is invalid. (Taking the contrapositive of either premise will not allow us to apply the transitive property.)
(C) No. *"Everyone who played volleyball at that party got badly sunburned"* can be symbolized as

Vb—>Sb

and *"no one at work today is even slightly sunburned"* is symbolized as

W—>~Sb

The conclusion, *"none of the volleyball players at yesterday's office beach party came to work today"* is symbolized as

Vb—>~W

with the overall structure of the argument being

Vb—>Sb
W—>~Sb
∴ Vb—>~W

Applying the contrapositive to the second statement shows that the argument is a valid application of the transitive property:

Vb—>Sb
Sb—>~W
∴ Vb—>~W

Now, the argument in this answer-choice can be symbolized as:

Donnely report —> Not completed in time
John's group —> Reputation for timely completion of assignments
∴ John's group —> Not contribute to Donnely report

This argument is invalid. It has two significant flaws: First, it wrongly equates having *"a reputation for getting assignments in on time"* to actually doing so. Perhaps in this instance the reputation was not fulfilled. Second, perhaps John's group did contribute to the Donnely report and did complete their portion on time, but someone else's contribution was late.
(D) Yes. *"Everyone who played volleyball at that party got badly sunburned"* can be symbolized as

Vb—>Sb

and *"no one at work today is even slightly sunburned"* is symbolized as

W—>~Sb

The conclusion, *"none of the volleyball players at yesterday's office beach party came to work today"* is symbolized as

Vb—>~W

with the overall structure of the argument being

Vb—>Sb
W—>~Sb
∴ Vb—>~W

Applying the contrapositive to the second statement shows that the argument is a valid application of the transitive property:

Vb—>Sb
Sb—>~W
∴ Vb—>~W

Now, the argument in this answer-choice can be symbolized as:

2nd floor —> Works for president
Works for president—> No vacation in July
∴ 2nd floor —> No vacation in July

Like the original passage, this argument is a valid, deductive argument based on the transitive property.
(E) No. *"Everyone who played volleyball at that party got badly sunburned"* can be symbolized as

Vb—>Sb

and *"no one at work today is even slightly sunburned"* is symbolized as

W—>~Sb

The conclusion, *"none of the volleyball players at yesterday's office beach party came to work today"* is symbolized as

Vb—>~W

with the overall structure of the argument being

$$\begin{array}{r} Vb \rightarrow Sb \\ W \rightarrow \sim Sb \\ \hline \therefore\ Vb \rightarrow \sim W \end{array}$$

Applying the contrapositive to the second statement shows that the argument is a valid application of the transitive property:

$$\begin{array}{r} Vb \rightarrow Sb \\ Sb \rightarrow \sim W \\ \hline \therefore\ Vb \rightarrow \sim W \end{array}$$

Now, the argument in this answer-choice is invalid. It presumes a causal relationship between two events—that people who are employed at MXM must have a stable employment history. However, nothing in the answer-choice indicates this must be so. The answer-choice presents only a correlation between two events that may or may not have a causal relationship. Perhaps everyone working at MXM likes their job so much that they choose not to change jobs.

Questions 13–14

(A) No. This is an explicit premise of the argument, not an assumption, of the argument: *"The only deans whom academics respect are those who hold doctoral degrees."*
(B) No. The passage merely states that the specific person selected must have a doctoral degree.
(C) No. The passage merely states that the specific person selected must hold a doctoral degree in computer science and really know about computers.
(D) No. The passage merely states that *"The only deans whom academics respect are those who hold doctoral degrees."* (Some deans could have doctoral degrees but not be respected.)
(E) Yes. The argument sets up three criteria for the dean of computing:

1) She must have a doctoral degree.
2) She must really know about computers.
3) She must be selected from among the university's staff.

The argument then concludes that the dean of computing must be a professor from this university's computer science department. This assumes that of people who meet criteria 1 and 3, only those from the university's computer science department meet criteria 2.

14. (A) Yes. The argument sets up three criteria for the dean of computing:

1) She must have a doctoral degree.
2) She must really know about computers.
3) She must be selected from among the university's staff.

The argument then concludes that the dean of computing must be a professor from this university's computer science department. However, this answer-choice states that there are people who satisfy all three criteria yet are not professors.
(B) No. The argument sets up three criteria for the dean of computing:

1) She must have a doctoral degree.
2) She must really know about computers.
3) She must be selected from among the university's staff.

This answer-choice does not meet criterion 1.
(C) No. The argument sets up three criteria for the dean of computing:

1) She must have a doctoral degree.
2) She must really know about computers.
3) She must be selected from among the university's staff.

This answer-choice does not meet criterion 3.
(D) No. This is irrelevant.
(E) No. The argument sets up three criteria for the dean of computing:

1) She must be respected by the academic staff (must have a doctoral degree).
2) She must really know about computers.
3) She must be selected from among the university's staff.

This answer-choice weakens the argument only if all members of the computer science department are not respected.

Questions 15–16

15. (A) Yes. The consumer advocate claims that manufacturers are misleading consumers precisely because they are not using the common meaning of "fresh": *"For example, a certain brand of juice is labeled 'fresh orange juice,' yet the product is made from water, concentrate, and flavor enhancers. Since 'fresh' as applied to food products is commonly understood to mean pure and unprocessed, labeling that orange juice 'fresh' is unquestionably deceptive."*

Whereas the manufacture claims that in the absence of government standards the meanings of words can be slightly altered: *"Using words somewhat differently than they are commonly used is not deceptive. After all, 'fresh' can also mean never frozen."*
(B) No. Ostensibly, both believe that truthful labeling practices which reflect common standards of usage can be established by the government.
(C) No. This is the consumer advocate's position: *"Since 'fresh' as applied to food products is com-*

monly understood to mean pure and unprocessed...." However, the passage does not indicate whether the manufacture agrees or disagrees with this statement.
(D) No. The passage does not indicate whether either party agrees or disagrees with this statement. Natural foods are not even discussed.
(E) No. This could be the consumer advocate's position—though it is a bit strong. However, the passage does not indicate whether the manufacture agrees or disagrees with this statement.

16. W(A) No. This contradicts the manufacturer's claim: *"Using words somewhat differently than they are commonly used is not deceptive."*
(B) No. This contradicts the manufacturer's claim: *"Using words somewhat differently than they are commonly used is not deceptive."*
(C) Yes. *"Manufacturer: Using words somewhat differently than they are commonly used is not deceptive.... We cannot be faulted for failing to comply with standards that have not been officially formulated."*
(D) No. Incompatibility between government standards and common standards for truthful labeling is not discussed in the passage.
(E) No. This does not address the manufacturer's claim that *"We cannot be faulted for failing to comply with standards that have not been officially formulated."*

17. (A) Yes. The strategy is to price the item high to maintain an aura of exclusivity. The counterproductive feature of pricing the item low is that it may lose its exclusivity: *"In fact, trying to sell such an item fast by asking too low a price is a serious error, since it calls into question the very thing—exclusivity—that is supposed to be the item's chief appeal."*
(B) No. The strategy is to price the item high. The advantages of the rejected alternative (pricing the item low) are not mentioned in the passage.
(C) No. The strategy is to price the item high, and the passage implies that this is the superior strategy because it preserves or increases the "exclusivity" of the item.
(D) No. This is not mentioned in the passage.
(E) No. The "error" is in pricing the item at other than the "right price." The passage does not indicate that an error in pricing the item high will go unnoticed, but does indicate that there is a greater disadvantage in pricing the item low.

18. (A) No. He does not assume this.
(B) No. This is irrelevant.
(C) No. He does not assume this.
(D) Yes. If female deer already contain 9 milligrams of the hormone, then injecting them with 10 milligrams more would bring the hormone level to 19 milligrams. In this case, by eating less than one entire deer a day, one could surpass the safe level of 10 milligrams of the hormone per day.
(E) No. He does not assume this, and appropriately so. Even if deer meat is rarely eaten, it must be safe in those few times it is consumed.

19. (A) No. This points out that the sample was flawed. Hence, it should not be accurate.
(B) No. If the people are lying, then it's not surprising that the election results would differ from the survey.
(C) No. The voters may have supported increased funding for schools by raising taxes but opposed the larger bill it was attached to.
(D) Yes. This would increase the apparent discrepancy since *"Seventy percent of the adults surveyed said they would pay higher taxes for drug treatment programs."*
(E) No. If the voters were confused by the wording of the proposition, some supporters of the proposition may have mistakenly voted against it.

Questions 20–21

20. (A) No. The passage criticizes the motives of the environmentalists; it does not attack the logical structure of their argument.
(B) Yes. The issue is whether the development would interfere with bird-migration patterns. Attacking the opposition's motives does not address this issue.
(C) No. Although the argument highlights the Golden Lake Development case, it also notes that the *"same people have raised environmental objections to virtually every development proposal brought before the council in recent years."* A few exceptional cases are not being used to misrepresent the general situation.
(D) No. Evidence for or against the environmentalists' claim is not presented in the passage.
(E) No. The environmentalists are addressed as a group, not as individuals.

21. (A) Yes. The point of the argument is that because the environmentalists almost always oppose development projects they cannot be merely concerned about the environment. This assumes that the environmentalists opposed some of the projects for other than environmental reasons.
(B) No. This is too strong. In other cases, opponents of development might be very forthright.
(C) No. This does not relate to the issue of the environment.
(D) No. Whether there are other reasons to oppose the development project is not mentioned in the passage. Besides, other independent reasons would not affect the environmentalists' argument.

(E) No. This is too strong. The point of the argument is that because the environmentalists almost always oppose development projects they cannot be merely concerned about the environment. The passage hinges on the pattern of opposition, not on opposition to any particular project.

22. (A) No. First, there is no discussion in the passage of conflicts between current psychological practices and traditional attitudes. Second, this choice is too strong since it concludes that every traditional attitude should be changed whereas the passage discusses only one issue: the psychology of advanced age.
(B) No. Although older people (the "second group") were previously middle-aged (the "first group"), the principle espoused in this choice does not establish that each group has its own distinct psychology.
(C) No. The author states that *"Most psychologists, however, persist in regarding people 70 to 90 years old as though they were 35 year olds ...."* Yet she argues against this approach.
(D) Yes. The author is tacitly appealing to this principle when she states, *"But old age is as fundamentally different from young adulthood and middle age as childhood is—a fact attested to by the organization of modern social and economic life. Surely it is time, therefore, to acknowledge that serious research into the unique psychology of advanced age has become indispensable."*
(E) No. This is irrelevant.

23. (A) No. Clearly, Emile would support this statement: *"Badly chosen words can make even the soundest argument a poor one."* Also, Sabina would probably support this statement: *"if the words are clearly defined and consistently used, the actual words chosen make no difference to an argument's soundness."*
(B) No. Sabina certainly allows for a "minimalist" definition of words, in which a word carries only its precise definition. Emile also allows for precise definitions, independent of social or political connotations, but also believes that these connotations can affect people's responses to the words. *"Many words have social and political connotations that influence people's response to claims expressed in those words, regardless of how carefully and explicitly those words are defined."*
(C) No. The dispute between Sabina and Emile is over the meanings of words used in an argument, not the structure of an argument.
(D) No. This goes a little beyond the scope of Sabina's and Emile's disagreement. They disagree whether the validity of an argument is affected by how it is expressed, not how one should express an argument.
(E) Yes. Sabina claims that *"words used in expressing facts affect neither the facts nor the conclusions those facts will support."* In other words, how an argument is presented has no affect on its soundness. However, Emile claims just the opposite: *"Badly chosen words can make even the soundest argument a poor one... Since whether people will acknowledge a fact is affected by how the fact is expressed, the conclusions they actually draw are also affected."*

24. (A) No. The argument concerns the amount of waste dumped into landfills, not the difference in cost between recycled plastics and new plastics.
(B) No. This represents an educational issue, not a structural flaw in the passage's plan.
(C) Yes. By refusing to purchase higher-numbered products, consumers are refusing to buy those very products most likely to be packaged in recycled materials! Hence, the plastics will most likely be discarded since there will be little market for recycled plastics.
(D) No. The argument concerns the amount of waste dumped into landfills, not the cost of using recycled plastics.
(E) No. This somewhat weakens the argument since it shows that there is a good-faith effort made to recycle the higher numbered products. However, there is a stronger answer-choice.

25. (A) No. Assuming that the poll is accurate, this would support the argument.
(B) Yes. This indicates that it was not the increase in television viewing that caused the decline in the percentage of people who read newspapers. Rather, there was a third factor that led both those who watch television and those who do not to spend less time reading newspapers.
(C) No. The argument concerns the declining number (percentage) of people who read newspapers, not the average amount of time they spend in this activity. Although there are fewer people reading newspapers, they may spend more time reading.
(D) No. This is irrelevant.
(E) No. The passage is referring to the past 20 years, whereas this answer-choice is referring only to the past 5 years. Further, the amount of time a television is on does not necessarily reflect the amount of time people actually spend watching it. For example, perhaps 5 years ago only young children were likely to watch much television, whereas now a whole family is likely to watch television.

LSAT
TEST III

SECTION I

Time—35 minutes
27 Questions

Directions: Each passage in this section is followed by a group of questions to be answered on the basis of what is stated or implied in the passage. For some of the questions, more than one of the choices could conceivably answer the question. However, you are to choose the best answer; that is, the response that most accurately and completely answers the question.

Many argue that recent developments in electronic technology such as computers and videotape have enabled artists to vary their forms of expression. For example, video art can now achieve images whose effect is produced by "digitalization": breaking up the picture using computerized information processing. Such new technologies create new ways of seeing and hearing by adding different dimensions to older forms, rather than replacing those forms. Consider *Locale,* a film about a modern dance company. The camera operator wore a Steadicam™, an uncomplicated device that allows a camera to be mounted on a person so that the camera remains steady no matter how the operator moves. The Steadicam™ captures the dance in ways impossible with traditional mounts. Such new equipment also allows for the preservation of previously unrecordable aspects of performances, thus enriching archives.

By contrast, others claim that technology subverts the artistic enterprise: that artistic efforts achieved with machines preempt human creativity, rather than being inspired by it. The originality of musical performance, for example, might suffer, as musicians would be deprived of the opportunity to spontaneously change pieces of music before live audiences. Some even worry that technology will eliminate live performance altogether; performances will be recorded for home viewing, abolishing the relationship between performer and audience. But these negative views assume both that technology poses an unprecedented challenge to the arts and that we are not committed enough to the artistic enterprise to preserve the live performance, assumptions that seem unnecessarily cynical. In fact, technology has traditionally assisted our capacity for creative expression and can refine our notions of any given art form.

For example, the portable camera and the snapshot were developed at the same time as the rise of Impressionist painting in the nineteenth century. These photographic technologies encouraged a new appreciation for the chance view and unpredictable angle, thus preparing an audience for a new style of painting. In addition, Impressionist artists like Degas studied the elements of light and movement captured by instantaneous photography and used their new understanding of the way our perceptions distort reality to try to more accurately capture reality in their work. Since photos can capture the "moments" of a movement, such as a hand partially raised in a gesture of greeting, Impressionist artists were inspired to paint such moments in order to more effectively convey the quality of spontaneous human action. Photography freed artists from the preconception that a subject should be painted in a static, artificial entirety, and inspired them to capture the random and fragmentary qualities of our world. Finally, since photography preempted painting as the means of obtaining portraits, painters had more freedom to vary their subject matter, thus giving rise to the abstract creations characteristic of modern art.

1. Which one of the following statements best expresses the main idea of the passage?

   (A) The progress of art relies primarily on technology.
   (B) Technological innovation can be beneficial to art.
   (C) There are risks associated with using technology to create art.
   (D) Technology will transform the way the public responds to art.
   (E) The relationship between art and technology has a lengthy history.

2. It can be inferred from the passage that the author shares which one of the following opinions with the opponents of the use of new technology in art?

   (A) The live performance is an important aspect of the artistic enterprise.
   (B) The public's commitment to the artistic enterprise is questionable.
   (C) Recent technological innovations present an entirely new sort of challenge to art.
   (D) Technological innovations of the past have been very useful to artists.
   (E) The performing arts are especially vulnerable to technological innovation.

GO ON TO THE NEXT PAGE.

3. Which one of the following, if true, would most undermine the position held by opponents of the use of new technology in art concerning the effect of technology on live performance?

(A) Surveys show that when recordings of performances are made available for home viewing, the public becomes far more knowledgeable about different performing artists.
(B) Surveys show that some people feel comfortable responding spontaneously to artistic performances when they are viewing recordings of those performances at home.
(C) After a live performance, sales of recordings for home viewing of the particular performing artist generally increase.
(D) The distribution of recordings of artists' performances has begun to attract many new audience members to their live performances.
(E) Musicians are less apt to make creative changes in musical pieces during recorded performances than during live performances.

4. The author uses the example of the Steadicam™ primarily in order to suggest that

(A) the filming of performances should not be limited by inadequate equipment
(B) new technologies do not need to be very complex in order to benefit art
(C) the interaction of a traditional art form with a new technology will change attitudes toward technology in general
(D) the replacement of a traditional technology with a new technology will transform definitions of a traditional art form
(E) new technology does not so much preempt as enhance a traditional art form

5. According to the passage, proponents of the use of new electronic technology in the arts claim that which one of the following is true?

(A) Most people who reject the use of electronic technology in art forget that machines require a person to operate them.
(B) Electronic technology allows for the expansion of archives because longer performances can be recorded.
(C) Electronic technology assists artists in finding new ways to present their material.
(D) Electronic technology makes the practice of any art form more efficient by speeding up the creative process.
(E) Modern dance is the art form that will probably benefit most from the use of electronic technology.

6. It can be inferred from the passage that the author would agree with which one of the following statements regarding changes in painting since the nineteenth century?

(A) The artistic experiments of the nineteenth century led painters to use a variety of methods in creating portraits, which they then applied to other subject matter.
(B) The nineteenth-century knowledge of light and movement provided by photography inspired the abstract works characteristic of modern art.
(C) Once painters no longer felt that they had to paint conventional portraits, they turned exclusively to abstract portraiture.
(D) Once painters were less limited to the Impressionist style, they were able to experiment with a variety of styles of abstract art.
(E) Once painters painted fewer conventional portraits, they had greater opportunity to move beyond the literal depiction of objects.

GO ON TO THE NEXT PAGE.

During the 1940s and 1950s the United States government developed a new policy toward Native Americans, often known as "readjustment." Because the increased awareness of civil rights in these decades helped reinforce the belief that life on reservations prevented Native Americans from exercising the rights guaranteed to citizens under the United States Constitution, the readjustment movement advocated the end of the federal government's involvement in Native American affairs and encouraged the assimilation of Native Americans as individuals into mainstream society. However, the same years also saw the emergence of a Native American leadership and efforts to develop tribal institutions and reaffirm tribal identity. The clash of these two trends may be traced in the attempts on the part of the Bureau of Indian Affairs (BIA) to convince the Oneida tribe of Wisconsin to accept readjustment.

The culmination of BIA efforts to sway the Oneida occurred at a meeting that took place in the fall of 1956. The BIA suggested that it would be to the Oneida's benefit to own their own property and, like other homeowners, pay real estate taxes on it. The BIA also emphasized that, after readjustment, the government would not attempt to restrict Native Americans' ability to sell their individually owned lands. The Oneida were then offered a one-time lump-sum payment of $60,000 in lieu of the $0.52 annuity guaranteed in perpetuity to each member of the tribe under the Canandaigua Treaty.

The efforts of the BIA to "sell" readjustment to the tribe failed because the Oneida realized that they had heard similar offers before. The Oneida delegates reacted negatively to the BIA's first suggestion because taxation of Native American lands had been one past vehicle for dispossessing the Oneida: after the distribution of some tribal lands to individual Native Americans in the late nineteenth century, Native American lands became subject to taxation, resulting in new and impossible financial burdens, foreclosures, and subsequent tax sales of property. The Oneida delegates were equally suspicious of the BIA's emphasis on the rights of individual landowners, since in the late nineteenth century many individual Native Americans had been convinced by unscrupulous speculators to sell their lands. Finally, the offer of a lump-sum payment was unanimously opposed by the Oneida delegates, who saw that changing the terms of a treaty might jeopardize the many pending land claims based upon the treaty.

As a result of the 1956 meeting, the Oneida rejected readjustment. Instead, they determined to improve tribal life by lobbying for federal monies for postsecondary education, for the improvement of drainage on tribal lands, and for the building of a convalescent home for tribal members. Thus, by learning the lessons of history, the Oneida were able to survive as a tribe in their homeland.

7. Which one of the following would be most consistent with the policy of readjustment described in the passage?

   (A) the establishment among Native Americans of a tribal system of elected government
   (B) the creation of a national project to preserve Native American language and oral history
   (C) the establishment of programs to encourage Native Americans to move from reservations to urban areas
   (D) the development of a large-scale effort to restore Native American lands to their original tribes
   (E) the reaffirmation of federal treaty obligations to Native American tribes

8. According to the passage, after the 1956 meeting the Oneida resolved to

   (A) obtain improved social services and living conditions for members of the tribe
   (B) pursue litigation designed to reclaim tribal lands
   (C) secure recognition of their unique status as a self-governing Native American nation within the United States
   (D) establish new kinds of tribal institutions
   (E) cultivate a life-style similar to that of other United States citizens

9. Which one of the following best describes the function of the first paragraph in the context of the passage as a whole?

   (A) It summarizes the basis of a conflict underlying negotiations described elsewhere in the passage.
   (B) It presents two positions, one of which is defended by evidence provided in succeeding paragraphs.
   (C) It compares competing interpretations of a historical conflict.
   (D) It analyzes the causes of a specific historical event and predicts a future development.
   (E) It outlines the history of a government agency.

GO ON TO THE NEXT PAGE.

10. The author refers to the increased awareness of civil rights during the 1940s and 1950s most probably in order to

    (A) contrast the readjustment movement with other social phenomena
    (B) account for the stance of the Native American leadership
    (C) help explain the impetus for the readjustment movement
    (D) explain the motives of BIA bureaucrats
    (E) foster support for the policy of readjustment

11. The passage suggests that advocates of readjustment would most likely agree with which one of the following statements regarding the relationship between the federal government and Native Americans?

    (A) The federal government should work with individual Native Americans to improve life on reservations.
    (B) The federal government should be no more involved in the affairs of Native Americans than in the affairs of other citizens.
    (C) The federal government should assume more responsibility for providing social services to Native Americans.
    (D) The federal government should share its responsibility for maintaining Native American territories with tribal leaders.
    (E) The federal government should observe all provisions of treaties made in the past with Native Americans.

12. The passage suggests that the Oneida delegates viewed the Canandaigua Treaty as

    (A) a valuable safeguard of certain Oneida rights and privileges
    (B) the source of many past problems for the Oneida tribe
    (C) a model for the type of agreement they hoped to reach with the federal government
    (D) an important step toward recognition of their status as an independent Native American nation
    (E) an obsolete agreement without relevance for their current condition

13. Which one of the following situations most closely parallels that of the Oneida delegates in refusing to accept a lump-sum payment of $60,000?

    (A) A university offers a student a four-year scholarship with the stipulation that the student not accept any outside employment; the student refuses the offer and attends a different school because the amount of the scholarship would not have covered living expenses.
    (B) A company seeking to reduce its payroll obligations offers an employee a large bonus if he will accept early retirement; the employee refuses because he does not want to compromise an outstanding worker's compensation suit.
    (C) Parents of a teenager offer to pay her at the end of the month for performing weekly chores rather than paying her on a weekly basis; the teenager refuses because she has a number of financial obligations that she must meet early in the month.
    (D) A car dealer offers a customer a $500 cash payment for buying a new car; the customer refuses because she does not want to pay taxes on the amount, and requests instead that her monthly payments be reduced by a proportionate amount.
    (E) A landlord offers a tenant several months rent-free in exchange for the tenant's agreeing not to demand that her apartment be painted every two years, as is required by the lease; the tenant refuses because she would have to spend her own time painting the apartment.

GO ON TO THE NEXT PAGE.

Direct observation of contemporary societies at the threshold of widespread literacy has not assisted our understanding of how such literacy altered ancient Greek society, in particular its political culture. The discovery of what Goody has called the "enabling effects" of literacy in contemporary societies tends to seduce the observer into confusing often rudimentary knowledge of how to read with popular access to important books and documents; this confusion is then projected onto ancient societies. "In ancient Greece," Goody writes, "alphabetic reading and writing was important for the development of political democracy."

An examination of the ancient Greek city Athens exemplifies how this sort of confusion is detrimental to understanding ancient politics. In Athens, the early development of a written law code was retrospectively mythologized as the critical factor in breaking the power monopoly of the old aristocracy: hence the Greek tradition of the "law-giver," which has captured the imaginations of scholars like Goody. But the application and efficacy of all law codes depend on their interpretation by magistrates and courts, and unless the right of interpretation is "democratized," the mere existence of written laws changes little.

In fact, never in antiquity did any but the elite consult documents and books. Even in Greek courts the juries heard only the relevant statutes read out during the proceedings, as they heard verbal testimony, and they then rendered their verdict on the spot, without the benefit of any discussion among themselves. True, in Athens the juries were representative of a broad spectrum of the population, and these juries, drawn from diverse social classes, both interpreted what they had heard and determined matters of fact. However, they were guided solely by the speeches prepared for the parties by professional pleaders and by the quotations of laws or decrees within the speeches, rather than by their own access to any kind of document or book.

Granted, people today also rely heavily on a truly knowledgeable minority for information and its interpretation, often transmitted orally. Yet this is still fundamentally different from an ancient society in which there was no "popular literature," i.e., no newspapers, magazines, or other media that dealt with sociopolitical issues. An ancient law code would have been analogous to the Latin Bible, a venerated document but a closed book. The resistance of the medieval Church to vernacular translations of the Bible, in the West at least, is therefore a pointer to the realities of ancient literacy. When fundamental documents are accessible for study only to an elite, the rest of the society is subject to the elite's interpretation of the rules of behavior, including right political behavior. Athens, insofar as it functioned as a democracy, did so not because of widespread literacy, but because the elite had chosen to accept democratic institutions.

14. Which one of the following statements best expresses the main idea of the passage?

(A) Democratic political institutions grow organically from the traditions and conventions of a society.
(B) Democratic political institutions are not necessarily the outcome of literacy in a society.
(C) Religious authority, like political authority, can determine who in a given society will have access to important books and documents.
(D) Those who are best educated are most often those who control the institutions of authority in a society.
(E) Those in authority have a vested interest in ensuring that those under their control remain illiterate.

15. It can be inferred from the passage that the author assumes which one of the following about societies in which the people possess a rudimentary reading ability?

(A) They are more politically advanced than societies without rudimentary reading ability.
(B) They are unlikely to exhibit the positive effects of literacy.
(C) They are rapidly evolving toward widespread literacy.
(D) Many of their people might not have access to important documents and books.
(E) Most of their people would not participate in political decision-making.

GO ON TO THE NEXT PAGE.

16. The author refers to the truly knowledgeable minority in contemporary societies in the context of the fourth paragraph in order to imply which one of the following?

    (A) Because they have a popular literature that closes the gap between the elite and the majority, contemporary societies rely far less on the knowledge of experts than did ancient societies.
    (B) Contemporary societies rely on the knowledge of experts, as did ancient societies, because contemporary popular literature so frequently conveys specious information.
    (C) Although contemporary societies rely heavily on the knowledge of experts, access to popular literature makes contemporary societies less dependent on experts for information about rules of behavior than were ancient societies.
    (D) While only some members of the elite can become experts, popular literature gives the majority in contemporary society an opportunity to become members of such an elite.
    (E) Access to popular literature distinguishes ancient from contemporary societies because it relies on a level of educational achievement attainable only by a contemporary elite.

17. According to the passage, each of the following statements concerning ancient Greek juries is true EXCEPT:

    (A) They were somewhat democratic insofar as they were composed largely of people from the lowest social classes.
    (B) They were exposed to the law only insofar as they heard relevant statutes read out during legal proceedings.
    (C) They ascertained the facts of a case and interpreted the laws.
    (D) They did not have direct access to important books and documents that were available to the elite.
    (E) They rendered verdicts without benefit of private discussion among themselves.

18. The author characterizes the Greek tradition of the "law-giver" (line 19) as an effect of mythologizing most probably in order to

    (A) illustrate the ancient Greek tendency to memorialize historical events by transforming them into myths
    (B) convey the historical importance of the development of the early Athenian written law code
    (C) convey the high regard in which the Athenians held their legal tradition
    (D) suggest that the development of a written law code was not primarily responsible for diminishing the power of the Athenian aristocracy
    (E) suggest that the Greek tradition of the "law-giver" should be understood in the larger context of Greek mythology

19. The author draws an analogy between the Latin Bible and an early law code (lines 46–48) in order to make which one of the following points?

    (A) Documents were considered authoritative in premodern society in proportion to their inaccessibility to the majority.
    (B) Documents that were perceived as highly influential in premodern societies were not necessarily accessible to the society's majority.
    (C) What is most revered in a nondemocratic society is what is most frequently misunderstood.
    (D) Political documents in premodern societies exerted a social influence similar to that exerted by religious documents.
    (E) Political documents in premodern societies were inaccessible to the majority of the population because of the language in which they were written.

20. The primary purpose of the passage is to

    (A) argue that a particular method of observing contemporary societies is inconsistent
    (B) point out the weaknesses in a particular approach to understanding ancient societies
    (C) present the disadvantages of a particular approach to understanding the relationship between ancient and contemporary societies
    (D) examine the importance of developing an appropriate method for understanding ancient societies
    (E) convey the difficulty of accurately understanding attitudes in ancient societies

GO ON TO THE NEXT PAGE.

The English who in the seventeenth and eighteenth centuries inhabited those colonies that would later become the United States shared a common political vocabulary with the English in England. Steeped as they were in the English political language, these colonials failed to observe that their experience in America had given the words a significance quite different from that accepted by the English with whom they debated; in fact, they claimed that they were more loyal to the English political tradition than were the English in England.

In many respects the political institutions of England were reproduced in these American colonies. By the middle of the eighteenth century, all of these colonies except four were headed by Royal Governors appointed by the King and perceived as bearing a relation to the people of the colony similar to that of the King to the English people. Moreover, each of these colonies enjoyed a representative assembly, which was consciously modeled, in powers and practices, after the English Parliament. In both England and these colonies, only property holders could vote.

Nevertheless, though English and colonial institutions were structurally similar, attitudes toward those institutions differed. For example, English legal development from the early seventeenth century had been moving steadily toward the absolute power of Parliament. The most unmistakable sign of this tendency was the legal assertion that the King was subject to the law. Together with this resolute denial of the absolute right of kings went the assertion that Parliament was unlimited in its power: it could change even the Constitution by its ordinary acts of legislation. By the eighteenth century the English had accepted the idea that the parliamentary representatives of the people were omnipotent.

The citizens of these colonies did not look upon the English Parliament with such fond eyes, nor did they concede that their own assemblies possessed such wide powers. There were good historical reasons for this. To the English the word "constitution" meant the whole body of law and legal custom formulated since the beginning of the kingdom, whereas to these colonials a constitution was a specific written document, enumerating specific powers. This distinction in meaning can be traced to the fact that the foundations of government in the various colonies were written charters granted by the Crown. These express authorizations to govern were tangible, definite things. Over the years these colonials had often repaired to the charters to justify themselves in the struggle against tyrannical governors or officials of the Crown. More than a century of government under written constitutions convinced these colonists of the necessity for and efficacy of protecting their liberties against governmental encroachment by explicitly defining all governmental powers in a document.

21. Which one of the following best expresses the main idea of the passage?

    (A) The colonials and the English mistakenly thought that they shared a common political vocabulary.
    (B) The colonials and the English shared a variety of institutions.
    (C) The colonials and the English had conflicting interpretations of the language and institutional structures that they shared.
    (D) Colonial attitudes toward English institutions grew increasingly hostile in the eighteenth century.
    (E) Seventeenth-century English legal development accounted for colonial attitudes toward constitutions.

22. The passage supports all of the following statements about the political conditions present by the middle of the eighteenth century in the American colonies discussed in the passage EXCEPT:

    (A) Colonials who did not own property could not vote.
    (B) All of these colonies had representative assemblies modeled after the British Parliament.
    (C) Some of these colonies had Royal Governors.
    (D) Royal Governors could be removed from office by colonial assemblies.
    (E) In these colonies, Royal Governors were regarded as serving a function like that of a king.

23. The passage implies which one of the following about English kings prior to the early seventeenth century?

    (A) They were the source of all law.
    (B) They frequently flouted laws made by Parliament.
    (C) Their power relative to that of Parliament was considerably greater than it was in the eighteenth century.
    (D) They were more often the sources of legal reform than they were in the eighteenth century.
    (E) They had to combat those who believed that the power of Parliament was absolute.

GO ON TO THE NEXT PAGE.

24. The author mentions which one of the following as evidence for the eighteenth-century English attitude toward Parliament?

(A) The English had become uncomfortable with institutions that could claim absolute authority.
(B) The English realized that their interests were better guarded by Parliament than by the King.
(C) The English allowed Parliament to make constitutional changes by legislative enactment.
(D) The English felt that the King did not possess the knowledge that would enable him to rule responsibly.
(E) The English had decided that it was time to reform their representative government.

25. The passage implies that the colonials discussed in the passage would have considered which one of the following to be a source of their debates with England?

(A) their changed use of the English political vocabulary
(B) English commitment to parliamentary representation
(C) their uniquely English experience
(D) their refusal to adopt any English political institutions
(E) their greater loyalty to the English political traditions

26. According to the passage, the English attitude toward the English Constitution differed from the colonial attitude toward constitutions in that the English regarded their Constitution as

(A) the legal foundation of the kingdom
(B) a document containing a collection of customs
(C) a cumulative corpus of legislation and legal traditions
(D) a record alterable by royal authority
(E) an unchangeable body of governmental powers

27. The primary purpose of the passage is to

(A) expose the misunderstanding that has characterized descriptions of the relationship between seventeenth- and eighteenth-century England and certain of its American colonies
(B) suggest a reason for England's treatment of certain of its American colonies in the seventeenth and eighteenth centuries
(C) settle an ongoing debate about the relationship between England and certain of its American colonies in the seventeenth and eighteenth centuries
(D) interpret the events leading up to the independence of certain of England's American colonies in the eighteenth century
(E) explain an aspect of the relationship between England and certain of its American colonies in the seventeenth and eighteenth centuries

S T O P

IF YOU FINISH BEFORE TIME IS CALLED, YOU MAY CHECK YOUR WORK ON THIS SECTION ONLY.
DO NOT WORK ON ANY OTHER SECTION IN THE TEST.

SECTION II
Time—35 minutes
25 Questions

Directions: The questions in this section are based on the reasoning contained in brief statements or passages. For some questions, more than one of the choices could conceivably answer the question. However, you are to choose the best answer; that is, the response that most accurately and completely answers the question. You should not make assumptions that are by commonsense standards implausible, superfluous, or incompatible with the passage.

1. Crimes in which handguns are used are more likely than other crimes to result in fatalities. However, the majority of crimes in which handguns are used do not result in fatalities. Therefore, there is no need to enact laws that address crimes involving handguns as distinct from other crimes.

   The pattern of flawed reasoning displayed in the argument above most closely resembles that in which one of the following?

   (A) Overweight people are at higher risk of developing heart disease than other people. However, more than half of all overweight people never develop heart disease. Hence it is unnecessary for physicians to be more careful to emphasize the danger of heart disease to their overweight patients than to their other patients.
   (B) Many people swim daily in order to stay physically fit. Yet people who swim daily increase their risk of developing ear infections. Hence people who want to remain in good health are better off not following fitness programs that include swimming daily.
   (C) Most physicians recommend a balanced diet for those who want to remain in good health. Yet many people find that nontraditional dietary regimens such as extended fasting do their health no serious harm. Therefore, there is no need for everyone to avoid nontraditional dietary regimens.
   (D) Foods rich in cholesterol and fat pose a serious health threat to most people. However, many people are reluctant to give up eating foods that they greatly enjoy. Therefore, people who refuse to give up rich foods need to spend more time exercising than do other people.
   (E) Many serious health problems are the result of dietary disorders. Yet these disorders are often brought about by psychological factors. Hence people suffering from serious health problems should undergo psychological evaluation.

2. Tall children can generally reach high shelves easily. Short children can generally reach high shelves only with difficulty. It is known that short children are more likely than are tall children to become short adults. Therefore, if short children are taught to reach high shelves easily, the proportion of them who become short adults will decrease.

   A reasoning error in the argument is that the argument

   (A) attributes a characteristic of an individual member of a group to the group as a whole
   (B) presupposes that which is to be proved
   (C) refutes a generalization by means of an exceptional case
   (D) assumes a causal relationship where only a correlation has been indicated
   (E) takes lack of evidence for the existence of a state of affairs as evidence that there can be no such state of affairs

GO ON TO THE NEXT PAGE.

3. Balance is particularly important when reporting the background of civil wars and conflicts. Facts must not be deliberately manipulated to show one party in a favorable light, and the views of each side should be fairly represented. This concept of balance, however, does not justify concealing or glossing over basic injustices in an effort to be even-handed. If all the media were to adopt such a perverse interpretation of balanced reporting, the public would be given a picture of a world where each party in every conflict had an equal measure of justice on its side, contrary to our experience of life and, indeed, our common sense.

Which one of the following best expresses the main point of the argument?

(A) Balanced reporting presents the public with a picture of the world in which all sides to a conflict have equal justification.
(B) Balanced reporting requires impartially revealing injustices where they occur no less than fairly presenting the views of each party in a conflict.
(C) Our experience of life shows that there are indeed cases in which conflicts arise because of an injustice, with one party clearly in the wrong.
(D) Common sense tells us that balance is especially needed when reporting the background of civil wars and conflicts.
(E) Balanced reporting is an ideal that cannot be realized, because judgments of balance are necessarily subjective.

4. Data from satellite photographs of the tropical rain forest in Melonia show that last year the deforestation rate of this environmentally sensitive zone was significantly lower than in previous years. The Melonian government, which spent millions of dollars last year to enforce laws against burning and cutting of the forest, is claiming that the satellite data indicate that its increased efforts to halt the destruction are proving effective.

Which one of the following, if true, most seriously undermines the government's claim?

(A) Landowner opposition to the government's antideforestation efforts grew more violent last year in response to the increased enforcement.
(B) Rainfall during the usually dry 6-month annual burning season was abnormally heavy last year.
(C) Government agents had to issue fines totaling over $9 million to 3,500 violators of burning-and-cutting regulations.
(D) The inaccessibility of much of the rain forest has made it impossible to confirm the satellite data by direct observation from the field.
(E) Much of the money that was designated last year for forest preservation has been spent on research and not on enforcement.

5. Advertisement: Northwoods Maple Syrup, made the old-fashioned way, is simply tops for taste. And here is the proof: in a recent market survey, 7 out of every 10 shoppers who expressed a preference said that Northwoods was the only maple syrup for them, no ifs, ands, or buts.

Of the following, which one is the strongest reason why the advertisement is potentially misleading?

(A) The proportion of shoppers expressing no preference might have been very small.
(B) Other brands of maple syrup might also be made the old-fashioned way.
(C) No market survey covers more than a sizable minority of the total population of consumers.
(D) The preference for the Northwoods brand might be based on such a factor as an exceptionally low price.
(E) Shoppers who buy syrup might buy only maple syrup.

6. In the summer of 1936 a polling service telephoned 10,000 United States voters and asked how they planned to vote in the coming presidential election. The survey sample included a variety of respondents—rural and urban, male and female, from every state. The poll predicted that Alfred Landon would soundly defeat Franklin Roosevelt. Nevertheless, Roosevelt won in a landslide.

Which one of the following, if true, best explains why the poll's prediction was inaccurate?

(A) The interviewers did not reveal their own political affiliation to the respondents.
(B) Only people who would be qualified to vote by election time were interviewed, so the survey sample was not representative of the overall United States population.
(C) The survey sample was representative only of people who could afford telephones at a time when phone ownership was less common than it is today.
(D) No effort was made to determine the respondents' political affiliations.
(E) Because the poll asked only for respondents' candidate preference, it collected no information concerning their reasons for favoring Landon or Roosevelt.

GO ON TO THE NEXT PAGE.

7. Waste management companies, which collect waste for disposal in landfills and incineration plants, report that disposable plastics make up an ever-increasing percentage of the waste they handle. It is clear that attempts to decrease the amount of plastic that people throw away in the garbage are failing.

Which one of the following, if true, most seriously weakens the argument?

(A) Because plastics create harmful pollutants when burned, an increasing percentage of the plastics handled by waste management companies are being disposed of in landfills.
(B) Although many plastics are recyclable, most of the plastics disposed of by waste management companies are not.
(C) People are more likely to save and reuse plastic containers than containers made of heavier materials like glass or metal.
(D) An increasing proportion of the paper, glass, and metal cans that waste management companies used to handle is now being recycled.
(E) While the percentage of products using plastic packaging is increasing, the total amount of plastic being manufactured has remained unchanged.

8. Most of the ultraviolet radiation reaching the Earth's atmosphere from the Sun is absorbed by the layer of stratospheric ozone and never reaches the Earth's surface. Between 1969 and 1986, the layer of stratospheric ozone over North America thinned, decreasing by about 3 percent. Yet, the average level of ultraviolet radiation measured at research stations across North America decreased over the same period.

Which one of the following, if true, best reconciles the apparently discrepant facts described above?

(A) Ultraviolet radiation increases the risk of skin cancer and cataracts; the incidence of skin cancer and cataracts increased substantially between 1969 and 1986.
(B) Between 1969 and 1986, the layer of stratospheric ozone over Brazil thinned, and the average level of ultraviolet radiation reaching the Earth's surface in Brazil increased.
(C) Manufactured chlorine chemicals thin the layer of stratospheric ozone.
(D) Ozone pollution, which absorbs ultraviolet radiation, increased dramatically between 1969 and 1986.
(E) Thinning of the layer of stratospheric ozone varies from one part of the world to another and from year to year.

Questions 9–10

The number of aircraft collisions on the ground is increasing because of the substantial increase in the number of flights operated by the airlines. Many of the fatalities that occur in such collisions are caused not by the collision itself, but by an inherent flaw in the cabin design of most aircraft, in which seats, by restricting access to emergency exits, impede escape. Therefore, to reduce the total number of fatalities that result annually from such collisions, the airlines should be required to remove all seats that restrict access to emergency exits.

9. Which one of the following, if true, provides the most support for the proposal?

(A) The number of deaths that occurred in theater fires because theater patrons could not escape was greatly reduced when theaters were required to have aisles leading to each exit.
(B) Removing the seats that block emergency exits on aircraft will require a costly refitting of aircraft cabins.
(C) In the event of fire, public buildings equipped with smoke detectors have fewer fatalities than do public buildings not so equipped.
(D) In the event of collision, passengers on planes with a smaller passenger capacity generally suffer more serious injury than do passengers on planes with a larger passenger capacity.
(E) The safety belts attached to aircraft seats function to protect passengers from the full force of impact in the event of a collision.

10. Which one of the following proposals, if implemented together with the proposal made in the passage, would improve the prospects for achieving the stated objective of reducing fatalities?

(A) The airlines should be required, when buying new planes, to buy only planes with unrestricted access to emergency exits.
(B) The airlines should not be permitted to increase further the number of flights in order to offset the decrease in the number of seats on each aircraft.
(C) Airport authorities should be required to streamline their passenger check-in procedures to accommodate the increased number of passengers served by the airlines.
(D) Airport authorities should be required to refine security precautions by making them less conspicuous without making them less effective.
(E) The airlines should not be allowed to increase the ticket price for each passenger to offset the decrease in the number of seats on each aircraft.

GO ON TO THE NEXT PAGE.

11. Recently discovered fossil evidence casts doubt on the evolutionary theory that dinosaurs are more closely related to reptiles than to other classes of animals. Fossils show that some dinosaurs had hollow bones—a feature found today only in warm-blooded creatures, such as birds, that have a high metabolic rate. Dinosaurs had well-developed senses of sight and hearing, which is not true of present-day cold-blooded creatures like reptiles. The highly arched mouth roof of some dinosaurs would have permitted them to breathe while eating, as fast-breathing animals, such as birds, need to do. Today, all fast-breathing animals are warm-blooded. Finally, fossils reveal that many dinosaurs had a pattern of growth typical of warm-blooded animals.

    The argument in the passage proceeds by

    (A) attempting to justify one position by demonstrating that an opposing position is based on erroneous information
    (B) establishing a general principle that it then uses to draw a conclusion about a particular case
    (C) dismissing a claim made about the present on the basis of historical evidence
    (D) assuming that if all members of a category have a certain property then all things with that property belong to the category
    (E) presenting evidence that a past phenomenon is more similar to one rather than the other of two present-day phenomena

12. Purebred dogs are prone to genetically determined abnormalities. Although such abnormalities often can be corrected by surgery, the cost can reach several thousand dollars. Since nonpurebred dogs rarely suffer from genetically determined abnormalities, potential dog owners who want to reduce the risk of incurring costly medical bills for their pets would be well advised to choose nonpurebred dogs.

    Which one of the following if true, most seriously weakens the argument?

    (A) Most genetically determined abnormalities in dogs do not seriously affect a dog's general well-being.
    (B) All dogs, whether purebred or nonpurebred, are subject to the same common nongenetically determined diseases.
    (C) Purebred dogs tend to have shorter natural life spans than do nonpurebred dogs.
    (D) The purchase price of nonpurebred dogs tends to be lower than the purchase price of purebred dogs.
    (E) A dog that does not have genetically determined abnormalities may nevertheless have offspring with such abnormalities.

13. Criticism that the press panders to public sentiment neglects to consider that the press is a profit-making institution. Like other private enterprises, it has to make money to survive. If the press were not profit-making, who would support it? The only alternative is subsidy and, with it, outside control. It is easy to get subsidies for propaganda, but no one will subsidize honest journalism.

    It can be properly inferred from the passage that if the press is

    (A) not subsidized, it is in no danger of outside control
    (B) not subsidized, it will not produce propaganda
    (C) not to be subsidized, it cannot be a profit-making institution
    (D) to produce honest journalism, it must be a profit-making institution
    (E) to make a profit, it must produce honest journalism

Questions 14–15

Lucien: Public-housing advocates claim that the many homeless people in this city are proof that there is insufficient housing available to them and therefore that more low-income apartments are needed. But that conclusion is absurd. Many apartments in my own building remain unrented and my professional colleagues report similar vacancies where they live. Since apartments clearly are available, homelessness is not a housing problem. Homelessness can, therefore, only be caused by people's inability or unwillingness to work to pay the rent.

Maria: On the contrary, all recent studies show that a significant percentage of this city's homeless people hold regular jobs. These are people who lack neither will nor ability.

14. Lucien's argument against the public-housing advocates' position is most vulnerable to which one of the following criticisms?

    (A) It offers no justification for dismissing as absurd the housing advocates' claim that there are many homeless people in the city.
    (B) It treats information acquired through informal conversations as though it provided evidence as strong as information acquired on the basis of controlled scientific studies.
    (C) It responds to a claim in which "available" is used in the sense of "affordable" by using "available" in the sense of "not occupied."
    (D) It overlooks the possibility that not all apartment buildings have vacant apartments for rent.
    (E) It fails to address the issue, raised by the public-housing advocates' argument, of who would pay for the construction of more low-income housing.

15. Maria responds to Lucien's argument by

(A) challenging the accuracy of the personal experiences he offers in support of his position
(B) showing that a presupposition of his argument is false
(C) presenting evidence that calls into question his motives for adopting the view he holds
(D) demonstrating that the evidence he offers supports a conclusion other than the conclusion he draws from it
(E) offering an alternative explanation for the facts he cites as evidence supporting his conclusion

16. Some people take their moral cues from governmental codes of law; for them, it is inconceivable that something that is legally permissible could be immoral.

Those whose view is described above hold inconsistent beliefs if they also believe that

(A) law does not cover all circumstances in which one person morally wrongs another
(B) a legally impermissible action is never morally excusable
(C) governmental officials sometimes behave illegally
(D) the moral consensus of a society is expressed in its laws
(E) some governmental regulations are so detailed that they are burdensome to the economy

17. Certain instruments used in veterinary surgery can be made either of stainless steel or of nylon. In a study of such instruments, 50 complete sterilizations of a set of nylon instruments required 3.4 times the amount of energy used to manufacture that set of instruments, whereas 50 complete sterilizations of a set of stainless steel instruments required 2.1 times the amount of energy required to manufacture that set of instruments.

If the statements above are true, each of the following could be true EXCEPT:

(A) The 50 complete sterilizations of the nylon instruments used more energy than did the 50 complete sterilizations of the stainless steel instruments.
(B) More energy was required for each complete sterilization of the nylon instruments than was required to manufacture the nylon instruments.
(C) More nylon instruments than stainless steel instruments were sterilized in the study.
(D) More energy was used to produce the stainless steel instruments than was used to produce the nylon instruments.
(E) The total cost of 50 complete sterilizations of the stainless steel instruments was greater than the cost of manufacturing the stainless steel instruments.

18. A local group had planned a parade for tomorrow, but city hall has not yet acted on its application for a permit. The group had applied for the permit well in advance, had made sure their application satisfied all the requirements, and was clearly entitled to a permit. Although the law prohibits parades without a permit, the group plans to proceed with its parade. The group's leader defended its decision by appealing to the principle that citizens need not refrain from actions that fail to comply with the law if they have made a good-faith effort to comply but are prevented from doing so by government inaction.

Which one of the following actions would be justified by the principle to which the leader of the group appealed in defending the decision to proceed?

(A) A chemical-processing company commissioned an environmental impact report on its plant. The report described foul odors emanating from the plant but found no hazardous wastes being produced. Consequently, the plant did not alter its processing practices.
(B) A city resident applied for rezoning of her property so that she could build a bowling alley in a residential community. She based her application on the need for recreational facilities in the community. Her application was turned down by the zoning board, so she decided to forego construction.
(C) The law requires that no car be operated without a certain amount of insurance coverage. But since the authorities have been unable to design an effective procedure for prosecuting owners of cars that are driven without insurance, many car owners are allowing their insurance to lapse.
(D) A real-estate developer obtained a permit to demolish a historic apartment building that had not yet been declared a governmentally protected historic landmark. Despite the protests of citizens' groups, the developer then demolished the building.
(E) A physician who had been trained in one country applied for a license to practice medicine in another country. Although he knew he met all the qualifications for this license, he had not yet received it one year after he applied for it. He began to practice medicine without the license in the second country despite the law's requirement for a license.

GO ON TO THE NEXT PAGE.

Questions 19–20

A university should not be entitled to patent the inventions of its faculty members. Universities, as guarantors of intellectual freedom, should encourage the free flow of ideas and the general dissemination of knowledge. Yet a university that retains the right to patent the inventions of its faculty members has a motive to suppress information about a potentially valuable discovery until the patent for it has been secured. Clearly, suppressing information concerning such discoveries is incompatible with the university's obligation to promote the free flow of ideas.

19. Which one of the following is an assumption that the argument makes?

(A) Universities are the only institutions that have an obligation to guarantee intellectual freedom.
(B) Most inventions by university faculty members would be profitable if patented.
(C) Publication of reports on research is the only practical way to disseminate information concerning new discoveries.
(D) Universities that have a motive to suppress information concerning discoveries by their faculty members will occasionally act on that motive.
(E) If the inventions of a university faculty member are not patented by that university, then they will be patented by the faculty member instead.

20. The claim that a university should not be entitled to patent the inventions of its faculty members plays which one of the following roles in the argument?

(A) It is the conclusion of the argument.
(B) It is a principle from which the conclusion is derived.
(C) It is an explicit assumption.
(D) It is additional but nonessential information in support of one of the premises.
(E) It is a claim that must be demonstrated to be false in order to establish the conclusion.

21. English and the Austronesian language Mbarbaram both use the word "dog" for canines. These two languages are unrelated, and since speakers of the two languages only came in contact with one another long after the word "dog" was first used in this way in either language, neither language could have borrowed the word from the other. Thus this case shows that sometimes when languages share words that are similar in sound and meaning the similarity is due neither to language relatedness nor to borrowing.

The argument requires that which one of the following be assumed?

(A) English and Mbarbaram share no words other than "dog."
(B) Several languages besides English and Mbarbaram use "dog" as the word for canines.
(C) Usually when two languages share a word, those languages are related to each other.
(D) There is no third language from which both English and Mbarbaram borrowed the word "dog."
(E) If two unrelated languages share a word, speakers of those two languages must have come in contact with one another at some time.

22. Politician: From the time our party took office almost four years ago the number of people unemployed city-wide increased by less than 20 percent. The opposition party controlled city government during the four preceding years, and the number of unemployed city residents rose by over 20 percent. Thus, due to our leadership, fewer people now find themselves among the ranks of the unemployed, whatever the opposition may claim.

The reasoning in the politician's argument is most vulnerable to the criticism that

(A) the claims made by the opposition are simply dismissed without being specified
(B) no evidence has been offered to show that any decline in unemployment over the past four years was uniform throughout all areas of the city
(C) the issue of how much unemployment in the city is affected by seasonal fluctuations is ignored
(D) the evidence cited in support of the conclusion actually provides more support for the denial of the conclusion
(E) the possibility has not been addressed that any increase in the number of people employed is due to programs supported by the opposition party

GO ON TO THE NEXT PAGE.

23. A poor farmer was fond of telling his children: "In this world, you are either rich or poor, and you are either honest or dishonest. All poor farmers are honest. Therefore, all rich farmers are dishonest."

The farmer's conclusion is properly drawn if the argument assumes that

(A) every honest farmer is poor
(B) every honest person is a farmer
(C) everyone who is dishonest is a rich farmer
(D) everyone who is poor is honest
(E) every poor person is a farmer

24. Journalist: Can you give me a summary of the novel you are working on?

Novelist: Well, I assume that by "summary" you mean something brief and not a version of the novel itself. The reason I write novels is that what I want to communicate can be communicated only in the form of a novel. So I am afraid I cannot summarize my novel for you in a way that would tell you what I am trying to communicate with this novel.

Which one of the following exhibits a pattern of reasoning that is most parallel to that used by the novelist?

(A) Only if a drawing can be used as a guide by the builder can it be considered a blueprint. This drawing of the proposed building can be used as a guide by the builder, so it can be considered a blueprint.
(B) Only a statement that does not divulge company secrets can be used as a press release. This statement does not divulge company secrets, but it is uninformative and therefore cannot be used as a press release.
(C) Watching a travelog is not the same as traveling. But a travelog confers some of the benefits of travel without the hardships of travel. So many people just watch travelogs and do not undergo the hardships of travel.
(D) Only a three-dimensional representation of a landscape can convey the experience of being in that landscape. A photograph taken with a traditional camera is not three-dimensional. Therefore a photograph taken with a traditional camera can never convey the experience of being in a landscape.
(E) A banquet menu foretells the content of a meal, but some people collect menus in order to remind themselves of great meals they have eaten. Thus a banquet menu has a function not only before, but also after, a meal has been served.

25. Medical research findings are customarily not made public prior to their publication in a medical journal that has had them reviewed by a panel of experts in a process called peer review. It is claimed that this practice delays public access to potentially beneficial information that, in extreme instances, could save lives. Yet prepublication peer review is the only way to prevent erroneous and therefore potentially harmful information from reaching a public that is ill equipped to evaluate medical claims on its own. Therefore, waiting until a medical journal has published the research findings that have passed peer review is the price that must be paid to protect the public from making decisions based on possibly substandard research.

The argument assumes that

(A) unless medical research findings are brought to peer review by a medical journal, peer review will not occur
(B) anyone who does not serve on a medical review panel does not have the necessary knowledge and expertise to evaluate medical research findings
(C) the general public does not have access to the medical journals in which research findings are published
(D) all medical research findings are subjected to prepublication peer review
(E) peer review panels are sometimes subject to political and professional pressures that can make their judgments less than impartial

S T O P

IF YOU FINISH BEFORE TIME IS CALLED, YOU MAY CHECK YOUR WORK ON THIS SECTION ONLY. DO NOT WORK ON ANY OTHER SECTION IN THE TEST.

SECTION III
Time—35 minutes
24 Questions

Directions: Each group of questions in this section is based on a set of conditions. In answering some of the questions, it may be useful to draw a rough diagram. Choose the response that most accurately and completely answers each question.

Questions 1–7

A florist is making three corsages from four types of flowers: gardenias, orchids, roses, and violets. Each of the corsages will contain exactly three flowers. The nine flowers used in the corsages must include at least one flower from each of the four types, and at least twice as many roses as orchids must be used. The corsages must also meet the following specifications:

Corsage 1 must contain exactly two types of flowers.
Corsage 2 must contain at least one rose.
Corsage 3 must contain at least one gardenia but no orchids.

1. Which one of the following is an acceptable selection of flowers for the three corsages?

	Corsage 1	Corsage 2	Corsage 3
(A)	2 gardenias 1 rose	1 orchid 1 rose 1 violet	1 gardenia 1 orchid 1 violet
(B)	2 orchids 1 rose	2 orchids 1 rose	2 gardenias 1 rose
(C)	2 orchids 1 rose	3 roses	1 gardenia 2 violets
(D)	1 gardenia 1 orchid 1 rose	1 gardenia 1 rose 1 violet	1 gardenia 1 rose 1 violet
(E)	1 orchid 2 roses	3 violets	3 gardenias

2. The maximum total number of roses that can be used in the three corsages is

(A) three
(B) four
(C) five
(D) six
(E) seven

3. If corsage 1 contains two orchids and one rose, what is the maximum total number of violets that the florist can use in making the three corsages?

(A) one
(B) two
(C) three
(D) four
(E) five

4. If corsage 2 is exactly the same as corsage 3, the nine flowers used in the corsages can include exactly

(A) two orchids
(B) three gardenias
(C) three roses
(D) five roses
(E) five violets

5. If two of the corsages contain at least one orchid each, then the flowers in corsage 2 must include at least

(A) one gardenia and one orchid
(B) one gardenia and one rose
(C) one orchid and one rose
(D) one orchid and one violet
(E) one rose and one violet

6. If the greatest possible number of violets is used in the three corsages, the florist must use

(A) exactly one rose and exactly one gardenia
(B) exactly one orchid and exactly four violets
(C) exactly two orchids
(D) exactly two roses
(E) exactly six violets

7. If corsage 1 contains at least one gardenia and at least one violet, and if corsage 3 contains three different types of flowers, which one of the following could be used to make corsage 2?

(A) one rose, one orchid, and one gardenia
(B) one rose and two orchids
(C) one rose and two violets
(D) two roses and one gardenia
(E) two roses and one violet

GO ON TO THE NEXT PAGE.

Questions 8–13

From a group of seven people—J, K, L, M, N, P, and Q—exactly four will be selected to attend a diplomat's retirement dinner. Selection must conform to the following conditions:

Either J or K must be selected, but J and K cannot both be selected.
Either N or P must be selected, but N and P cannot both be selected.
N cannot be selected unless L is selected.
Q cannot be selected unless K is selected.

8. Which one of the following could be the four people selected to attend the retirement dinner?

(A) J, K, M, P
(B) J, L, N, Q
(C) J, M, N, Q
(D) K, M, P, Q
(E) L, M, N, P

9. Among the people selected to attend the retirement dinner there must be

(A) K or Q or both
(B) L or M or both
(C) N or M or both
(D) N or Q or both
(E) P or Q or both

10. Which one of the following is a pair of people who CANNOT both be selected to attend the retirement dinner?

(A) J and N
(B) J and Q
(C) K and L
(D) K and N
(E) N and Q

11. If M is not selected to attend the retirement dinner, the four people selected to attend must include which one of the following pairs of people?

(A) J and Q
(B) K and L
(C) K and P
(D) L and P
(E) N and Q

12. If P is not selected to attend the retirement dinner, then exactly how many different groups of four are there each of which would be an acceptable selection?

(A) one
(B) two
(C) three
(D) four
(E) five

13. There is only one acceptable group of four that can be selected to attend the retirement dinner if which one of the following pairs of people is selected?

(A) J and L
(B) K and M
(C) L and N
(D) L and Q
(E) M and Q

GO ON TO THE NEXT PAGE.

Questions 14–18

Three boys—Karl, Luis, and Miguel—and three girls—Rita, Sarah, and Tura—are giving a dance recital. Three dances—1, 2, and 3—are to be performed. Each dance involves three pairs of children, a boy and a girl partnering each other in each pair, according to the following conditions:

Karl partners Sarah in either dance 1 or dance 2.
Whoever partners Rita in dance 2 must partner Sarah in dance 3.
No two children can partner each other in more than one dance.

14. If Sarah partners Luis in dance 3, which one of the following is a complete and accurate list of the girls any one of whom could partner Miguel in dance 1?

(A) Rita
(B) Sarah
(C) Tura
(D) Rita, Sarah
(E) Rita, Tura

15. If Miguel partners Rita in dance 2, which one of the following could be true?

(A) Karl partners Tura in dance 1.
(B) Luis partners Sarah in dance 2.
(C) Luis partners Sarah in dance 3.
(D) Miguel partners Sarah in dance 1.
(E) Miguel partners Tura in dance 3.

16. If Miguel partners Sarah in dance 1, which one of the following is a pair of children who must partner each other in dance 3?

(A) Karl and Rita
(B) Karl and Tura
(C) Luis and Rita
(D) Luis and Tura
(E) Miguel and Tura

17. If Luis partners Sarah in dance 2, which one of the following is a pair of children who must partner each other in dance 1?

(A) Karl and Rita
(B) Karl and Tura
(C) Luis and Rita
(D) Luis and Tura
(E) Miguel and Rita

18. If Miguel partners Rita in dance 1, which one of the following must be true?

(A) Karl partners Rita in dance 2.
(B) Karl partners Sarah in dance 3.
(C) Karl partners Tura in dance 1.
(D) Luis partners Rita in dance 2.
(E) Luis partners Tura in dance 3.

GO ON TO THE NEXT PAGE.

Questions 19–24

Six cities are located within the numbered areas as follows:

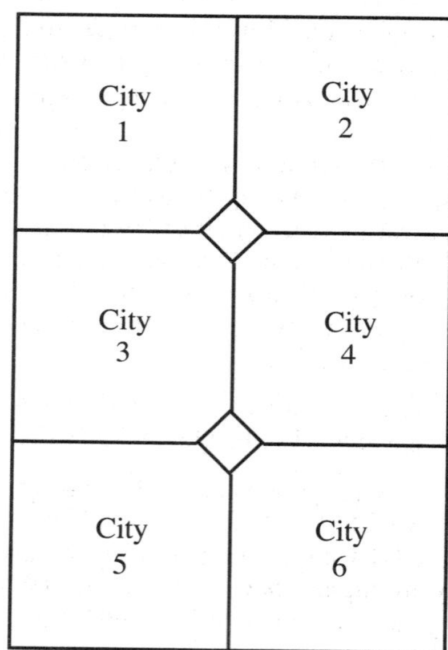

Within the six-city area there are exactly four hospitals, two jails, and two universities. These eight institutions are located as follows:

No institution is in more than one of the cities.
None of the cities contains more than one jail, and none contains more than one university.
None of the cities contains both a jail and a university.
Each jail is located in a city that contains at least one hospital.
The universities are located in two cities that do not share a common boundary.
City 3 contains a university, and city 6 contains a jail.

19. Which one of the following could be true?
    (A) City 5 contains a university.
    (B) City 6 contains a university.
    (C) City 2 contains a jail.
    (D) City 3 contains a jail.
    (E) City 3 contains a hospital.

20. Which one of the following could be true?
    (A) City 1 contains exactly one hospital.
    (B) City 1 contains exactly one university.
    (C) City 2 contains exactly one jail.
    (D) City 5 contains exactly one university.
    (E) City 6 contains exactly one university.

21. Which one of the following is a complete and accurate list of the cities any one of which could contain the jail that is not in city 6?
    (A) 1, 4
    (B) 2, 4
    (C) 4, 5
    (D) 1, 4, 5
    (E) 1, 2, 4, 5

22. If each of the six cities contains at least one of the eight institutions, then which one of the following must be true?
    (A) There is a jail in city 1.
    (B) There is a hospital in city 2.
    (C) There is a hospital in city 3.
    (D) There is a hospital in city 4.
    (E) There is a jail in city 4.

23. In which one of the following cities must there be fewer than three hospitals?
    (A) 1
    (B) 2
    (C) 4
    (D) 5
    (E) 6

24. If one of the cities contains exactly two hospitals and exactly one university, then which one of the following lists three cities that might, among them, contain no hospital?
    (A) 1, 3, 5
    (B) 1, 4, 5
    (C) 2, 3, 5
    (D) 2, 4, 6
    (E) 4, 5, 6

S T O P

IF YOU FINISH BEFORE TIME IS CALLED, YOU MAY CHECK YOUR WORK ON THIS SECTION ONLY.
DO NOT WORK ON ANY OTHER SECTION IN THE TEST.

SECTION IV

Time—35 minutes
25 Questions

Directions: The questions in this section are based on the reasoning contained in brief statements or passages. For some questions, more than one of the choices could conceivably answer the question. However, you are to choose the best answer; that is, the response that most accurately and completely answers the question. You should not make assumptions that are by commonsense standards implausible, superfluous, or incompatible with the passage.

1. People who accuse the postal service of incompetence and inefficiency while complaining of the proposed five-cent increase in postal rates do not know a bargain when they see one. Few experiences are more enjoyable than reading a personal letter from a friend. Viewed in this way, postal service is so underpriced that a five-cent increase is unworthy of serious debate.

   The reasoning in the argument is flawed because the argument

   (A) suggests that the postal service is both competent and efficient, but does not establish how competence and efficiency should be measured
   (B) claims that the proposed increase is insignificant but does not say at what level the increase would be worthy of serious debate
   (C) confuses the value of the object delivered with the value of delivering that object
   (D) appeals to an outside authority for support of a premise that should be established by argument
   (E) fails to establish whether or not the critics of the postal service are employees of the postal service

2. When a study of aspirin's ability to prevent heart attacks in humans yielded positive results, researchers immediately submitted those results to a medical journal, which published them six weeks later. Had the results been published sooner, many of the heart attacks that occurred during the delay could have been prevented.

   The conclusion drawn above would be most undermined if it were true that

   (A) the medical journal's staff worked overtime in order to publish the study's results as soon as possible
   (B) studies of aspirin's usefulness in reducing heart attacks in laboratory animals remain inconclusive
   (C) people who take aspirin regularly suffer a higher-than-average incidence of stomach ulcers
   (D) the medical journal's official policy is to publish articles only after an extensive review process
   (E) a person's risk of suffering a heart attack drops only after that person has taken aspirin regularly for two years

3. It might seem that an airline could increase profits by reducing airfares on all its flights in order to encourage discretionary travel and thus fill planes. Offers of across-the-board discount fares have, indeed, resulted in the sale of large numbers of reduced-price tickets. Nevertheless such offers have, in the past, actually cut the airline's profits.

   Which one of the following, if true, most helps to resolve the apparent discrepancy described above?

   (A) Fewer than 10 percent of all air travelers make no attempt to seek out discount fares.
   (B) Fares for trips between a large city and a small city are higher than those for trips between two large cities even when the distances involved are the same.
   (C) Across-the-board discounts in fares tend to decrease revenues on flights that are normally filled, but they fail to attract passengers to unpopular flights.
   (D) Only a small number of people who have never before traveled by air are persuaded to do so on the basis of across-the-board discount fares.
   (E) It is difficult to devise an advertising campaign that makes the public aware of across-the-board discount fares while fully explaining the restrictions applied to those discount fares.

4. Only if the electorate is moral and intelligent will a democracy function well.

   Which one of the following can be logically inferred from the claim above?

   (A) If the electorate is moral and intelligent, then a democracy will function well.
   (B) Either a democracy does not function well or else the electorate is not moral or not intelligent.
   (C) If the electorate is not moral or not intelligent, then a democracy will not function well.
   (D) If a democracy does not function well, then the electorate is not moral or not intelligent.
   (E) It cannot, at the same time, be true that the electorate is moral and intelligent and that a democracy will not function well.

GO ON TO THE NEXT PAGE.

5. Infants younger than six months who have normal hearing can readily distinguish between acoustically similar sounds that are used as part of any language—not only those used in the language spoken by the people who raise them. Young adults can readily distinguish between such sounds only in languages that they regularly use. It is known that the physiological capacity to hear begins to deteriorate after infancy. So the observed difference in the abilities of infants and young adults to distinguish between acoustically similar speech sounds must be the result of the physiological deterioration of hearing.

The reasoning in the argument is flawed because the argument

(A) sets an arbitrary cutoff point of six months for the age below which infants are able to distinguish acoustically similar speech sounds
(B) does not explain the procedures used to measure the abilities of two very different populations
(C) ignores the fact that certain types of speech sounds occur in almost all languages
(D) assumes that what is true of a group of people taken collectively is also true of any individual within that group
(E) takes a factor that might contribute to an explanation of the observed difference as a sufficient explanation for that difference

6. The economies of some industrialized countries face the prospect of large labor shortages in the decades ahead. Meanwhile, these countries will have a vast number of experienced and productive older workers who, as things stand, will be driven from the work force upon reaching the age of sixty-five by the widespread practice of requiring workers to retire at that age. Therefore, if the discriminatory practice of mandatory retirement at age sixty-five were eliminated, the labor shortages facing these economies would be averted.

The argument assumes that

(A) older workers have acquired skills that are extremely valuable and that their younger colleagues lack
(B) workers in industrialized countries are often unprepared to face the economic consequences of enforced idleness
(C) a large number of workers in some industrialized countries would continue working beyond the age of sixty-five if workers in those countries were allowed to do so
(D) mandatory retirement at age sixty-five was first instituted when life expectancy was considerably lower than it is today
(E) a substantial proportion of the population of officially retired workers is actually engaged in gainful employment

7. The incidence in Japan of most types of cancer is remarkably low compared to that in North America, especially considering that Japan has a modern life-style, industrial pollution included. The cancer rates, however, for Japanese people who immigrate to North America and adopt the diet of North Americans approximate the higher cancer rates prevalent in North America.

If the statements above are true, they provide the most support for which one of the following?

(A) The greater the level of industrial pollution in a country, the higher that country's cancer rate will tend to be.
(B) The stress of life in North America is greater than that of life in Japan and predisposes to cancer.
(C) The staple foods of the Japanese diet contain elements that cure cancer.
(D) The relatively low rate of cancer among people in Japan does not result from a high frequency of a protective genetic trait among Japanese people.
(E) The higher cancer rates of Japanese immigrants to North America are caused by fats in the North American diet.

8. A translation invariably reflects the writing style of the translator. Sometimes when a long document needs to be translated quickly, several translators are put to work on the job, each assigned to translate part of the document. In these cases, the result is usually a translation marked by different and often incompatible writing styles. Certain computer programs for language translation that work without the intervention of human translators can finish the job faster than human translators and produce a stylistically uniform translation with an 80 percent accuracy rate. Therefore, when a long document needs to be translated quickly, it is better to use a computer translation program than human translators.

Which one of the following issues would be LEAST important to resolve in evaluating the argument?

(A) whether the problem of stylistic variety in human translation could be solved by giving stylistic guidelines to human translators
(B) whether numerical comparisons of the accuracy of translations can reasonably be made
(C) whether computer translation programs, like human translators, each have their own distinct writing style
(D) whether the computer translation contains errors of grammar and usage that drastically alter the meaning of the text
(E) how the accuracy rate of computer translation programs compares with that of human translators in relation to the users' needs

GO ON TO THE NEXT PAGE.

Questions 9–10

Myrna: People should follow diets in which fat represents no more than 30 percent of total calories, not the 37 percent the average diet in this country contains.

Roland: If everyone in the country followed your recommendation during his or her entire life, just 0.2 percent would lengthen their lives at all, and then only by an average of 3 months. Modifying our diet is not worthwhile. A lifetime of sacrifice spent eating an unappealing low-fat diet is too high a price to pay for the chance of extending that sacrifice for 3 months.

Myrna: But for everyone who dies early from a high-fat diet, many more people suffer from serious chronic diseases because they followed such diets.

9. Myrna responds to Roland by

(A) disputing the correctness of the facts cited by Roland and offering facts that she considers correct
(B) showing that the factors considered by Roland are not the only ones relevant in evaluating her recommendation
(C) demonstrating that the statistics used by Roland to dispute her recommendation are inaccurate
(D) suggesting that Roland's evidence derives from unreliable sources
(E) pointing out that Roland's argument assumes the very proposition it sets out to prove

10. Roland's argument assumes that

(A) it is desirable to live in such a way as to lengthen life as much as possible
(B) a low-fat diet cannot readily be made appealing and satisfying to a person who follows it regularly
(C) diet is the only relevant factor to consider in computing influences on length of life
(D) the difference in tastiness between a diet in which fat represents 30 percent of total calories and one in which it represents 37 percent is not noticeable
(E) not everyone in the country eats the average diet

11. Some critics claim that it is unfair that so many great works of art are housed in huge metropolitan museums, since the populations served by these museums already have access to a wide variety of important artwork. But this criticism is in principle unwarranted because the limited number of masterpieces makes wider distribution of them impractical. Besides, if a masterpiece is to be fully appreciated, it must be seen alongside other works that provide a social and historical context for it.

Which one of the following, if established, could most logically serve as the principle appealed to in the argument countering the critics' claim?

(A) In providing facilities to the public, the goal should be to ensure that as many as possible of those people who could benefit from the facilities are able to do so.
(B) In providing facilities to the public, the goal should be to ensure that the greatest possible number of people gain the greatest benefit possible from them.
(C) It is unreasonable to enforce a redistribution of social goods that involves depriving some members of society of these goods in order to supply others.
(D) For it to be reasonable to criticize an arrangement as unfair, there must be a more equitable arrangement that is practically attainable.
(E) A work of art should be displayed in conditions resembling as closely as possible those in which the work was originally intended to be displayed.

12. Some accountants calculate with simple adding machines, and some use complex computers. One can perform more calculations in less time with a computer than with an adding machine. Therefore, assuming the costs of using the two types of machines are equal, an accountant who uses a computer generally can earn more per hour than an accountant who uses an adding machine.

Which one of the following is an assumption that would make the conclusion in the passage a logical one?

(A) More accountants use computers than use adding machines.
(B) The more hours an accountant spends on the job, the more money he or she will earn.
(C) The more calculations an accountant performs, the more money he or she will earn.
(D) An accountant who uses an adding machine can charge a higher hourly rate than one who uses a computer.
(E) In general, accountants vary in terms of the number of calculations they make and the amount of money they earn.

GO ON TO THE NEXT PAGE.

13. This summer, Jennifer, who has worked at KVZ Manufacturing for just over three years, plans to spend with her family the entire four weeks of paid vacation to which she is entitled this year. Anyone who has worked at KVZ Manufacturing for between one and four years is automatically entitled to exactly three weeks paid vacation each year but can apply up to half of any vacation time that remains unused at the end of one year to the next year's vacation.

    If the statements above are all true, which one of the following must also be true on the basis of them?

    (A) Jennifer did not use two weeks of the paid vacation time to which she was entitled last year.
    (B) If Jennifer continues to work for KVZ Manufacturing, she will only be entitled to three weeks paid vacation next year.
    (C) The majority of KVZ's employees use each year all of the paid vacation time to which they are entitled.
    (D) Last year Jennifer took only one week of the paid vacation time to which she was entitled.
    (E) KVZ Manufacturing sometimes allows extra vacation time to employees who need to spend more time with their families.

14. A careful review of hospital fatalities due to anesthesia during the last 20 years indicates that the most significant safety improvements resulted from better training of anesthetists. Equipment that monitors a patient's oxygen and carbon dioxide levels was not available in most operating rooms during the period under review. Therefore, the increased use of such monitoring equipment in operating rooms will not significantly cut fatalities due to anesthesia.

    A flaw in the argument is that

    (A) the evidence cited to show that one factor led to a certain result is not sufficient to show that a second factor will not also lead to that result
    (B) the reasons given in support of the conclusion presuppose the truth of that conclusion
    (C) the evidence cited to show that a certain factor was absent when a certain result occurred does not show that the absence of that factor caused that result
    (D) the evidence cited in support of the conclusion is inconsistent with other information that is provided
    (E) the reason indicated for the claim that one event caused a second more strongly supports the claim that both events were independent effects of a third event

15. New types of washing machines designed to consume less energy also extract less water from laundry during their final spin cycles than do washing machines that consume somewhat more energy. The wetter the laundry, the more energy required to dry it in an automatic dryer. Thus using these new types of washing machines could result in an overall increase in the energy needed to wash and dry a load of laundry.

    In which one of the following is the pattern of reasoning most parallel to that in the argument above?

    (A) The more skill required to operate a machine, the harder it is to find people able to do it, and thus the more those people must be paid. Therefore, if a factory installs machines that require highly skilled operators, it must be prepared to pay higher wages.
    (B) There are two routes between Centerville and Mapletown, and the scenic route is the longer route. Therefore, a person who is not concerned with how long it will take to travel between Centerville and Mapletown will probably take the scenic route.
    (C) The more people who work in the library's reading room, the noisier the room becomes; and the noisier the working environment, the less efficiently people work. Therefore, when many people are working in the reading room, those people are working less efficiently.
    (D) Pine is a less expensive wood than cedar but is more susceptible to rot. Outdoor furniture made from wood susceptible to rot must be painted with more expensive paint. Therefore, building outdoor furniture from pine rather than cedar could increase the total cost of building and painting the furniture.
    (E) The more weights added to an exercise machine, the greater the muscle strength needed to work out on the machine. Up to a point, using more muscle strength can make a person stronger. Thus an exercise machine with more weights can, but does not necessarily, make a person stronger.

GO ON TO THE NEXT PAGE.

Questions 16–17

G: The group of works exhibited in this year's Metropolitan Art Show reveals a bias in favor of photographers. Equal numbers of photographers, sculptors, and painters submitted works that met the traditional criteria for the show, yet more photographs were exhibited than either sculptures or paintings. As you know, each artist was allowed to submit work in one medium only.

H: How could there have been bias? All submitted works that met the traditional criteria—and only those works—were exhibited in the show.

16. If both G's assertions and H's assertion are true, which one of the following must also be true?

(A) More photographers than sculptors or painters submitted works to be considered for exhibition in the Metropolitan Art Show.
(B) All the works submitted for the Metropolitan Art Show met the traditional criteria for the show.
(C) The quality of photographs exhibited in the Metropolitan Art Show was inferior to the quality of the sculptures or paintings exhibited.
(D) Some of the photographs submitted for the Metropolitan Art Show did not meet the traditional criteria for the show.
(E) More works that met the traditional criteria for the Metropolitan Art Show were submitted by photographers than by sculptors or painters.

17. Which one of the following, if true, most strongly supports G's allegation of bias?

(A) If an artist has had one of his or her works exhibited in the Metropolitan Art Show, that artist has an advantage in getting commissions and selling works over artists who have never had a work exhibited in the show.
(B) The fee for entering photographs in the Metropolitan Art Show was $25 per work submitted, while the fee for each painting or sculpture submitted was $75.
(C) The committee that selected from the submitted works the ones to be exhibited in this year's Metropolitan Art Show had four members: one photographer, one sculptor, one painter, and one who works in all three media but is the least known of the four members.
(D) Reviews of this year's Metropolitan Art Show that appeared in major newspapers and magazines tended to give more coverage to the photographs in the show than to the sculptures and paintings that were exhibited.
(E) In previous years, it has often happened that more paintings or more sculptures were exhibited in the Metropolitan Art Show than photographs, even though the total number of works exhibited each year does not vary widely.

Questions 18–19

Marcus: For most ethical dilemmas the journalist is likely to face, traditional journalistic ethics is clear, adequate, and essentially correct. For example, when journalists have uncovered newsworthy information, they should go to press with it as soon as possible. No delay motivated by the journalists' personal or professional interests is permissible.

Anita: Well, Marcus, of course interesting and important information should be brought before the public—that is a journalist's job. But in the typical case, where a journalist has some information but is in a quandary about whether it is yet important or "newsworthy," this guidance is inadequate.

18. The point made by Anita's statements is most accurately expressed by which one of the following?

(A) Marcus' claim that traditional journalistic ethics is clear for most ethical dilemmas in journalism is incorrect.
(B) A typical case illustrates that Marcus is wrong in claiming that traditional journalistic ethics is essentially correct for most ethical dilemmas in journalism.
(C) The ethical principle that Marcus cites does not help the journalist in a typical kind of situation in which a decision needs to be made.
(D) There are common situations in which a journalist must make a decision and in which no principle of journalistic ethics can be of help.
(E) Traditional journalistic ethics amounts to no more than an unnecessarily convoluted description of the journalist's job.

19. In order to conclude properly from Anita's statements that Marcus' general claim about traditional journalistic ethics is incorrect, it would have to be assumed that

(A) whether a piece of information is or is not newsworthy can raise ethical dilemmas for journalists
(B) there are circumstances in which it would be ethically wrong for a journalist to go to press with legitimately acquired, newsworthy information
(C) the most serious professional dilemmas that a journalist is likely to face are not ethical dilemmas
(D) there are no ethical dilemmas that a journalist is likely to face that would not be conclusively resolved by an adequate system of journalistic ethics
(E) for a system of journalistic ethics to be adequate it must be able to provide guidance in every case in which a journalist must make a professional decision

GO ON TO THE NEXT PAGE.

Questions 20–21

Of every 100 burglar alarms police answer, 99 are false alarms. This situation causes an enormous and dangerous drain on increasingly scarce public resources. Each false alarm wastes an average of 45 minutes of police time. As a result police are consistently taken away from responding to other legitimate calls for service, and a disproportionate share of police service goes to alarm system users, who are mostly businesses and affluent homeowners. However, burglar alarm systems, unlike car alarm systems, are effective in deterring burglaries, so the only acceptable solution is to fine burglar alarm system owners the cost of 45 minutes of police time for each false alarm their systems generate.

20. The statement that burglar alarm systems, unlike car alarm systems, are effective in deterring burglaries plays which one of the following roles in the argument?

(A) It justifies placing more restrictions on owners of burglar alarms than on owners of car alarms.
(B) It provides background information needed to make plausible the claim that the number of burglar alarms police are called on to answer is great enough to be a drain on public resources.
(C) It provides a basis for excluding as unacceptable one obvious alternative to the proposal of fining owners of burglar alarm systems for false alarms.
(D) It gives a reason why police might be more inclined to respond to burglar alarms than to car alarms.
(E) It explains why a disproportionate number of the burglar alarms responded to by police come from alarm systems owned by businesses.

21. On the basis of the premises advanced, which one of the following principles, if established, would provide the most justification for the concluding recommendation?

(A) No segment of a community should be permitted to engage in a practice that has been shown to result in a disproportionate share of police service being devoted to that segment of the community.
(B) When public resources are in short supply, any individual who wants special services from public agencies such as police and fire departments should be required to pay for those services if he or she can afford to do so.
(C) Police departments are not justified in improving service to one segment of the community at the expense of other segments of the community unless doing so reduces the crime level throughout the entire area served.
(D) Anyone who directly benefits from a service provided by public employees should be required to reimburse the general public fund an amount equivalent to the average cost of providing that service.
(E) If receipt of a service results in the waste of scarce public resources and people with other legitimate needs are disadvantaged in consequence, the recipient of that service should compensate the public for the resources wasted.

GO ON TO THE NEXT PAGE.

22. When butterfat was considered nutritious and healthful, a law was enacted requiring that manufacturers use the term "imitation butter" to indicate butter whose butterfat content had been diminished through the addition of water. Today, it is known that the high cholesterol content of butterfat makes it harmful to human health. Since the public should be encouraged to eat foods with lower rather than higher butterfat content and since the term "imitation" with its connotations of falsity deters many people from purchasing products so designated, manufacturers who wish to give reduced-butterfat butter the more appealing name of "lite butter" should be allowed to do so.

Which one of the following, if true, most seriously undermines the argument?

(A) The manufacturers who prefer to use the word "lite" instead of "imitation" are motivated principally by the financial interest of their stockholders.
(B) The manufacturers who wish to call their product "lite butter" plan to change the composition of the product so that it contains more water than it now does.
(C) Some individuals who need to reduce their intake of cholesterol are not deterred from using the reduced-butterfat product by the negative connotations of the term "imitation."
(D) Cholesterol is only one of many factors that contribute to the types of health problems with which the consumption of excessive amounts of cholesterol is often associated.
(E) Most people deterred from eating "imitation butter" because of its name choose alternatives with a lower butterfat content than this product has.

23. Farm animals have certain behavioral tendencies that result from the evolutionary history of these species. By imposing on these animals a type of organization that conflicts with their behavioral tendencies, current farm-management practices cause the animals more pain and distress than do practices that more closely conform to the animals' behavioral tendencies. Because the animals tend to resist this type of organization, current practices can also be less efficient than those other farm-management practices.

If the statements above are true, which one of the following can be properly inferred from them?

(A) Some of the behavioral tendencies of farm animals can be altered by efficient farm-management practices.
(B) In order to implement efficient farm-management practices, it is necessary to be familiar with the evolutionary history of farm animals.
(C) In order to create farm-management practices that cause less pain and distress to farm animals, a significant loss of efficiency will be required.
(D) Farm-management practices that cause the least amount of pain and distress to farm animals are also the most efficient management practices.
(E) Some changes in farm-management practices that lessen the pain and distress experienced by farm animals can result in gains in efficiency.

GO ON TO THE NEXT PAGE.

24. It now seems clear that the significant role initially predicted for personal computers in the classroom has not become fact. One need only look to the dramatic decline in sales of computers for classroom use in the past year for proof that the fad has passed. Which one of the following arguments contains flawed reasoning parallel to that in the argument above?

(A) Clearly, government legislation mandating the reduction of automobile emissions has been at least partially successful, as is demonstrated by the fact that the air of the 20 largest cities now contains smaller amounts of the major pollutants mentioned in the legislation than it did before the legislation was passed.
(B) Mechanical translation from one language into another, not merely in narrow contexts such as airline reservations but generally, is clearly an idea whose time has come. Since experts have been working on the problem for 40 years, it is now time for the accumulated expertise to achieve a breakthrough.
(C) Sales of computers for home use will never reach the levels optimistically projected by manufacturers. The reason is that home use was envisioned as encompassing tasks, such as menu planning and checkbook reconciliation, that most homemakers perform in much simpler ways than using a computer would require.
(D) It is apparent that consumers have tired of microwave ovens as quickly as they initially came to accept this recent invention. In contrast to several years of increasing sales following the introduction of microwave ovens, sales of microwave ovens flattened last year, indicating that consumers have found relatively little use for these devices.
(E) Creating incentives for a particular kind of investment inevitably engenders boom-and-bust cycles. The evidence is in the recent decline in the value of commercial real estate, which shows that, although the government can encourage people to put up buildings, it cannot guarantee that those buildings will be fully rented or sold.

25. Scientists attempting to replicate certain controversial results reported by a group of experienced researchers failed to get the same results as those reported. The conclusion drawn from this by the scientists who conducted the replication experiments was that the originally reported results had been due to faulty measurements.

The argument of the scientists who conducted the replication experiments assumes that

(A) the original experiments had not been described in sufficient detail to make an exact replication possible
(B) the fact that the originally reported results aroused controversy made it highly likely that they were in error
(C) the theoretical principles called into question by the originally reported results were themselves based on weak evidence
(D) the replication experiments were not so likely as the original experiments to be marred by faulty measurements
(E) the researchers who originally reported the controversial results had themselves observed those results only once

STOP

IF YOU FINISH BEFORE TIME IS CALLED, YOU MAY CHECK YOUR WORK ON THIS SECTION ONLY. DO NOT WORK ON ANY OTHER SECTION IN THE TEST.

Test III

Answers

Section I

1.	B	7.	C	13.	B	19.	B	25.	E
2.	A	8.	A	14.	B	20.	B	26.	C
3.	D	9.	A	15.	D	21.	C	27.	E
4.	E	10.	C	16.	C	22.	D		
5.	C	11.	B	17.	A	23.	C		
6.	E	12.	A	18.	D	24.	C		

Section II

1.	A	6.	C	11.	E	16.	A	21.	D
2.	D	7.	D	12.	A	17.	B	22.	D
3.	B	8.	D	13.	D	18.	E	23.	A
4.	B	9.	A	14.	C	19.	D	24.	D
5.	D	10.	B	15.	B	20.	A	25.	A

Section III

1.	C	6.	D	11.	B	16.	B	21.	D
2.	D	7.	A	12.	C	17.	C	22.	D
3.	B	8.	D	13.	E	18.	D	23.	B
4.	A	9.	B	14.	D	19.	E	24.	A
5.	C	10.	B	15.	B	20.	A		

Section IV

1.	C	6.	C	11.	D	16.	E	21.	E
2.	E	7.	D	12.	C	17.	B	22.	E
3.	C	8.	C	13.	A	18.	C	23.	E
4.	C	9.	B	14.	A	19.	A	24.	D
5.	E	10.	B	15.	D	20.	C	25.	D

Score Conversion Chart

Directions:

1. Use the Scoring Worksheet below to compute your raw score.

2. Use the Score Conversion Chart to convert your raw score into the 120–180 scale.

Scoring Worksheet

1. Enter the number of questions you answered correctly in each section.

	Number Correct
SECTION I	______
SECTION II....................	______
SECTION III	______
SECTION IV	______

2. Enter the sum here: ______

This is your Raw Score

Conversion Chart

For Converting Raw Score to the 120-180 LSAT Scaled Score

Reported Score	Raw Score Lowest	Raw Score Highest
180	98	101
179	97	97
178	96	96
177	95	95
176	94	94
175	93	93
174	92	92
173	90	91
172	89	89
171	88	88
170	86	87
169	85	85
168	83	84
167	82	82
166	80	81
165	78	79
164	77	77
163	75	76
162	73	74
161	71	72
160	70	70
159	68	69
158	66	67
157	64	65
156	63	63
155	61	62
154	59	60
153	58	58
152	56	57
151	54	55
150	53	53
149	51	52
148	49	50
147	48	48
146	46	47
145	45	45
144	43	44
143	42	42
142	40	41
141	39	39
140	37	38
139	36	36
138	35	35
137	33	34
136	32	32
135	31	31
134	29	30
133	28	28
132	27	27
131	26	26
130	25	25
129	24	24
128	23	23
127	22	22
126	21	21
125	20	20
124	19	19
123	18	18
122	17	17
121	—*	—*
120	0	16

* There is no raw score that will produce this scaled score for this form.

Test III
Section I
Solutions

Questions 1–6

1. (A) No. This is too strong—there may be other factors that drive progress in art. The passage merely argues against viewing technology as a threat to art.
(B) Yes. This is the gist of the final paragraph, where the author points out that photography was a boon to painting because it opened new perspectives to viewing the world: *"Since photos can capture the 'moments' of a movement, such as a hand partially raised in a gesture of greeting, Impressionist artists were inspired to paint such moments in order to more effectively convey the quality of spontaneous human action."* Further, *"since photography preempted painting as the means of obtaining portraits, painters had more freedom to vary their subject matter, thus giving rise to the abstract creations characteristic of modern art."*
(C) No. These sentiments are expressed in the opening lines of paragraph two, but there the author is summarizing the arguments of her detractors. Her opinion is expressed at the end of paragraph two: *"In fact, technology has traditionally assisted our capacity for creative expression and can refine our notions of any given art form."*
(D) No. Although this is a natural deduction from the passage, it is not the main idea. Rather, the point of the passage is that technology will not negatively affect the way the public responds to art.
(E) No. The historical references are made merely to illustrate the main idea.

2. (A) Yes. The opponents of the use of new technology in art value live performances: *"...musicians would be deprived of the opportunity to spontaneously change pieces of music before live audiences. Some even worry that technology will eliminate live performance altogether."* Furthermore, the author apparently values live performances: *"But these negative views assume ... that we are not committed enough to the artistic enterprise to preserve the live performance."*
(B) No. This statement is contradicted by the sentence *"But these negative views assume both that technology poses an unprecedented challenge to the arts and that we are not committed enough to the artistic enterprise to preserve the live performance, <u>assumptions that seem unnecessarily cynical.</u>"*
(C) No. The author holds that new technology is a boon, not a challenge, to art.
(D) No. This is the author's opinion. And since her opponents *"claim that technology subverts the artistic enterprise,"* it is reasonable to assume they believe that technology has subverted art in the past.
(E) No. The point of the passage is that the arts are invigorated by technological innovation, not made vulnerable by it.

3. (A) No. The opponents fear that the loss of live performances will deprive artists of *"the opportunity to spontaneously change pieces of music before live audiences"* and *"abolish the relationship between performer and audience."* Although increased knowledge about different performing artists may be beneficial, this would not alleviate the opponents' concerns.
(B) No. This could support the opponents' position. Those people who *"feel comfortable responding spontaneously to artistic performances when they are viewing recordings of those performances at home"* may become less inclined to attend live performances.
(C) No. The opponents fear that the loss of live performances will deprive artists of *"the opportunity to spontaneously change pieces of music before live audiences"* and *"abolish the relationship between performer and audience."* Although artists may benefit financially if sales of their recordings increase, this would not alleviate the opponents' concerns.
(D) Yes. If recordings and other products of technology attract new people to live performances, then the opponents' concerns that *"technology [may] eliminate live performance altogether"* will prove unfounded.
(E) No. Opponents are concerned that *"The originality of musical performance, ... might suffer, as musicians [are] deprived of the ability to spontaneously change pieces of music before live audiences."* If recordings are less spontaneous than live performances, opponents would presumably conclude that recorded performances are less original and therefore less valuable.

4. (A) No. The example of the Steadicam™ is used to illustrate the statement *"Such new technologies create new ways of seeing and hearing by adding different dimensions to older forms, <u>rather than replacing those forms.</u>"*
(B) No. Although the Steadicam™ may be *"an uncomplicated device,"* this is of less concern to the author than the fact that new technology may offer new ways of viewing and achieving art.
(C) No. The author never mentions that the interaction of art and technology will change attitudes toward technology.
(D) No. Although the author would probably agree with this statement, it is not why the example of the Steadicam™ is introduced.
(E) Yes. The example of the Steadicam™ is used to illustrate the statement *"Such new technologies create new ways of seeing and hearing by adding different dimensions to older forms, <u>rather than replacing those forms.</u>"*

5. (A) No. This is not mentioned in the passage.
(B) No. This is not mentioned in the passage.
(C) Yes. This is a paraphrase of the statement *"Such new technologies create new ways of seeing and hearing by adding different dimensions to older forms, rather than replacing those forms."*
(D) No. This is not mentioned in the passage.
(E) No. Although modern dance is used to illustrate a benefit of new technology, the passage does not state or imply that modern dance benefits most from new technology.

6. (A) No. The passage is discussing the effects of technology, not the results of artistic experiments.
(B) No. This knowledge gave rise to a more accurate view of the world, not a more abstract view. *"Impressionist artists like Degas studied the elements of light and movement captured by instantaneous photography and used their new understanding of the way our perceptions distort reality to try to more accurately capture reality in their work."*
(C) No. This is too strong. Notice the absolute word "exclusively."
(D) No. The passage implies that it was photography that begat abstract art.
(E) Yes. This is the thrust of the closing line of the passage *"Finally, since photography preempted painting as the means of obtaining portraits, painters had more freedom to vary their subject matter, thus giving rise to the abstract creations characteristic of modern art."* Abstract art does not rely on the literal depiction of objects.

Questions 7–13

7. (A) No. The policy of readjustment *"encouraged the assimilation of Native Americans as individuals into mainstream society."* A tribal system would not be part of mainstream society.
(B) No. The policy of readjustment *"encouraged the assimilation of Native Americans as individuals into mainstream society."* Preserving Native American language would work against assimilation.
(C) Yes. The policy of readjustment *"encouraged the assimilation of Native Americans as individuals into mainstream society."*
(D) No. The policy of readjustment *"encouraged the assimilation of Native Americans as individuals into mainstream society."*
(E) No. The policy of readjustment *"encouraged the assimilation of Native Americans as individuals into mainstream society."*

8. (A) Yes. This is stated in the last paragraph: *"As a result of the 1956 meeting, the Oneida rejected readjustment. Instead, they determined to improve tribal life by lobbying for federal monies for postsecondary education, for the improvement of drainage on tribal lands, and for the building of a convalescent home for tribal members."*
(B) No. This is not mentioned in the passage.
(C) No. This is not mentioned in the passage.
(D) No. This is not mentioned in the passage.
(E) No. This is not mentioned in the passage.

9. (A) Yes. As is often the case with reading passages, the first paragraph sets the stage for the discussion to follow. It presents two opposing social policies without indicating a preference.
(B) No. The first paragraph does present two conflicting positions. However, the rest of the passage recounts an example illustrating the conflict rather than defending one position as better than the other.
(C) No. The first paragraph introduces two policies for Native American relations. These are distinct social policies, not interpretations of a historical conflict. Furthermore, the passage does not compare the policies.
(D) No. There is no analysis nor prediction in the first paragraph. It is merely introducing two competing social movements.
(E) No. The first paragraph merely outlines the relationship between the Bureau of Indian Affairs and the Oneida tribe in the 1940s and 1950s. It does not outline the history of the BIA.

10. (A) No. The passage does not mention any social phenomena other than the readjustment movement.
(B) No. *"...the increased awareness of civil rights in these decades helped reinforce the belief that life on reservations prevented Native Americans from exercising [their Constitutional] rights...."* As this belief grew, the U.S. Government proposed a change in its policies toward Native Americans. However, the passage does not say that this belief influenced the position of the Native American leaders.
(C) Yes. It shows that the "readjustment" policy was probably well meaning: *"Because the increased awareness of civil rights in these decades helped reinforce the belief that life on reservations prevented Native Americans from exercising the rights guaranteed to citizens under the United States Constitution, the readjustment movement advocated the end of the federal government's involvement in Native American affairs and encouraged the assimilation of Native Americans as individuals into mainstream society."*
(D) No. This is the second-best choice. The passage does explain the impetus for the readjustment movement, but not necessarily the motives of the BIA bureaucrat. They may have been merely following social trends or they may have been in the vanguard of the movement. We can't determine from the passage.
(E) No. The final paragraph makes it clear that the author opposes the policy. The author refers to the increased awareness of civil rights in order to set the

tone of passage: that the "readjustment" policy was probably well meaning, but wrong.

11. (A) No. The purpose of the readjustment policy was to assimilate Native Americans into mainstream society. That is, to encourage Native Americans to move off the reservations.
(B) Yes. The purpose of the readjustment policy was to assimilate Native Americans into mainstream society.
(C) No. The purpose of the readjustment policy was to assimilate Native Americans into mainstream society. Once assimilated, they would receive no more government services than other assimilated groups.
(D) No. The purpose of the readjustment policy was to assimilate Native Americans into mainstream society and to reduce the Federal Government's involvement.
(E) No. The passage indicates that proponents of the readjustment policy advocated changing the nature of the Canandaigua Treaty between the Federal Government and the Oneida.

12. (A) Yes. *"The Oneida were then offered a one-time lump-sum payment of $60,000 in lieu of the $0.52 annuity guaranteed in perpetuity to each member of the tribe under the Canandaigua Treaty.... Finally, the offer of a lump-sum payment was unanimously opposed by the Oneida delegates, who saw that changing the terms of a treaty might jeopardize the many pending land claims based upon the treaty."*
(B) No. It granted them certain rights and privileges: *"The Oneida were then offered a one-time lump-sum payment of $60,000 in lieu of the $0.52 annuity guaranteed in perpetuity to each member of the tribe under the Canandaigua Treaty.... Finally, the offer of a lump-sum payment was unanimously opposed by the Oneida delegates, who saw that changing the terms of a treaty might jeopardize the many pending land claims based upon the treaty."*
(C) No. Presumably, the Oneida already had such an agreement with the Federal Government as specified by the Treaty. The Government hoped to change the provisions of the Treaty.
(D) No. Recognition of independent status is not mentioned in the passage.
(E) No. They saw it as valuable and relevant: *"the offer of a lump-sum payment was unanimously opposed by the Oneida delegates, who saw that changing the terms of a treaty might jeopardize the many pending land claims based upon the treaty."*

13. (A) No. In rejecting the scholarship, the student did not retain benefits that had already been granted by the university. However, in rejecting readjustment, the Oneida tribe still retained the benefits that had already been granted by the Canandaigua Treaty.
(B) Yes. The company offered a bonus to the employee if he would retire (in lieu of his regular salary), but acceptance of the offer might harm his position in his pending worker's compensation suit. Similarly, *"The Oneida were then offered a one-time lump-sum payment of $60,000 in lieu of the $0.52 annuity guaranteed in perpetuity to each member of the tribe under the Canandaigua Treaty.... The offer of a lump-sum payment was unanimously opposed by the Oneida delegates, who saw that changing the terms of a treaty might jeopardize the many pending land claims based upon the treaty."*
(C) No. The teenager still received payment. However, the Oneida tribe forfeited the $60,000.
(D) No. The customer received proportionate compensation for the $500. However, the Oneida tribe forfeited the $60,000 without any other compensation.
(E) No. This is a good answer; but choice (B) more closely parallels the passage.

Questions 14–20

14. (A) No. The passage argues against the claim that literacy gave rise to democratic institutions in ancient Greece, but does not state that the traditions and conventions of a society give rise to democratic institutions.
(B) Yes. The main idea of the passage is summed up in the closing line: *"Athens, insofar as it functioned as a democracy, did so not because of widespread literacy, but because the elite had chosen to accept democratic institutions."*
(C) No. The passage does imply that the medieval Church guarded access to the Latin Bible by discouraging its translation it into everyday language. However, this is not the main idea of the passage. The passage argues against Goody's claim that literacy contributed to the rise of democratic institutions in ancient Greece.
(D) No. Though this may be true, it is not mentioned in the passage.
(E) No. This is not mentioned in the passage.

15. (A) No. In fact, the author implies that knowing a society's literacy rate does not help determine its degree of political advancement: *"Direct observation of contemporary societies at the threshold of widespread literacy has not assisted our understanding of how such literacy altered ancient Greek society, in particular its political culture."*
(B) No. This is too strong. From the passage, we can only say that literate people do not necessarily have access to politically important documents and books. The passage does not discuss how literacy may assist people in other areas of life—for example, business and health.
(C) No. The passage never discusses the rate of increase or decrease in literacy.

(D) Yes. This follows from the second sentence: *"The discovery of what Goody has called the 'enabling effects' of literacy in contemporary societies tends to seduce the observer into confusing often rudimentary knowledge of how to read with popular access to important books and documents; this confusion is then projected onto ancient societies."*
(E) No. In fact, the passage states that *"in Athens the juries were representative of a broad spectrum of the population, and these juries, drawn from diverse social classes, both interpreted what they had heard and determined matters of fact."*

16. (A) No. The passage indicates that contemporary societies, like ancient societies, depend heavily on the knowledge of experts: *"People today also rely heavily on a truly knowledgeable minority for information and its interpretation."*
(B) No. The passage does not state or imply that contemporary popular literature often contains specious information.
(C) Yes. *"Granted, people today also rely heavily on a truly knowledgeable minority for information and its interpretation, often transmitted orally. Yet this is still fundamentally different from an ancient society in which there was no "popular literature," i.e., no newspapers, magazines, or other media that dealt with sociopolitical issues.... When fundamental documents are accessible for study only to an elite, the rest of the society is subject to the elite's interpretation of the rules of behavior, including right political behavior."*
(D) No. The passage does not discuss how people become members of the governing elite.
(E) No. The passage does not state or imply that a certain level of educational achievement is attainable only by a contemporary elite.

17. (A) Yes. *"True, in Athens the juries were representative of a broad spectrum of the population, and these juries, drawn from diverse social classes, both interpreted what they had heard and determined matters of fact."*
(B) No. *"Even in Greek courts the juries heard only the relevant statutes read out during the proceedings, as they heard verbal testimony, and they then rendered their verdict on the spot, without the benefit of any discussion among themselves."*
(C) No. *"True, in Athens the juries were representative of a broad spectrum of the population, and these juries, drawn from diverse social classes, both interpreted what they had heard and determined matters of fact."*
(D) No. *"True, in Athens the juries were representative of a broad spectrum of the population, and these juries, drawn from diverse social classes, both interpreted what they had heard and determined matters of fact. However, they were guided solely by the speeches prepared for the parties by professional pleaders and by the quotations of laws or decrees within the speeches, rather than by their own access to any kind of document or book."*
(E) No. *"Even in Greek courts the juries heard only the relevant statutes read out during the proceedings, as they heard verbal testimony, and they then rendered their verdict on the spot, without the benefit of any discussion among themselves."*

18. (A) No. The author implies that others, such as Goody, have mistakenly labeled ancient Greek society the "law-giver" merely because it had a set of written laws. But, according to the author, this was not enough to break the power monopoly of the old aristocracy. People must also control interpretation of the laws. This is illustrated by the following sentence *"But the application and efficacy of all law codes depend on their interpretation by magistrates and courts, and unless the right of interpretation is 'democratized,' the mere existence of written laws changes little."*
(B) No. The author implies that others, such as Goody, have mistakenly labeled ancient Greek society the "law-giver" merely because it had a set of written laws. But according to the author this was not enough to break the power monopoly of the old aristocracy. People must also control interpretation of the laws. This is illustrated by the following sentence *"But the application and efficacy of all law codes depend on their interpretation by magistrates and courts, and unless the right of interpretation is 'democratized,' the mere existence of written laws changes little."*
(C) No. The author implies that others, such as Goody, have mistakenly labeled ancient Greek society the "law-giver" merely because it had a set of written laws. But according to the author this was not enough to break the power monopoly of the old aristocracy. People must also control interpretation of the laws. This is illustrated by the following sentence *"But the application and efficacy of all law codes depend on their interpretation by magistrates and courts, and unless the right of interpretation is 'democratized,' the mere existence of written laws changes little."*
(D) Yes. The author implies that others, such as Goody, have mistakenly labeled ancient Greek society the "law-giver" merely because it had a set of written laws. But according to the author this was not enough to break the power monopoly of the old aristocracy. People must also control interpretation of the laws. This is illustrated by the following sentence *"But the application and efficacy of all law codes depend on their interpretation by magistrates and courts, and unless the right of interpretation is 'democratized,' the mere existence of written laws changes little."*
(E) No. The myth the author refers to is the modern interpretation that sees the early written code of law as the catalyst for democracy in Athens.

19. (A) No. Although both the Latin Bible and the early law codes were inaccessible to most members of the societies, the authority of these documents was not due to their inaccessibility.
(B) Yes. The Latin Bible is referred to as a "closed book" because only the elite who studied Latin were able to read it. Similarly, the legal documents in ancient Greek society were read only by the elite.
(C) No. Like ancient law codes, the Latin Bible was inaccessible to most people. However, the passage does not discuss the similarities in the misinterpretations of these types of documents.
(D) No. Although this answer-choice may be true, the analogy is drawn between the Latin Bible and an early law code in order to illustrate how an influential document can be inaccessible to most people.
(E) No. The passage does state that the Latin Bible was inaccessible because it was not written in the common language. However, the passage does not state that ancient law codes were not written in the common language.

20. (A) No. The passage is criticizing attempts to compare the effects of literacy on modern societies to its effects on ancient societies. This is indicated by the opening sentence: *"Direct observation of contemporary societies at the threshold of widespread literacy* has not assisted our understanding of how such literacy altered ancient Greek society, *in particular its political culture."*
(B) Yes. The passage is criticizing attempts to compare the effects of literacy on modern societies to its effects on ancient societies. This is indicated by the opening sentence: *"Direct observation of contemporary societies at the threshold of widespread literacy* has not assisted our understanding of how such literacy altered ancient Greek society, *in particular its political culture."*
(C) No. The passage is criticizing attempts to compare the effects of literacy on modern societies to its effects on ancient societies. This is indicated by the opening sentence: *"Direct observation of contemporary societies at the threshold of widespread literacy* has not assisted our understanding of how such literacy altered ancient Greek society, *in particular its political culture."* The passage is not concerned with understanding the relationship between ancient and modern societies but with the problem of using modern societies to understand an ancient society.
(D) No. The passage is criticizing attempts to compare the effects of literacy on modern societies to its effects on ancient societies. This is indicated by the opening sentence: *"Direct observation of contemporary societies at the threshold of widespread literacy* has not assisted our understanding of how such literacy altered ancient Greek society, *in particular its political culture."* The passage is not so directed toward developing a method to understand ancient societies as it is toward criticizing one particular method.
(E) No. The passage is criticizing attempts to compare the effects of literacy on modern societies to its effects on ancient societies. This is indicated by the opening sentence: *"Direct observation of contemporary societies at the threshold of widespread literacy* has not assisted our understanding of how such literacy altered ancient Greek society, *in particular its political culture."* Though it may be true that ancient societies are difficult to understand, the passage is a critique of one particular method used to understand the effects of literacy on these societies.

Questions 21–27

21. (A) No. The passage does imply the colonials thought they shared a common political vocabulary with the English: *"Steeped as they were in the English political language, these colonials failed to observe that their experience in America had given the words a significance quite different from that accepted by the English with whom they debated; in fact, they claimed that they were more loyal to the English political tradition than were the English in England."* However, there is no indication in the passage that the English thought they shared a common political vocabulary with the colonials.
(B) No. Although the passage points out that they shared many political institutions, the main point of the passage is that they viewed the institutions differently.
(C) Yes. This is summed up by the sentence, *"To the English the word 'constitution' meant the whole body of law and legal custom formulated since the beginning of the kingdom, whereas to these colonials a constitution was a specific written document, enumerating specific powers."*
(D) No. The passage does not state that Colonial attitudes toward English institutions were hostile.
(E) No. In fact, seventeenth-century English legal development diverged from colonial attitudes toward constitutions. *"English legal development from the early seventeenth century had been moving steadily toward the absolute power of Parliament,"* while *"the citizens of these colonies ...[did not] concede that their own assemblies possessed such wide powers."*

22. (A) No. *"In both England and these colonies, only property holders could vote."*
(B) No. *"Moreover, each of these colonies enjoyed a representative assembly, which was consciously modeled, in powers and practices, after the English Parliament."*
(C) No. *"By the middle of the eighteenth century,* all of these colonies except four were headed by Royal Governors *appointed by the King and perceived as*

bearing a relation to the people of the colony similar to that of the King to the English people."
(D) Yes. This problem is best solved by elimination:

Choice (A) is supported by the passage: *"In both England and these colonies, only property holders could vote."*
Choice (B) is supported by the passage: *"Moreover, each of these colonies enjoyed a representative assembly, which was consciously modeled, in powers and practices, after the English Parliament."*
Choice (C) is supported by the passage: *"By the middle of the eighteenth century, all of these colonies except four were headed by Royal Governors appointed by the King and perceived as bearing a relation to the people of the colony similar to that of the King to the English people."*
Choice (E) is supported by the passage: *"By the middle of the eighteenth century, all of these colonies except four were headed by Royal Governors appointed by the King and perceived as bearing a relation to the people of the colony similar to that of the King to the English people."*

Hence, by process of elimination, the answer is (D).
(E) No. *"By the middle of the eighteenth century, all of these colonies except four were headed by Royal Governors appointed by the King and perceived as bearing a relation to the people of the colony similar to that of the King to the English people."*

23. (A) No. The passage implies that the Parliament existed before the seventeenth century but was less powerful then.
(B) No. This is not stated or implied by the passage.
(C) Yes. *"For example, English legal development from the early seventeenth century had been moving steadily toward the absolute power of Parliament. The most unmistakable sign of this tendency was the legal assertion that the King was subject to the law."*
(D) No. Just the opposite is implied. Since Parliament became more powerful in the seventeenth and eighteenth centuries, it would have then been better able to institute legal reforms.
(E) No. This is not stated or implied by the passage.

24. (A) No. This contradicts the passage: *"By the eighteenth century the English had accepted the idea that the parliamentary representatives of the people were omnipotent."*
(B) No. This is not stated in the passage.
(C) Yes. *"Together with this resolute denial of the absolute right of kings went the assertion that Parliament was unlimited in its power: it could change even the Constitution by its ordinary acts of legislation."*
(D) No. This is not stated in the passage.
(E) No. This is not stated in the passage.

25. (A) No. They were unaware that they gave different values to political terms than did the English: *"Steeped as they were in the English political language, these colonials failed to observe that their experience in America had given the words a significance quite different from that accepted by the English with whom they debated ..."*
(B) No. Although the colonials did not look upon the English Parliament with "fond eyes," this does not necessarily imply that the English were staunch supports of the Parliament. Indeed, the passage implies that the Parliament increased its power due to internal struggles, not through the support of the masses. The masses may have supported a more powerful Parliament, but we cannot determine that from the passage.
(C) No. They did not realize that their experience in America was not an "English experience": *"Steeped as they were in the English political language, these colonials failed to observe that their experience in America had given the words a significance quite different from that accepted by the English with whom they debated....*
(D) No. They did, in fact, adopt English political institutions.
(E) Yes. *"Steeped as they were in the English political language, these colonials failed to observe that their experience in America had given the words a significance quite different from that accepted by the English with whom they debated; in fact, they claimed that they were more loyal to the English political tradition than were the English in England."*

26. (A) No. *"To the English the word 'constitution' meant the whole body of law and legal custom formulated since the beginning of the kingdom, whereas to [the] colonials a constitution was a specific written document....This distinction in meaning can be traced to the fact that the foundations of government in the various colonies were written charters granted by the Crown."* Presumably then, the foundation of government in the English Kingdom was not the written body of law and legal custom.
(B) No. This choice is too narrow. The English viewed the English Constitution as the total of all customs and laws. *"To the English the word "constitution" meant the whole body [corpus] of law and legal custom formulated since the beginning of the kingdom, whereas to these colonials a constitution was a specific written document, enumerating specific powers."*

(C) Yes. *"To the English the word "constitution" meant the whole body [corpus] of law and legal custom formulated since the beginning of the kingdom, whereas to these colonials a constitution was a specific written document, enumerating specific powers."*
(D) No. Although the constitution was alterable by Parliament, there is no mention that royal authority (i.e., the King) could alter it.
(E) No. This is not mentioned in the passage.

27. (A) No. Whatever misunderstandings existed occurred in the seventeenth and eighteenth centuries, *"the colonials failed to observe that their experience in America had given the words a significance quite different from that accepted by the English."* The passage does not mention any current misunderstandings.
(B) No. The way England treated the colonies is not discussed much in the passage.
(C) No. There is no mention of an ongoing debate in the passage.
(D) No. This is too broad. Although the passage does discuss differences between the English and the American colonies, it does not mention American independence.
(E) Yes. The passage discusses the conflicting interpretations of their common language and common institutional structures.

Test III
Section II
Solutions

1. (A) Yes. The problem with the argument is that as much as 49 percent of crimes involving handguns could result in fatalities yet still be less than a majority. Similarly, the problem with this answer-choice is that as many as 49 percent of overweight people could develop heart disease yet still be less than half.
(B) No. The problem with the argument is that as much as 49 percent of crimes involving handguns could result in fatalities yet still be less than a majority. However, this answer-choice is not discussing the percentage or faction of people who are better off not following fitness programs that include swimming daily.
(C) No. The problem with the argument is that as much as 49 percent of crimes involving handguns could result in fatalities yet still be less than a majority. However, this answer-choice is not discussing the percentage or faction of people who need not avoid nontraditional dietary regimens.
(D) No. The problem with the argument is that as much as 49 percent of crimes involving handguns could result in fatalities yet still be less than a majority. However, this answer-choice is not discussing the percentage or faction of people who need to spend more time exercising.
(E) No. The problem with the argument is that as much as 49 percent of crimes involving handguns could result in fatalities yet still be less than a majority. However, this answer-choice is not discussing the percentage or faction of people who should undergo psychological evaluation.

2. (A) No. An individual is not mentioned.
(B) No. The conclusion (that which is to be proved) is mentioned only once—at the end of the passage.
(C) No. While several generalizations are made (e.g., *"Tall children can generally reach high shelves easily."*), no specific cases are mentioned that refute these principles.
(D) Yes. This is a false causal argument. It falsely assumes that the difficulty short children have in reaching high shelves is what stunts their growth.
(E) No. The argument errs in falsely establishing a causal relationship between two items—difficulty reaching shelves as a child and short height as an adult—that are actually both effects of a third, independent cause. True, no specific evidence is given, but its lack is not used as a basis for any conclusion.

3. (A) No. Just the opposite. Balanced reporting sometimes presents one side of a conflict in worse light than the other side: *"This concept of balance ... does not justify concealing or glossing over basic injustices in an effort to be even-handed."*

(B) Yes. The passage argues that balanced reporting contains two equal parts:

1) The facts must be presented accurately, with each side's view represented.
2) Any facts that reflect more poorly on one side than the other must also be presented.

(C) No. Although this statement is made in the passage, it is done to support the main idea: In an accurate representation, balanced reporting sometimes presents the two sides in a conflict as having unequal justification.
(D) No. Civil wars and conflicts are used to illustrate the illustrate the main idea.
(E) No. The passage does not state or imply that balanced reporting cannot be achieved. Further, there is no discussion of the subjectiveness of the balanced reporting.

4. (A) No. This would probably increase the deforestation rate. If the landowner's opposition to the government's program grew more violent, then the government should have more difficulty implementing the program.
(B) Yes. We are looking for an agent (other than the government's program) that might cause the deforestation rate to decrease. Rainfall is one such agent. Heavy rainfall during the burning season might prevent the burning of the forest or at least hinder it.
(C) No. This information can be interpreted as either supporting the government's claim or undermining it. If during the previous year the government issued fines totaling only \$1 million, then increasing the fines to \$9 million was probably effective. However, if during the previous year the government issued fines totaling \$8.5 million, then increasing the fines to \$9 million was probably irrelevant.
(D) No. Although this does somewhat weaken the government's claim, it is just as possible that direct observation might show that the deforestation rate was even lower than what the satellite data indicated. Besides, there is a more direct answer-choice offered.
(E) No. It's conceivable that the money spent on research was more effective that the money spent on enforcement. Perhaps the money spent on research showed the government how to better enforce the laws.

5. (A) No. This strengthens the claim. Had the proportion of shoppers expressing no preference been very large, it would have weakened the claim.
(B) No. The shoppers still prefer Northwoods particular old-fashioned way.
(C) No. Usually, surveys only cover a small minority of the total population. For example, most political surveys poll less than 5,000 people, yet the potential electorate is over 100 million.
(D) Yes. The advertisement implies that shoppers choose Northwoods Maple Syrup because of the taste, but does not state that taste was why shoppers choose the syrup. There may be many other reasons for choosing Northwoods Maple Syrup. One possibility is a low price.
(E) No. The claim is expressly made about maple syrup, not about any other types of syrup.

6. (A) No. This would increase the poll's credibility. Had the interviewers revealed their political affiliations, it would have decreased the poll's credibility because their opinions might have influenced the people they were interviewing.
(B) No. This would increase the poll's credibility. The opinions of those unqualified to vote were irrelevant since they did not vote.
(C) Yes. We are looking for something that might have caused the poll to be unrepresentative of the general population. Now, in 1936, phones were not as common as today. If most of the phones were in the homes of the wealthy who held opinions that differed from those of most of the population, then the poll would not have been based on a good cross section of the electorate.
(D) No. Asking for the respondents' political affiliations would probably help determine how representative the poll was. However, if a disproportionate number of respondents were supporters of Alfred Landon, this choice does not explain why the selection process was skewed.
(E) No. This might somewhat explain the inaccuracy of the poll: Perhaps the support for Landon was weak or very volatile. Nevertheless, there is a much stronger explanation offered.

7. (A) No. The passage claims that the amount of plastic being thrown away by the public is not decreasing. How the waste management companies handle the disposal is irrelevant.
(B) No. The passage claims that the amount of plastic being thrown away by the public is not decreasing. Whether this plastic is recyclable or not is irrelevant.
(C) No. This should decrease the percentage of plastic waste discarded by the public. In spite of this, the percentage is actually increasing.
(D) Yes. Suppose an increasing proportion of paper, glass, and metal cans are being recycled. Then even if people are throwing away less plastic than before, the percentage could still increase since there could be considerably less of the other materials being thrown away.
(E) No. The argument is about the amount of plastic people throw away, which is only loosely related to the total amount of plastic manufactured. Perhaps industry uses plastic more efficiently in equipment that is not disposed in landfills. Then consumers will use a greater percentage of the total amount of plastic produced.

8. (A) No. This contradicts what the passage implies. If the amount of ultraviolet radiation reaching the Earth decreased, then the incidence of skin cancer and cataracts should also decrease, not increase.
(B) No. This makes the discrepant facts in the passage even more puzzling. Why did the radiation reaching the Earth's surface in Brazil increase as expected while it decreased under similar conditions in North America?
(C) No. The passage states that the layer of stratospheric ozone has thinned. Knowing why it thinned does not explain why the expected increase in radiation reaching the Earth's surface did not occur.
(D) Yes. If the amount of ozone in the lower atmosphere increased dramatically, then it may more than offset the decrease in ozone in the upper atmosphere.
(E) No. The passage is about the average ozone layer in North America, not about the Earth's general layer of ozone.

Questions 9–10

9. (A) Yes. This draws a strong analogy between what happens in two similar situations. Since aisles leading to the exits allowed more people to escape fires in theaters, it is reasonable to expect a similar result if aisles are formed to the exits on aircraft.
(B) No. The cost of refitting could be so high that the proposal would be impractical.
(C) No. This would a strong answer-choice if the proposal were to install smoke detectors, not to install aisles to the exits.
(D) No. This does not address the issue of removing seats to increase access to the exits.
(E) No. This does not address the issue of removing seats to increase access to the exits.

10. (A) No. The given proposal already covers this situation: the obstructing seats in the new aircraft would be removed.
(B) Yes. The passage states *"The number of aircraft collisions on the ground is increasing because of the substantial increase in the number of flights operated by the airlines."* So increasing the number of flights should also increase the number fatalities.
(C) No. Although this might reduce the amount of time passengers have to wait at airports, it would not affect the likelihood of on-ground aircraft collisions so long as the number of flights remains unchanged.
(D) No. This may be a wise business policy, but it does not increase safety.
(E) No. This does not increase safety. In fact, it might decrease safety: if ticket prices are allowed to rise, the number of tickets sold might decrease, which in turn would decrease congestion at the exits.

11. (A) No. None of the evidence mentioned in the passage is refuted.
(B) No. This is the second-best answer. Although the passage does state several general principles (e.g., *"all fast-breathing animals are warm-blooded)*, this is done as part of a series of evidence rather than directly used to deduce the conclusion of the argument.
(C) No. The passage is casting doubt on a present claim about the past.
(D) No. This is too strong. The passage merely implies, *"fossil evidence casts doubt on the evolutionary theory that dinosaurs are more closely related to reptiles than to other classes of animals."*
(E) Yes. The passage presents a sequence of evidence indicating that dinosaurs were similar to modern birds and dissimilar to modern reptiles.

Characteristics	Dinosaurs	Birds	Reptiles
hollow bones	yes	yes	no
well-developed senses	yes	yes	no
arched mouth roof	yes	yes	no
growth pattern typical of warm-blooded animals	yes	yes	no

12. (A) Yes. Perhaps the abnormalities can be as benign as splotches of color in a dog's white coat. Since such cases would have no effect on a dog's health, there would be no medical need for costly surgery.
(B) No. At first glance, this choice seems good. But the passage already implies that both purebred and nonpurebred dogs suffer genetically determined abnormalities. The more important issue is the percentage of purebred dogs who have genetically determined abnormalities versus the percentage of nonpurebred who have genetically determined abnormalities.
(C) No. This should not affect health care costs for the dogs. The key phrase in this answer-choice is *"natural life spans."*
(D) No. The argument concerns only the avoidance of costly medical bills.
(E) No. Even if the offspring of nonpurebred dogs are as likely to have abnormalities as the offspring of purebred dogs, the passage implies the current generation of nonpurebred dogs is less likely to have the abnormalities.

13. (A) No. The passage states only that if the press is subsidized then there will be outside control. The conditional statement in this answer-choice does not allow us to infer anything if there is no subsidy. Perhaps there is outside control for political, not financial, reasons.
(B) No. The passage states only that if the press is subsidized then there will be outside control. The conditional statement in this answer-choice does not allow us to infer anything if there is no subsidy. Perhaps the press produces propaganda for political reasons.

(C) No. The passage states only that if the press is subsidized then there will be outside control. The conditional statement in this answer-choice does not allow us to infer anything if there is no subsidy. Perhaps the press makes a profit through the use of sound business practices.
(D) Yes. The passage presents a chain of implications:

Not profit-making —> Subsidies —> Outside control —> Not honest journalism

This answer-choice then negates the conclusion (*"if the press is to produce honest journalism"*). By using the contrapositive, we can then conclude the negation of the premise of the above chain, *"the press must be a profit-making institution."*
(E) No. Just the opposite: if the press is to produce honest journalism, it must make a profit.

<u>Questions 14–15</u>

14. (A) No. Lucien does offer justification; it's just flawed.
(B) No. Although the evidence is anecdotal, Lucien does not give it the weight of knowledge gained through scientific study.
(C) Yes. The issue is whether the "available" housing is affordable. Since Lucien identifies himself and his colleagues as professionals, the apartments that are available in their buildings probably are not affordable to the working class.
(D) No. Lucien does not need to argue that all apartment buildings have vacant apartments for rent, just that his and his colleagues' apartment buildings have vacancies and that this situation is not uncommon.
(E) No. Lucien argues that there is no need to construct more low-income housing.

15. (A) No. Maria does not respond to Lucien's personal experiences.
(B) Yes. Lucien states *"Homelessness can, therefore, only be caused by people's inability or unwillingness to work to pay the rent."* Maria shows that this statement is false by pointing out *"that a significant percentage of this city's homeless people hold regular jobs"* and that *"These are people who lack neither will nor ability."*
(C) No. Maria never directs her argument toward Lucien.
(D) No. Maria does not respond to the evidence presented by Lucien.
(E) No. This is the second-best answer. Maria indirectly provides another explanation for Lucien' observations, but does so by directly attacking one of his premises.

16. (A) Yes. If *"law does not cover all circumstances in which one person morally wrongs another,"* then there is a situation in which a person can legally commit an immoral act against another person. But this directly contradicts the statement: *"it is inconceivable that something that is legally permissible could be immoral."*
(B) No. This is consistent with the statement: *"it is inconceivable that something that is legally permissible could be immoral."*
(C) No. This is irrelevant.
(D) No. This is consistent with the statement that *"something that is legally permissible [is not] immoral."* In other words, the law reflects the morals of society.
(E) No. This is irrelevant.

17. (A) No. The passage establishes a relation between the amount of energy used to sterilize nylon instruments and the amount of energy required to produce these instruments. It also establishes a relation between the amount of energy used to sterilize stainless steel instruments and the amount of energy required to produce these instruments. However, the passage gives no information to compare nylon and steel instruments to one another. Therefore, <u>it can be true</u> that it takes more energy to sterilize nylon instruments than to sterilize steel instruments.
(B) Yes. The passage states that <u>50</u> complete sterilizations of nylon surgical instruments takes 3.4 times more energy than manufacturing those instruments. Making the reasonable assumption that each sterilization requires the same amount of energy, <u>one</u> complete sterilization should require 3.4/50 (a number less than one) times the energy required to produce the instruments. In other words, <u>it can not be true</u> that *"more energy was required for each complete sterilization of the nylon instruments than was required to manufacture the nylon instruments."*
(C) No. Nothing indicates the total number of instruments of either type used in the study. Therefore, <u>it can be true</u> that more nylon instruments were used in this study than stainless steel instruments.
(D) No. The passage establishes a relation between the amount of energy used to sterilize nylon instruments and the amount of energy required to produce these instruments. It also establishes a relation between the amount of energy used to sterilize stainless steel instruments and the amount of energy required to produce these instruments. However, the passage gives no information to compare nylon ;and steel instruments to one another. Therefore, <u>it can be true</u> that more energy was used to produce the steel instruments the nylon instruments.
(E) No. While the passage implies that the energy costs of 50 complete sterilization of stainless steel instruments is greater than the energy costs of manufacturing them, nothing in the passage indicates the total costs of manufacturing the instruments. Perhaps the raw materials for the instruments are expensive, or

maybe labor costs for manufacturing are much greater than for sterilization.

18. (A) No. The principle states that in certain cases the letter of the law need not be followed. However, this answer-choice never mentions a law.
(B) No. The principle states *"citizens need not refrain from actions that fail to comply with the law if they have made a good-faith effort to comply but are prevented from doing so by government inaction."* In this answer-choice, the resident did refrain from actions that fail to comply with the law—she stopped construction. Further, there was government action—it actively refused to rezone the property.
(C) No. The principle states *"citizens need not refrain from actions that fail to comply with the law if they have made a good-faith effort to comply but are prevented from doing so by government inaction."* In this answer-choice, the citizens did not make a good-faith effort to comply with the law.
(D) No. The principle states *"citizens need not refrain from actions that fail to comply with the law if they have made a good-faith effort to comply but are prevented from doing so by government inaction."* In this answer-choice, the government did act—it issued the permit.
(E) Yes. The principle states *"citizens need not refrain from actions that fail to comply with the law if they have made a good-faith effort to comply but are prevented from doing so by government inaction."* In applying for the license one year earlier, the doctor made a good faith effort to comply with the law, but government inaction prevented him from getting the license.

Questions 19–20

19. (A) No. The passage refers to only universities. So any assumption does not need to exclude other institutions that are not universities.
(B) No. The passage explicitly refers to "potentially valuable" discoveries. So the argument does not need to assume that most inventions by university faculty members would be profitable, nor even that some inventions would be profitable. It needs to assume only that there are some discoveries by faculty members.
(C) No. The passage is about the suppression of information, not about how to best disseminate information.
(D) Yes. The passage states that universities have a motive to suppress information about potentially valuable discoveries until patents have been secured. It then states, *"suppressing information concerning such discoveries is incompatible with the university's obligation to promote the free flow of ideas."* This assumes that on at least one occasion universities will act on their motives.
(E) No. The passage does not allude to any struggle between the faculty and the university regarding who should get the patents, so this assumption is not needed.

20. (A) Yes. The conclusion is stated in the opening of the passage (*"A university should not be entitled to patent the inventions of its faculty members"*). The rest of the passage presents an argument to support that conclusion.
(B) No. It is the conclusion.
(C) No. It is the conclusion of the argument, not a premise (i.e., assumption) of the argument.
(D) No. It is the conclusion.
(E) No. It is the conclusion.

21. (A) No. In fact, if English and Mbarbaram share other words besides "dog" then the conclusion is strengthened.
(B) No. In fact, this could weaken the argument because it makes it more likely that both English and Mbarbaram borrowed the word "dog" from a third language.
(C) No. This directly attacks the conclusion of the argument: *"Thus this case shows that sometimes when languages share words that are similar in sound and meaning the similarity is due neither to language relatedness nor to borrowing."*
(D) Yes. The argument needs to assume that the word "dog" is native to both languages. Otherwise, perhaps ancient travelers had contact with both languages and introduced the word "dog" to both languages.
(E) No. This directly attacks the conclusion of the argument: *"Thus this case shows that sometimes when languages share words that are similar in sound and meaning the similarity is due neither to language relatedness nor to borrowing."*

22. (A) No. The politician only needs to support the conclusion that *"fewer people now find themselves among the ranks of the unemployed"*; He is not required to specifically refute the opposition's position. Even so, he does implicitly address the opposition, which apparently claims that a greater or equal number of people are unemployed now than four years ago.
(B) No. This is irrelevant. The politician's claim is about *the "number of people unemployed city-wide"* and does not concern differences in employment that might exist among different neighborhoods in the city.
(C) No. This is irrelevant. Since both the politician's party and the opposition's party held office for four years, annual seasonal fluctuations should have no impact on overall employment.
(D) Yes. Although the percentage increase in unemployment was less than it was under the previous administration, it still did increase. So by definition, there are now more people unemployed than before.

(E) No. The politician's claim concerns programs that were implemented under the leadership of his party. Whatever programs were supported by the opposition is irrelevant.

23. (A) Yes. The passage defines categories: everyone is poor or rich, honest or dishonest, a farmer or a non-farmer. It then states that all poor farmers are honest; in other words, there are no dishonest poor farmers. It then concludes that all rich farmers are dishonest; in other words, there are no honest rich farmers. We can represent these statements as follows (where the crossed-out boxes indicate those combinations that do not exist):

	HONEST	DISHONEST
POOR	farmer	farmer
	non-farmer	non-farmer
RICH	farmer	farmer
	non-farmer	non-farmer

From the table, we see that the passage assumes that every farmer who is honest is also poor.

(B) No. The passage defines categories: everyone is poor or rich, honest or dishonest, a farmer or a non-farmer. It then states that all poor farmers are honest; in other words, there are no dishonest poor farmers. It then concludes that all rich farmers are dishonest; in other words, there are no honest rich farmers. We can represent these statements as follows (where the crossed-out boxes indicate those combinations that do not exist):

	HONEST	DISHONEST
POOR	farmer	farmer
	non-farmer	non-farmer
RICH	farmer	farmer
	non-farmer	non-farmer

From the table, we see that the passage allows for honest people who are not farmers—namely, some poor and rich non-farmers).

(C) No. The passage defines categories: everyone is poor or rich, honest or dishonest, a farmer or a non-farmer. It then states that all poor farmers are honest; in other words, there are no dishonest poor farmers. It then concludes that all rich farmers are dishonest; in other words, there are no honest rich farmers. We can represent these statements as follows (where the crossed-out boxes indicate those combinations that do not exist):

	HONEST	DISHONEST
POOR	farmer	farmer
	non-farmer	non-farmer
RICH	farmer	farmer
	non-farmer	non-farmer

From the table, we see that the passage allows for dishonest people who are not rich farmers—namely, some poor and rich non-farmers).

(D) No. The passage defines categories: everyone is poor or rich, honest or dishonest, a farmer or a non-farmer. It then states that all poor farmers are honest; in other words, there are no dishonest poor farmers. It then concludes that all rich farmers are dishonest; in other words, there are no honest rich farmers. We can represent these statements as follows (where the crossed-out boxes indicate those combinations that do not exist):

	HONEST	DISHONEST
POOR	farmer	farmer
	non-farmer	non-farmer
RICH	farmer	farmer
	non-farmer	non-farmer

From the table, we see that the passage allows for people who are both poor and dishonest—namely, some non-farmers).

(E) No. The passage defines categories: everyone is poor or rich, honest or dishonest, a farmer or a non-farmer. It then states that all poor farmers are honest;

in other words, there are no dishonest poor farmers. It then concludes that all rich farmers are dishonest; in other words, there are no honest rich farmers. We can represent these statements as follows (where the crossed-out boxes indicate those combinations that do not exist):

		HONEST	**DISHONEST**
POOR		farmer	farmer
		non-farmer	non-farmer
RICH		farmer	farmer
		non-farmer	non-farmer

From the table, we see that the passage allows for poor people who are not farmers.

24. No. The Novelist's argument can be paraphrased as follows:

If a work is to express the content of a novel, then it must be a novel
A summary is not a novel
∴ A summary cannot express the content of a novel

This answer-choice can be paraphrased as follows:

If this drawing is a blueprint, then it is a guide
This drawing is a guide
∴ This drawing is a blueprint

Clearly, this paraphrase does not have the same structure as the paraphrase of the Novelist's argument.

(B) No. The Novelist's argument can be paraphrased as follows:

If a work is to express the content of a novel, then it must be a novel
A summary is not a novel
∴ A summary cannot express the content of a novel

This answer-choice can be paraphrased as follows:

If this is used as a press release, then it does not divulge company secrets
This does not divulge company secrets (but is uninformative)
∴ This cannot be used as a press release

This argument does not have the same structure as the original argument. In the original argument, the second statement negates the "then" portion of the first statement, while in this choice, the second statement affirms the "then" portion of the first statement.

(C) No. The Novelist's argument can be paraphrased as follows:

If a work is to express the content of a novel, then it must be a novel
A summary is not a novel
∴ A summary cannot express the content of a novel

This answer-choice can be paraphrased as follows:

If you are watching a travelogue, then you are not traveling
A travelogue has some of the benefits of traveling without the hardships
∴ Many people watch travelogues and do not suffer the difficulties of travel

Clearly, the structure of this paraphrase is very different from the Novelist's argument.

(D) Yes. The Novelist's argument can be paraphrased as follows:

If a work is to express the content of a novel, then it must be a novel
A summary is not a novel
∴ A summary cannot express the content of a novel

This answer-choice can be paraphrased as follows:

If a representation conveys the experience of a landscape, it must be 3D
A photograph is not 3D
∴ A photograph cannot convey the experience of a landscape

Clearly, the two arguments have the same structure.

(E) No. The Novelist's argument can be paraphrased as follows:

If a work is to express the content of a novel, then it must be a novel
A summary is not a novel
∴ A summary cannot express the content of a novel

In the way that the original argument contrasts a summary and a novel, this answer-choice contrasts two functions of a menu: as a list of contents of a meal, and as a reminder of a meal. However, there is no similar pattern of reasoning used in both the argument and this answer-choice.

25. (A) Yes. There may be ways other than medical journals for researchers to get their work reviewed by their colleagues.
(B) No. This is too strong. The passage only assumes that <u>most people</u> who don't serve on medical review panels (i.e., the public) do not have the knowledge to evaluate research findings.
(C) No. The argument is about the delay of research <u>before</u> publication, not about access <u>after</u> publication.
(D) No. This is too strong. The passage does not assume that <u>all</u> research findings are subject to peer review, only that those findings that have been reviewed do not contain erroneous or potentially harmful information.
(E) No. This would weaken the argument. If non-medical reasons influence the review panels, then peer review may not *"to protect the public from making decisions based on possibly substandard research."*

Test III
Section III
<u>Solutions</u>

<u>Questions 1–7</u>

1. (A) No. This choice violates the condition *"Corsage 3 must contain at least one gardenia but no orchids."*
(B) No. This choice violates the condition *"At least one of each flower."* There are no violets.
(C) Yes. All the conditions are satisfied: There is one of each type of flower. There are 4 roses, which is twice the number of orchids, 2. Corsage 1 contains exactly two types of flowers. Corsage 2 contains at least one rose. Finally, Corsage 3 does contain at least 1 gardenia and does not contain an orchid.
(D) No. This choice violates the condition *"Corsage 1 must contain exactly two types of flowers."*
(E) No. This choice violates the condition *"Corsage 2 must contain at least one rose."*

2. (A) No. The following arrangement has 4 roses and satisfies all the conditions:

<u>Corsage 1</u>	<u>Corsage 2</u>	<u>Corsage 3</u>
2 roses	1 rose	2 gardenias
1 orchid	1 gardenia	1 rose
	1 violet	

Note, since the question asks for greatest number possible, you should start with choice (E)—the greatest number.
(B) No. The following arrangement has 5 roses and satisfies all the conditions:

<u>Corsage 1</u>	<u>Corsage 2</u>	<u>Corsage 3</u>
2 roses	1 rose	1 gardenia
1 orchid	1 gardenia	2 roses
	1 violet	

Note, since the question asks for greatest number possible, you should start with choice (E)—the greatest number.
(C) No. The following arrangement has 6 roses and satisfies all the conditions:

<u>Corsage 1</u>	<u>Corsage 2</u>	<u>Corsage 3</u>
2 roses	3 roses	1 rose
1 orchid		1 gardenia
		1 violet

Note, since the question asks for greatest number possible, you should start with choice (E)—the greatest number.
(D) Yes. The following arrangement has 6 roses and satisfies all the conditions:

Corsage 1	Corsage 2	Corsage 3
2 roses 1 orchid	3 roses	1 rose 1 gardenia 1 violet

Furthermore, there cannot be more than 6 flowers of any one type since there is a total of 9 flowers, and at least 1 from each of the 4 types of flowers must be chosen.
(E) No. There is a total of 9 flowers, and at least 1 from each of the 4 types of flowers must be chosen. Hence, there cannot be more than 6 flowers of any one type.

3. (A) No. The following arrangement has 2 violets and satisfies all the conditions:

Corsage 1	Corsage 2	Corsage 3
1 rose 2 orchids	3 roses	1 gardenia 2 violets

(B) Yes. Since *"at least twice as many roses as orchids must be used,"* at least 4 roses must be used (we are given that Corsage 1 contains two orchids and one rose). Now, from the original conditions, Corsage 3 must contain at least one gardenia. This determines seven of the nine flowers, none of which are violets. Hence, there can be at most two violets. Furthermore, the following arrangement has 2 violets and satisfies all the conditions:

Corsage 1	Corsage 2	Corsage 3
1 rose 2 orchids	3 roses	1 gardenia 2 violets

(C) No. Since *"at least twice as many roses as orchids must be used,"* at least 4 roses must be used (we are given that Corsage 1 contains 2 orchids and 1 rose). Now, from the original conditions, Corsage 3 must contain at least one gardenia. This determines seven of the nine flowers, none of which are violets. Hence, there can be at most two violets.

(D) No. Since *"at least twice as many roses as orchids must be used,"* at least 4 roses must be used (we are given that Corsage 1 contains 2 orchids and 1 rose). Now, from the original conditions, Corsage 3 must contain at least one gardenia. This determines seven of the nine flowers, none of which are violets. Hence, there can be at most two violets.

(E) No. Since *"at least twice as many roses as orchids must be used,"* at least 4 roses must be used (we are given that Corsage 1 contains two orchids and one rose). Now, from the original conditions, Corsage 3 must contain at least one gardenia. This determines seven of the nine flowers, none of which are violets. Hence, there can be at most two violets.

4. (A) Yes. Since Corsage 2 is identical to Corsage 3, it too must contain a gardenia:

Corsage 1	Corsage 2	Corsage 3
	1 gardenia	1 gardenia

Now, suppose Corsage 1 contains two orchids and one violet:

Corsage 1	Corsage 2	Corsage 3
2 orchids 1 violet	1 gardenia	1 gardenia

Now, since there are 2 orchids, there must be 4 roses (*at least twice as many roses as orchids must be used*). The roses can be arranged without violating any conditions as follows:

Corsage 1	Corsage 2	Corsage 3
2 orchids 1 violet	1 gardenia 2 roses	1 gardenia 2 roses

This diagram satisfies all the conditions. Hence, the corsages can include exactly two orchids.

(B) No. Since Corsage 2 is identical to Corsage 3, it too must contain a gardenia:

Corsage 1	Corsage 2	Corsage 3
	1 gardenia	1 gardenia

Now, if there is to be a third gardenia, it must be in Corsage 1 (Why?):

Corsage 1	Corsage 2	Corsage 3
1 gardenia	1 gardenia	1 gardenia

Since Corsage 3 cannot contain an orchid, neither can Corsage 2. Hence, Corsage 1, which contains exactly two types of flowers, must contain 2 orchids:

Corsage 1	Corsage 2	Corsage 3
1 gardenia 2 orchids	1 gardenia	1 gardenia

Since there are *"at least twice as many roses as orchids,"* there must be at least 4 roses. However, this arrangement already has 9 flowers selected and the violets are yet to be selected. Hence, the arrangement cannot include exactly 3 gardenias.
(C) No. Corsage 1 cannot contain all three roses since it must contain two types of flowers. Hence, each corsage must contain exactly 1 rose (neither Corsage 2 nor Corsage 3 could contain two roses [why?]):

Corsage 1	Corsage 2	Corsage 3
1 rose	1 rose	1 rose

Since Corsage 3 cannot contain an orchid, neither can Corsage 2. Hence, Corsage 1 must contain 2 orchids:

Corsage 1	Corsage 2	Corsage 3
1 rose 2 orchids	1 rose	1 rose

Since there are *"at least twice as many roses as orchids,"* there must be at least 4 roses. However, this violates our assumption that there are exactly 3 roses. Hence, the arrangement cannot include exactly 3 roses.

(D) No. There cannot be 3 roses in Corsage 1 since it must contain two types of flowers. Hence, there must be one rose in Corsage 1, two roses in Corsage 2, and two roses in Corsage 3:

Corsage 1	Corsage 2	Corsage 3
1 rose	2 roses	2 roses

Since Corsage 3 cannot contain an orchid, neither can Corsage 2. Hence, Corsage 1 must contain 2 orchids:

Corsage 1	Corsage 2	Corsage 3
1 rose 2 orchids	2 roses	2 roses

Now, Corsage 3 *"must contain at least one gardenia,"* so Corsage 2 does as well. However, this leaves all nine flowers chosen with no violet selected. Hence, the arrangement cannot include exactly 5 roses.

(E) No. There cannot be 3 violets in Corsage 1 since it must contain two types of flowers. Hence, there must be one violet in Corsage 1, two violets in Corsage 2, and two violets in Corsage 3:

Corsage 1	Corsage 2	Corsage 3
1 violet	2 violets	2 violets

Since Corsage 3 contains a gardenia, so does Corsage 2:

Corsage 1	Corsage 2	Corsage 3
1 violet	2 violets 1 gardenia	2 violets 1 gardenia

The rose and the orchid must fill the remaining two spaces in Corsage 1. However, this violates the condition *"Corsage 1 must contain exactly two types of flowers."* Hence, the arrangement cannot include exactly 5 violets.

5. (A) No. Since Corsage 3 cannot contain an orchid, the two corsages containing at least one orchid each must be Corsage 1 and Corsage 2. Now, arranging the remaining flowers as follows will not violate any condition:

Corsage 1	Corsage 2	Corsage 3
1 orchid 2 roses	1 orchid 2 roses	2 violets 1 gardenia

In this valid arrangement, Corsage 2 does not have a gardenia.

(B) No. Since Corsage 3 cannot contain an orchid, the two corsages containing at least one orchid each must be Corsage 1 and Corsage 2. Now, arranging the remaining flowers as follows will not violate any condition:

Corsage 1	Corsage 2	Corsage 3
1 orchid 2 roses	1 orchid 2 roses	2 violets 1 gardenia

In this valid arrangement, Corsage 2 does not have a gardenia.

(C) Yes. Since Corsage 3 cannot contain an orchid, the two corsages containing at least one orchid each must be Corsage 1 and Corsage 2. Further, the initial conditions state *"Corsage 2 must contain at least one rose."* Thus, Corsage 2 contains both an orchid and a rose.

(D) No. Since Corsage 3 cannot contain an orchid, the two corsages containing at least one orchid each must be Corsage 1 and Corsage 2. Now, arranging the remaining flowers as follows will not violate any condition:

Corsage 1	Corsage 2	Corsage 3
1 orchid 2 roses	1 orchid 2 roses	2 violets 1 gardenia

In this valid arrangement, Corsage 2 does not have a violet.

(E) No. Since Corsage 3 cannot contain an orchid, the two corsages containing at least one orchid each must be Corsage 1 and Corsage 2. Now, arranging the remaining flowers as follows will not violate any condition:

Corsage 1	Corsage 2	Corsage 3
1 orchid 2 roses	1 orchid 2 roses	2 violets 1 gardenia

In this valid arrangement, Corsage 2 does not have a violet.

6. (A) No. From the initial conditions, each of the 4 types of flowers must be used and there must be at least twice as many roses as orchids. Hence, any arrangement must contain at least 2 roses.

(B) No. From the initial conditions, each of the 4 types of flowers must be used and there must be at least twice as many roses as orchids. Hence, any arrangement must contain at least

2 roses
1 orchid
1 violet
1 gardenia

If arranged properly, the 4 remaining flowers can all be violets. Hence, the greatest possible number of violets is 5. The following diagram illustrates one possible arrangement:

Corsage 1	Corsage 2	Corsage 3
1 orchid	2 roses	1 gardenia
2 violets	1 violet	2 violets

(C) No. From the initial conditions, each of the 4 types of flowers must be used and there must be at least twice as many roses as orchids. Hence, any arrangement must contain at least

2 roses
1 orchid
1 violet
1 gardenia

If arranged properly, the 4 remaining flowers can all be violets. Hence, the greatest possible number of violets is 5, which corresponds to exactly 1 orchid. The following diagram illustrates one possible arrangement:

Corsage 1	Corsage 2	Corsage 3
1 orchid	2 roses	1 gardenia
2 violets	1 violet	2 violets

(D) Yes. From the initial conditions, each of the 4 types of flowers must be used and there must be at least twice as many roses as orchids. Hence, any arrangement must contain at least

2 roses
1 orchid
1 violet
1 gardenia

If arranged properly, the 4 remaining flowers can all be violets. Hence, the greatest possible number of violets is 5, which corresponds to exactly 2 roses. The following diagram illustrates one possible arrangement:

Corsage 1	Corsage 2	Corsage 3
1 orchid	2 violets	1 gardenia
2 violets	1 rose	1 rose
		1 violet

(E) No. From the initial conditions, each of the 4 types of flowers must be used and there must be at least twice as many roses as orchids. Hence, any arrangement must contain at least

2 roses
1 orchid
1 violet
1 gardenia

If arranged properly, the 4 remaining flowers can all be violets. Hence, the greatest possible number of violets is 5. The following diagram illustrates one possible arrangement:

Corsage 1	Corsage 2	Corsage 3
1 orchid	2 violets	1 gardenia
2 violets	1 rose	1 rose
		1 violet

7. (A) Yes. Since Corsage 3 cannot contain an orchid, it must contain 1 gardenia, 1 violet, and 1 rose:

Corsage 1	Corsage 2	Corsage 3
1 gardenia		1 gardenia
1 violet		1 violet
		1 rose

Since Corsage 1 contains exactly two flowers and each type of flower must be used, Corsage 2 must contain both an orchid and a rose:

Corsage 1	Corsage 2	Corsage 3
1 gardenia	1 orchid	1 gardenia
1 violet	1 rose	1 violet
		1 rose

The third flower in Corsage 2 can be a gardenia without violating any condition.

Corsage 1	Corsage 2	Corsage 3
1 gardenia	1 orchid	1 gardenia
1 violet	1 rose	1 violet
	1 gardenia	1 rose

Finally, if the third flower in Corsage 1 is either another gardenia or another violet, then all the conditions will be satisfied.

(B) No. Since Corsage 3 cannot contain an orchid, it must contain 1 gardenia, 1 violet, and 1 rose:

Corsage 1	Corsage 2	Corsage 3
1 gardenia		1 gardenia
1 violet		1 violet
		1 rose

Since Corsage 1 contains exactly two flowers and each type of flower must be used, Corsage 2 must contain both an orchid and a rose:

Corsage 1	Corsage 2	Corsage 3
1 gardenia	1 orchid	1 gardenia
1 violet	1 rose	1 violet
		1 rose

Now, if a second orchid is chosen for Corsage 2, then at least two more roses would need to be selected (*at least twice as many roses as orchids must be used*). However, this scenario has 10 flowers being selected.

(C) No. Since Corsage 3 cannot contain an orchid, it must contain 1 gardenia, 1 violet, and 1 rose:

Corsage 1	Corsage 2	Corsage 3
1 gardenia		1 gardenia
1 violet		1 violet
		1 rose

Since Corsage 1 contains exactly two flowers and each type of flower must be used, Corsage 2 must contain both an orchid and a rose:

Corsage 1	Corsage 2	Corsage 3
1 gardenia	1 orchid	1 gardenia
1 violet	1 rose	1 violet
		1 rose

Clearly, there is no room in Corsage 2 for two violets.
(D) No. Since Corsage 3 cannot contain an orchid, it must contain 1 gardenia, 1 violet, and 1 rose:

Corsage 1	Corsage 2	Corsage 3
1 gardenia		1 gardenia
1 violet		1 violet
		1 rose

Since Corsage 1 contains exactly two flowers and each type of flower must be used, Corsage 2 must contain both an orchid and a rose:

Corsage 1	Corsage 2	Corsage 3
1 gardenia	1 orchid	1 gardenia
1 violet	1 rose	1 violet
		1 rose

Now, adding a gardenia and an additional rose to Corsage 2 would bring the total number of flowers in Corsage 2 to four.
(E) No. Since Corsage 3 cannot contain an orchid, it must contain 1 gardenia, 1 violet, and 1 rose:

Corsage 1	Corsage 2	Corsage 3
1 gardenia		1 gardenia
1 violet		1 violet
		1 rose

Since Corsage 1 contains exactly two flowers and each type of flower must be used, Corsage 2 must contain both an orchid and a rose:

Corsage 1	Corsage 2	Corsage 3
1 gardenia	1 orchid	1 gardenia
1 violet	1 rose	1 violet
		1 rose

Now, adding a violet and an additional rose to Corsage 2 would bring the total number of flowers in Corsage 2 to four.

Questions 8–13

The statement *A unless B* means that A is true in all cases, except when B is true. In other words, if B is false, then A must be true. That is, if not B, then A.

(A unless B) = (If not B, then A)

This can be symbolized as ~B—>A.

Symbolizing the condition *"N cannot be selected unless L is selected"* yields

~L—>~N

Applying the contrapositive to this diagram yields

N—>L

Next, the condition *"Either J or K must be selected, but J and K cannot both be selected"* can be symbolized as

J or K

Note, we won't indicate in the symbol that *"J and K cannot both be selected"*—just keep it in mind. Symbolizing the remaining conditions in like manner yields

J or K
N or P
N—>L
Q—>K

8. (A) No. This violates the condition *"J and K cannot both be selected."*
(B) No. This violates the condition **Q—>K** since Q is selected but K is not.
(C) No. This violates the condition **Q—>K** since Q is selected but K is not.
(D) Yes. All the conditions are satisfied: Since K is selected, the condition **J or K** is satisfied. Since P is selected, the condition **N or P** is satisfied. Since N is not selected, the condition **N—>L** does not apply. Since both Q and K are selected, the condition **Q—>K** is satisfied.

(E) No. This violates the condition *"N and P cannot both be selected."*

9. (A) No. The following group contains neither K nor Q and does not violate any of the conditions:

J, L, P, M

(B) Yes. Suppose neither L nor M is selected. Then applying the contrapositive to the condition **N—>L** shows that N cannot attend. This leaves only J, K, P, and Q. But *"J and K cannot both be selected."*
(C) No. The following group contains neither N nor M and does not violate any of the conditions:

K, L, P, Q

(D) No. The following group contains neither N nor Q and does not violate any of the conditions:

K, L, M, P

(E) No. The following group contains neither P nor Q and does not violate any of the conditions:

K, L, M, N

10. (A) No. The following group contains both J and N and does not violate any of the conditions:

J, L, M, N

(B) Yes. Suppose both J and Q are selected. Then from the condition **Q—>K**, K must be selected. However, this violates the condition *"J and K cannot both be selected."*
(C) No. The following group contains both K and L and does not violate any of the conditions:

K, L, M, N

(D) No. The following group contains both K and N and does not violate any of the conditions:

K, L, M, N

(E) No. The following group contains both N and Q and does not violate any of the conditions:

K, L, N, Q

11. (A) No. The following group does not contain M or J and does not violate any of the conditions:

K, L, N, Q

(B) Yes. Since M is not selected, 6 people remain in the selection pool—J, K, L, N, P, and Q. Now, exactly one of either J and K must be selected. This leaves 4 people in the pool—L, N, P, and Q. Next, exactly one of either N and P must be selected. This leaves 2 people in the pool—L and Q. Since 4 people are to be selected, both L and Q must be selected. Further, from the condition **Q—>K**, we know that K must be selected. Thus, both K and L must be selected.

(C) No. The following group does not contain M or P and does not violate any of the conditions:

K, L, N, Q

(D) No. The following group does not contain M or P and does not violate any of the conditions:

K, L, N, Q

(E) No. The following group does not contain M or N and does not violate any of the conditions:

K, L, P, Q

12. (A) No. Both of the following groups satisfy all the conditions:

K, L, N, M　　　K, L, N, Q

(B) No. All three of the following groups satisfy all the conditions:

K, L, N, M　　　K, L, N, Q　　　J, L, N, M

(C) Yes. If P is not selected, then from the condition **N or P** we know that N must be selected. Now, from the condition **N—>L,** we know that L must also be selected. Next, along with N and L, we must select either J or K, but not both. This yields two groups:

Group I	Group II
J, L, N	K, L, N

In Group I, Q cannot be selected because the condition **Q—>K** would force K into the group—violating the condition *"J and K cannot both be selected."* Hence, Group I is uniquely determined:

J, L, N, M

However, either M or Q can join Group II without violating any conditions:

K, L, N, M　　　K, L, N, Q

Thus, there are only 3 acceptable groups.
(D) No. If P is not selected, then from the condition **N or P** we know that N must be selected. Now, from the condition **N—>L,** we know that L must also be

selected. Next, along with N and L, we must select either J or K, but not both. This yields two groups:

Group I	Group II
J, L, N	K, L, N

In Group I, Q cannot be selected because the condition **Q—>K** would force K into the group—violating the condition *"J and K cannot both be selected."* Hence, Group I is uniquely determined:

J, L, N, M

However, either M or Q can join Group II without violating any conditions:

K, L, N, M   K, L, N, Q

Thus, there are only 3 acceptable groups.

(E) No. If P is not selected, then from the condition **N or P** we know that N must be selected. Now, from the condition **N—>L,** we know that L must also be selected. Next, along with N and L, we must select either J or K, but not both. This yields two groups:

Group I	Group II
J, L, N	K, L, N

In Group I, Q cannot be selected because the condition **Q—>K** would force K into the group—violating the condition *"J and K cannot both be selected."* Hence, Group I is uniquely determined:

J, L, N, M

However, either M or Q can join Group II without violating any conditions:

K, L, N, M   K, L, N, Q

Thus, there are only 3 acceptable groups.

13. (A) No. The following two groups contain both J and L, and they do not violate any of the conditions:

J, L, N, M   J, L, M, P

(B) No. The following two groups contain both K and M, and they do not violate any of the conditions:

K, L, N, M   K, L, M, P

(C) No. The following two groups contain both L and N, and they do not violate any of the conditions:

J, L, N, M   K, L, N, M

(D) No. The following two groups contain both L and Q, and they do not violate any of the conditions:

K, L, P, Q   K, L, N, Q

(E) Yes. Suppose both M and Q are selected. Then from the condition **Q—>K**, we know that K must be selected. This yields the following partial group:

K, M, Q

Now, we must select either N or P. Suppose N is selected. Then from the condition **N—>L**, L must also be selected. This, however, puts 5 people—K, M, Q, N, and L—in the group. Hence, N cannot be selected, so P must be selected, and the group is uniquely determined:

K, M, Q, P

<u>Questions 14–18</u>

14. (A) No. The following diagram satisfies all the conditions and has Miguel paired with Sarah in dance 1:

Dance 1	Dance 2	Dance 3
Karl/Rita	Karl/Sarah	Karl/Tura
Miguel/Sarah	Miguel/Tura	Miguel/Rita
Luis/Tura	Luis/Rita	Luis/Sarah

(B) No. The following diagram satisfies all the conditions and has Miguel paired with Rita in dance 1:

Dance 1	Dance 2	Dance 3
Karl/Sarah	Karl/Tura	Karl/Rita
Miguel/Rita	Miguel/Sarah	Miguel/Tura
Luis/Tura	Luis/Rita	Luis/Sarah

(C) No. The following diagram satisfies all the conditions and has Miguel paired with Rita in dance 1:

Dance 1	Dance 2	Dance 3
Karl/Sarah	Karl/Tura	Karl/Rita
Miguel/Rita	Miguel/Sarah	Miguel/Tura
Luis/Tura	Luis/Rita	Luis/Sarah

(D) Yes. Miguel can partner with Rita in dance 1:

Dance 1	Dance 2	Dance 3
Karl/Sarah	Karl/Tura	Karl/Rita
Miguel/Rita	Miguel/Sarah	Miguel/Tura
Luis/Tura	Luis/Rita	Luis/Sarah

Further, Miguel can partner with Sarah in dance 1:

Dance 1	Dance 2	Dance 3
Karl/Rita	Karl/Sarah	Karl/Tura
Miguel/Sarah	Miguel/Tura	Miguel/Rita
Luis/Tura	Luis/Rita	Luis/Sarah

Now, suppose Miguel partners Tura in dance 1. Since Luis partners Sarah in dance 3, the condition *"Whoever partners Rita in dance 2 must partner Sarah in dance 3"* force Luis to partner Rita in dance 2:

Dance 1	Dance 2	Dance 3
Miguel/Tura	Luis/Rita	Luis/Sarah

However, this leaves no partner for Luis in dance 1: Luis cannot partner Tura because Miguel already does. Luis cannot partner Rita because he already did in dance 2, and Luis cannot partner Sarah because he already did in dance 3. Hence, a complete and accurate list of the people who could partner Miguel in dance 1 is Rita and Sarah.

(E) No. The following diagram satisfies all the conditions and has Miguel paired with Sarah in dance 1:

Dance 1	Dance 2	Dance 3
Karl/Rita	Karl/Sarah	Karl/Tura
Miguel/Sarah	Miguel/Tura	Miguel/Rita
Luis/Tura	Luis/Rita	Luis/Sarah

15. (A) No. Since Miguel partners Rita in dance 2, the condition *"Whoever partners Rita in dance 2 must partner Sarah in dance 3"* forces Miguel to partner Sarah in dance 3.

Dance 1	Dance 2	Dance 3
Karl/Tura	Miguel/Rita	Miguel/Sarah

Since Miguel partners Rita in dance 2 and Sarah in dance 3, he must partner Tura in dance 1 (*No two children can partner each other in more than one dance*). However, this answer-choice already has Karl paired with Tura.

(B) Yes. Since Miguel partners Rita in dance 2, the condition *"Whoever partners Rita in dance 2 must partner Sarah in dance 3"* forces Miguel to partner Sarah in dance 3. Now, suppose Luis partners Sarah in dance 2:

Dance 1	Dance 2	Dance 3
	Luis/Sarah	Miguel/Sarah

This diagram satisfies the first two conditions, and the following pairs can be added to the diagram without violating the last condition:

Dance 1	Dance 2	Dance 3
Karl/Sarah	Miguel/Rita	Miguel/Sarah
Luis/Rita	Luis/Sarah	Luis/Tura
Miguel/Tura	Karl/Tura	Karl/Rita

(C) No. Since Miguel partners Rita in dance 2, the condition *"Whoever partners Rita in dance 2 must partner Sarah in dance 3"* forces Miguel to partner Sarah in dance 3.

(D) No. Since Miguel partners Rita in dance 2, the condition *"Whoever partners Rita in dance 2 must partner Sarah in dance 3"* forces Miguel to partner Sarah in dance 3. Hence, Miguel cannot partner Sarah in dance 1 (*No two children can partner each other in more than one dance*).

(E) No. Since Miguel partners Rita in dance 2, the condition *"Whoever partners Rita in dance 2 must partner Sarah in dance 3"* forces Miguel to partner Sarah in dance 3.

16. (A) No. Since Miguel partners Sarah in dance 1, the condition *"Karl partners Sarah in either dance 1 or dance 2"* forces Karl to partner Sarah in dance 2:

Dance 1	Dance 2	Dance 3
Miguel/Sarah	Karl/Sarah	

Since Miguel and Karl have partnered Sarah, Luis must partner Sarah in dance 3—otherwise the condition *"No two children can partner each other in more than one dance"* would be violated:

Dance 1	Dance 2	Dance 3
Miguel/Sarah	Karl/Sarah	Luis/Sarah

From *"whoever partners Rita in dance 2 must partner Sarah in dance 3,"* Luis must partner Rita in dance 2. This leaves Tura as the only person he hasn't danced with, so he dances with her in dance 1:

Dance 1	Dance 2	Dance 3
Miguel/Sarah	Karl/Sarah	Luis/Sarah
Luis/Tura	Luis/Rita	

Now, in dance 1, Karl must dance with Rita. Since Karl already dances with Sarah in dance 2, which leaves Tura as Karl's partner in dance 3.

(B) Yes. Since Miguel partners Sarah in dance 1, the condition *"Karl partners Sarah in either dance 1 or dance 2"* forces Karl to partner Sarah in dance 2:

Dance 1	Dance 2	Dance 3
Miguel/Sarah	Karl/Sarah	

Since Miguel and Karl have partnered Sarah, Luis must partner Sarah in dance 3—otherwise the condition *"No two children can partner each other in more than one dance"* would be violated:

Dance 1	Dance 2	Dance 3
Miguel/Sarah	Karl/Sarah	Luis/Sarah

From *"whoever partners Rita in dance 2 must partner Sarah in dance 3,"* Luis must partner Rita in dance 2. This leaves Tura as the only person he hasn't danced with, so he dances with her in dance 1:

Dance 1	Dance 2	Dance 3
Miguel/Sarah	Karl/Sarah	Luis/Sarah
Luis/Tura	Luis/Rita	

Now, in dance 1, Karl must dance with Rita. Since Karl already dances with Sarah in dance 2, which leaves Tura as Karl's partner in dance 3.

(C) No. Since Miguel partners Sarah in dance 1, the condition *"Karl partners Sarah in either dance 1 or dance 2"* forces Karl to partner Sarah in dance 2:

Dance 1	Dance 2	Dance 3
Miguel/Sarah	Karl/Sarah	

Since Miguel and Karl have partnered Sarah, Luis must partner Sarah in dance 3—otherwise the condition *"No two children can partner each other in more than one dance"* would be violated:

Dance 1	Dance 2	Dance 3
Miguel/Sarah	Karl/Sarah	Luis/Sarah

(D) No. Since Miguel partners Sarah in dance 1, the condition *"Karl partners Sarah in either dance 1 or dance 2"* forces Karl to partner Sarah in dance 2:

Dance 1	Dance 2	Dance 3
Miguel/Sarah	Karl/Sarah	

Since Miguel and Karl have partnered Sarah, Luis must partner Sarah in dance 3—otherwise the condition *"No two children can partner each other in more than one dance"* would be violated:

Dance 1	Dance 2	Dance 3
Miguel/Sarah	Karl/Sarah	Luis/Sarah

(E) No. Since Miguel partners Sarah in dance 1, the condition *"Karl partners Sarah in either dance 1 or dance 2"* forces Karl to partner Sarah in dance 2:

Dance 1	Dance 2	Dance 3
Miguel/Sarah	Karl/Sarah	

Since Miguel and Karl have partnered Sarah, Luis must partner Sarah in dance 3—otherwise the condition *"No two children can partner each other in more than one dance"* would be violated:

Dance 1	Dance 2	Dance 3
Miguel/Sarah	Karl/Sarah	Luis/Sarah

From *"whoever partners Rita in dance 2 must partner Sarah in dance 3,"* Luis must partner Rita in dance 2. This leaves Tura as the only person he hasn't danced with, so he dances with her in dance 1:

Dance 1	Dance 2	Dance 3
Miguel/Sarah	Karl/Sarah	Luis/Sarah
Luis/Tura	Luis/Rita	

Now, in dance 1, Karl must dance with Rita. Since Karl already dances with Sarah in dance 2, which leaves Tura as Karl's partner in dance 3.

17. (A) No. Since Luis partners Sarah in dance 2, the condition *"Karl partners Sarah in either dance 1 or dance 2"* forces Karl to partner Sarah in dance 1.

(B) No. Since Luis partners Sarah in dance 2, the condition *"Karl partners Sarah in either dance 1 or dance 2"* forces Karl to partner Sarah in dance 1.

(C) Yes. Since Luis partners Sarah in dance 2, the condition *"Karl partners Sarah in either dance 1 or dance 2"* forces Karl to partner Sarah in dance 1:

Dance 1	Dance 2	Dance 3
Karl/Sarah	Luis/Sarah	

This forces Miguel to partner Sarah in dance 3, which in turn forces Miguel to partner Rita in dance 2 (*Whoever partners Rita in dance 2 must partner Sarah in dance 3*).

Dance 1	Dance 2	Dance 3
Karl/Sarah	Luis/Sarah	Miguel/Sarah
	Miguel/Rita	

Now, if Luis partners Tura in dance 1, then Miguel must partner Rita in dance 1. However, Miguel has already been paired with Rita in dance 2. Hence, Luis must be paired with Rita in dance 1.

(D) No. Since Luis partners Sarah in dance 2, the condition *"Karl partners Sarah in either dance 1 or dance 2"* forces Karl to partner Sarah in dance 1:

Dance 1	Dance 2	Dance 3
Karl/Sarah	Luis/Sarah	

This forces Miguel to partner Sarah in dance 3, which in turn forces Miguel to partner Rita in dance 2 (*Whoever partners Rita in dance 2 must partner Sarah in dance 3*).

Dance 1	Dance 2	Dance 3
Karl/Sarah	Luis/Sarah	Miguel/Sarah
	Miguel/Rita	

Now, if Luis partners Tura in dance 1, then Miguel must partner Rita in dance 1. However, Miguel has already been paired with Rita in dance 2.

(E) No. Since Luis partners Sarah in dance 2, the condition *"Karl partners Sarah in either dance 1 or dance 2"* forces Karl to partner Sarah in dance 1:

Dance 1	Dance 2	Dance 3
Karl/Sarah	Luis/Sarah	

This forces Miguel to partner Sarah in dance 3, which in turn forces Miguel to partner Rita in dance 2. Since *"No two children can partner each other in more than one dance,"* Miguel cannot partner Rita in dance 1.

18. (A) No. If Karl partners Rita in dance 2, then the condition *"Whoever partners Rita in dance 2 must partner Sarah in dance 3"* forces Karl to partner Sarah in dance 3. However, this violates the condition *"Karl partners Sarah in either dance 1 or dance 2."*
(B) No. Since *"No two children can partner each other in more than one dance,"* this violates the condition *"Karl partners Sarah in either dance 1 or dance 2."*
(C) No. The following arrangement satisfies all the conditions and has Karl paired with Sarah in dance 1:

Dance 1	Dance 2	Dance 3
Karl/Sarah	Karl/Tura	Karl/Rita
Miguel/Rita	Miguel/Sarah	Miguel/Tura
Luis/Tura	Luis/Rita	Luis/Sarah

(D) Yes. Since Miguel partners Rita in dance 1, either Luis or Karl must partner Rita in dance 2. Suppose Karl partners Rita in dance 2. Then the condition *"Whoever partners Rita in dance 2 must partner Sarah in dance 3"* forces Karl to partner Sarah in dance 3. However, this violates the condition *"Karl partners Sarah in either dance 1 or dance 2."* Hence, Luis partners Rita in dance 2.
(E) No. The following arrangement satisfies all the conditions and has Luis paired with Sarah in dance 3:

Dance 1	Dance 2	Dance 3
Karl/Sarah	Karl/Tura	Karl/Rita
Miguel/Rita	Miguel/Sarah	Miguel/Tura
Luis/Tura	Luis/Rita	Luis/Sarah

Questions 19–24

Applying the conditions to the diagram yields

City 1	City 2
City 3 **U**	City 4
City 5	City 6 **JH**

Since *"None of the cities contains both a jail and a university"* and *"The universities are located in two cities that do not share a common boundary,"* the remaining university must be in City 2:

City 1	City 2 **U**
City 3 **U**	City 4
City 5	City 6 **JH**

19. (A) No. Since there is a university in City 3, this would violate the condition *"The universities are located in two cities that do not share a common boundary."*
(B) No. Since there is already a jail in City 6, this would violate the condition *"None of the cities contains both a jail and a university."*
(C) No. The original diagram has a university in City 2. Hence, placing a jail in City 2 would violate the condition *"None of the cities contains both a jail and a university."*
(D) No. Since there is a university in City 3, this would violate the condition *"None of the cities contains both a jail and a university."*
(E) Yes. In the original diagram, place a hospital in City 3:

City 1	City 2 **U**
City 3 **UH**	City 4
City 5	City 6 **JH**

Now, the remaining jail can be placed in City 1 along with one of the remaining hospitals, and the last remaining hospital can be placed in City 4—all without violating any conditions:

City 1	City 2
JH	**U**
City 3	City 4
UH	**H**
City 5	City 6
	JH

20. (A) Yes. The follows diagram satisfies all the conditions:

City 1	City 2
H	**U**
City 3	City 4
UH	**JH**
City 5	City 6
	JH

(B) No. The original diagram has the two universities in Cities 2 and 3.
(C) No. The original diagram has a university in City 2. Hence, placing a jail in City 2 would violate the condition *"None of the cities contains both a jail and a university."*
(D) No. The original diagram has the two universities in Cities 2 and 3.
(E) No. The original diagram has the two universities in Cities 2 and 3.

21. (A) No. A jail cannot be in City 2 because the original diagram has a university in City 2, which would violate the condition *"None of the cities contains both a jail and a university."* This eliminates choices (B) and (E). Next, a jail can be in City 1 as the following diagram illustrates:

City 1	City 2
JH	**U**
City 3	City 4
UH	**H**
City 5	City 6
	JH

This eliminates choice (C)—it doesn't contain 1. Since both of the remaining answer-choices contain City 4, we need not check whether a jail can be placed in City 4—it can be. Suppose City 5 contains a jail. Then the remaining 3 hospitals can be placed in City 5, without violating any of the conditions:

City 1	City 2
	U
City 3	City 4
U	
City 5	City 6
JHHH	**JH**

Thus, the additional jail can be in only cities 1, 4, or 5.
(B) No. A jail cannot be in City 2 because the original diagram has a university in City 2, which would violate the condition *"None of the cities contains both a jail and a university."* This eliminates choices (B) and (E). Next, a jail can be in City 1 as the following diagram illustrates:

City 1	City 2
JH	**U**
City 3	City 4
UH	
City 5	City 6
	JH

This eliminates choice (C)—it doesn't contain 1. Since both of the remaining answer-choices contain City 4, we need not check whether a jail can be placed in City 4—it can be. Suppose City 5 contains a jail. Then the remaining 3 hospitals can be placed in City 5, without violating any of the conditions:

City 1	City 2
	U
City 3	City 4
U	
City 5	City 6
JHHH	**JH**

Thus, the additional jail can be in only cities 1, 4, or 5.

(C) No. A jail cannot be in City 2 because the original diagram has a university in City 2, which would violate the condition *"None of the cities contains both a jail and a university."* This eliminates choices (B) and (E). Next, a jail can be in City 1 as the following diagram illustrates:

City 1 JH	City 2 U
City 3 UH	City 4 H
City 5	City 6 JH

This eliminates choice (C)—it doesn't contain 1. Since both of the remaining answer-choices contain City 4, we need not check whether a jail can be placed in City 4—it can be. Suppose City 5 contains a jail. Then the remaining 3 hospitals can be placed in City 5, without violating any of the conditions:

City 1	City 2 U
City 3 U	City 4
City 5 JHHH	City 6 JH

Thus, the additional jail can be in only cities 1, 4, or 5.

(D) Yes. A jail cannot be in City 2 because the original diagram has a university in City 2, which would violate the condition *"None of the cities contains both a jail and a university."* This eliminates choices (B) and (E). Next, a jail can be in City 1 as the following diagram illustrates:

City 1 JH	City 2 U
City 3 UH	City 4 H
City 5	City 6 JH

This eliminates choice (C)—it doesn't contain 1. Since both of the remaining answer-choices contain City 4, we need not check whether a jail can be placed in City 4—it can be. Suppose City 5 contains a jail. Then the remaining 3 hospitals can be placed in City 5, without violating any of the conditions:

City 1	City 2 U
City 3 U	City 4
City 5 JHHH	City 6 JH

Thus, the additional jail can be in only cities 1, 4, or 5.

(E) No. A jail cannot be in City 2 because the original diagram has a university in City 2, which would violate the condition *"None of the cities contains both a jail and a university."* This eliminates choices (B) and (E). Next, a jail can be in City 1 as the following diagram illustrates:

City 1 JH	City 2 U
City 3 UH	City 4 H
City 5	City 6 JH

This eliminates choice (C)—it doesn't contain 1. Since both of the remaining answer-choices contain City 4, we need not check whether a jail can be placed in City 4—it can be. Suppose City 5 contains a jail. Then the remaining 3 hospitals can be placed in City 5, without violating any of the conditions:

City 1	City 2 U
City 3 U	City 4
City 5 JHHH	City 6 JH

Thus, the additional jail can be in only cities 1, 4, or 5.

22. (A) No. The following diagram satisfies all the conditions and does not have a jail in City 1:

City 1 H	City 2 U
City 3 U	City 4 JH
City 5 H	City 6 JH

(B) No. The following diagram satisfies all the conditions and does not have a hospital in City 2:

City 1	City 2
H	**U**
City 3	City 4
U	**JH**
City 5	City 6
H	**JH**

(C) No. The following diagram satisfies all the conditions and does not have a hospital in City 3:

City 1	City 2
H	**U**
City 3	City 4
U	**JH**
City 5	City 6
H	**JH**

(D) Yes. City 4 cannot contain a university since the original diagram has the two universities in Cities 2 and 3. So City 4 must contain either a hospital or a jail. But if it contains a jail, then it must also contain a hospital (*Each jail is located in a city that contains at least one hospital*). So in all cases, City 4 contains a hospital.

(E) No. The following diagram satisfies all the conditions and does not have a jail in City 4:

City 1	City 2
JH	**U**
City 3	City 4
U	**H**
City 5	City 6
H	**JH**

23. (A) No. The following diagram has three hospitals in City 1 and does not violate any of the conditions:

City 1	City 2
JHHH	**U**
City 3	City 4
U	
City 5	City 6
	JH

(B) Yes. Suppose there are three hospitals in City 2. Then the original diagram becomes

City 1	City 2
	UHHH
City 3	City 4
U	
City 5	City 6
	JH

The remaining jail cannot be placed in City 6 since that would violate the condition *"None of the cities contains more than one jail."* The remaining jail cannot be placed in City 2 since that would violate the condition *"None of the cities contains both a jail and a university."* The remaining jail cannot be placed in Cities 1, 4, or 5 since that would violate the condition *"Each jail is located in a city that contains at least one hospital"* (all four hospitals have already been placed on the diagram). Thus, there is no room to place the remaining jail. Hence, there must be fewer than three hospitals in City 2.

(C) No. The following diagram has three hospitals in City 4 and does not violate any of the conditions:

City 1	City 2
	U
City 3	City 4
U	**JHHH**
City 5	City 6
	JH

(D) No. The following diagram has three hospitals in City 5 and does not violate any of the conditions:

City 1	City 2
	U
City 3	City 4
U	
City 5	City 6
JHHH	**JH**

(E) No. The following diagram has three hospitals in City 6 and does not violate any of the conditions:

City 1	City 2
JH	**U**
City 3	City 4
U	
City 5	City 6
	JHHH

24. (A) Yes. The following diagram satisfies all the conditions and does not contain a hospital in Cities 1, 3, or 5:

City 1	City 2 **UHH**
City 3 **U**	City 4 **JH**
City 5	City 6 **JH**

(B) No. Referring to the original diagram, we see that the remaining jail cannot be placed in Cites 2 or 3 because that would violate the condition *"None of the cities contains both a jail and a university."* Further, since *"None of the cities contains more than one jail,"* the remaining jail cannot be placed in City 6. Hence, the remaining jail must be placed in City 1, 4, or 5. Since *"Each jail is located in a city that contains at least one hospital,"* City 1, 4, or 5 must contain a hospital.
(C) No. The original diagram has the two universities placed in Cities 2 and 3. Hence, the city that contains exactly two hospitals and exactly one university must be either City 2 or City 3.
(D) No. The original diagram has a hospital in City 6.
(E) No. The original diagram has a hospital in City 6.

Test III
Section IV
Solutions

1. (A) No. The author implies that other people accuse the postal service of incompetence and inefficiency and does not dispute that accusation. Instead, he states that the result of the postal service's function—for example, a personal letter from a friend—is worth the increased cost.
(B) No. This is irrelevant to those who believe a five-cent increase is significant.
(C) Yes. The argument is confusing the emotional value of a letter from a friend with the monetary value of delivering the letter (i.e., the price of the stamp).
(D) No. There is no outside authority mentioned in the passage.
(E) No. *Who* makes the criticism is not relevant; the issue is the *truthfulness* of the criticism.

2. (A) No. Regardless of the reason, the delay still occurred and the argument's validity remains unaffected.
(B) No. This is irrelevant. The passage states that aspirin is effective in tests with humans.
(C) No. The conclusion does not state that the general health of people who take aspirin would be better, just that their risk of heart attack would be lessened.
(D) No. Regardless of the reason, the delay still occurred and the argument's validity remains unaffected.
(E) Yes. If aspirin must be taken regularly for two years before any benefits are realized, then taking aspirin during the six-week delay would have had no affect on reducing the risk of heart attacks during the delay.

3. (A) No. This doesn't provide enough information about the 90 percent of the travelers who seek discount fares. Are they new travelers who would not have otherwise purchased tickets except at a discount? Or are they travelers who were intending to pay full-fare but took advantage of a good deal?
(B) No. This is irrelevant.
(C) Yes. If across-the-board discounts attract passengers who displace full-fare travelers on filled flights, then revenues will decrease on those flights. Further, if no new passengers are attracted to usually unfilled flights, there will be no corresponding increases in revenue elsewhere. The net effect is a decrease in revenues and thus profits.
(D) No. This is actually a pretty good choice, but it's not the answer for two reasons: 1) There is a stronger answer-choice. 2) It has a flaw: Although only a small number of people who had never flown before were persuaded to do so, it's possible that people who already travel by air greatly increased the number of trips they take.
(E) No. This is irrelevant.

4. (A) No. Given the statement *"Only if the electorate is moral and intelligent will a democracy function well,"* we know that if a democracy is functioning well, then the electorate must be moral and intelligent. This can be diagrammed as follows:

FW—>(M & I)

where the arrow means "If ..., then ...." Now, this answer-choice states, "If the electorate is moral and intelligent, then a democracy will function well," which can be diagrammed as follows:

(M & I)—>FW

This is clearly the fallacy of affirming the conclusion (see ARGUMENTS, page 242).
(B) No. Given the statement *"Only if the electorate is moral and intelligent will a democracy function well,"* we know that if a democracy is functioning well, then the electorate must be moral and intelligent. This can be diagrammed as **FW—>(M & I)**, where the arrow means "If ..., then ...."

Now, an *if-then* statement is false only when its premise is true and its conclusion is false—in all other cases it is true. The following "truth-table" illustrates all four possible cases for the original argument:

Premise	Conclusion	If-then Statement
FW	M & I	FW—>(M & I)
T	T	T
T	F	F
F	T	T
F	F	T

Now, the opposite of Choice (B) is

The democracy functions well and the electorate is moral and intelligent.

This is the first row of the truth-table in which the original *if-then* statement is true. Since the opposite of Choice (B) is consistent with the original argument, Choice (B) does not necessarily follow from the original argument.
(C) Yes. Given the statement *"Only if the electorate is moral and intelligent will a democracy function well,"* we know that if a democracy is functioning well, then the electorate must be moral and intelligent. This can be diagrammed as follows:

FW—>(M & I)

where the arrow means "If ..., then ...." Applying the contrapositive yields

~(M & I)—>~FW

Now, saying that the electorate is not both moral and intelligent, ~(M & I), is equivalent to saying that the electorate is either not moral or not intelligent, ~M or ~I.

(~M or ~I)—>~FW

In other words, if the electorate is not moral or not intelligent, then a democracy will not function well.
(D) No. Given the statement *"Only if the electorate is moral and intelligent will a democracy function well,"* we know that if a democracy is functioning well, then the electorate must be moral and intelligent. This can be diagrammed as follows:

FW—>(M & I)

where the arrow means "If ..., then ...." Applying the contrapositive (see GAMES, page 28) yields

~(M & I)—>~FW

In other words, if the electorate is not both moral and intelligent, then a democracy will not function well. Now, this answer-choice states *"a democracy does not function well."* This affirms the conclusion in the last diagram. The answer-choice then commits the fallacy of affirming the conclusion (see ARGUMENTS, page 26) by concluding *"the electorate is not moral or not intelligent."*
(E) No. Given the statement *"Only if the electorate is moral and intelligent will a democracy function well,"* we know that if a democracy is functioning well, then the electorate must be moral and intelligent. This can be diagrammed as follows:

FW—>(M & I)

where the arrow means "If ..., then ...." Now, recall that an *if-then* statement is false only when its premise is true and its conclusion is false. Hence, it is possible for the premise to be false (democracy will not function well) and the conclusion to be true (the electorate is moral and intelligent) simultaneously.

5. (A) No. While the passage discusses infants younger than six months, there is nothing in the passage that states this ability disappears immediately at six months of age.
(B) No. This is irrelevant. The passage is about similar but *different* speech sounds.
(C) No. This is irrelevant.
(D) No. There is no discussion of individuals in the passage.
(E) Yes. There might be several factors that contribute to the observed difference in ability to distinguish similar sounds. For example, perhaps the por-

tion of the brain that identifies and interprets sounds responds differently in infants than in adults.

6. (A) No. The argument does not need this assumption. The problem is not that the younger workers are not skilled, it's that there are not enough younger workers.
(B) No. The passage is about the size of the labor pool, not about the plight of retired workers.
(C) Yes. If the people would retire regardless of whether they were forced to, then abolishing the practice of mandatory retirement would have no affect on the size of the labor pool.
(D) No. This is irrelevant.
(E) No. This would weaken the argument. If many retired workers were already in the labor pool, those remaining may not be sufficient to make up for the coming labor shortages.

7. (A) No. In fact, the passage implies that Japan and North America have similar levels of industrial pollution.
(B) No. In fact, the passage states that Japan has a modern life-style. Therefore, it is reasonable to assume that the levels of stress are equivalent to those in North America.
(C) No. This choice is tempting, but it has a flaw. Instead of the Japanese diet curing cancer, perhaps the North American diet causes cancer.
(D) Yes. That Japanese who immigrated to North America soon developed the same rate of cancer as other North Americans is strong evidence that the lower cancer rate in Japan is due to diet, not genetic or environmental factors.
(E) No. This is too strong. Although the passage provides support for arguing that the different cancer rates in Japan and North America are due to the different diets, it does not state or imply that any particular factor in the North American diet causes cancer.

8. (A) No. If stylistic differences between human translators could be reduced by providing guidelines for writing, there would be fewer reasons to use a computer for translation. This answer-choice provides an alternate solution to the stated problem.
(B) No. To determine the relative accuracy of computer versus human translations, numerical evaluations would be very useful.
(C) Yes. The issue is the different writing styles *within* a given document. The argument advocates using a *single* computer program to translate a given document—thus, insuring the writing style will be consistent throughout the document.
(D) No. The argument presumes that accurate translation is important. It is certainly relevant to determine whether a translation program makes errors that change the meaning of the text.
(E) No. Knowing how the translation is used is important for determining whether the style of the translation is more important than its accuracy.

Questions 9–10

9. (A) No. Myrna does not dispute Roland's statements. Rather, she expands the scope of the discussion from mortality to overall health.
(B) Yes. While Roland considers only the changes in life-span that would result from a change in diet, Myrna considers the overall health benefits.
(C) No. Myrna does not dispute Roland's statements. Rather, she expands the scope of the discussion from mortality to overall health.
(D) No. Myrna does not dispute Roland's statements.
(E) No. Myrna does not say that Roland's argument is circular. Rather, she expands the scope of the discussion from mortality to overall health.

10. (A) No. In fact, Roland argues that the slightly lengthened life-span is not worth the sacrificial changes in diet.
(B) Yes. Roland's argument is based on the comparative value of two possibilities:

1) A higher-fat diet and a shorter life-span.
2) An "unappealing low-fat diet" and a longer life-span.

However, he does not consider a third possibility—that a low-fat diet can be appealing and still increase life-span.
(C) No. Nothing indicates that Roland makes this assumption. The argument mentions only diet because it is the particular factor that Myrna and Roland are discussing.
(D) No. Just the opposite. Roland states that a low-fat diet would be *"unappealing"* and would require a *"lifetime of sacrifice."*
(E) No. This is irrelevant: Roland's argument is directed toward those who do have a higher-fat diet. In fact, if many people have a low-fat diet instead of the "average" diet, his argument could be weakened if those people found their nutritional lifestyle to be worthwhile.

11. (A) No. The argument challenges those critics who believe that more great works of art should be displayed outside large metropolitan areas. The basis of this challenge is twofold: 1) since only a limited number great works of art exists, distribution of these works of art outside of metropolitan museums is impractical; 2) masterpieces are best appreciated in the context of other works of art of the same era, which is more likely in *"huge metropolitan museums."* The principle in this answer-choice is not espoused by the author of the argument. It is the critics who would likely hold this principle since they

believe it is unfair that *"the populations served by [metropolitan] museums already have access to a wide variety of important artwork."*
(B) No. This is the second-best choice. The argument challenges those critics who believe that more great works of art should be displayed outside large metropolitan areas. The basis of this challenge is twofold: 1) the critic's position *"is in principle unwarranted because the limited number of masterpieces makes wider distribution of them impractical"*; 2) masterpieces are best appreciated in the context of other works of art of the same era, which is more likely in *"huge metropolitan museums."* The principle in this answer-choice is not espoused by the author of the argument. It is the critics who would likely hold this principle since they believe it is unfair that *"the populations served by [metropolitan] museums already have access to a wide variety of important artwork."* Although this answer-choice might support the second point, does not serve as the principle of the first point.
(C) No. The argument challenges those critics who believe that more great works of art should be displayed outside large metropolitan areas. The author responds to these critics by claiming that their desire to redistribute masterpieces is *"in principle unwarranted because the limited number of masterpieces makes wider distribution of them impractical."* In other words, no matter how inequitable a situation is, criticism of that situation is warranted only if a better arrangement is practical. The appropriateness of redistribution that deprives some people for the benefit of others is not discussed.
(D) Yes. The argument challenges those critics who believe that more great works of art should be displayed outside large metropolitan areas. The author responds to these critics by claiming that their desire to redistribute masterpieces is *"in principle unwarranted because the limited number of masterpieces makes wider distribution of them impractical."* In other words, no matter how inequitable a situation is, criticism of that situation is warranted only if a better arrangement is practical.
(E) No. Although the author does believe that great works of art are best seen in surroundings that depict the social and historical situation in which they were created, such surroundings are not necessarily those that the artist had intended. Regardless, this point is not relevant to the principle the author uses to establish her position.

12. (A) No. The argument is concerned with comparisons between accountants who use adding machines and those who use computers. It is not concerned with comparisons of the relative number of accountants in each group.
(B) No. This does not relate to computers.
(C) Yes. Since the passage states that a computer can perform more calculations is less time than an adding machine (in other words, more calculations per hour) and that an accountant can earn more per hour using a computer, the passage needs to assume that the more calculations an accountant performs, the more money he or she will earn.
(D) No. This contradicts the argument. The argument concludes that "*an accountant who uses a computer generally can earn more per hour than an accountant who uses an adding machine*" whereas this answer-choice states the opposite.
(E) No. This is irrelevant. The argument is concerned with two categories of accountants—those who use adding machines and those who use computers.

13. (A) Yes. This year, she earned 3 weeks of vacation time but took a 4-week vacation. Now, she can use only up to half of any vacation time she did not use last year. Since she took one additional week of vacation this year, she must not have used at least 2 weeks of vacation last year.
(B) No. The passage only states *"Anyone who has worked at KVZ Manufacturing for between one and four years is automatically entitled to exactly three weeks paid vacation each year"* and that Jennifer has worked at KVZ just over three years. The passage tells us nothing about the vacation time earned by employees who have worked with the company for more than four years.
(C) No. This is independent of the issue in the passage, which is concerned about Jennifer.
(D) No. Although Jennifer had to have <u>at least</u> two weeks of vacation time available at the end of last year (to apply one week to this year), conceivably she could have taken no vacation time last year.
(E) No. Though this might be true, it cannot be concluded from the passage.

14. (A) Yes. That better training of anesthetists improved safety in no way implies that new equipment would not have a similar result. The argument cannot validly make a conclusion about equipment that was not studied.
(B) No. The argument is not circular. In fact, the argument is flawed because it takes too big of a leap in logic.
(C) No. The passage does not argue that the absence of a certain factor (monitoring devices) caused a certain result (increase in safety). Rather, it states that the presence of better-trained anesthetists resulted in a better safety record. The argument then invalidly concludes that the presence of the monitoring devices would not also improve the safety record.
(D) No. Only one piece of evidence is cited—a review of hospital fatalities due to anesthesia during the last 20 years. No evidence is cited to support the

conclusion regarding the use of monitoring equipment.

(E) No. The argument states that one event (better training of anesthetists) resulted in another event (an improved safety record in hospital anesthesia use). Nothing in the passage suggests that both of these results were independently caused by a third event.

15. (A) No. The argument describes a situation in which an alternative designed to produce savings in an area may have side effects that counteract these savings, and the overall impact of the change may actually require more resources than another alternative.

New washing machines —> less energy but wetter clothes
Wetter clothes —> more energy to dry
∴ New washing machines —> may consume more energy overall

This answer-choice can be paraphrased as follows:

Machines that require greater skill —> harder to find operators
Harder to find operators —> more they must be paid
∴ Machines that require greater skill —> higher wages for operators

This valid application of the transitive property is not parallel to the original argument.

(B) No. The argument describes a situation in which an alternative designed to produce savings in an area may have side effects that counteract these savings, and the overall impact of the change may actually require more resources than another alternative.

New washing machines —> less energy but wetter clothes
Wetter clothes —> more energy to dry
∴ New washing machines —> may consume more energy overall

In this answer-choice, there are two alternatives: a scenic route between Centerville and Mapletown, and a more direct route. However, there is no discussion of unexpected side-effects from choosing either route.

(C) No. The argument describes a situation in which an alternative designed to produce savings in an area may have side effects that counteract these savings, and the overall impact of the change may actually require more resources than another alternative.

New washing machines —> less energy but wetter clothes
Wetter clothes —> more energy to dry
∴ New washing machines —> may consume more energy overall

This answer-choice can be paraphrased as follows:

More people in reading room —> Noisier the room becomes
Noisier the room becomes —> Less efficient people work
∴ More people in reading room —> Less efficient people work

This valid application of the transitive property is not parallel to the original argument.

(D) Yes. The argument describes a situation in which an alternative designed to produce savings in an area may have side effects that counteract these savings, and the overall impact of the change may actually require more resources than another alternative.

New washing machines —> less energy but wetter clothes
Wetter clothes —> more energy to dry
∴ New washing machines —> may consume more energy overall

This answer-choice can be paraphrased as follows:

Pine furniture —> less expensive but more susceptible to rot
Susceptible to rot —> more expensive paint
∴ Pine furniture —> may cost more overall

Like the original argument, this answer-choice describes an alternative that costs less initially but may end up costing more in the long run.

(E) No. The argument describes a situation in which an alternative designed to produce savings in an area may have side effects that counteract these savings, and the overall impact of the change may actually require more resources than another alternative.

New washing machines —> less energy but wetter clothes
Wetter clothes —> more energy to dry
∴ New washing machines —> may consume more energy overall

This answer-choice can be paraphrased as follows:

More weights on machine —> more muscle strength needed
More muscle strength needed —> person becomes stronger
∴ More weights on machine —> can make a person stronger

Although this choice is not strictly a deductive argument, it has the same structure as a transitive argument and is not parallel to the original argument.

Questions 16–17

16. (A) No. G states *"Equal numbers of photographers, sculptors, and painters submitted works that met the traditional criteria for the show."* However, this allows the photographers to submit more items each than the sculptors and painters.
(B) No. H's statements imply that some works submitted for the Metropolitan Art Show did not meet the traditional criteria for the show: *"All submitted works that met the traditional criteria—and only those works—were exhibited in the show."*
(C) No. We know only that the quality of objects displayed—photographs, sculptures, and paintings—met or surpassed the traditional criteria. We are given no information about the relative quality of the different types of works.
(D) No. H's statements imply that some works submitted for the Metropolitan Art Show did not meet the traditional criteria for the show: *"All submitted works that met the traditional criteria—and only those works—were exhibited in the show."* However, we do not have enough information to determine whether any of these works were photographs.
(E) Yes. G states only that equal numbers of photographers, sculptors, and painters submitted works. This allows the photographers to submit more items each than the sculptors. For example, each photographer may have submitted 10 photographs, whereas each sculptor may have submitted only 1 sculpture.

17. (A) No. The passage concerns the number of works submitted and displayed at the Art Show, not the rate of sales of the art.
(B) Yes. Clearly, putting a larger financial burden on painters and sculptors shows a bias.
(C) No. This shows that the committee was balanced.
(D) No. This is irrelevant. G's allegation of bias is directed toward those who selected the works of art to be displayed, not toward the news coverage of the show.
(E) No. This suggests that the imbalance is not intentional.

Questions 18–19

18. (A) No. This is the second-best choice. Anita states that traditional journalistic ethics do not provide sufficient guidelines for journalists to make professional decisions. ("*But in the typical case, where a journalist has some information but is in a quandary about whether it is yet important or 'newsworthy,' this guidance is inadequate.*") Rather than object to Marcus' assertion that traditional ethics are clear, she objects to his claim that these ethics are adequate.
(B) No. She does not believe that traditional journalistic ethics are incorrect for most ethical dilemmas ("*Well, Marcus, of course interesting and important information should be brought before the public—that is a journalist's job*"), just that the precepts are inadequate ("*But in the typical case, where a journalist has some information but is in a quandary about whether it is yet important or "newsworthy," this guidance is inadequate*").
(C) Yes. Anita does not disagree with the journalistic principles that Marcus cites, she just believes that they are not sufficient guidelines for typical situations journalists encounter.
(D) No. This is too strong. She merely believes that the particular principle of journalistic ethics Marcus cited is inadequate for typical cases.
(E) No. She does not reject traditional journalistic ethics as unnecessary and convoluted ("*Well, Marcus, of course interesting and important information should be brought before the public—that is a journalist's job*"). Rather, she believes that traditional journalistic ethics are insufficient to guide journalists.

19. (A) Yes. Anita argues that traditional journalistic ethics is not sufficient for *"the typical case, where a journalist has some information but is in a quandary about whether it is yet important or "newsworthy"* Now, if deciding whether a piece of information is or is not newsworthy does not raise ethical dilemmas for journalists, then her argument is moot.
(B) No. She agrees with Marcus that *"when journalists have uncovered newsworthy information, they should go to press with it as soon as possible."* This is seen from her opening line *"Well, Marcus, of course interesting and important information should be brought before the public—that is a journalist's job."*
(C) No. The discussion is limited to typical cases, not other types of professional dilemmas.
(D) No. Anita discusses only the traditional system of journalistic ethics. She does not mention whether a different, adequate system of journalistic ethics could be designed.
(E) No. This is too strong. She is merely implying that a system of journalistic ethics should at least cover a typical case.

Questions 20–21

20. (A) No. It would justify placing fewer restrictions on owners of burglar alarms than on owners of car alarms since burglar alarms at least occasionally deter crime.
(B) No. One obvious solution to the problem is to outlaw the use of burglar alarms. The statement heads off this suggestion by implying that outlawing burglar alarms would be unacceptable.
(C) Yes. One obvious solution to the problem is to outlaw the use of burglar alarms. The statement heads off this suggestion by implying that outlawing burglar alarms would be unacceptable.
(D) No. Although this is true, it is not needed for the purpose of the argument.

(E) No. The statement appears to apply equally to both businesses and homes.

21. (A) No. As Question 20 established, the arguer does not want to banish burglar alarms, just require that their owners compensate the public for the loss of police time in responding to false alarms.
(B) No. The arguer merely wants burglar alarm owners to reimburse the public for the police costs of responding to false alarms, not legitimate alarms.
(C) No. There is no mention in the passage of reducing the crime level throughout an area.
(D) No. The arguer merely wants burglar alarm owners to reimburse the public for the police costs of responding to false alarms, not legitimate alarms.
(E) Yes. *"This situation causes an enormous and dangerous drain on increasingly scarce public resources ..., and a disproportionate share of police service goes to alarm system users, who are mostly businesses and affluent homeowners ... the only acceptable solution is to fine burglar alarm system owners the cost of 45 minutes of police time for each false alarm their systems generate."*

22. (A) No. This is irrelevant. The argument is about health, not profits.
(B) No. This would strengthen the argument. The argument's intent is to lower the public's intake of butterfat, and increasing the water content in a product would decrease the amount of butterfat.
(C) No. Although this does weaken the argument, there is a stronger answer-choice that applies to most, not just some, individuals.
(D) No. This is irrelevant.
(E) Yes. The purpose of the recommendation is to lower the amount of butterfat that people eat. But *"Most people deterred from eating 'imitation butter' because of its name choose alternatives with a lower butterfat content than this product has."* So if the labeling change prompted people to return to the original product, they would actually increase their butterfat intake.

23. (A) No. The passage implies that some behavioral tendencies of farm animals cannot be altered: the opening line of the argument implies that some behavioral tendencies are instinctive, and the closing line of the argument implies that the animals will resist changing these tendencies.
(B) No. This is too strong. The passage merely states that current farm-management practices *"can also be less efficient than those other farm-management practices."*
(C) No. The passage implies just the opposite: that farm-management practices that cause less pain and distress to farm animals can increase efficiency.
(D) No. This goes too far. The passage merely states that current farm-management practices *"can also be less efficient than those other farm-management practices."*
(E) Yes. *"Because the animals tend to resist this type of organization, current practices can also be less efficient than those other farm-management practices."*

24. (A) No. Although this argument also fails to account for other possible explanations for the observed situation, there is another answer-choice that is more similar to the original argument.
(B) No. This is more of a prediction than an argument.
(C) No. Unlike the passage, this is a reasonably valid argument.
(D) Yes. Like the original this argument fails to consider that other factors may have caused the drop in sales. Perhaps there was a recession during the past year, or perhaps the manufactures were able maximize their profits by selling their products at a price that the average consumer or school district could not afford.
(E) No. Unlike the passage, this is a reasonably valid argument.

25. (A) No. They are, in fact, assuming that the original experiments had been described in sufficient detail to make an exact replication possible.
(B) No. The scientists attempted the replication to determine whether the original results were in error. However, the controversy may have increased the desire to attempt the replication.
(C) No. If anything, this would support the original results.
(D) Yes. Both sets of experiments are subject to faulty measurements. So for the argument to be valid, it must assume that original experiments were more likely to have been marred by faulty measurements than were the replication experiments.
(E) No. The scientists do not need to assume this to make their conclusion. Besides, it's difficult to conclude anything from the statement that the original researchers observed their results only once. Perhaps the observation was a false artifact, or perhaps the single observation indicates the difficulty of the experiment and explains the failure to replicate the result.

LSAT Writing Sample
(Test 1)
Time—30 minutes

The city of Stockton must choose an event to inaugurate its new auditorium, an open-air stage with seats for about 15,000 people and a surrounding lawn with room for 30,000 more. Write an argument in favor of hiring either of the following performers with these considerations in mind.

- The city hopes the inaugural performance will raise as much money as possible to pay off the auditorium's construction loans.
- The city wants to obtain considerable positive publicity for the new auditorium.

Astrani, one of the legends of popular music, is giving a farewell concert tour before retiring. He has proposed holding the final three concerts in Stockton; because of his elaborate sets and costumes, tickets would be sold only for the auditorium's seats and no lawn seating would be available. Astrani never allows souvenirs to be sold at his concerts, but the city will receive 20 percent of the proceeds form ticket sales. If the tour ends in Stockton, a well-known director will film the historic event and plans to release a full-length feature which will share the final shows with fans around the world.

A number of prominent bands have organized "Animal-Aid" to raise money for endangered species. The concert has already generated significant attention in the press and a number of important arenas competed for the privilege of hosting the event. Stockton's new auditorium is the organizer's first choice as the site for the all-day concert and the city would be allowed to design and sell souvenirs commemorating the event. While tickets would be available for both the seats and surrounding lawn, all of the proceeds from ticket sales would go to "Animal-Aid." The auditorium's security expert is concerned that the facility's novice staff may not yet have the experience to handle a large crowd during an all-day event.

LSAT Writing Sample
(Test 2)
Time—30 minutes

The English department at Corbett University must choose a text for the college's first-year composition course. Write an argument in favor of selecting either of the following texts with these consideration in mind:

- The department has a strong commitment to teach basic writing skills, such as grammar and essay organization.
- The department wants to increase the students' enthusiasm for and interest in writing.

During the three years that the department has used *The Standard Textbook of English*, instructors in other departments have reported significant improvement in students' writing skills. Nicknamed "The Best and the Dullest," the text contains classic essays from both ancient and modern authors and is organized to illustrate the various forms of the essay—such as narration, exposition and persuasion. The essays average more than 10 pages, and almost all are written in a formal style. While students find some of the subjects foreign, they feel the materials covered are often useful in their other coursework.

A new text, *The Modern Writer*, contains both an introduction describing the basics of grammar and a number of journalistic essays by contemporary authors. The pieces are typically short (only 2 to 3 pages) and explore topics of interest to most college students, such as popular music and career planning. The style of the essays tends to be informal, even colloquial. Each chapter contains several essays on a given topic and exercises designed to aid students in developing essays of their own. Although the introduction provides an adequate overview of basic grammar, the text does not discuss the essay form.

LSAT Writing Sample

(Test 3)

Time—30 minutes

The large publishing firm that owns financially troubled Westerly Books has allocated $50,000 to the small company in one major effort to save it. Write an argument for spending the money on one of the following plans. The publishing firm has set the following conditions for keeping Westerly in business:

- Westerly must show a profit within one year by significantly increasing total sales.
- Westerly must change its image from an elite literary press to one with a broader audience appeal.

The Series Plan calls for contracting with a commercial artist who designs covers and book jackets. Westerly primarily publishes fiction by young and little-known writers whose names are recognized by only a small reading audience. This artist successfully launched a series of biographies for another small press by designing distinctive covers that became a trademark for the series. She believes that she can do something similar for Westerly by developing individual cover designs that will also become recognized trademarks. Book stores have told Westerly that its covers lack visual appeal and estimate that sales of its twenty current titles could jump at least 50 percent with better designs. The artist wants a $50,000 contract to undertake this project.

The Star Plan calls for spending the money on promotion of one promising novel. Westerly's books are generally well received by the critics but rarely sell more than five thousand copies. Westerly usually does not have the resources for extensive national advertising. As a result, young writers who start out with Westerly usually sign with larger publishing houses once they achieve some success. Westerly has published two novels by a writer whose popularity has grown steadily. He is about to complete his third novel and claims that, with the right promotion, sales of this novel alone will exceed those of Westerly's entire line. Though optimistic, Westerly's staff has a more conservative estimate of expected sales. To remain with Westerly, the author wants a promotional campaign costing the entire $50,000.

Score Conversion Chart (For the section tests)

Directions:

1. Use the Scoring Worksheet below to compute your raw score.
2. Use the Score Conversion Chart to convert your raw score into the 120–180 scale.

Scoring Worksheet

1. Enter the number of questions you answered correctly in each section.

	Number Correct
SECTION I	______
SECTION II....................	______
SECTION III	______
SECTION IV	______

2. Enter the sum here: ______

This is your Raw Score

Conversion Chart

For Converting Raw Score to the 120-180 LSAT Scaled Score

Reported Score	Raw Score Lowest	Raw Score Highest
180	100	101
179	99	99
178	98	98
177	97	97
176	__*	__*
175	96	96
174	95	95
173	94	94
172	93	93
171	92	92
170	91	91
169	89	90
168	88	88
167	87	87
166	85	86
165	84	84
164	82	83
163	81	81
162	79	80
161	77	78
160	75	76
159	74	74
158	72	73
157	70	71
156	68	69
155	66	67
154	65	65
153	63	64
152	61	62
151	59	60
150	57	58
149	55	56
148	54	54
147	52	53
146	50	51
145	48	49
144	47	47
143	45	46
142	43	44
141	42	42
140	40	41
139	38	39
138	37	37
137	35	36
136	34	34
135	33	33
134	31	32
133	30	30
132	29	29
131	28	28
130	27	27
129	25	26
128	24	24
127	23	23
126	__*	__*
125	22	22
124	21	21
123	20	20
122	19	19
121	18	18
120	0	17

* There is no raw score that will produce this scaled score for this form.

Law Schools: Average Scores

The following list contains the average scores for 154 ABA approved law schools. The average individual LSAT score is 150. However, due to intense competition, the average scores of only a few schools are below 150. The average LSAT score for schools that release their scores is 157. However, the actual average LSAT score is probably around 155 since more schools with lower scores refuse to release their scores than schools with higher scores.

171 Yale
169 Duke University
168 Columbia University
167 Stanford University
167 University of California—Berkeley
167 University of Michigan
166 Georgetown University
165 Boston College
165 University of California—Los Angeles
165 University of Pennsylvania
165 University of Southern California
164 University of California—Davis
164 University of Colorado—Boulder
164 University of Virginia
164 Vanderbilt University
164 Northewestern University
163 Fordham University
163 George Washington University
163 University of California—Hastings
163 University of Georgia
163 University of Minnesota
163 University of North Carolina
163 University of Washington
163 Washington and Lee University
162 Boston University
162 Brigham Young University
162 Emory University
162 University of Arizona
162 University of Cincinnati
162 University of Texas
162 Wake Forest University
161 Arizona State University
161 Lewis and Clark
161 Loyola Law School—Los Angeles
161 Rutgers University—Newark
161 University of Florida
161 University of Illinois
161 University of Oregon
161 University of Richmond
161 University of Utah
160 Baylor University
160 Benjamin N. Cardozo School of Law
160 Case Western Reserve University
160 Chicago Kent College of Law
160 George Mason University
160 Indiana University—Bloomington
160 Pepperdine University
160 Tulane University
160 University of Alabama
160 University of Hawaii
160 University of Iowa
160 University of Kentucky
160 University of Maryland
160 University of Pittsburgh
160 University of San Diego
160 University of Wisconsin
160 Villanova University
160 Washington University
159 Georgia State University
159 Indiana University—Indianapolis
159 Loyola University Chicago
159 Northeastern University
159 Pace University
159 Santa Clara University
159 Southern Methodist University
159 University of Houston
159 University of Kansas
159 University of Puget Sound
159 University of San Francisco
159 Vermont Law School
158 Catholic University of America
158 DePaul University
158 Florida State University
158 Golden Gate University
158 John Marshall School of Law
158 Suffolk University
158 Texas Tech University
158 University of Connecticut
158 University of Denver
158 University of Missouri—Columbia
158 University of New Mexico
158 University of the Pacific
158 Wayne State University
157 Marquette University
157 McGeorge School of Law
157 Mercer University
157 Northern Illinois University
157 Rutgers—The State University—Camden
157 St. John's University
157 University of Maine
157 University of South Carolina
157 University of Toledo
157 Williamette University
156 California Western School of Law
156 Campbell
156 Dickinson School of Law
156 Louisiana State University
156 Ohio Northern University
156 Saint Louis University
156 Temple University

156	University of Louisville
156	University of Nebraska
156	University of South Dakota
155	Albany Law School
155	Bridgeport School of Law—Quinnipiac College
155	Drake University
155	Hamline University
155	Stamford University
155	Seton Hall University
155	South Texas College of Law
155	Southern Illinois University
155	University of Baltimore
155	University of Detroit
155	University of Montana
155	University of Tulsa
155	University of Wyoming
155	Valparaiso University
155	Whittier College
155	Widener University
154	Capital University Law & Graduate Center
154	Creighton University
154	Detroit College of Law
154	Franklin Pierce Law Center
154	Gonzaga University
154	Memphis State University
154	Mississippi College
154	New York Law School
154	St. Mary's University
154	Syracuse University
154	University of Missouri—Kansas City
154	University of Oklahoma
153	Regent University
153	St. Thomas University
153	University of Arkansas—Fayetteville
153	Washburn University
153	Western New England College
152	Howard University
152	Loyola University—New Orleans
152	New England School of Law
152	University of Arkansas at Little Rock
152	University of Idaho
152	University of Mississippi
152	University of North Dakota
151	Northern Kentucky University
151	Nova University
151	Touro College
150	City Univ. of New York—Queens College
150	North Carolina Central University
150	Oklahoma City University
148	Thomas M. Cooley Law School
146	University of Puerto Rico
145	Texas Southern University
144	Southern University Law Center
139	Inter American University

Software

(Windows and Mac Classic)

INSTALLATION DIRECTIONS FOR MASTER THE LSAT SOFTWARE

Windows:

1. Insert the disk into the CD-ROM drive.
2. From the Start menu, select Run and then select Browse.
3. Select your CD-ROM drive from the Browse menu.
4. Select the file lsatprep.exe
5. Click Open and then click OK.

Macintosh Classic:

1. Insert the disk into the CD-ROM drive.
2. If necessary, double click the disk icon.
3. Double click the icon: LSAT.sea
4. Select a folder into which you would like to place the file.
5. Click Save.

SOFTWARE ORIENTATION

If you are familiar with computers and software, you are unlikely to need to read this orientation: We put considerable thought into making the software as simple and intuitive as possible.

A. Main Menu

You start a test by clicking either the Mentor Mode or Test Mode button of the test you want to take. In Mentor Mode, you can immediately see a solution to each problem and you will not be timed. Select this mode for studying. In Test Mode, you will not see solutions of the problems and you will be timed. Select this mode for practice at taking timed LSATs.

1. **Select Section Screen**
   When you click Mentor Mode, the Select Section Screen appears. On this screen, click the section of the test you want to study. If you have chosen Test Mode instead of Mentor Mode, this screen will not appear and you will be taken directly to the first section of the test.
2. **Section/Direction Screen**
   After clicking the section you want to study, the program takes you to the first page of the section—the Directions page. To see the first question, click Next.
3. **Selecting an Answer**
   You select an answer by clicking its letter (or typing its letter). This highlights the letter, and, if you are in Mentor Mode, presents a feedback box that explains why your selection is correct or incorrect. You can change your answers as often as you like. Some solutions to the questions are too long to display all at once in the feedback box. In these cases, use the scroll bar to scroll through the solution. When there is more text to be viewed, the scroll bar will be highlighted.

B. Navigation

There are three ways to reach other questions.

1. **Questions Near By**
   If the question is near by, merely click Next (or Back) the appropriate number of times.
2. **Questions Moderately Far Away**
   If the question is farther away, press the Right Arrow Key on the keyboard the appropriate number of times (this is available only on extended keyboards). If you are on Question 3 and want to go to Question 7, then press the Right Arrow Key four times
3. **Questions Far Away**
   If the question is far away, click the Status Button, which takes you to the Status Display. From there, you can go to any question by merely clicking the question. If you are on Question 3 and want to go to Question 26, click the Status Button and then click Question 26.

C. The Navigation Strip

The Navigation Strip is present at the bottom of the screen when questions are present.

1. **Status Button**

   Clicking the Status Button takes you to the Status Display which lists the questions you have answered correctly or incorrectly (in Test Mode, it states only whether the questions have been answered). The Status Display is also a convenient and fast way to reach far away questions. If you are on Question 21 and want to go to Question 2, then click the Status Button and then click Question 2.

2. **Time Button**

   The Time Button displays the time you have been working on a section and the time you have remaining.

3. **Stop Button**

   The Stop Button gives you access to your current score (and from there access to the Score Conversion Chart). It also allows you to navigate to other sections of the test or to return to the Main Menu.

   A. Return to the Section Button

   The Return to the Section Button takes you back to the question you were working on.

   B. Switch Sections (Go to Next Section)

   The Switch Sections Button takes you to the Switch Sections Screen from which you can choose another section of the test.

   In Test Mode, the Switch Sections Button is labeled Go to Next Section, and it takes you directly to the next section. If you want to skip that section, just click the Stop Button and then click the Go to Next Section Button. By doing this, you will be unable to return to the skipped section. Although this is inconvenient, it is how the paper and pencil test is administered.

   C. Return to Main Menu Button

   The Return to Main Menu Button takes you back to the Main Menu. When you select this option, the Are You Sure dialog box will appear reminding you that your current score and status will be erased. (Note, changing sections within a test does not erase your score or status.)

   D. Show Score Button

   The Show Score Button takes you to the Score Display which shows your current score for the entire test and for each section.

Online Course

To register for your Personal Online LSAT Course, go to

myg360.com

Then click the Register button and fill in all required information. In the field marked Promotional Code, enter the following code: AF16978RP. Then click Continue. Finally, click the Account link at the top right to access your course. Note: You must have the book with you when you first register because you will be asked a question from the book.

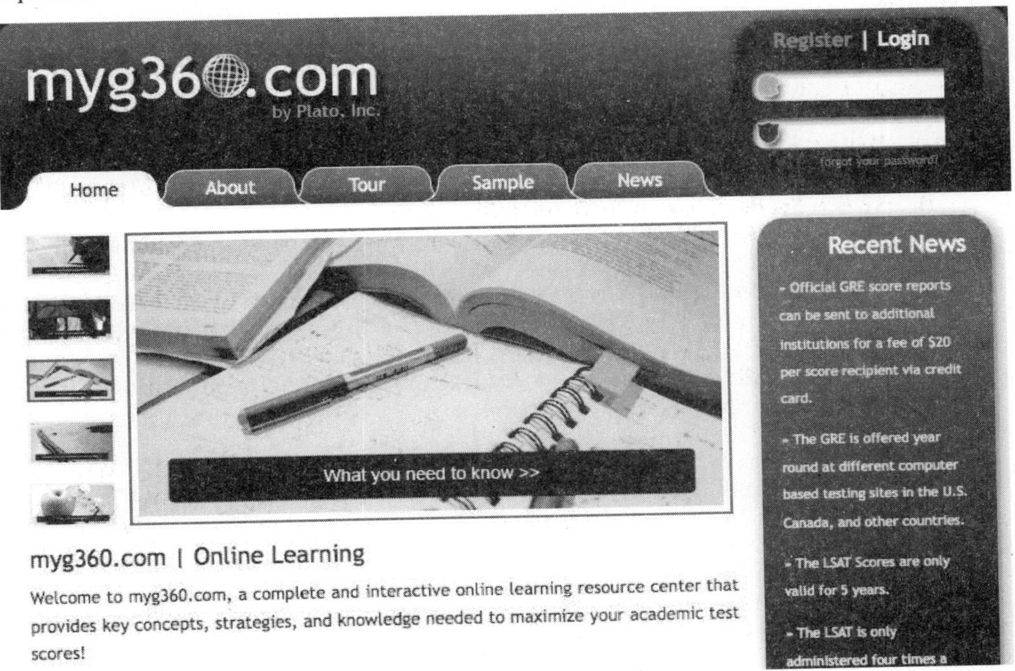

This is your gateway to all the interactive features of your Personal Online LSAT Course.

Course Tour

The course presents short chapters of text along with exercises like a prep book does. But it also offers many powerful, interactive features. Such as,

Ask Questions!

During regular business hours, questions are usually answered in real time. And all questions are answered within 24 hours. On each page, there is a tab titled "Ask" where you can ask questions. If there is a specific sentence or paragraph that you don't fully understand, just paste it into the field and click Ask A Question. The course will first search its database of questions that have been asked by students in the course. It will then present any answers that may have been previously written on the issue, and it will relay the question to us.

Monitoring

The course monitors your progress and directs you to weak areas that you need to study more.

Feedback

When you answer a question, you are told immediately whether you answered it correctly and you can elect to return to the question, view a solution, or proceed to the next question.

Rank

You can compare your performance in the course to other students who are taking the course.

The following illustrated tour will give you a good idea of what expect from your Personal Online LSAT Course.

The Courses Tab

This is where you choose an activity: Study a lesson, take an exercise, check a report, etc.

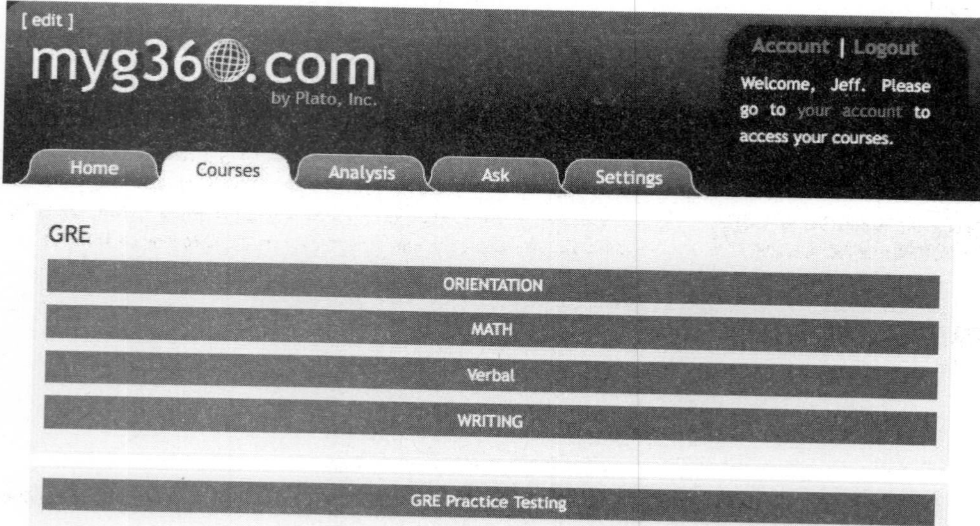

Practice Testing Tab

This is where you access the exercises and tests. The exercises and tests are also presented in the core of the course; but they are collected here so that you may conveniently and quickly find an exercise or test.

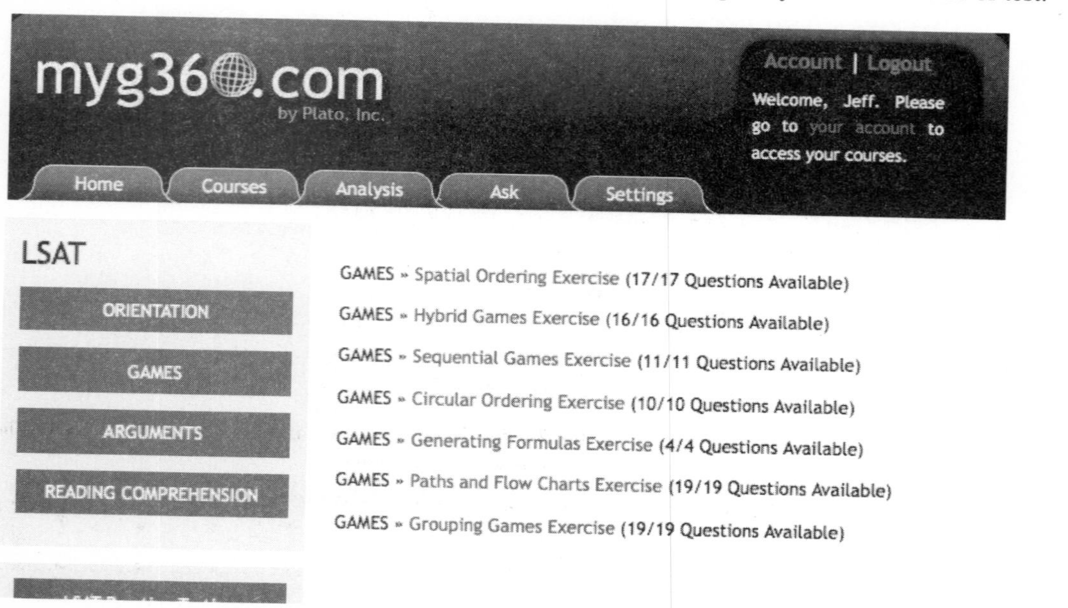

Analysis Tab

This is where you can view stats on your performance in the course and compare it to others taking the course.

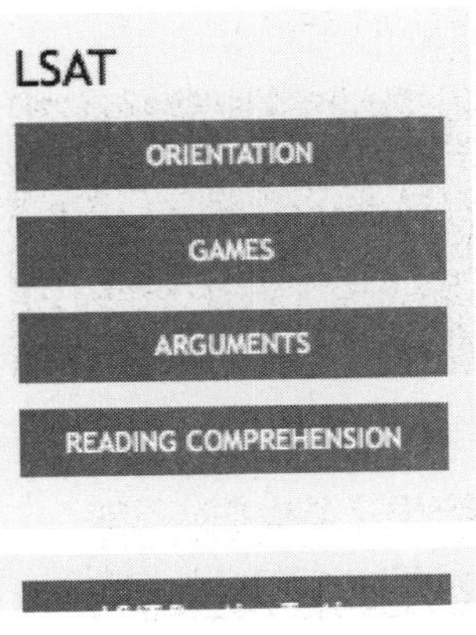

Spatial Ordering Exercise » Questions

You have answered the questions listed below.

Questions 13-17

Seven children are to be seated in seven chairs arranged in a row that runs from west to east. All seven children will face north. Four of the children are boys: Frank, Harry, Ivan, and Joel. Three are girls: Ruby, Sylvia, and Thelma. The children are assigned to chairs according to the following conditions:

Exactly one child sits in each chair.

No boy sits next to another boy.

Ivan sits next to and east of the fourth child in the row.

Sylvia sits east of Ivan.

Frank sits next to Ruby.

17. If Frank sits east of Ruby, which one of the following pairs of children CANNOT sit next to each other?

The correct answer is D. You chose answer A.

(100% chose answer A)

(A) Frank and Thelma

(0% chose answer B)

(B) Harry and Ruby

(0% chose answer C)

(C) Harry and Sylvia

(0% chose answer D)

(D) Ivan and Ruby

Note: For reference, the setup for this game is reproduced at the bottom of this screen.

(A) No. The following diagram satisfies all the conditions and has Frank seated next to Thelma:

1	2	3	4	5	6	7
[illegible]	R	F	T	I	S	H